·DISTANCE POINTS·

The MIT Press   *Cambridge, Massachusetts*   *London, England*

·DISTANCE POINTS·

Essays in Theory and Renaissance Art and Architecture

JAMES S. ACKERMAN

First MIT Press paperback edition, 1994

© 1991 Massachusetts Institute of Technology

This book was set in Sabon, Centaur, Arrighi, and Optima by Graphic Composition, Inc. and printed and bound in the United States of America.

Library of Congress Cataloging-in-Publication Data

Ackerman, James S.

    Distance points : essays in theory and Renaissance art and architecture / James S. Ackerman.

      p.   cm.

    Published in honor of the author's seventieth birthday.

    Includes bibliographical references and index.

    ISBN 0-262-01122-0 (HB), 0-262-51077-4 (PB)

    1. Art, Renaissance. 2. Art—Philosophy.   I. Title.

N6370.A26   1991

709'.02'4—dc20

90-44210

CIP

For Jill

Contents

Preface

These papers of the past forty years were selected by a group of my former doctoral students on the occasion of my seventieth birthday. They suggested that I should write a postscript to each piece, in emulation of the volume of studies by my teacher Richard Krautheimer, of which I was a coeditor, and they arranged for the publication of the volume.

The title *Distance Points* refers to a point selected in constructing a Renaissance—specifically Albertian—perspective image that fixes the distance of the observer from the object. I mean it to refer in this context to the position the historian or critic takes in relation to his or her object—as it were, the point of viewing.

I want to thank especially those of the organizing committee who sent me critical bibliographies for the several chapters: Joseph Connors, David Friedman, Marcia Hall, Andrée Hayum, Carolyn Kolb, Elizabeth McDougall, Linda Pellecchia, John Pinto, Myra Nan Rosenfeld, Jeffrey Ruda, Leon Satkowsky, Natasha Staller, Stephen Tobriner, and Franklin Toker. In addition, Professors Friedman, Pinto, Rosenfeld, and Toker have energetically taken on important organizational tasks. I am honored and delighted by the warm introduction by my dear friends Kathleen Weil-Garris Brandt and Richard Krautheimer, and I am most grateful to The MIT Press for their helpful assistance in the production.

I am moved by this enterprise, and proud to have contributed in some way to the impressive careers of those involved in it.

J.S.A.

Xenion: A Bread and Butter Letter

The essays that make up this book span Jim's work from 1949 to 1985. They cover his contributions to architectural history, his search for the links between art and science in the
Renaissance, and his concerns as a critic for the intellectual, social, and moral foundations
of art and scholarship. They mirror his anxiety regarding the responsibility of artists, architects, critics, and scholars toward their public, their students, and primarily toward themselves. It is significant that Jim throughout has shown a strong predilection for the essay as
his vehicle. His bibliography lists five books; we all know them and each has been a model
of its kind: the architectural monograph, the artist's biography, the building type in its
historical, social, and economic contexts. Alongside such major scholarly achievements,
however, stand close to a hundred papers, ranging from long scholarly articles to essays of
but a few pages, essays distributed over publications read at times less by scholars than by
artists, critics, and their public. Reaching out to a broad and varied spectrum of readers
and listeners has always been a major goal of the teacher, author, and lecturer Jim
Ackerman.

The writers of this introduction are grateful for the chance given them to preface this selection of essays: R.K. as Jim's teacher half a century ago; K.W.G.B. as his student at Harvard in the early sixties; and both as his friends ever since. This selection from among his
many papers is typical, but necessarily leaves out much we might have liked to include. But
since he approved the choice, we take it as presenting a recognizable portrait of the man.
It is, moreover, a portrait in time. It mirrors the changes he has gone through, the modifications of his views, the facets of his nature, at times his moods. It is the image of a man
who thoughtfully reflects on his work and his life. In these introductory pages we have
quoted him often to let him speak with his own inimitable voice. We are presuming on the
privilege of old friendship in offering this interpretation and response to the image his
work shows us. We may sometimes be more frank than is usual in an encomium. It seems
to us, though, that anything less would ignore Jim's own values.

To get the externals out of the way: James Sloss Ackerman was born in San Francisco on
November 8, 1919. He graduated from Yale, class of 1941, went on to the Institute of Fine
Arts, New York University, and there took his M.A. in 1949, his Ph.D. in 1952. That year he
started teaching at the University of California, Berkeley, joined the Harvard faculty in 1969,
and taught there till his retirement in 1990. The number of his activities, affiliations, and
academic honors is large. That much the *Directory of American Scholars* tells. What it does

not tell is that Jim served in the army from 1942 to the late spring of 1945, in North Africa and through the Italian campaign; nor can official biographies record the qualms that beset him before and after his return to graduate study. Doubt about the validity of scholarly pursuits and of academic life is, to be sure, a reaction not uncommon among thoughtful academics returning from a war; but, for Jim, such questioning foreshadowed an enduring concern. He never tries to keep himself out of his work or his talk. Reading Jim, we share his insights and—like it or not—his painful doubts.

Reading the essays, we are struck first by what they have in common. For all their range of subject matter, they exhibit the kind of powerful underlying consistency both of style and content that often characterizes the achievement of important artists and thinkers. We are struck by the dazzling intelligence and elegance of mind revealed in the radical questions Jim poses, by the subtlety of their treatment, and by the lucid felicity and pith of his phrasing: "It becomes apparent that the fervor of its defense is a sign not of superior confidence, but exceptional ignorance"; or "The St. Peter's crossing piers had to be fattened, much to the detriment of their handsome profile." Yet this gift for clever exposition and striking formulation is used not for sheer display but as a necessary expression of a profound responsibility to his audience.

As Jim, the art historian, has grown over these past forty years, we believe we see, broadly speaking, three successive (Eriksonian) stages: one of mastering, a second of exploration, a third centered on reflections about fundamentals of the field, on criticism rather than on a primarily historical approach. Needless to say, these stages are in no way strictly chronological. They overlap and they interweave with each other as well as with the persistent continuities in Jim's thinking.

On reading "Ars Sine Scientia Nihil Est" four decades after its publication, one fancies Jim sprung like Athena from the head of Zeus fully formed and armed. It stands to reason that this cannot have been so; such mastery must have been preceded by some formative years. To show us that Jim *ante litteram,* we take it, this self-portrait-in-time includes the paper on "The Certosa of Pavia" published that same year of 1949, though written two or three years before. In "Ars Sine Scientia Nihil Est," Jim is puzzled by the conflict that, in the 1390s at Milan, sets Gothic theoreticians from beyond the Alps against local practitioners. Both sides defend procedures of construction long established but without examining their validity. Behind Jim's mild surprise at such an emotional and unreasonable approach, however, one senses a deeper uneasiness: the forecast of an inquiry, as yet unformulated, into the irrational cussedness of human beings. (He is disturbed by questions rarely posed in the profession.) In any case, when Jim wrote "Ars Sine Scientia" he was already preparing that model of an architectural monograph *The Cortile del Belvedere.* By that time he handled the tools of the craft with superb ease and grace: hunting down and interpreting documents; reading in the building the successive phases of construction and the *penti-menti;* and presenting a lucid picture of the monument and its growth from the patron's and architect's *primi pensieri* to the drafting table and to their completion or noncompletion. Concurrently and subsequently he dealt with the broader spectrum of Renaissance architecture, its character and history, in a number of studies, some chosen by him for this volume. All start from concrete situations and all show his enviable gift for using precise and plain language to pin down the essentials of a building, the problems faced by the architect, and the context in which they should be viewed. The Cortile del Belvedere is astutely interpreted as reflecting a villa of antiquity as the Renaissance would have viewed it, guided by Pliny's descriptions and by Roman wall paintings apparently known at the time ("The Belvedere as a Classical Villa"). Nor is there much comparable to Jim's description of the *area capitolina* as designed by Michelangelo ("The Capitoline Hill"): the historical context that, by the early sixteenth century, had led architects "to regard a given environment not merely as a neutral repository for a work of art, but as something that might be formed and controlled by the manipulation of voids and the coordination of masses"; the site, the saddle of the hill between two hillocks; the trapezoid predetermined by the old structures reused; the oval inscribed into that trapezoid and its stellar pavement; the lateral palaces, the mass and weight of their walls played down and denied by the colossal order of pilasters: the balance of verticals and horizontals through the counterplay of piers, pilasters, entablatures, and cornices; and the overall design involving the observer in the architectural setting. It is vintage art historical scholarship at its very best.

In a number of studies published successively during the sixties and seventies, Jim goes beyond such a classical approach to architectural history. He focuses on the figure of the architect and on his need to cope with intersecting forces and pressures. The architect may view himself as a free agent distrustful of bureaucratic organization, of an office, impatient with heaps of lengthily evolved preparatory drawings down to the smallest detail. Untrammeled by architectural theories; alternatively, he may subdue his ego, get things under control, build up a disciplined staff, plan far ahead, and establish ("Architectural Practice in the Italian Renaissance"). Bramante and Palladio are Jim's leading antithetical examples. To this day the architect has to choose at these crossroads. The spectrum broadens and deepens as Jim probes the complex network of demands that directly or indirectly press on the architect and to which his design must provide the answer. He is the linchpin of the entire process. In planning the Gesù, the funding patron Cardinal Farnese, the Jesuit fathers, and the architect Vignola each start out with a vision of their own. Through negotiation, the financial restrictions, the demands of the cardinal, the liturgical requirements of the users (the Jesuit fathers), and the spiritual demands of the Counter-Reformation are brought together and given shape by the architect's sensitive responses ("The Gesù in the Light of Contemporary Church Design").

In "The Geopolitics of Venetan Architecture," written in the late seventies, Jim broadens the perspective. His questions turn more ambitious: the architectures of Venice and of the Veneto in the sixteenth century are compared and contrasted; so are the widely different political aims pursued in the capital and in the towns and countryside of the *Terraferma* and their equally diverging economic background and interests. The tasks are differentiated—villas (agriculturally oriented), town palaces, public buildings, churches. The clients are introduced, both as private patrons and as members of public bodies cooperating with others of similar or different background, education, and training—Alvise Cornaro, Giangiorgio Trissino, Girolamo Chiericati; and the architects take the stage—Sansovino, Sanmicheli, Palladio. They all serve to illustrate the challenge Jim has set himself and architectural historians: to explore and reconstruct the "programs" that brought these buildings into being; programs framed by the client interacting with the architect. These agendas stem from unconscious ideologies. So the critic-historian is bound to use historical perspective based on thorough exploration of the sociocultural climates from which clients, architects, and the users of the building have sprung. It is in these years that Jim reaches out to Marxist and neo-Marxist thinking in his quest to establish a justifiable place for art and scholarship in the overall order of things.

Where in "The Geopolitics of Venetan Architecture" he explores a comparatively uncomplicated situation in the past with a limited number of actors on the scene, he turns in "Transactions in Architectural Design" to the present and deliberately chooses as a paradigm the planning and designing of a school. Architecture, so says Jim, borrowing from the social sciences and from psychology, is a social artifact arising from a great number of transactions in which conflicts are resolved. There are the demands of the client, a many-faceted public body—the city fathers, the budget director, educators, health officials. Their voices are complemented and complicated by those of the users—teachers, students, parents—and by the demands of the wider community: taxpayers, financing institutions, public transportation, neighbors. Then there are the claims of the contractors who are to provide the materials obtainable within the means available. And there are the concepts, possibly widely diverging, preconceived by the client, the users, and the general public, as well as the architect's own concept of how a school should function and what it should look like. To respond successfully to such manifold demands and challenges, to balance them against each other and against his own integrity, is up to the architect. Jim's "aim in this essay" is "to suggest a framework within which the autonomy and authority given to the designer by the tradition of European aesthetics might be restrained in the interests of the community. This has involved both the pragmatic formulation of the design process as a transactional field and the moral formulation of a complementarity between the designer's power of free imagination and his responsibility toward the whole company of those affected by his invention."

A second large group of these essays explores encounters between the visual arts and science in fifteenth-century Italy. Far from the physical and intellectual solidities of architectural history, Jim turned to a set of less palpable and familiar problems that stood in the Renaissance in confused and uneasy relation to each other, as they do now. On the one hand, optics and color theory; on the other, the traditions and requirements of artistic practice. In "Alberti's Light" and "Leonardo's Eye," Jim charted an essential redefinition of the transactions between the seer and the seen that are at the core of vision and of pictorial representation in the Renaissance. This theme is expressed still more synthetically in "On Early Renaissance Color Theory and Practice," researched like the other two articles in the mid-seventies but published only in 1980.

The choice of problem is interesting in itself. Color studies had, notwithstanding pioneering work done by Gombrich, Shearman, Edgerton, and others, been relatively neglected by modern scholars. Such wariness of color as a subject of art historical inquiry has deep roots: Vasari's Tuscan belief in the superiority of *disegno* and *rilievo* over *colore*; a long western philosophical tradition that identified matter, form, and space but not color as the prime categories of being; the lack of agreement on a serviceable vocabulary and on adequate methods to describe and record colors and their effects. (The recent advent, costliness, and unreliability of color photographs have also played their part.) Jim's decision to concentrate on an area that combined the dauntingly scientific and technical with the potentially subjective, in the wake of the late 1960s, seems to us to suggest an attempt to transform and justify the scholar and his field: a way to overcome the isolation of art history, to challenge its claims to objectivity, and to heal the rift between the "two cultures," notorious since the 1950s and today even more acute and dangerous. Recently, moreover, as the cleaning of so many of the great Renaissance wall and easel paintings reveals a whole new world of color, Jim's articles take on still greater interest.

Jim showed how Alberti's recourse to the study of optics and color was, like the better-known Renaissance study of linear perspective, an attempt to rationalize the visual arts on the basis of science and thus to raise them to the status of "liberal," intellectual pursuits. Jim presents this endeavor against the foil of constraints and ambiguities inherent in early color theory and defines the tensions among its often contradictory precepts and workshop traditions and what artists actually observed and painted. The implicit goal was to imitate nature more "correctly" to give a more convincing illusion of *rilievo*, but both theory and practice were essentially schematic and hampered by false ideals of objectivity. ("Alberti wrongly believed that color is a property of the object that is conveyed to the eye; actually, the color sensation is generated in the eye from external light stimuli. It is not entirely an 'objective' phenomenon.")

Leonardo's optics accommodated precisely this more subjective view of the relation between vision and its object, a view that gave new power to the observing eye and mind of the imaginative artist. Leonardo's innovations were to make possible a greater "range of emotional and sensual interplay between the viewer and the figures and objects in a picture." This reciprocity also encouraged the development of a new working method, allowing the artist to "offer different rules for different occasions" and to record innumerable observations of specific local conditions of light and color."

Jim understands the intellectual shift between Alberti and Leonardo in the context of scientific progress, but the changes wrought by Leonardo were essential also to the more convincing, unified *look* of his art that, since the cinquecento, has been distinguished as "High Renaissance." This is not an attempt to explain stylistic change by a single and external cause. Jim proposes, rather, that in specific circumstances of fifteenth-century culture, intellectual activities perceived as "science" could engender states of mind and practical decisions in the visual arts that were "not always conscious."

In the conclusion to "Early Renaissance Color Theory and Practice," Jim tests his historical image against received, current notions of Renaissance art and art history. Why, he asks, do historians today permit the notion of "improvement" in the sciences but shy away from this concept when discussing art—even though "Renaissance artists themselves did agree on a 'fixed standard of perfection' (rational and convincing illusion of *rilievo* and space)? This question leads to a nuanced reformulation of notions of progress and improvement in both art and science and thus, implicitly, also in scholarship. Jim asks us to be vigilant to observe more closely what people actually thought and did in the past in order to monitor our own assumptions in the same way or, at least, to realize that we are making them.

"Early Renaissance 'Naturalism' and Scientific Illustration," published in 1985, is a little, almost Mozartian gem. Ideas long held and matured, deeply felt, are projected through new, agreeable motifs, perceived in fresh relationships, with a chastened simplicity of diction that asks to be mistaken for informality. Castiglione and Montaigne, one feels, would have liked the content and the *sprezzature* of the piece. Jim starts from a provocative observation: whereas the humanities depended on traditional verbal culture, the emerging natural sciences increasingly relied on detailed visual observation, on visualizations of concepts and of mathematical order. The dissemination of these scientific images by means of the new medium of print required and stimulated collaboration with artists. Conversely, the "painter, who was trained to record visual evidence, was able not only to aid scientific work, but to pursue it himself."

The heroic protagonist of these essays, for all their difference in subject, is Leonardo. To the natural world he pays a new degree and kind of attention: more discriminating, more varied in detail, more powerful and concentrated in concept. He seeks to unite feeling and reason, mind and eye. Leonardo's world view and working methods seem to become, for Jim, a mandate, a metaphor of a more empirical and flexible model of scholarship as well as of art.

All four of the pieces on Renaissance art and science voice common themes that we find throughout Jim's other work as well. Jim assumes high value for art, for its visual, concrete, sensuous, and emotional qualities. At the same time, though, he is—willy-nilly—highly rational. As an art historian, he deals with words and he studies a period when high art was closely related to verbal culture. Here is a dilemma for many scholars of Jim's generation and others who grew up with the traditional modernist assumption that art is defined as what takes place precisely beyond and outside words. By the same token, Jim's work increasingly seems to reflect doubt that the privileges that the academic humanities—the verbal establishment—arrogate to themselves can simply be taken for granted in a post–World War II world. This mental set allows Jim to look beyond both much Renaissance theory and an underlying endeavor of iconology: to lend the visual arts intellectual prestige by linking them to professional humanism; that is, to the written, verbal tradition. Ingeniously and perhaps "not always consciously," Jim can rescue Renaissance art by stressing, instead, its links with a science that ideally combines the visual and nonverbal with the rational and empirical. This conjunction also validates the craft aspect of Renaissance art, an impediment, from the standard humanist viewpoint, to the intellectual claims made for the visual arts. This neat switch of affiliation also releases art from its embarrassing client status in relation to verbal culture. Unlike the humanities, as Jim shows, Renaissance science actually needed what artists had to offer, and their skills allowed artists to do real science. Wed to science, Renaissance art thus takes on a new centrality, if not a new value from a twentieth-century standpoint.

Jim is, to be sure, more sophisticated a thinker than our simplification suggests. He knows that not all definitions of visual art exclude words. He is well aware of the linguistic approach that has gained such dominance in recent art history and that to some extent flavors the essays on theory ("Style"; "Interpretation, Response"). Yet especially in a postmodern intellectual climate, his insistence on the concrete, on individual visual observations and flexible method, his alertness to differences between theory and practice are a *monitum* of the highest relevance.

An instinctive skepticism of all solutions haunts Jim's desire to find them and so he is sensitive to the contradictions, alibis, and limitations that attended the encounter of Renaissance art and science and that live on today. We are deeply sympathetic with his theme, found throughout his work, that artists like others may believe one thing and do another: that things are very seldom what they seem or what we had been taught they were. Jim is quick to point out the irony that Leonardo "was no more able than Alberti to reconcile [his practice] with the vision of science." Elsewhere he notes that "in the end he failed to formulate a valid optical theory" and to consummate the wedding between observation and the painted image. "Still," he concludes in what might be a credo, "it is fascinating to follow

. . . the probing of an intriguing mind toward a new scientific empiricism, [to see it] as a demonstration of the importance of challenging questions—even those whose answers do not work."

The third group of articles gathers writings on art theory, criticism, and methods of art history. They were published in non–art historical journals and addressed primarily to a meta–art historical audience. It is significant that he agreed to include them in this volume. At the same time, they seem until now to have played a secondary role in shaping most art historians' views of Jim's achievement. We ourselves found these critical pieces especially valuable because in them the moral, intellectual agenda that underlies his art historical work is stated most freely and directly precisely because he is not speaking primarily to art historians.

In these papers, Jim brings out the human factors mirrored in the intricate transactions that link artists, critics, and historians of art, whether in today's world or in the past. He searches for ways of "judging art without absolutes," a phrase he will use to entitle an essay of 1979, not included here.

The earliest paper in our group is "Style," published in a first version as "A Theory of Style" in 1962. Jim's concerns in this piece have also been voiced by others and, today, they have been integrated in much art historical thinking; but in 1962–63 the points Jim made were by no means to be taken for granted. Then, although some at Harvard, like John Coolidge and Jim himself, emphasized the function and context of architecture, the analysis and differentiation of styles in cinquecento art had reached its apogee with works like Freedberg's monumental *Painting of the High Renaissance*. Most students assumed that individual and period styles were real entities and that they were the prime subjects of study in the visual arts; Jim plunges in: "It is meaningless to ask, as we usually do, 'What is style?' The relevant questions is rather 'What definition of style provides the most useful structure for the history of art?'" Style is not an objective description of qualities inherent in the works of art themselves. It is only a useful tool invented by art historians to help understand certain kinds of relationships among works of art. Jim tailors for art historical use the anthropological concept of style as "a complex of behavior patterns within a society." Resolutely he rejects all determinist or teleological concepts of style, whether based on biological, cyclical, or dialectical models. The traditional notion of style in art history is inseparable from the biological fallacy: a predetermined linear evolution. Individual works are valued in terms of their supposed contribution to this development; works that fail to participate cannot be described in a positive way. If the biological model creates a bogus standard for quality on the basis of the standards of the past, the "myth of the avant-garde" simply displaces the goal of artistic development to the future. Both concepts judge the value of any work by its fit in a linear evolution and both judge significance in terms of the work's innovations. In fact, though, innovation per se does not make an artist great. Jim shows how these models for describing style as development were nourished and shaped by both idealist philosophy and Darwinism in its various forms. Ultimately he concludes that the "history of art has been fashioned into another version of the materialist success story." Jim seems to moot the notion that traditional art history is at least unconsciously shaped by repressive and totalitarian values. They coerce works of art and therefore our thinking about them into a putatively objective and unitary narrative. Jim instead proposes an open pluralistic (and thus implicitly more democratic) model for the discussion of style. Its development is "a succession of complex decisions as numerous as the works by which we have defined the style . . . a constant incidence of probings [by artists] into the unknown, not a sequence of steps toward the perfect solution." Style, for Jim, is "the manifestation rather of the imagination of individual artists than of historical forces"; the idea that a period or group may "embody a creative expressive will (I am recalling Riegl's 'Kunstwollen') . . . I find incomprehensible and distasteful." This is not to say that Jim denies the impact of external factors on the artist's imagination. He voices early support for a contextual approach to individual works of art. Like Gombrich and Thomas Kuhn, he also reminds us that there may indeed be "progress" of a certain kind in art, once a specific artistic goal is defined, for instance the illusionistic representation of objects in space. Some works of art may be seen by the artist's contemporaries or by ourselves as more satisfactory solutions to a given problem, but that does not make one work "better" than another. Styles, thus, overlap and interact, they are confluent and concurrent rather than strictly chronological. Throughout, however, "the individual work of art, and not the force of some vague destiny, [should] be seen as the prime mover of the historical process."

"Interpretation, Response: Toward a Theory of Art Criticism" sums up Jim's most recent position. To us, this piece is also one of his finest, most personal, and most moving statements to date. In this essay, he strives for a new systematic approach to an issue that had always preoccupied him, how to reconcile the rational with the intuitive, in life and in scholarship. Jim takes a citation from Roland Barthes for his text and applies it to art history and criticism—two activities that, as we have seen, are no longer divisible in his mind. "Il faut affirmer," wrote Barthes in 1973, "le plaisir du texte contre les indifférences de la science et la puritanisme de l'analyse idéologique." Jim does not advocate abandoning "interpretation," which deals with import and function, but wants to give salutary emphasis instead to "response," the personal subjective experience of the viewer. In the article, these two elements of criticism are shown to be inextricable, as he seeks to "bind interpretation to response in a single critical method."

From this base, Jim calls up a wide range of themes, many of which we have met earlier. Thus, "intimacy with the art of the past gives us, in turn, a perspective on the present"; "the pretense of speaking on behalf of the work of art is a disingenuous attempt to make critical statements without accepting responsibility for them"; "the dullness and sameness of most critical and historical writing in this country is due partly to the concentration of intellectual life in universities, where imagination is constrained by a reductive ideal of scholarly objectivity supported by an obsolete ideology." Above all, it is idealist criticism with its hierarchical "immanent standards of value" that receives here the soundest of many thrashings Jim has administered to it.

Lévi-Strauss's *La pensée sauvage* of 1962 offers Jim a paradigm for the desired fusion of two modes of thought—actually, it is a model of tripartite structure. Where the anthropologist placed "artistic creation midway between mythic thought and science," however, Jim sees "criticism as occupying a position midway between interpretation and response." This new "responsive criticism" opens up "a cornucopia of pleasures." We need not necessarily reject our idealist cultural heritage but become open to a pluralism of standards. "The proper task of criticism is to offer not authoritative judgments of works of art but insights into how an experienced and informed individual who holds certain stated convictions responds to the work of art he or she is discussing."

Characteristically, Jim ends by reaching out to analogies between the elements of criticism and research on the bicameral brain. Response is the work of the right brain that processes and synthesizes sense data, whereas interpretation is the sphere of the intellectual, analytical left brain. Our culture privileges left-brain characteristics to its detriment. Jim urges us to be "concerned not with the separateness but with the collaboration of the two sides of the brain just as we should focus not on the distinction but on the synthesis of interpretation and response in criticism."

These papers, it seems to us, flesh out Jim's self-portrait. They show us the man pondering matters more weighty to him than professional questions proper. He searches within himself for the roots of human behavior as it impinges on the attitudes and the work of scholars, artists and architects, critics and their audiences. There lurk in his mind queries we all ask ourselves or ought to ask. Jim has the courage to ask aloud. Haunted, he haunts his public. The most considerate of men, he yet exhorts us to clear our conscience, as, without self-pity, he seeks to clear his own.

A sense of moral accountability implicitly or explicitly pervades all of his work, born of an acute awareness of the tensions and contradictions that underlie the scholar's life. He strives to overcome them by social commitment, action, and ultimately liberation. None of these themes can be seen in isolation. They are the very texture of his thought. They all are there, it seems to us, from the outset. But looking again at this choice of papers we perceive a progression. As the years go by, ideas change in coloring, shading, and strength. They are louder at times, *in sordina* at others. For some time he explored German and Italian neo-Marxist criticism with its dominant emphasis on social function. But by 1979

("Art without Absolutes") he no longer felt able "to believe categorically that one value criterion could be applied universally without restricting receptivity to the variety of experiences available in art." Freudian concepts also inevitably color his work. More recently, the insights of family and individual therapy and, indeed, a notion of the therapeutic model generally have informed his work. These changes, we feel, mirror Jim's *peregrinatio*.

Paramount is his sensitivity to and his respect for the conflicts between emotion and intellect. This conflict exists, of course, in all our lives. But for Jim, it becomes a subject to integrate in scholarship. In early pieces, like "Ars Sine Scientia" and "Sources of the Renaissance Villa," he proposes the scholar's rational faculties as instruments to understand and thus to disarm harmful nonrational behavior. It is the scholar's job to search out tacit assumptions, unexamined habits of thought and feeling, in one's self and others in the past and the present. *Vox clamantis in deserto*, Jim speaking in 1961 before the International Congress of Art History raises the warning cry: the foundations of the discipline are being betrayed. Students of the Renaissance, he claims, have been blinded by their bias against the Middle Ages and late antiquity and by a restrictive focus on Florence. The Renaissance villa, rather than having evolved through recourse to classical antiquity or through innovation, goes back to late antique villa types and their medieval offspring in the Veneto. Prevailing prejudices on the subject have sprung from a rigid habit deeply rooted in the profession of dividing the indivisible course of events into strict periods. We have been blinded also by the subsconscious and irrational assumption that novelty is more praiseworthy than tradition.

To harmonize the dichotomy between reason and feeling is Jim's basic desire. He approaches this task through different subjects and strategies at different times. In the early "Ars Sine Scientia," the irrational was to him an obstacle to straight thinking and architectural achievement. Later, throughout the nineteen sixties and seventies, he consistently tried to find room in the house of art history for the subjective and unconscious elements that belong to artistic creativity and are too often absent from scholarship. The personal and emotional immediate reaction, the "gut response" to a work of art or to a "fact" of history, is and must be at the basis of our judgment: "We start with a response and then try to articulate it," he had said in "Art without Absolutes." Response and responsibility have a common root deeper than philology. We need to ask why we privilege the art of Raphael or for that matter El Greco; what our value judgments stem from; how we can look beyond the persistent apotheosis of Renaissance idealism that favored the evolution in our days of nonobjective art and of formalist criticism as exemplified by Clement Greenberg. That insight is also a demand. One is reminded of Paul Klee's "Art does not render the visible, it renders visible." Over time, Jim tries to work out narrative structures in which the nonrational is increasingly given its due and is shown to be inseparable from its opposite ("Theory of Art Criticism").

Creativity in the humanities or the arts is bound up with other kinds of nagging doubts: how do I square my political, social, economic, my ethical beliefs with my lifelong commitment to my work? Are my words seducing my students and readers, my public? Are not the sciences, sociology, perhaps philosophy or politics more important? Who cares for my research, for the paintings I have done, the buildings I have designed, the books I have written? How can I justify my life's work before my own conscience?

Jim is profoundly suspicious of the relevance and value of art history as it has been and is being practiced. He is a poignant figure to all of us because he is so aware of the marginality of the intellectual in today's life. He suspects this social emargination is all too often justified. Skepticism is essential, but it must not be allowed to become an excuse for evasion for someone who is, like Jim, instinctively attached to the very values he questions. One might even say that the seriousness of Jim's challenge is the measure of the importance he assigns to them. Clear exposition of one's values and anxieties is ultimately a social act. He has sought to transcend doubts and guilts about the value of our profession by exploring means to give art history a dimension of social usefulness. Jim is not, of course, the only scholar to feel unease about the place and practice of the humanities, or to be aware of the need to reintegrate them with society. Many different approaches have been tried to resolve this dilemma and Jim has employed many of them. But, for us, the greatest qualities of Jim's work reside less in his methods than in the urgency of his engagement and in the special flavor of his scholarly and human personality.

Responsibility and commitment must turn into action. Persuasion is the scholar's tool to that end. For all teachers and writers work to persuade students, listeners, readers, and in the end a broader public of their findings, ideas, and underlying beliefs. Their aim is to bring their audience to set right what they deem wrong: unstated and mistaken assumptions; the artist's or the architect's failure to produce work responsive and committed; the critic's and the art historian's correlative failure in judging such work. It is Jim's special contribution to have applied this notion both to past and present. The functions of the critic and historian are indivisible and have moral force. To pretend to historical objectivity is a hollow conceit. Whether the critic-historian confronts postmodern architecture, its practitioners and public, or the builders of the Renaissance and their use of the Tuscan order and of rustication, he is bound by his moral and social commitment: "What an impressive metaphorical burden the language of architecture supported in the Renaissance. An architectural order was seen as an expression of actual or virtual structure and as an affirmation of the traditions and capacity for invention of a social group and of its culture. It seems to me timely to ponder this message at this moment, when many . . . architects . . . are employing the classical orders as if they were intended merely for decoration and diversion" ("The Tuscan/Rustic Order").

Jim's own involvement in present-day art, architecture, and art criticism is not a superficial trendiness but an act of conviction. Reconciling past and present, response and interpretation, the social and personal, duty and pleasure, are all part of the task Jim sets himself. Would he agree with Peter Brown on St. Augustine: "The healed man enjoys a more acute sense of responsibility, clearer knowledge, a greater ease of choice"?

Jim will never be free of a thinking man's inner disquiet. But the most recent essays chosen for this collection suggest an increasingly liberating intuition that duty and responsibility flourish best when nourished by a direct and intimate appreciation of "le plaisir du texte." By the same token, his author's voice, which had a didactic and exhorting tone, despite its modesty, has taken on a more personal and flexible timbre. He speaks unblushingly as "I." His long-time teaching that even the most objective investigation is determined by subjective factors has been put into practice. He allows himself to speak with a new directness and intimacy and to find a scholarly outlet for his natural human warmth. This makes his friends and admirers happy and it gives us permission to search for something like it in our own labors.

His work has always been so moving because it evoked a clear, eloquent image of our own innermost concerns and reminded us that we should listen to their promptings. Jim's most recent writing offers us an invitation to value individuality and pleasure. Potential in Jim's approach may also be the hope that scholarship and the history of art need not be marginal at all but could provide an intersection where ideas and emotions, imagination and discipline can meet. If so, Jim's radical questions and searching honesty will have helped to point the way.

Jim's pioneering contributions to the history of architecture have changed our angle of vision on the field. His work on art and science in the Renaissance has helped to define a new province. He has made us look at scholarship itself anew. He has taught us to bind together history and criticism, the once and the now. As to the future, no one is more keenly aware than he that it remains an open field. The *peregrinatio* is by no means over. Notwithstanding Jim's hard-won conquest of subjective response and the bent of recent theories of criticism, we doubt he is temperamentally inclined to pursue subjectivity to its limits. We would guess that he still finds it hard to deny that the external world—and art with it—do exist apart from our perceptions of them and we wonder whether he would or could abandon his troublesome faith in the priority of reason. So we could imagine that Jim might experience new conflicts in times to come; and that, as in the past, will be good for our profession and probably also for him as he continues the questing that is the sign of a youthful mind and that makes it hard to remember that we are celebrating his seventieth birthday this year.

Kathleen Weil-Garris Brandt
Richard Krautheimer

James S. Ackerman:
Selected Bibliography

1949   "The Certosa of Pavia and the Renaissance in Milan," *Marsyas,* 5, 23–37.

"'Ars Sine Scientia Nihil Est': Gothic Theory of Architecture at the Cathedral of Milan," *The Art Bulletin,* 31, 84–111.

1951   "Bramante and the Torre Borgia," *Pontificia Accademia di Archeologia, Rendiconti,* 25/26, 247–265.

"The Belvedere as a Classical Villa," *Journal of the Warburg and Courtauld Institutes,* 14, 70–91.

1954   *The Cortile del Belvedere* (Vatican City).

"Tradition and the Future of Architecture," *California Monthly,* 44 (April), 42–44.

"Architecture" and "Leon Battista Alberti," in *Encyclopaedia Britannica,* 14th ed.

"Architectural Practice in the Italian Renaissance," *Journal of the Society of Architectural Historians,* 13, no. 3, 3–11.

1955   "California Buildings," University of California Department of Architecture, limited edition.

1956   "Report on California," *Architectural Review,* 120, no. 717, 237–239.

1957   "Marcus Aurelius on the Capitoline Hill," *Renaissance News,* 10, 69–75.

1958   "On American Scholarship in the Arts," *College Art Journal,* 17, 357–362.

"Art History and the Problems of Criticism," *Daedalus* (Winter), 253–263. Republished in *The Visual Arts Today* (Middletown, Conn., 1960).

1959   "Bramante" and "Michelangelo," in *Les architectes célèbres,* ed. Pierre Francaste, vol. 2 (Paris).

1961   *The Architecture of Michelangelo* (London and New York).

1962 "A Theory of Style," *The Journal of Aesthetics and Art Criticism*, 20, 227–237.

"One Culture or None," *Current*, 22, 67–72.

"Abstract Art and the Critics," *Atlantic Monthly* (Oct.), 73–78. Reprinted by Graham Gallery; The Singer Corporation, *American Journal*, 3 (1963), 199–208.

"Vignoliana," with Wolfgang Lotz, in *Essays in Memory of Karl Lehmann* (New York; *Marsyas*, 1, suppl. 1), 1–24.

1963 *Art and Archaeology*, with Rhys Carpenter (Englewood Cliffs, N.J.).

"Art and Social Responsibility," *Rhode Island School of Design Alumni Bulletin* (Sept.), 2–5.

"Sources of the Renaissance Villa," in *Studies in Western Art: Acts of the Twentieth International Congress of the History of Art*, ed. Millard Meiss, 2 vols. (Princeton), 2: 6–18.

1964 "Palladio e l'architettura del '700 negli Stati Uniti; il Presidente Jefferson e il palladianismo americano," *Bollettino del Centro Internazionale di studi d'architettura A. Palladio*, 6, 29–48.

1965 "Della Porta's Gesù Altar," in *Essays in Honor of Walter Friedlaender*, ed. Walter Cahn et al. (New York), 1–2.

"Art and Evolution," in *The Nature and Art of Motion*, ed. Gyorgy Kepes (New York), 32–40.

"Notes on Larsen Hall," *Connection*, 1 (Fall), 16–20.

"On Scientia," *Daedalus* (Winter), 14–23.

"The Future of Humanistic Studies in America," in *Humanistic Scholarship in America*, ed. John Higham, Leonard Krieger, and Felix Gilbert (Princeton), 12–15.

1966 *Palladio* (Harmondsworth).

"Preface," *Harvard Art Review*, 1 (Winter), 8.

"Editorial: Rx for Art Criticism," *Art in America* (Mar.–Apr.), 29.

"Palladio's Vicenza: A Bird's-eye Plan of ca. 1571," in *Studies in Renaissance and Baroque Art Presented to Anthony Blunt*, ed. Jeanne Courtauld et al. (London and New York), 53–61.

1967   *Palladio's Villas* (New York).

"Palladio's Lost Portico Project for San Petronio in Bologna," in *Essays in the History of Architecture Presented to Rudolf Wittkower*, ed. Douglas Fraser, Howard Hibbard, and Milton J. Lewine (London and New York), 110–115.

Views of Florence by Giuseppe Zocchi (New York).

1969   "Two Styles: A Challenge to Higher Education," *Daedalus* (Summer), 855–869.

"Listening to Architecture," *Harvard Educational Review*, 39, no. 4, 4–20.

"Concluding Remarks: Science and Art in the Works of Leonardo," in *Leonardo's Legacy*, ed. Charles D. O'Malley (Berkeley and Los Angeles), 205–225.

"The Demise of the Avant Garde: Notes on the Sociology of Recent American Art," *Comparative Studies in Society and History*, 11, 371–384; reduced version in *L'Arte*, 6, 4–11.

"Education of Vision," in *The Arts on Campus: The Necessity for Change*, ed. Margaret Mahoney (New York), 63–80.

1972   "The Gesù in the Light of Contemporary Church Design," in *Baroque Art: The Jesuit Contribution*, ed. I. Jaffe and R. Wittkower (New York), 15–28.

"Toward a New Social Theory of Art," *New Literary History*, 4, 315–330.

1973   "The Arts in Higher Education," in *Content and Context*, ed. Carl Kaysen (New York), 219–266.

1974   "Notes on Bramante's Bad Reputation," in *Studi bramanteschi, Atti del Convegno internazionale* (1970) (Rome), 339–350.

"Transactions in Architectural Design," *Critical Inquiry*, 1, 229–243.

1975   "The History of Design and the Design of History," *Psicon* 2/3, 138–146 (Italian version).

"Il contributo dell'Alessi alla tipologia della chiesa longitudinale," in *Galeazzo Alessi e l'architettura del Cinquecento, Atti del Convegno internazionale* (1974), ed. Corrado Maltese (Genoa), 461–466.

1977   "Palladio e lo sviluppo della concezione della chiesa a Venezia," *Bollettino del Centro Internazionale di Studi di Architettura*, 19, 9–26 (published 1980).

"L'architettura religiosa veneta in rapporto a quella toscana del Rinascimento," *Bollettino del Centro Internazionale di Studi di Architettura*, 19, 135–164.

Introduction to Wolfgang Lotz, *Studies in Italian Renaissance Architecture* (Cambridge, Mass.), xvii-xxiv.

Review article, "Leonardo da Vinci, The Madrid Codices," *Journal of the Society of Architectural Historians*, 36, 46ff.

1978   "Palladio Revisited," *The John Williams Lawrence Memorial Lectures*, Tulane University School of Architecture, New Orleans.

Introduction to Sebastiano Serlio, *On Domestic Architecture: The Sixth Book* (New York and Cambridge).

"Alberti's Light," in *Studies in Late Medieval and Renaissance Painting in Honor of Millard Meiss*, ed. Irving Lavin (New York), 1–27.

"On Rereading 'Style,'" *Social Research*, 45, 153–163.

"Leonardo's Eye," *Journal of the Warburg and Courtauld Institutes*, 41, 108–146.

1979   "On Judging Art without Absolutes," *Critical Inquiry*, 5, 441–469.

"Worldmaking and Practical Criticism," *Journal of Aesthetics and Art Criticism*, 39, 249–254.

"Notes and Exchanges," *Critical Inquiry*, 5, 795–799.

1980   "On Early Renaissance Color Theory and Practice," *Studies in Art History: American Academy in Rome*, 1, 11–38.

"The History of Design and the Design of History," *Via*, 4, 19–28.

"Observations on Renaissance Church Planning in Venice and Florence," in *Florence and Venice, Comparisons and Relations*, ed. Sergio Bertelli, Nicolai Rubinstein, and Craig Hugh Smyth, 2 vols. (Florence), 2: 287–308.

"The Cloisters of San Zaccaria," in John MacAndrew, *Venetian Architecture of the Early Renaissance* (Cambridge), 554–559.

1981   "The Arts Require Government Aid," *Yale Alumni Magazine*, 45, no. 1, 8f.
       "La storia dell'architettura e l'architettura della storia," *Spazio e società*, 4,
       no. 14, 25–37.
       "Dürer's Crab," in *Ars Auro Prior: Studia Ioanni Bialostocki Sexagenario
       Dicata*, ed. Juliusz A. Chroscicki et al. (Warsaw), 291–295.

1982   "The Geopolitics of Venetan Architecture in the Time of Titian," in *Titian:
       His World and His Legacy,* ed. David Rosand (New York), 41–71.
       "In Memoriam, Wolfgang Lotz," *Journal of the Society of Architectural
       Historians*, 41, 5–6.
       "The Planning of Renaissance Rome, 1480–1580," in *Rome in the
       Renaissance: The City and Its Myth*, ed. P. A. Ramsey (Binghamton), 3–18.

1983   "Palladio Revisited: Civic Architecture," *Spazio e Società*, 6, no. 21, 8–19.
       "The Tuscan/Rustic Order: A Study in the Metaphorical Language of
       Architecture," *Journal of the Society of Architectural Historians*, issue in
       honor of John P. Coolidge, 42, 15–34.
       "Palladio Revisited: The Churches," *Spazio e Società,* 6, no. 22, 62–75.
       "Palladio Revisited: The Villas," *Spazio e Società,* 6, no. 23, 8–19.

1984   "Interpretation, Response: Toward a Theory of Art Criticism," in *Theories of
       Criticism,* with M. H. Abrams (Washington, D.C.), 33–53.
       "The Faces of Palazzo Chiericati," in *Interpretazioni veneziane: studi in onore
       di Michelangelo Muraro,* ed. David Rogand (Venice), 213–220.

1985   "Il paradigma della villa," *Casabella*, 49, 53–65.
       "Early Renaissance 'Naturalism' and Scientific Illustration," in *The Natural
       Sciences and the Arts,* Acta Universitatis Upsaliensis: Figura, n.s. 22, ed.
       Allan Ellenius (Uppsala), 1–17.
       "The Involvement of Artists in Renaissance Science," in *Science and the Arts
       in the Renaissance,* ed. John W. Shirley and F. David Hoeniger (Washington),
       94–128.

1986   "Why Classicism?," *Harvard Architectural Review*, 5, 78f.
       "The Villa as Paradigm," *Perspecta*, 22, 10–31.
       "Pellegrino Tibaldi, San Carlo Borromeo e l'architettura ecclesiastica del loro
       tempo," in *San Carlo e il suo tempo: Atti del Convegno internazionale*, ed.
       Giovanni Testori (Rome), 574–586.

1987   Contribution to "Seminar I: Transitional Periods," *Harvard Architectural Review,* 6, 10–12.

Introduction to Michelangelo Muraro, *Venetian Villas: The History and Culture* (Udine), 7–8.

"The Medici Villa in Fiesole," in *"Il se rendit en Italie": Etudes offertes à André Chastel* (Rome), 49–56.

1989   "Renaissance," in *International Encyclopedia of Communications* (Philadelphia), 3: 447–452.

"Social Stratification in Renaissance Urban Planning," with Myra Nan Rosenfeld, in *Urban Life in the Renaissance,* ed. Susan Zimmerman and Ronald F. E. Weissman (Newark), 21–49.

"The Visual Arts Collections: Manifold Resources," in *The Invention of Photography and Its Impact on Learning,* ed. Louise Todd Ambler and Melissa Banta (Cambridge, Mass.), 62–71.

"Rudolf Wittkower's Influence on the History of Architecture," *Source,* 8/9, 87–90.

1990   "Social Concern and Architectural Discourse," *Places,* 6, 68–71.

The Villa: Form and Ideology of Country Houses (London and Princeton).

"Gli studi palladiani degli ultimi trent'anni," in *Andrea Palladio: Nuovi contributi,* ed. R. Cevese and A. Chastel (Milan), 122–126.

I

Historical and Critical Theory

I

Style

Art historians are especially preoccupied with defining the nature and behavior of style.[1] For history to be written at all we must find in what we study factors that at once are consistent enough to be distinguishable and changeable enough to have a "story." In political-social history these factors are sometimes institutions, sometimes persons or groups—units that retain their identity over a span of time or shift of locale, yet change and develop as they react to their environment and its changes.

In the study of the arts, works—not institutions or people—are the primary data; in them we must find certain characteristics that are more or less stable, in the sense that they appear in other products of the same artist(s), era or locale, and flexible, in the sense that they change according to a definable pattern when observed in instances chosen from sufficiently extensive spans of time or of geographical distance. A distinguishable ensemble of such characteristics we call a style.

We use the concept of style, then, as a way of characterizing relationships among works of art that were made at the same time and/or place, or by the same person or group. If we do not know where, when, or by whom works of art were produced, then the process may be inverted to allow hypotheses that works of the same style are from the same time, place, or person(s). In this second role, style is an indispensable historical tool; it is more essential to the history of art than to any other historical discipline.

From James S. Ackerman and Rhys Carpenter, *Art and Archaeology* (Englewood Cliffs, N.J.: Prentice-Hall, 1963), 164–186.

Because works of art are preserved for reasons other than their historical or biographical significance, they often lose all extrinsic evidence of their historical position, so that no record survives of the artist(s), era, or locale that produced them. Without such evidence—coordinates of time and space—it is impossible to plot the graphs of consistency and change that are a prerequisite for the writing of history. But isolated fragments of evidence may be extended into a credible historic account by conclusions based on style; one signed work may be sufficient to construct the whole production of an artist, one dated work to associate a type of art with an epoch.

Style thus provides a structure for the history of art. Other structures are possible (e.g., the biography of artists), but that of style is the most comprehensive, since it is the only one that can be built with minimal external documentation on the evidence of works of art alone. Because our image of style is not discovered but created by abstracting certain features from works of art for the purpose of assisting historical and critical activity, it is meaningless to ask, as we usually do, "What is style?" The relevant question is rather "What definition of style provides the most useful structure for the history of art?"

I suggested that the concept of style is a means of establishing *relationships* among individual works of art. In this it resembles the concepts of society and culture, which are based on similar definitions of relationships; anthropologists also use the word *style* to designate a complex of behavior patterns within a society. There is no objective correlative for our image of a style; we may observe and define certain traits or characteristics in a single work of art, but we cannot call them traits of Rembrandt's style, Gothic style, or Tuscan style without summoning our experience of other works by Rembrandt, or the "Gothic period" (which is itself a historian's invention), or from Tuscany. A particular work of art therefore may represent or exemplify characteristics of a style in the way that a person may represent a society, but to say that it has a style, as we often do, is not illuminating. The word *style* defines a certain currency—distinguishable in the work (or in some portion of the work) of an artist, a place, or a time—and it is inefficient to use it also to define the unique traits of single works of art; uniqueness and currency are incompatible. The virtue of the concept of style is that by defining *relationships* it makes various kinds of order out of what otherwise would be a vast continuum of self-sufficient products.

In using an image of style to establish orderly relationships among works of art, we follow the path of the artist, who—by accepting or altering certain features of the arts around him—establishes a relationship that is the predominant factor in the formation of his individual style. For the artist and for his audience, style is a protection against chaos; it serves the same purpose as do cultural patterns and institutions in society. A class of works of art of any kind—pyramids, portraits of rulers, still lifes—is orderly and distinguishable because it is necessary to human beings not only to express themselves within established patterns, but to experience the world around them in accordance with such patterns; our perceptual mechanisms cause us to interpret what we see in terms of what we know and expect. The factor of stability in style can be traced to a sort of inertia; presumably, if natural inclinations were undisturbed by imagination, ambition and other desires, society and language would remain fixed and art would have a history of more or less competent copies of the work of some Daedalic demigod. But we are mercifully favored with passions that struggle with—though they never quite overcome—that inertia, and these contribute the flexible factor in style.

The artist submits to this tension between stability and change, between the reproduction of existing forms and the invention of new ones, by necessity, not by choice. Unlike a machine, he cannot reproduce without inventing, for when change is not prompted by inventiveness it is prompted by boredom. So art has never been static; when it is not vital, it actively degenerates. Conversely, the artist cannot invent without reproducing; in order to make a meaningful innovation he must be able to concentrate his forces upon the few aspects of his work where circumstances favor fresh departures; for the rest, he relies on the support of his tradition and of his environment. An artist cannot invent himself out of his time and, if he could, he would succeed only in making his work incomprehensible by abandoning the framework in which it might be understood.

The relationship of stability and change varies according to the pace and degree of individualization of a culture; in recent art a powerful factor of flexibility causes radical shifts of style in the course of a generation, while in ancient Egypt stability predominated to the point that barely perceptible innovations were sufficient to secure the vitality of a style for three millennia.

In the tradition of modern Western criticism, the forces that make for change in art have been praised more warmly than those that make for stability. Since the Romantic period the military hero has been admired more for his adventurousness than for his caution, and the artist-hero more for his innovations than for his ability to sustain tradition. This preference exemplifies a "progressive" view of art opposed, presumably, to a conservative view that would favor the forces of stability. Neither is really relevant to criticism. Change and stability simply are primeval forces in style and cannot be invested with value except in terms of some preconceived image of man's destiny.

If the characteristics of the work of art that contribute to a definition of style must exhibit some stability and flexibility, then all of its possible characteristics cannot contribute in equal measure. Conventions of form and of symbolism yield the richest harvest of traits by which to distinguish style. I mean by conventions an accepted vocabulary of elements—a scale of color, an architectural order, an attribute of a god or a saint—and a syntax by which these elements are composed into a still life, a temple, or a frieze. We get an image of the style of an individual by observing the interaction of his private conventions and the public conventions of his time and place. Since conventions, like language, are the basic vehicle for the communication of meaning, society aids the artist in promoting their stability and in controlling the rate, the degree, and even the nature of their change. Religious symbolism, for example, is determined by religious establishments as well as by artists, and other less utilitarian conventions, such as those of landscape painting or of recent abstract art, are sustained, if not formulated, by the needs of an economically powerful class.

Other inherent characteristics help less in determining style; aspects of the work of art as a material object change so little in the course of history that they might appear almost anywhere at any time. So to say that a painting is done on wood, that a statue weighs three hundred pounds, or that a building is thirty feet high is to make a statement that, for all its precision, conveys little of style.

Technique, or the process by which matter is given form, is a more sensitive gauge of style than the strictly material aspect of the work of art, but less sensitive than the conventional character. To say that a temple is constructed of doweled ashlar blocks and that its trussed roof rests on lintels supported by columns is to reveal more of its style than to say that it is built of marble, wood, and iron; but it does not distinguish a Greek temple from a Roman or Neoclassic one.

Yet technique may be a fundamental stylistic determinant; this occurs because usually it is not merely a means, but serves important formal or symbolic functions. In Gothic architecture the ribbed vault, which represents a substantial advance in engineering, is not just a device for achieving an expressive form; it is itself an expressive form, whereas in the skyscraper design of the last generation, the aim to "reveal" the skeletal steel frame in the exterior design had a symbolic motivation. (The skeleton, in fact, had to be covered for fire protection; its reflection in the façade design, often achieved artificially, symbolized "honesty.") Gothic and early twentieth-century architects were uncommonly interested in structure, and their interest promoted an extraordinary flexibility in technique. Structural change in Gothic architecture was so rapid and so rational that it can be traced systematically in a succession of cathedrals started within the same generation; vaulting or buttressing methods alone are sufficient to provide a key to chronology. By contrast, the technical change in other great phases of European architecture—from 550 to 350 BC or from AD 1450 to 1650—was negligible, almost an insignificant component of style.

One of the most stubborn and challenging problems of art history is to explain the motivations and behavior of change in style. While this involves concentration on flexible factors, we could not separate one style from another, or speak of a style, without first defining it in terms of stable factors. We created classes such as Impressionism, Baroque art, or Picasso's Blue Period on the assumption that a certain complex of elements common to a group of works is sufficiently stable, distinct, and relevant to justify characterizing it as a style. In a similar way, political historians distinguish "periods" within the constant flux of human action—the Middle Ages, the Reformation, or the Colonial Era—in terms of what they believe to be cohesive and significant social events. This definition of a style in terms of its stable factors is a hypothesis (and one that we must challenge constantly) that makes it possible to study change. While style usually can be defined in reference to a more or less fixed block of historical time, the study of its processes of change requires reference to the succession of events within that block.

For most of the five hundred years of modern art history the patterns of change have been described in biological metaphors. Vasari, the most scholarly historian of the Renaissance, believed that style, "like human bodies, has a birth, a growth, an aging and a death." The scheme survived into the last century, when it got refinements from Darwin and his colleagues and when terms such as *the evolution* (or *life*) *of style* entered our vocabulary.[2] Most of Vasari's followers before 1850 were interested chiefly in the art of two epochs—antiquity and the Renaissance—which were susceptible to being fit into the biological life cycle, and even those who turned from Classicism toward the Gothic found that the formula still could be used. Toward the end of the last century, scientific scholarship and the broadening of taste encouraged a more specific and less normative model of evolution from an archaic to a classic to a baroque phase. There remained, however, a bias in favor of the classic; the Parthenon, Amiens, and Raphael were thought to be peaks of the cycle (as expressed in the terms *High Gothic; High Renaissance)* toward which earlier artists aspired and from which later artists retreated.

At the turn of the century, Alois Riegl, who supported his theory of style with studies of nonclassical phases (late Roman, early Baroque art), was influential in persuading colleagues to grant equality to all phases. He promoted a principle that typifies art history in this century, that the best solution to an artistic problem is the one that best fulfills the artist's aim. But this relativism in the sphere of value was accompanied by determinism in explaining the dynamics of style; in place of the biological metaphor, Riegl put cycles of evolution from an early "haptic" to a later "optic" phase. At the same time, Heinrich Wölfflin offered a still more influential theory of preordained evolution from classical to baroque form in terms of polar formal categories: closed-open, linear-painterly, etc. As compared to the biological tradition, which had the disadvantage of being applicable to only three of the major styles of Western art, that of Riegl and Wölfflin describes more universal patterns of style, though eras remain—among them Carolingian and nineteenth-century art—that give little support to their systems. In the past half century no new theories of style have taken root; in this country none was even proposed until quite recently.[3] This is not due so much to satisfaction with earlier theories as to the rise of a narrow scientism that has made philosophical speculation suspect. Although we cannot work without a theory of style, and although we continue to speak of classical, baroque, or painterly forms, we have allowed the systems that give meaning to these terms to slip into the unconscious, where they operate without the benefit of our control, as a barrier against new perceptions.

All of the major theories of style have been determinist in the sense that they define a preordained pattern of "evolution": the earlier phase of a style is *destined* to move toward the later. This is to say that at any stage in the process some force other than the will of artists must be at work directing invention toward the goal that ultimately is to be achieved. Twentieth-century scholars do not grant a priority of value to any phase of the evolution, but a value concept lurks in the shadows; if it is the destiny of styles to evolve as they did, then those works of art that promoted that evolution are destiny-fulfilling and those that did not are destiny-denying. The implication that the former are superior cannot be avoided. So, in our handbooks of the history of styles it appears that the chief function of any work of art is to contribute toward the works that follow it in a sequence; and the greater the contribution the more "significant" the work. The history of art has been fashioned into another version of the materialist success story.[4]

It is easy to understand how historians studying Greek, Gothic, or Renaissance art first formulated a biological model and later a more sophisticated theory of an innate dynamics of style; in those periods the sequence of works is so evident, the number of "unsuccessful" productions so few, that it appears almost inevitable that the Temple of Hera at Olympia should have led ultimately to the Parthenon, or the portal sculpture of the façade of Chartres to that of Rheims and finally to that by Claude Sluter. The process is orderly; it is similar in ancient Greece and late medieval Europe, which otherwise are dissimilar civilizations, and finally it is so much like biological growth that we are tempted almost irresistibly to define it as natural or necessary. At the least it would seem that the designer of Olympia and the sculptors of Chartres were making the first steps toward the goal that was gained by their successors.

But the account of a sequence of increasingly successful solutions to a problem contains a concealed germ of determinism. It introduces a trap into which historians habitually fall, as a result of the benefits of hindsight. When we review the surviving evidence of a process in the past we can see the effects as well as the causes of any event within the process. We can, for example, designate a work from a later moment as a "classic" solution and judge any earlier work according to what it contributed or failed to contribute to that solution. Or, with Wölfflin, we can praise—or cite as especially significant—solutions in the classic phase that contributed most to the making of the baroque phase.

We cannot erase our image of the totality of a style process in the past, but this need not discourage us from trying to interpret a work of art in terms of its proper context rather than its effects by gaining perspectives *within* the process at points short of its termination. At any one of these points we shall find an artist making a statue or designing a cathedral. He, too, is aware of works preceding his, and of works being made by his contemporaries, and these constitute an important source in the formation of his style. Given our habits of hindsight, it is necessary to add that he is not aware of the works that will follow his; he knows only past and present. He accepts and rejects aspects of what he finds in things about him and he adds something of his own. By his choice and by his contribution he moves a step—sometimes a leap—away from the past. Are we, then, justified in saying that he has moved toward the future?

In his terms the future is a void—how can he move toward it? If he dreams of its wonders, the dreams themselves, like his art, are creations of the present. He may happen to contribute to the future, but only by having concentrated primarily on the making of something intrinsically worthwhile in the present. If the sculptors at Chartres had visualized as the ultimate goal of their effort something like the Rheims figures, they surely would have carved something like the Rheims figures. Anyone who seeks to alter or to accelerate the change of style primarily in the hope of anticipating the future is likely to become, like the fashion designer, an expert in and purveyor of taste.[5]

What ultimately prevents an artist from controlling the future is the unpredictable behavior of his successors. His effect upon them is partly a matter of chance. It depends on his work being seen by someone and, if it is, on the receptivity of those who see it. Powerfully expressive works are more likely to be influential than weaker ones, but often they are rejected vigorously even by artists—not only when they are considered too radical (Michelangelo's late pietàs; William Blake's paintings) but even when they are considered not radical enough (Botticelli in 1505, Ingres in 1860).

These observations suggest a different approach to defining the process of change in style. What is called evolution in the arts should not be described as a succession of steps toward a solution to a given problem, but as a succession of steps away from one or more original statements of a problem. Each step, for the artist who takes it, is a probe that reaches to the limits of his imagination; he cannot consciously make a transition to a succeeding step, for if he visualizes something he regards as preferable to what he is doing, he presumably will proceed to do it, unless he is constrained in some way. So we cannot speak properly of a sequence of solutions to a given problem, since with each solution the nature of the problem changes.

We might visualize a style as a great canvas on which generations of artists have painted. The earliest ones set out a composition; later ones keep some of it, rub some out, and add some of their own; the next do the same and so on. At any moment in the process there is a complete picture, but no indication of what it will look like after the succeeding artist has done his share. At the close of the process, when some artists have started on another picture, this one is abandoned. But the final image, although composed of contributions from every artist, cannot be said to represent the aims of the earlier ones, or to represent a solution to the problem posed by the first of them.

The pattern of style change, then, is not determined by any destiny or by a common goal, but by a succession of complex decisions as numerous as the works by which we have defined the style. We can detect a pattern or distinguish a common problem because each decision in turn, by its choice of elements that are to be retained or rejected, and by its innovations, gives to the whole a determinable configuration. The configuration may *appear* purposeful or predestined because each successive work retains something of those that precede it and because its innovations, though not anticipated in earlier works, are coherently related to them. But what actually motivates the process is a constant incidence of probings into the unknown, not a sequence of steps toward the perfect solution.

So we return to an earlier observation that the pattern of change is a product of the tension in society and in the artist between the instinct for the stability and security of established schemes and the human capacity (resulting partly from biological and psychological differences) for creating something unique and individualized. Change is slow when the former is stronger, rapid when the latter prevails. As a rule, the factor of stability gets more support from society and its institutions, and the factor of change from the individual imagination; creative vision seldom is granted to groups. On the rare occasion when inspired patronage (Emperor Frederick II, Louis XIV) does more than the artist to motivate a style, the patron proves to be a creative individual who deserves to be called an artist. Given our background in the dialectic of German art history, it is necessary to emphasize that a nation, a religion, a *Zeitgeist,* is likely, except in its formative stage, to *resist rather than to promote* change in style. The idea that Germans, Roman Catholics, or Baroque Man embody a creative expressive will (I am recalling Riegl's "Kuntswollen") apart from the contributions of their artists I find incomprehensible and distasteful. If German art is German, it is not because any creative innovation in it has been produced by a mystical German Spirit, but because the nation and its artists show a tendency to keep certain kinds of innovation and to cast out other kinds. It is by this conservative, post facto, pressure that society affects art.

In proposing an alternative to current interpretations of patterns of change in style, I do not want to overrate the significance of chronological succession. To do so is to imply that each work necessarily is related more closely to its immediate predecessors than to others of an earlier stage of a style or in what we have defined as different styles. Indeed, the demands of society and the inclinations of artists make the innovations of the latest work by contemporaries in the same culture especially interesting, because they represent attempts to solve in a familiar language the kind of problem that is challenging at the moment. But the creative process is complex enough to be stimulated at many points; often the art of earlier times or of foreign places offers solutions to such problems, too—it even may suggest new problems, since its language is less familiar. So inspiration may come from far as well as from near; sometimes, especially in the formulation of a new problem, the distant past is actually closer than yesterday, as Roman art was closer than Gothic to the early Renaissance or primitive sculpture closer than Impressionism to some painters of the early 1900s.

In visualizing a style process, then, we must keep in mind that the individual innovations that give it pattern may be motivated as easily from outside as from within the style itself. Since the artist may experience and put to use in making a work of art anything in his environment, the historian must reconstruct as much of that environment as possible. Each work of art can be considered a repository of experiences entering from every direction in the artist's surroundings. That it owes a special debt to great predecessors in the same tradition, to the artist's teachers and colleagues, is no more than a plausible hypothesis; the role of these likely contributors must be weighed against that of all the works of art and other possible visual and nonvisual stimuli available to the artist.

This contextual approach—establishing an open, as opposed to a closed, system—has been used by the best modern historians and need not be described in detail, but the absence of it in a majority of studies, particularly those devoted to the work of individual artists, causes the assumption of an internal "evolution" from one work to the next to gain precedence over a deep analysis of the genesis of each work in succession.

My primary aim is to explain change in style as the manifestation rather of the imagination of individual artists than of historical forces that guide the actions of men and nations. But if we attributed every aspect of change to the operation of individual free will, we should not be able to explain the crucial phenomenon that originally encouraged deterministic and evolutionary theories: that sequences in quite different cultures may reveal similar patterns of change. In Greek, Gothic, and Renaissance art there appears to be a phase of equilibrium (usually described as *classic*) preceded by a more formalized, and followed by a freer phase. The fact that this pattern cannot be found in every sequence (e.g., Roman, Carolingian, nineteenth-century art) does not lessen our responsibility to explain it where it can be found, if it really is, as I believe, justified by the evidence of the monuments themselves. The problem is to discover an explanation of recurrent patterns that avoids on the one hand the tyranny of external historical forces or laws, and on the other hand the anarchy of mere chance.

Perhaps the clearest instance of a recurrent pattern in art is in the development of techniques from a stage of crudity and exploration to a stage of refinement. Sculptors, for example, may learn to carve with greater finesse or to cast more and more complex forms up to a point at which they attain—within the requirements of their style—a maximal potential for their body, tools, and materials. But technique does not always behave in this way; desire for progress in finesse occurs with variable intensity and even may be absent. Nor is it always possible, for some problems are solved at the start of a style, as when the Van Eycks, the first great painters to adopt oil glazes, achieved in their earliest surviving pictures a technical perfection that was never surpassed and rarely equaled.

There is no predetermined law of technical progress any more than there is a law of stylistic evolution. Even where we find techniques systematically refined to a point at which they reach their maximal potential, the succeeding steps cannot be predicted; at that point, artists may abandon the benefits of finesse (Manet as against the Salon painters); maintain the level achieved (Renaissance sculpture after Donatello) or be unable to sustain a high level of performance (mosaics and stained glass after 1300).

But while technique need not progress in refinement, it often does progress, and where technical problems are similar in different styles, the pattern of the progress is similar. Figural stone sculpture in the round is found in many diverse cultures; the typical pattern of change begins with stiff, frontal, and blocky figures and passes on to more mobile and rounded ones. One reason for this is that the technique of carving stone with a metal instrument does not change fundamentally; in any epoch the beginner has difficulty in turning a block into a human figure without retaining a blocklike character. The stone and the chisel impose their own laws that the artist must obey, and this is true at the most refined as well as at the most primitive level; there is a limit to freedom, to the length an unsupported arm can be extended without breaking, to the amount that can be cut from the lower position of the block without weakening the superstructure. Such limits—together with the classical heritage—explain certain similarities between highly developed techniques in different eras (the figure in Hellenistic sculpture, Bernini, Canova).

We find another example of the pressures exerted on the artist by technique in the development of skeletal structure in Gothic architecture. The invention of the rib vault and the flying buttress made it possible to lighten vaults and walls, which had been uniformly massive in Romanesque building, by concentrating stresses in chosen points. The lightening process was barely noticeable in the first experiments with bulky members, but once conceived, it was continued to the limit of the structural strength of stone (and even beyond, as demonstrated by the collapse of the choir of Beauvais Cathedral). A similar development of skeletal structures occurred with the introduction of the steel frame in the last century, in that it encouraged a systematic development away from massiveness and a metamorphosis of the masonry wall into glass, as in Gothic architecture.

In discussing figural sculpture and skeletal structure I have implied that there is something about the posing of the technical problem that suggests the direction in which a succession of solutions is likely to move. But what that something is cannot be explained in terms of technique alone; it is also a matter of formal and symbolic aims. What impels an artist along the path toward finesse is not so much a love of skill for its own sake as the conception of forms that are beyond the reach of existing skills. In figural sculpture this conception often has something to do with imitation; the style is drawn from its blocky beginnings to freer and more rounded forms because the human body is freer and more rounded than a block. So long as each artist in turn is intrigued by the problem of mimesis the process is likely to continue along the scale from the blocky to the illusionistic. The aims seldom are so simple; in one sense archaic Greek figural sculptors followed such a path, but at the same time they became increasingly intrigued by a sophisticated linear refinement that was not illusionistic; sculptors of the early fifth century BC had to reject that refinement vigorously in order to resume the mimetic process; but they in turn were drawn to idealization and generalization as well as to imitation of the human body.

The appeal of illusion best illustrates how the acceptance of a problem directs the artist, for he continually may adjust his art to conform to his perceptions of the world about him. The notebooks of Leonardo da Vinci are evidence of just this process of adjustment; nature is taken to be an objective goal toward which art can and should strive, and minute observations of it are systematically translated into the terms of painting. But the example of Gothic architecture proves how problems that cannot be solved by models in nature may still guide the process of solutions. The development of the skeletal structure was motivated, among other things, by a continuing desire to get more light. So long as this desire prevailed, the revision of forms was bound to be in the direction of substituting glass for stone—first, by concentrating stresses in the skeleton, and second by reducing the mass of the skeleton itself.

These observations do not modify my earlier strictures against predetermined patterns. The artist involved in such a process need not be striving toward a distant and unobtainable goal; he merely may be refining the solution of his predecessor. So the Gothic architect might say "At Soissons they managed to get more glass and thinner piers than at Paris but I shall do still better." He did not have the "classic" solution of Amiens in mind. The same psychology would apply even in cases where it might be said that there is only one correct solution, for example, the geometrical projection of a three-dimensional figure onto a two-dimensional plane in Renaissance painting.

One plausible explanation, then, for patterns of change in style is that where a certain problem posed at the start of a style continues to challenge artists over an extended span of time, and only where it suggests one type of solution rather than another, the process will show progressive refinement toward the preferred type of solution. When similar patterns are exhibited in different cultures, it is likely that the preferred type of solution is in some way similar. Refinement of this kind is neither inevitable nor necessarily desirable. The stability of Egyptian art is due to the fact that the solutions found at an early stage were considered optimal for centuries; by contrast, Roman and nineteenth-century art tended to shift often from one problem to another. In short, the psychology of artistic production admits but does not demand systematic and recurrent patterns of change in style.

On what grounds may we establish the limits or extent of a style, and differentiate it from other styles? Sometimes the question is partially answered by social-historical phenomena, as in epochs when a new style is started abruptly to satisfy a new need (early Christian architecture) or terminated by disaster or acculturation (Aztec, Northwest Indian art); or when it is coextensive with a closed political or geographical unit (ancient Egypt). Most of Western art, however, from Greek antiquity to the present day is a great mega-style within which we attempt to find plausible subdivisions that help to clarify the historical process.

Style is not the only framework within which historical process can be studied in the arts. Classes of works exemplifying a particular technique or a formal or symbolic convention reveal processes that may span several styles (e.g., the history of the dome, of perspective, of landscape painting, of the iconography of the immaculate conception). Another kind of framework is formed by the entire body of work produced within an arbitrarily chosen span of time such as a decade, a century, or a political reign. But limits of this kind, which presume some special significance to mere contemporaneity, are less likely to prompt fresh perceptions than those suggested by criteria of style deduced from works of art themselves. The framework most highly favored by students of Renaissance and modern art—life work of a single artist—is subject to similar deficiencies. It has the apparent advantage that its limits are inexorably fixed by mortality, and that it normally is coextensive with a consistent personal style that behaves as a minuscule echo of larger styles. But the presumption of consistency in human beings is unwarranted; the life span of an individual can be almost as insensitive a measure of style as any arbitrarily chosen segment of time. One artist or the artists of a century may adhere to a single style or shift from one style to another, and in our time such shifts are more the rule than the exception.

We distinguish one style from another by noting differences in the use of conventions, materials, and techniques. We do this by referring to an image of the norms of a style as a whole—style in the stable sense; but the image does not help to determine chronological or geographical limits. We can easily define generic differences between a Gothic and a Renaissance statue without being able to specify which statues are the first works of Renaissance sculpture.

We cannot find a specific moment at which one style gives way to another because the creative process involved in contributing to the formation of a new style is not of a different order from other creative acts. Both radical and conservative artists choose what they want to retain and what they want to reject from their tradition and contribute something of their own. When the balance favors retention, styles survive; when it favors rejection, they dissipate—though they may flourish, particularly in the provinces, long after desertion by the adherents of a new current. Since the extinction of one style is neither the prerequisite for nor, necessarily, the result of the initiation of another, old and new styles may exist side by side and mutually influence one another; and several new ones may coexist even in the same locale. (Paris of the early twentieth century harbored Cubism, Fauvism, Futurism, etc.)

A style, then, may be thought of as a class of related solutions to a problem— or responses to a challenge—that may be said to begin whenever artists begin to pursue a problem or react to a challenge that differs significantly from those posed by the prevailing style or styles. It is easy to detect a "significant" difference when artists vigorously reject major features of a traditional style and consciously aim to eliminate them from their work (Carolingian and Renaissance architecture, most early twentieth-century movements); but the distinction is quite unclear when the inventions of an artist who thinks of himself as a faithful bearer of tradition become the nucleus of a wholly new style, and one style flows into another without perceptible deflections. I think of Giotto and Duccio; they represent the flowering of the late Middle Ages and/ or the origins of the Renaissance, according to the historian's needs—to his definition of what is significant.

If we accept, then, a theory of confluent, overlapping, and interacting styles in place of a cyclical-evolutionary theory, the problem of fixing limits becomes much less urgent. The cycles of traditional art history must have beginnings and ends and new cycles need to be started by somebody; but the limits of confluent styles such as Gothic-Renaissance or Renaissance-Baroque can be fixed wherever the problem at hand requires, since they admittedly have no objective reality.

So long as it matters a great deal when and by whom a new style is initiated, it is difficult to distinguish the innovator from the genius, for the premium tends to be placed rather on novelty than on quality. While the two are not necessarily antithetical, a theory that exaggerates the importance of the initiation of styles cannot admit a dispassionate examination of the relationship of novelty to quality. The great artist is often an innovator, but his genius does not consist so much in the innovations themselves as in his ability to make them expressive and forceful. Innovations can be made by anyone, and often minor artists have conceived novelties that gained significance and force only in the hands of their betters. It is useful to designate as the start of a style the work of a great master, but often he is only one, and not always the first, to employ the new elements that characterize the style. But by the power of his art he frames the innovations into problems or challenges that continue to absorb his successors for generations. These successors are expressing their respect, not for the novelty but for the quality and authority of certain works of art. Being artists and not chroniclers, they tend to be indifferent to the question of whether those works were the first of their kind.

By taking a neutral position with respect to innovation, we awaken our perceptions to the realm of qualities that distinguished artists evoke from traditional elements in their art. Equally important is the evaluation of "minor" and "unsuccessful" styles, which are forced into the background by cyclical or dialectic theories that allow only one "major development" at one time. Because Leonardo and Raphael were so effective around 1505, the powerful and original art of Botticelli and Piero di Cosimo at the same period has been relegated to obscurity. It is revealing that this art, at the close of the Florentine early Renaissance, should have suffered more from our historical biases than other comparable terminal expressions—the late Michelangelo, El Greco, Vermeer, Turner. I believe that the members of this second group, who had little following in their time (younger artists could not emulate or understand their achievements), were "successful" in modern times because our own art had trained us to appreciate them. A theory that properly accredits the so-called minor and terminal expressions by accentuating the complexity of the context of any work of art should promote a subtler and more penetrating criticism.

If our image of a style is formed about a succession of works that develops the potential of a given problem, then styles of a relatively modest extension make the most rewarding frame for study. Grand, epochal frames such as Renaissance and Baroque are too large to help in making critical distinctions; we cannot agree on defining their problem. Renaissance scholars generally recognize this difficulty, but the monolithic image of the Baroque still causes works of radically opposed styles (Bernini and de Hooch!) to be forced into a single category. At the opposite extreme, the channel of works by a single artist may be too constricted, for reasons that I have already stated.

The subdivision of large epochs into lesser spans (Early and High Renaissance, Mannerism) is a compromise—partly a hangover of the old biological metaphor— which confuses criteria of style (*Mannerism* is a style term) with vague chronological measures (*Early Renaissance* means c. 1400–1500 in Italy and something else in other countries). Categories that are created for the purpose of making distinctions of style should be built logically on criteria of style. Furthermore, since the selection of a style as the object of study inevitably involves a presumption of cohesiveness, it should follow and not precede the hypothesis that a certain group of works is closely integrated and clearly distinguished from other groups. If we assume the existence of a style at the start (a danger with pat concepts such as "classic" and "romantic" periods, etc.) we shall delude ourselves into crowding into it what does not belong.

In this study I have tried to define principles based as far as possible on the examination of the creative process, so that the individual work of art, and not the force of some vague destiny, might be seen as the prime mover of the historical process revealed by style. So I have interpreted the concept of a style and of its limits as a generalization that we form, by comparing individual works, into shapes that are convenient for historical and critical purposes. I hope that my image of confluent and concurrent styles, by avoiding the implication of a predetermined evolution and hierarchy of values, may admit a method that is sensitive to the actual causes and effects of works of art, and that it may encourage the interpretation of any creative act in terms of the total context in which it was performed.

Notes

1.   Since this chapter appeared as "A Theory of Style" in the *Journal of Aesthetics and Art Criticism*, 20 (1962), 227–237, I have taken the opportunity to make some changes prompted by the cordial and penetrating criticisms of Herbert Blau, Donald Egbert, Walter Hipple, Timothy Kitao, Thomas Parkinson, and Leo Steinberg.

2.   Historians of the last century who adopted evolutionary metaphors generally misapplied them in support of deterministic theories of history (aided by some evolutionists who also were teleologists and "vitalists"). But modern evolutionary theory discourages all such efforts, and indeed offers the most convincing support for the nondeterminist kind of interpretation I am proposing here. See, e.g., George G. Simpson, *The Meaning of Evolution* (New Haven, 1949, 1960).

3.   See Vincent Scully, "The Nature of the Classical in Art," *Yale French Studies*, 19/20 (1957), 107ff.; J. S. Ackerman, "Art History and the Problems of Criticism," *Daedalus* (Winter 1960), 253ff. (reprinted in *The Visual Arts Today*, ed. Gyorgy Kepes [Middletown, Conn., 1960]); Lincoln Rothschild, *Style in Art* (New York, 1960); and George Kubler, *The Shape of Time* (New Haven, 1962).

4.   See Meyer Schapiro's classic survey and critique of style theory in *Anthropology Today*, ed. A. L. Kroeber (Chicago, 1953), 287–312; reprinted in *Aesthetics Today*, ed. Morris Philipson (Cleveland, 1961), 81–113. My earlier statement on this subject, "Art History and the Problems of Criticism" (see note 3), was criticized by Thomas Munro in the *Journal of Aesthetics and Art Criticism*, 19 (1961), 414f.

5.   I received some warranted criticism of my initial phrasing of this idea (article cited in note 3), which suggested that artists are not prophets, that they communicate present experience, not hope for the future. I should have seen that artists, like most of the rest of us, are eager to leave an imprint on the future, and that, unlike many of us, they may, if they are gifted and win an audience, be effective prophets. Many works of art, particularly since the Renaissance, have been motivated in part by the artist's desire to change the world. In my eagerness to attack historical determinism I failed to point out that while the ability of a particular work of art to compel a following is not *necessarily* a sign of its greatness, it can be. Thus historians and critics are justified in pointing to the impact of masterpieces on future generations as material evidence of their stature, so long as they do not invert the argument to use the quantity of influence of a given work as a measure of its quality.

Postscript

This paper was written during the year that I spent in Princeton, N.J. (1960–61), as a fellow of the Council of the Humanities, a group that had been formed to produce a set of volumes defining and assessing the role of each of the humanistic disciplines in education and scholarship. Rhys Carpenter and I shared the writing of the volume *Art and Archaeology*. "Style"—an earlier version of which I had published separately—was one of my five chapters.

Reading it again, I felt good about its style and persuasiveness and by the recollection that it upset a lot of fixed notions that prevailed at the time. I believe that much of its message is still relevant; but neither I nor anyone else would write anything like it today. At the time the concept of style seemed central to the practice of art history; it does not seem to be so important today. The impact of structuralism, post-structuralism, neo-Marxism, feminism, and other intervening critical modes on interpretation in the humanities helped us to see other dimensions of consciousness and of social structure affecting the form and content of works of art. Coming to terms with the radical attitudes of the late '60s was an anguishing process for me and for others of my generation who chose to do so (witness the gap in my bibliography between 1969 and 1972). The contrast between this essay and the one that follows demonstrates something of what it meant.

I have found George Kubler's book *The Shape of Time* (which appeared at the same time as ours) and his later refinements of his position the most challenging response to the issues of constancy and change in form, content, and technique that are central to all discussions of style. Kubler's system encompassed not only objects of fine arts but all artifacts. It represented on the one hand a reaction against the biological-evolutionary system of *La vie des formes*, by his mentor Henri Focillon (which he had translated), and on the other a by-product of his interest in pre-Columbian art, which brought him into a discipline dominated by anthropologists, whose systems of ordering material differed markedly from those of art historians.

Kubler's theory attempted to avoid using the concept of style as a basis for characterizing periods or sequences in anthropology and the history of art on the grounds that "different styles coexist at the same time [and] style is more synchronic than diachronic, consisting of acts undergoing change" (1979, p. 122). I had characterized the unfolding of a style as "a succession of steps away from one or more original statements of a problem"; Kubler proposed that "instead of the idea of style, which embraces too many associations, [I] have outlined the idea of a linked succession of prime works with replications, all being distributed in time as recognizably early and late versions of the same kind of action" (1962, p. 130) (which was strikingly close in its basic image to Thomas Kuhn's concurrent identification of "paradigms" and their effect on scientific sequences [*The Structure of Scientific Revolutions,* 1962]). I should say in retrospect that a weakness of both systems is that "original statements" or "prime objects" are easily identified in some classes of artifacts and impossible to identify in others.

A major contribution of Kubler's 1979 paper was the identification of two etymological sources of the term "style," the one from Greek *stylos,* adapted by Vitruvius to the modes of architecture, and the other from Latin *stilus,* which refers to writing. His interpretation of the Greek term as representing "the arts of spatial organization" and the Latin "the arts of temporal form" is nice, but it strikes me as too orderly.

Morris Weitz, in demonstrating the "irreducible vagueness" of definitions of Mannerism as a style, showed that my definition of style in terms of "a succession of steps away from one or more original statements of a problem" was problematic, at least in the case of sub-styles that, as in the case of Mannerism, are satellites of or responses to preceding styles.

The decline of interest in style on the part of historians of the arts indicates changes in approach not only within these disciplines but in recent art itself; the pluralism of contemporary art defeats efforts to define the style or styles of our times; the most frequently used label, Postmodern, inherently avoids a style inference and refers rather to an attitude toward the goals of modernism. While in this respect it resembles Mannerism, much Postmodern art rejects the concept of style with the same decisiveness as it rejects traditional critical values.

In the course of the 1960s, Structuralist criticism and history encouraged a shift from diachronic to synchronic treatments of past cultures that tended to take the focus off of style definitions. Recent critical directions, particularly deconstruction, have emphasized the futility or presumptuousness of efforts to establish style definitions with any degree of objectivity.

None of the critics of the uses of the concept of style has proposed how we might redesignate the sequences we know as Hellenistic, Gothic, Renaissance, Baroque, or Impressionism, and they are probably too well rooted to change. But the intense discussion of the issue has called attention to the problems inherent in the use of labels that imply a unity, that encourage unwarranted exclusions, and that discourage the formulation of new and better ways to place artifacts in time.

Ackerman, James A. "Art and Evolution," in Gyorgy Kepes, ed., *The Nature and Art of Motion* (New York, 1965), 32–40.

Ackerman, James S. "On Rereading 'Style'," *Social Research,* 45 (1978), 153–163. A discussion of Meyer Schapiro's celebrated article in Alfred Krober, ed., *Anthropology Today* (Chicago, 1953), 287–312.

Alpers, Svetlana. "Style Is What You Make It: The Visual Arts Once Again, " in B. Lang, ed., *The Concept of Style* (Philadelphia, 1979), 95–118. Suggests that our concept of style is grounded in classical and Italian Renaissance studies and that it is misleading when applied to northern European art.

Frankl, Paul. *Zu Fragen des Stils* (1962), ed. Ernst Ullman (Leipzig, 1988). A systematic study, allied to the author's monumental *System der Kunstwissenschaft* (Brünn and Leipzig, 1938); it is a pity that it could not have entered the arena when it was completed, shortly before the author's death, contemporaneously with Kubler's book and ours. It might have further stimulated the lively interest in the subject at that moment.

Gombrich, E. H. "Style," *International Encyclopedia of Social Sciences* (New York, 1968), 15: 352–361. Especially valuable for a section on the influence of ancient rhetorical literature on the formation of the concept of style in the Italian Renaissance.

Goodman, Nelson. "The Status of Style," *Critical Inquiry,* 1 (1975), 799–811.

Kubler, George. *The Shape of Time* (New Haven, 1962).

Kubler, George. "Towards a Reductive Theory of Visual Style," in B. Lang, ed., *The Concept of Style* (Philadelphia, 1979), 119–128.

Meyer, Leonard. "Toward a Theory of Style," in B. Lang, ed., *The Concept of Style* (Philadelphia, 1979), 3–44.

Meyer, Leonard. *Style and Music: Theory, History, and Ideology* (Philadelphia, 1989).

Miles, Josephine. "Toward a Theory of Style and Change," *Journal of Aesthetics and Art Criticism,* 22 (1963), 63–67.

Prown, Jules David. "Style as Evidence," *Winterthur Portfolio,* 15 (1980), 197–210. A stimulating discussion of the issues involved in applying the concept of style to objects of material culture.

Weitz, Morris. "Genre and Style," in *Contemporary Philosophic Thought: The International Philosophy Year Conferences at Brockport* (Albany, 1970), 3: 183–218.

Wollheim, Richard. "Pictorial Style: Two Views," in B. Lang, ed., *The Concept of Style* (Philadelphia, 1979), 129–148.

2

Transactions in Architectural Design

Vitruvius, writing in the first century, BC, set out three essential components of architectural design: *firmitas, commoditas, and venustas* (which his Elizabethan translator rendered as Firmness, Commodity, and Delight), and ever since they have remained the cornerstones of design and criticism.[1] But the forces at work in the design process seem to me to be too complex to be so neatly categorized, and I propose in the following the image of an open field system in which architectural decisions are made through an unlimited number of transactions among a variety of people who are or should be interested in the making of particular buildings.

The most obvious way in which a work of architecture differs from other works of art is that it is always made to order. It has a client who asks the architect to design something to fit a stated need. That need is defined—sometimes clearly, sometimes vaguely—by the social organization of the moment and by the client's particular concerns, and is articulated in a program which is a definition of the anticipated functions of the desired building. It is a basic precept of the relationship between the client and the architect that the latter's primary obligation is to provide forms and spaces that best accommodate the letter and the spirit of the program. And much historical and critical writing evaluates works of architecture according to this precept: the fulfillment of the client's needs is as much a criterion of success as the proper calculation of stresses that keeps a building from collapsing.

It may seem reasonable, even inevitable, that architectural practice should be based on an understanding that architects, like lawyers and doctors, should discover their clients' needs and accommodate them to the best of their abilities. But current discussion within the legal and medical professions of the conflict between service to private individuals who can pay, and to the public who cannot, suggests an expanded or altered definition of professional responsibility. Actually, the conflict between public and private interest may be more acute in architecture than in other professions: the kind of buildings architects design are costly and are made possible only by the wealth

From *Critical Inquiry* 1, no. 2 (December 1974), 229–243.

of a small segment of the population or the state, yet every one raised affects the lives of people other than the one who makes the program and pays the architect for his services. Furthermore, the decisions of architects are embodied in buildings that last for generations, even for millennia, so that the overwhelming majority of people in our culture live and work in places designed not only for other people but for other times and conditions. For this reason, even the "private" practice of architecture involves responsibilities to a widespread constituency.

The complexity of the client-architect relationship and of the transactions involved in defining a program can be illustrated by a hypothetical example: let us imagine that the members of the Board of Education of a certain town have voted to build a new school.[2] They select a particular site, and an individual or a group designated by them gathers data and defines the nature of the facilities needed—a certain number of classrooms, a library, washrooms, athletic and recreational areas, offices for administration, a teachers' room, and so on, with estimates of the amount of space required by each and of the desirable interrelationship of one with another. A separate set of more general directives is embodied in local law, with its zoning and planning regulations and its standards for the minimal amount of space, light, air, insulation, sanitation facilities, fire protection, and the like for the several components of the project. Finally, on the most general and least negotiable level, there is the character and position of the site—on one hand its natural topography, soil conditions, exposure to sun and wind, etc., and on the other its man-made environment, particularly access to communication, transportation, and public services; both require particular design responses. These constitute the core of the quantifiable factors in the program, some of which the architect may help to clarify or modify, but which for purposes of discussion may be accepted as the givens of a project.

Beyond this lies the large area of cultural, social, and aesthetic desiderata in which the client and architect must negotiate for a determining voice. They involve choices of form—the nature of the masses and spaces of a building, materials, colors, textures—and of symbol—the way in which a building expresses its purpose and intent, as in the choice between a historical and avant-garde style. In practice, formal and symbolic aspects are intricately interwoven. In the Vitruvian tradition, such considerations are assigned to the aesthetic category and are discussed independently of utilitarian considerations, but no separation is justified. A particular theory of education, for example, influences not only the size and arrangement of classrooms but their quality as well: a school system that seeks to make elementary pupils feel at home and protected will be predisposed to an intimacy of scale, warmth of materials, casualness of arrangement, etc. Can such choices be called aesthetic rather than practical?

Criteria for the selection of an architect usually harmonize with the cultural-social-aesthetic aspects of the program. In the public school system, the selection is ordinarily made, however, at a level higher than that of the programming committee for a particular school (by the board, the superintendent, or even the mayor or city council): in one case because officials take seriously the duty to provide safe, economical, and pleasing public edifices; in another because they seek to control the assignment of lucrative commissions. In any event, the choice of the architect has as great an influence on the ultimate character of the school as the choices made by the architect, because professionals well enough established to be contenders for a public commission usually have a reputation for a certain style of design and/or for certain administrative or technological skills.

To whom is the architect responsible? Each constituency within the school system has different interests at stake. A program for the school as written by a group of administrators would be wholly different from one prepared by teachers, pupils, maintenance staff, or by parents (e.g., the administrators and maintenance staff might choose concrete floors as being inexpensive and easy to maintain, while the teachers would seek a material that would be easier on the feet and would reduce noise). The architect in our society usually feels a moral responsibility to accommodate the needs of each of these groups, but in the many instances where they are incompatible the decision and the program will reflect the balance and imbalance of power within the system. Decision-making power is always in the hands of those who control the money; in public schools they are the administrators, watched over by higher public officials and by the taxpayers; in private schools, the more committed members of the Board of Trustees, usually parents. In addition, banks and other mortgage-granting institutions influence design decisions because of their concern that the proposed structure satisfy not only the needs and taste of the borrower but of potential purchasers in the event that the borrower should default. This predisposes them toward conservative designs and against experiment.

The architect produces, first for the client and ultimately for the builder, projects in the form of drawings and models representing the translation of the program into physical spaces and masses. This takes time: the client is not usually experienced enough to conceive a usable or complete program without extensive help and persuasion from the architect, and physical planning cannot begin until the program is minutely articulated. According to their respective principles and personalities, architects may involve the client in every step of this process, urging him to define his needs and intuiting his unexpressed desires, or the architect may impose his own conception on the client. There are no clear rules to guide the relationship. Conflict between the client's and the architect's vision of what a building ought to be is inevitable. It can arise from the latter's commitment to personal interest and career (style of design, desire to produce a prize-winning building) or from his orientation to conflicts of interest between the client and the intended users, neighbors, etc. (E.g., an architect who wished to maximize the well-being of inmates in designing a prison might be opposed by the warden, the Department of Correction and its officers, and even a majority of taxpayers.) Such conflict can be minimized only when the architect seeks to represent exclusively the interest of the client who pays the bills and to ignore any incompatible interests of those who are to use or to be affected by the building.

In determining their responsibility toward society as distinct from the demands of their clients, the architects may not be concerned only with the interests of the actual users of projected buildings. A building alters the natural and man-made environment physically, socially, and economically, and can have an impact on the lives of people who never have cause to enter it: it may increase traffic congestion by bringing more people into the neighborhood, require a change in the public service systems such as water supply and sewage, lower or raise property values in the surrounding area, increase or decrease the city's tax revenues, affect neighbors' access to light or a view, accelerate or retard a large-scale movement of population, and so on. But the attitudes of interested nonusers may not always be in harmony; for example, an improvement leading to increased rents is likely to be favored by landlords, financers, and city officials, and opposed by tenants; architects may find themselves in the position of arbitrating such conflicts.

As the program matures, design decisions begin to be accommodated to another body of participants, the manufacturers and building trades. In electing particular methods of construction and specific architectural elements, the designer and client have to consider first the availability of the products, the materials, and the labor skills required, and second the cost of available options in relation to the benefits promised. Decisions of this kind cannot, however, be made simply with the catalog and slide rule because the easiest and most economic solution may be unsatisfactory for a variety of other reasons. Conflicts between aesthetic and economic considerations are among the most frequent; the designer may elect brick exterior walls rather than exposed concrete because he thinks they look better and harmonize with surrounding buildings, but he may be unable to justify the high cost of the hand labor involved in masonry work as against formwork for concrete. Or practical and community considerations may generate the conflict: medieval architects and communities had to decide whether the economy of roofing their churches in wood as against the far more costly cut-stone vaulting justified the greater risk of fire. Decisions of this kind do not, however, always involve simply the balance of cost against benefit, because the range of choice offered by a given market and labor force is restricted. In our time, the number of elements that can be made to order is steadily decreasing; the execution, for example, of hand-carved ornament is virtually a lost art; increasingly the choice of architectural detail is limited to what is offered in manufacturers' catalogs. Finally, the relationship of the designer to the contractors and building craftsmen is a transaction involving as much diplomacy and negotiation as his relationship to the client. He must adjust his conceptions to their way and rate of work, often including guild rules that inhibit innovation.

Finally, in addition to the legitimate interests of those nonusers affected by the building at the time it is completed, the interests of unborn generations warrant an advocate, since buildings last longer than people and frequently longer than the institutions they are designed to serve. A building program sensitive to future users would provide an equilibrium between the potential life span of the design solution and the life span of the social functions to be accommodated. There is a disequilibrium when a function that may be short-lived is housed in a specialized building permanently fixed in indestructible steel and reinforced concrete construction (such as elementary schoolrooms being built today of uniform size with permanent interior walls and fixed rows of seats facing the teacher at a time when the institution of the "open classroom" requiring flexible space may be widely adopted), and conversely when a relatively unchanging function is accommodated by tacky, impermanent structures. Many of the earliest Christian churches still serve as well after 1,600 years, partly because they were designed as simple and well-built meeting halls without integral accommodation to the liturgical practice of the moment of construction, and partly because, unlike most other institutions, the Church—particularly the Catholic church—has resisted drastic change in its functions.

Few institutions in our culture will enjoy the long-range permanence of the church. Modern institutions not only change rapidly in nature and function but in location as well: office buildings and stores located in the center of great cities have been made obsolete by the migration of the commercial market and rapid deterioration of their environment. Even without such unfavorable conditions, the structure of financing and taxation (e.g., short-term tax shields extended by city governments to attract and hold business) has encouraged the construction of new commercial buildings and the destruction of others only one generation old. Architects and planners have not adjusted to the mobility of modern life to the extent of offering acceptable alternatives to fixed and permanent building: the mobile home, an imaginative response both to the migratory character of a large segment of our population and to the demand for inexpensive mass-produced single-family shelter, is scorned by the architectural profession and its design left to the market-research process that determines the style of automobiles. The result is that the environment is marred rather than enhanced by a type of structure destined to cover the land.

Many buildings have survived millennia after being abandoned by the institution for which they were first designed. This testifies in some cases to their flexibility (as the second-century Temple of Hadrian, which serves as the Rome Stock Exchange), but more often to the values embodied in their design—typically aesthetic (the Parthenon, the Alhambra) but also historical and associational (Independence Hall, the House of Seven Gables). Although the latter values cannot be anticipated in a design, they can enter the planning process indirectly, as when a program requiring the destruction of old buildings puts aesthetic-historic values against the validity for modern functions of the intended replacement. And it occurs whenever the decision to preserve an old building involves remodeling it to serve functions that may be inimical to integral features of the original design: the issue had been raised by a project to put a new west front on the U.S. Capitol. In resolving these conflicts, the interest of future generations is again relevant; values change, and the old eyesore we might want to demolish today could become tomorrow's paragon of beauty; respect for the past and for the future go hand in hand.

These instances illustrate the relevance of aesthetic and associational values in coming to what in traditional design and criticism are regarded as utilitarian decisions. In some cases these values prove to be even more "functional" than so-called practical considerations in design: many modern public housing projects embodying a high standard of convenience and space have produced overall a lower quality of life for the tenants than the old and decayed dwellings they replaced that may have had such unquantifiable amenities as humane scale, continuity with a tradition, and a neighborhood with variety and unique character. The distinction between "use" values and "surplus" values, to interpolate the Marxian terms, may be dependent on cultural conditioning and economic status: the urban middle class (which provides the decision makers in public housing enterprises) tends to regard a fully equipped and private bathroom, hot running water, and elevators as being more essential than intercourse with neighbors and apartment blocks of limited height.

The poor, who have to sacrifice physical safety and a sense of belonging somewhere for these amenities, are less likely to perceive them as basic (though in our society the attitudes of all economic strata are becoming homogenized into the bourgeois mold of the mass media). In fact, a high-rise federal housing project (Pruitt-Igoe),[3] well-equipped, of good construction, and conveniently sited in central Saint Louis was completely evacuated less than twenty years after its completion because it had been made uninhabitable by the vandalism of its own tenants, apparently in response to its impact on their lives. Decision making in such situations involves weighing the cost of remodeling a restricted number of units in old neighborhoods, which is almost always higher than building new mass housing, against providing a greater amount of shelter for people in need. A decision between quality of environment and quantity plus efficiency is hard to make on behalf of a nonhomogeneous and usually unidentified body of other people.

The difficulties arising from the different values of designers and users in public housing have led to much discussion and experiment over the last decade of strategies for giving the prospective tenants a voice in design decisions. The results have been poor, first because those whose opinions are sought have no conception of the possible options and are forced to formulate their expectations within the mold of the inadequate housing they have seen around them, and second because the major decisions are ultimately made on the administrative level without consultation. These efforts, which, incidentally, have not been made in planning places of work or other public facilities, have served only to demonstrate that the environment is shaped by those who possess or are invested with wealth and power, whether or not they wish to be responsive to the desires of those whom their projects are intended to serve.

To some extent they show also that the problem is not that the architect fails to give people what they want but that people don't know how to want—that is, how to formulate their real needs and to distinguish what they perceive as needs from mere habits of behavior and clichés of expression. The architect cannot compensate for this failure because both he and his clients are molded by the existing social and ideological structure; the building they seek to realize is the shell of some social institution and cannot relevantly be more successful in design than the institution can be in function. Truly imaginative architecture that has worked has usually been built for vigorous, confident, and creative institutions. The uncertainties of our present institutions are revealed by the meaningless formalism of their new buildings, and the fault does not lie more with the designers than with the clients and users.

A work of architecture is a social artifact arising from a great number of transactions in which conflicts are resolved. The architect stands near the center of a network of interactions that initially involves the client or his representatives but also, and not less significantly, others who will be users of the building, who may fall into a number of different groups with different and at times opposed interests, others who will not use the building but whose lives will be affected by it (or by the loss of what it replaces)—officers of the law or of government, building contractors and the building trades and manufacturers, funding agencies, and, finally, on a different plane, and as if by proxy, those in the near and far future who will use and be affected by his decisions. Although the architect is a key figure in many of these transactions, many other transactions affecting the nature of the building take place among the other participants— as when the client negotiates with the contractor and the banker, the contractor with the trades and the public works department, and so on.

Still, the architect has a wide latitude of choice, particularly in our time, when the institutions that build are too insecure and uncertain about the future to define precisely what they want their buildings to do or to express. Left without guidance, the architect is forced to choose between (1) trying to imagine what the client needs, (2) making a striking building that will call attention to himself, and (3) attending to needs of others than his client, or some mixture of the three. This choice is moral (assuming that those others are less powerful than the client): it involves the option of acting on a sense of responsibility to society with the consequent risks incurred by departing from a pragmatic position of self-interest. And it makes moral criteria become relevant for the critic or historian assessing his achievement. When the architect takes a position on a conflict between the interests of the client and of those of the prospective user or banker in favor of one or the other party, we must judge whether the decision was right or wrong. Although Ruskin found no obstacle to this conclusion, in our times historians and critics have claimed to make judgments on "purely" aesthetic grounds, uncontaminated by moral commitments. (The claim is hypocritical: International Style architecture was praised by critics as being pure, clean, honest, etc., etc.)

The root of the resistance to moral criteria in the criticism of architecture is the fear that they are so easily subsumed into social-political commitments, with the result that the criticism of architecture becomes a tool of political propaganda. I believe that the risk is inescapable but that intelligent criticism will not be trapped by it; we are better off confronting it consciously than being unconscious pawns of a traditional morality. A criticism that avoids the issue of moral options simply fails to account for the actual nature of the transactions involved in designing buildings. The historian faces the additional difficulty of having to assess the moral options in past choices in the light of the value system within which they were made: to represent the Egyptian pyramids as unsuccessful because they glorified despotism would be to impose our (irrelevant) value on the assessment of a choice made on quite other criteria.

I do not underestimate the difficulties involved in applying moral criteria: they are illustrated in the incapacity of Marxist theory to deal with architecture. Because capital and a position of privilege are prerequisites for building, existing architecture can be seen as an instrument and a symbol of repression. Consequently, criticism is pointless until social change gives to the "people," the users, the decision-making power. But whether or not this view of society is valid, it is possible to consider how in imperfect or even deplorable social conditions there may be ways of making better rather than worse architectural decisions.

The better decisions have been made in situations where parties to the transactions involved were in harmony, where individual interests were subsumed into a communal interest. They emerged not because power shifted from one group to another but because it became relatively diffused. The most obvious instances are cases of communal building in which there is no identifiable architect, and exceptional designing and building skills are scattered among the participants—the precincts of the Dogon people, the Greek settlements of the Aegean Islands, the Italian communes of the thirteenth and fourteenth centuries, or some New England towns of the post-Revolutionary period. Harmony of that degree is harder to achieve when an architect is involved because his presence injects into the group a figure who must to some extent remain distinct. He is called upon because distinctiveness or distinction is expected: the anonymity of the communal settings I have cited may be good and the totality pleasing but, like all results achieved by consensus, it works precisely because of the lack of focus, contrast, and other characteristics of designs conceived by the individual imagination. Moreover, even the best vernacular expressions are conservative and unlikely to adjust to changing culture. The individual is needed to invent new contexts for the expression of the communal spirit; without him the vernacular would lack even a vocabulary.

The architect's power to formulate has caused him at times in the past to be deified as was Imhotep, the designer of the first surviving pyramid, and Michelangelo, who was called "divino." The very term "creativity" was first applied to artistic conception in the Renaissance to suggest a parallel to God's creation. Since the Renaissance, the architect often has been celebrated not as the member of the community charged with providing a shape to serve its needs and to convey its message but rather as an aesthetic shaman whose inventions might be visited upon a populace grateful for his fortuitous concessions to its wishes and hopes. My aim in this essay has been to suggest a framework within which the autonomy and authority given to the designer by the tradition of European aesthetics might be restrained in the interests of the community. This has involved both the pragmatic formulation of the design process as a transactional field and the moral formulation of a complementarity between the designer's power of free imagination and his responsibility toward the whole company of those affected by his invention.

Notes

The author's concept of transactions is indebted to that of John B. Spiegel, *Transactions: The Interplay between Individual, Family, and Society* (New York, 1972).

1.   In today's terminology they appear as the technological, the utilitarian or functional, and the aesthetic components of architecture.

2.   The choice of a public administrative body as the client in this illustration does not mean that decisions will be in the public interest.

3.   See Lee Rainwater, "The Lessons of Pruitt-Igoe," in *Housing in Urban America*, ed. J. Pynoos, R. Schafer, and C. Hartman (Cambridge, Mass., 1973).

Postscript

This paper was written in the aftermath of the 1960s, a decade of increased awareness of social inequalities that inevitably affected architectural discourse. The urban renewal and public housing achievements of the preceding decade were encountering criticism for their failure to preserve what was represented as being the familial, humane environment of traditional urban communities. Many architects experimented with "advocacy" design— roughly equivalent to the work of public defenders in law—which invited potential users to share in the process of designing public spaces and accommodations.

"Transactions" was one evidence of a widespread awareness among critics of architecture that the modern movement was at a crossroads. Architectural modernism had a resolutely moral/behavioral program that promised on the one hand the liberation of bourgeois life and work from the formal constraints of traditional architecture, and on the other the amelioration of the oppressive urban conditions of the industrial age. In the years following the First World War, socialist governments in Europe supported urban redevelopment and mass housing on an unprecedented scale, with apparently successful results. The Congrès International d'Architecture Moderne was founded by Le Corbusier and other leading European architects in the late 1920s to provide a forum for the discussion of urban planning and housing issues. When I first became aware of modernist buildings and ideas as a student in the '30s, I was swept away in the almost religious fervor of the belief that architecture could make a better world.

It was only after the Second World War that modernist ideals were put into practice widely in the United States, in federally supported redevelopment and mass-housing projects. Results fell far short of expectations, for reasons discussed in my essay. In the same period, the aesthetic principles of modernism triumphed, filling city cores with abstract glass boxes that, one generation removed from their European origins, seemed bland and expressively mute. This helped to bring about two divergent reactions against modernist claims and achievements—one socially and the other formally oriented.

The first (which this essay and another cited below of 1980 represent) still focused on urban and public design, retaining the ameliorative goals of modernism but rejecting the abstract, totalitarian approach that completely cleared away the older portions of cities in order to start afresh with new utopias. This approach had been taken by Team Ten, a group of younger architects that broke away from the CIAM (it survives in the journal *Spazio e So-*

cietà, an Italian-American collaborative publication), and by the practitioners of advocacy design. But, from the 1960s on, governments in Europe and America greatly reduced support for urban renewal and housing, and the cultural mood of the '70s and '80s has discouraged an architecture of social amelioration.

The second, a counterrevolution that became known as Postmodernism, proceeds on the premise that architectural design has proven to be incapable of resolving problems that are at root essentially political. Insofar as Postmodern theory addresses the social dimension, it holds that the social contribution architects are best qualified to make is in the realm of expression, by communicating cultural values through symbolism and affect. Postmodernist thinking encompasses widely divergent positions, from that of Peter Eisenman, who approaches architectural design as an abstract syntax of self-referential form, to that of Leon Krier, who seeks to recreate environments of classical purity with the literal vocabulary of ancient Rome; but none of the positions is directed toward amelioration.

The neglect in current discourse of the social implications of architecture is in sharp contrast to the evolution of architectural history since the modernist period, and this contrast is a sign of disarray in our intellectual life. Architectural history in the course of the thirty-five years that I have been practicing it has moved steadily toward the interpretation of the architecture of past times in terms of social, political, and economic forces. The constricted formalism of Hitchcock and Johnson's *The International Style* of 1932, which focused on individual and period style evolving in an autonomous architectural culture, was characteristic of both the historical and the critical stance of that time. It took me two decades of writing before I quite shook that mode. My book on Michelangelo (see chapter 13, below) was rather formalist. The one on Palladio turned to social, economic, and theological interpretations, but it was still a single-personality monograph, which is in a way a survival of formalist interpretation, since it focuses attention on the sequence of an individual's achievements rather than on the context in which particular works were created. Today I work more with context and ideologies as the background for history and criticism.

The current situation in historical interpretation is the outcome of a remarkable flowering of ideas in Europe during the '60s and '70s, involving structuralism and its analog, semiology, the *Annales* group of historians in France, and neo-Marxism, notably that of the Frankfurt school.

Though the impact of this diverse development cannot be characterized in a sentence, the general thrust was to focus attention on the synchronic study of events or buildings in the light of the complexity of ideas and the social, economic, and political conditions of their moment rather than to see them in diachronic terms, as part of a sequence of like occurrences or buildings. Further, the neo-Marxist achievement was not simply to reveal the significance of the material economic base supporting the superstructure of cultural activity, but to open up the sphere of ideological interpretation. This suggested to the historian that architectural works might be seen in terms of the ways in which they fulfilled not only the stated needs of the client, that is, the program, but also those ideological needs that were subliminal—the unconscious requirements so intimately tied to the social and class structure that only an outsider like a historian or anthropologist could perceive them. This made it possible to subject the program itself, as well as the design of a building, to criticism.

It seems paradoxical that criticism and the writings of architects have moved away from references to the societal contexts while historians—not to speak of psychiatrists and anthropologists—have been moving toward them. We are all subject to the same intellectual influences, and we are all addressing the built environment. The fact that designers, now that they are employing motives from the past and from vernacular architecture, have become much more sympathetic to history than they were at the end of the modernist period ought to make for a community of outlook. But history as it is seen in a Postmodern mode is not the same as ours: it is rather one of free-floating motives unrooted in culture, while we have become increasingly interested in roots.

In one sense, the new history is isolated from, and the new architecture is attuned to, present-day society. In politics there has been a retreat from efforts to define and to deal in modern ways with major social pathologies such as the inadequacy of housing and health care and racial and sexual inequality. The socialist parties abroad and the left at home are in disarray; all of the major Western governments are now headed by leaders suspicious of social programs and oriented to individual entrepreneurial initiative. The condition is reflected in architecture, which has retired from the public arena to seek engagement with the individual client. We ought, however, to be able to come together in support of an architecture capable of transforming, as great architecture has done in earlier centuries, those traditional aspects that arouse a response and stimulate the imagination today. This means seeking a deeper knowledge of the forces that formed past architecture and a committed search for the forms that embody our communal aspirations today.

Can we ask architects to take on problems that no one is putting before them? Yes. Le Corbusier's Citrohan house or Ville Radieuse and Wright's Usonian houses were not conceived on commission but as a way of articulating their ideas about the accommodation of modern life. It was an ethical dimension to their careers—an effort to serve not simply the fortuitous client but the whole of humanity—that is less in evidence today.

Architects, as specialists of the man-made physical environment, have the opportunity and responsibility to suggest solutions that under more hospitable political conditions could ultimately stimulate further experiment in an abandoned area.

Ackerman, James. "The History of Design and the Design of History," *Via*, 4 (1980), 19–28.

Ackerman, James. "Social Concern and Intellectual Discourse," *Places*, 6 (1990), 68–71.

Broady, Maurice. "Social Theory in Architectural Design," *Arena: The Architectural Association Journal*, 81 (1966), 149–154.

Broady, Maurice, ed. *People and Buildings* (New York, 1972).

Gans, Herbert. *People and Plans: Essays on Urban Problems and Solutions* (New York, 1968).

Gutman, Robert. "Human Architecture, a View of the Profession," *Journal of Architectural Education*, 21 (1978).

Gutman, Robert. "Patrons or Clients?," *Harvard Architectural Review*, 6 (1987), 148–159.

Kieran, Stephan. "The Architecture of Plenty: Theory and Design in the Marketing Age," *Harvard Architectural Review*, 6 (1987), 102–113.

Lang, Jon. "The Built Environment and Social Behavior: Architectural Determinism Reexamined," *Via* 4 (1980), 147–153.

Sommer, Robert. *Personal Space: The Behavioral Basis of Design* (Englewood Cliffs, N.J., 1969).

Tafuri, Manfredo. *Progetto e utopia* (Bari, 1973). (I do not cite the English translation because it is incomprehensible.)

Tzonis, Alexander. *Toward a Non-oppressive Environment* (New York, 1972).

Woods, Shadrach. *The Man in the Street* (Harmondsworth, 1975).

3

Interpretation, Response: Toward a Theory of Art Criticism

Il faut affirmer le plaisir du texte contre les indifférences de la science et la puritanisme de l'analyse idéologique; il faut affirmer la jouissance du texte contre l'aplatissement de la littérature à son simple agré-
ment. [It is necessary to emphasize the pleasure of the text in opposition to the indifference of scientific
(criticism) and the puritanism of ideological analysis. It is necessary to affirm the enjoyment of the text in
opposition to the leveling of literature simply to a question of comprehension.]
Roland Barthes, *Le plaisir du texte*, 1973

Barthes's challenge to his literary colleagues is equally applicable to art historians and
critics. We, too, have nearly analyzed away the enjoyment that makes our work worthwhile. We have not yet faced the limitations of that positivistic interpretation that traces
meanings and forms to their sources, or the coercions of idealist and materialist theory
descending from Kant and Marx. Barthes did not imply that interpretation should be
abandoned in order to allow historians and critics to respond to works of art as entities
of value in themselves but rather that the best criticism emerges from an equilibrium of
interpretation and response.[1]

Art criticism comes out of interactions between a subject and an object. Interpretation in its simplest sense focuses critical attention on the import and function of
the object, while the articulation of response focuses on the experience of the subject.
Interpretation is not by this definition "objective." It inevitably is colored by the perspectives and personality of the subject. It could be called the object-oriented aspect of
criticism.

An analogy to personal relationships may clarify these distinctions. In interacting with a friend or someone we love, we try to understand his motivations and
feelings and what he means to tell us by behaving in a certain way, saying certain things,
or making certain gestures. This is like some aspects of interpretation. At the same
time, we try to articulate our reactions and feelings to the other as a particular person-

From James S. Ackerman and M. H. Abrams, *Theories of Criticism* (Washington, D.C.: Library of Congress, 1984), 33–53.

ality and to find how best to implement them in the relationship, which is like response. The two processes are too intricately intertwined to grant either priority over the other. We are drawn to people and to works of art because of both their nature and ours.

I intend in what follows to comment only briefly on interpretation because its character is defined in the practice of most critical and historical writing today. My primary aim is to define response, since what I mean by that term has not been much attended to recently. And I shall conclude with observations on some illuminating parallels between the practice of interpretation and response and the workings of the brain in processing perceptions by a collaboration of the left and right hemispheres.

I

Interpretation has to be built on documentation.[2] Its validity depends on a command of the accessible data relating to the object. The purpose of interpretation is to help others to understand the object through discussing the conditions in which it was made, its function, its message, its relation to other works of a similar kind, the intentions of the maker, and other factors affecting its genesis and mode of presentation.

The interpretation of past art involves both the attempt to recreate the interaction between the work and its original viewers and an assessment of its potential impact at the present moment. These aims cannot be definitively fulfilled because every interpreter employs a different mix of evidence and draws from it his peculiar conclusions; but such pluralism is a distinguishing feature of the *sciences humaines* and should not make the effort suspect. One of the chief pleasures of studying the art of the past is that it admits us into the consciousness and sensibilities of people who thought and felt differently from ourselves. Being removed from it in time, we have the kind of perspective—however skewed by accumulated attitudes—that distance allows. Intimacy with the art of the past gives us, in turn, a perspective on the present.

Interpreters of contemporary art, however, are unable to get the same kind of perspective in the immediate environment in which a work is produced. The artists and the interpreter share a culture and an ideology, and it is in the nature of ideology that it be unconsciously accepted, that its norms be perceived as truths rather than as choices. For this reason, an interpretation of a current work of art has to establish a fixed position, as one does in calculating the height of a tower by triangulating from a point paced off to a certain distance from its base. That position is a philosophical commitment that may be made to a certain critical tradition, as in the postulation by Clement Greenberg of a modernist main line exerting pressure on the present and future or Vasari's commitment to a classicism enshrined in Roman art and revived by Michelangelo and Raphael. This favors a particular style tradition and permits its principles to be applied to the interpretation of any new work.

Recent critical perspectives have been derived from contemporary philosophical or methodological positions that give shape to interpretation without necessarily predisposing the critic to one type of art over another. Marxism, psychoanalytic theory, structuralism, semiotics, and phenomenology have all contributed to the contemporary critical consciousness. Their impact on literary criticism has been incalculable, but American art historians and even many art critics have remained suspicious of consciously avowed theoretical interests. This isolation has prevented us from formulating points of view that would give fresh perspectives on our studies and would bring them into sustained contact with stimulating thinkers working within similar frameworks outside the field and in other countries.

The effort of American scholars to remain theoretically innocent is rooted in the belief that one can approach works of art without predispositions and interpret them "on their own terms." The pretense of speaking on behalf of the work of art is a disingenuous attempt to make critical statements without accepting responsibility for them. The illusory nature of this aspiration has been clear to philosophers of history and the social sciences for almost a century. The interpreter operates either from an unarticulated position of which he himself is likely to be unaware (which denies to his audience any means of orienting itself), or he works from an explicit position of the kind I have described.

The critic or historian, no matter whom he actually is addressing, feels the eyes of colleagues and cognoscenti glaring over his shoulder, imagined rightly or wrongly as searching not for an original revelation but for possible departures from orthodoxy and conformity. His fear of displeasing the established authorities is the bane of criticism and the curse of academic writing of all kinds. It is reinforced by powerful economic incentives because advancement and success, especially in academic careers, may depend on adherence to favored modes of interpretation. Critics of contemporary art are particularly influenced by the prevailing consensus, though it follows a vacillating course imposed by the needs of the market and the dictates of fashion. But this weakness has at least the advantage of being more obvious than that of the art historians, which is more effectively veiled by the prevailing ideology. Historians for the most part do not elect to follow the current fashion: they assume it without even knowing it is a fashion, in the conviction that this is the way one does history. From historians of this sort we learn only more of what we already know.

Radical innovation in the art of the last twenty years shattered the consensus of the 1950s and 1960s and helped to reveal the inadequacy of traditional methods of interpretation. Artists stopped trying to work within the deeply rooted principles of Renaissance/modernist art and criticism and repeatedly challenged our conception of what qualifies an object as a work of art. Their work articulated a powerful and intentional criticism of criticism. I shall return to the implications of this challenge in discussing response.

The dullness and sameness of most critical and historical writing in this country is due partly to the concentration of intellectual life in universities, where imagination is constrained by a reductive ideal of scholarly objectivity supported by an obsolete ideology. Objectivity is marginally attainable only on the most primitive plane of raw data, the plane of documentation. There can be an objective reporting of the date and signature on a letter or a canvas; it could be made by a machine as well as by a person. But the moment we attempt to make anything of the data, the result becomes an amalgam of our feelings, our experience, our knowledge, and a host of physical and emotional responses that resist labeling. In most cases, even the supposed objective grounds of history—the "hard" facts—are identifiable only through the process of interpretation. If one sets out to gather material for a study on the work of a particular artist, that decision is based on the unstated and often unconscious conviction that meaningful statements about art can be made by selecting out of the whole range of possible objects those done by one person over the span of his working years; in such cases the treatment is normally chronological, which makes the establishment of sequences essential. But the traditional evolutionary treatment of the history of art as a process moved forward by a succession of masters each of whom hands on the legacy to the next is only one of many interpretative options. The "objective" data we gather to support it might be completely useless in pursuing an alternative approach. Ruskin's treatment of Venice, for example, is a classic of criticism that depends hardly at all on names and dates. I wonder if Ruskin would get tenure in an American university.

Innovative historical methods, responding to the stimulus of modern linguistics and structuralism in the last three decades, have put more emphasis on the synchronic and less on the diachronic mode.[3] Emphasis on the evolutionary flow of events—history as the unfolding of a story—has been giving way to penetrations into particular moments of time. The diachronic mode continues to be useful in tracing the genesis of the style, symbols, and other conventions of objects, but the synchronic permits an enriched understanding by revealing systematic structures linking art with contemporaneous political theory and practice, social and economic organization, and scientific and literary achievement.

While the structuralist model that supports contextual interpretation has provided expanded understanding of the ways in which works of art are formed by the social milieu, it is in its nature to emphasize the links that connect works of art to institutions, traditions, and individuals. This focus on external bonds inevitably diverts attention from the uniqueness of the individual work of art and from the peculiar function of art objects as distinct from institutions, customs, tools, and other historical artifacts. Works of art normally are treated by contextual and particularly by Marxist critics and historians primarily as social documents. The contextual approach, developed to reveal the interactions of the object and its milieu, is confounded by the relationship between the object and the interpreter. We need a structure capable of accommodating both the object-milieu axis and the object-observer axis—of binding interpretation to response in a single critical method.

Interpretation must remain basic to such a coordinated criticism. To adequately understand a work of art, we ought to find out what we can about the context in which it was produced and the symbolic and formal conventions which it observes or rejects. The critic of contemporary art may expect his reader to have some grasp of that context, because he shares it with the artist. But the majority of potential viewers are as alien from the concerns and conventions of avant-garde artists as they are from those of medieval manuscript illuminators, so his task is not fundamentally different from that of the historian. Yet the revelations of historical research do not inevitably contribute anything of value. Historians exhume and publish a mass of information that does not facilitate understanding.

One can be absorbed and challenged by works of art without the help of historical research. I have been intrigued by works of African sculpture and of Sung painting without knowing anything of their context and content. But enjoyment of this sort—response unenlightened by interpretation—is necessarily partial. It cuts one off from a wide range of potential communication that more understanding would make accessible—communication about the sensibility, modes of perception and knowledge of people distant in time and space, and about the production and function of their artifacts, that can intensify the direct response to the work of art. The innocent observer is confined to a cloistered sensuous world where art is removed from life.

II

Traditional method isolates interpretation from response by accepting an overarching hierarchy of values that determines what art is and what is good art. The standards were first determined by the idealist critical philosophy formulated in the Renaissance, fortified in the baroque and neoclassical periods—especially by Kant—and refurbished in later times by the doctrine of art-for-art's-sake and the metaphor of the avant-garde. Idealist criticism measures the work of art against abstract principles and isolates it in a perfect realm divorced from that of everyday experience. Because of its commitment to abstraction, it focuses on the formal characteristics of works of art—structure, space, the plane, color, line, shape and so on—separating them from content. Subject matter and symbols are treated as "literary" aspects imported into the visual object from the everyday world. The final disengagement of art from depiction and narration in modern abstract art represented the natural destiny of idealist theory and not, as the popular account would have it, a revolution against the principles of the past. Cubism, International Style architecture, and their descendants in the 1950s were the modern restatements of the classical tradition. Critical theory perfectly complemented the asceticism and purism of early twentieth-century art in enjoining the critic and the historian from engaging with the art object. The element of individual personality and perception in the subject was to be suppressed in addressing the self-realizing work of art.

In classical critical practice, an individual reaction that conformed with tradition was justified as a value judgment. One that failed to conform, as in the discussion of a controversial contemporary work or of an overlooked artist of the past, had to be validated by the claim that the work was of great value. To state the basic case, one had to prove that one liked or was interested in a work of art because it was good: it would not do to assert simply that one liked or was interested in it regardless of value considerations.

Value judgments are fundamental in much of the literature of art though they are never overtly stated. Historians and critics favor French over German or Russian nineteenth-century painting, Michelangelo over Bandinelli, early rather than late Picasso, and late rather than early Pollock, without justifying their choice or even confessing that one has been made. The choice is accepted because it conforms to the prevailing consensus, which in turn is buttressed by the value of paintings and sculptures as market commodities. It is said to have "passed the test of time." The very formats for interpretation—the national style of one century, the work of an individual artist, the art produced for the dominant classes—are based on unexamined precepts of classical critical thought. Interpretation could continue on the same trajectory forever if it were not redirected by individual responses and convictions uncomplicated by overt or covert judgments of value.

Interpretation could be represented as the analytic-intellectual component and response as the synthetic-perceptual component of criticism. But the two modes of construction interact. Methods of interpretation, guided by principles, give us a particular insight into certain works of art and predispose us to respond to them. Conversely, works of art may affect us that do not conform to that disposition and may draw us into an effort to reconcile our interpretative stance with actual experience. This accommodation is necessary to the vitality of criticism. Without it, interpretation would become impervious to change, particularly to the kind of change generated by the strongest contemporary art.

A paradigm for such a fusion of two modes of thought has been suggested by Claude Levi-Strauss in his book *The Savage Mind*.[4]

Here he distinguishes a "mythic" from a scientific response to the worlds of culture and nature. Mythic reflection, which he calls "prime" rather than "primitive," is spontaneous and works on the material presented to the senses. "The elements of mythic reflection," Levi-Strauss says, are "midway between percepts and concepts," and he places artistic creation midway between mythic thought and science. I am suggesting a similar view of criticism as occupying a position midway between interpretation and response.

The insight given by a work seen for the first time can alter our view of all other works. This is more likely to occur in encountering contemporary work because we see it without preparation. New perceptions of past art occur less readily because our relationship to it is set by convention. In recent times new art has often brought about the rediscovery of works buried under centuries of indifference. El Greco, Piero della Francesca, and Romanesque sculptures were brushed aside by eighteenth- and nineteenth-century viewers and re-illuminated by the perceptions made possible through the experience of cubist and expressionist artists. New art also forced us to extend the limits of our definition of art by revealing the claims of work previously excluded, as Manet and his contemporaries extracted Japanese wood-block prints from oblivion and as the following generation did the same for African tribal art. Recently, the reaction of the "postmodern" architects to the purism of the International Style has stimulated a positive reassessment of beaux-arts and other classically inspired design.

The extent to which fresh responses to art can guide the evolution of one's interpretation is limited, however, by conflicts of values. One can have a vivid response to a work that cannot be made to conform to the principles of one's philosophical commitment. The finest critics of the abstract art of the 1950s could not accept even the best of pop or minimal art, while some Marxist critics condemned abstract works and their supporters as formalist. Ruskin, if he ever caught himself about to be stirred by a Renaissance building, tried to suppress the feeling because his principles told him that Renaissance goals were corrupt. The philosophical commitment has to win out, otherwise the critic could not convey a credible structure of values. The validity of this rule is evident in the writing of Ruskin and a number of more recent committed critics, who have conveyed a more illuminating and powerful insight into the character and quality of the works they approved of than those who have tried to take every work of art "on its own terms."

The principal differences between the criticism I propose and idealist criticism stem from the rejection of immanent standards of value. Those standards defined characteristics and qualities regarded as praiseworthy in the abstract, in advance of the subject's contact with the object. Since the object of idealist criticism possesses inherent values, there can be only a correct or an incorrect assessment of it (whoever is bored by the Sistine ceiling or the Villa Savoie simply needs more education). A criticism open to response, by contrast, does not undertake to reveal the inherent value or the character of the object because the attributes of the object cannot be apprehended apart from their reception by a subject. It must start with an account of the encounter of a subject with an object. In responsive criticism, one may communicate the experience of viewing a particular work of art; this communication is relevant to the experience of other works only to the extent that it expands the viewer's horizon.

Once having rejected idealist absolutes we can understand the evolution of our response to particular works of art over time: what moved us once may no longer do so, and we may now find stimulating what we once found distasteful or boring (this is especially likely to happen with radical contemporary art that most of us assimilate slowly). Such changes are not a matter of "losing touch" or of "seeing the light" but instances of normal human inconstancy and growth that enrich life.[5]

Idealist criticism determined not only the preferred orientation of the work of art, it set down standards by which we could judge the worth of one properly oriented work over another. The great work of art was one that exhibited creativity, that is, originality of technique and style, though within the framework of the ongoing historical evolution of art. It had to have a variety of elements organized in a unified and rational structure and, in the case of visual art, it normally had to be a stable physical object. Objects from the real world, actual or closely imitated, could be incorporated only if given an artistic purpose other than or in addition to their normal one. Finally, particularly in the criticism of abstract art, the work was enjoined from reaching out to involve the viewer physically or psychologically.

These rules of idealist art were not simply ignored by the dadaists and by many artists since the early sixties: they were overtly broken, as if freedom of artistic endeavor required their abolition. Evidence of individual facture was eliminated by pop and minimal artists; the barrier between art and everyday life was violated in both directions; variety was rejected in paintings of one color and texture; unity as well as permanence was ignored, as in the casting by chance of materials of different kinds onto gallery and museum floors and walls; and finally, in some conceptual art, the physical object itself was eliminated. There may be no precept proposed by Vasari, Bellori, de Piles, Reynolds, or Greenberg that has not been violated by some artist in recent times. The implications are more radically disturbing to traditional criteria than has been grasped, at least by critics of past art. Recent art compels us to commit ourselves as never before. Either much of recent art is not art at all or the standards we have inherited are no longer valid. To reject the message of contemporary art is to state that what is art is determined by historians and critics rather than by artists, which has always been a ridiculous proposition. Every time critics have made that claim in the past they have been proven wrong.

The traditional way of judging works of art is to apply to them criteria formed from our past education and experience. Why not assume that any work of art has the potential of expanding our knowledge and experience and of altering our criteria? This alternative again suggests social intercourse. While we may measure the people we meet against standards of virtue, appearance, or manners we have formed beforehand, that is not the most satisfactory basis for a relationship. A more rewarding interchange is likely to result from taking people as they are and seeking out ways to become acquainted. We do not choose our friends because they conform to a set of requirements.

The most difficult aspect of such an open criticism is that we shall not know in advance which of all the objects and actions in the world qualify as works of art. But having no prior knowledge of which of all the strangers in the world will become our friends does not disorient us. We come to know the work of art and the friend through our experience of them. Criticism is the practice of sharing the experience with an audience. And we do not operate in a vacuum of discrimination: others guide us—museums, galleries, books, past custom—in selecting objects for our consideration as works of art, as we make friends through other friends or at work or recreation. But in both cases we may make discoveries on our own that perhaps do not conform to those encountered in our normal patterns of life.

In a system free of absolutes we rid ourselves of the unbecoming elitism imposed by traditional criticism that makes it possible to believe that we understand what art is and that this understanding confers the authority to teach or to browbeat others into accepting our position. As the role of high priest of art is eliminated, the complementary role of philistine will also disappear. The person who likes pictures that have yellow in them or that tell amusing stories may in time find more resonant relationships to art, or he may not, just as people who are attracted to blondes or to storytellers may or may not come to grips with the personalities of those they meet rather than with just their surface characteristics. Both alternatives have their rewards.

The rejection of idealist standards liberates us to enjoy a cornucopia of pleasure formerly denied us. Naturalism and narrative head the list; they have always been denigrated by idealist criticism, though there is no question of their capacity to excite interest.[6] For most people, they are the initial and primary access to art: the reputation of Andrew Wyeth attests to that power. I recall my struggle as a teenager to give up such indulgences in order to qualify as a proper art lover. And almost forgotten, even by populists, are the delights to be had from the exhibition of consummate skill or from finely wrought precious materials like the gold Scythian burials or of the tomb of Tutankhamen exhibited not long ago in this country.

The abandonment of idealist critical method does not imply a denigration of works or aspects of works that observe its principles. The principles are internally valid, even if they are dethroned from absolute authority. I cannot imagine, for example, interpreting a painting by Raphael, Poussin, or Mondrian without trying to show that a balanced relationship of forms and colors and a perfected image of reality is fundamental to its effectiveness. Most viewers in the West European cultural tradition respond positively to ordered structure among other forms of organization. Idealist principles may not be rooted in our psychological makeup as is often claimed, but they are certainly part of our cultural inheritance. We can incorporate them into our critical responses without excluding other principles.

The pluralism does not invite chaos. Critics who accept it do not become sponges disposed to absorb everything they see; their opinions do not lose consistency. They continue to be integrated people who are in many ways the product of a tradition in which idealism was dominant. They have beliefs, prejudices, principles, and other equipment with which to distinguish what they like and find interesting from what they do not, and which things they find adapted to effective interpretation. Critics establish in their interpretation criteria of their own based on their convictions and, if they have enough self-confidence, are ready to alter their criteria as their experience widens and their likes and dislikes change. This change, however, unlike the path defined by idealism, is not a gradual ascent to an ultimate Berensonian seat of authority but a symptom of the normal evolution of a personality within an environment. In replacing absolute values with values of openness and freedom of choice, our criticism can become suited to a democratic society as the absolutes of idealist criticism were suited to an authoritarian society.

The danger of pluralistic criticism from a traditional point of view is that, as every critic follows his own responses of the moment, we shall lose a grip on values of any kind. But precisely for the reason that critics cannot assume assent from their audience, they will be impelled to be explicit in articulating their principles. Paradoxically, it is the traditional critics, with their commitment to absolute values, who have been unwilling or unable to articulate them and to face the responsibility to justify their choices. The proper task of criticism is to offer not authoritative judgments of works of art but insights into how an experienced and informed individual who holds certain stated convictions responds to the work of art he or she is discussing.

III

The distinction I have proposed between interpretation and response has an analog in the different roles of the left and right hemispheres of the brain. In the past two decades, research has dramatically extended our understanding of the way the two sides of the human brain process visual and other sense stimuli.[7]

Over a century ago the study of aphasic subjects led to the observation that the seat of language and of our analytic capacities was in the left hemisphere. Since damage to the left hemisphere ordinarily results in at least partial loss of the ability to communicate verbally (while damage to the right ordinarily does not), early researchers believed that the right hemisphere was not only mute but inferior in capacity; the left came to be called the "major" or "dominant" hemisphere and the right the "minor."

Interest in this aspect of brain research revived after the Second World War and accelerated following the initiation in 1960 of a procedure, called commissurotomy, for the treatment of severe epileptics that involved cutting through the corpus callosum, the fibrous tract interconnecting the left and right hemispheres through which signals normally pass from side to side. Those on whom the operation was performed, who continued to lead relatively normal lives, became ideal subjects for tests to determine the differential functions of the hemispheres. Researchers could direct information exclusively to one side or the other of the brain simply by presenting stimuli intended for the right hemisphere to the left eye and for the left hemisphere to the right eye.

Repeated tests confirmed earlier suppositions that the mute right hemisphere performs essential functions in processing the data coming through the five senses, organizing and synthesizing visual, oral, and other perceptions. In the words of R. W. Sperry, who has studied split-brain subjects since the start of this research, "Though predominantly mute and generally inferior in all performances involving language or linguistic or mathematical reasoning, the minor hemisphere is nevertheless clearly the superior cerebral member for certain types of tasks. . . . Largely they involve the apprehension and processing of spatial patterns, relations and transformations. They seem to be holistic and unitary rather than analytic and fragmentary, and orientational more than focal, and to involve concrete perceptual insight rather than abstract, symbolic, sequential reasoning."[8]

The designation of the left hemisphere as "dominant" then is explained by the fact that its special capacities are those most prized in our culture. The transactions we consider most essential and all activities of our educational system are carried on conceptually and verbally while few advantages accrue from exceptional development of our visual, aural, and other perceptual faculties or from the imaginative constructs of myth and ritual.[9] In consequence, the potentialities of the right hemisphere of the brain are developed particularly by artists and, since art is so little integrated into the everyday activities of our society, they remain relatively dormant in the average individual. Indeed, they might become virtually atrophied were it not for the fact that in the first years of human development, prior to the acquisition of speech and to the specialization of function in the two hemispheres, the ambient world is structured primarily through the senses. Just as the experiences of infancy affect the balance of ego and id in adult life, so it may be our earliest response to the environment that helps us to retain and sometimes even to give priority to the structures of sense perception.

I must emphasize, however, that the specialization of the two sides of the brain has been greatly exaggerated both by those involved in brain research and by nonscientists eager to find alternatives to our analytic culture. The significance of work in this discipline is not that it indicates a physiological base for the distinction of the "artistic" from the "conceptual" aspects of our minds, but that it suggests how culture puts its stamp on the way we coordinate input and output of the senses on one hand and of symbols on the other. We should be concerned not with the separateness but with the collaboration of the two sides of the brain just as we should focus not on the distinction but on the synthesis of interpretation and response in criticism.

I do not intend the import of my observations on criticism to stand or fall on the relevance of research on brain lateralization. In fact, they were developed before I became aware of the nature of that research. But what must be incorporated into future discussions of critical theory is the knowledge that visual (or aural) form is experienced not as some diffuse and primitive sensation bathed in emotion and evasively described in the past as "aesthetic" but as highly articulated thinking which is absolutely essential to structuring and synthesizing visual (aural) percepts. Maybe the so-called "aesthetic" enjoyment we get from works of art comes from the process of synthesizing (it surely does not derive from analyzing and interpreting), which could relate to the "creative" synthesis of the artist in initially constructing an object. But the roots of enjoyment are not a concern of criticism. What I hope to have accomplished in this study is to call attention to the essential role of that spontaneous grasp of form and structure which develops more acutely in one half of our brain, and its inevitable integration in criticism with the verbal accommodation to culture that we call analysis and interpretation.

How much right-hemisphere response can find articulation in language remains to be seen as we attempt to communicate our visual experience with an increased awareness of capacities we have been refusing to acknowledge. With sufficient effort we may perhaps be able to acquire some of the responsiveness of the "savage mind."

Appendix: Some Reports on Brain Lateralization Relevant to "Interpretation" and "Response"

One of the best-known early experiments that may have contributed to the foregoing conclusions required the subject to copy before and after commissurotomy a simple drawing of a box drawn in perspective (fig. 3.1). The tests made before show an average performance by someone not accustomed to sketching. The postoperative tests showed the subject able to repeat the essential structure of the earlier performance when drawing with the left hand what he had perceived with the right hemisphere but that the right hand, in reporting the perception of the left hemisphere, showed a total loss of spatial response.[10]

3.1 *Drawing of a cube before and after commissurotomy. Cube 1 drawn by the left hand preop; 2 by the right hand pre-op; 3 by the left hand post-op; and 4 by the right hand post-op. From Gazzaniga and Le Doux,* The Integrated Mind.

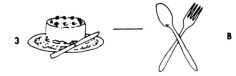

MATCHED BY APPEARANCE   MATCHED BY FUNCTION

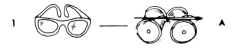

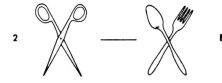

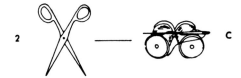

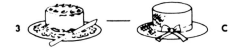

3.2 *Appearance-function matching test. From Levy and Trevarthen, "Metacontrol of Hemispheric Function in Human Split-Brain Patients."*

We can infer from this that in grasping the spatial constructs so essential to the making and criticism of works of art, the mute right hemisphere is dominant and the articulate verbal side of the brain receives the information at least partly as communicated across the corpus callosum.

One test administered to the subjects who had undergone commissurotomy is of critical importance to our assessment of the respective roles of the two hemispheres in processing formal and conceptual information. In a paper published in 1976, Levy and Trevarthen reported on the results of an experiment in perception involving the association of pairs of images displayed on a card, ingeniously designed so that each might be associated with one other image that resembled it in form and one that resembled it in function. The images are illustrated in figure 3.2 where it is apparent that the scissors can be paired formally with the knife and fork and functionally with the spools of thread; the knife and fork are functionally paired with the cake on a platter, which in turn is visually associable with the hat, and so on. When these images were directed at the right hemisphere of split-brain subjects they chose the formal pairings, and when they were offered to the left hemisphere the functional pairings predominated. When the test was administered to normal subjects who were asked, ambiguously, to pair "similar" images they chose to make the pairing on the basis of formal appearance (though they subsequently could account for all the functional associations).[11]

The relevance of this experiment to those of us who are concerned with visual art and criticism diverges somewhat from what concerned the researchers who performed it. They were interested in the predisposition of normal people to choose one type of response over another. We, on the other hand, are likely to be most fascinated by the discovery that not only is the mute hemisphere dominant in our grasp of form and structure, but it also differs from the verbal hemisphere precisely according to the dialectic of form and function that has long been central to critical discourse.

This experiment was followed by the same researchers with a series that demonstrated a superiority of the right hemisphere in color perception, leading to the observation that "An 'object' for the right hemisphere should be represented by its form, size, texture and color, but for the left hemisphere the same 'object' may only be represented by a symbol, poor in information regarding the physical characteristics of the thing symbolized."[12]

Subjects asked to identify the ink color shown on a card on which the word "blue" was printed in green showed right hemisphere dominance when asked to match the color to the green on a color chart and left hemisphere dominance when asked to select the word "green" from a list of written color names. While the left hemisphere showed a capacity to identify colors in this and other tests, its memory for color and capacity to form images of colors appeared limited.

The report concludes: "The artistic capacities of the right hemisphere almost certainly result not only from its superiority in being able to generate representations of form, but also from its superiority in being able to generate the infinite variety of colors that fill the human perceptual world."

Notes

This essay has been greatly improved by the advice of Mark Ashton, Leon Kirchner, Rosalind Krauss, James Rosen, and Barbara Herrnstein Smith.

1.   Recent literary criticism, as discussed in the accompanying paper by M. H. Abrams [published in *Theories of Criticism*, Washington, D.C., 1984], has been involved with comparable issues, and a concept similar to "response" has been developed in the "reception aesthetics" of Germany and Poland. See *Poétique* 39 (September 1979), *Théorie de la reception en Allemagne;* H. R. Jauss, *Kleine Apologie der ästhetischen Erfahrung* (Constance, 1972); Michael Glowinski, "Reading, Interpretation, Reception," *New Literary History* 11, no. 1 (1979), 75–82. I found the German studies soggy—a debility that sometimes affects German theory that attempts to moderate vigorous analysis with sensibility. Susan Sontag was perhaps the first critic in this country to focus on the need to avoid the extremes of analytic detachment, but her prescription tipped the scale excessively in the opposite direction, as did much writing of this kind in the late 1960s: "In place of a hermeneutics we need an erotics of art" (*Against Interpretation,* [New York, 1966], 14).

2.   Documentation is the discovery and presentation of the data required for describing and identifying the object of criticism. These data relate to the physical, the historical, and the semantic nature of the work being examined. Physical documentation involves the identification of the materials and techniques used, the intended placement of the work, its condition, and so on. Histor-

ical documentation involves fixing the basic parameters of time and space by answering the queries when? where? why? by whom? and how? Semantic documentation deals with the aspects of content that have a public meaning existing independently of the work, such as generally established symbols. Obviously, some aspects of documentation require in certain cases the support of interpretation, as often happens in attributing works of art.

3.   See Annette Michelson, "Art and the Structuralist Perspective," in *On the Future of Art* (New York, 1970), 37–59; Sheldon Nodelman, "Structuralist Analysis in Art and Anthropology," in *Structuralism*, ed. J. Ehrmann (New York, 1970), 79–93.

4.   *La pensée sauvage* (Paris, 1962). The translation published in this country (Chicago, 1966) does not consistently communicate the subtleties of the original.

5.   For an acute exposition of the way our responses to works of art we know well change with time, see Barbara Herrnstein Smith, "Fixed Marks and Variable Constancies: A Parable of Literary Value," *Poetics Today,* 1 (1979), 7–22.

6.   A useful survey of recent research on brain lateralization is Sally P. Springer and Georg Deutsch, *Left Brain, Right Brain* (San Francisco, 1981).

7.   On the barriers to the appreciation of realist art since the Renaissance, see Linda Nochlin, "The Realist Criminal and the Abstract Law," *Art in America,* no. 5 (1973), 54–61; no. 6 (1973), 96–103.

8. R. W. Sperry, "Lateral Specialization in the Surgically Separated Hemispheres," in *The Neurosciences Third Study Program,* ed. F. O. Schmitt and F. G. Worden (Cambridge, Mass., 1974), 11. See also Sperry and D. Zaidel, "Performance on the Raven's Colored Progressive Matrices Test by Subjects with Cerebral Commissurotomy," *Cortex,* 4 (1973), 34–39.

9. These observations are inspired by Gazzaniga and Le Doux, *The Integrated Mind* (New York, 1978).

10. M. S. Gazzaniga, "The Split Brain in Man," *Scientific American,* 217, no. 2 (1967), 24–29; reproduced by R. Ornstein, *The Nature of Human Consciousness* (New York, 1973), 87–100. The subject of the initial test showed marked improvement in executing the same task months later. Comparable results were reported by J. E. Bogen, "The Other Side of the Brain: An Appositional Mind," *Bulletin of Los Angeles Neurological Societies,* 34 (1969), 135–162, consulted in Ornstein, *Nature of Human Consciousness,* 101–125 and discussed by Ornstein in *The Psychology of Consciousness* (San Francisco, 1977), 26ff. In later tests (reported by Le Doux et al., "Manipulospatial Aspects of Cerebral Lateralization: Clues to the Origin of Lateralization," *Neuropsychologia,* 15 [1977], 744), Gazzaniga and his associates showed that a split-brain subject who was unable to draw a cube was able to recognize the image of one and to select it in preference to his own drawing, demonstrating that spatial perception is not lacking in the left hemisphere.

11. Jerry Levy and Colwyn Trevarthen, "Metacontrol of Hemispheric Function in Human Split-Brain Patients," *Journal of Experimental Psychology: Human Perception and Performance,* 2 (1976), 299–312. They conclude (p. 310): "In summary, our results show that the right and left hemispheres are specialized for detecting structural and functional similarities respectively; that task instructions selectively activate one or the other side of the brain as well as appropriate strategies, and finally that such instructions do not necessarily activate both together. . . . We conclude that a hemisphere's dominance over behavior depends only indirectly on specialization of capacity. We suggest that the hemispheres are also specialized with respect to intentions to act in particular ways."

   The recent studies of Gazzaniga and Le Doux have likewise modified the view that visuospatial processing is a specialty of the right hemisphere, showing it to be represented to some degree also in the left. See Le Doux et al., "Manipulospatial Aspects," 743–750, which suggests that a dependence on tests involving manual activities led earlier investigations of lateralization to overemphasize the specialization of the two hemispheres; they conclude: "While studies clearly demonstrate that functional asymmetry is a salient feature of human brain organization, these studies also demonstrate that there are inherent similarities in the types of processing that occur in the left and right half-brains." See also Le Doux et al., "Left Hemisphere Visual Processes in a Case of Right Hemisphere Symptomatology," *Archives of Neurology,* 37 (1980), 157–159; Gazzaniga and Le Doux, *The Integrated Mind,* 69: "The qualitatively superior manipulospatial and the relatively superior perceptual skills of the right hemisphere arise as a by-product of the fact that language is usually in the left, and thus does not represent evolved specializations of the right."

12. J. Levy, "Lateral Differences in the Human Brain in Cognition and Behavioral Control," *Cerebral Correlates of Conscious Experience* (Amsterdam, N.Y., 1978), 291. Earlier, Gazzaniga (1967) reported on an experiment in which a green or a red light was directed to the left eye (right hemisphere) of the commissurotomized subject, who was then asked to identify verbally which light had been shown. The verbal response was random, but when the subject guessed wrong, he would frequently frown or shake his head, signaling his ability to make a correct identification after hearing the sound of the incorrect one. Recently, more detailed tests by Levy and Colwyn Trevarthen have reported that split-brain subjects who were shown colored figures of familiar objects could name the color but not the object and that while both half-brains could identify colors, the strategies employed are quite different, and the right hemisphere performs better in recognizing colors "resistant to verbal description." "Color-matching, Color-naming and Color Memory in Split-Brain Patients," *Neuropsychologia,* 19 (1981), 523–541; this paper modifies the earlier hypotheses of B. E. Pennal, "Human Asymmetry in Color Discrimination," *Neuropsychologia,* 15 (1977), 563–568.

Postscript

This paper, which was presented at a meeting of the Council of Scholars of the Library of Congress, was later published by the Library in a special pamphlet that enjoyed only a limited circulation before going out of print. It escaped the notice of art historical colleagues, most of whom wouldn't have liked it anyhow, but was generally well received by artists and writers.

It was prompted by ruminations on the assault upon traditional standards by the art of the past twenty years, and by my conviction that critics and historians had to account for this situation in judging the art of the past as well as that of the present. The essay proposed a relativist approach to the assessment of works of art on the model of human relations, an approach that fused interpretation and response in critical discourse. It failed, however, to account for the fact that the many works of art by Dadaists as well as by contemporary artists do not call for and cannot sustain a responsive reaction.

I became conscious of this deficiency in reading a paper by Arthur Danto. Danto cites the case of a piece exhibited by Marcel Duchamp entitled ambiguously "In Advance of the Broken Arm." This piece was a simple snow shovel, an industrial product similar in concept to other Duchamp objects offered as works of art and transformed by the situation of the exhibit and by the application of a title. He posits an exhibit in which there would be three identical snow shovels, one of which would be a work of art while the other two would be merely utilitarian objects from the hardware store, and raises the question of what it is that differentiates the "Duchamp." It is emphatically not formal or structural affects of the shovel of the sort that call for response in the sense I intend: to point to the delicate modeling of the wood grain of the handle or the gleaming surface of the metal would be inappropriate because these are characteristics of the non-art shovels, and in any event the artist did not undertake to select his shovel by aesthetic criteria. A more extreme instance may be found in the photographs exhibited by Sherrie Levine in the 1970s, which were reproduced photographically from original prints by Walker Evans (a paradigmatic instance of "appropriation" art), for in this case one's response could be only to Evans's work. In sum, there are works of art that can be identified and accepted as such only through interpretation; response simply does not enter the process.

Reading *The Judgment of Sense* by David Summers alerted me to the mysteriously obscured fact that a differentiation of two aspects of criticism—one more rational and the other more sensible—is as old as Aristotle (in *De Anima* and *De Motu Animalium*) and is commonly alluded to in the Renaissance. Our interpretation of Renaissance theory and criticism has blinded us to the many instances in which unsupported, nonrationalized judgments made by the (trained) eye or ear are taken to be plausible alternatives to those based on reason or derived from rules. For example, Michelangelo was said to have *il sesto nell'occhio* (a compass in his eye), and Vasari wrote "one may use no better measure than the judgment of the eye, which, should a thing be well measured and the eye offended by it, will for this reason not cease to censure it" (quoted in Summers, pp. 30, 140).

I sent this essay to my colleague Helen Vendler, who, as a practicing critic, raised a number of questions, of which the most relevant to this postscript concerned the rigidity of my demand that the critic articulate his or her position. She asked whether a single, fixed position is necessary, and also pointed to a fact of which I have always been aware but neglected in this case, that too much tolerance can make for boring criticism. She also suggested that I emphasize that standards are not made only by critics and theorists but by works of art and by their patrons.

Hans Belting in his book *The End of the History of Art?* has proposed that the phenomena of recent art and their demand for revised critical positions also call for a reassessment of art historical principles. He proposes that previous paradigms of art history involved the construction of systems to explain the unfolding of patterns of change. He identifies as a major paradigm in the formulation of modern art history the model of Vasari, who saw the arts as evolving almost biologically from a primitive condition in which artists like Giotto first struggled to represent convincingly the world around them to a mature state represented by Raphael and Michelangelo in which the capacity to imitate nature is fully realized while being subjected to revision according to ideal norms.

In my view, the modern paradigm of art history is represented by the hypothesis of the avant-garde, which views the succession of works of art in the light of an evolutionary system. According to avant-gardist historical theory, art evolves through the stimulus of works of art the originality and individuality of which place them ahead of the art of their time, while they retain at the same time certain features of established art. It was this paradigm that prompted Clement Greenberg to justify his praise of certain works of Abstract Expressionism and Color Field painting on the grounds that, while strikingly innovative, they sustained or took off from certain precepts of Cubism. I had discussed the decline of the concept of the avant-garde in my 1969 essay "The Demise of the Avant Garde," but that was before its definitive disruption in postmodernist work from the 1970s on, in which the necessity of originality was repeatedly challenged. As Rosalind Krauss pointed out in a stimulating reassessment of the avant-garde tradition, "In deconstructing the sister notions of origin and originality, postmodernism establishes a schism between itself and the conceptual domain of the avant-garde, looking back at it from across a gulf that in turn establishes a historical divide. The historical period that the avant-garde shared with modernism is over" (1985, p. 170). As a consequence of this situation, the premises of history making as well as of criticism must be radically revised.

While the study of brain lateralization has progressed significantly since I wrote this essay, researchers are concerned that laymen have distorted and exaggerated evidence for the specialization of the functions of the left and right hemispheres. I had tried to avoid this temptation, and I hope that, even if I cited as evidence (in figs. 3.1 and 3.2) tests made on subjects who had undergone a drastic operation that altered their brain function, the modest claims I made for the right hemisphere in the organization of space, form, and color are justified.

Ackerman, James. "The Demise of the Avant Garde: Notes on the Sociology of Recent American Art," *Comparative Studies in Society and History,* 11 (1969), 371–384; reduced version in *L'Arte,* 6 (1970), 4–11.

Belting, Hans. *The End of the History of Art?* (Chicago, 1984).

Danto, Arthur C. *The Transfiguration of the Commonplace* (Cambridge, Mass., 1981).

Danto, Arthur C. "The Appreciation and Interpretation of Works of Art," *The Philosophical Disenfranchisement of Art* (New York, 1986), 23–46.

Gardner, Howard. *Art, Mind, and Brain: A Cognitive Approach to Creativity* (New York, 1982).

Krauss, Rosalind. "The Originality of the Avant-Garde," in *The Originality of the Avant-Garde and Other Modernist Myths* (Cambridge, Mass., 1985 [first published 1981]), 151–170.

Segalowitz, Sid J. *Two Sides of the Brain* (Englewood Cliffs, N.J., 1983).

Summers, David. *The Judgment of Sense* (Cambridge, 1987).

II

Art and Science

4

Alberti's Light

I

The closest bond between art and science in the fifteenth century developed in the field of optics. Optics was the foundation on which rationalist painters and sculptors in relief could build a technique for conveying the illusion of consistent and rational space and of three-dimensional objects within that space in correct proportion to one another. It suggested to the painters, in particular, ways of imitating the action of natural light to give the effect of relief. Thus in both of the first two theoretical writings of the Renaissance, Leon Battista Alberti's *De pictura* of 1435[1] and Lorenzo Ghiberti's *Commentarii* of 1447–48, one of the three parts was devoted to a discussion of the application of optics to art.

Since Ghiberti's third commentary has been shown in recent times to consist almost entirely of notes and transcriptions from medieval optical tracts,[2] the key to the assimilation of this science into art is found in Alberti's small but tightly packed treatise; it was the first Renaissance book on art, and possibly the most influential and imaginative one of all time.

"In writing about painting in these short books," Alberti begins, "we will, to make our discourse clearer, first take from mathematicians those things which seem relevant to the subject. When we have learned these, we will go on, to the best of our ability, to explain the art of painting from the basic principles of nature."[3] And so he begins by defining a point, a line, and a surface, and from there proceeds to the effects

From *Studies in Late Medieval and Renaissance Painting in Honor of Millard Meiss,* edited by Irving Lavin and John Plummer (New York: New York University Press, 1978), 1–27. Copyright © 1978 New York University.

of light and how it is transmitted to the eye by rays. The exclusively geometrical approach of ancient and medieval science to the study of optics, which postulated rays of light traveling in straight lines between the object seen and the eye, made it possible for Alberti and his contemporaries to rationalize vision through mathematics, and thereby to produce an illusion of the complex three-dimensional world on the two-dimensional surface of a painting. Because the science was dominated by mathematics, physiological optics—the study of the implications of vision with two eyes, the effects of the motion of the head and eyeball, distortions in peripheral vision, and the like—was not a factor in Alberti's system, though some medieval writers were aware of the physiology of vision, and it began to preoccupy Leonardo.

The medieval term for optics, *perspectiva,* survives in the modern "perspective," but what we understand by this term is only half of the discipline as defined by Alberti. He divides Book I of *De pictura* into two parts (see table 4.1). The first (i–iii, §§ 2–12) is an exposition of the operation of light in transmitting images of objects to the eye, a review of the tradition of *perspectiva* as it had been transmitted to scholars of the early fifteenth century, with observations on its application to the practice of painting. The second (iv, §§ 13–22) is a description of the method of constructing on a two-dimensional surface by geometrical means an illusionary three-dimensional spatial framework in which the dimensions of any object could be made proportional to its distance from the observer; this, by contrast to the foregoing, was entirely an invention of Alberti's, aided by the earlier researches of his older contemporary Filippo Brunelleschi, but not anticipated (except insofar as it was based on optical theory) in ancient or medieval art or science.[4] By way of differentiation, the traditional study of optics was referred to in the Renaissance as *perspectiva naturalis* or *communis,* and Alberti's invention—perspective as we understand it today—*perspectiva artificialis.*[5]

Though Alberti meant the two parts to be complementary, modern readers of his book have focused almost exclusively on the second. A very large literature testifies to the fascination that artificial perspective holds for twentieth-century scholars (among whom there is still warm controversy over the interpretation of Alberti's description of his method and even over whether Renaissance perspective is "correct").[6] But the study of light and color in optics and its application to painting, which Alberti necessarily placed first and treated at greater length, has been neglected.[7] I think there are two reasons for this bias: one, that the mathematical clarity of the perspective box appeals to the positivistic attitude of modern art history and is easily taught and discussed, particularly at a time when art is studied primarily from photographs; and two, that perspective could be represented as the paradigmatic invention of the Renaissance, in that it literally brought all of perceived space under rational control, whereas Alberti's optical exposition was dependent on medieval sources and focused on issues of light and color that were not resolved in his time. I intend to demonstrate that though Alberti's theory may not have been new, it is essential for understanding the genesis of perspective, and that his perception of its relevance for the future of painting is incalculably important.

Table 4.1

Outline of Alberti's Optical System in Book I of *De Pictura*

(paragraph numbers in parentheses refer to the Grayson edition)

I. Geometry: point; line; surface (§§2, 3, 4)

II. Properties of objects (§5)
   A. *Permanent*
      1. edge
      2. surface or skin
   B. *Accidental*
      1. changes due to place
      2. changes due to light

III. Light: the ray theory
   A. *Rays* (explained in two dimensions) (§§5, 6)
      1. extrinsic
      2. median
      3. centric
   B. *The visual pyramid* (§§7, 8): functioning of the three types of ray in three dimensions
   C. *Color* (§§9, 10): relation to light; the four primaries and black and white
   D. *Light* (§11)
   E. *Application of the theory to painting* (§12)

IV. Artificial perspective: the surfaces (§13); proportionality, two-dimensional (§14) and three-dimensional (§15); exceptional angles of vision (§§16, 17); scale (§18); the method of constructing perspective image (§19–21)

V. Conclusion (§§22–24)

Optics was one of the most highly developed of the ancient and medieval sciences, both because it could be pursued to a sophisticated level with the mathematical tools available, and because the processes of sense perception concerned all philosophers who addressed problems of epistemology. Already in antiquity, however, the optics of ordinary vision had been expanded by the investigation of reflection (using mirrors) and refraction.[8] Though many ancient scientist-philosophers wrote on optical problems, three were particularly influential in the later development of the science: Euclid and Ptolemy, who wrote treatises specifically on the subject, and Galen, whose interest was anatomical. These writers, all of whom were known throughout the Middle Ages, and most other ancient students of optics, proceeded on the hypothesis that vision is made possible by rays of light emanating from the eye to reach the object of vision (fig. 4.1B); the concept of the "light of the eye" is pervasive in Western culture and has survived linguistically the withdrawal of scientific support. Because the rays were assumed to extend in straight lines from a point source within the eye, the study of optics could be closely allied with that of geometry, since the basic visual percept could be represented as a triangle, cone, or pyramid with its apex in the eye, its sides formed by rays, and its base by the object viewed. By this means the study of vision was translated from the experiential to the mathematical realm and, thus abstracted, could be pursued accurately and to a complex level without resolving the question of whether the eye really emits or receives the rays of light. Thus most of Euclid's work, for example, remained valid after the abandonment of the extromission hypothesis, while the opposing theories of Aristotle and the Epicureans, in which the image originates in the object, did not generate an alternative optical literature. [See the fuller exposition of this tradition in section II of the essay "Leonardo's Eye," reprinted below.]

As in other fields of the mathematical and physical sciences, it was the Arab scholars who preserved and added to the work of the ancients.[9] In optics, Ibn-al-Haitham (d. ca. 1039), known in the later Middle Ages as Alhazen, dominated the future course of the discipline. In a number of separate studies passed on to the Renaissance under the title *Perspectiva* or *De aspectibus,* he rejected the metaphysical interpretations of light that had entered optics in late-antique and Neoplatonic texts and had survived even in Avicenna, returning to the empirical tradition of Euclid and Ptolemy. He gave it a more materialist base, however, by postulating that light rays emanate from the object and are received by the eye (fig. 4.1A), and that they are in a sense corporeal, each issuing from a point on the perceived object and traveling from there to the eye. He offered two persuasive proofs for the first theory (intromission): first, that light rays "wound" the eye (one feels pain and can suffer burns from looking straight at the sun), and second, that we experience an afterimage when we close our eyes after looking at a well-lit object in a dark environment. Neither of these phenomena would occur if the eye emitted rays of light. In addition, he studied the effects of atmosphere and of the structure of the eye on the refraction of light and raised, without solving, the problem of where and how images are projected within the eye. Alhazen accepted the Galenic theory that images are sensed on the surface of the crystalline or glacial humor, rather than on the retina, as we believe today. This was the result of an effort to suppress the evidence of geometrical laws and of the camera obscura (which Alhazen knew) that a retinal image would have to be inverted (see fig. 4.4)—evidence which is so hard to adjust to common-sense experience that even today laymen are confused by it.

Virtually all later writing on optics was indebted to Alhazen; the most widely read works, the *Perspectiva* of the Polish scholar Witelo and the *Perspectiva communis* by John Pecham of Oxford, both composed in the 1270s, owe much to their predecessor for empirical data and to a great extent for theoretical positions. Witelo in particular, however, was affected by the earlier thirteenth-century Oxford scholar Robert Grosseteste, and perhaps also by his older contemporary Roger Bacon, in injecting a Neoplatonic strain that represented light in a metaphysical as well as a physical sense as the manifestation of God (Bacon's optics, for example, focused on the "multiplication of species," associating the infinite number of images projected by objects in light with the principle of generation). Pecham closely followed Bacon; both were Franciscans and pursued their studies at Oxford and Paris.

Around 1390 the Parmesan scholar and professor Biagio Pelacani used problems raised in Pecham's text as the basis for a penetrating commentary, *Quaestiones de perspectiva,* which, for the first time since Alhazen, returned to a strictly empirical method. We do not know for sure whether Alberti read Pelacani, but it is significant that the recently published transcription of the manuscript was taken from a copy executed in Florence in 1428.[10] Alberti, like Pelacani, entirely eliminated the metaphysical element from his exposition of optical principles; he favored the strictly mathematical theories and must have read Euclid, possibly Ptolemy, and have known Alhazen either in the original or through a later intermediary. This was not an exceptional achievement in his circle: Book Three of Ghiberti's *Commentarii* has been shown to be, apart from a short discussion on some antique sculptures, a compilation of quotations from the works of Vitruvius, Alhazen, Avicenna, Averroes, Witelo, Pecham, and Bacon.[11]

This interest in ancient and medieval science and technology was widespread in Florence in Alberti's generation. Though it represented a countercurrent to the mainstream of humanist culture, it shared with it an eagerness to discover and interpret the surviving texts. Alberti's interest in the arts was one of the factors that allied him to a group of liberal intellectuals with strong scientific interests that may have gathered around Ambrogio Traversari and Niccolò Niccoli and was supported by the library and other resources of Cosimo de' Medici—a group that must have included Brunelleschi, to whom the Italian translation of *De pictura* was dedicated, the mathematician and cartographer Paolo Toscanelli, and perhaps the other rationalist artists mentioned in the dedication as the author's friends: Donatello, Ghiberti, Luca della Robbia, and Masaccio. Its physical center was the cloister of Santa Maria degli Angeli, where Traversari taught moral philosophy to provide a counterbalance to the conservative education of the Studio (University), which was supported by the old, anti-Medicean oligarchy.[12] Alberti must have been attracted to the Medici orbit partly because he was born and raised in exile, owing to his family's political stance in opposition to the late fourteenth-century oligarchy. His contact with the scientific tradition outlined here was surely not entirely through self-education; the members of this circle must have come together often to announce and discuss their discoveries. The astonishing variety of subjects covered in Alberti's writings must have been encouraged by the group, which was a sort of precursor of the Parisian café communities of the nineteenth century.

II

An outline of the major ideas presented in Book I of *De pictura* should make it easier to discuss Alberti's approach. The first section presents geometry, in Euclidean terms, as the basis of painting, and gives a definition of a point, a line, and a surface. But the descriptions differ a little from Euclid's because Alberti makes no reference to abstractions or to infinite extensions; "things which are not visible," he says, "do not concern the painter, for he strives to represent only the things that are seen." Thus he defines the surface in terms of "many lines joined closely together like threads in cloth," whereas in Euclid it is "that which has length and breadth only."[13]

Intertwined with this geometrical introduction there appears an essential optical proposition, injected so inconspicuously that one easily misses it on first reading. Surfaces have two properties that are "permanent" (*perpetua*): their outline and their skin; these quantifiable physical properties are to be distinguished from their accidental qualities (which are of no concern to mathematicians but are of great importance to

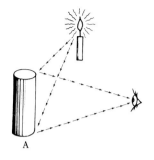
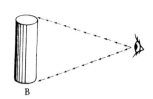

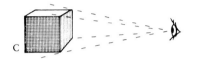

4.1   *Ray theories of vision. (A) the triangle of vision: intromission; (B) the triangle of vision: extromission; (C) the pyramid of vision.*

painters).[14] The latter are of two kinds, those that result first from the position in which an object is placed (and presumably from which it is viewed), and second from the light that falls on it: "these matters are related to the power of vision; for with a change of position surfaces will appear larger, or of a completely different outline from before, or diminished in color; all of which we judge by sight."

This leads to the exposition of the optics of normal vision based on "the opinion of philosophers" (that is, scientists). The ray theory is methodically explained first in terms of plane geometry—that is, of a triangle whose base is the line from the top to the bottom of an observed object and whose apex is in the eye (figs. 4.1A, 4.1B)—and then in the more complex terms of a pyramid of vision formed by rays joining the eye to all points in an observed continuum (fig. 4.1C).[15] It is understood that, for purposes of this theory, one sees with one eye at a fixed position, as through a peephole:

These rays, stretching between the eye and the surface seen, move rapidly with great power and remarkable subtlety, penetrating the air and rare and transparent bodies until they encounter something dense or opaque where their points strike and they instantly stick. Indeed among the ancients there was considerable dispute as to whether these rays emerge from the surface or from the eye. This truly difficult question, which is quite without value for our purposes, may here be set aside.

In spite of this profession of neutrality with respect to the alternative theories of extromission and intromission, Alberti proceeds to describe a number of phenomena in a way that makes it clear that he thinks of visual rays as coming to us unaided, and not as being grasped and carried in by ocular exertion. It may be that he evaded an overt statement of this position because it could be interpreted as too materialistic, eliminating as it did the participation of the *anima,* or integral agent, in the visual process.

But the rays are not all of the same sort; there are three kinds, classified according to their function. *Extrinsic rays* communicate the outlines of objects, *median rays* the surface or skin, and the *centric ray* is the single axis of vision that emanates from the center of the object as viewed and enters the center of an eye at a right angle to its vertical axis. This distinction can be traced to the Greek anatomist Galen, who applied it specifically to seeing the circumference, the plane, and the center of a circle.[16] It then appears in Alhazen and other medieval writings on optics in the Euclidean-Galenic tradition, with the primary emphasis being placed on distinguishing the centric ray from the others.[17]

Alberti tells us that the *extrinsic rays,* "which hold on like teeth to the whole of the outline, form an enclosure around the entire surface like a cage." When we form a triangle or a circle, the lines we draw form this outline, which is made up of the points from which such rays emanate. The function of the rays is to permit measurement and the definition of shape: "we use these *extrinsic rays* whenever we apprehend by sight the height from top to bottom, or width from left to right, or depth from near to far, or any other dimensions." In normal vision, or course, these measurements are relative, since a given object looks larger when we see it close up than when it is far away. As Alberti puts it, "the more acute the angle within the eye, the less will appear the quantity."

The *median rays* are defined as:

the mass of rays which is contained within the pyramid [*of vision*] *and enclosed by the* extrinsic rays. *These rays do what they say the chameleon and other like beasts are wont to do when struck with fear, who assume the colors of nearby objects.*[18] *These* median rays *behave likewise; for, from their contact with the surface to the vertex of the pyramid, they are so tinged with the varied colors and lights they find there, that at whatever point they were broken, they would show the same light they had absorbed and the same color.*

Thus, the *median rays* transmit the qualities of things as we see them—color, light, and texture, and *extrinsic rays* the quantities. Alberti does not confront the problem of whether *extrinsic rays* convey light and color, but they obviously do not because they come from one-dimensional lines.

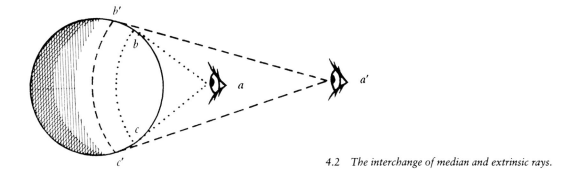

4.2   *The interchange of median and extrinsic rays.*

We should keep in mind that the two types of ray are generated by the two permanent properties of objects described at the start: outline and skin. But the rays do not give conclusive evidence of the permanent properties because they communicate only the accidental appearance of things seen from a certain position and in a certain light. Alberti emphasizes the contingent nature of the evidence when he says: "anyone who has properly understood the theory behind this, will plainly see that some *median rays* sometimes become *extrinsic,* and *extrinsic* ones *median.*"

This interchange occurs when we move toward or away from an object like a ball (fig. 4.2). If we hold the ball close to one eye, we see less of the whole, and the *extrinsic rays* encompass a smaller area of *median rays;* if we hold it farther off to see more of the whole, the points from which *extrinsic rays* were generated close-up are now the source of *median rays.*[19] The phenomenon is much easier to understand if we imagine ourselves moving *around* an object so that its outline and surface constantly change place (but Alberti does not use this illustration because, perhaps unconsciously, he believed that a single, frontal viewpoint was the correct one for a painting or a sculpture; accordingly his perspective system provided only straight-on views with all planes parallel to the picture plane, and no objects seen at an angle).

The *centric ray* alone is supported in their midst, like a united assembly, by all the others, so that it must rightly be called the leader and prince of rays. In asserting its preeminence, Alberti is simply transmitting a principle of medieval optics. The traditional emphasis was due to the fact that all other rays had to be refracted by the lens of the eye in order to reach the apex of the visual pyramid (see fig. 4.3).[20] This meant that they arrived by a less direct route and therefore, it was said, with correspondingly

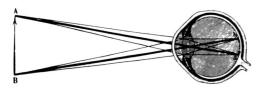

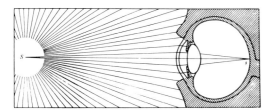

4.3   *Diagram of the reception of light by the eye. From M. H. Pirenne,* Optics, Painting and Photography. *Above: The retinal image ab of an object AB, in focus on the retina. This diagram illustrates a simplified construction, which in any case is valid only for retinal images close to the optical axis of the eye. All the* main *rays, such as the straight lines* Aa *and* Bb, *are taken to cross at one optical center, inside the crystalline lens, to define the position of the retinal images of the different points of the object. Below: Light convergence in the vertebrate eye. Some of the divergent rays emitted by a point source* S, *having entered the eye, are made convergent by the optical system of the eye and are reunited at a point* s *on the retina.*

less effectiveness. Furthermore, because it enters the eye directly rather than at an angle, the *centric ray* was more distinct and less distorted—in Alberti's words "more keen and vigorous." Leonardo made this point vividly by a sort of reversed ballistic metaphor:

The pupil transmits nothing perfectly to the intellect except when the objects presented to it through the light reach it by the line (perpendicular to the pupil); these objects act like the archers who wish to shoot through the bore of a carbine; the one among them who finds himself in a straight line with the bore will be most likely to touch the bottom of the barrel.[21]

An allusion to the field of mechanics lurks just below the surface and is brought out elsewhere in Leonardo's notes,[22] the *centric ray* being visualized as having the virtues of a force applied to a body along the axis in which the body is to be moved. Finally, Alberti points out, "a quantity will never appear larger than when the *centric ray* rests upon it," which is to say that anything seen at an angle is more or less foreshortened and hence diminished in size.[23]

Since the abandonment of the ray theory of light propagation, the hypothesis of a *centric ray* with special powers no longer has validity, but there is a justification in the physiology of the eye for the conception that the image is sharper at the center of the visual field. In the center of the retina, there is a "yellow spot," the *fovea centralis*, instead of the more even distribution of cones and rods that occurs elsewhere in the retina, a small area alongside the intersection of the retina and the optic nerve where, instead of the more even distribution of cones and rods that occurs elsewhere in the retina, there is a concentration of cones that contributes to sharpening the center of the visual image; the periphery of the retina has much reduced receptivity. Thus the old Italian saying, "se non è vero, è ben trovato," applies to the medieval and Albertian hypothesis. Like many other subsequently superseded principles of earlier science and technology, this one not only fitted the system for which it was conceived but also provided a metaphorical, prescientific explanation of a significant phenomenon, the actual causes of which were not yet accessible to the investigatory method of the time.

It is easy to see how Alberti's description of light propagation based on Euclidean geometry produced this particular triadic system of rays: each of the three is the conduit of one of the basic geometrical elements—the *centric ray* of the point, *extrinsic rays* of the line, and *median rays* of the plane.

In summing up his description of the *centric ray* (§8), Alberti emphasizes that the two geometrical elements that determine the nature of a visual image are the *position* of the *centric ray* (e.g., where the center of the image is) and the *distance* of the observer from the object(s) seen (figs. 4.4B, 4.4C). "There is also a third condition in which surfaces present themselves to the observer as different or of diverse form. This is the reception of *light*." An object seen from a particular position and distance will, for example, look one way when lit from above or from the right, and another when lit from below or from the left (fig. 4.4A). Further (§9), "colors vary according to light, as every color appears different when in shade and when placed under rays of light. Shade makes a color look dark, and light makes it bright and clear."

III

What Alberti does not say about his basic variables is that the third, light/color, draws him out of the sphere that can be controlled by the mathematics and science of his time: whereas the effects of light from a particular fixed source, such as cast shadow (merely mentioned by Alberti), were reproduced later with the aid of geometry, many aspects of light and color of interest to painters could be discussed only in terms of experience and could not be quantified. Alberti, in fact, drops his Euclidean mode, apparently unconsciously, the moment he makes an observation about color. In the earlier passage in which he says that the *median rays* carry color, he adds:

We know for a fact about these median rays *that over a long distance they weaken and lose their sharpness. The reason why this occurs has been discovered: as they pass through the air, these and all other visual rays are laden and imbued with lights and colors; but the air too is also endowed with a certain density, and in consequence the rays get tired and lose a good part of their burden as they penetrate the atmosphere. So it is rightly said that the greater the distance, the more obscure and dark* [suboscurioram et magis fuscam] *the surface appears.*

This remarkable passage attempts to deal with common-sense observation of what, since Leonardo's time, has been called "aerial perspective," a phenomenon that could not be predicted or explained by a purely mathematical model of vision such as that of Euclid. The problem did, however, arise in the studies of Aristotle and Ptolemy, who were more concerned with sensation. Their explanation involved the hypothesis, first, that light is not propagated instantaneously but travels with a finite velocity, and second, the air is not a vacuum but a medium that has a density which affects vision. From the latter assumption they concluded that the denser the air intervening between an object and the eye, the more it would obstruct vision. But Alberti's explanation of this phenomenon—a mixture of vitalism with mechanics (the rays, physically worn down, lose their intensity as they encounter friction)—is unconvincing, and though he states that it "has been discovered," presumably by scientists, it has never been found in another writer. Furthermore, the passage concludes with a statement on the darkening of distant surfaces that appears to be in conflict with normal visual experience.

Alberti was not the only one to have found aerial perspective difficult to explain. To begin with, Aristotle and Ptolemy, though they describe a similar phenomenon, attribute it to quite different causes. In Aristotle, "Dark color is a kind of negation of vision, the appearance of darkness being due to the failure of our sight; hence objects seen at a distance appear darker because sight fails to reach them." [24] And, in Ptolemy, "That which is far off we see less well because the visual rays as they proceed carry with them something of the darkness (*nigretudine*) of the air through which they travel, and thus a thing in the remote air appears as if it were under a veil." [25] What is paradoxical in this comparison is that while Aristotle (in *De anima* and *De sensu*) was the most vigorous opponent in antiquity of the extromission theory (whereby visual rays are cast out from the eye) and attributed a major role in the transmission of images to the action of the medium, this statement from the *Meteorologica* clearly implies extromission, while Ptolemy, who was a supporter of that theory, offers an explanation based on the coloration of the atmosphere that could work equally well whether the rays originated in the eye or the object. The confusion was perpetuated into the Middle

Ages, when Witelo, who accepted Alhazen's demolition of the extromission theory, repeated the Aristotelian explanation almost verbatim.[26] Nicholas Oresme, the great physicist and philosopher of the fourteenth century, resolved the problem by attributing the phenomenon simply to the difficulty of seeing through great quantities of air, the cause being, as Ptolemy had said, in the nature of the medium rather than in the power of the eye.[27] While his explanation was oversimplified, it cleared the way for a more effective approach by later investigators; Biagio Pelacani, for example, discussed the effects of varying densities in the atmosphere.[28]

Alberti tried, in a sense, to accommodate the various arguments by suggesting that the rays, rather than the observer, possessed a kind of vital force that was spent by the effort of traveling through a dense medium. This had no foundation elsewhere in his theory and certainly was not sustained by common-sense experience.[29] The only possible explanation is that, in spite of his avowed neutrality in the conflict over the extromission theory, he wanted to establish once and for all the concept that the rays originated in the object, and he tried to adjust this position to the Aristotelian-Witelian idea that physical exhaustion was somehow involved.

But why did the early authors and Alberti say that objects seem darker at a distance, when everyday experience confirms the fact that the effect of the atmosphere is to make them seem lighter? While in normal light the atmosphere lowers the intensity of colors, it heightens their value, and Aristotle was too keen an observer of nature to have overlooked the fact that frequently distant mountains seem to fade toward a light blue or purple. The apparent contradiction is due, as Edgerton has shown, to a disjunction between ancient and modern color terminology. In Alberti's vocabulary (which follows Aristotle in this respect, but reduces the number and nature of the primaries), cool colors such as blue and purple are dark no matter how high in value they may be, and this results in descriptions that do not make sense in our terms: the lightest blue would be spoken of as darker than the deepest red. Distinctions were not made between hue and value. Alberti used the term *fuscus,* which roughly means muddy, to refer to the loss of intensity of colors in shadows and at a distance. It implies a dark brownish or neutral tone and, while it does not correspond to later perceptions of the effects of the atmosphere, it is consistent with his other statements.[30]

But §9, which is about color, repeats from earlier sources a number of empirical observations that seem in hindsight to teeter on the brink of the discovery of value and intensity (though the account of "the four true kinds of colors," or primaries associated with earth, air, fire, and water, is medieval-symbolic in character). "It is evident," Alberti says, "that colors vary according to light, as every color appears different when in shade and when placed under rays of light. Shade makes a color look dark (*fuscus*), and light makes it bright and clear." This seems a common-sense base on which to proceed with a color theory, but it sets up an unresolved contradiction with the Aristotelian tradition: if those distant bluish mountains are well lit, is their color bright or *fuscus?* In the two passages cited here, Alberti's answers are in apparent conflict.

From theory, Alberti turns to what he presents as practice:

My own view about colors, as a painter, is that from the mixture of colors there arises an almost infinite variety of others, but that for painters there are four true kinds of colors corresponding to the number of elements, and from these many species are produced. There is fire color, which they call red, and the color of air, which is said to be blue or blue-grey, and the green of water, and the earth is ash-colored. So, there are four kinds of colors, of which there are countless species according to the admixture of white and black. For we see verdant leaves gradually lose their greenness until they become white. We also see the same thing with the air, how, when, as is often the case, it is suffused around the horizon with whitish mist, it gradually changes back to its true color.

Though, in telling us that "we see" the described phenomena, Alberti may seem to be recording visual experiences, he is in fact still adhering to the written texts—not texts on optics in this case, since they were not concerned with particular colors, but perhaps a short Peripatetic essay, *De coloribus*, believed in the Renaissance to be by Aristotle. Here the phenomenon of the whitening sky at the horizon is discussed and attributed to the "densification" of the air, while the deep blue of the sky is caused by the air's rarity, which permits the passage of more powerful rays of light.[31] Alberti's preceding observation on the whitening of green leaves usually has been taken as a similar instance of atmospheric perspective; but the extended discussion in *De coloribus*—which could be his source—of such phenomena in plants and animals is concerned with their actual color change from one season to another rather than with the effects of atmosphere on appearances. "The leaves of most trees turn yellow in the end," it says, "because owing to the failure of nutriment, they become dried up before they change to their natural color."[32] Why did Alberti say "white" when both this text and common-sense experience dictate the yellowing of leaves? Apparently because, in his four-color system, yellow is not a primary, but one of the "species" produced, presumably from green, by the "admixture of white." It is hard to reconcile this with Alberti's emphasis that he is speaking here as a painter: a few hours' experience with pigments would persuade a much lesser intelligence than his that the yellows used in the tempera panels of his time could not have been produced by the mixture of any other colors. This passage, then, is one of the many instances in which humanist writers refused to permit empirical evidence to shake the authority of established theory.[33]

More on the palette appears in Book II (§30) of *De pictura*, in which the art of painting is defined:

We divide painting into three parts, and this division we learn from Nature herself. As painting aims to represent things seen, let us note how in fact things are seen. In the first place, when we look at a thing, we see it as an object which occupies space. The painter will draw around this space, and he will call this process of sketching the outline, appropriately, circumscription. *Then, as we look, we discern how the several surfaces of the object seen are fitted together; the artist, when drawing these combinations of surfaces in their correct relationship, will properly call this* composition. *Finally, in looking we observe more clearly the colors of surfaces; the representation in painting of this aspect, since it receives all its variations from light, will aptly here be termed the* reception of light.

In the studio, then, the study of light focuses on the practice of coloring. When, in the closing paragraphs of Book II (§§ 46–49), Alberti expands on this third part of painting, he begins by stating that "colors contribute greatly to the beauty and attraction of a painting," but proceeds to discuss only the employment of white and black as the essential factor in the application of pigment. White represents light, and black, shadow; they occur on opposite sides of any body, and skill in their use consists in mixing them with the color of the things painted in order imperceptibly to create transitions from light to shadow, and in employing them sparingly and subtly, never allowing them to be seen in pure state except for the brightest highlights or night shadows. "With such balancing, as one might say, of black and white, a surface rising in relief becomes still more evident." The importance of relief is such that special praise is assigned to pictures in which the faces "seem to stand out . . . as if they had been sculpted." The painter is even advised to begin by drawing the outlines of the light areas as well as of the figures themselves.

Most Italian painters from Masaccio to Leonardo shared Alberti's preoccupation with the illusion of relief; but none accepted his color theory. In spite of its scientific basis, it was quite inapplicable in the workshop, and the prescriptions of Cennino Cennini, the recorder of late-medieval shop practice, continued to be a much closer guide to the color principles of most artists working in tempera before 1500. The reasons for this will be discussed at the close of this article.

IV

Alberti's last word on light and color in Book I, in §11, is a brief recital of a number of kinds of shadows and reflections of special interest to painters—a subject that, like the principles of color, was not treated extensively in most of the ancient and medieval texts on optics. "Some [lights] are of stars, such as the sun and the moon, and the morning-star, others of lamps and fire. There is a great difference between them, for the light of stars makes shadows exactly the same size as bodies, while the shadows from fire are larger than the bodies."

Again, these observations prove to be not the result of Alberti's own investigation: ancient and medieval contributions to the subject are found in the literature on astronomy.[34] Alberti's reference to stars—which were of no more import for painters than for writers on optics—strengthens the likelihood of his dependence on astronomical sources. The science of shadows, based on the study of the gnomon, was essential to the development of sundials and provided the foundation for essential astronomical measurements, such as that of the size of the sun and its distance from the earth; it was basic to Ptolemy's geographical research and perhaps even to his invention of orthographic and stereographic projection.

The only ancient text on shadows is in the introduction to Theon of Alexandria's recension of Euclid's *Optics*.[35] Theon used shadows to prove that light rays are rectilinear, explaining that an object illuminated by light from a small fire (i.e., artificial light) throws a large shadow and vice versa, while a source the same size as the object makes a shadow equal to it in size. It was probably from this text that later writers, including Alberti, got the idea of classifying shadows by relative size and of creating them by "fire." The most penetrating investigations of cast shadows were made by Alhazen, the father of medieval optics, in a study devoted exclusively to the subject in the context of astronomy; he experimented with a candle and made significant observations of shadows cast by the sun, but his work was not translated and does not seem to have been read until recent times.[36]

When Alberti states that celestial light creates shadows of the same size as the intercepting body, he is accepting a tacitly held (and, from a painter's point of view, valid) assumption of ancient astronomers that the rays of the sun, or of other celestial lights, are parallel, as distinct from the divergent rays emitted by a point source such as a candle or lamp.[37] All in all, there is nothing in Alberti's passage to indicate that he had a lively interest in the matter that might have prompted him to study the postclassical literature on it.[38]

Alberti then turns from shadows to reflected rays, informs us that the angle of reflection equals that of incidence, and concludes by observing that reflected rays carry color from the surface on which they originate: "We see this happen when the faces of people walking about in meadows appear to have a greenish tinge." Even this observation appears to have a textual stimulus; the author of *De coloribus,* after stating that firelight, moonlight, and torchlight alter the character of colors, continues, "For if light falls on a given object and is colored by it [say] crimson or herb-green, and then the light reflected from the object falls on another color, it is again modified by this second color, and so gets a new chromatic blend."[39]

The perfunctory nature of Alberti's passage on shadows and the lack of adjustment to the interests of the painter suggest that Alberti did not believe that cast shadows were a significant means for achieving a persuasive illusion of the visual world, or for creating links between parts of a picture. His study of light and shadow concentrated on the modeling of bodies by the addition of white and black—the mode of relief.[40] He was predisposed to thinking about composition as the arrangement of autonomous bodies by the fact that his geometrical-optical theory defined light and vision in terms of rays that delimit and describe the surfaces of people and things, and by the fact that Early Renaissance artists and theorists who turned to ancient art for models found only sculpture and were prompted to think of painting in sculptural terms. But history nonetheless made Alberti an unwitting pioneer in the development of the technique of rendering cast shadows. When Dürer showed for the first time how to calculate geometrically the shadows cast by an object lit from a point source, he simply adopted the technique of perspective projection first proposed in *De pictura* (which he had adjusted and simplified): he represented the pyramid of rays extending from a candle to a depicted object and beyond it to form a shadow as the analogue of the pyramid formed between the object and the eye and intercepted by the plane of the picture.[41]

V

Paragraph 12, which follows, is the conclusion of Alberti's study of light and color and the transition to the exposition of the *costruzione legittima.* It begins with a review of what had gone before and continues with a spirited effort to counter the resistance he anticipates from artists who might have preferred a book of this sort to consist, like Cennino Cennini's, of recipes covering the details of daily workshop practice within the established style. Alberti says, in effect, that it is practical as well as intellectually rewarding to approach painting from a theoretical-scientific foundation. The implication is that painters who fail to do so are missing an opportunity to participate in a challenging new enterprise.[42] With this, the argument is summed up:

They [the painters] should understand that, when they draw lines around a surface, and fill the parts they have drawn with colors, their sole object is the representation on this one surface of many different forms of surfaces, just as though this surface which they color were so transparent and like glass, that the visual pyramid passes right through it from a certain distance and with a certain position of the centric ray and of the lights established in their proper places in the air. Painters prove this when they move away from what they are painting and stand further back, seeking to find by the light of nature the vertex of the pyramid from which they know everything can be more correctly viewed. . . . Therefore, a painting will be the intersection of a visual pyramid at a given distance, with a fixed center and certain position of lights, represented skillfully within lines and colors on a given surface.[43]

Twice in this quotation, and once at the beginning of the paragraph, Alberti declares that there are three basic processes of orientation to perform in laying out a painted version of a visual image. Two of them refer to the viewer's relationship to the object—his distance away from it, and the position of his eye directly opposite a chosen point on the object (establishing the centric ray means orienting with respect to the up/down and left/right axes)—and the third to the position of the light source(s) illuminating the object. Alberti has been working toward this conclusion from the very start; in §5, he defined accidental qualities as determined by the same three factors (fig. 4.4). The reason for the redundant emphasis on these points is that, except in the work of two of Alberti's colleagues, Donatello and Masaccio, who contributed to the formulation of the method, they were not yet a part of artistic practice. No earlier artist had oriented himself precisely in relation to his object: his distance would have been the product of roughly how big or small the parts of his object looked to him, his center of vision would have been higher when he looked up at the ceiling than when he looked down at the floor, and his light, while normally coming from a vaguely defined area to the left or right, would often have shifted from figure to figure.[44] If painters stood back from their paintings to get a better look at relationships of parts to the whole, none of them prior to Masaccio and one or two of his emulators at the time of *De pictura* was being composed would have done it for the reason Alberti states in this passage (i.e., that they were seeking the vertex of the visual pyramid). To understand what he means by this, we must realize that this passage contains his most influential and revolutionary contribution to the history of art.

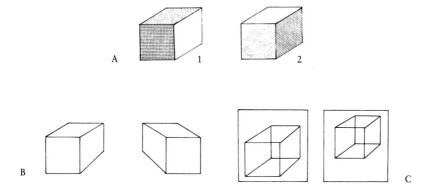

4.4 *Variables in seeing or depicting an object.* (A) *effect of change of light source: (1) source on lower right; (2) source on upper left.* (B) *effect of change of position.* (C) *effect of change of distance.*

Up to this point, Alberti has been presenting a rationalized account of the process of seeing, with an emphasis on issues of interest to painters. Here, however, he is concerned for the first time with transferring the image we see onto a flat painted surface with absolute mathematical accuracy, which is the ultimate purpose of all his scientific research. At this point, where the accumulated wisdom of ancient and medieval writers on optics was of no help, Alberti had an inspiration—prompted, it appears, by looking out the window:[45] if the image of the outside world comes to the eye via a pyramid of light rays, the same image could be hypothetically caught at any point between the object and the eye by interposing a vertical screen, or intersection of the pyramid.[46] The look out the window made this highly abstract notion concrete: there, within a frame, is a view of the outside world that could be thought of as projected onto the glass, though it passes through this "screen" to the eye (windows and paintings looked remarkably alike in Alberti's time, when picture frames were modeled on architectural forms).[47] If one took a brush and pigments and painted onto the window glass all the outside objects visible there, one would have a picture that was a geometrically precise imitation of what was seen through the window. But the experiment works only if one stays in an absolutely fixed position, because the view out the window alters as one moves toward or away from the glass, left or right, up or down. Once the painting is done, and one can no longer see the real world beyond, one could indeed look at the picture from any position within the room, but only one position would correspond precisely to the view out the window, and only in that position would the picture be fully illusionistic.

There need be no difference between the painted window glass and a painted panel, except that the former was transparent to start with. In painting a panel, one simply transfers the intersection of the pyramid from a preparatory sketch done on a transparent sheet—Alberti called it a "veil" (fig. 4.5)[48]—or one concocts a fictive scene according to the rules of the view-out-the-window. Either way, *the illusion works only if the picture is viewed from exactly the same point as the scene was viewed or imagined to begin with*. That is why the painter in Alberti's explanation moves back to locate the vertex of the visual pyramid (that is, the point from which the perspective is constructed), and why we, in looking at Renaissance pictures, should also make an effort to locate it, remembering, of course, to shut one eye.[49] The reader who still finds Alberti's text and my explanation of it baffling is advised to make some sketches in a transparent, and preferably water-soluble, medium on his windowpane.[50]

If all pictures could be made through a window or a veil, there would have been no need for inventing perspective; everything could have been done by eye. But Alberti's was a period in which painting was rarely done from nature, which meant that a system had to be devised that created an imaginary world in which events could be staged. This involved reversing the initial procedure in a sense; with the window or veil the artist began (as in fig. 4.5) by delineating people or objects and, if he wished, arrived finally at a convincing representation of a whole environment. But to make an illusionistic imaginary scene it was necessary to first invent a consistent space in which it would take place; otherwise the relationship between the people and objects, and between both of these and the observer, would be arbitrary and unconvincing. So the primary purpose of the invention of artificial perspective was to concoct a measurable void that could subsequently be peopled. It was an abstract geometrical problem, unrelated to the questions of vision (we do not actually see space, but only the objects that fill it) that had occupied Alberti in the first twelve paragraphs. But the solution of the problem was wholly dependent on three postulates affirmed in §12: The picture must be regarded as the intersection of the visual pyramid, and the observer must be at a fixed distance, and his eye at a fixed centric point. The centric point became, in fact, the focus of Alberti's perspective construction—the terminus, later called the "vanish-

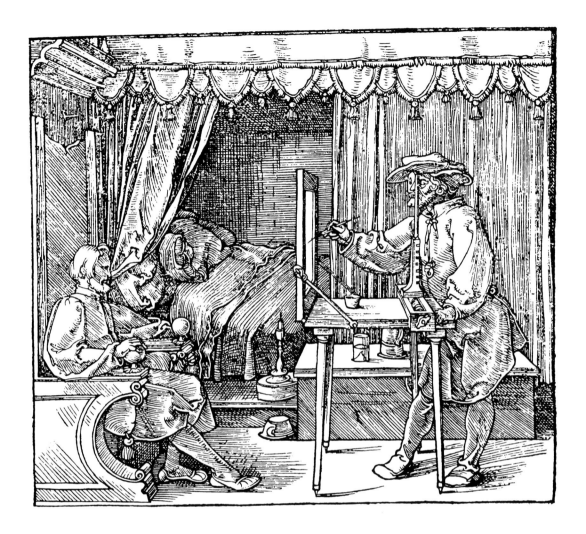

4.5   *Albrecht Dürer, painter using a version of*
Alberti's "veil." From Underweysung der Messung . . . ,
1525.

ing point," toward which all orthogonals converge. Its focal position is conceptually based on the superior powers of the centric ray; indeed, the "vanishing point" is nothing other than the centric ray viewed end-on, or, to put it another way, the point where the centric ray strikes. Because the *costruzione legittima* creates an abstract space, Alberti did not perceive that its procedures could be adapted to his fourth principle, the establishment of a fixed source of light; it was to be ninety years before Dürer announced a method of projecting shadows that was based on an analogy between the pyramid of light rays emanating from the sun and the pyramid entering the eye.[51]

Artificial perspective is relevant here only because of its great debt to Alberti's study of ancient and medieval optics as recorded in the first half of Book I of *De pictura*. The book moves with impressive purpose and logic through the applicable hypotheses of the optical scientists toward a climax in Alberti's unique contribution, the intersection of the visual pyramid, which made it possible to translate the scientific data into the practice of painting, and concludes with the application of the intersection to perspective construction.

VI

The immediate and widespread impact of artificial perspective on Early Renaissance painting is well known, but the effect of the precepts dissolved here, which led to its invention, have not been examined.

Alberti's basic hypothesis, that light is propagated by rectilinear rays of three distinct kinds (extrinsic, median, and centric) had direct and indirect implications for the practice of painting. The most obvious was the separation of the outline of objects from their surfaces by the extrinsic rays, which Alberti described (in §2) as constituting a "brim or fringe" serving to measure quantities. Median rays differ by being propagated from the surface of the object and by carrying the color and light from their points of origin. Since the extrinsic rays are by inference not modified by local color or light, a painter reading the passage would conclude that they should be recorded by a thin line of neutral color that retains the same character whether it was on the shaded or the lit side of the object to be portrayed. In Book II (§30), wherein Alberti defines the nature of painting, he shows circumscription, the application of the concept of the extrinsic ray, to be one of the cornerstones of the art. The other two parts of painting are then defined as composition and coloring, which is termed "reception of light." The following paragraph expands on the concept of circumscription, the "process of tracing the outlines in the painting":

I believe one should take care that circumscription is done with the finest possible, almost invisible, lines like those they say the painter Apelles used to practice and vie with Protogenes at drawing. Circumscription is simply the recording of the outlines, and if it is done with a very visible line, they will look in the painting, not like the edges of surfaces, but like cracks. I want only the outlines to be sketched in circumscription; and this should be practiced assiduously. No composition and no reception of light will be praised without the presence of circumscription. But circumscription by itself is very often most pleasing.[52]

The outlining of figures in the way described here was indeed the standard practice of Florentine painters throughout the fifteenth century (fig. 4.6) and was still used by Michelangelo in the Doni tondo of 1506, and in fresco painting for a much longer time. It was so much the rule that Leonardo launched numerous attacks on it, for example in the *Trattato:* "The outline of one object impinging on another is like a mathematical line, but it is not a line because the limit of one color is the beginning of another color, and must not be called a line because nothing intervenes between the outlines of one color which is placed opposite another color except the outline that is invisible even close up. Therefore, painter, do not accentuate it in distant things."[53]

Alberti had used his scientific hypothesis to support a theoretical position that provided the justification for the Florentine emphasis on *disegno,* and particularly for a style of drawing with a continuous closed outline separating the figure from the ground.[54] Florentine *disegno* does not, however, stem from Alberti, nor is it even substantially indebted to his formulation—it was already well established in the preceding century.[55] But Alberti's formulation affirmed that the primacy of drawing and the concept of composition as an assembly of distinct objects were consistent with the ideal of art in the new era. The historical role of art theory is not only to invent new practices and set new goals but also to indicate which traditional practices remain valid.

The color transmitted by the median rays is what might be called the "real" color of an object as it is affected by light and shadow. Other factors influence color perception, such as atmosphere and reflected light/color, but Alberti presents these as special cases, with somewhat negative overtones, as if they were obstacles to perceiving things rightly, and he provides no encouragement to painters to take pleasure in or to record the kind of special environmental effects that were to be so important in later painting. The practical effect of his advice was to encourage painters to assign a particular hue to the area within the circumscribed outline and then to modulate this by raising its value (with white) on the side toward the light and to lower it (with black) on the opposite, shadowed side. This is discussed in §46 of Book II, where Alberti expands on the third part of painting, "reception of light." He also suggests that

4.6 *Domenico Veneziano*, Resuscitation of the Child,
Cambridge, Fitzwilliam Museum.

you may change the color with a little white applied as sparingly as possible in the appropriate place within the outlines of the surface, and likewise add some black in the place opposite to it. With such balancing, as one might say, of black and white a surface rising in relief becomes still more evident. Go on making similar sparing additions until you feel you have arrived at what is required.

Modeling of each object individually to achieve relief was the practice followed by quattrocento painters, but neither Alberti nor any other writer or practitioner of the period was able to translate "light" and "shadow" into pigment equivalents in a way that fulfilled his aspirations both to realism and to effective color design.[56]

Alberti failed in this area because he did not differentiate between the behavior of light, as defined scientifically or as experienced optically, and the behavior of pigment. This difference invalidates two of his fundamental principles: first, that white and black are the palette equivalents of light and shadow respectively, and second, that all other colors can be produced by mixing the four primaries with white and black. The second of these principles perpetuated a mistake that originated in Aristotle:[57] we have already seen that Alberti's primaries (blue, red, green, earth color) were excessively limiting, since yellow was excluded. Further, mixing a hue with black and white does not alter it but merely raises or lowers its value. If white is mixed with a pure blue, the resulting pigment is a paler state of the same blue. The term "paler" is more indicative than "lighter" because in the process the blue loses some of its intensity or impact; the majority of colors are neutralized almost as much by the addition of a bit of white as by a comparable amount of black.

The modeling of all objects toward white on the light side and toward black on the dark, which results from the first proposition, is not, on the other hand, unacceptable, but it was rejected by the mass of quattrocento painters because it was not to their taste. They, like the Impressionists, did not mind neutralizing their colors with white, but they found that an equal application of black produced a somber and deadening effect that was particularly uncongenial to the tempera medium.[58] They preferred to make individual experiments based on the old-fashioned formula detailed by Cennino Cennini in his *Libro dell'arte* of about 1390, in which black is not used for modeling at all; the deepest shadows are established by pigment in its purest, and most intense, state, and modeling is done entirely with white.[59] This entirely ignores the neutralizing effect of shadow in nature, on which Alberti insists, and makes areas the most vivid where they ought to be the least: it accounts in large part for the unreal appearance of much quattrocento painting. In Alberti's system, the pure pigment would appear along a band just on the light side of a line that he advises the painter to draw at the start, dividing the light part of the figure from the dark.[60] Of the two practices, Alberti's was actually the more realistic and, for outdoor lighting in the full sunlight, the more capable of producing an acceptable illusion, because in that situation the combined effect of glare, reflection, and the adjustment of the eye to brightness does lower color perception and may make it seem that the most intense color appears roughly midway between the highest and the lowest value.

Neither Alberti nor the painters differentiated between value and intensity; it did not matter, for example, that yellow has a high value at full intensity and ultramarine blue a low one, so that, in either Alberti's or Cennini's system, the blue cloak of a figure could not be modeled in the same way as the yellow shirt without making them appear to be in two different conditions of lighting. Consequently, not only was each object or figure kept distinct, but each color area within the figure seems to pull away from its neighbors, which can produce stimulating color patterns but inhibits tonal harmony.

Finally, the Albertian system, in conceiving the value range as creating an equilibrium between light and dark, assumes that the objects in a painting will be illuminated by rays traveling parallel to the picture plane at 90° to the centric rays coming to the eye. Thus, discounting variations in their surface, each will appear half in the light and half in the shadow (because cast shadows are rarely used, objects in quattrocento paintings are almost all lit directly). Each figure is to be modeled in relief, in the nearest possible approximation of the sculptural relief of Ghiberti and Donatello (in §46, Alberti praises "those faces which seem to stand out from pictures as if they were sculpted"); indeed, relief is actually more modified by atmosphere in Donatello's *schiacciato* panels than in any painting done in Alberti's lifetime, with the exception of some frescoes of Masaccio.[61]

VII

In bringing the hypotheses of medieval optics into the painter's workshop, Alberti necessarily accepted and promoted a particular philosophical position that influenced the goals and the criticism of art. His theory posits the existence of objects out there in the world that light makes it possible for us to see; rectilinear beams that retain the color and the value of the source transmit data from the surface of the objects to the eye. Under exceptional conditions, these data may be altered by the intervening environment, but it is assumed that they enter the eye and pass through it to the mind without being further affected; every eye and mind processes the data in the same way. Philosophically the approach is purely materialist; reality is immanent in the objects of the external world, and our percepts of them are undistorted reflections of that reality.

Alberti's text contains none of the idealist principles that came to the fore with the revival of Neoplatonism and were to dominate later theories of art, according to which the objects of perception are imperfect versions of a pure idea, compromised by their earthliness. In idealist theory, the percept is different for different viewers: the common man sees nothing behind the crass surface of objects, while the more elevated spirit (of the artist, connoisseur, or philosopher) penetrates nearer to the perfection of the idea.[62] Alberti's system did not provide this effective formula for differentiating the artistic imagination or vision from the ordinary. In fact, it appears to call for a purely naturalized art—though one modified by mathematical order.[63] Book III of *De pictura* faces the problem of reconciling this with a concept of beauty (*pulchritudo*) formulated with the help of the Aristotelian principle of selection:[64] "The early painter Demetrius failed to obtain the highest praise because he was more devoted to representing the likeness of things than to beauty. Therefore, excellent parts should all be selected from the most beautiful bodies, and every effort should be made to perceive, understand and express beauty" (§55). This leads to an account of the legend of the "Maids of Croton," in which the painter Zeuxis devised a perfect female type by taking the best features from the five most beautiful girls of the town in which he was working, a device by which *mimesis* could be reconciled with the idea of beauty. The principle, however, has an obvious and serious flaw, in that the standard by which Zeuxis or Alberti selects the girls to begin with, and then finds their comeliest parts, is kept secret, though it is the key to the whole argument. From what Alberti says, we can conclude only that it emerges as an endowment of upright and well-educated artists (§52).

But quite apart from standards of aesthetic value, Alberti's epistemology poses problems for painters because it fails to account for the experience of anyone trying to work from nature: that things do not always look "the way they are" (in a dim light, for example, the shaded part of a head or body may be indistinguishable from the obscurity of the environment or of a body alongside it). Whatever the causes of differences between the object and the percept, the artist has to choose between portraying things "as they are" (a distinct, definable body in full relief with an outline) and things as they seem. The quattrocento artist almost invariably joined Alberti in preferring the former. Though Alberti was aware that deprivation of light and atmospheric conditions inhibit clarity of vision, he obviously believed that one simply did not make pictures of objects unless their modeling was discernible and their entire outline visible, and every quattrocento painting affirms the same conviction until the moment when it is challenged by Leonardo's *sfumato* technique in the last decade of the century.

Most quattrocento painters avoided the conflict between reality and appearance by not drawing or painting from nature. Because their pictures were totally invented, things could be rendered as if they were solids lit in the way most favorable to bringing out their fullest relief.[65] Figures, objects, and even flora were conceived almost as sculptures; and it is symptomatic that in some of the earliest Florentine life drawings, apprentices are sketched in poses taken from antique statues.[66] This helps to explain why landscape painting was not much cultivated—the appeal of landscape is primarily in textures of indefinite form and effects of atmosphere—and why Mantegna, who was the first particularly to emphasize landscape settings, invented exceptionally stony countrysides with sharp contours edged by curving roads. It also explains how an age committed to realism in art got much farther in creating illusions of space and mass than illusions of color: a completely abstract and intellectual construct such as Uccello's *Mazzocchio* could be made to look like a solid object in three-dimensional space, but the abstract-intellectual treatment of color, even when based on what the artist knew to be the "real" colors of objects, did not produce a convincing illusion and led to decorative, abstract color composition rather than to naturalism.

It would be misleading to suggest either that fifteenth-century painting followed this course because it conformed to the optical theory of Alberti and the scientists or, conversely, that Alberti's optics remained strictly geometrical because the Early Renaissance mode of perception avoided appearances. The art and the science were simply different manifestations of one outlook on the nature of the material world. But without Alberti, they would not have been brought together so that they could be perceived as part of the same conceptual structure, and that, as much as any originality of thought, is the significant contribution. We have seen that the optics are those of the era from Alhazen to Pelacani, and the concepts of color and modeling are not far from the practice of Giotto, but out of these medieval components emerged a new alloy that showed artists the relevance of science as a way of making sense out of the experience of nature. No particular precept in the first part of *De pictura* had as pervasive an impact as the following section on perspective construction; the specific recommendations on color and shadow were ineffectual and, until Leonardo, artists continued to examine those problems by the old hit-or-miss methods. But the incalculable change that Leonardo wrought was directly dependent on Alberti's vision of art as a branch of natural science and particularly of optics: the debt is acknowledged by the opening lines of Leonardo's *Trattato*, which, in the context of establishing painting as a science, repeat the same Euclidean demonstrations as those at the start of *De pictura*.

Notes

In homage to the major contributions of Millard Meiss to the study of light in quattrocento painting: "Light as Form and Symbol in Some Fifteenth-Century Paintings," *Art Bulletin*, 27 (1945), 175–181; "Some Remarkable Early Shadows in a Rare Type of Threnos," *Festschrift Ulrich Middeldorf* (Berlin, 1968), 112–118.

1. *On Painting and On Sculpture: The Latin Texts of De Pictura and De Statua*, edited and translated by C. Grayson (London and New York, 1972): I have not yet seen the more richly annotated edition of the Italian text published by Grayson as vol. 3 of Alberti, *Opere volgari* (Bari, 1973). The new editions will doubtless supersede that of J. Spencer, *On Painting* (New Haven, 1956 and 1966), done from the Italian text, and the earlier German and Italian editions.

Grayson dates the text of *De pictura* from a note of August 26, 1435, in one of the manuscripts and proposes 1436 for the Italian translation executed by the author ("The Text of Alberti's De Pictura," *Italian Studies*, 23 [1968], 71–92; see also Grayson's "Studi su L. B. Alberti," *Rinascimento*, 4 [1953], 54–62). Before receiving galleys, I was alerted (by Prof. D. C. Lindberg) to the study of M. Simonelli, "On Alberti's Treatises of Art and Their Chronological Relationship," *Yearbook of Italian Studies* (1971), 75–102, which offers persuasive testimony that the Latin version is a later expansion and correction of the Italian.

2. As accounted by G. Ten Doesschate, "De derde Commentaar van Lorenzo Ghiberti in Verband met de middeleeuwsche Optiek," dissertation, Utrecht, 1940; summarized in his "Over de Bronnen van de derde Commentaar van Lorenzo Ghiberti," *Tijdschrift voor Geschiednis*, 47 (1932), 432–438. Cf. J. White, *The Birth and Rebirth of Pictorial Space* (London, 1957), 126ff.

3. The location in the Grayson edition of passages from the optical section of Book I of *De pictura* is given below in table 4.1 and is therefore not indicated separately in the notes.

4. For the Brunelleschian system, see n. 46, below.

That Alberti may have been aided in his refinement of artificial perspective by an ancient scientific treatise in a quite different field—Ptolemy's *Geografia* (brought to Florence ca. 1400 and translated from the Greek ca. 1406)—is suggested by Samuel Edgerton in his forthcoming book on Renaissance perspective and its origins. Cartographers have problems in common with painters in reducing three-dimensional reality to a flat image. This study owes much to conversations with Professor Edgerton, and to his careful reading of it in manuscript; I discovered after completing it that it duplicates in part his chapter entitled "Alberti's Optics." An essay by him concerning religious symbolism and Albertian perspective appears on pp. 115–130 of *Studies in Late Medieval and Renaissance Painting in Honor of Millard Meiss*, ed. Irving Lavin (New York, 1978).

5. Called *costruzione legittima* in modern literature (I was unable to answer Professor Edgerton's query as to whether the term originated in the Renaissance). I believe the Latin term would apply to any Renaissance perspective construction and the Italian to Alberti's and its descendants.

6. A basic bibliography is given in Grayson's edition of *De pictura*, 26ff., and M. Dalai, "La questione della prospettiva, 1960–1968," *L'arte*, 2 (1968), 96–105. Some issues of the continuing controversy are mentioned in n. 50, below.

7. Except for H. Siebenhüner, *Über den Kolorismus in der Frührenaissance,* dissertation, Leipzig (Schramberg, 1935), which first alerted me to the importance of Alberti's text, and recently, S. Y. Edgerton, "Alberti's Colour Theory: A Medieval Bottle without Renaissance Wine," *Journal of the Warburg and Cortauld Institutes,* 32 (1969), 109–134. See also no. 58, below.

8. A good survey of ancient writing on the subject is A. E. Haas, "Antike Lichttheorien," *Archiv für Philosophie,* n.s. 20 (1907), 345ff. See also V. Ronchi, *The Nature of Light* (Cambridge, Mass., 1970), 1–39.

9. The medieval authors are closely analyzed with extensive quotations in the fundamental study by G. F. Vescovini, *Studi sulla prospettiva medievale.* Pubblicazioni della Facoltà di Lettere e Filosofia, Università di Torino, XVI, I (Turin, 1965), 89–124, and more superficially by Ronchi, *The Nature of Light,* 39ff. See also D. C. Lindberg, "Alhazen's Theory of Vision and Its Reception in the West," *Isis,* 58 (1967), 321ff., and Lindberg, "Lines of Influence in 13th-Century Optics: Bacon, Witelo and Pecham," *Speculum,* 46 (1971), 66–83. I have not yet seen Lindberg's introduction to a new facsimile of the Basel 1572 edition of the optical texts of Alhazen and Witelo.

10. On Pelacani, see G. F. Vescovini, "Le questioni di 'perspectiva' di Biagio Pelacani da Parma," *Rinascimento,* ser. 2, 1 (1961), 163–243; idem, *Studi sulla prospettiva medievale,* 239–267. Vescovini transcribed portions of the Laurenziana MS. Plut. 29, 18, of 1428. The transcription of another manuscript is cited in n. 28, below. The text was composed ca. 1390 while the author was teaching at Pavia and expanded by him in 1403 by the addition of a section on phenomena of refraction, such as the rainbow, and on optical illusions.

Though not cited by Ghiberti, Pelacani may have been one channel by which the Florentine community became aware of the science of *perspectiva.* His text on Question 16, on the relationship of the apparent size of objects to the angle of vision and to their distance from the eye, may have helped Alberti with his interpretation of perspective construction in paragraphs 14–18 of Book I, which discuss the problem of proportion in perspective (see n. 19, below).

Though the question discussed by Pelacani had already been raised by Pecham, his work goes beyond earlier authors, particularly in its empirical method and its abandonment of the metaphysical component of the majority of late medieval writings. The form is still scholastic, but the spirit is of the new rationalism of the Renaissance. Passages of the *Quaestiones* coordinate optical studies with astronomy and geometrical with physiological/psychological optics.

11. Ten Doesschate, "De derde Commentaar," 4ff.

12. See M. Adriani, "Note sulla cultura protoquattrocentista fiorentina," *Un' altra Firenze: l'epoca di Cosimo il Vecchio* (Florence, 1971), 469–528. Adriani represents the conservative-liberal conflict as an early instance of the battle of the ancients and the moderns; his focus on political-moral philosophy tends, however, to deemphasize the technological-scientific interests of the liberal circle and its debt to the Middle Ages. For different interpretations of early quattrocento intellectual life in Florence, see L. Olschki, *Geschichte der neusprachlichen wissenschaftlichen Literatur,* vol. 1 (Leipzig, 1919), 1–107; R. Krautheimer and T. Krautheimer-Hess, *Lorenzo Ghiberti* (Princeton, N.J., 1956), chaps. XIX–XII, 294–334; E. H. Gombrich, "From the Revival of Letters to the Reform of the Arts: Niccolò Niccoli and Filippo Brunelleschi," *Essays Presented to Rudolf Wittkower* (London, 1967), 71–82.

13. *The Thirteen Books of Euclid's Elements,* translated, with introduction by Sir Thomas L. Heath, 2d ed. (New York, 1956), 153. Alberti may have been influenced in his departures from Euclid by the earliest of the surviving Arabic optical treatises, Alkindi's *De aspectibus* (ninth century), which argues that visual rays must be corporeal in order to be visible, since we cannot see abstractions (cf. Vescovini, *Studi sulla prospettiva medievale,* 5f.). The issue is raised also in an anonymous fourteenth-century commentary on Euclid's *De visu* in Florence (Biblioteca Nazionale, San Marco, Conv. Soppr. j. x. 19; ibid., 223 ff.), which contains similarities in vocabulary as well as in content to Alberti's text and may have been consulted by him. Both these connections are noted by Grayson in his edition of *On Painting and On Sculpture,* 108.

14. The Aristotelian-Thomistic term "accident" appears only later in Book I (§18), where Alberti is explaining the basic principle of perspective, that objects appear to change in size proportionally with their distance from the eye: "large, small, long, short, high, low, wide, narrow, light, dark, bright, gloomy, and everything of the kind, which philosophers termed accidents, because they may or may not be present in things—all these are such

as to be known only by comparison." Here, at the start, he is referring to the more limited case of "properties which, even when there is no change in the surface itself, do not always present the same aspect."

15. Alberti, like most medieval and Renaissance writers, calls this matrix of rays a "pyramid," electing the image invented by Ptolemy rather than the "cone" of Euclid and Galen (see n. 16, below). According to Edgerton, the terms were regarded as synonymous by Alberti and his predecessors, though the pyramid metaphor is suited to a time when nonmural pictures began to be made on rectangular surfaces, and is easier to employ in geometrical operations.

16. The relevant passage from *De usu partium*, X, 12, is quoted by Edgerton, "Alberti's Colour Theory," 125: "Circulique circumferentiam sic per visiones illas videri, ipsiusque centrum per aliam visionem in axe coni locatam, omnemque circuli planitiem per multas quasdam visiones ad ipsam pervenientes" (from ed. G. Kühn [Leipzig, 1822], III, 817).

17. Though the axial ray is defined as more powerful and effective than the others by all authors in this tradition (cf. the works cited in n. 9, above), Alhazen says that it communicates an even higher level of understanding of the thing seen; the totality of rays produces an *aspectus* of the object, while the axial ray gives an *intuitio* or *obtutus*: "Vision *per aspectu* is had by any ray of the optical pyramid, but vision *per obtutum* is had only by the axis. . . . The comprehension of visible things is therefore had in two ways, one superficial comprehension, which is the first impression, and the other comprehension by intuition. The former is uncertified, while comprehension by intuition is that by which the form of visible things is certified" (from *De aspectibus* in *Opticae Thesaurus*, ed. Risner [Basel, 1572], II, 65 and 64, quoted in Vescovini, *Studi sulla prospettiva medievale*, 120).

18. The case of the chameleon was cited by Ptolemy (*L'Optique de Claude Ptolémée . . .* , ed. A. Lejeune [Louvain, 1956], II, paragraph 15, p. 18) as an exception to his rule that the color of an object remains fixed so long as it is seen in the same light from the same position.

19. The proposition is a product of the reasoning adduced by Biagio Pelacani in Question 16 of his *Quaestiones,* which examines whether the size of things seen is in direct proportion to the angle of the visual triangle. In proving this not to be the case, he argues that as the eye approaches a

sphere, the angle of vision increases, but a smaller portion of the sphere is seen (Vescovini, "Le questioni di 'perspectiva,'" 221ff.). Alberti confronts the issue of the visual angle more overtly in §13–17, at the beginning of his exposition of artificial perspective.

20. Thus, in Alhazen: "The form that comes [to the eye] perpendicularly may be distinguished from other forms in two ways: the first is that it reaches from the surface of the thing seen to the center of the glacial humor by a straight line, whereas the others come by refracted lines; the second is that it is not only perpendicular to the surface of the thing seen, but perpendicular to the surface of the glacial humor . . . while the other lines are bent in relation to the surface. And the impact of light coming perpendicularly is stronger than the impact of light coming on inclined lines." (Quoted by Vescovini, *Studi sulla prospettiva medievale,* 118n., from the Basel 1572 ed. of *Opticae Thesaurus,* I, 18, p. 10.)

A similar statement is made by John Pecham (1230s–1292), who observes as well that one of the reasons for moving the eye about is that we thus direct the central ray to various parts of the observed object; cf. D. C. Lindberg, *John Pecham and the Science of Optics* (Madison, 1970), 120f.; the passage was called to my attention by Prof. Edgerton.

21. Codex Atlanticus, 270r, v. In quoting these observations, K. D. Keele, "Leonardo da Vinci's Physiology of the Senses," in *Leonardo's Legacy,* ed. Charles S. O'Malley (Berkeley and Los Angeles, 1969), 44ff., points out that the metaphor of the gun barrel probably was generated by Leonardo's thesis that the visual image was transmitted to the brain along the optic nerve which, like all nerves in Galenic physiology, was "perforated." It also suited his attempt to apply the principles of percussion to the action of light rays.

22. Keele, ibid., passim.

23. The point was ultimately challenged by Leonardo, who was the first writer on perspective to perceive the contradictions and limitations of the *costruzione legittima,* though the issue had been raised in a theoretical context by Pelacani (see n. 10, above; Vescovini, *Studi sulla prospettiva medievale,* 262f.). Leonardo cited and drew a row of columns seen at a right angle to their axis (see fig. 5.2); given a fixed eye, the column opposite the eye will appear to be the thinnest, and those on either side will appear to increase in width with distance (MS. A., fol. 41a; cf. J. P. Richter, *The Notebooks of Leonardo da Vinci* [London, 1883],

§544; cf. also Richter, §§86, 109, 543, 545). The problem is discussed in a modern context by M. H. Pirenne, *Optics, Painting and Photography* (Cambridge, 1970), chap. 9.

24. *Meteorologica*, ed. and tr. by H. D. P. Lee, Loeb Classical Library (Cambridge and London, 1952), III, iv, 374b, pp. 258f. The weakening of the sight with distance is mentioned previously in the same passage, in relation to the appearance of rainbows. This passage was cited by Edgerton in his article "Alberti's Colour Theory," 119. I think it is unlikely that Alberti would have gone to this source for information on vision and more probable that he would have seen Witelo's version of the passage cited in n. 26, below. The Early Renaissance is more likely to have used as sources for Aristotle's theory of vision the better-known passages from *De sensu*, II, 437b and *De anima*, II, 7 (ed. Lee, 418f.); the latter states in polemic style the author's refutation of the extromission theory.

25. *L'Optique . . .* , ed. Lejeune, II, chap. 19, p. 20, ll. 13ff.

26. ". . . ideo accidit quod ea, quae longe videntur, propter visus debilitationem omnia nigriora apparent" (*Perspectiva*, ed. Risner, 1572, IV, 159, as cited in Edgerton, "Alberti's Colour Theory," 133n.).

27. From *De visione stellarum*, Florence, San Marco, Conv. Soppr., j. x. 19, vol. 33, as quoted in Vescovini, *Studi sulla prospettiva medievale*, 202 n. 19: "Magna aeris quantitas interposita visui valde debilitat visionem . . . unde si tanta spissitudo aeris esset inter lunam et stellas fixas quanta est corpulentia intermedii caeli, stellae non possent a nobis videri." The passage is cited in this connection by Grayson, *On Painting and On Sculpture*, 109.

28. *Questione perspectivae*, Vienna, Österreichische Nationalbibliothek, cod. lat. 5447, fols. 58vff., ed. F. Alessio, "Questioni inedite di ottica di B. P. da Parma," *Rivista critica di storia della filosofia*, 16 (1961), 215f., and paraphrased by Vescovini "Le questioni di 'perspectiva,'" 195. These concurrent publications of portions of Pelacani's work are based on different versions, of which Vescovini's, dated 1428, is probably later. Pelacani does not state his opposition directly: he posits a dual nature of the atmosphere (*medium*): "quoddam est susceptivum actionis agentis et quoddam non est susceptivum," but gives an instance of a cloudlike opacity that "fortius evanescat" toward its edges, permitting a partial vision of an object beyond it.

29. Alberti, nevertheless, may have had also a vitalist principle in the back of his mind when he referred to the centric ray as "vivacissimus" (§8).

30. See the slightly different interpretations of Edgerton, "Alberti's Colour Theory," 132f., and Grayson, *On Painting and On Sculpture*, 109. In night scenes, of course, distant objects are enveloped in a darkness nearing black that perfectly illustrates the word *fuscus* and that may be found in Piero della Francesca's *Dream of Constantine* in San Francesco at Arezzo, as pointed out by E. Battisti, "Note sulla prospettiva rinascimentale," *Arte lombarda*, 16 (1971), 96.

31. *De coloribus*, IV, 794a (*The Works of Aristotle*, translated under the editorship of W. D. Ross, vol. 6 [Oxford, 1913]). This source was proposed by Edgerton ("Alberti's Colour Theory," 121, 128), whose implication that Alberti was referring in the quoted passage to the effects of atmospheric perspective—making the sky whiter near the horizon and a more intense blue overhead—is challenged by Grayson (*On Painting and On Scupture*, 110): "I see it as a far more bland statement: when there is white mist on the horizon, the sky looks pale; when the mist disperses, the sky appears blue again." Grayson may be correct, but I imagine the artists who read Alberti's text took it in the former sense.

32. Ibid., IV, 797a.

33. Cennino Cennini, in his *Libro dell'arte* of ca. 1390 (ed. D. V. Thompson, Jr. [New Haven, Conn., 1933], chaps. XLV–L) gives recipes for the manufacture of six different yellows for fresco and panel painting, made from mineral, vegetal, and chemical sources. The one surviving fifteenth-century book of instructions on pigment manufacture (*Il libro dei colori*, ed. O. Guerrini and C. Ricci [Bologna, 1887]), however, has no recipe for the making of a pure yellow. The only yellow mentioned is made from "spingerbino" and "ramoverde," and must be a high-value yellow-green (p. 96). The recipe is preceded by twenty-three recipes for making greens, none of which involve the mixture of yellow and blue.

34. I am indebted to Thomas da Costa Kaufmann for this review of the history of cast shadows, and particularly for his discovery of the crucial role of Dürer in first associating shadows in painting with perspective. Kaufmann's study, originally presented as a M. Phil. thesis at the Warburg Institute of the University of London under the direction of Sir Ernst Gombrich, has since been published as "Perspective of Shadows: The His-

tory of the Theory of Shadow Projection," *Journal of the Warburg and Courtauld Institutes,* 38 (1975), 258–287.

35. *Euclidus Optica, Opticorum Recensio Theonis,* ed. J. L. Heiberg (Leipzig, 1895), 144ff., cited by Kaufmann, "Perspective of Shadows," and by Grayson, *On Painting and On Scupture,* 109.

36. I have not been able to find the analysis of this manuscript, cited by Kaufmann; E. Weidermann, "Über einer Schrift von Ibn al Haitam, 'Über die Beschaffenheit des Schattens,'" *Beiträge zur Geschichte der Naturwissenschaften, Berichte der physikalisch-medizinisch Sozietäten Erlangen,* 39 (1907), 226–248.

37. John Pecham (Lindberg, *John Pecham,* 100f.) wrote that, since the sun is larger than the earth, it must throw light on more than half of the globe at any time; but he did not apply this observation to its effects on local bodies on earth. Alberti's assumption of parallel rays is valid for the processes of normal vision and representation, the actual angle being too small to perceive (see Pirenne, *Optics, Painting and Photography,* 57f.).

38. The work on optics that was most accessible to Alberti, however, had the most complete and original passages on cast shadows: Pelacani's *Quaestiones de Perspectiva* (see n. 10, above). His interest in astronomical problems led him to original experiments with shadows cast by a die and a gnomon, and he even explains a method for producing optical illusions through stereographic projection based on Ptolemy's method (Kaufmann, from MS. Ashburnham 1042, fols. 54v–59v; Vescovini, "Le questioni di 'perspectiva,'" 242f.).

39. *De coloribus,* ed. Ross, IV, 793b.

40. "The mode of relief" is a term applied to the tonal approach of pre-Leonardesque quattrocento painting by A. Pope, *The Painter's Modes of Expression: An Introduction to the Language of Drawing and Painting,* vol. 2 (Cambridge, Mass., 1939), 71–85. Pope's valuable analysis, made on the basis of surviving works of art without reference to Alberti's theory, indicates an identity of purpose in practice and theory, though, as will appear, the means used by the painters are not those suggested by Alberti.

41. Albrecht Dürer, *Die Underweysung der Messung mit dem Zirckel . . .* (Nuremberg, 1525), unnumbered pages (marked 164–175 in the Fogg Museum copy); cf. E. Panofsky, *Dürers Kunsttheorie* (Berlin, 1915), 26ff. Kaufmann in his dissertation (see n. 34, above) shows that Leonardo,

though he made intensive studies of cast shadows from a point source, failed to arrive at a functional method of shadow projection based on perspective, such as Dürer's.

42. "Even so, someone may ask what practical advantage all this enquiry brings to the painter. It is this: he must understand that he will become an excellent artist only if he knows well the outlines of surfaces and their proportions, which very few do; for if they are asked what they are attempting to do on the surface they are painting, they can answer more correctly about everything else than about what in this sense they are doing. So I beg studious painters to listen to me. It was never shameful to learn from any teacher things that are useful to know." In *De re aedificatoria* Alberti also pauses halfway through his exposition to defend his theoretical approach against anticipated criticism (Book VI, introduction). He may have had models for this sort of defense in ancient and medieval didactic literature.

43. The passage contains one difficulty that I have met by eliminating rather than solving it: midway, the phrase "positione cominus in aere suis locis constitutis," which I have translated as "established in their proper places in the air." Grayson's translation reads: "established at appropriate points nearby in space." The problematic word is "cominus" (*comminus*), for which "nearby" is the proper translation, but it is not consistent with Alberti's perspective system to require the distance point and the light source to be near the hypothetical window or to be near one another. Grayson (*in litteris,* and in the notes to his 1973 Bari edition [p. 334], which I have not yet seen), points out that the Basel 1540 edition has "eminus" (at a distance), while the Italian has "altrove" (which would suggest that the light source and distance point each has its own place). Prof. Grayson agrees that either of these alternatives would be preferable as a clarification of the method.

44. Practices in perspective and lighting in the century between Giotto and Alberti are outlined in E. Panofsky, *Renaissance and Renascences in Western Art,* 2d ed. (New York, 1969), chap. III.

45. The metaphor of the window actually appears further on, in §19, where Alberti explains how he sets about to construct a perspective: "But as it is relevant to know, not simply what the intersection is and what it consists in, but also how it can be constructed, we must now explain the art of expressing the intersection in painting. Let me

tell you what I do when I am painting. First of all, on the surface on which I am going to paint, I draw a rectangle of whatever size I want, which I regard as an open window through which the subject to be painted is seen; and I decide how large I wish the human figures in the painting to be . . ."

46. The conception of the intersection of the visual pyramid and the invention of a method of combining the plan and elevation of a perceived or imagined space in a single geometrical construction are what I believe differentiated Alberti's perspective from Brunelleschi's. What we know of the Brunelleschian system, recorded in the *Life* of the architect by Manetti (ed. H. Saalman [University Park, Md., 1970], 43–47, ll. 167–227), suggests that it provided the necessary catalyst by postulating an intersection of the visual rays; but as I read it, Brunelleschi got his three-dimensional effect by superimposing two two-dimensional constructions, so that he might be said to have intersected the visual *triangle*. The evidence provided by Manetti is not quite sufficient to confirm hypotheses about the essential differences between the two systems. The Brunelleschian method is explained by R. Krautheimer and T. Krautheimer-Hess in *Lorenzo Ghiberti*, 229–253, and in numerous other commentaries, though with flaws.

The idea of a pane of glass interposed between the object and the eye may have been suggested by medieval optical experiments. Biagio Pelacani, for example, used colored panes of glass to illustrate points in his discussion of the "mixture of the species," or the faculty of light rays to pick up characteristics of the media through which they pass (Vienna, Österreichische Nationalbibliothek, cod. lat., 5447, fol. 42v B, in Alessio, "Questioni inedite," 188f.).

47. This cultural phenomenon is not restricted to the Late Gothic period; the rectangular picture and window frame became popular simultaneously during Alberti's lifetime, ovals in the sixteenth and eighteenth centuries, and in our own time the expanses of plate glass (sometimes symptomatically called "picture windows") made possible by steel and concrete construction have been paralleled by huge canvases similarly provided with only the vestiges of a frame, frequently made of metal.

48. Alberti describes the *velo* in Book II, §31, when he is discussing "circumscription," the first of the three parts of painting: "I believe that noth-

ing more convenient can be found than the veil, which among my friends I call the intersection, and whose usage I was the first to discover. It is like this: a veil loosely woven of fine thread, dyed whatever color you please, divided up by thicker threads into as many parallel square sections as you like, and stretched on a frame. I set this up between the eye and the object to be represented, so that the visual pyramid passes through the loose weave of the veil. This intersection of the veil has many advantages, first of all because it always presents the same surfaces unchanged, for once you have fixed the position of the outlines, you can immediately find the apex of the pryamid you started with, which is extremely difficult to do without the intersection."

49. This involves first placing one'e eye opposite the center point, which in Albertian constructions is nearly always midway between the left and right borders of the picture on the horizon. The horizon is by definition at eye level; if its position is not obvious, as it is, say, in a picture of the sea, it can be located by finding the point at which the receding orthogonals converge. Often one cannot make this first step, as the picture may be painted or hung high on a wall above one's head. Early Renaissance painters were not hesitant in presenting illusions that could not be viewed from the point at which they were constructed; but the center point of the most explicit first instance of the *costruzione legittima*, Masaccio's *Trinity* (ca. 1427–28), was placed exactly at the eye level of an observer standing in the church in which it was frescoed (at the bottom of the picture, to give the illusion that one looks up at the scene).

The second procedure is to find how far away to stand or, in technical terms, to locate the distance point. Although this can be done mathematically by reconstructing the perspective system in reverse, it is more practical to do it by "feel," moving back and forth at a distance somewhere between half the width of the picture and the full width, until the perspective looks right. For an excellent demonstration, see B. A. R. Carter and R. Wittkower, "The Perspective of Piero della Francesca's *Flagellation*," *Journal of the Warburg and Courtauld Institutes*, 16 (1953), 292–302, and F. Casalini, "Corrispondenze fra teoria e practica nell'opera di Piero della Francesca," *L'arte*, 2 (1968), 62–95.

50. Some of the literature on perspective continues to perpetuate the misconception that the Albertian method and its Renaissance variants is

invalidated by the fact that we see with two eyes rather than one, that in the process of seeing we move the body, the head, and the eyeball, and that there is distortion at the periphery of vision. But none of these physiological conditions could be used to draw or paint a more accurate perspective construction on a flat surface than Alberti proposes. The painting is indeed like the view out the window, and if it were altered to account for physiological effects—if, say, the building and the tree at the far edge were distorted as in peripheral vision—then in looking at the picture, our peripheral vision would *distort the distortion,* and the effect would be less illusionistic than Alberti's. The point has been repeatedly and decisively made by Sir E. H. Gombrich (for example, in *Art and Illusion* [New York, 1960], chap. VIII, especially 242–258).

Another canard that occasionally recurs is justified neither on physiological nor on perspectival grounds: that the curvature of the eyeball or of the retina causes us to see curves where there are straight lines. This argument is quite without substance; the eye is constructed, like the camera lens, which is also curved, to give as accurate an image of things as possible; second, in Pirenne's words, "the retinal image is not what we see: we see the external world"; and third, to repeat the foregoing argument, if the shape of our eye did cause us to see straight lines as curved, and if pictures were accordingly made with curvilinear "perspective," our eyes would curve the lines further in looking at them (see Pirenne, *Optics, Painting and Photography,* 145 ff.).

The instances of "synthetic" or curved "perspective" adduced by White, notably in the miniatures of Jean Fouquet (*The Birth and Rebirth of Pictorial Space,* 207–235), do not produce more accurate records of things, but the device can be a forceful means of emphasis in the same way that photographs made with a wide-angle or "fisheye" lens can. They were probably inspired by convex mirrors, which were common household appurtenances in the fifteenth century.

What keeps the controversy over curvature alive is that whereas Albertian perspective is the only accurate way of transferring certain kinds of data about the world onto a picture plane, it is not necessarily the most convincing, because vision is affected by our bodies, our movements, and our psyches. If the artist wants to communicate as precise a record of fact as he can, he should follow Alberti; if he wishes to communicate the way

things look to him, he is not obliged to follow anyone, but he might be attracted to the solutions of Fouquet, or of the Impressionists, etc.

51. See n. 41, above.

52. The advice is contradicted by the proposition cited in §9: "Philosophers say that nothing is visible that is not endowed with light and color." The contradiction is inevitable, since the hypothesis of extrinsic rays is an abstraction borrowed from mathematics and does not correspond to visual experience.

53. *Treatise on Painting,* ed. A. P. McMahon (Princeton, N.J., 1956), §506. A similar statement is made in MS. G, fol. 37 (Richter, *Notebooks,* I, § 49): "wherefore, O painter, do not surround your bodies with lines." I cannot explain the apparent illogicality of Leonardo's application of his precept specifically to "distant things" (the passage starts with proposing that objects in the fourth and fifth plane be less sharply distinguished than those in the first and second); it would seem to apply at any distance.

54. John White has perceptively discussed the evolution of drawing style in the post-Albertian generation in "Aspects of the Relationship between Sculpture and Painting," *Art, Science and History in the Renaissance,* ed. C. Singleton (Baltimore, 1967), 43–108.

55. Centuries earlier, Vincent of Beauvais (d. 1264) had written: "Painters first draw lines around the images as if around shadows and then fill them up with color" (*Speculum doctrinale,* edition Donai, 1624, II, ii, chap. XIX, col. 1005, as quoted by I. Galantič, "The Sources of Leon Battista Alberti's Theory of Painting," dissertation, Harvard, 1969, 152). The parallel with Alberti is probably fortuitous, since Vincent was simply describing a shop convention, whereas Alberti was applying to painting what he held to be a natural law.

56. Modeling practice in the fifteenth century is discussed by Pope, *The Painter's Modes of Expression,* and by Sir E. H. Gombrich, "Light, Form and Texture in Fifteenth-Century Painting," *Journal of the Royal Society of Arts,* 112 (1964), 826–849, who cites as an example of Albertian modeling a predella of Fra Angelico with scenes from the Life of St. Nicholas in the Vatican (his fig. 13). Gombrich discusses modeling in relation to highlights and sheen, effects which were more cultivated in fifteenth-century Flemish painting than in Italian.

57. *De sensu,* chap. II.

58. On the quattrocento palette, see Siebenhü-ner, "Über den Kolorismus in der Frührenaissance"; T. Hetzer, *Tizian, Geschichte seiner Farbe* (Frankfurt a. M., 1935); J. Shearman, "Leonardo's Colour and Chiaroscuro," *Zeitschrift für Kunstgeschichte,* 25 (1962), 13–47; S. Cowardin, "Some Aspects of Color in Fifteenth-Century Florentine Painting," dissertation, Harvard, 1962.

59. Cennino Cennini, *Il libro dell'arte,* ed. Thompson, chap. LXXI: "The Way to Paint a Drapery in Fresco: . . . get three little dishes. Take one of them, and put into it whatever color you choose, we will say red. Take some cinabrese and a little lime white; and let this be one color, well diluted with water. Make one of the other two colors light, putting a great deal of lime white into it. Now take some out of the first dish, and some of this light, and make an intermediate color; and you will have three of them. Now take some of the first one, that is, the dark one; and with a rather large and fairly pointed bristle brush go over the golds of your figure in the darkest areas; and do not go past the middle of the thickness of your figure. . . ." When these three levels of relief have been smoothly modeled, the final touches are added first in a still lighter mixture and finally in pure white for the highest lights and pure cinabrese for the deepest shadow. This method results in the use of a great deal more white than Alberti recommends in his discussion of modeling in §47, in which he says, "no surface should be made so white that you cannot make it a great deal whiter still," and "those painters who use white immoderately and black carelessly, should be strongly condemned."

Cennino also discusses in chaps. LXXVIII–LXXX the use of the color "shift," which represents shadows not by a low value of the color of the drapery itself, but by a quite different color of lower value. In Alberti's time the latter frequently was ultramarine in practice, as in the first of Cennino's examples.

60. Book II, §47: "But if, as I explained, the painter has drawn the outlines of the surface correctly and clearly sketched the border-line between lighter and darker, the method of coloring will then be easy."

61. The *schiacciato* relief style was first used by Donatello in the relief beneath the statue of St. George in Orsanmichele in Florence, ca. 1417, and reached its culmination in the *Ascension and Delivery of the Keys to St. Peter* in the Victoria and Albert Museum in London, of the late 1420s.

62. For idealist theory in the Renaissance and its sources, see E. Panofsky, *Idea, ein Beitrag zur Begriffsgeschichte der älteren Kunsttheorie* (Leipzig and Berlin, 1924; English ed., Columbia, S.C., 1968); Sir Anthony Blunt, *Artistic Theory in Italy, 1450–1600* (Oxford, 1940).

63. Alberti's concept of the imitation of nature and its roots in Aristotle's theory of *mimesis* as presented in the *Poetics* is ably discussed by Galantič, "The Sources of Leon Battista Alberti's Theory of Painting," chaps. II, III.

64. A clear statement of Aristotle's position on artistic criteria is found in the *Politics,* 1281b, 10: "the superiority . . . of handsome men, so it is said, over plain men and of the works of the painter's art over the real objects, really consists in this, that a number of scattered good points have been collected together into one example; since if the features be taken separately, the eye of one real person is more beautiful than that of the man in the picture, and some other feature of somebody else."

65. But generally this was true only of the figures: for reasons of tonal balance and emphasis, full relief and value contrast was avoided in architectural and landscape backgrounds.

66. Cf. B. Degenhart and A. Schmitt, *Corpus der italienischen Zeichnungen, 1300–1450,* I–II (Berlin), xxxi and cat. nos. 336, 338–340, 342–343, 452–453, 461–463, 472, 475–476, attributed to Domenico Veneziano and to the workshop of Benozzo Gozzoli. Also, J. Bialostocki, "The Renaissance Concept of Nature and Antiquity," *Acts of the Twentieth International Congress of Art History,* vol. 2 (Princeton, N.J., 1963), 19–30.

Postscript

This study came from the same enterprise as those on color and on Leonardo's studies of the eye, as an outcome of my extended interest in the use and revision of medieval optics by early Renaissance painters and theoreticians. In hindsight I feel that I would have gained from giving relatively greater weight to the works of art themselves as against the texts, as Paul Hills has done. But I also realize that to some extent textual interpretation is an adaptive mechanism of American scholars between sabbaticals, a response to the frustrations of trying to pursue research on original works of art that are far away, and an exploitation of the capacities of great American libraries to support the kind of research that can be done from books and journals: on theory, iconography, and socio-historical issues.

Paul Hills's book reveals the extent to which Alberti's effort to rationalize the workings of light in geometrical terms worked to limit rather than to attain naturalism in light and color, especially through tonal balance. He points specifically to Alberti's distinction of "median" light rays, which carry the colors of objects to the eye, and "extrinsic" rays, which are colorless and are to be represented in painting by "circumscription" in gray or black outlines. This distinction did not appear in medieval optics: Bacon and Pecham had stated that objects are certified visually as we move our eyes and head, shifting the centric ray over their surfaces (Hills, p. 71). In Albertian terms, that would involve a constant change of the extrinsic rays.

Alberti's method implies a rigidly fixed viewing point for light and dark composition as well as for constructing perspective, and favors the assumption of a single light source projecting rays over the object in an analogy to the pyramid of rays that culminates in the eye.

My study identified Leonardo as primarily responsible both in theory and in practice for overcoming the limitations of Alberti's dicta, particularly by abandoning circumscription and permitting objects to merge in shadow and in hue with one another and with the environment. Hills, in his admirable chapter on Masaccio (pp. 129–44), demonstrates how these achievements predate the publication of Alberti's text, notably in the Brancacci Chapel frescoes, where Leonardo's tonal and color balance is already adumbrated and neutral outlines are avoided. Masaccio even abandoned the tradition of identifying the edges of his *giornate* with the borders of figures so that he could paint portions of the environment at the same time as the figures.

Barasch, Moshe. *Light and Color in Italian Renaissance Theory of Art* (New York, 1978).

Edgerton, Samuel Y. *The Renaissance Rediscovery of Linear Perspective* (New York, 1975).

Hills, Paul. *The Light of Early Italian Painting* (New Haven and London, 1987).

Kemp, Martin. "Science, Non-Science and Nonsense: The Interpretation of Brunelleschi's Perspective," *Art History*, 1 (1978), 134–161.

Maltese, Corrado. "Colore, luce e movimento nello spazio albertiano," *Commentari*, 27 (1976), 238–247.

See also the bibliography that follows the essay "Leonardo's Eye," below.

5

Leonardo's Eye

I

The eye whereby the beauty of the world is reflected by beholders is of such excellence that whoso consents to its loss deprives himself of the representation of all the works of nature. Because we can see these things owing to our eyes the soul is content to stay imprisoned in the human body; for through the eyes all the various things of nature are represented to the soul. Who loses his eyes leaves his soul in a dark prison without hope of ever again seeing the sun, light of all the world; and how many there are to whom the darkness of night is hateful though it is of but short duration; what would they do if such darkness were to be their companion for life?[1]

For Leonardo the eye was the window of learning. He spoke of it as the instrument that makes possible direct contact with the natural environment and the uncovering of truths that before his time had been obscured by the authority of the printed word. As the eye was the organ fundamental to his work in painting as well as in descriptive science, it became an important subject, as well as an essential tool, for investigation. Notes on vision and on the physiology and anatomy of the eye appear in his earliest manuscripts of the late 1480s and in his latest of 1513–14, and throughout the intervening period. He planned a treatise on optics, and at an early stage quoted as it if were his own the introduction to John Pecham's *Perspectiva communis,* stating his intention to present "natural and mathematical demonstrations, sometimes determining the effects in terms of the causes, and sometimes the causes in terms of the effects."[2] In fact Leonardo came closer in optics than in other scientific fields to achieving the balance

From *Journal of the Warburg and Courtauld Institutes,* 41 (1978), 108–146.

of deductive and inductive method he sought. But in the end he failed to formulate a valid optical theory, and his work had no following. Still, it is fascinating to follow as the probing of an intriguing mind toward a new scientific empiricism, and as a demonstration of the importance of challenging questions—even those whose answers do not work.

Leonardo's scientific projects normally began with a study of the authorities. The earliest manuscripts are, at least partly, notes on—or reviews of—reading, and one cannot always be sure that a statement made in them represents Leonardo's own conviction. In the next stage he often confronts the traditional view of a subject with his own experience or experiments, rejecting elements of the former that do not harmonize with the latter. Finally, he attempts to formulate his own partly theoretical, partly descriptive system, in many cases in the form of a projected treatise. If any such treatise was completed it has not survived, but the one on vision had progressed farther than most: in addition to many scattered notes, Leonardo made a small separate notebook devoted entirely to the physiology of the eye—MS. D of the Institute of France, written around 1508–9.[3] That manuscript, as will appear, leaves unresolved many traditional problems and creates new ones, in some cases unnecessarily. Leonardo's work on vision was far from complete when he abandoned it.

As Leonardo's approach developed from an early dependence on tradition toward increasing originality and empiricism, he shifted from more static to more dynamic interpretations of nature. Even Euclidian geometry, which was fundamental to all his investigations, began in his late writings to assume a dynamic aspect:

the point may be compared with an instant in time, and the line may be likened to the length of a certain quantity of time. And just as points are the beginning and end of the line, so instants are the end and beginning of any given space of time.[4]

This simile recalls a roughly contemporary group of physiological notes in MS. K, for example:

If a brand of fire is drawn in a circle or from under the eye upwards, this brand will appear as a line of fire. . . . If the eye that looks on a star shifts quickly, it will seem that the star continues on in an opposite direction in a linear fiery course.[5]

These observations indicate dissatisfaction with the strictly geometrical descriptions of light and vision in traditional optics or in texts on perspective, where the eye is posited as a fixed point. Leonardo was starting to seek out instances of phenomena of perception that appeared to frustrate the geometrical rationalization of vision. Observations such as:

If the eye is in the middle of a course with two horses running to their goal along parallel tracks, it will seem that they are running towards each other

and

If a bird flies along a level line separating itself from the eye, it will seem to be descending stage by stage with the stages of its movement[6]

are meant to suggest that while traditional perspective is capable in many cases of producing a convincing illusion, it can also lead to distorted perceptions.[7]

Leonardo must have written a book—now lost—on painters' perspective as well as the one on the physiology of the eye.[8] Benvenuto Cellini owned a perspective manuscript which he said was by Leonardo and described it as "the most beautiful a man ever made, showing how objects foreshorten not only in depth but also in breadth and height"; Lomazzo mentioned the work as "written very obscurely." Whatever it contained—I believe it was chiefly devoted to illusionistic wall and ceiling paintings— it was surely not in the tradition of the writings of Alberti and Piero della Francesca, the major codifiers of fifteenth-century *costruzione legittima*, or painters' perspective.

Although several notes in Leonardo's early MS. A (ca. 1492) are formulated as propositions of the *costruzione legittima*, which he must have learned in Verrocchio's workshop, the mass of his later observation and experiment on the subject tends to devalue, or reveal the limitations of the method. Moreover, though very numerous, they are restricted almost exclusively to the problem of diminishing the size of objects in relation to their distance from the observer. His focus on this aspect led him to observe a fundamental flaw in the system and to attempt an explanation.

The flaw derives from the geometrical construction of perspectives from a point representing the eye: to be properly illusionistic, the construction should be looked at from this point. But observers move around, and even when stationary move heads and eyes. This movement does not cause bothersome distortions in most pictures, but the exception that concerned Leonardo was when the construction point is so close to the object that the picture surface itself becomes foreshortened to the eye. His example of depicting two adjacent squares on the ground—say the tiles of a floor— illustrates the problem vividly. In the lower sketch of figure 5.1, the tiles are *ov* (the nearer) and *vx* (the farther) and *no* is the surface on which the picture is to be painted:

The object that is nearest to the eye always seems larger than another of the same size at greater distance.

The eye m, *seeing the spaces* ovx, *hardly detects the difference between them, and the reason of this is that it is close to them; but if these spaces are marked on the vertical plane* no *the space* ov *will be seen at* or, *and in the same way the space* vx *will*

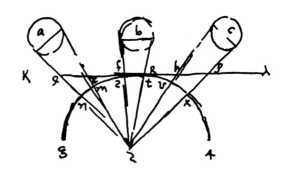

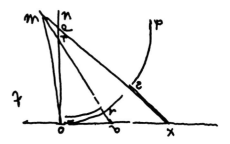

5.1   *Two demonstrations of perspective distortions.*
Institut de France, MS. A, fol. 38r.

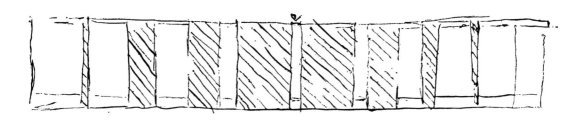

5.2   *Demonstration of the perspective distortion of a*
row of columns seen from a fixed point close to the
central column with one eye. Institut de France, MS. A,
fol. 41r.

appear at rq. *And if you carry this out in any place where you can walk round, it will look out of proportion by reason of the great difference in the spaces* or *and* rq. *And this proceeds from the eye being so [near] the plane that the plane foreshortens them. Hence, if you wanted to carry it out, you would have [to arrange] to see the perspective through a single hole which must be at the point* m, *or else you must go to a distance of at least 3 times the height of the object you see. The plane* op *being always equally remote from the eye will reproduce the objects in a satisfactory way, so that they may be seen from place to place.*[9]

In the same manuscript Leonardo draws another instance of distortion occurring from a close viewpoint.[10] Figure 5.2 shows a row of columns extending laterally across the field of vision from so close a position that normal relationships are upset and the nearest seems smallest while the farther ones expand in size. As drawn here, the row is not—if one looks at the drawing from a normal distance—illusionistic; but, Leonardo says, if the picture were large enough and if one had to see it through an eyehole fixed at the point of construction, the columns and the intervals between them would "deceive beholders."

Alternatively, the artist could start constructing a picture from a position far enough away to avoid the foreshortening of the picture surface, which in this case, in Leonardo's estimate, would be ten times the size of the object.[11] A third drawing (fig. 5.1, top), which appears together with the first in both the earliest and the latest (ca. 1513–14) notes on perspective, clarifies the cause of the distortion.[12] The three circles can be thought of as part of the row of columns seen in plan; if they are projected onto a picture surface *ed*, the two outer columns become wider than the center one. An arc is drawn (fig. 5.1, bottom), upon which the objects projected are all of the same size (*nm, st, vx*) as they look when one turns one's head or eyes in an arc. The arcs also indicate the extent of the foreshortening of the picture surface: as the viewpoint gets farther from the picture the arc will flatten out and soon become indistinguishable from the plane of the picture, at which distance there will be no distortion of the sort that concerned Leonardo.

In his later manuscripts, particularly MS. E of 1513–14, Leonardo discusses the problem in terms of three different kinds of perspective. The first, the *costruzione legittima,* he calls "simple" because the artist constructs it from a point far enough away from the picture surface to avoid foreshortening; here the observer "is not obliged to stay more in one place than in another" except to avoid a position from which the picture itself becomes distorted.[13] The second, *prospettiva composta,* is constructed "parte dell'arte e parte della natura" (partly artificially and partly naturally) from the close-up viewpoint, and pictures in which it is used have to be seen through a fixed eyehole.[14] Though Leonardo advised that "it is well to avoid" this type, since pictures ought to be visible in the right way by more than one person at a time, he realized that it offered a potential for intriguing optical tricks. His experiments led to the invention of a new kind of image we call anamorphic, in which the object is projected from a point so close to the painted surface that it is unrecognizable from a normal viewing distance and can be read only by putting one's eye up to the right point near the surface.[15] Anamorphic pictures were popular in the sixteenth and seventeenth centuries, the best-known example being the skull placed in the otherwise normally constructed *Ambassadors* by Hans Holbein as a cryptic reference to the frailty of life.

Leonardo's third perspective, which he called "natural," is just the way normal vision operates and is not presented as an artist's device. In the early notes Leonardo did not differentiate between painter's perspective and normal perception: he refers in one passage to the "simple and natural method, that is, how things, without any other medium, appear to the eye."[16] At that time he still believed that fifteenth-century geometric perspective method represented the workings of the eye. But later, for reasons I shall shortly explain, he came to regard simple perspective as no more than a workshop device, and natural vision as operating quite differently, with light impulses being registered in the eye not at a point, as required by the simple method, but all over the surface of the eye. In his last notes on the subject Leonardo proposes a geometrical method of approximating natural perspective by projecting the curvature of the eye onto a flat surface "near the surface of the pupil,"[17] but this would have grossly distorted the image in the same way as his demonstration of composite perspective in figure 5.2: he ended by challenging the tradition without offering a viable alternative.[18] The hypothesis of image formation on the entire front surface of the eye was not a forward step in science, but it did constitute progress in consciousness, because it was the first modern effort to mark the borderline between mathematical optics,[19] on which painters' perspective had been grounded, and the physiology and even the psychology of everyday vision.

II

Although many of Leonardo's ideas on the physiology of vision were original, his study of the subject was grounded in ancient and medieval theory and will be more easily understood if we first review briefly what he was likely to have known of traditional treatments.[20]

Ancient scientists were divided on the nature of the fundamental workings of vision: whether the eye was passive and simply received emanations from the outer world (theory of intromission); or whether it was active and cast out rays or a spirit to touch the seen object, either directly or by causing the intervening atmosphere in some way to conduct information (theory of emission). Among the proponents of intromission, the atomists and Lucretius held that an integral image (*eidola*) is cast off by the object and enters the eye, while Aristotle and his followers attributed to the atmosphere the power to collect the data of color and light and to convey it to the eye. By late antiquity the emission principle, maintained by the Stoics, Plato, Euclid, Ptolemy, and Galen, prevailed—not so much, perhaps, because it was more convincing, as because the most substantial and useful optical texts were written by its adherents. Euclid and Ptolemy established the outlines of optics as a science and quantified it so that it could be pursued entirely by geometrical operations with no more than a passing nod to the mechanisms of vision and of light propagation, and the physician Galen extensively treated the anatomy, and to a lesser extent the physiology, of the eye. Thus the former pair became the ultimate ancestors of Renaissance perspective, and Galen of Leonardo's and the anatomists' study of the structure and function of the eye.

When Arab scholars initiated the renaissance of ancient science from the ninth to the eleventh centuries, virtually their only source on human anatomy and physiology was Galen (ca. 129–ca. 199 AD), whose most thorough discussions on the eye occur in two works, *De placitis Hippocratis et Platonis* and *De usu partium corporis humani*.[21] Galen's knowledge probably derived chiefly from the dissection of animals. He describes seven tunics—or concentric outer coats—of the eye; and three humors filling the inner volume: the albuminoid surrounding the iris, the crystalline, and the vitreous. The crystalline is the locus of image reception and the function of the vitreous is to nourish it. The image forms on the lenticular forward surface of the crystalline humor (which we now call a lens) and is passed through it to the hollow optic nerve. The surface of the crystalline is only slightly curved in front, as it is represented today, since this shape requires less refraction of rays passing to and from the outer world. Medieval writers gave it the same form; but Leonardo, who did not believe that the crystalline was the sensitive organ, represented it as spherical. To explain perception, Galen proposes a complex system through which the "visual spirit" can pass from the brain to the sensitive anterior surface of the crystalline, where it picks up images, and to the pupil. The retina is not described as a tunic, but as a spreading-out of the optic nerve and the source of vessels that nourish the anterior portions of the eye and also transmit the spirit. The "visual spirit," which functions only inside the eye, is distinct from the "shining pneuma," which the eye emits in order to establish contact with the object of vision. Galen altered Stoic theory, which had represented the pneuma as reaching out to contact the perceived object, proposing instead that the pneuma transforms the intervening air, with the aid of light, into a sentient instrument. This aspect of Galenic theory did not survive in medieval and Renaissance writings, partly because it was demolished—along with other versions of the emission theory—by the penetrating logic of Avicenna (Abū-ibn-Sīnā, 980–1037); and partly because the future course of both geometrical optics and the physiology of vision came to be dominated by the theory based on intromission of Avicenna's contemporary Alhazen (Ibn-al-Haitham, 965–ca. 1040).[22]

Of some nineteen works on optics by Alhazen about half were lost; and many of the others were neglected during the Middle Ages. The major treatise, however, was translated into Latin around 1200 as *De aspectibus* or *Perspectiva*, and was known (in later interpretations if not in the original) and to a greater or lesser extent followed by every writer on the subject from the thirteenth century to the time of Kepler. It has been compared in importance to the optical works of Ptolemy, Kepler, Descartes, and Helmholtz.[23] Most later medieval and Renaissance writers knew Alhazen's theories indirectly through the medium of one of three thirteenth-century treatises on optics based upon them—those of Roger Bacon, whose "Perspectiva" forms a part of his encyclopedic *Opus maius*, of Witelo, or of John Pecham.

Alhazen's account is more physiological and less anatomical than Galen's. As in Galen, two primary hollow nerves emerge from the two sides of the anterior portion of the brain and join together at a point, the "common nerve" (chiasma), from which the two secondary optic nerves, also hollow, emerge and extend to the eye cavity where they spread out, funnel-like (fig. 5.3).[24] The exterior skin of the optic nerve then merges into the cornea, or exterior sphere of the eye, and the interior skin becomes the uvea, or interior sphere. Alhazen's uvea, like Leonardo's, is the modern retina in locus but not in function: the term *retina* does not appear. Within the spheres there are three humors. The foremost, behind the cornea, is the *albugeneous* or white of the eye, named from the white of the egg. The two posterior humors are held together in a single internal sphere, the front portion of which, right behind the "hole" of the eye (Alhazen's term for pupil is *foramen*), is the *glacial* or crystalline, and the rear the *vitreous* humor, the purpose of which is to nourish the *crystalline* and to convey the image formed by it to the optic nerve. The front part of the sphere, which is the actual

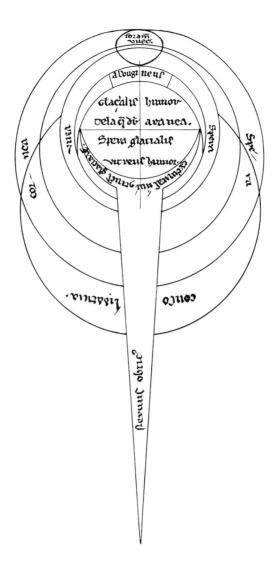

5.3 *Horizontal section of the eye, from an early, inaccurate Latin manuscript of the optics of Alhazen. From S. Polyak,* The Retina.

locus of sensation, is less sharply curved than the rear because the geometry of Alhazen's system requires that it be concentric with the anterior surface of the eye (cornea). A thin membrane called the *tela aranea* separates the sphere from the albugeneous humor.

Alhazen decisively refutes ancient theories requiring the emission of a spirit from the eye. In his description, rays come from the object to the eye in a pyramid; they are received to the entire surface of the eye in such a way that any point on the eye can receive a light impulse from any point on the object.[25] From here they pass on to the entire surface of the crystalline humor, the primary seat of sensation (without being refracted, since the two surfaces are concentric). The pupil or "hole" apparently has no significant function, though it must at least have cut off the more peripheral rays. Innumerable impulses thus reach every point on the cornea and crystalline, but confusion is avoided because the latter admits only those rays that are *perpendicular to the points on its surface* where they strike.[26] The eye's constant scanning movements assure the complete registration of all points on the object.[27]

Behind the "hole" the image is spread in precisely the form and proportions of the object viewed on the anterior surface of the crystalline humor, which is the effective sensory organ. Though Alhazen knew from experiments with the *camera obscura* that the image would be inverted in passing through the hole,[28] he could not bring himself to apply the analogy directly to the eye, because that would require the image sensed on the crystalline humor to be inverted—and Alhazen, followed by everyone prior to Kepler, could not accept the implication of an inverted image being transmitted to the brain. Even after penetrating the surface, the rays are not permitted to cross: they diverge again because, on the analogy of light passing from air into water, they are refracted into divergent paths by passing from the "rarer" crystalline humor to the denser vitreous. Thus the crystalline was prophetically defined as a lens; but, since it had also to serve as a sense organ, the implications of this concept could not be developed correctly.[29]

Alhazen is ambivalent about the next step. "It is said," he observes, referring to Galen, "that the visual spirit is sent forth from the anterior part of the brain and fills the two channels of the two primary nerves joined to the brain and passes to the common nerve and fills its channel and thence to the secondary optic nerves and fills them and thence to the crystalline humor and gives it the faculty of vision."[30] But, reading further, one comes to doubt whether Alhazen actually believed in the existence of the spirit he attributed to other authors. Further references seem to indicate that the image is conveyed to the brain by strictly mechanical means, with the aid of a *corpus sentiens*. The process is summarized in one passage:

The forms of light and color of the object came to the surface of the eye and are projected on the surface of the glacial humor according to determined paths, that is, according to the proper relationships of figure and form [e.g., not inverted]. From here they proceed to the hollow common nerve [chiasma] and are perceived by the sensitive faculty after their arrival in the glacial body. And after their arrival in the whole sensitive body [in corpore sentiente], *the judgmental faculty judges all intentions in them, and the form of light and of color do not come to the hollow nerves except by virtue of the sentient body spread over the hollow nerve.*[31]

The mechanical alternative to the visual spirit raised the issue of how the impulses of light and color could reach the brain when they could no longer travel in straight lines, and he specifically explains in another section that "all the paths curve according to the curvature of the nerves and end up after their curving (*gyrationem*) arrayed in the same order as they were before on account of the quality of the sensitivity of this body."[32]

As A. I. Sabra has shown,[33] Alhazen went beyond this description of the mechanics of vision to offer in his second book a theory of perception which distinguished pure sensation—registration by the eye of light and color—from the apprehension of a true form (*forma vera*), which requires not simply an open eye but extended contemplation to grasp and verify all parts of the object. At the same time awareness of such characters as similarity, difference, and relationship requires the faculty of judgment (*virtus distinctiva*); and the recognition (*cognitio*) of objects calls on the faculties of memory and comparison. All are beyond the capacities of pure sensation.

What made Alhazen's theory and its descendants dominate optics for so many centuries, in spite of the errors and loose ends, was primarily that—starting from the hypothesis that rays are propagated in straight lines from every point on an object to every point on the eye—it fused into one science two distinct traditions of antiquity: those of geometrical optics and of the anatomy and physiology of the eye.[34]

Ancient and Arabic scientific learning penetrated Western Europe gradually and during the twelfth century at an accelerated rate, as manuscripts were acquired and translated into Latin, mainly in the monasteries. The great resurgence of research and writing on optics occurred in the thirteenth century, stimulated initially by a philosophy and theology that represented light as a manifestation of divinity, and thus gave vision a privileged position among the senses. The English Franciscan Robert Grosseteste (ca.

1168–1253) was the first major Western scholar of optics. Though unaware of Alhazen, he knew most of the major literature and adapted the Platonic theory of emission to his neo-Platonic theology. Basic to Grosseteste's system was the concept of the "multiplication of species": all physical objects radiate their *species* (the Latin word means "form," "image," "sight") which through the mediation of light—itself a radiation of divine character—become potentially visible. Thus optics was made fundamental to all science. The eye also projects not only its species but, as in Plato, "a substance shining and radiating like the sun, the radiation of which, when coupled by radiation from the exterior shining body, entirely completes vision."[35]

While Grosseteste's radiation theory gave a religious justification for the practice of geometrical optics, it affected theology more than science, partly because his younger contemporary Roger Bacon (1214?–94), also a British Franciscan whose career was spent mostly in Paris, absorbed it into a more flexible, less metaphysical system. Bacon not only knew Alhazen thoroughly, but intended his *Perspectiva* (part V of his *Opus maius*) to be an interpretation of Alhazen's theory in the light of other major optical works. He found no conflict between the doctrine of the multiplication of species and Alhazen's emanation of rays from point sources, and he glossed over the irreconcilable differences between Alhazen's passive eye, which merely accepts and refracts light rays, and the Platonic eye, which sends out welcoming spirits.[36] The eye diagrams in manuscripts of Alhazen and Bacon are essentially alike,[37] and most of the passages in the *Perspectiva* gave no hint of any modification of a strict intromission theory: rays enter the eye, are recorded in the crystalline humor, but are perceived in the optic nerve, and are transmitted for use and storage to the "sensus communis" in the anterior ventricle of the brain. This location of Aristotle's hypothetical common sense—where evidence from all the senses is organized—was taken up by Leonardo in his early writings, perhaps directly from Bacon.

Bacon believed that since there was one universal truth all serious scientific work must ultimately be in harmony, and so he sought to make a concordance of all earlier writers which minimized or suppressed conflicting hypotheses. Yet, like the first writings that conveyed in great detail and with creative extensions the contributions of Alhazen to the West, his *Perspectiva* and *De multiplicatione specierem* (which expands the concept of the *species* to cover all aspects of transmittable character, including but not restricted to the visible) were incalculably influential.

The tradition of Bacon was continued in two younger scholars whose treatises on optics appeared in the 1270s, John Pecham and Witelo, the first of whom, another British Franciscan, was with Bacon in the Parisian monastery in the 1260s, and later became Archbishop of Canterbury. The philosophical-theological implications of the work of Bacon and Grosseteste had placed optics near to the core of the university curriculum, and Pecham's *Perspectiva communis* and Witelo's *Perspectiva* were to become (and probably were designed as) the textbooks of the subject for the following two and a half centuries.[38] The former is essentially Baconian, though it clarifies and corrects some of Bacon's difficult innovations and is very little concerned with theology. Witelo's text is closest of all to being a summary of *De aspectibus* (a misconception reinforced by the publication of the two in the Risner edition of 1572 with mutual cross-references in every paragraph). Though Witelo, as indicated in his prefatory letter to his mentor William of Morbeke, was open to concepts derived from neo-Platonic light theory, his text is the most straightforward presentation (far less repetitive and inconsistent than Alhazen's) of quasi-mechanistic intromission theory. It calls on the visual spirit only to convey the image from the crystalline humor to the brain.

In the two centuries between the treatises of Pecham and Witelo and that of Leonardo, optics continued to be an important university subject. After 1400 the discipline nourished a rapidly increasing number of practical applications to technologies such as surveying, navigation, cartography, lens making, and, as we have seen, painter's perspective. But theory remained static. This was due chiefly to a change of intellectual style in the fourteenth century, the great period of scholasticism. The Aristotelian tradition coming to dominate the natural sciences caused a shift of interest toward subjects that had occupied Aristotle: in the study of vision, not geometrical optics but cognition and perception (*De anima, De sensu et sensato*).[39] And all the demands of pedagogy turned scholars to the criticism of texts. Almost all fourteenth-century optical literature is presented in the form of *quaestiones* addressed to the theories of earlier writers, with extended answers distinguished more for their logic and rhetoric than for their substance. The most important work in this genre was the *Quaestiones super perspectivam* by Biagio Pelacani of Parma (1390, with later emendations), a commentary on Pecham's *Perspectiva communis*. The work contains many ingenious and some original arguments; and, as it was surely available to fifteenth-century Florentine scholars and artists, it may have served as a stepping-stone to the major works discussed here.[40]

There are no significant optical works in the fifteenth century; given the interest in the subject in both schools and workshops, it is odd that not even the revered medieval optical texts were published for an entire century after the invention of printing. Leonardo's work was done in complete isolation—even the physicians and anato-

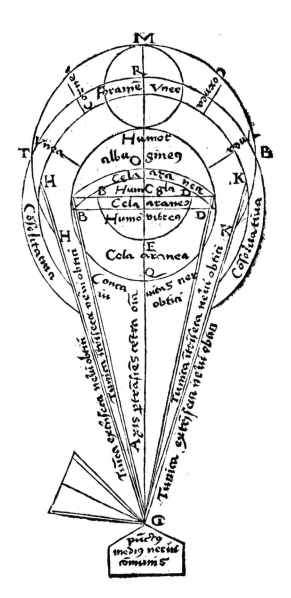

5.4   *Horizontal section of the eye, from Witelo,*
Opticae Thesaurus, *ed. F. Risner (Basel, 1572).*

mists were halted at the level of commenting on Galen or on the fourteenth-century anatomist Mondino de' Luzzi. "The eye," Leonardo said, "which so clearly reveals its function, has been defined by an infinite number of authors up to my own time in one way, while I find by experiment [experience?] that it is another."[41]

Leonardo's work remained in note form and had no impact on the future of optics except through his disciples, in the area of painters' perspective. The scientists of his time, and indeed throughout the sixteenth century, made no substantial innovations in theory, though they did begin to chip away at isolated misconceptions and habits of thought that had caused stagnation in the field.[42] Vesalius's *De humani corporis fabrica* of 1543, though it represents the cross-section of the eye much as it would appear in a medieval manuscript (fig. 5.5), makes a statement (that the optic nerves are solid), expresses a doubt (whether the crystalline humor is really the sensitive organ), and reports a current minority opinion (that the retinal area is the locus of visual reception), any one of which could have shaken the very foundations of traditional optics.[43] But Vesalius refused to get more involved at that point with the physiology of vision, promising to tackle it later.

Felix Plater's *De corporis humani structura et usu* of 1583 is the first published work in which the retina is identified as the essential receptor, a conclusion Plater supports by citing the similarity of its appearance to that of the brain. His illustration, though based on Vesalius's, incorporates the discovery of Vesalius's successor in the chair of anatomy at Padua, Realdo Colombo, that the crystalline humor is not in the center, but near the front of the eye. But the book is a diagrammatic atlas of anatomy, and has no text to explain the effect of this discovery on the workings of sight. There are other individual observations of the kind in the later sixteenth century, tending in the direction of Kepler's *Ad Vitellionem paralipomena* . . . of 1604, in which the fundamentals of the modern view of the physiology of vision are laid out: the humors are defined as lenses, the retina as the receptor, and the system is wholly mechanical. Kepler's great achievement was his capacity to abandon a mental set as basic, as firmly planted, and as long-lived as that of geocentrism: the conviction that an inverted image could not be delivered to the brain. The problem that stumped Leonardo and all his predecessors began to be resolved in a diagram (fig. 5.6, from Descartes, which shows light rays intersecting in the crystalline lens and projecting an inverted image), and in a sentence and a half of text:

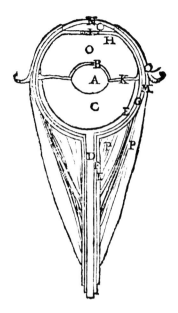

5.5 *Horizontal section of the eye. From Andreas Vesalius,* De humanae corporis fabrica libri septem *(Basel, 1543).*

5.6 *Horizontal section of the eye, based on Kepler, from R. Descartes,* La dioptrique *(Leiden, 1637).*

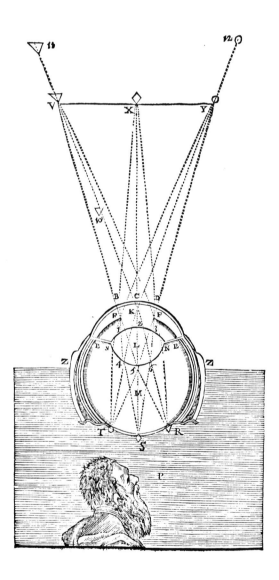

I say that vision occurs when the image of the whole hemisphere of the world in front of the eye, and a little more, is formed on the reddish white concave surface of the retina. I leave it to natural philosophers to discuss the way in which this image or picture is put together by the spiritual principles of vision residing in the retina and in the nerves.[44]

III

With the means at his command, Leonardo's effort to found a new physiology was perhaps doomed from the start. But having once suggested that ordinary vision might differ from that described in the optical and perspective literature, he characteristically and persistently tried to find anatomical and physiological support for the proposition.[45]

While the issue for Alberti and other perspective theorists had been "How can the phenomena revealed by light rays be projected onto a picture panel so that they seem as convincing as possible to the eye?," for Leonardo it was "How are the phenomena revealed by light rays received into the eye(s) and transmitted to the brain?" Very early in his studies, perhaps before any of his research, Leonardo listed the key questions to which he wanted to find answers:[46]

Why the eye goes varying hour by hour, enlarging and lessening.

Why the pupil in proportion as it has a greater light in front of it becomes less, and why on the other hand it increases in the dark.

Why the things seen by the eye when continuing are small within the eye and appear large.

Why a thing seen through a chink with both the eyes becomes double and is transposed; that is to say the thing seen on the right hand goes to the left eye, and similarly that on the left hand goes to the right.

Why a building among clouds appears greater.

Why the eye cannot see perfectly except in a straight line.

Why pyramidal lines which start from the eyes come to a point in the thing seen.

Why when the said pyramid proceeds from the eyes and comes to a point in an object that is in water the lines bend as they reach the water and do not keep their straightness.

How the things seen form a pyramid only in the eye.

How the two eyes form a pyramid in the thing seen.

Clearly he was motivated to study the physiology of vision not only by reading ancient and medieval writers on optics (who discussed issues such as the special power of the central ray and refraction in water) but by original observations and experiments that initially may have been prompted by questions about painting. He says, in fact, that it was "isperienza" that caused him to challenge his predecessors.[47]

Leonardo's terminology is considerably looser than Alberti's. He refers to visual impressions as *simulacri, similitudini, idoli, species,* or *radii.*[48] The variety reveals the fluid state of Leonardo's thought, even his vacillation about the nature of perception as his study of optics proceeded. The first three terms, usually translated as "images," refer to percepts of whole objects, and the last one to stimuli from point sources; while *species* is a Baconian term that can be interpreted either way according to context. An instance of the concept of the integral image is the passage and diagram (fig. 5.7) from the early Ashburnham manuscript of 1492, which Kemp[49] cites as an early instance of Leonardo's gradual assimilation of medieval optics: the diagram[50] is derived from that of John Pecham:[51]

every body in light and shade fills the surrounding air with infinite images [similitudini] *of itself; and these, through infinite pyramids projected by it, represent this body throughout space and in every direction. Each pyramid that is composed of an extended concourse of rays includes within itself an infinite number of pyramids and each has the same power as all, and all as each. A circle of equidistant pyramids of vision* [*the starlike extension of fig 5.7*] *will convey the object at equal angles, and an eye at each point will see the object at the same size. The body of the air is full of infinite pyramids composed of radiating straight lines, which are produced from the external outlines of bodies in light and shade existing in the air, and the farther they are from the object* [f, e, d, c, *in fig. 5.7*] *which produces them, the more acute they become, and although in their distribution they intersect and cross they never mingle together but pass through all the surrounding air, independently converging, expanding and penetrating . . . and each pyramid, in itself, includes in each minute part, the whole form of the body causing it.*[52]

The purpose of this passage is to demonstrate that the air is packed with potentially visible images; and that (1) at a given distance an object like a sphere will always appear to have the same size and shape (the starlike ring); and (2) the farther away one goes the less the angle of vision and the apparent size (pyramids *f, e, d, c*). Reflecting on the fact that every object in the world emanates infinite images in a 360-degree arc and that these all crisscross through the universe without being mixed or deflected, Leonardo expanded elsewhere into a panegyric on the mysterious order of Creation, concluding, "it is this that guides human discourse to the consideration of divine things."[53]

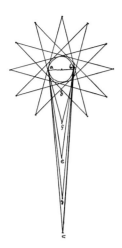

5.7   *The propagation of light rays from an illuminated*
object. British Library, MS. Ashburnham 2038, fol. 6v.

But the concept—although geometrically valid—raises problems that were already detected by ancient and Arabic critics of Democritus, Epicurus, and Lucretius, who established the theory of *eidola:* that is, whole and invisible images that emanate from objects and enter the eye as complete entities. By what agency would such an image shrink just the right amount to get into the eye, and how would the proportion be maintained between the amount of shrinkage of a mountain and of a molehill?[54] Leonardo was aware of the problem, and in his early years in Milan he attempted to resolve it by appealing in turn to the two principal ancient explanations of the hypothetical force that carries light from the object to the eye: Aristotle's theory that it was the nature of atmosphere to draw images from the object, and—an opposing theory, closer to Plato and Galen—that it was in the nature of the eye to attract *spetie* "as a target and magnet."[55]

The *eidola* hypothesis had been dropped by the major medieval writers; Leonardo must have returned to it because the alternative—stimulation by point sources—posed another knotty problem which in modern times became a focus of Gestalt psychology: how, if light impulses are transmitted from points on the object as innumerable individual stimuli, do we reassemble them into whole images inside the brain? Ultimately, however, the difficulties inherent in the first hypothesis appeared greater to him than those in the second; the struggle can be followed in his use of the term *spetie,* which appears in the notes as synonymous with the triad of terms connoting "image" but also repeatedly in the sense of *radii,* as in a reference to "all the species of things placed before the eye travel by radiating lines to the surface of that eye."[56] Almost all

5.8   The reception of light rays by the eye. Windsor Castle, 19152r.

diagrams of light propagation other than figure 5.7 have lines that stand for rays from point sources (e.g., fig. 5.8). *Spetie,* following the doctrine of the multiplication of species stated by Grosseteste and Bacon, is also given a broader meaning, as in a passage in which Leonardo says that the sun "sends out from itself two sorts of species, the first luminous and the second of heat."[57]

The proliferation of terms and concepts in Leonardo's optical notes demonstrates a broad knowledge of the tradition: he could present the atomists' hypothesis and the two ancient responses to it; he knew Alhazen's theory and the variations on it by Bacon and Pecham, whose terms he adopted. Moreover, it shows that he accepted the risk of confusion because his experiments led him to reject the simple geometric optics of Alberti, and this opened the basic historic issues in the field. At the root of his difficulty was the fact that neither he nor anyone else in the Renaissance had separated the psychology of vision (which would deal with the perception of whole objects) from the physiology.

Figure 5.7 can be interpreted to imply that the images emanating from objects in every direction move out from their source in a uniform progression; and indeed Leonardo on several occasions paralleled the propagation of images with the succession of waves set up when a pebble is thrown into a still body of water:

Just as a stone flung into the water becomes the center and cause of many circles, and as sound diffuses itself in circles in the air: so any object, placed in the luminous atmosphere, diffuses itself in circles, and fills the surrounding air with infinite images of itself. And is repeated, the whole everywhere, and the whole in every smallest part. This can be proved by experiment, since if you shut a window that faces west and make a hole . . .[58]

Another passage extends the simile to sound:

The air likewise fills itself with circles the centers of which are the sounds and voices made in it.[59]

Leonardo's effort to develop a general, mechanistic theory of the propagation of sense impulses appears to have been made early in his career when he was more attracted to grand unitary theories, and to have been abandoned in his later work when experience and experiment had diminished their credibility.[60] The paralleling of the images of objects with the wave motion generated by the pebble in the pond, and the voices, has led to the inference that Leonardo had proposed a wave theory of light centuries before it was accepted. This is unwarranted: the "waves" are merely a succession of hypothetical points at which the rays emanating from an object could be halted;[61] actually the lines joining these points would resemble the circular ripples in the pond only in the unique case where the object considered is, as in figure 5.7, itself circular or spherical.

At the start of his work on vision Leonardo had revived the question of whether the eye perceives by receiving light stimuli from the external world or by emitting visual rays—the question hotly debated in antiquity and, as mentioned before, brushed aside by Alberti.[62] In one of the anatomical sheets at Windsor Castle, which contain the earliest surviving notes on vision (ca. 1483–85), Leonardo appears as a supporter of the Euclidian-Galenic theory of emission that had been decisively refuted by Alhazen and subsequent medieval writers:

I say the eye projects an infinite number of lines, and these attach themselves to or mingle with those that come toward it which emanate from the things seen.[63]

Some time later Leonardo wrote out an extended dialogue in which he takes the part of the defender of the emission theory; one of the sections entitled "how radiating lines carry the visual faculty with them to the point of repercussion" reads:

This mind of ours, or common sense, which scientists claim resides in the middle of the head, maintains its spiritual extension for a great distance away from itself, and this is clearly seen in the fact that the lines of visual rays which terminate in the object immediately give to the seat of reason the character of the form of [the object] they hit.[64]

After each defense of this position in the dialogue the opposing argument is presented (*openione contrarie*): the eye that emits rays would be consumed in the effort to grasp the distant stars; a colored light source casts forth its color to everything around it, proving that visual rays originate in the object; the *camera obscura* receives images without sending anything forth. Finally Leonardo cites the power of the eye according to folk myths: the glance of the wolf can give men hoarse voices; the ostrich and spider are said to hatch their eggs by looking at them, etc. This crowded sheet from the Codex Atlanticus is a *jeu d'esprit* in which the writer fantasizes around traditional theories and superstitions. There was a precedent for its odd mixture of affirmation and negation of extromission in the *Liber de anima* of Avicenna, the great eleventh-century Arab authority on the sciences, which contains the fullest and most effective argument *against* extromission and yet comments in closing that animals, particularly the lion and the serpent, see in the dark by projecting the light of the eye.[65] That belief was still strong enough in Leonardo's time to prompt him explicitly to reject it in a later sheet than the one just mentioned; he points out ingenuously that one's cat is more likely to knock the vase off the shelf at night than during the day.[66]

Yet, around 1490, Leonardo did commit himself to emission: as in many other scientific fields his first notes were more records of somewhat capricious reading and listening (e.g., in optics he first hit upon early authors like Galen and missed more recent ones) than of investigation; his mature work increasingly showed the evidence of experiment and deduction and of wider reading. Emission is entirely absent from the later work, and instead demonstrations of the opposite view appear, as early as 1492, among them Alhazen's citation of the afterimage that appears when one looks at a strong light and then closes one's eyes.[67] But once he had accepted Alhazen's view that the eye simply receives impulses from the outside, he rejected, as we see in the following section, the traditional explanation of what happened next.

IV

Alhazen and all his followers up to Leonardo had had another reason for rejecting the Euclidian point-within-the-eye: that the light rays could not stop at that point but would inevitably intersect and pass beyond, inverting the image (fig. 5.6).[68] So they represented the humors of the eye as lenses that refract the rays away from the crossing point and preserve a right-side-up image. On the grounds of medieval optics alone, painters' perspective could not have been invented.

One of Leonardo's major achievements, as Dr. Kemp has shown, was the abandonment of this hypothesis. It must have been work with the *camera obscura* and other applications of projection through a pinhole that persuaded him that the rays have to cross. He describes experiments in which he places a piece of heavy paper or sheet metal with a small hole cut into it against an otherwise blacked-out window in a darkened room and observes the image cast on the opposite wall.[69] The image is inverted because the rays, as they pass through the hole, intersect, those entering from beneath being cast on the upper part of the projected indoor image, those from above in the lower part, and the same for right and left. Ironically this technique, probably invented by the ancient Greeks, had been used and reported by Alhazen himself and by the other *Perspectiva* writers, but none of them before Leonardo had been able to overcome their prejudice about inversion sufficiently to realize that the pinhole image is a simple model of the eye (in figure 5.9, from MS. D, Leonardo draws the *camera obscura* right under the eye to make his case).[70] It receives the rays or species from the outside and projects them accurately—with the proper colors and relationships—on a surface inside. There would indeed be a *point* at the aperture (not outside it, as in Leonardo's freehand fig. 5.9) at which they cross; but images are not recorded at that point either in the camera or in the eye: they are cast onto a surface or screen somewhere behind it.

It may seem a simple step from observing the function of the *camera obscura* to assuming that the images passing through the pupil are sensed on the *rear* inner surface of the eye. But Leonardo was not able to move that far from tradition: he, too, could not believe that an inverted image would be righted by the brain. And he was too much of a mechanist to fall back on the "visual spirit" or other mysterious force to solve the new dilemma he had created. This left him with only one possible solution: the image would have to be *reinverted* before reaching the optic nerve. The eye diagram of figure 5.8 shows an image entering from various points on the surface of the crystalline sphere in the center of the eye. The sphere is a second lens which reinverts the image and reduces it to the size of the optic nerve (compare this to the seventeenth-century version of figure 5.7, where the crystalline humor—in the front of the eye, not the center—functions as a focusing lens, but not as an image inverter. Leonardo's crystalline lens, as he pointed out, works like a glass sphere filled with water;[71] it is no longer a sense organ as in Galen and all the medieval anatomists and optical writers. But also its anterior surface is no longer lenticular in shape, and in this respect it is a step farther from the actual eye than Galen's.[72]

Leonardo's image could not be sensed on the crystalline lens because at that point it had not been righted (figs. 5.8, 5.9, and 5.14). We would expect him, then, to move the locus of sensation to the rear surface of the eye—to the retina or the optic nerve—but, for reasons we shall discover, he rejected this possibility and identified instead the anterior surface of the eye, which we call the cornea and he called the *popilla* or *luce,*[73] as the initial sensor. Its function is the same as the surface of the crystalline humor in earlier optics, and there remains the medieval ambiguity as to what aspect of the sensing occurs on this surface and what in the optic nerve to which the surface transmits the image.

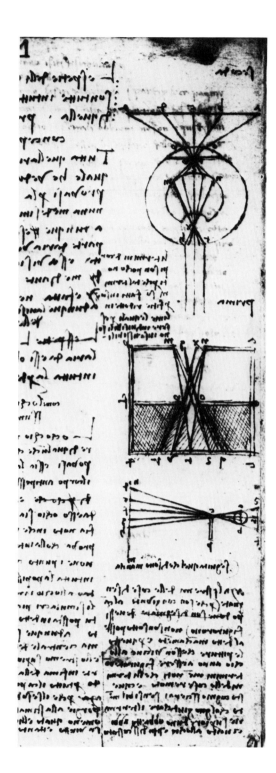

5.9 Leonardo da Vinci, *reception of light rays by the eye* (top) *and by the* camera obscura (middle). *Paris, Institut de France, MS. D, fol. 10v.*

This hypothesis is affirmed in a statement which appears with slightly different phrasing throughout the later optical writings:

The visual faculty is distributed in equal strength through the whole popilla [= cornea] *of the eye, so that the visual act is whole throughout the* popilla *and whole in every part of it,*

and again:

Every point on the popilla *sees the whole object, and every point on the object "sees" the whole* popilla.[74]

The two statements are almost paraphrases of Alhazen's descriptions:

Any part or any point of the visible form multiplies itself through the atmosphere to the whole surface of the eye, and the whole surface of the thing seen to a single point on the eye.

Since, when it [the eye] grasps [comprehenderit] the color of one point [on the object] from any given point on its [the eye's] surface, it must grasp the color of one part of the object from one part of its [the eye's] surface and grasp the color of another part [of the object] from another part of its [the eye's] surface.[75]

How is it that Alhazen, who placed sensation on the surface of the crystalline humor, implied—by using the verb *comprehendere* (and in the same paragraph, *sentire*)[76]—that the image is sensed also on the surface of the cornea? His choice of words must have been metaphorical in the same way that Leonardo's was in stating that the object "sees" the eye: in fact, in the following paragraph he affirms that the "surface" merely transmits and does not sense.[77] But whatever the explanation, the Arab scholar—or his translator—left a loose end that Leonardo picked up, or rather tripped over.[78]

Leonardo compared the image-receiving capacity of the anterior surface of the eye to that of a convex mirror:

The spaces between the images of the stars on the surface of the eye have the same proportion among themselves as the spaces between the stars in the sky; the images cover the whole eye . . . as [they] would on a mirror surface.[79]

While he may have arrived at the hypothesis of the sentient cornea partly by the logic I suggested and partly with the support of Alhazen's ambiguity, he discovered what he believed to be experimental proof in phenomena that appeared to contradict the theory of point-to-point propagation of light that was basic to Euclidian optics and to Renaissance perspective. An obstruction—notably a small one placed near the eye—can be put between the eye and an observed object without blocking vision. How could this happen if all rays move direct from the source to the eye? The modern answer, involving the hypothesis of light waves and the phenomenon of diffraction, is that they don't; but for Leonardo the only conceivable answer was that if vision is inhibited in one part of the eye, another part must pick up the stimuli:

the whole popilla [= *cornea*] *has the capacity for vision, but not uniformly, because the part most distant from the center discerns things less well. Since the visual faculty is distributed evenly throughout the* popilla, *no object which is less large than it* [*the* popilla] *and which is placed at a short distance before it, can block* [occupare] *any part of a distant object. You can prove it this way* [*fig. 5.10*]: *let* op *be the* popilla *and* f *the small object before it. Draw line* oe *and likewise* nb *over the object, and you will see that the half-pupil* on *sees everything in the area* bc; *likewise, the other half sees everything in the area* ac. *One demonstrates by this that if point* n *alone saw object* f, [*that object*] *would block from the eye all of the area* bc *of the second object. Again it is confirmed that all the species of objects enter the eye upside down; behind* f, *you see* b, *which is on top, as if it were underneath, in* p, *and* e, *on the bottom, corresponds to* o, *on top.*[80]

Figure 5.10 shows how the theory upsets the principles of painters' perspective.[81] Perspective presumes that from any one point on the object only one ray emanates to a point in the eye, and if the ray is blocked by a nearby object it cannot be seen. But Leonardo interprets his experiment as showing that if there is an uninterrupted line from any part of the eye to the point on the object, it will be seen. By that rule, even the centric ray, which establishes the crucial vanishing point of perspective, could be blocked from the eye without impairing vision.[82]

The result of replacing the point to which the rays of perspective converge by the whole surface of the eye was to make the latter the effective intersection of the "visual pyramid," as Leonardo himself once observed.[83] One could still interpose a plane intersection at some distance from the eye (see fig. 5.1, where two intersections are indicated) if one wanted to use it for constructing pictures—since the spherical intersection of the eye would alter it exactly as it would alter the real world—but it no longer had the authority that Alberti had given it by implying that the intersection would receive the same image as the mind, and, indeed, that artificial and natural perspective were the same. Leonardo's conclusion therefore reduced perspective to the status of a workshop device (whereas his predecessors believed that it revealed the order of the universe) and made it more possible to elect whether to use it or to paint "by eye" (a term to which his reasoning gave a literal as well as a metaphorical meaning).

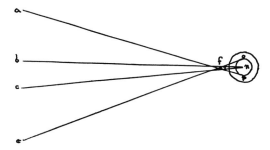

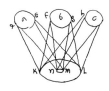

5.10 *Demonstration of the capacity of the eye to "see through" a small nearby object* f. *Milan, Codex Atlanticus, fol. 250v.*

5.11 *Simulation of the function of the pupil* (nm) *in receiving the image of three stars* (a, b, c). *Institut de France, MS. F, fol. 32v.*

In committing himself to the hypothesis that the whole front surface of the eye is sensitive, Leonardo was propelled into other errors. The most misleading was the idea that as the aperture of the eye contracts, objects look smaller, and as it expands, they look larger. A diagram in MS. F, 32v, illustrates the point (fig. 5.11).[84] You are looking at three stars (*a, b,* and *c*) in the night sky. If you see them with your whole eye *kl,* they look proportionally bigger than if you put a card with a little hole (representing the contracted aperture) *nm* before the eye, which allows you to see just as much of the sky, but over a greatly restricted area of the eye. The approach is logically consistent if the original hypothesis is accepted, and if one follows Leonardo in comparing what the eye registers to what a convex mirror reflects: a given object seen in a large convex mirror looks bigger than it does in a small mirror.

Leonardo did not choose stars for his demonstration of the theorem by chance. He believed that if one carried out the instructions for figure 5.11 the geometrical proof would be sustained by experience. A bright light on a dark ground will indeed seem smaller if viewed through a tiny hole—though only because of the reduction of the spread of diffraction and the increased sharpness of focus.

I have referred to the "aperture" of the eye rather than the "pupil" because Leonardo's *popilla* is usually the whole cornea which, if not controlled by such artificial means as the hole in the card, presumably is contracted by narrowing the eyelids. But

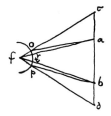

5.12   *Demonstration of refraction by the cornea of the*
eye. Institut de France, MS. D, fol. 2r.

at one point in the mid-1490s Leonardo identifies the pupil in the modern sense, and
correctly defines an important aspect of its function without, however, coordinating
the observation into his own system:

Everything we see looks bigger at midnight than at midday and bigger in the morning
than at midday.

   This happens because the pupil of the eye is a great deal smaller at midday
than at any other time.

   As much as the eye or pupil of the owl is bigger in proportion to the animal
than that of man, so much more light can it see at night than man can; so at midday it
can see nothing if its pupil does not diminish; and, in the same way, it sees things as
bigger at night than by day.[85]

   Had he tried to reconcile his many experiments and observations on the expansion and contraction of the pupil in men and animals with his ideas about size
perception, he might have taken more literally his comparison of the eye to the *camera*
obscura, rather than seeking analogies to the mirror.

   In one respect, however, the eye is unlike the typical *camera obscura* of Leonardo's time: it contains lenses (fig. 5.6). Many of Leonardo's late eye diagrams illustrating the passage of light rays into the interior of the eye show the rays refracted by
the cornea. In MS. D Leonardo demonstrates geometrically how "the straightness of
the concourse of the species bends on entering the eye" (fig. 5.12):

the eye receives on itself the section of the species ab *in* op, *while the perspectivist,*
imagining the rays to be straight, cuts the rays at rt *and thereby finds the things pro-*
duced in his perspective to be considerably less [large] than the eye judges them to be.[86]

The reason for the refraction by the eye, Leonardo says, "is proven in optics when
species pass from the density of water to the rarity of air."[87] This observation might
have put Leonardo on the track of a mechanical definition of the cornea as a lens if he
had not been blocked by his theory that the image is formed on its front surface. In
fact, at one point, he actually compares the eye to the lens of eyeglasses, but records
what we regard as the wrong evidence:

The glass of spectacles shows how the images of objects are held on the surface of the eye and from there penetrate, bending.[88]

The experiments recorded in figures 5.10 and 5.11 led to the threshold of a major discovery in optics that would ultimately demolish the ray theory of light. This was the phenomenon of diffraction. One type had already been observed by Roger Bacon in a manuscript (*De multiplicatione specierum*) that does not seem to have been known to Renaissance writers.[89] Diffraction phenomena were described first in print by F. M. Grimaldi in 1665, but were not accounted for until Constantin Huygens proposed a wave theory of light propagation later in the seventeenth century. Huygens showed that if light from a candle passes through a hole, as in one of Leonardo's cards, a new circular wave front is generated on the viewer's side of the hole because each point in a wavefront is the source of its own wavefront. Thus the new front sends the image of the candle off in directions diverging from the central axis of vision so that it can be seen even if direct vision through the hole is blocked.

Leonardo sensed that this hole, which he had used for the *camera obscura*, was the clue to an important discovery, and he devised an experiment which, when reported with certain clarification by Christoph Scheiner in 1621, was recognized as a milestone for modern optics. He proposed piercing a card with a needle,[90] holding it a short distance off, and moving the needle up and down (or right and left) very close to the eye, at which point, "you'll see in the air on the other side of the hole the image of the needle making all motions contrary to that which you are making with the needle between your eye and the small hole." A geometrical proof and diagram follow and are accompanied by a second diagram and text showing how the traditional convergence of rays to a point fails to account for the phenomenon, and how the only possible explanation is again that "the visual faculty is distributed over the whole *popilla* of the eye and in every point of it."

Several diagrams and notes in MSS. D and F of 1508–9 represent another effort by Leonardo to explain, with the simple means at his disposal, phenomena that were to be understood only much later. They show three rays emanating from an object: one from the center of the object to the center of the eye, and the others to the upper and lower eyelids respectively.[91] These purport to illustrate, as Leonardo put it on D, 9v, "why luminous bodies show their outlines full of straight luminous rays." The answer is that

the rays that show us the outlines of luminous bodies do not have their origins from those bodies but from their image in the thickness of the eyelids of the observing bodies.

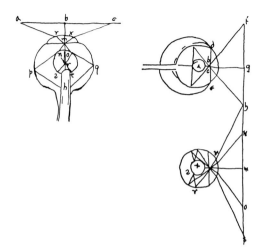

5.13 *Demonstrations of the reception of light rays by the eye and the inversion of the image, first at the pupil and subsequently in the crystalline sphere. Institut de France, MS. D, fol. 10r.*

5.14 *Demonstration of the theory (rejected by Leonardo) that light rays penetrate to the retina and are reflected back to the sensitive crystalline sphere. Institut de France, MS. D, fol. 7v.*

The upper and lower rays bounce off the inside convex surface of the lids—aided by moisture that builds up there by capillary action—casting "secondary" rays into the eye, so that the edges of the observed object appear more "luminous."[92] I am unable to tell from his few notes on the subject whether Leonardo meant to explain more than the irradiation that appears to surround the sources of bright light in a dark environment.[93] In any case, the implication of the eyelids in visual functions had a long history: Averroes, commenting on Aristotle's *De sensu,* reported that the eyelids, besides protecting the eye, aid in long-distance vision; and that many animals see farther than men because they have thicker eyelids: he was quoted by Roger Bacon who, however, offered no opinion on the question.[94]

In two long passages in MS. D, Leonardo undertakes to answer an unnamed expert in optics who claims that images are formed not on or in the crystalline sphere, but on the surface at the rear of the eye that we call the retina and he called the "concavity of the uvea."[95] The argument is hard to follow unless one accepts two erroneous assumptions shared by Leonardo and his "adversary." The first, a heritage of medieval optics, is that the optic nerve penetrates into the crystalline humor in the center of the eye as illustrated in figure 5.13 (cf. figs. 3, 4, 8).

The second is a corollary, that rays of light may indeed penetrate to the uvea-retina, but since the image has to arrive at the optic nerve right-side-up, they would somehow have to be *reflected back to the center of the eye* (fig. 5.14). Consequently Leonardo represents the uvea as: "The terminus and covering of the vitreous humor [which] provides the darkness behind the transparency of the vitreous humor as lead provides mirrors with darkness behind the transparency of glass." The concept of the reflecting uvea is necessary not only to bring the rays of light to the front of the optic nerve for transmission to the brain, but to solve the original and nagging problem of inversion: the image received on the uvea-retina would have to be reflected back to another surface in order to be righted. The mechanism of this process is just too complicated: Leonardo disposes of it by showing in figure 5.13 that the rays hitting the uvea (at p and q) would not bounce back to the front of the optic nerve. "I'm sure," he says, "that the *idola* doesn't get reflected in the faculty of sight by being on the concavity of the uvea, since the angle of incidence would not equal the angle of reflection." Figure 5.14 shows how the rays would have to reflect backward at impossible angles.

The final problem to be solved was how the image righted by the crystalline sphere was to be perceived by the brain. The ancient and medieval system of perception involved a visual spirit that issues from the brain through the optic nerves, captures the image at the crystalline humor, and returns with it to the juncture of the optic nerves (chiasma) where the evidence from the two eyes is coordinated. From here, according to Aristotle, it passes via the brain to the common sense, where evidence from all the single senses is collated.[96] Aristotle's common sense is in the heart; later writers, when they refer to it at all, imply that it is at the front of the brain.

In Leonardo's earliest anatomical study of the cranial nerves, he illustrates the physical elements of the system. A drawing of ca. 1493–94 in Windsor (fig. 5.15), showing the brain in vertical and horizontal cross section, has the optic nerves running from the rear of each eyeball directly to the anterior ventricle, which is the first of three globular organs that process information received from the senses.[97] The drawing does not indicate what functions each performs, though they are labeled with letters.

The theory that the three ventricles were thus specialized in function appears in commentaries on Aristotle's *De anima*.[98] The medieval and Renaissance tradition can be traced to Avicenna's *De anima,* where the *sensus communis* or *fantasia* is located in the forward ventricle, the *imaginatione* and *vis aestimationis* in the middle ventricle, and the *vis memorialis* in the rear. This disposition was taken over by Albertus Magnus, some of whose work was known to Leonardo.[99] Leonardo's drawings, in which the three ventricles are identified, depart from the tradition in identifying the anterior ventricle as the *imprensiva,* the middle one as the Common Sense, and the rear as the seat of Memory.[100]

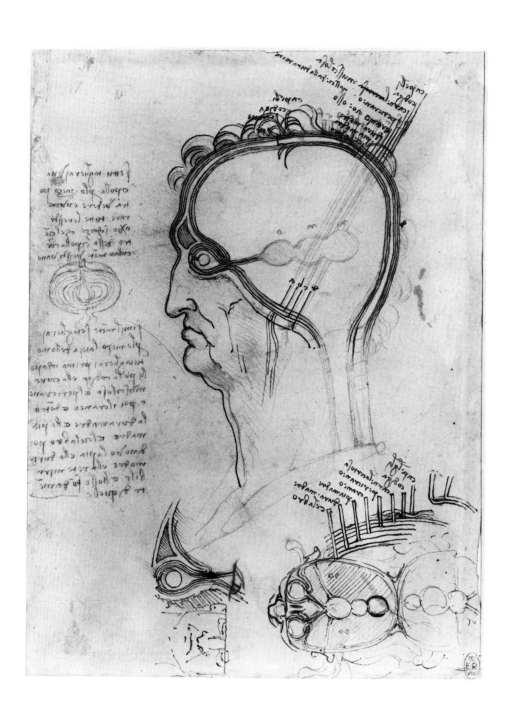

5.15   *Leonardo da Vinci, cross section of the human head, showing the ventricles of the brain. Windsor Castle, 12603.*

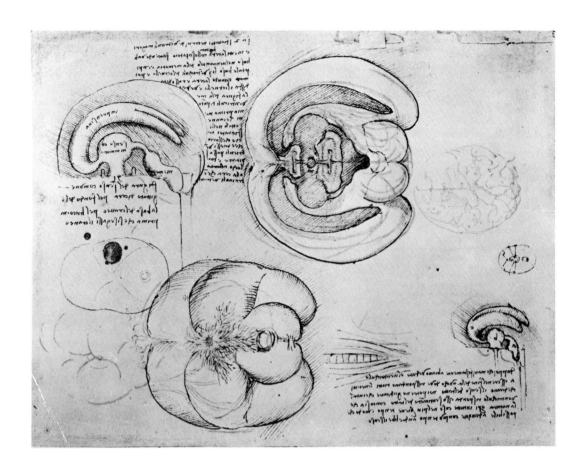

5.16   *Leonardo da Vinci, structure of the brain,*
showing the ventricles. Windsor Castle, 19127.

Leonardo put the *imprensiva*, an actual physical organ of perception, in the forward position so that it could process visual stimuli before passing them to the Common Sense, now displaced to the middle. He always sought mechanical explanations and distrusted reliance on mysterious powers such as the visual spirit:

there can be no instrument without a body; and this being so, a spirit can have neither voice, nor form nor strength . . . where there are neither nerves nor bones there can be no force exercised in any kind of movement made by such imaginary spirits.[101]

After 1500, when Leonardo invented a method of investigating the form of the brain ventricles by reversing the lost-wax process of casting sculpture and injecting wax to obtain models (fig. 5.16), he realized that the anterior ventricle was actually divided into two lateral cavities, which he again labels *imprensiva*.[102] Elsewhere he explained the function:

The Common Sense is activated by the imprensiva, *which is placed between it and the senses. The* imprensiva *is activated by the images* [similitudini] *of things given it by the surface instruments, that is, the senses, which are placed between external things and the* imprensiva.[103]

By about 1508, when Leonardo was drawing figure 5.16, he was already aware of a serious flaw in the hypothesis: that there is no way within a system of geometrical optics—without the help of incorporeal spirits—to get rays of light from the eye to an *imprensiva* in the brain. If an infinite number of single light stimuli have to travel through the hollow channels of the optic nerves by an angular or curved route (from the two eyes to a confluence at the chiasma, and branching out from there to meet a second time in the brain) they would necessarily be blocked or distorted, and geometrical optics can no longer accommodate the theory. A drawing in the Arundel manuscript of 1506–8 (fig. 5.17) shows the eye with the nerve emerging from it at an angle, and the text explains:

If the imprensiva *were outside the eye straight lines would not reach it. Though* b *comes straight to eye* f *and from* f *goes to* d, *nevertheless, the line that goes to the* imprensiva *is straight and oblique so it is necessary that the* imprensiva *be in the eye. The nerve that goes from the eye to the brain is like the perforated cords that are interwoven with many branches through the skin of bodies and carry* [sensations] *through their hollows to the common sense.*[104]

This conclusion, to which Leonardo apparently arrived independently, happened to bring his thinking into line with that of Alhazen—whose theory of perception had been pushed aside in the Middle Ages by Aristotle. Alhazen proposed that incoming light

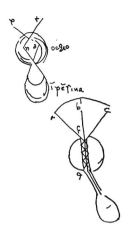

5.17   Two demonstrations of the passage of light rays through the eye to the imprensiva, *or organ of perception. London, British Library, MS. Arundel, fol. 171v.*

impulses are simultaneously selected and structured by the crystalline humor, so that an integrated image could be transmitted to the brain.[105]

Another passage, presumably of the same period, bears a title which suggests that Leonardo was on the track of the modern view of ocular function: "The *imprensiva,* placed behind the spherical glacial humor, rights the images [*ridriza le specie*]." [106] But the text and drawing that follow, while they put the *imprensiva* in the area where the optic nerve touches the rear of the crystalline sphere, still insist that the image must be righted by the sphere. In spite of the confusion, the passage concludes with an important departure from ancient and medieval dependence on spirits: "Now think about the eye, and you will realize that necessity, mistress of all things, has been properly foresighted, providing within the eye all the instruments for its function." The *imprensiva* is perhaps no more material than the visual spirit, but it is significantly different in being passive—in awaiting stimulation[107]—rather than an active force that emanates from the brain, presumably whether or not there is anything for it to do.

The disarray in which Leonardo left the problem of vision was probably unavoidable before the confirmation of the function of the retina by Felix Plater in 1583. Seen in retrospect, the theory of the *imprensiva* was an effort to explain functions that we now attribute partly to the retina and partly to the psychology of perception, the workings of which are still not entirely clear. Much of Leonardo's confusion over the processes of perception was inevitable for a searching mind in his generation.

V

Leonardo's extensive studies of vision have remained virtually ignored during almost a century of exhaustive scholarship on his thought because of the strong element of progressivism in its historical attitude, especially in the history of science. Scholars have been put off by finding that, in groping toward a new physiology of the eye, Leonardo stumbled into unworkable hypotheses. His failure to advance science—in the sense of improving the state of knowledge of his time and contributing to the discoveries of his successors—obscured the fact that in many aspects his approach to the subject was extraordinarily inventive and open-minded in its empiricism, radically different from that of his predecessors and contemporaries, and that it produced discoveries which, when repeated a century later, contributed to a new era in optics.

Before Leonardo the study of vision was restricted to summary description of the structure of the eye and extensive demonstrations in geometrical optics—the material of physics rather than of physiology. Reference was rarely made to the observable functions and appearance of the eye, to the experience of vision (as when Alhazen cited the afterimage impressed on the eye by a bright light as evidence against the extromission theory), or to experiments devised for solving specific problems. Leonardo brought the discipline from an abstract plane to concrete issues that could be investigated experimentally: he sought to explain the expansion and contraction of the pupil in response to light stimuli and its effect on vision, the phenomena of diffraction, the workings of refraction within the eye, binocular vision and the coordination of the movements of the two eyes, the near and far limits of the range of normal vision, the role of the brain in perception, and other phenomena. In the process he demonstrated the distinction between the physiology of vision and the anatomy of the eye and optics. None of these achievements directly affected the future as they were never published or even collected together. Since there is no evidence of other innovative work in the field during the fifteenth century, the generation following Leonardo—notably Vesalius, Sylvius, and Maurolycus—had to begin where late medieval optics and anatomy had left off.

Granted that Leonardo's answers to many of the radical questions he raised were wrong, his contribution deserves attention and respect because the kind of questions he posed and the experimental methods he devised for answering them represent a great contribution to scientific consciousness—the new consciousness that within the subsequent century and a half produced what we now hold to be the right answers to most of the questions.

It is ironical that Leonardo should have been deflected from a clear conception of ocular function primarily by his incapacity to accept the evidence of an inverted image on the rear surface of the eye. He was the only scientist who ever recorded all his observations and made all his demonstration sketches in inverted writing, proceeding from right to left (though not also upside-down like the retinal image). He surely could read his notes without recourse to a mirror, and this act would by itself be sufficient proof that the brain can right an inverted image. But the evidence so readily (and so literally) at hand escaped him. Liberated though he was from traditional mental tenets, in this fundamental respect Leonardo could not shake their grip.

In the sphere of art, as in science, the significance of Leonardo's studies of vision must be sought more in the point of view and in the approach to problem-solving than in specific solutions and hypotheses. The perspective construction of fifteenth-century painting, for example, would have lost some of its quasi-moral authority over the structuring of pictures without Leonardo's critique, but the critique gave philosophical support to the trend.

Leonardo expressed three reservations about the strict *costruzione legittima*: first, that it did not permit the observer of an object to move freely about but required him to observe with one fixed eye from a fixed position; second, that it was geometrically questionable, since it required everything seen by the observer to be reduced to a point, which by definition has no extension; and third, that the eye, being sensitive everywhere on the convex anterior surface, does not receive images the same way as the hypothetical screen intersecting the visual pyramid (which, for fifteenth-century perspectivists, was equivalent to the picture plane). The eye, as Leonardo described it in his later manuscripts, works like a convex mirror, in that the relative size of objects recorded on it changes according to the angle at which they are received (fig. 5.12); given two identical figures at the same distance, the one nearer the center axis of the eye or mirror will appear "disproportionately" larger (a phenomenon we experience when we see our face reflected in a silver bowl, the nose unbecomingly enlarged in relation to the eyes, etc.). Leonardo did not, however, propose a new perspective method for ordinary pictures based on these reservations, because he knew that the picture image comes to the eye the same way as the world image (so that if the picture is distorted in an effort to compensate for visual disproportions, it will look distorted). His reform of perspective was restricted on the one hand to warning against constructions that bring the viewer too close to the picture surface (fig. 5.2), and on the other hand to inventing two new perspective devices based on his careful analysis of the problems of close-up views and odd angles of vision: anamorphosis and the foreshortening of images painted on curved or angled surfaces. The first of these laid the foundation for centuries of trick images; but the second had a more stimulating and far-reaching impact on the future evolution of painting, by formulating procedures for the foreshortening of images on curved or angled surfaces, that sparked the era of illusionistic ceiling, vault, and dome decoration.

There is nothing in the critique to discourage painters from continuing to organize pictorial space by the boxlike constructions of the fifteenth century (though Leonardo's major applications of the *costruzione legittima* in the *Adoration of the Magi* and the *Last Supper* are far from being legitimately constructed).[108] But the effect was to demystify perspective, to represent it as a potentially fallible workshop device which, although the only way to assure accurate relationships of size in most situations, had no special authority, and was not a reflection of the order of the universe. By calling the geometrical method "simple" perspective, and the processes of ordinary vision "natural" perspective, Leonardo left the impression that the painter might as well return to representing things empirically, as they look to him. His use of the term "natural" in this context must have been intended subtly to affect the meaning of "*perspectiva naturalis*," the medieval designation for the science of optics, implying that ordinary visual perception may be as close to nature as the mathematical study of light propagation, or at least that it deserves the same name.

This shift of emphasis had implications far beyond perspective construction; in giving the processes of perception a new rational—even proto-scientific—validity, Leonardo lent authority to the effort on the part of contemporary and later painters to represent things as they seem as distinct from the quattrocento tendency to represent things as they are. His observations on optical illusions, loss of distinction of distant objects, diffraction phenomena, the indistinctness of objects seen by peripheral vision, and the appearance of objects in motion demonstrated that the illusion of reality is not necessarily secured by pictures based on objective measurement. He even went too far in this direction in claiming that the apparent size of objects alters with the expansion and contraction of the pupil and with the objects' position in relation to the axis of the eye.

A revaluation of perception was also involved in Leonardo's abandonment of the theory of the *idola*—the transmission of whole images as illustrated in figure 5.7—because that theory presupposes the objective existence of an object of a determined shape and color that is conveyed to the ambient atmosphere and thence to the wholly passive eye. Only the alternative theory of point sources would explain the many different ways in which the same object can be perceived. It is self-evident that this choice was as significant for art as it was for physiology.

The effect of Leonardo's perception theories was to prompt painters to observe the visual world closely in all its vast variety of lights, colors, and shapes without regard for whether what they experienced was really out there or whether it was altered by the atmosphere, the eye, even the eyelids, or the *imprensiva*. This attitude underlies the hundreds of observations that Leonardo noted for inclusion in his *Trattato* on the optical effect of light, shadow, reflection, and atmosphere on colors and forms. These observations further emphasize that for the painter, objects in the outer world do not "have" a particular color and shape as they seem to in most fifteenth-century paintings, but rather that conditions of the environment and of vision at a particular moment give them a unique appearance. Moreover, since the appearance is not necessarily an indication of the way things really are, the painter can produce illusionistic images without being constrained to imitate what he sees before him; he can invent a wide range of atmospheric and optical conditions without departing from the possible, and this permits him to manipulate light, color, and form for expressive purposes.

Leonardo's *Madonna of the Rocks* (fig. 6.6), started at the beginning of his optical researches, shows the dawn of the new consciousness most obviously in the treatment of light and shadow (*chiaroscuro*). The scene is set in a place suggesting a cave for symbolic reasons, but also because this establishes a dark, shadow-pervaded environment out of which parts of the figures are selected by a light which, in such a place, is necessarily mysterious, whether it is natural or divine. The light, without being capricious, falls on the expressive surfaces—faces, hands and limbs, or draperies that emphasize significant movement. As the surrounding darkness moves in on the illuminated surfaces, it swallows the edges of people and things, so that the *chiaroscuro*, instead of describing objects in their number and dimensions, as in quattrocento pictures, molds them together in one expressive moment. For rhetorical-formal purposes, the limits of the figures are distinguished less from each other than they are from the landscape: the four are drawn into a single conical shape. Because Leonardo wanted the *chiaroscuro* to be cohesive, he represented it as hazy (*sfumato*—smoky—was the term he coined). The gentle transitions on soft surfaces eliminate the sharp breaks that a brighter, cleaner light would cause; they also add a subtlety and mystery to a scene which is, in any case, poetic rather than historical.

Finally, the pervasive shadow neutralizes, as it does in our perception of nature, the bright colors of fifteenth-century painting, and with them an air of festivity and tendency to decorativeness. In this picture Leonardo began to use his intense observation of nature and the hypothesis of his physiology of vision to attain for art both a heightened verisimilitude and an expanded range of expressive means.[109]

Postscript on Leonardo's Notebooks

I was baffled, when I first tried to understand Leonardo's views on a particular subject, by the complexity and disorder of his surviving writings, and by the failure of most modern commentators acquainted with the material to help their readers to understand what is involved in determining Leonardo's opinion. I hope here to lessen the difficulty, at least to the extent of explaining my references to the sources.

All Leonardo's surviving theoretical writing, scientific notes, and other literary production, is preserved in single-sheet notes and drawings and in notebooks of various dimensions and bulk. None was published during his lifetime. The notes were inherited by a student, Francesco Melzi, who compiled from them, toward the middle of the sixteenth century, the *Treatise on Painting*. Leonardo had meant to publish such a treatise, as well as others on a variety of subjects; and much of what appeared in Melzi's version is probably what Leonardo thought of as being in final form. However, the bulk of the *Trattato* is assembled more or less in subject categories from many disconnected sheets, and appears somewhat chaotic. Modern editors have rearranged the material from the Melzi manuscript (Vatican, Cod. Urb. lat. 1270). The standard English edition is that of A. Philip McMahon (Princeton, 1956) which includes a facsimile of the Vatican manuscript; most scholars cite the paragraph numbers of the German edition by H. Ludwig (Vienna, 1882 and later editions).

In spite of the loss of a major part of the manuscripts willed to Melzi (in the Madrid MS. II Leonardo listed fifty volumes completed by 1505, while only some twenty-five survive from his entire career) many of the over one thousand propositions in the *Trattato* appear also in one of the surviving original manuscripts preserved in libraries of various western European cities. In many cases, the same or similar statements appear in different manuscripts, as Leonardo frequently repeated and copied observations. Carlo Pedretti has undertaken the enormous task of tracing and tentatively dating the source of every proposition (*Leonardo da Vinci on Painting: A Lost Book* [Berkeley and Los Angeles, 1964], pp. 176–221; the study includes a good survey of the lost portions and of the vicissitudes of the *Trattato*).

Leonardo made notes on a vast variety of subjects other than painting. Compilations of translated selections from these were made by J. P. Richter (*The Literary Works of Leonardo da Vinci* [London, 1883; rev. eds. Oxford, 1939, New York, 1970]) and by Edward MacCurdy (*The Notebooks of Leonardo da Vinci* [New York, 1938 and later eds.]) as well as by various editors in different languages. But students seeking the full range of Leonardo's writings on any subject must go ultimately through the editions of the original manuscripts, which began to be reproduced in facsimile at the end of the last century and which, with the publication of the recently rediscovered two volumes in Madrid, now make records of all of Leonardo's known writings and drawings accessible in larger libraries. Leonardo's work on some subjects has been studied sufficiently by modern scholars that the essential notes are all compiled in secondary sources. But on others, such as the physiology of the eye, it remains difficult even to locate relevant notes.

Recent research on the writings has been directed increasingly to the problem of chronology. Leonardo changed his mind on many issues as his curiosity drove him to question traditional explanations; and, in the many cases where two of his statements on a subject are in conflict, one often represents an opinion based on or even quoted from reading or on incomplete research, and another a revision based on further examination. Where this occurs, as it does in his work on the physiology of the eye, it is essential to know which was the later and thus, in most cases, the definitive view.

On the subject of the eye, as on a few other themes, there exists a separate small notebook written in 1508–9, toward the end of Leonardo's study of the subject (MS. D of the Institute of France, ed. A. Corbeau). The date is estimated on the grounds of handwriting, the composition of the page, and comparison with treatments of the same subject in earlier and contemporary manuscripts. An even greater number of notes on the eye from the early 1490s and later years are found in books with other material or in the so-called Codex Atlanticus in the Ambrosiana Library in Milan (published 1894–1904 by the Accademia dei Lincei, Milan; a new facsimile is in process of publication); this is not really a codex, but a collection of several hundred single sheets of varying sizes produced during Leonardo's whole career and pasted by a later owner without order in a bound volume.

In this essay I have accepted the prevailing opinion that Leonardo's first notes on vision (in MS. A of the Institute of France, in some of the Windsor Castle Library anatomical drawings, and elsewhere), which adhere to Albertian perspective, were made during Leonardo's early years in Milan after 1490, and that his final views are represented in MS. E of the Institute, written in 1513–14.

The following dates for manuscripts frequently quoted in this essay are largely those of Pedretti and represent, with minor variations, the current opinion of Leonardo scholars:

MS. A   ca. 1492 (Cod. Ashburnham I [Paris, Bibliothèque Nationale 2038] was originally part of this manuscript: fols. 81–114; fols. 54, 65–80 are lost)

Cod. Arundel   1495/97–1505

MS. C   1490–91

MS. D   1508/9

MS. E   1513/14

MS. F   1508/9

MS. H   1493/95

MS. K   before 1500–6/7

Madrid II   ca. 1503/5

Notes

This paper was submitted to the Editors in 1976, shortly after their receipt of Martin Kemp's exemplary "Leonardo and the Visual Pyramid," *Journal of the Warburg and Courtauld Institutes,* 40 (1977), 138–149. It was agreed that the articles should be printed in consecutive volumes. I am grateful to Dr. Kemp for making this typescript available to me and for his observations on my original draft; also to the National Endowment for the Humanities for a fellowship and to the American Academy in Rome.

1.   Leonardo da Vinci, *Trattato,* paragraph 24 (12). The numbering is that of H. Ludwig (Vienna, 1882 and later editions); the numbers in parenthesis refer to the edition of A. Philip McMahon (Princeton, 1956).

2.   Cod. Atl. 203ra; Edward MacCurdy, *The Notebooks of Leonardo da Vinci* (New York, 1941), 989. For the original passage by Pecham see David C. Lindberg, *John Pecham and the Science of Optics* (Madison, 1970), 60. The source was identified by D. Strong, *"Leonardo da Vinci on the Eye: MS D in the Bibliothèque de l'Institut de France . . . ,"* dissertation, UCLA 1967 (University Microfilms 68–246), 101. Pecham's work appears, as *Prospettiva comune,* in the list of books that Leonardo put in storage in 1504/5 and listed on fol. 2v of Madrid II (identified in the volume of commentary by the editor, Ladislao Reti, pp. 91f.). See my postscript on Leonardo's notebooks at the end of this article.

3.   Support for placing MS. D in 1508/9 (and reasons for rejecting the date of ca. 1513 proposed by A. Corbeau in the facsimile edition of 1964) is convincingly given by K. Clark and C. Pedretti in the catalogue entry on the contemporary drawing, Windsor 19117, *Leonardo Drawings at Windsor Castle* (London, 1969). A more detailed justification of the date is given by Strong, "Leonardo da Vinci on the Eye," chap. II; Strong's dissertation was written under the direction of Prof. Pedretti.

4.   Cod. Arundel, 190v; J. P. Richter, *The Literary Works of Leonardo da Vinci* (London, 1883; rev. eds. Oxford 1939, New York 1970), paragraph 916 (hereafter "R" followed by the paragraph number).

5. MS. K 119v, 120r.

6. MS. K 120v, 121r.

7. Leonardo cites numerous other instances of the inadequacy of perspective construction: the painted face will look larger than that of the model, even when its measurements are the same (MS. A 2); the painted object seems larger than the one in relief (*Trattato*, paragraph 439 [489]; Cod. Ash. I, 19r); "among objects of equal height which are higher than the eye, that which is farthest from the eye will seem the lowest, and if the object is below the eye, that nearest to the eye will seem lowest" (*Trattato*, paragraph 476 [493]; "the line of the horizon must be curved since the earth is spherical" (ibid., paragraph 936 [988ff.].) A detailed discussion of Leonardo's differences with painters' perspective is given in Strong, "Leonardo da Vinci on the Eye," chap. V. The interpretation of Leonardo's perspective notes has been hotly debated in modern literature. I find most convincing the treatments of M. H. Pirenne, "The Scientific Basis of Leonardo da Vinci's Theory of Perspective," *British Journal for the Philosophy of Science*, 3 (1952–53), 169–185; D. Gioseffi, *Perspectiva artificialis* (Trieste, 1957), 106–120; C. Maltese, "Per Leonardo prospettico," *Raccolta vinciana*, 19 (1962), 303–314; and C. Pedretti, "Leonardo on Curvilinear Perspective," *Bibl. de l'Humanisme et de la Renaissance*, 25 (1963), 69–87. These, I believe, put right a confusion introduced into perspective studies by Panofsky's theory of a curvilinear perspective based on the curvature of the eyeball (*Die Perspektiv als symbolische Form*, Vorträge der Bibliothek Warburg [1924–25], 258–330), partly preserved in John White's interpretation (*The Birth and Rebirth of Pictorial Space* [London, 1957], especially 207ff.). The problem is reviewed by P. Sanpaolesi, "Studi di prospettiva," *Raccolta vinciana*, 17 (1960), 188–202.

8. The evidence for a discourse on perspective is gathered by C. Pedretti, *Leonardo da Vinci on Painting, a Lost Book (Libro A)* (Berkeley and Los Angeles, 1964), 167ff.

9. MS. A 38r; R paragraph 86.

10. MS. A 41r; R paragraph 544: "if you place yourself in the middle of a straight row [of objects], and look at several columns arranged in a line, you will see, beyond a few columns separated by intervals, that the columns touch; and beyond where they touch they cover each other, till the last column projects but very little beyond the last but one [fig. 5.2]. Thus the spaces between the columns are by degrees entirely lost. So, if your

method of perspective is good, it will produce the same effect; this effect results from standing near the line in which the columns are placed. This method is not satisfactory unless the objects seen are viewed from a small hole in the middle of which is your point of sight; but if you proceed thus your work will be perfect and will deceive the beholder, who will see the columns as they are here figured."

11. In the former quotations from MS. A 38r, Leonardo says it should be three times the size of the object; and elsewhere (A 41v; R paragraph 545), alongside the discussion of the columns, he says twenty times. Evidently he had not calculated beyond the need to get far enough away to take in everything at a glance (or, in terms of figure 5.1, to eliminate the effective distance between the image as projected on the flat plane and that projected on the arc).

12. As the three balls in figure 5.1 are projected onto a flat surface, the two outer ones, which are farther away than the one in the center, take up more space, which is to say they look bigger (like the columns in figure 5.2). Leonardo comments (MS. E 16r; R paragraph 108; MacCurdy, pp. 997ff.): "Nature, in its perspective, acts in the opposite way, for the greater the distance the smaller does the thing seen appear, and the less the distance the larger it appears. But this invention constrains the beholder to stand with his eye at a small hole, and then with this small hole it will be seen well. But since many eyes come together to see at the same time one and the same work produced by this art, only one of them will have a good view of the function of this perspective and all the others will only see it confusedly. It is well therefore to shun this compound perspective, and to keep to the simple which does not purport to view plans fore-shortened but as far as possible in exact form. And of this simple perspective in which the plane intersects the pyramid that conveys the images to the eye that are at an equal distance from the visual faculty, an example is afforded us by the curve of the pupil of the eye upon which these pyramids intersect at an equal distance from the visual faculty." Cod. Atl. 353rb has a similar diagram and note.

13. MS. E 16v; R paragraph 107; and 16r; R paragraph 108 (in that order); MS. G 13v: Richter corrects Ravaisson-Mollien's mistranscription of the quoted phrase, which eliminated the negative.

14. In the passage cited in n. 13 and in MS. A 62r (R paragraph 109), the term "accidentale" is used as a synonym for "composta." Cf. Pedretti,

Leonardo da Vinci on Painting, 170f.; Corrado Maltese, "Per Leonardo prospettico," *Raccolta vinciana,* 19 (1962).

15. The geometrical principle of anamorphosis is stated briefly with a diagram of a square seen in "simple" and "compound" perspective in MS. Ar. 62r (R paragraph 109). Two lightly sketched anamorphic heads without an accompanying text appear on Cod. Atl. 35va—probably the first of their kind. For the history of anamorphic pictures, see J. Baltrušaitis, *Anamorphoses ou perspectives curieuses* (Paris, 1955); on Leonardo's drawings, ibid., pp. 35f.; C. Pedretti, "Ricordi di G. P. Lomazzo e un soggetto anamorfico," *Studi vinciani* (Geneva, 1957), 68–75.

16. MS. A 35r; R paragraph 86.

17. MS. E 15v; R paragraph 869, 1513–14 (illustrating Leonardo's method): "Possibile è fare che l'occhio non vedrà le cose remote molto diminuite, come fa la prospettiva naturale, le quali diminuiscono mediante la curvità del l'occhio, che è costretto a tagliare sopra di se le piramidi con angoli retti vicino alla superfitie di tal popilla" (for the term "popilla," see n. 73). The "method" is to put the intersection of the visual pyramid at eyelash distance, thinking thus to eliminate the difference between the image as cast on the eyeball and the picture surface. This would repeat the distortion of *perspectiva composta* to an exaggerated degree, but in his representation of the result on the same page, Leonardo claims that it would merely cut down on the range of sight so one could depict only one star rather than all the stars one can see in the night sky with the naked eye.

18. Maltese (op. cit., 309) pointed out that on fol. 105r of the Codex Huygens, a treatise on perspective and proportion by a close follower of Leonardo who used the master's sketches (E. Panofsky, *The Codex Huygens and Leonardo's Art Theory* [New York, 1940], fig. 61), figures represented as seen from below are foreshortened in "doi modi": orthogonal-infinite (following *prospettiva semplice*) and curvilinear, according to the angle of vision (corresponding to *prospettiva naturale*). Panofsky apparently missed the distinction, though the second figure would have provided him with the best (perhaps the only) Renaissance illustration of a method involving curvature or the angle of vision. To project a figure in this way on a curved intersection of the visual pyramid does not, however, involve procedures or conceptions different from projections on flat intersections, and does not imply the capacity to depict a three-dimensional space by a curvilinear method.

19. The hypothesis had been proposed in the Middle Ages by Alhazen; see section IV below.

20. The physiology of the eye in medieval and Renaissance writing has been reviewed recently by S. L. Polyak, *The Retina* (Chicago, 1961), part II; G. F. Vescovini, *Studi sulla prospettiva medievale* (Turin, 1965); A. C. Crombie, "The Mechanistic Hypothesis and the Scientific Study of Vision," *Historical Aspects of Microscopy,* ed. S. Bradbury (Cambridge, 1967), 3–112 (extensive bibliography); and, most completely, in D. C. Lindberg, *Theories of Vision from Al-kindī to Kepler* (Chicago, 1976), which the author was kind enough to send me in typescript. The subject was virtually abandoned after an initial probing by scholars, principally German, in the generation before the First World War.

21. *De usu partium* was the more influential in the Middle Ages and Renaissance because *De placitis* was not translated into Latin until the sixteenth century (Lindberg, *Theories,* chap. III, n. 6, citing R. J. Darling, "A Chronological Census of Renaissance Editions and Translations of Galen," *Journal of the Warburg and Courtauld Institutes,* 24 [1961], 285). See also Polyak, *The Retina;* and Crombie, "Mechanistic Hypothesis," 12ff.

22. Cf. *Avicenna latinus liber de anima seu sextus de naturalibus,* I–III, ed. S. Van Riet (Louvain and Leiden, 1972), with an excellent introductory essay on Avicenna's psychology and on ancient and medieval writings on the *Anima* by G. Verbeke; E. Wiedemann, "Ibn Sīnā's Anschauung vom Sehvorgang," *Archiv für Gesch. der Naturwissenschaften und der Technik,* 4 (1913), 239ff.; Lindberg, *Theories,* chap. III.

23. By A. C. Crombie, "Mechanistic Hypothesis," 17; cf. D. C. Lindberg, "Alhazen's Theory of Vision and Its Reception in the West," *Isis,* 58 (1967), 321–341; A. I. Sabra, "Ibn al-Haytham . . . ," *Dictionary of Scientific Biography,* 6 (1972), 189–210, with bibliography and a checklist of original works. Also Sabra's forthcoming "Sensation and Inference in Alhazen's Theory of Visual Perception," *Studies in Perception: Interrelations in the History of Philosophy and Science* (Ohio State University Press, in press). Alhazen and Witelo are published together in *Opticae thesaurus,* ed. Risner (Basel, 1572), with cross references. The illustration in this edition purportedly representing Alhazen's anatomy of the eye is, as earlier commentators noted, unrelated to the text and seems to be indebted to the woodcut in Vesalius's *Fabrica.* A facsimile edition of this edition with a commentary by Lindberg has been announced; Sa-

bra is preparing an edition of the Arabic text with an English translation [cited in the bibliography that follows this essay].

24. The description of the eye, the chief subject of book I and the first chapters of book II, pp. 1–34 in the 1572 edition, appears in scattered places throughout the treatise.

25. Passages are quoted in n. 75 below. This could be the original stimulus for Leonardo's expanded version of the same theory. Leonardo, however, makes the outer surface, the cornea, the primary sensory receptor, since he realized that the pupil would invert the image received by the crystalline. As suggested in n. 78 Alhazen's discussion of the role of the cornea might have encouraged readers to believe that it, too, was a sensory receptor.

26. Witelo explains more clearly than Alhazen that perpendicular rays penetrate because they are not refracted: "quia tamen oculorum tunicae sunt alterius diaphanitatis quam aer extrinsicus, solae illae lineae formarum a superficie rei visibilis ad superficiem oculi productae, quae protractae centrum oculi productae, quae protractae centrum oculi penetrant, cum sint perpendiculares super superficiem oculi, non refringuntur in medio diaphani ipsius corneae" (*Opticae thesaurus*, Witelo, III, 18, p. 93; cf. Alhazen, I, 19, p. 12). However, the process is psychological as well as mechanical: the power of sensation in the crystalline gives it the capacity to select the perpendicular rays and thus to receive an image of the object that is structured in the same order as the object itself (Sabra, manuscript cited in n. 23: part of this theory is stated in the Latin edition, but Sabra adds a translation of a key passage which is missing there).

27. Book II, 42–44, pp. 57f. The process is not satisfactorily explained and seems not to have been understood by Alhazen's interpreters. The scanning introduces the possibility of a constant change in the image that is inconsistent with other aspects of the theory, though it conforms superficially to modern perception theory.

28. D. C. Lindberg, "The Theory of Pinhole Images from Antiquity to the Thirteenth Century," *Archive for the History of Exact Sciences*, 5 (1968), 154ff., quoting Alhazen, *De aspectibus*, book I, ch. 27, p. 17 in the 1572 edition.

29. Book II, 1, p. 24. The lens function is interpreted by Crombie, pp. 19ff., who points out that the geometry of the system requires the centers of curvature of the cornea, the albugeneous and the anterior surface of the glacialis to be identical (which does not occur in figure 5.3). Cf. Lindberg, *Theories*, 68f.

30. Book I, 4, p. 4.

31. Book II, 16, p. 34: "formae lucis et coloris istius rei visae perveniunt ad superficiem glacialis et extenditur secundum verticationes determinatus quas diximus secundum suam ordinationem & figuram & formam, quousq. perveniant ad concavum nervi communis & comprehendentur a virtute sensitiva apud perventum earum in corpore glacialis & apud perventum earum in toto corpore sentiente & virtus distinctiva distinguet omnes intentiones quae sunt in eis & forma lucis et forma coloris non perveniunt ad concavum nervi nisi quia corpus sentiens extensum in concavo nervi." My translation of the last sentence departs from the literal in order to approximate what I take to be the meaning, adding a stop after *corpore glacialis* and omitting *et* before *virtus distinctiva*.

32. Book II, 6, p. 26.

33. Sabra, manuscript cited; the core of the psychological argument is in book II, 4, pp. 67ff.

34. Cf. Lindberg, *Theories*, 85f.

35. The translation from Grosseteste's *De iride* is from Lindberg, *Theories*, 100. On Grosseteste, see A. C. Crombie, *Robert Grosseteste and the Origins of Experimental Science, 1100–1700* (Oxford, 1953), esp. 116ff., where Bacon's optics are also discussed.

36. Bacon says that the species of the everyday world cannot act unaided on sight because of the "nobility" of vision: "therefore these species must be aided and excited by the species of the eye, which proceed through the locale of the visual pyramid, altering and ennobling the medium and rendering it commensurate with sight . . .". Cited and translated by Lindberg, *Theories*, 115, from *Opus maius* V, 1, diss. 7, ch. 4 (Bridges edition II, 52).

37. Several illustrations from Bacon manuscripts are reproduced by Crombie, "The Mechanistic Hypothesis," figs. 7–9, 11, 12.

38. See D. C. Lindberg, "Lines of Influence in Bacon, Witelo and Pecham," *Speculum*, 46 (1971), 66–83; Lindberg, *John Pecham*, passim.

39. Aristotle's *Meteorologica* also played a part because its discussion of the rainbow (sections 374a ff.) deals with the issues of whether color and light are propagated independently, and of the nature and perception of color.

40. On Pelacani, see G. F. Vescovini, "Le questioni di 'perspectiva' di Biagio Pelacani da Parma," *Rinascimento*, n.s. 1 (1961), 163–243; Vescovini, *Studi sulla prospettiva medievale* (Turin, 1965), 239–267; F. Alessio, "Questioni inedite di ottica di Biagio Pelacani da Parma," *Riv. critica di storia della filosofia*, 16 (1961), 215ff.

41. Cod. Atl. 119va.

42. An example is Francesco Maurolyco, who wrote a treatise on light in 1521 (*The Photismi de Limine of Maurolycus, a Chapter in Late Medieval Optics,* tr. Henry Crew [New York, 1940]) and a major optical work in 1554 (*Diaphanorum partes seu libri tre* [Naples, 1611]). He diverged from medieval optics in only one respect, in proposing that the crystalline "humor" functions like a lens with two convex faces, and that its shape affects near- and farsightedness (*Diaphanorum,* III, p. 77 in the London 1613 edition: cf. the translation by Crombie, "Mechanical Hypothesis," 43ff.). But in saying that the purpose of the shape is to keep the incoming rays from intersecting and inverting the image, he only confirms medieval theory. Maurolyco used the word *pupilla* to designate the crystalline humor (he also used the latter term and *glacialis*), whereas Leonardo used it alternately for the cornea—or, as Kemp suggests, more vaguely the surface of the crystalline sphere (but see n. 25 above); and occasionally for what we call the pupil, as did the major text of Leonardo's time, Mondino de' Luzzi's. This sort of terminological chaos played its part in frustrating scientific progress.

43. *De humani corporis fabrica* (Basel, 1543), 32f., 649f. Galen had made the optical nerves hollow in order to provide a channel for the passage of the visual spirit. The purely empirical discovery through dissection that the nerves are solid was the first substantial blow to a hypothesis that had been sustained by all schools of thought in ancient and medieval optics. The antecedents or contemporaries of Vesalius who held the retina to be the receiver of visual images ("praecipuum visus organum a multis habeatur") have not been identified.

44. Translation from Kepler, *Ges. Werke,* II, 151ff. by Crombie, "The Mechanistic Hypothesis," 55. See also Richard Held, "Object and Effigy," *Structure in Art and Science* (New York, 1965), 42–54.

45. The fullest treatment of Leonardo's work on optics and vision is that of Donald Strong (see n. 2). The subject is well surveyed by D. Argentieri, "L'ottica di Leonardo," *Leonardo da Vinci* (Novara, 1940), 405–436, and by David C. Lindberg, *Theories,* 154–168. A more superficial treatment is V. Ronchi, "Leonardo e l'ottica," *Leonardo, saggi e ricerche* (Rome, 1954), 158–185.

46. Cod. Atl. 360; MacCurdy, *Notebooks of Leonardo,* p. 240. It is apparent from the handwriting that the note was written early in Leonardo's career.

47. See above, at n. 41.

48. On Leonardo's concept of rays, see A. M. Brizio, *Raggi incidenti e raggi refressi,* Terzo lettura vinciana 1963 (Florence, 1964). The comparison to Alberti is made in Kemp, n. 42.

49. Kemp, p. 133.

50. Kemp, pl. 1.

51. Kemp, pl. 2.

52. Cod. Ash. I 6v, R paragraph 63 (I have revised Richter's translation): also Cod. Atl. 101vb, R paragraph 64. Similar descriptions appear too often in the notes to warrant a full roster; some instances are Ash. I 13r, R paragraph 61; 179, R paragraph 67; Windsor 19150v, R paragraph 66, which ingeniously demonstrates the same principle by showing that a *camera obscura* with two small apertures placed one above the other will record two images of the complete object.

53. Cod Atl. 345vb.

54. Richard Held ("Object and Effigy") examined the history of theoretical writing on this problem in relation to the study of the physiology of the eye.

55. The Aristotelian explanation appears in Cod. Atl. 135vb, R paragraph 70, and 138vb, R paragraph 60, and eye as a "bersaglio e calamita" in MS. A 27r, R paragraph 58.

56. Cod. Atl. 120rd: "Tutte le spezie delle cose all'occhio antiposte concorrano per linie radiose alla superfizie di tale occhio"; or (Ar. 221v): "Il concorso delle linie create dalle spetie delli obbietti antiposti all'occhio." Richter's translation of the latter (R paragraph 74), "The lines sent forth by the *image* of the object to the eye," clouds the distinction I am making, as do other translations of his. Leonardo made this distinction explicitly in a passage (Cod. Atl. 179vc, R paragraph 67) where both *spezie* and *similitudine* appear: "Tutti i corpi anno infuse e miste tutte loro spetie e similitudine in tutta la quantità dell'aria a se controposta. La spetie di ciascun punto delle corporee superfizie è in ciascun punto dell'aria."

57. Cod. Atl. 138vb.

58. MS. A 9v, R paragraph 69.

59. Cod. Atl. 373rb compares visual and auditory wave propagation in circles with the stone thrown into water. Codl Atl. 126ra is a sheet of drawings apparently of ca. 1490, which illustrate and compare a number of tests devised to prove that uniform laws control the propagation of such waves; MS. H 67r, in a note entitled "De anima," compares the gradual subsiding of the circular waves in water as they are farther from the percussion to comparable weakening of the effects of the voice, fire (e.g., light), and "the mind."

60. See Kenneth Keele, "Leonardo da Vinci's Physiology of the Senses," *Leonardo's Legacy*, ed. C. D. O'Malley (Berkeley and Los Angeles, 1969), 35–56; and "Leonardo da Vinci on Vision," *Proceedings of the Royal Society of Medicine*, 48 (1955), 384–390.

61. Lindberg (*Theories*, 161) came to a similar conclusion.

62. The discussion in this and the following paragraph parallels that of Kemp, pp. 133f.

63. Windsor Castle 19148 (R paragraph 130; MacCurdy, *Notebook of Leonardo*, 982). The passage concludes: "and only the center line of this perceptive faculty is that which knows and judges bodies and colors; all the others are false and deceitful." Cf. K. Clark and C. Pedretti, *The Drawings of Leonardo da Vinci at Windsor Castle*, III, p. 56, dated 1483–85 on the grounds of the handwriting and association with other sheets of secure date.

64. Cod. Atl. 270vb; see also Cod. Atl. 270vc, MacCurdy, pp. 234ff., and 138rb. The latter appears from the handwriting to be several years later.

65. *Avicenna latinus liber de anima . . . ,* III, 7, 257, lines 42–45.

66. Cod. Atl. 90r; R paragraph 834.

67. Cod. Atl. 204r (undated); R paragraph 54; MacCurdy, p. 95f. An argument of 1492 is that the hypothetical rays emitted by the eye would take more time to perceive very distant objects like stars than nearby ones (Ash. I, ir, R paragraph 68). A passage in the late optical treatise, D 9v, which appears to affirm extromission, proves on closer reading to be restricted to a phenomenon of diffusion, as Strong makes clear (*Leonardo da Vinci on the Eye*, 84, 128f.).

68. An essential point of Kemp's argument (pp. 135ff.) is that Leonardo, in abandoning the hypothesis of the convergence of light rays in a point in the eye, rejected the Albertian perspective he had espoused in his early notes. Kemp shows that the change came as early as 1492, in a portion of MS. A that was lost in the nineteenth century. Many similar notes date from ca. 1508, as MS. F 34r; R paragraph 81a: "If all the *simulacri* that come to the eye were to converge in an angle, by the definition of that angle they would converge in a mathematical point which is proven to be indivisible. Therefore everything seen in the universe would seem to be one thing and indivisible and there would be no space between one star and another as judged in that angle. And if experience shows us all things separate with the spaces [be-

tween them] proportionate and intelligible, then that faculty [*virtù*] on which the *spezie* of things imprint themselves is itself divisible in as many greater and smaller parts as are the *simulacri* of the things seen. We therefore conclude that the sense [of sight] takes the *simulacri* that are mirrored on the surface of the eye, and then judges them within, and thus they do not converge in a point or, in consequence, an angle." Similar statements are made in Cod. Atl. 222v (translated in n. 106 below); B 25r; D 4v (R paragraph 81c); F 28r, 36r (R paragraph 81b); Cod. Atl. 237r.

69. The *camera obscura* is described in an early folio of Cod. Atl. 135vb (R paragraph 70), and experiments with it are cited in many notes over the whole period of Leonardo's work on optics (e.g., the experiment cited in n. 52). D. Strong, *Leonardo on the Eye*, cites several other instances from the period 1492–95: Cod. Atl. 125vb, 144ra, 187ra, 337ra. Early writers on Leonardo believed that he, or a contemporary, invented the *camera obscura;* but its essential feature—the casting of an image onto a plane surface through a small aperture—appears in Alhazen and throughout the Middle Ages (cf. Lindberg, "The Theory of Pinhole Images"). Leonardo may have been the first to experiment with a lens at the aperture of the camera, as noted by D. Argentieri, "L'ottica di Leonardo," 428, discussing a diagram from Cod. Atl. 337ra.

70. The drawing, which is not explained in Leonardo's text, shows a camera with a light section above and a dark section below; the upper has an aperture too large to invert the image, like a wall with a window. MS. D 8r (R paragraph 71; MacCurdy, 227) has another diagram of a—one-celled—camera with an explanation of its operation that recommends the use of a thin iron plate for the aperture and transparent paper at the rear, so the image could be looked at from behind.

71. In MS. D 3v Leonardo describes how to make a model to simulate the process by putting one water-filled glass sphere (representing the crystalline humor) inside another (representing the uvea), the outer one having a hole cut at the top large enough to insert the face (thus putting the eyes in the position of the optic nerve). A screen with a central hole to function as a pupil would be put at the bottom of the larger sphere. A drawing shows the image entering through the hole and being reversed in the inner sphere (it neglects to show the intersection of rays at the "pupil," thus defeating its purpose).

72. It is strange that Leonardo, who was experienced in anatomy, was less concerned with anatomical accuracy in his description of the interior of the eye than the ancient and medieval authors who had never seen a cadaver. He invented the spherical crystalline humor for purely geometrical reasons, and eliminated the vitreous, making it one with the albugeneous.

73. I translate *popilla* and *luce* as "cornea" because in most cases Leonardo does not distinguish the anterior parts of the eye (e.g., in MS. A 10r he refers to "quel punto nero che si vede in mezzo della popilla"), and because drawings such as figure 5.8 show the entire exposed surface to be equally sensitive. In a few places, however, "popilla" is indeed used as it is today (as Madrid II 127v: "La popilla posta nel mezo della luce dell'occhio"; MS. K 119r: "This *luce* being part of a sphere takes all the images of objects and sends them by the *popilla* inside the eye where vision is formed"). Cf. n. 42. The function of the pupil in the modern sense is ambiguous in Leonardo's writings. He seems to know that it works like the hole in the *camera obscura,* as the place where light rays penetrate and cross, and he draws it that way in his late notebooks (fig. 5.10); but he never quite integrates it into his theory of image formation on the cornea. In some early notes, the *popilla* is the terminus of a "nervo forato che va dentro alle intrinsiche virtù" (Cod. Atl. 270rb; MacCurdy, 237)—a kind of pipe or, as Leonardo says in the same passage, the barrel of a shotgun, which conducts the stronger centric ray direct to the brain: something of the sort is drawn in figure 5.17.

74. Cod. Atl. 237ra: "Le spezie della cosa minore dell'occhio non concorron piramidalmente in esso occhio. La virtù visiva è infusa con equal potenzia in tutta la popilla dell'occhio, onde l'operazione visiva è tutta per tutta la popilla, e tutta in ogni parte di quella." MS. D 2v: "Ogni punto della pupilla vede tutto l'obietto e ogni punto del obietto vede tutta la pupilla." A similar statement appears in MS. D 4v.

75. *Opticae thesaurus,* III, 18, p. 93: "Quaelibet pars formae visibilis & punctus se multiplicet per medium extrinsecum ad oculi superficiem totam: & tota superficies rei visae ad unum punctum oculi"; ibid., I, 15, p. 8: "Quoniam quando comprehenderit colorem puncti unius ex uno puncto tantum superficiei eius, comprehendet colores unius partis rei visae ex una parte superficiei suae, & comprehendet colorem alterius partis ex alia parte superficiei suae."

76. Ibid., I, 15, p. 8: "si ergo visus senserit ex tota eius superficie formes coloris et lucis, quae veniunt ex aliquo puncto superficiei rei visae, sentiet tota eius superficiei, formam cuiuslibet puncti superficiei rei visae."

77. Ibid., I, 16, p. 8: "Ergo non per superficiem visus sentiet visus istam formam, sed postquam transierit superficiem visus et pervenerit ad glacialem."

78. The implication that the cornea records images does not reappear in Alhazen's followers. This raises the question whether Leonardo came to the conclusion independently or somehow had access to a mansucript of Alhazen directly; Kemp (his nn. 35, 37) gives another instance of a borrowing from Alhazen that does not appear in intervening writers.

79. MS. F 31v (ca. 1508); MacCurdy, 246. On fol. 32r of MS. F there is a diagram with a geometrical proof of the proposition. A similar observation is made in MS. E 15v (ca. 1513–14). The mirror simile is not new to Leonardo; Alberti, in *De pictura* (ed. Grayson, 1972, 40f.) says: "this is not the place to argue whether sight rests, as they say, at the juncture of the inner nerve of the eye, or whether images are created on the surface of the eye, as it were in an animate mirror." There is no way of telling whether this statement is evidence for a party of specialists holding the second of the two theories prior to Leonardo, or whether Alberti was giving a shorthand version of the medieval theory.

80. Cod. Atl. 250va; MS. D 6v (Kemp, fig. 4). In the last phrase of the translation I have substituted the letter "p" for "n" which appears in the transcription, since the latter was obviously an error. Similar observations and diagrams appear in MSS. F 28r (MacCurdy, 244), C 27r, D 8rv, E 15r; and Cod. Atl. 222ra and 347va. Kemp cites the lost fol. 77 of MS. A, ca. 1492, as the earliest instance (his fig. 3).

81. When Leonardo first noted the phenomenon of seeing through the small nearby object in MS. C 19v, 26r, and 27v, of 1490–91, he still adhered to the traditional convergence of the visual pyramid in a point, and thus devised the term "trasparente occupazione"; for example, on fol. 19v: "the thing placed before the eye that is smaller than the cornea will occupy with transparent occupation as much of its field as the amount of the base made by the pyramid caused after the intersection that is found between the eye and the object."

82. He overlooked one consequence of the option that might have raised doubts: that if a particular point on the eye can register any point on the object, it would have to *select* the unique point that it actually does register and would have to avoid interference from all others. This would involve the *popilla* in psychological and physiological functions beyond the mechanical faculty attributed to it. Alhazen had avoided this difficulty by claiming that only the one ray that enters the eye perpendicularly will register, but Leonardo must have rejected this unlikely proposition from the start.

83. MS. E 15v (1513–14); R paragraph 869. "It is possible to find means by which the eye shall not see remote objects as much diminished as in natural perspective, which diminishes them by reason of the convexity of the eye, which necessarily intersects on its surface the pyramid of every image conveyed to the eye by a right spherical triangle."

84. The text of MS. F 32v accompanying figure 5.13 is: "Let the whole of the larger circle *kl* which receives the impression of the three stars *abc* be the eye or *luce,* which receives along the lines *dkel, fkgl, nkil.* But if the eye cannot make use of more than the part *nm* for the reason that it has to look at those stars through the hole in the piece of paper, it will still see in the part *nm* the images of these three stars, but they will be seen as much smaller as *nm* is smaller than *kl,* and the images of the three stars will come along the six lines *dnem, fngm, hnim."* Similar statements appear in MS. F 32r and D 7r, with different diagrammatic proofs.

85. MS. H 86r; R paragrah 828; cf. Madrid II, 25v, 27r. (Cf. Kemp, 137 and n. 36.)

86. MS. D 2r. Leonardo's demonstration does not discredit artificial perspective (which has no concern with the function of the eye), but it appears to do so, and indeed persuaded many modern scholars to believe that it did.

87. In Cod. Arundel 221v Leonardo drew a stick refracted in a glass of water. Alongside, he showed in two sketches light rays entering and diverging within the eye (according to the theory of medieval optical writers) instead of converging as they should. It was possible for him to be aware that refraction occurs without realizing the similarity of the interior part of the eye to a lens or the relationship between the kind of refraction and the shape of the lens. Several drawings (fig. 5.14) show the corneal bulge, which underscores the lens function, but it is not mentioned in the text and may have slipped into the illustrations unconsciously from Leonardo's anatomical experience.

88. MS. D 2r, following the passage cited above (n. 86).

89. Roger Bacon, *De multiplicatione specierum,* II, iii, p. 464. Bacon speaks of the four normal light rays—direct, refracted, reflected, and tortuous (because these pass through the curved optic nerve)—and a fifth "super quam vadit species, differt ab omnibus praedictis quia scilicet non venit ab agente, sed ab aliqua praedictarum linearum quattuor, et idea non venit a re faciente speciem, sed a specie verum species super eam decurrens est species speciei sicut luxum angulo domus venit a ratio solari cadente per fenestram. Nam radius ille venit a sole super lineam rectam fractam vel reflexam et ideo est multiplicatio principalis . . . per hoc quod oculus per eam non videbit agens principale, sed eius speciem principalem rectam vel fractam reflexam, quoniam oculus in angulo domus non videt solem, sed radiam cadentem per foramen vel fenestram vel aliam aperturam." The idea of the *species speciei* is closer to the solution of Huygens than is that of any intervening author.

90. Kemp, fig. 6; MS. D 2v, 4v; discussed by Kemp, 141f. Leonardo's anticipation of Scheiner is noted by previous commentators. Scheiner's experiment is reported in his *Oculus: hoc est fundamentum opticum* (Freiburg i. B., 1621), p. 32: "res per foramen minutum visuntur radiis decussatis . . .". He employs a small plate or card rather than a needle to block part of the eye. A number of his other experiments on the same principle must have given Huygens a base for his hypothesis on the propagation of light by waves.

91. MS. D 1v; MacCurdy, 217; the most extensive treatment of the hypothesis, with several diagrams, is on D 9v. Similar evidence is interpreted in MS. F 29r–30r, K 36, and Cod. Atl. 125rb. In the diagrams of the phenomenon an X is sketched over or just before the eye to indicate that the rays to the upper eyelid reflect downward and vice versa. The detailed discussion of the evidence by D. Strong, *Leonardo on the Eye,* 191ff., caused me to drop my original belief that Leonardo was attempting to account in this way for Mach bands.

92. The increased sharpness of the image seen with the eyelids narrowed is also cited to support the theory (MSS. F 30r, D 9v).

93. As it is in Roger Bacon, *Opus maius,* V, iii, v (ed. Bridges, ii, 560). Strong, *Leonardo on the Eye,* 97f., identified this source of Leonardo's reflecting eyelids (in Bacon, only lashes) and related Leonardo's interest in it to his current interest in mirror images.

94. Bacon, *Opus maius: perspectivae,* II, i (ed. Bridges, ii, 85): "Averroes in libro suo de Sensu et Sensato ponit causam vicendi a remotis custodiam palpebrarum . . . ," referring to the passage in Averroes: "Et ideo qui grossiorem habent palpebram magis inspicient in remoto, quia conservant illam partem a calore extrinseco et a frigore extrinseco. Et ideo multa animalia inspiciuunt in remoto plusquam homo propter grossitiem palpebrarum." (*Averrois cordubensis compendia librorum Aristotelis qui Parva naturalia vocantur,* ed. A. L. Shields [Cambridge, Mass., 1949], 7f.). Averroes's commentaries on Aristotle's *Parva naturalia* (which include *De sensu*) were published first in Padua, ca. 1474, and again in the *Opera omnia* (Venice, 1496), ed. Leonardo Aretino; they would have provided the easiest access to Aristotle as well as to Averroes.

95. MS. D 7v (fig. 5.14; MacCurdy, 226) and 10r, referring to figure 5.13: "One has doubts about the situation of the *idolo* in the eye, that is, whether it appears on the concavity of the uvea, *p,* or on the convexity of the crystalline sphere, *n.* But soon I became convinced that this *idolo* does not get reflected in the faculty of sight by being impressed on the concavity of the uvea, since the angle of incidence would not be equal to the angle of reflection, and anyhow one can judge that *idolo c,* coming to the cornea by line *cx,* enters the pupil by line *xm* and strikes the crystalline sphere by line *nrt.* And point *t* is at the front of the optic nerve *st,* which penetrates some into the crystalline sphere. Thus *c* at the left sends its image to *t* at the left, which could not happen if it was impressed on the concavity of the uvea at *p.*" The passage on D 7v is confused by Leonardo's failure to indicate when he is giving the opinion of the "tale ottico" (a scholar who sustains the theory of image reception on the uvea), and when he is speaking for himself. A diagram of the eye in which rays go through the pupil and strike the retina first without passing through the crystalline "sphere" is given in MS. K 119v.

96. See the review of Aristotle's cognition-perception theories by C. H. Kahn, "Sensation and Consciousness in Aristotle's Psychology," *Archiv für Gesch. der Philosphie,* 48 (1966), 43–81. The Aristotelian tradition is summarized by Leonardo in Cod. Atl. 90rb; R paragraph 836. The impact of Aristotle's theories of perception, cognition, imagination, and memory on medieval and Renaissance thought was even greater than his pervasive influence on other scientific fields because he was the only ancient writer who treated

these subjects extensively. Almost all writing on them prior to Descartes took the form of commentary on Aristotle.

97. Windsor 12603 (C. B. O'Malley and J. B. Saunders, *Leonardo da Vinci on the Human Body* [New York, 1952], no. 142). The drawing seems to be based on a misunderstanding of the textual tradition rather than on observation: the optic nerves do not meet at the chiasma but go straight to the anterior ventricle. Clark and Pedretti date it 1493–1494.

98. I have not tried to find which of the Peripatetics first presented the ventricle theory. Dr. Kemp writes that he has traced it to *Stoicorum veterum fragmenta,* II, p. 230, 38–39; Alexander of Aphrodisias, *De anima,* ed. Bruns, p. 68, 31–69; Nemesius, *De natura nominis liber unus,* and Augustine, *De spiritu et anima.* See his paper tracing the origins of the Renaissance theory of creation and genius, *Viator,* 7 (1977), 347–398.

99. Avicenna's theory is developed in his *De Anima,* I, v, 19, 44; III, viii, 60 (ed. cit., 87ff., 269ff.). Albertus Magnus repeats it with credit to Avicenna in *Isagoge in libros de anima,* xv–xix, *Opera omnia,* ed. Borgnet (Paris, 1890–99), 5:518–522.

100. The drawings illustrating the *imprensiva* are Windsor 12626 (O'Malley and Saunders, no. 159) and Windsor 12627 (O'Malley and Saunders, no. 160), both of ca. 1487; in the latter the middle ventricle is labelled "comō sēso," not *comocio* as transcribed by the authors quoted (Kemp, *in litteris*). The *imprensiva* appears also on the single sheet in the Weimar Schlossmuseum (illustrated by Crombie, "The Mechanistic Hypothesis," fig. 16, and *Léonard de Vinci, dessins anatomiques,* ed. P. Huard [Paris, 1961]). Neither Kemp nor I have found the concept of the *imprensiva* in other writers.

101. MS. B 4v; R paragraph 1212. Cf. also R paragraph 1211, 1214ff.; Windsor 12603 dated ca. 1487.

102. Windsor 19127, dated by Clark and Pedretti 1508 and by O'Malley and Saunders (no. 147) 1504–7. The drawing is accompanied by a text explaining the casting procedure (MacCurdy, 183).

103. Cod. Atl. 90rb; R paragraph 836; MacCurdy, 200f.; Madrid II, 25v and 27r, compares the human *imprensiva* to that of an owl, and proposes that, as the owl's pupil enlarges as much as forty times more than the human pupil, so the human *imprensiva* (evidently an organ of the brain) is larger than the owl's by the same degree.

104. Cod. Ar. 171v: "Neciessaria cosa sarebbe se la inprensiva fussi fori del'ochio che le linee rette non avessino loco. Inperochè benchè *b* venga per linea retta all'ochio *f,* e da *f* vada in *d,* non di meno la linea che va alla inprensiva sia nel'ochio; el nervo che si parte da l'ochio e va al cielabro, è simile alle corde perforate che con infinite rami tessano la pella de' corpi, e per lor vacui si porta al comune senso."

105. Sabra, manuscript cited, referring to *Opticae thesaurus,* I, 6 and II, 2.

106. Cod. Atl. 222va; the passage continues: "If the eye did not make a point, no object, no matter how small, would diminish at no matter how great a distance. If it has a point, that is indivisible, and in the indivisible part no *species* can be understood; rather, they become mixed up with one another. And if objects are to be well seen without confusion, and everything, no matter how small, is to diminish with distance, it is necessary that the lines of the *species* intersect at a point and, passing it, begin to spread out; and if it were this way, and if the *imprensiva* were in [the path of] this spreading out, every object would appear upside down. Since they do not appear thus, it is necessary that these *species* pass through a spherical and transparent body that turns in the opposite direction what comes to it in front, so that everything presented to it right side up on one side is turned on the other side upside down. So, if the *imprensiva* is there [on the rear side], it will be able to see objects well. Now think about the eye and you will see that necessity, mistress of all things, has provided well; you will see that the eye has within itself the instruments necessary to its job." The passage is repeated in MS. D 2v, with the addition that the *imprensiva* sends the data to the common sense.

107. Cod. Atl. 90rb, 258r; R paragraph 836: "la inprensiva si muove mediante le similitudini delle cose a lei date dalli strumenti superfitiali."

108. Leo Steinberg has shown the subtle complexities and the deviations from accepted practice in the perspective construction of the Last Supper in "Leonardo's *Last Supper,*" *The Art Quarterly,* 36 (1973), 297–410.

109. Two contributions essential to the study of Leonardo's physiology of vision became available to me too late for inclusion: A. Borsellino and C. Maltese, "Leonardo, un'agucchia e un foro, uno studio sull'ottica Leonardiana," *Physis,* 17 (1976), 221–244, and Carlo Pedretti, *Commentary to the Literary Works of Leonardo da Vinci Compiled and Edited by Jean Paul Richter* (Berkeley and Los Angeles, 1977).

Postcript

Two chapters of Kenneth Keele's book of 1983 on Leonardo's anatomical and physiological notes deal with writings on vision and the eye that provide a substantial expansion of our understanding of this subject: chapter II, "To Know How to See," pp. 43–78, and chapter VIII, "Leonardo's Anatomy of the Eye and Physiology of Vision," pp. 201–214. Dr. Keele, a distinguished historian of the medical disciplines, shows how Leonardo's observations related to his ancient and medieval predecessors and to modern science. Dr. Keele does not deal with Leonardo's inconsistency in sometimes using the term *popilla* to mean "cornea" as well as what we call "pupil" (he also uses *luce* for "cornea"). In order to explain how light rays can enter the eye in a spectrum of 180° or more (fig. 5.13 in my text), Leonardo had to postulate that they entered not only through what we call the pupil but through the entire curved surface of the cornea ("la popila è specchio cavo" [C.A. 309r–b; Richter/Pedretti, I, 127]; "This *luce* forming part of a sphere takes all the images of the objects and transmits them by the pupil within to the place where vision is formed"; [E. MacCurdy, *The Notebooks of Leonardo da Vinci*, New York, 1939, p. 253]).

In the peculiar history of scholarship on perspective every contribution is demolished by the one that follows, which is particularly remarkable because many intelligent people have made what appear to be wholly convincing interpretations. This may be due to the fact that the human mind is incapable of wholly separating the experience of seeing from the rationalization of sight. The first section of my study concerns three different kinds of perspective identified by Leonardo: simple, compound, and natural. "Simple" I identified with the *costruzione legittima,* descended from the Albertian system; "compound" with constructions having a close viewpoint, in which nearer objects appear to be smaller than more distant ones; and "natural" with normal subjective viewing not accommodated to geometrical rationalization. In this I differed from a number of my predecessors and from the most recent treatments of the subject. Kim Veltman duly differs from what I proposed (though without reference to my paper). Veltman, whose book of 1986 is an exhaustive treatment of Leonardo's perspective studies that covers more of the relevant notes and drawings than any other, proposes (especially on pp. 165–169) that Leonardo used "natural" as a synonym of "simple" and did not differentiate between them. Veltman's position is tied to his conviction that—apart from instances of compound, anamorphic perspective at exceedingly close range (figs. 5.1, 5.2)—there was no curvilinear or angular perspective in the Renaissance, as Panofsky had proposed. Maltese, writing in the recent volume that contains Veltman's criticism of Panofsky, affirms Leonardo's long involvement with curvilinear/angular perspective. Most recently, Günter Janowitz convincingly reverses my definitions of "simple" and "natural," calling the latter equivalent to the *costruzione legittima;* the former he calls subjective and effectively unrealizable in constructing the space of pictures.

The distinction can be seen in the light of Leonardo's physiology of vision. As indicated above, Leonardo's cornea, the whole surface of which operates as a receptor of light impulses, takes in images from a sweep of over 180° around the eye (fig. 5.8; compare these to the modern diagram, fig. 4.3). That meant that in order to be registered in the brain, most of Leonardo's light rays would have had to be bent (refracted) to pass through the pupil, and at sharper angles as they reached the periphery. Rays entering at sharper angles could not be accommodated to the precepts of the *costruzione legittima* (the angles of the rays closer to the center could be ignored as insignificant).

In this regard, Leonardo wrote in MS. D, 10b, of ca. 1508 (Richter/Pedretti I, 194; alternative version in *Treatise on Painting,* ed. McMahon [Princeton, 1956], §806): "the visual virtue is not at a point as the painters who deal with perspective would have us believe, but is in the whole of the pupil [here I believe *popilla* is intended, as in numerous other passages, to mean cornea] through which the species of objects penetrate into the eye to a space larger than that of such a pupil. But these simulacra are more clearly perceived in proportion as they are further removed from this center." While this passage refers only to the issue of the clarity of peripheral vision, it indicates Leonardo's awareness of the limitations of painters' perspective in conforming to the physiology of vision. Further, by denying that light rays converge directly on a point in what we call the pupil, it calls into question the relevance of the *camera obscura* as an analogy of the eye. Leonardo did not propose a perspective system to accommodate this principle, but he did differentiate—as "natural"—the experience of seeing from the making of painter's perspective.

Eastwood, Bruce. "Alhazen, Leonardo and Late-Medieval Speculation of the Inversion of Images in the Eye," *Annals of Science,* 43 (1986), 413–446.

Elkins, James. "Did Leonardo Develop a Theory of Curvilinear Perspective?" *Journal of the Warburg and Courtauld Institutes,* 51 (1988), 190–196.

Janowitz, Günter J. *Leonardo da Vinci, Brunelleschi, Dürer, ihre Auseinandersetzung mit der Problematik der Zentralperspective* (Einhausen, 1986). The clearest and most succinct exposition of Leonardo's principal writings on perspective, with a revealing discussion of central perspective.

Keele, Kenneth D. *Elements of the Science of Man* (New York, 1983).

Keele, Kenneth D., and Carlo Pedretti. *Leonardo da Vinci: Corpus of the Anatomical Studies in the Collection of Her Majesty the Queen at Windsor Castle* (New York, 1979), especially the drawings on 115r and 118r.

Kemp, Martin. *The Science of Art: Optical Themes in Western Art from Brunelleschi to Seurat* (New Haven and London, 1990).

Maltese, Corrado. "La prospettiva curva di Leonardo da Vinci e uno strumento di Baldassarre Lanci," in Marisa Dalai Emiliani, ed., *La prospettiva rinascimentale: codificazioni e trasgressioni* (Florence, 1980), 1: 417–425.

The Optics of Ibn al Haytham: Books I–III on Direct Vision, translated with introduction and commentary by A. I. Sabra (Studies of the Warburg Institute, 40), 2 vols. (London, 1989).

Richter, Jean Paul, ed. *The Literary Works of Leonardo da Vinci,* with commentary by Carlo Pedretti (Berkeley and Los Angeles, 1977); cited above as Richter/Pedretti.

Veltman, Kim. "Panofsky's Perspective: A Half Century Later," in Marisa Dalai Emiliani, ed., *La prospettiva rinascimentale: codificazioni e trasgressioni* (Florence, 1980), 1: 565–584. Discusses and contests Panofsky's hypothesis that Leonardo advocated a curvilinear or angular perspective, and gives a thorough review of subsequent writings on the subject and an extensive bibliography of studies of Leonardo's perspective studies in general.

Veltman, Kim. *Studies in Leonardo da Vinci, I: Linear Perspective and the Visual Dimensions of Science and Art* (Munich, 1986). See the review by Martin Kemp in *Burlington Magazine*, 129, no. 1013 (Aug. 1987), 540f.

6

On Early Renaissance Color Theory and Practice

I
Cennini and Alberti

Leone Battista Alberti's *De pictura*, written in 1435, was the major treatise on painting of the early Renaissance.[1] While the first of its three books, an application of ancient and medieval optics to painting, refers in passing to the influence of atmosphere and reflected light on the appearance of colors,[2] the practical instructions to the painter on the use of pigments in the closing paragraphs of the second book (46–50) are not concerned with such local phenomena. The color transmitted by rays of light from the surface of an object is assumed to be its "real" color as affected by direct light and shadow only, and cases of interference by surrounding conditions are looked on as special, with slightly negative overtones, as if they were obstacles to perceiving things rightly. Artists are not encouraged to take pleasure in or to record the kind of special environmental effects that were to be so important in later painting. The practical outcome of the advice was to encourage painters to assign a particular hue to the area within the circumscribed outline and then to modulate this by raising its value (with white) on the side toward the light and to lower it (with black) on the opposite, shadowed side. This is discussed in §46, where Alberti expands on the "third part" of painting, "reception of light." He also suggests that

you may change the color with a little white applied as sparingly as possible in the appropriate place within the outlines of the surface, and likewise add some black in the place opposite to it. With such balancing, as one might say, of black and white, a

From *Studies in Art History: American Academy in Rome*, 1 (1980), 11–38.

surface rising in relief becomes still more evident. Go on making similar sparing addi-
tions until you feel you have arrived at what is required.

Modeling of each object singly to achieve relief was the practice followed by quattrocento painters, but neither Alberti nor any other writer or practitioner of the period was able to translate "light" and "shadow" into pigment equivalents in a way that fulfilled his aspirations both to realism and to effective color design.[3]

Alberti failed in this area because he did not differentiate between the behavior of light as defined scientifically or as experienced optically, and the behavior of pigment. This difference invalidates two of his fundamental principles: first, that white and black are the palette equivalents of light and shadow respectively, and second, that all other colors can be produced by mixing the four primaries with white and black. The second of these perpetuated the tradition that originated in Aristotle, who, however, was not concerned with pigments (see Appendix). Alberti's primaries (blue, red, green, earth color), like Aristotle's, were excessively limiting since yellow was excluded. [See the revision of this statement in the postscript to this essay.] Besides, mixing a hue with black and white normally does not alter it but merely raises or lowers its value. If white is mixed with a pure blue, the resulting pigment is a paler state of the same blue. The term "paler" is more indicative than "lighter" because in the process, the blue loses some of its intensity or impact; the majority of colors are neutralized almost as much by the addition of a bit of white as by a comparable amount of black.[4]

The modeling of all objects toward white on the light side and toward black on the dark, which results from the first proposition, is not, on the other hand, unacceptable, but it was rejected by the mass of quattrocento painters because it was not to their taste. They, like the Impressionists, didn't mind neutralizing their colors with white, but they found that an equal application of black produced a somber and deadening effect that was particularly uncongenial to the tempera medium. Alberti recognized this preference, and though he emphatically cautions (in §47) against the excessive use of either white or black, he regards white as more dangerous, since the experienced painter will "hate work that is dark and horrid" in any case, while "we all by nature love things that are open and bright; so we must the more firmly block the way in which it is easier to go wrong."

In Alberti's procedure, the paint appears in its pure and most intense state along a band just to the light side of a line which he advises the painter to draw at the start dividing the light side of the figure from the dark.[5] This effect corresponds most closely to outdoor lighting in the full sunlight when the combined effect of glare, reflection, and the adjustment of the eye to brightness lowers color perception and may make it seem that the most intense color appears roughly midway between the highest and the lowest value.

Alberti's instructions, in implying that light and dark should be kept in equilibrium, assume that objects in paintings will be illuminated by rays traveling parallel to the picture plane at 90 degrees to the centric ray coming to the eye. Thus, discounting surface variations, objects appear half in the light and half in the shadow (because cast shadows are rarely used in quattrocento paintings, all objects are assumed to receive full direct light). Each figure is to be modeled in relief, in the nearest possible approximation of the sculptural relief of Ghiberti and Donatello (in §46, Alberti praises "those faces which seem to stand out from pictures as if they were sculpted"); paradoxically, relief is actually more modified by "atmosphere" in the *schiacciato* panels of Donatello—which antedate the writing of *De pictura*—than in any painting done in Alberti's lifetime.

Alberti's application of ancient and medieval optics to the problems of pictorial light and color affected the way his contemporaries thought about painting more than the way they practiced it. In this respect, *De pictura* was the opposite of Cennino Cennini's *Libro dell'arte*, written in about 1390, a manual that recorded many of the techniques practiced and taught to apprentices in late medieval workshops.[6] Alberti, though he claimed to have experimented in painting, would not have been able to give such practical advice. Anyhow it would have been contrary to his purpose to step down from the level of natural philosophy to what he would have regarded as merely "mechanical" concerns; he was trying among other things to raise the intellectual level of art and the social status of the artist.[7]

Cennini's *Libro dell'arte* may be read as a compendium of standard practices in the Florentine workshops of the later fourteenth and early fifteenth centuries; a few masters at that time might have differed with it in certain respects, but a majority would have accepted it as more or less representative of their practice. Most of its information on color relates to making and mixing pigments, but in one passage where Cennini tells how color is used to model figures in fresco painting, he gives the key to his system and the basis for a comparison to Alberti's:

The Way to Paint a Drapery in Fresco
Now let us get right back to our fresco-painting. And, on the wall, if you wish to paint a drapery any color you please, you should first draw it carefully with your verdaccio; and do not have your drawing show too much, but moderately. Then, whether you

want a white drapery or a red one, or yellow, or green, or whatever you want, get three little dishes. Take one of them, and put into it whatever color you choose, we will say red: take some cinabrese and a little lime white; and let this be one color, well diluted with water. Make one of the other two colors light, putting a great deal of lime white into it. Now take some of the first one, that is, the dark one; and with a rather large and fairly pointed bristle brush go over the folds of your figure in the darkest areas; and do not go past the middle of the thickness of your figure. Then take the intermediate color; lay it in from one dark strip to the next one, and work them in together, and blend your folds into the accents of the darks. Then, just using these intermediate colors, shape up the dark parts where the relief of the figure is to come, but always following out the shape of the nude. Then take the third, lightest color, and just exactly as you have shaped up and laid in the course of the folds in the dark, so you do now in the relief, adjusting the folds ably, with good draftsmanship and judgment. When you have laid in two or three times with each color, never abandoning the sequence of the colors by yielding or invading the location of one color for another, except where they come into conjunction, blend them and work them well in together. Then in another dish take still another color, lighter than the lightest of these three; and shape up the tops of the folds, and put on lights. Then take some pure white in another dish, and shape up definitively all the areas of relief. Then go over the dark parts, and around some of the outlines, with straight cinabrese; and you will have your drapery, systematically carried out. But you will learn far better by seeing it done than by reading. When you have finished your figure or scene, let it dry until the mortar and the colors have dried out well all over. And if you still have any drapery to do in secco, you will follow this method.[8]

These instructions would be valid for most panel painting as well, but the artist particularly concerned with color effects had more flexibility on the panel: first, he could vary the thickness of his surface, letting the underlying preparation show through in the thin portions to affect the value or the tone of the surface, and second, he could more easily mix colors directly on the painting, by hatching strokes of different hues; for the most part fresco painters were constrained to mix the chosen color on the palette, or, as Cennini would suggest, in a dish.

In one respect, Cennini's practice resembled Alberti's: the problem is conceived as one of creating an illusion of relief by assuming a figure to be illuminated from one side (from at least a right angle, as indicated by the phrase "do not go past the middle of the thickness of your figure"), so that the light tones will predominate on the half toward the light and the darks on the half away from it. But while Alberti proposed that the darks be made by mixing the basic color of the figure with black, Cennini advises in this passage only the base (red, in his example) and white.[9] His deepest shadow is represented by the pigment at its greatest intensity—and even this has a little white in it. Transitions to more illuminated parts are made by progressive additions of white. This method, with minor variations (e.g., in panel painting, white was not widely used in the deep shadows) was followed in almost all Florentine pictures prior to the writing of *De pictura,* and in a large number of later quattrocento works. It produced paintings of a high value range—partly because it evolved in a period of gold-ground painting when color areas had to compete with the reflective brilliance of burnished metal—in which each figure stood out from its neighbors and from the background by virtue of its uniformity of hue. It preserved some of the character of what Hetzer called the "absolute" color of medieval painting, in which the hue remains unaltered by the position or conditions in which the object is placed. The resplendent compositions of vigorously colored figures emphasized surface patterns (the reflectivity of the high-value color patches tended to hold them to the surface), and failed to satisfy Alberti's demand for the illusion of relief in a number of other ways:

1. The least illuminated portion of the surface (the shadow) receives the most intense or saturated color, while the well-illuminated parts are progressively lessened in intensity by the addition of white. Thus the most vibrant tones occur in areas where, in the actual world in normal conditions, they appear inhibited—neutralized by the deprivation of light. As a result, the painted shadows attract the eye, and seem to advance, while the neutralized lights recede. This effect conflicts with the modeling effort, especially in the drapery of figures, where the lighter portions are always intended to advance and the darker to recede.

2. Pigments of different hues in their pure, unmixed form (e.g., at their most intense) have different values: yellow and orange are bright—yellow a little more so—and blue and violet are dark. It is not just that they look respectively more bright and dark; if one tests them with a photometer they register a higher and lower reflection of light. To make a yellow of the same value as a blue, one mixes in some black or some violet, which reduces its intensity while it lowers its value; conversely, to make a blue the same value as a yellow, one adds white, again reducing intensity. Cennini and most early Renaissance Florentines did not worry about balancing values in this way; they usually used pure pigment for every shadow regardless of hue. But they did encounter many occasions on which it was necessary to represent a rose or light blue robe which,

according to their system, required a great deal of white in its deepest shadows. Consequently, the difference between light and shadow in such a robe would be far less than the light-shadow difference in a neighboring figure whose robe would be far less than the light-shadow difference in a neighboring figure whose robe might be deep red or blue, with the result that two adjoining figures could appear to be in different lighting conditions, or of different degrees of solidity. And because the under and outer garments of figures were usually of quite different hues, there could be violent value contrasts within a single figure.

3.   In addition to the difference in value between one hue and another, there is also a differential of intensity due to the physical nature of the pigments. This is particularly noticeable in the unique vividness of the ultramarines made from lapis lazuli, which is much greater than that of blues made from other materials and attracts the eye in spite of the lower value of blues in relation to other colors. The ultramarines usually overwhelm the greens, for example, which tend to be rather flaccid. Furthermore, ultramarine often held a dominant position; it was used for the sky and for the outer robe of the Virgin in altarpieces. Patrons often specified its extensive use because its preciousness, in a mercantile society, made such liberality a token of piety.[10]

4.   White objects and draperies could not be treated consistently with those done in color for the obvious reason that white can be only darkened and not lightened. The shadows of white objects were therefore down-modeled by the admixture of some low-value neutral such as blue-gray or a variety of mixtures with earth colors. The neutralization of the shadows tended to make white objects look more natural than colored objects with their brilliant shadows, and in some mid-fifteenth-century pictures, such as those of Piero della Francesca, white-robed figures seem to move in a more light- and atmosphere-filled ambience than their colored companions.

For all of these reasons, the work of Lorenzo Monaco, Fra Angelico, often Mantegna and Piero della Francesca, and many other early Renaissance Italians seems to be a patchwork of intense colors, each isolated from its neighbor and involved in a competition that inevitably is won by those of higher value. If this treatment of light-shadow-color had been consistently used, and carried over into landscape and domestic settings when they began to replace gold as a ground for panels, the competition and contrast would have been excessive. It would have inhibited the communication of the content of pictures and have clashed with the illusion of recession given by linear perspective.[11] But painters subdued the tones of the background, which avoided that problem of competition but caused another, by perceptually separating the people depicted from the surrounding world of nature and buildings.

Cennini recommends a second mode of modeling that was widely practiced from the later fourteenth century into the sixteenth: the color shift.[12] This involved using a low-value color such as blue to render the shadows of a red drapery, or red as the shadow of a green drapery, etc. It rarely was used to depict anything but folds of cloth, and Cennini even proposed that its purpose was to represent shot silk, the fabric woven in two colors in such a way that it appears to change from one hue to another when seen at different angles. Albrecht Dürer, writing in ca. 1512–13, suggested that color shifts were still in use, but he disapproved of them as a shading device except where shot silks were to be represented.[13] That artists would have sought for more than a century to represent this exceptionally luxurious modern industrial product as the garb of a great variety of figures seems less likely than that they welcomed a further change to enrich the color pattern and to escape the pervasiveness of local color. Cennini's statement can be taken, however, as an engaging document in support of the economic interpretation of art, coming as it does from the foremost silk-producing town in the western world in which the silkmakers' guild, the Arte della Seta, was one of the three most powerful political and social institutions, and a major patron of the arts.

Alberti wanted to change these practices by recommending the use of black for shadows in symmetry with the use of white for lighter portions. This presented in one respect an advance in verisimilitude over the prevailing method. It kept the shadows from competing in interest with the highlights by lowering their intensity, neutralizing them with black, and this made for convincing modeling. It did not, however, resolve the value contrasts in the overall composition because even though black would bring the shadows of a yellow drapery closer to those of a blue, the parts of the figures halfway between the darkest and lightest portion would be executed in pure pigment and create sharp value contrasts. But the chief obstacle was that the method threatened to destroy the decorative qualities of the Cenninesque tradition without achieving the chiaroscuro that Leonardo demanded. As white neutralized the lights, and blacks the darks, Albertian pictures would have approached the character of tinted drawings—while lacking the spontaneity of drawing—and have lost much of the expressive potential of rich color.

Dürer, in the passage just cited, appears to have held essentially to an Albertian system (though he wrote later than Leonardo) in recommending cautious modeling up and down of a basic drapery color with white and black, while warning against the danger of destroying the basic color:

6.1   *Masaccio*, Madonna and Child with Angels.
London, National Gallery.

6.2 *Masaccio,* Crucifixion. *Naples, Museo del Palazzo di Capodimonte.*

Moreover, take care, when painting anything in one color, whether it be red, blue, brown, or mixed color, not to put so much light in the highlights that it departs from its own nature. For example: an uneducated person looking at your painting with a red drapery in it says: "Look, my good friend, how the drapery is such a brilliant red in one part and in the other it's white or pale colored." That is improper, and you have not done right. In such a case, you should paint a red object so that it is red all over, and the same for all colors. And the same goes for the shadows, so that it cannot be said that a brilliant red is soiled with black.[14]

Although Alberti was much concerned with the behavior of light and Cennini was not, his prescription for painted chiaroscuro was only another, slightly more mimetic formula for modeling, equally unrelated to the unique experience of perceiving a particular object or scene at a particular time or place. Both systems could be practiced by the rule without looking at anything, just as a fictive space could be constructed in perspective without a model in actual experience. Both writers, and most quattrocento painters, concentrated on modeling each figure in a composition separately, as a relief sculptor would have to do. As a method of painting it was therefore inescapably bound to drawing.[15] This had radical implications for the illumination of pictures: it favored a light entering the picture from left or right at a right angle to the axis of vision which would illuminate one side of the figure and put the other side in shadow. Unlike sunlight, the source is thus not localized at a specific point overhead; light, if it is consistent at all, simply blows in from the side like a gentle, steady breeze, touching all the objects alike. One figure or object does not block this effluvium from another, casting a shadow—partly because shadows are impossible to plot unless there is a specific light source,[16] and partly because they would alter the color consistency of the individual figure, and upset the whole color system. Quattrocento figures sometimes cast shadows of an unspecific sort on the ground, but rarely on each other. Shadows often are more precisely delineated on furniture and architecture because these belong to an already neutralized setting and the neutralizing effect of shadow does not disturb the color system, and because the flat planes simplify the problem of shadow projection. Masaccio's Pisa altarpiece of 1427 (figs. 6.1 and 6.2) may be the first instance of both procedures: the figures in the central panel cast imprecisely defined shadows and receive light from a vague area to the left and somewhat above, and the gray throne is lit from a definable point source at the upper left (note especially the rosettes on the forward face).[17]

The rare instances in quattrocento art of illumination by sources other than the sun were the cause of remarkable innovations in the representation of shadow and in color practice, perhaps because they forced the painter out of the mold of uniform modeling. The light that comes from a torch (as in Piero della Francesca's *Dream of Constantine* at Arezzo) or from a supernatural source within the picture necessarily originates at a defined point and impels the artist to paint strong and inevitably dramatic chiaroscuro contrasts and low-value shadows.[18] Gentile da Fabriano, in the Nativity predella of the Strozzi Altarpiece of 1423, combined divine light emanating from the Christ child with moonlight to produce a doubled cast shadow in a notable fusion of naturalism with the supernatural. Piero again, in the predella of the Perugia altarpiece with the Stigmatization of St. Francis (fig. 6.3), where the Crucifix is the source of light, completely abandoned the Cenninesque color practice he normally applied to figures to produce an astonishingly naturalistic vision of a sharp cold light descending on the figures from above, modeling them from a wholly unfamiliar angle and throwing the surroundings into a deep neutral obscurity that appears almost nowhere else in Florentine art; this work is closer in sensibility to the naturalistic illuminations of the *Coeur de l'amour épris* (fig. 6.4), a French work of the third quarter of the century,[19] than to the Florentine tradition of supernaturally lit narratives launched by Taddeo Gaddi with his starlit *Annunication to the Shepherds* in the Baroncelli Chapel of Sta. Croce in Florence. The *Stigmatization* stands virtually alone in its time in its awareness of the interaction of light, shadow, and color.

6.3 *Piero della Francesca,* Stigmatization of St. Francis. *Perugia, Gallery.*

6.4 *René d'Anjou (attr.), episode from* Coeur de l'amour épris. *Österreichische Nationalbibliothek, MS. 2597, fol. 15 (late 1450s).*

Such paintings show that the painter does not simply identify the color of each object to be represented, match it with a pigment, and apply it to his picture, as Alberti seems to imply. First, the effects of light and shadow on color perception vary with the character of the environment. The shadows of a given object seen outdoors at a distance on a sunny summer's day may appear to be a brilliant blue tinged by the color of neighboring objects, while those of the same object seen indoors and lit from a single source may appear an indescribable dark mud color. In the first instance, modeling with black would probably misrepresent the nature of the light, and in the second, it might seem true to life. Further, the colors of pigments not only behave differently from those in nature, but are entirely dependent on the color setting in which they are used: a patch of blue paint looks to be one color when it is mixed on the palette, another when it is placed by a red, and a third when yellows are added alongside. This is one demonstration of the final point that the perceptual process itself influences our experience: Alberti wrongly believed that color is a property of the object that is conveyed to the eye; actually, the color sensation is generated in the eye from external light stimuli. It is not entirely an "objective" phenomenon.

Alberti, though he spoke of the effects of atmosphere and of reflection, was not prepared psychologically or philosophically to deal with ambiguities of this order. He would have thought it unscientific to offer different rules for different occasions. This is exactly what Leonardo decided was necessary to break out of the confines of early Renaissance color practice, and it meant for him recording innumerable observations of specific local conditions of light and color. But he was no more able than Alberti to reconcile this with his vision of science, though he was as eager to do so.

II

Color and Content

While early Renaissance painters thought about light and color principally in terms of the problems of representing the visible world and of making internally harmonious compositions, their decisions, not always conscious, influenced a third fundamental aspect of their work, the content.

Three consequences of the prevailing and conservative color style of the quattrocento inhibited the gravity of the message conveyed by paintings:

First, the practice of modeling (in which the pure pigment used for shadows tended to come forward because of its intensity) reduced the solidity and denseness of figures and made them what we call colloquially "light-weight"; the lack of an appearance of physical gravity suggests a lack of dramatic gravity. This was a factor contributing to the rejection of the practice by Leonardo, who asked:

What is more important, that a figure abound in brilliance of colors or display high relief? *Only painting presents itself to its observers as if it were in relief and causes what has no substance to project from the walls. But colors honor only the masters who make them, for in them there is no cause for wonder except their brilliance* [bellezza], *and their brilliance is not to the credit of the painter, but of him who has generated them. A subject can be dressed in ugly colors and still astound those who contemplate it, because of the appearance of relief.*[20]

Second, the need to distinguish figures in a continuum of bright, uniformly lit colors led to differentiating each one—and usually the separate garments of any single one—by hue, so that multifigured compositions often covered the entire range of the palette. Alberti approved this:

I should like all the kinds and species of colors to appear in painting with a certain grace and amenity . . . if you are painting Diana leading her band, it is appropriate for this nymph to be given green clothes, the one next to her white, and next red, and another yellow, and the rest should be dressed successively in a variety of colors, in such a way that light colors are always next to dark ones of a different kind. (§48)[21]

Finally, the high values resulting from modeling entirely with white, and strong intensities, gave the surface a bright, candid appearance. "White," Alberti adds in the same passage, "lends gaiety [*hilaritatem*] not only when placed between gray and yellow, but almost to any color," which is one reason why he recommended caution in its use.

In the Middle Ages, when colors frequently were chosen for established symbolic inferences or for the economic value of the material, their value and intensity did not affect their message. But a new generation, seeking to give painting a psychological as well as a representational validity, and to gain dramatic impact in narrative, must have been frustrated by the cheerfulness and excitation of the traditional palette. The mood it generated was unsuited to commissions that called for the depiction of key events in the Bible and lives of the Virgin and saints, altarpieces, and subjects from ancient poetry, normally of a sober nature. It was particularly incongruous in representations of the Passion of Christ, Fra Angelico's *Deposition from the Cross* now in San Marco in Florence (fig. 6.5) being a notable example, with its festive, exhilarating color range. Alberti, in discussing the appropriate treatment of the *historia* (narrative theme) at the end of Book II and the start of Book III, chose almost exclusively dramatic events of intense emotional content and sobriety—the scene of Diana mentioned above being

6.5   Fra Angelico, Deposition from the Cross.
Florence, Museo San Marco (ca. 1441).

an exception. The discussion is dependent entirely on Roman rhetoric, particularly Ciceronian.[22] It is consequently concerned with *decorum,* or appropriateness of the style to the theme, and gives the impression that the author is on the verge of formulating a theory of genres that would have involved, *inter alia,* different color ranges for different types of theme, as Nicolas Poussin, another painter absorbed in rhetoric, attempted to do two centuries later.[23] Whether nor not this was the case, Alberti's rejection of the exclusively high-value palette must have been related to an effort to find a suitable tonal range for tragic themes.

I believe that one reason why critics of the nineteenth century classed quattrocento painters together with those of the previous century as "primitives" is that they found the products of the high-value color system emotionally naive. But even Early Renaissance commentators appear to have responded similarly. The modern popular image of Fra Angelico as a simple soul, cheerfully singing praises of the Lord, does not really clash with that of Cristoforo Landino, who, describing in 1480 the Florentine painters of his century, called Angelico "vezoso [blithe] divoto et ornato molto con grandissima facilità," while Masaccio was "optimo imitatore di natura, di gran rilievo universale, buono compositore, et puro sanzo ornato."[24] I'm not sure that Angelico's religious sensibility was as shallow as it has looked to later generations. He learned his craft at a time when nobody dreamed of a psychological use of color and, being of a conservative disposition, he was insufficiently inventive to create a new palette. If there had been clear leadership, Angelico and others addicted to high values might have adopted a new color system. But, in contrast to the treatment of other formal features in quattrocento painting, every leading master struck out independently with his own experiments in color and no consensus emerged.

III

Leonardo da Vinci

Nearly everything Leonardo wrote about painting can be found in the *Trattato della pittura,* which his heir Francesco Melzi efficiently compiled from scattered statements in the mass of notebooks left by the artist. Leonardo had given no form to the notes, and Melzi and modern editors attempted to arrange them roughly by theme but without overcoming the lack of structure, the repetitiveness, or the contradictions.[25] Any attempt to present a consistent theory based on this evidence is therefore likely to be somewhat arbitrary. Yet Leonardo's notes on color, while they constitute neither a practice manual like Cennini's nor an element in a theoretical system like Alberti's, clarify the profound differences that distinguish his approach to color from that of his predecessors.

The notes are less concerned with the way color is used in painting than with the way it looks in nature. They are short and empirical, recording effects as perceived under different conditions, primarily in terms of light and shadow, and only secondarily in terms of hue. The method is simple—to look around without preconceptions, attending to the way in which three-dimensional effects may be translated into two-dimensional terms illusionistically. Past theory and practice are seldom cited. It is as if Leonardo wished to begin the art again from scratch, without so much as a bow to those predecessors—chiefly northern Europeans—who had pioneered in representing in art the phenomena in nature that most interested him.

The basic difference between Leonardo's approach and that of his Italian predecessors is that while they aimed in a painting to represent objects as they knew them to be, he sought to represent the effect of things on the eye. For Leonardo, the object seen could be altered entirely in form and color by changes in the light and the surrounding atmosphere and, where it differed, in the light and atmosphere of the observer's surroundings. This distinction was of fundamental importance for Leonardo's painting, but paradoxically his actual painting is not naturalistic in the sense that the notes would suggest. Leonardo had many aims as an artist that did not get recorded on paper because they were not empirical. Conversely, many of the natural effects that he advises using for paintings occur in scenes that neither he nor other Italian Renaissance painters depicted.

Had the *Trattato* been published in Leonardo's lifetime, its chief impact would probably have been to reinforce criticism of the non-naturalistic results of quattrocento color practice, and to urge painters to look more closely at nature. It could not have helped contemporaries to articulate an alternative color system or to integrate the empirical naturalism it champions with the theoretical ideals of Renaissance painting—classic form, proportions, and imitation in the sense of idealization.

Leonardo's description of the illusion of relief as the fundamental goal of painting echoes Alberti's, and the following passage is only one of many in the *Trattato* that suggest on first reading that his color system was no more than an expanded and more sophisticated version of the one presented in *De pictura*:

The primary purpose of the painter is to make a plane surface look like a body in relief detached from the plane, and he who in that art most surpasses others deserves most praise, and this particular investigation, which is the crown of the science of painting, originates in the shadows and lights or, if you wish, brightness and darkness. Therefore whoever avoids shadows avoids what is the glory of the art for noble imaginations, but gains glory with the ignorant public, who want nothing in painting but brilliance [bellezza] of color, altogether forgetting the brilliance and marvel of depicting a relief on what in reality is a plane surface. (T. 412 [434])[26]

But there are radical differences which focus on what is meant by "shadows and lights." Alberti's concept of relief could be called *modeling*, in that he visualized raising each individual figure and object from the picture plane by working down toward black or shadow on one side and up toward white or light on the other. The composition has a consistent lighting only to the extent that the light sides of all the figures face the same way. Leonardo's concept can be called the relief of *chiaroscuro*, since light, rather than body, is the fundamental element and, so far as the painter is concerned, bodies and things do not exist until they are illuminated. As light falls, it reveals color, brings parts of objects forward in relief, and reflects from one object to another. Light has its own color which it casts onto objects and which mixes with the color of the objects. As light takes precedence over body, unity takes precedence over diversity, for in Alberti's system, the whole can be conceived only as a collection of modeled parts. Chiaroscuro was the cornerstone of a new, more harmonious and unified style of painting.

The painter who "avoids shadows" in the passage quoted, and is scorned by Leonardo, represents the fifteenth-century practitioner whose distaste for the dulling effects of black and for large neutralized areas led to the retention of Cenninesque shadows rendered in full or only slightly moderated intensity. Probably the "ignorant public" to which Leonardo refers in this connection encouraged many of his contemporaries to retain what he regarded as an absurd practice that flouted the evidence of everyday experience. Quattrocento painters are implicitly berated in other passages in the *Trattato*—most memorably in the one quoted above at the start of section II—and always for the reason that they prefer the excitement of colors in their full intensity to the satisfaction of representing the three-dimensionality of nature. He appears, in that statement, to regard the attraction of the picture in which all colors appear in high intensities as being comparable to that of precious stones (some colors being ground from rare minerals) and to be unworthy of an artist. He proposes to overcome the tyranny of brilliant colors by introducing the neutralization of color in a naturalistic way.

In the *Trattato*, the only form of neutralization approved is the admixture of black in shadows. In practice, however, Leonardo normally toned down the lights as well by mixing colors on the palette, sometimes with black but also with lower-value hues, and often, as in the clothing of the *Mona Lisa*, to the extent that the hue is virtually indescribable (at least, under the present screen of varnish), and changes in response to the play of light. In the *Madonna and Child with St. Anne* (fig. 6.7), the color passes beyond the stage represented by the *Trattato*; the shadows are a chromatic gray rather than black, and seem as alive and as transparent as the lights; objects no longer have a basic color but become a field for a subtle play of varied colors.

In Alberti's treatise, light is a simple phenomenon that varies only according to the nature and the direction of its source (the sun, moon, lamplight, etc.). Leonardo's light is infinitely more complex. Not only does it have its own color according to the nature of its source, which it casts onto the objects it strikes, but it reflects from every object and takes the color from it to whatever other objects stand facing it.[27] Furthermore, the atmosphere itself is a vehicle of light as particles or "atoms" of humidity near the earth's surface catch and reflect the rays of the sun. The blueness of the sky and the blue cast given by the thickness of the atmosphere to distant objects results from our seeing the illuminated particles against a dark background—pure unhumidified air being by nature dark (an explanation based on Aristotle).[28] Thus the color of an object can be made up of its own "natural" color, the color of the source of illumination, reflections from one or more facing objects, and the atmosphere between it and the viewer.[29]

An even more significant contribution to the painter's vision was linked to Leonardo's work on the physiology of vision: the statement that the light perceived varies according to the conditions of viewing. The best illustration cited in the *Trattato* is the room that looks brightly lit when one is inside it but seems dark (and objects within it virtually colorless) when it is seen "from the piazza."[30] The reason given—correctly—is that the pupil of the eye enlarges in the reduced light of the interior and contracts in the bright light of the outdoors.

Because of Leonardo's concentration on chiaroscuro relief, black and white are much more important than colors in his thinking.

His black, like Alberti's, is used to represent the absence of light (black is "tenebre" in T. 213 [178]), to neutralize shadows, and discourages the general practice of shading with low-value neutrals made from colors such as the mixture of complementaries:

The shadow of bodies ought not to take on any other color than that of the body to which it is attached. Therefore, since black is not counted in the number of colors, the shadows of all the colors are taken from it. As the colors of bodies are in greater or lesser shadow, they require more or less black, provided that the color of the body is never entirely lost, except in the complete darkness contained within the boundaries of the opaque body.

Therefore, painter, if you would copy nature, tinge somewhat the walls of your studio with white mixed with black, because white and black are not colors.   (T. 703 [803])

There are two reasons for this rule: first, the "natural" color of the object is the only color that can appear in its shadows unless another color is reflected onto it from a facing object (or coloration is caused by the light source or the atmosphere);[31] second, since in this theory shadow is the absence of light and color, there is no justification for using even neutralized color to represent it; only the non-color black is equivalent to shadow.[32]

In practice this simple precept could be carried out only in the artificial conditions of the studio, where a given object could be isolated from other objects that might reflect on it, where the effect of atmosphere could be minimized, and where, by devices like painting the studio walls as recommended in the quoted passage, even the color of natural light could be controlled.

Leonardo explained what makes reflected color objectionable in the following:

Never will the color of the shadow of any body be a true, proper shadow, unless the object opposite, which casts the shadow, is of the same color as the body to which the shadow is given.

Let us suppose, for example, that I have a room whose walls are green. I say that if a blue object is seen in such a place, illuminated by the bright blueness of the air, then the illuminated side will be a very intense blue. But the shadow of such an intense blue will be ugly and not a true shadow of an intense blue because it is spoiled by green, which reverberates in it. It would be worse if the walls were tan.   (T. 239 [202])[33]

Since Leonardo would have conceded that reflected and atmospheric colors of all kinds occur in the natural environment, his dicta on black shadows represent a departure from his generally naturalistic and empirical position. He accepted this inconsistency because an uncompromising naturalism would make it impossible to achieve harmonious and balanced color compositions, while consistent black shadowing could produce tonal consistency throughout a picture.

The role of white in Leonardo's theory is entirely different from its function in the quattrocento; white is a wholly passive non-color "more receptive to any color than the surface of any other body except a mirror":

For that reason we shall say that because white is empty, devoid of color, when it is illuminated with the color of any luminous body it takes on the color of that luminous body. Black would not do so, for black is like a broken vessel, which is deprived of the capacity to contain anything. (T. 215 [205])

Thus, while black was made equivalent to shadow, white was not, as it had been for earlier painters, equivalent to light. That is because light in nature is colored and, when it falls on a white object, gives it a hue.[34] Leonardo cites the instance of a lady in white "in the country" whose dress will have the brightness of the sun in one part, the blue of the air in another, and the green of the fields where they were reflected.[35] Leonardo's thinking about black and white is so far from being symmetrical that, while he advises using black non-naturalistically in order to permit the kind of tonal balance he sought in his pictures, he advises a completely naturalistic use of white, citing an example—reminding us of an Impressionist canvas—of a subject and a setting one cannot imagine his choosing for a painting. Almost every comment in the *Trattato* on the use of white is about depicting white objects.[36] I have not found any reference to the use of white to raise the value of other colors, which was the chief concern of Cennini and Alberti.

I believe, however, that Leonardo was the first writer to differentiate value from intensity, but his reticence about mixing white with other colors kept him from pursuing the issue. The term *chiarezza* appears to be the equivalent to our use of "value," as (T. 485 [460]).[37]

The edge of that illuminated object will seem darkest that is seen on the lightest [più chiaro] *ground, and similarly that will seem lightest which is seen on a dark ground. And if that edge is flush with—and seen on—a light ground of the same lightness* [chiarezza] *as itself, it will be imperceptible.*[38]

The choice of the terms *chiaro, chiarezza*—both suggestive of light—to discuss value contrasts reminds us that in the many passages where Leonardo refers to the admixture of black to represent shadow, he never differentiates the lowering of value-*chiarezza* from the lowering of intensity-*bellezza*. This produces a dilemma that is the reverse of that of the quattrocento, since achieving a tonal balance between a naturally high-value yellow and naturally low-value blue is difficult whether they are in shadow or in light. But it is not *as* difficult in the darks. In his paintings, Leonardo was able to capitalize on the fact that black minimizes such contrasts while the earlier use of white had maximized them.

The early *Madonna of the Rocks* in the Louvre (fig. 6.6) is a bold realization of the new ideas; the dark setting and the directed light throw much of the picture into a shadow that helps to unify it. Although the draperies of the Virgin and angel are still conceived as having particular local colors—in fact, Leonardo's four primaries—the competition between them is reduced by the pervasiveness of shadow. In the later (London) version of the same picture, more complex chromatic means are used to draw the different colors together; the yellow drapery, for example, is modeled down with browns picked up from the landscape, and in similar ways the diverse hues are bound together coloristically rather than simply in terms of value as in the earlier picture.

In his passages relating to the effect of light and shadow on color, Leonardo was the first of the theorists to present a clearly articulated concept of color intensity (or saturation, brilliance). John Shearman first pointed this out,[39] showing that Leonardo used the term *bellezza* to convey the concept; earlier scholars, mistranslating *bellezza* as "beauty,"[40] had been misleading enough to deprive it of precision but not enough to have revealed the error. The following quotation is typical (T. 242 [189]):

Color found between the shadowed and the illuminated parts of shadowed bodies is of less bellezza *than that which is entirely illuminated, so that the prime* bellezza *of colors is to be seen in the principal lights.*

This principle is diametrically opposed to Cennini's placement of the most intense hue in the deepest shadow; and, in that it operates against using white in the highlights, it is opposed to Alberti as well. In a related passage, Leonardo openly states his opposition to the Cenninists by casting them as "the adversary" (T. 245 [193]):

Colors placed in shadow will partake more or less of their natural intensity [bellezza] *depending on whether they are in greater or lesser obscurity; but if the colors are located in luminous space, they will look the more intense the greater the splendor of the source of light.*

THE ADVERSARY: *The differences of color in shadow are as numerous as are the differences of color in the things shadowed.*

REPLY: *Colors placed in shadow will differ less and less as the shadows in which they are situated grow deeper. For this there is the testimony of those who from the squares look inside the doors of shadowed temples, where the paintings covered with different colors all appear to be enveloped in obscurity.*

This concept is modified in T. 206 (190):

Different colors have their bellezza [*greatest intensity*] *in different parts of themselves, and this is seen in black, which has its* bellezza *in the shadows, white in the light, and blue green and tan in half shadows, and yellow and red in the light, gold in reflections, and lake in half shadow.*

The statement appears in a context that makes it ambiguous whether Leonardo is referring to colors in nature or to pigments. This is not the only ambiguity in Leonardo's system: another arises in the conflict between the two precepts (1) that a hue reaches its greatest intensity when it is most lit, and (2) that light is itself colored. In many instances the color of the light would reduce the intensity of the color of the object, as would occur in carrying out the instructions of T. 756 (869).[41] Here, in a fashion reminiscent of Cennini's mixing in little bowls, the painter is advised to use mixing spoons to measure out the relative amounts of body-color and light-color for representing the illuminated portions of a body: the amounts are determined by figuring the angle of incidence of the light source, up to a maximum of two parts light-color to one part body-color.

In practice, Leonardo tended to modify such precepts to improve the tonal harmony of pictures; the strongly illuminated yellow drape at the center of the Louvre *Madonna of the Rocks* (fig. 6.6) is toned down from full intensity to keep it from seeming inconsistent with its surroundings. In the *Madonna and Child with St. Anne* (fig. 6.7), the red undergarment of the Virgin, most intense in the middle tones, is paler in the yellow-white highlights.

Another innovation in Leonardo's treatment of the effect of light and shadow on color was his emphasis on the changes caused by the displacement of the observer from the immediate environment of the object to be depicted to a more (or less) illuminated environment. I have mentioned passages that cite the case of the well-illuminated room in which the objects appear to an indoor observer brightly colored while they seem to an observer standing outdoors in the sunlight dark and colorless; that is due partly to "a defect of the eye which, overcome by the excessive light of the air, contracts the size of its pupil a good deal and so loses much of its visual power."[42] The expansion and contraction of the pupil is also cited as accounting partly for the differing brilliance of the moon in day and night: these passages are the only ones I have found in which Leonardo put to use his extensive studies in the physiology of the eye in developing his painting theory. The consideration both of the observer's ambience and of its potential physiological effect represents a radically different attitude

6.6   *Leonardo da Vinci*, Madonna of the Rocks. *Paris,*
Louvre (1492).

6.7 *Leonardo da Vinci*, Madonna and Child with St.
Anne. *Paris, Louvre.*

from that of the quattrocento. In one passage Leonardo suggests the practical implications of his observation, instructing the painter never to mix colors in a light different from that of the object to be depicted; he goes on (T. 819 [872]):

Suppose . . . I represent a mountain in the west, which is half shadowed and half luminous, but I wish to depict only the luminous part. I take a little piece of paper covered with that color which seems to me similar to that of the mountain, and I put it alongside the real color in such a way that there is no space between the true and the simulated, exposing it to the sun's rays, and adding different colors until each seems true, and I will continue thus with respect to every kind of shadowed and luminous colors.

The simple-minded naturalism of this proposal was not one that Leonardo followed in his painting; in fact, it wouldn't work, because as soon as other colors were added alongside the one matched they would alter its appearance, and it would no longer look like the mountains.

Neither of the two passages in the *Trattato* that identify the primary colors (*colori semplici*) is based on studio practice. One repeats a reduced Aristotelian list (T. 254 [176]) of six: white, black, yellow, green, blue, and red, the last four standing for earth, water, air, and fire: T. 237 (213) adds two to that number, as Aristotle had (though the specific colors are different) lion-colored or tan and blackberry-colored, and discusses the making of "composite" colors from the mixture of the primaries, first one with one, then two with two, and so on.[43] In what seems to be a footnote to these lists, Leonardo adds (T. 255 [177]):

Blue and green are not in themselves simple colors because blue is composed of light and darkness, as in the case of air; that is, it is composed of most perfect black and purest white. Green is composed of a simple and compound color . . . blue and yellow.

In the case of green, the apparent contradiction is due to the fact that the Aristotelian system, which did not purport to apply to pigments, conflicted with studio experience (where green results from mixing yellow and blue). The reservation about blue is more complicated. It originates in Aristotle's claim that *all* colors are made up of black and white (or darkness and light) in different proportions; I think Leonardo singled out blue because, in addition to being the color of certain objects in nature, it is the color of the sky and atmosphere as well, as discussed above,[44] and his explanation of that phenomenon involved the simple mixture of lightness and darkness.

In spite of this conservative approach to the fundamentals, Leonardo produced a remarkable new precept of color composition. It is the first to identify complementary colors and to perceive that in juxtaposition they intensify each other (T. 258 [180]):

Among colors of equal perfection the one which will appear to be the most excellent is that which is seen in the company of the direct opposite color [retto contrario]. *A direct opposite is a pale color with red, black with white . . . azure blue and golden yellow, green and red.*[45]

The term *retto contrario*, implying that the colors are laid out according to a geometric figure, suggests the color wheel.[46] The advantage of juxtaposing complementary fields is that it emphasizes relief; as an alternative, Leonardo suggests (T. 190 [185]): "If you wish the proximity of one color to make another which it borders attractive, observe the rule which is seen in the rays of the sun that compose the rainbow." The image of a picture employing hues aligned according to the spectrum is curiously inconsistent with Leonardo's surviving paintings.

The notes do not show much interest in the effects of one color on another other than as a way of separating bodies: Leonardo did not investigate in his written work the way particular pigments are affected by different chromatic settings in which they may be placed.

Remarkably few of Leonardo's notes on painting deal with actual colors apart from the conditions that light, shade, atmosphere, and reflection exert on colors generically. What is revealing about the corpus of color notes is the context in which they were conceived, the approach that made Leonardo the first to differentiate the workings of intensity and value and that helped him to achieve a new and radical chromatic and tonal composition. Although Leonardo was an irrepressible experimenter with pigments and media, there are not more than half a dozen notes on technical processes in the manuscripts. He overlooked even the issue that from hindsight seems to have been the most crucial in Italian painting of his generation: the differing coloristic effects and potentialities of the oil and tempera media.

IV

Conclusion

In writing of color theory and practice from Cennini to Leonardo, I may have made it appear that there occurred a steady progress from a relatively unsophisticated level to a relatively mature level. In the early days of art history, the thesis that art advanced from the early fifteenth century to an apex in the early sixteenth century was taken for granted, and memorialized by identifying the style of Leonardo, Raphael, and Michelangelo as "High Renaissance." Modern historical theory has rejected the concept of progress in art; it is now generally agreed that what matters in a work of art is its validity as an aesthetic object and as an expression of its time and place rather than the degree to which it approaches a fixed standard of perfection. But there is some ambiguity in the present subject. First, color practice is in part a theoretical and applied science, and we agree that it is proper to speak of progress in science and technology—fifteenth-century artists unquestionably improved the potential range of coloristic and chiaroscuro effects in the tempera and oil media and expanded their means of achieving tonal balance. Second, early Renaissance artists did agree on a "fixed standard of perfection": a major task of painting was held to be the representation of the three-dimensional effects of nature—and the color practice of 1500 was better able than that of 1400 to produce the desired impression of relief.

But there is also a different basis on which future generations regarded the art of the early 1500s as an advance over that of Cennini's time. The color and chiaroscuro of Leonardo and Giorgione intensified the interaction of the artist with his subject, and of the viewer with the picture in two ways—in providing means to dramatize the actors and the environment by manipulating light and dark for emotional effect, accenting one area or part of the body and suppressing another, and in developing the means of presenting the visual world perceptually rather than conceptually, as when a group of trees or a range of mountains is presented as a pattern of light and shadow rather than as a collection of autonomous objects.

These innovations deeply affected the future course of painting, since they made possible a kind and a range of emotional and sensual interplay between the viewer and the figures and objects in a picture beyond the reach even of such great dramatists as Masaccio and Giotto. And over the centuries, the artist's ability to bring us into this sort of relationship to the work of art (which was associated in the Renaissance with the art of poetry and has been called "literary" in modern criticism, but which is easier to understand as an effort to appeal to our perceptions and experiences of people and of nature) has been held to be a primary index of value in art, and constituted the fixed standard by which the Renaissance of the early sixteenth century became "High."

The fact that this is no longer the case, that twentieth-century art and taste shifted emphasis to abstract expression in form and color, has helped to restore the art of the quattrocento in critical esteem. When we concede today that Leonardo had a better control of color and chiaroscuro than Alberti's contemporaries, we do not imply that he could therefore make better pictures, but simply that he was better able to make the kind of pictures he wished.

Notes

Research on this paper was done largely at the American Academy in Rome in 1974/75 during my term as Resident, when I was supported by a grant from the National Endowment for the Humanities. I am grateful to both institutions for providing one of the most rewarding years of my life.

As the basic vocabulary of color theory applied to pigments is not standardized, I explain my use of the three essential terms:

Hue is the specific color identification, as: ultramarine blue.

Value is the place of a given area of pigment on a scale from light (high value) to dark (low value).

Intensity (also called brilliance or saturation) is the degree of vividness of a given area of pigment. The pigment is its pure form is usually as its highest intensity.

1. Citations are from Leon Battista Alberti, *On Painting and On Sculpture: The Latin Texts of De Pictura and De Statua*, ed. and tr. by Cecil Grayson (London and New York, 1972). Grayson ("The Text of Alberti's De Pictura," *Italian Studies*, 23 [1968], 71–92) dates the text from a note in one of the manuscripts of August 26, 1435, and proposes 1436 for the Italian translation done by the author. Maria Simonelli, "On Alberti's Treatises of Art and Their Chronological Relationship," *Yearbook of Italian Studies* (1971), 75–102, persuasively argues that the Latin text is a later expansion and correction of the Italian.

2. I have discussed the first book (except for the much-studied section on painters' perspective) in a sequel to this essay, "Alberti's Light," *Studies in Late Medieval and Renaissance Painting in Honor of Millard Meiss* (New York, 1978), pp. 1–27 [reprinted in this volume]. The two are part of an eventual book on Renaissance art and science.

3. The literature on quattrocento color and modeling is limited; I am greatly indebted to the following works, which stimulated my interest in the subject: Herbert Siebenhüner, *Über den Kolorismus in der Frührenaissance*, dissertation, Leipzig (Schramberg, 1935); T. Hetzer, *Tizian, Geschichte seiner Farbe* (Frankfurt a. M., 1935); John Shearman, "Leonardo's Colour and Chiaroscuro," *Zeitschrift f. Kunstgeschichte*, 25 (1962), 13–47; Samuel Cowardin, "Some Aspects of Color in Fifteenth Century Florentine Painting," dissertation,

Harvard, 1962; Sir E. H. Gombrich, "Light, Form and Texture in Fifteenth Century Painting," *Journal of the Royal Society of Arts*, 112 (1964), 826–849. Cf. the discussion of "the mode of relief" based on an empirical study of quattrocento paintings by Arthur Pope, *The Painter's Modes of Expression (An Introduction to the Language of Drawing and Painting, II)* (Cambridge, Mass., 1939), 71–85, from which I have taken my color terms.

See also the valuable technical contributions of H. Ruhemann, "Technical Analysis of an Early Painting by Botticelli," *Studies in Conservation*, 2 (1945), 26ff.; and M. Johnson and E. Packard, "Methods in the Identification of Binding Media in Italian Paintings of the Fifteenth and Sixteenth Centuries," *Studies in Conservation*, 16 (1971), 145–164. Filippo Lippi alone is discussed by Ernst Strauss, *Koloritgeschichtliche Untersuchungen zur Malerei seit Giotto* (Kunstwissenschaftliche Studien, XLVII) (Munich, 1972), 60ff.

4. It is practical to assume that pigments are at their most intense in a pure form, though Cowardin, "Some Aspects of Color," 26, points out that due to the physical constitution of ultramarine and the red lakes, the addition of a little white causes a slight rise in intensity. The effect is to increase the impression of relief in objects painted with these pigments.

5. Book II, 47: "But if, as I explained, the painter has drawn the outlines of the surface correctly and clearly sketched the border-line between lighter and darker, the method of coloring will then be easy."

6. Cennino d'Andrea Cennini, *The Craftsman's Handbook, The Italian "Il Libro dell'arte,"* ed. D. V. Thompson, 2 vols. (New Haven, 1933; volume of translation only, New York, 1954, 1960). The "arte" of the title should be translated "craft," not "art." A manuscript of this kind is not likely to have been used in the workshop, since it records just the essential practices that every master would have taught to his apprentices. But this sort of recording of basic practical information for the illumination of the amateur, for posterity, or for the sheer pleasure of it became increasingly frequent in the later Middle Ages; the relaxation of guild control over trade secrets may have been a factor in this case and in comparable northern European manuals on Gothic building.

7. His description of perspective construction, however, was an instructive exception because, while it met his criteria in being the proof of a scientific theory and a paradigm of the mathematical rationalization of art, it could be read by contemporary painters as a set of instructions not yet available in the workshops for the application of a radically new technique—they could even use it without understanding the theory behind it.

8. Cennini, *The Craftsman's Handbook,* ch. 71, pp. 49f.

9. In other notes, Cennini advised the use of black in deep shadows, notably in the instructions for modeling the Virgin's mantle in ultramarine, in fresco (ch. 83, pp. 54f; see also chs. 78, 81, 85). I am emphasizing the passage quoted as the standard Cenninesque practice, however, because it is standard in panel painting of his time and in much of the quattrocento.

10. The economic value of gold and of the constituents of pigments—particularly ultramarine, which was made from lapis lazuli, a semi-precious stone—continued to be a factor in the appreciation and commissioning of pictures during the quattrocento, and contracts often stipulated the quality and quantity of precious materials. The phenomenon is discussed by Michael Baxandall, *Painting and Experience in Fifteenth Century Italy* (Oxford, 1972), 1–27, whose observation that emphasis gradually shifted in the course of the century from the value of the materials to the value of the painters' skill is amply supported from Alberti (49) advising against the use of gold to represent gold jewelry and other objects: "I would try to represent with colors rather than with gold this wealth of rays of gold . . . there is greater admiration and praise for the artist in the use of colors." Cowardin, "Some Aspects of Color," 51ff., suggests that ultramarine was less modeled than ordinary colors to avoid diluting it and to keep it from emerging too vigorously from the plane.

11. Hetzer, *Tizian,* 26ff., shows that Giotto broke with this tradition, using color to achieve a unity of intensity and of value between foreground and background.

12. Cennini, *The Craftsman's Handbook,* ch. 77ff., pp. 53f. Cennini's term for the shift is *colore cangiante.*

13. In his short note, "vom Farben," *Dürer: Schriftlicher Nachlass,* ed. H. Rupprich (Berlin, 1966), 2: 393f.

14. Ibid. An English translation of the passage is given by M. Conway, *Literary Remains of Albrecht Dürer* (Cambridge, 1889), 173f. While Dürer is negative about excessive use of white and black in modeling, the implication of the passage is that a moderate use is expected, since he warns against shading one color with another, as yellow with blue or green.
Here, as in the Leonardo passages (cf. note 30), I understand the word usually translated as "beautiful" (*schön, bella*) to mean "brilliant" or "intense" (Conway, who attempted to translate into Renaissance English, used "fair").

15. The point is emphasized by Shearman, "Leonardo's Colour and Chiaroscuro," 16.

16. See Thomas Kaufmann, "The Perspective of Shadows: The History of the Theory of Shadow Projection," *Journal of the Warburg and Courtauld Institutes,* 36 (1975), 25. The appearance of cast shadows in paintings purportedly illuminated by natural light (e.g., fig. 6.1) is contemporaneous with the emergence of linear perspective, the reason being that the method of projection is similar. However, as Kaufmann demonstrates, a geometric system of casting shadows from a point source was not worked out until the late writings of Dürer.

17. John Shearman has proposed, partly on the basis of the distinctness of the cast shadows, a reconstruction of the altarpiece with additional figures of saints to the right and left ("Masaccio's Pisa Altar-piece: An Alternative Reconstruction," *Burlington Magazine,* 108 [1966], 449–455).

18. A number of such cases from the early 1400s on are discussed by Millard Meiss in "Some Remarkably Early Shadows in a Rare Type of Threnos," *Festschrift Ulrich Middeldorf* (Berlin, 1968), 112–118.

19. The *Coeur* manuscript is discussed by O. Paecht, "René d'Anjou et les van Eycks," *Cahiers de l'Association internationale des études françaises,* 8 (1956), 41–57.

20. Leonardo da Vinci, *Treatise on Painting,* paragraph 123 (108); see also paragraph 236 (110). My numbering of passages in the treatise is explained in note 25.

21. The juxtaposition of "light" and "dark" colors is further explained in what follows in the same paragraph: "There is a kind of sympathy among colors, whereby their grace and beauty is increased when they are placed side by side. If red

stands between blue and green, it somehow enhances their beauty as well as its own." Alberti, showing an unaccustomed firsthand familiarity with pictorial effects, is referring to the intensification that results from the juxtaposition of complementary colors, though the concept of complementary only began to be grasped by Leonardo (see below, at n. 45).

Piero della Francesca treats the clothing of the angels in the London *Baptism* as if he were attempting to carry out Alberti's instructions.

22. For Alberti's roots in rhetoric, see John Spencer, "Ut Rhetorica Pictura," *Journal of the Warburg and Courtauld Institutes,* 20 (1959), 26–44; Michael Baxandall, *Giotto and the Orators* (Oxford, 1971), 121–139; H. Mühlmann, "Über den humanistischen Sinn einiger Kerngedanken der Kunsttheorie seit Alberti," *Zeitschrift für Kunstgeschichte,* 33 (1970), 127–142.

23. A theory of genres seems to me to emerge naturally from a concern for *decorum* in painting as it does in rhetoric (and in architecture, with the orders). For lack of it, Alberti seems inconsistent when he advises (paragraph 40): "The first thing that gives pleasure in a *historia* is a plentiful variety. . . . I would say a picture was richly varied if it contained a properly arranged mixture of old men, youths, boys, matrons, maidens, children, domestic animals, dogs, birds, horses, sheep, buildings and provinces . . . provided it is appropriate to what is going on in the picture," and a moment later, "Perhaps the artist who seeks dignity above all in his *historia* ought to represent very few figures." The two statements might be harmonious if one were taken as describing the comic genre and the other the tragic, but Alberti also says, "In a *historia* I strongly approve of the practice I see observed by the tragic and comic poets, of telling their story with as few characters as possible," which leaves the purpose of "variety" undefined. Baxandall ("Guarino, Pisanello and Manuel Chrysalorus," *Journal of the Warburg and Courtauld Institutes,* 28 [1965], 200f.) offers the suggestion that Alberti is here tactfully expressing his debt to the less articulated rhetorical aesthetics of the previous generation of humanists, particularly Guarino of Verona; in that event, his next step would not have been to develop a system of genres, but to subordinate *varietas* to *dignitas.* The paradox is discussed in a still different light by Mühlmann, "Über den humanistischen Sinn einiger Kerngedanken," 135ff.

24. Landino's critique (from his Commentary on Dante's *Divine Comedy,* 1481) is discussed and analyzed in detail by Baxandall, *Painting and Experience,* 114ff. Since Baxandall has justifiably devoted almost a page to defining each of the characterizing terms, I felt that providing a translation here would distort the meaning.

25. Quotations from Leonardo's *Trattato* follow the accepted practice of English publications, giving the paragraph number first from the standard German edition of H. Ludwig (Vienna, 1882 and several later editions) and then again, in parenthesis, from the English translation of A. P. McMahon (Princeton, 1956). The latter is indispensable because it includes a facsimile of Melzi's original manuscript transcription from Leonardo's notebooks, Cod. Urb. Lat. 1270, but it greatly complicated Leonardo studies by needlessly rearranging the numeration of the paragraphs so that the double-reference system is required.

26. "Brilliance" in the closing lines of the passage is a translation of "bellezza," which Leonardo does not use in the modern sense of "beauty" (as McMahon translated it). As John Shearman first pointed out ("Leonardo's Color," 31): "It cannot be too strongly emphasized that *bellezza di colori* does not mean 'beauty of color' in the modern sense, but the harsh brilliance of pure pigment." Elsewhere I use the term "intensity," which is inappropriate here because of Leonardo's play on the word.

27. In *De pictura,* Alberti discusses (paragraph 11) how reflected light carries the color of the object from which it is reflected, citing the case of a person walking in an open field receiving a green reflection on the face; but this is an isolated observation not integrated into his precepts for painting.

28. *Trattato* 243 (225); 226 (226); 490 (519). The theory also explains why the sky seems less blue at the horizon: in 226, Leonardo demonstrates geometrically that when we look at the horizon—along a line tangent to the earth's surface—the eye has to penetrate a greater segment of the sphere of humidified air surrounding the earth than when we look straight upward in a line perpendicular to the earth's surface.

29. The assumption that a particular object has an intrinsic color independent of conditions of illumination and environment is Leonardo's and need not be challenged here.

30. See below, at n. 42.

31. J. P. Richter, *The Notebooks of Leonardo da Vinci* (London, 1883, 1970), paragraph 306, from MS. G, fol. 153v: "The surface of every object partakes of the color of the [source of] illumination and of the color of the air that is interposed between the eye and that object, that is, of the color of the transparent medium."

32. The statement in T. 905 (980), "The shadow of verdure always takes on blue, and so does every shadow of all other objects, and it becomes more blue the farther from the eye it is and less blue the nearer it is," is not a contradiction of the precept about black shadows, but deals with the effects of the intervening atmosphere and is a special case of Leonardo's "perspective of color." T. 630 (814) also treats blue shadows and explains: "This happens because of the brightness of the air . . .". Cf. T. 646 (816).

33. Also in the Madrid Codex II, fol. 127, where green reflections on a red body are disapproved. The passage was not transcribed into the *Trattato*.

34. While emphasis on the color of light and on the independence of light from illuminated objects was new to theory, it had a history in naturalistic painting starting in the first years of the fifteenth century in some of the illuminations of the Boucicault master and the Limbourg brothers, Jan van Eyck, and the majority of the major northern European masters. The progress of the latter was encouraged by the fact that white diminishes the transparency of glazes, as Leonardo noted (Richter, 277: "no white or black is transparent"), which is particularly deleterious in oil painting. Italian masters working in tempera generally avoided the problem of colored light unless they were depicting superior non-natural light, such as an apparition or an artificially lit night scene, which made these exceptions paradoxically more "naturalistic."

35. T. 785 (786).

36. I am discounting the two passages on the primary colors cited below (T. 254 [176] and 237 [213]), in which white is associated with light, because both are paraphrases of Aristotelian and post-Aristotelian theory and are not related to studio practice.

37. Cf. T. 154 (260): "Li colori di che tu vesti le figure sieno tali che dieno gratia l'uno al altro e quando l'un colore si fa campo del altro sia tale che non paino congionti et appichati n' sieme anchora che fussino di medesima natura di colore ma sien vari di chiarezza . . .". If we read *natura di colore* as "hue," then the different *chiarezza*

("value") is achieved by adding or subtracting white. Another instance occurs in the passage T. 226, paraphrased in n. 28, explaining that the sky seems *"più chiaro"* at the horizon than overhead: this obviously means "lighter" in the sense of higher in value, as against the great intensity of the overhead blue, which Leonardo would call *"più bella."*

38. This passage, besides dealing with the issue of value, is one of several that refer to optical effects on the borderlines between hues of different value, or between black and white (e.g., T. 204 [151]). The observations of this phenomenon, known today as Mach bands, are presented abstractly, without reference to practice; in fact, all of the passages cite black and white as the contrast causing the effect, though the two are almost never juxtaposed in paintings of Leonardo's time.

Recent research on Mach bands has demonstrated that they are caused by the inhibition of individual receptors in the retina due to competition from neighboring receptors. See Floyd Ratliff, "Contour and Contrast," *Scientific American* (June 1972), 90–101, which discusses a number of works of art as well as recent experimental achievements. The paper is based on one of the same title in *Proceedings of the American Philosophical Society*, 115, no. 2 (1971), 150–163.

39. See note 26 above.

40. In T. 210 (188), the term *qualità* is used rather than *bellezza*: "The true quality of colors is known through light . . .". The passage was taken from Cod. Ashburnham, fol. 33, which is dated 1492. I assume that at this date Leonardo's vocabulary was not fixed.

41. "Sia tolto un colore simile al colore del corpo che tu voi imitare, e sia tolto il colore del principale lume col quale voi aluminare esso corpo, di puoi se tu trovi che il sopra detto maggior angolo sia duplo al angolo minore, allora tu torrai una parte del colore naturale del corpo che voi imitare, e dagli due parti del lume che tu voi ch'esso riceva, et harai posto il lume duplo al lume minore di puoi per fare il lume sub duplo, togli una sola parte d'esso colore naturale del già detto corpo, e aggiongieli solo una parte del detto lume; et cosi harai fatto sopra un medesimo colore un lume il quale sara doppio l'uno à l'altro, perchè sopra una quantità d'esso colore è datto una simil quantità di lume, e l'altra quantità è datto due quantità di tale lume. E se tu voi misurare di punto esse quantità di colori habbi uno piccolo chuchiaro col quale tu possi pigliare le tue quantità eguali come

posto quivi in margine [sketch of spoon]. E quando tu hai con esso tolto il tuo colore e tu lo radi colla piccola riga come far si sole alle misure delle biade quando si vende esse biade."

42. See T. 202 (195); 700 (815); 628 (753), and also MS. E, 17v, and L. 41v. The manuscripts are cited in Leonardo, *Scritti scelti*, ed. A. M. Brizio (Turin, 1952), 407, 453 (as noted by Carlo Pedretti, *Leonardo da Vinci on Painting: A Lost Book* [Berkeley and Los Angeles, 1964], 206; this volume is an indispensable source book for *Trattato* studies).

43. In his *Treatise on Architecture* of ca. 1460 (ed. J. Spencer, New Haven, 1965, fols. 180r ff.), Antonio Averlino, il Filarete, includes a section on drawing and painting largely borrowed from Alberti's *De pictura*, but adjusted in specifics to observations that the author had made in the studios of painters (that he was not himself trained in painting is suggested by his open admission of ignorance with respect to the manufacture of several pigments). The treatise cannot have influenced later painting theory.

Filarete lists the same six *principali et più degni* colors as Leonardo for his basic palette (fol. 181v): white (= light), black (= shadow), red (fire), blue (air), green (grass), and yellow (gold, flowers, grass). The last two associations with nature show that Filarete had lost the thread of the tradition of aligning colors with the elements, which Leonardo sustained.

Filarete's comments on making and mixing pigments in this passage, though inexpert, are unique in the quattrocento. Especially interesting is his apparent preference for oil as a medium (fol. 182r): "but this is another practice and another mode which is beautiful for anyone who knows how to do it. In Germany they work well in this technique, especially Master Jan of Bruges [van Eyck] and Master Roger [van der Weyden]."

44. See above, at n. 28.

45. Slightly different lists of favored harmonies are offered in T. 190a (183), 238 (184), and 253 (182).

46. See also T. 258c (181): "ogni colore si conosce meglio nel suo contrario che nel suo simile." The term *eccellentia* used in the first passage is rare: *bellezza* being more common. The reason is probably that the notes were taken from an early manuscript of ca. 1492, according to Pedretti, *Leonardo da Vinci on Painting*, p. 188.

Postscript

This paper was prepared some time before its publication in 1980, which explains the lack of reference to several important studies published during the '70s. It often occurs that a subject that has been relatively dormant for decades or generations suddenly gets "hot," as did this one, partly perhaps as a result of innovations in contemporary art and criticism. These and subsequent contributions have altered my view of significant aspects of the subject, and prompt the following corrections and additions.

The major deficiency in my treatment of Alberti, detected by Maltese and by Gavel (pp. 47ff.) and best explained by Parkhurst (Hall volume, pp. 162f. and n. 7) is in the interpretation of the color scale. In addition to the Baconian primaries, red, green, and blue (celeste), Alberti proposed as a fourth bigio and cenericcio (Latin cinereus color), which I translated as "earth color." Earlier writers, including some sixteenth-century theorists, had understood the terms to mean grayish, ashen. What Alberti must have meant was an earthy, unsaturated yellow. He wanted to reduce the intensity of this primary color in order to bring it closer in value to the other primaries, to keep yellow objects from jumping forward simply because of the reflectivity of the pure pigment. Hills (p. 137) illustrates the point in his discussion of the ocher cloaks of two apostles in Masaccio's *Tribute Money* in the Brancacci Chapel. I cannot accept Maltese's proposition (1976, p. 244) that cenericcio can indeed be translated as gray, and that Alberti, rather than intending it to constitute another primary hue, meant in this way to introduce into color theory the modern concept of color value on the light-dark axis.

Alberti's blue (celeste) is defined as sky-blue for a complementary reason—to lower the intensity of ultramarine or other deep blues presumably by the mixture of white (Alberti was less concerned with the purity of his primaries than with their traditional association with the four elements—yellow standing for earth and blue for sky), and thus bring it closer in value to the other primaries. This was the first step toward the tonal balance achieved by Leonardo.

Hall, concentrating on practice rather than theory, defines four phases of fifteenth-century color, the Cenninesque, to which only Angelico of Alberti's contemporaries adhered, the Albertian, which dominated the mid-century, the Eyckian technique of oil glazing with pure colors, and the late-century technique of Leonardo and his contemporaries, which sought tonal balance through underpainting and glazing, often with mixed colors. Her comments on specific paintings add a new dimension to my overview.

Barasch, Moshe. *Light and Color in Italian Renaissance Theory of Art* (New York, 1978).

Gage, J. "A Locus Classicus of Color Theory: The Fortunes of Apelles," *Journal of the Warburg and Courtauld Institutes*, 45 (1981), 1–26. A study of ancient and medieval color theory and its impact on the Renaissance, with a bibliography of early sources.

Gavel, Jonas. *Colour: A Study of Its Position in the Art Theory of the Quattro- and Cinquecento* (Stockholm, 1978).

Hall, Marcia B. "From Modeling Techniques to Color Modes," in *Color and Technique in Renaissance Painting . . .*, ed., M. B. Hall (New York, 1987), 1–30, with rich bibliography.

Hills, Paul. *The Light of Early Italian Painting* (New Haven and London, 1987).

Kemp, Martin, "Yellow, Red and Blue: The Limits of Colour Science in Painting: 1400–1730," *The Natural Sciences and the Arts: Aspects of Interaction from the Renaissance to the Twentieth Century* (*Figura*, n.s. 22; Uppsala, 1985), 98–105.

Leonardo da Vinci. *The Codex Atlanticus of Leonardo da Vinci* (New York, 1978–79, and Florence, ca. 1973–75).

Maltese, Corrado. "Colore, luce e movimento nello spazio albertiano," *Commentari* 27 (1976), 238–247.

Maltese, Corrado. "Tra Leonardo e Land: qualche interazione tra arte e scienza," *Storia dell'arte*, 38–40 (1980), 419–423.

Maltese, Corrado. "Leonardo e la teoria dei colori," *Römische Jahrbuch für Kunstgeschichte*, 20 (1983), 211–219. Focuses on the mixing of natural light.

Parkhurst, Charles. "Leon Battista Alberti's Place in the History of Color Theories," in *Color Technique in Renaissance Painting*, ed. M. B. Hall, 161–204.

Parkhurst, Charles. "Roger Bacon on Color: Sources, Theories and Influences," in *The Verbal and the Visual: Essays in Honor of William Sebastian Heckscher*, ed. K.-L. Selig and Z. Sears (New York, 1990), 151–193.

Ruda, Jeffrey. "Color and Spatial Structure in Paintings by Filippo Lippi," in *Color Technique in Renaissance Painting*, ed. M. B. Hall, 41–53.

Shearman, John. "Isochromatic Color-Compositions in the Italian Renaissance," in *Color Technique in Renaissance Painting*, ed. M. B. Hall, 151–160.

I am grateful for the criticisms and bibliographical assistance of Marcia Hall and Charles Parkhurst and for their generosity in sharing their unpublished studies.

7

Early Renaissance "Naturalism" and Scientific Illustration

Early in the introduction to Leonardo da Vinci's *Treatiste on Painting,* there appears the following title and paragraph:

Whoever disparages painting loves neither philosophy or nature
If you disparage painting which alone is the imitator of all the works to be seen in nature, you most surely will disparage an invention which, with philosophic and subtle speculations, examines all qualities of forms: the sea, lands, animals, plants, flowers, which are surrounded by shadow and light. This is truly science and the legitimate daughter of nature, because painting is born of nature herself or, to put it more correctly, let us say granddaughter of nature because all things we sense are born of nature and painting is born of all those things.[1]

Leonardo was able to refer to painting as a path to science or natural philosophy because he was writing at a time when almost all scientific activity was empirical, and more specifically descriptive. Those sciences that progressed most effectively in the course of the fifteenth century were anatomy, geography and cartography, botany, optics, zoology, and astronomy, all of which were to some extent dependent on visual observation. Thus, the painter, who was trained to record visual evidence, was able not only to aid scientific work, but to pursue it himself, and Leonardo contributed to virtually all the disciplines I have mentioned.[2]

From *The Natural Sciences and the Arts,* Acta Universitatis Upsaliensis: *Figura,* n.s. 22 (Uppsala, 1985), 1–17.

Artists, in fact, virtually preempted the fields of scientific investigation because the equivalents of modern professional scientists, the scholastic and humanist scholars who published books and taught in the universities, were exclusively concerned with the written tradition. The scholastics adhered to the texts of Aristotle, Euclid, Galen, and others in the tradition of Greek empirical science and had made impressive contributions to theoretical physics during the late Middle Ages, though quite without the aid of experiment. The humanists significantly expanded the corpus of scientific texts by their energetic combing of libraries and their enterprise as editors and translators for the new printing presses. Forgotten manuscripts of Ptolemy and Archimedes were among their more dramatic discoveries. But members of both these groups were set in the conviction that knowledge of nature was to be gained only through the liberal arts, the sphere of intellectual activity, and not through the mechanical arts, which encompassed those manual activities demanded by scientific experiment (e.g., dissection, the collection of specimens, the making and use of scientific instruments) or by painting.[3]

Painting could constitute a proper support of scientific investigation only when its practice involved efforts to reliably depict the phenomena of nature that present themselves to the eye. This was not the case during most of the Middle Ages, though there are sufficiently numerous exceptions from the thirteenth and fourteenth centuries to challenge Jacob Burckhardt's claim that a rediscovery of the world and of man was a characteristic achievement of the Renaissance. Indeed it was in secular, mostly courtly, imagery between 1250 and 1400 that the close investigation of natural objects and phenomena for their own sake made its first reappearance since antiquity,[4] encouraged by the interest of feudal patrons in the birds and animals of the hunt and the flora of which an agricultural society would be more aware than would city dwellers.

I want in this paper to study three quite distinct ways in which studio artists furthered the aims of science in the early Renaissance. The first, which I shall call naturalistic, required a refinement of the techniques of mimesis. It involved improving the means of presenting visually the kind of evidence from natural objects and phenomena that was of interest to the scientific investigator and to the naturalist.[5] The second, which I shall call conceptual, involved adjusting visual evidence to an ideal, external concept of order, usually mathematical. Early Renaissance writers were keenly conscious of this distinction and referred to the first as *natura naturans* and the second as *natura naturata*.[6] The third, which I shall call conventional, involved the preservation of traditional representational imagery; this paradoxically characterized the illustration of scientific texts.

The fourteenth-century studio sourcebook of a Lombard painter Giovannino de' Grassi may stand as characteristic of the earliest modern naturalistic imagery.[7] It contains renditions of birds and beasts, evidently intended for reference by artists in the shop on the occasions when they would be called upon to depict a creature of a particular species in a manuscript or printed panel. The manuscript does include a hunting scene with lively action, but most of the images depict animals in strict profile so as to reveal as much as possible of their characteristic form, coloring, and texture, precisely as they appear in today's field guides for naturalists. The appearance of many of de' Grassi's drawings in other workbooks of the period indicates that drawings made directly from nature would be mixed in with copies from other volumes. Such images were made because the society of the time had developed the interest and the visual capacity to make fine discriminations among beings in the physical environment but, in turn, the development of the skills necessary to produce these images must have made people observe nature more closely and better.[8] The image-making capacity thus became a stimulus to scientific classification.

This capacity was greatly refined in the ensuing century, as demonstrated in the drawings of another artist of the north Italian courts, Pisanello (fig. 7.1). They are the direct ancestors of the drawings from life by Leonardo da Vinci and Dürer (figs. 7.2–5), who often chose the same kind of subject and treated it in a quite similar manner in spite of the great differences in their work as painters; naturalism is not deeply affected by the style changes of high culture.[9] While Pisanello's animals, like those of de' Grassi, cannot be located in a measurable space (in contrast to Dürer's *Crab*, which casts a shadow), they are observed with care—with such care, in fact, that the drawing does not correspond to any real experience of foxes because it is impossible to focus attention on all parts of such a complex object simultaneously. The artists observed the fox and crab over a span of time during which their attention shifted from one part to another, with the result that the image is composite rather than being an approximation of a momentary visual event. We see the record of a process of observation rather than of a *Gestalt* perception. It would be hard to imagine a setting for these drawings that would not detract from their power and make them seem less real (Dürer, conscious of this problem, keeps his indication of setting to a minimum). Surrounding flora, for example, would call attention to the fact that the *Fox* is encircled by a silhouette line, and this would cause him to flatten out; further, the lighting, which is selected specifically to bring out details in the animal, would have to be adjusted to an overall lighting scheme with conflicting functions, and compromises would be necessary.

Finally, the psychology and physiology of vision differentiate what we see from what we can depict. If we focus on an object as intently as Pisanello and Dürer did, the environment is indistinct, or we are unconscious of it. But a painter cannot reproduce this effect by depicting a fuzzy setting because the fuzz is not in nature but in the "mind." On the other hand, if the minute rendering of the *Fox* and the *Crab* were to be extended over the whole sheet to include details of the setting, the gap would widen between the time and effort required to gather and record the information and the momentary percept of the same scene. In short, the greater the area of detailed investigation, the less the image would correspond to ordinary experience.

What permits us to call such an image "objective" is that the artist has established the equivalent of what we call "laboratory" conditions, which reduce variables affecting its appearance and permit him to standardize procedures. The principal external variables for an artist—color, light and dark, atmosphere, and spatial differentials—can be controlled by eliminating the effects of an environment, by moving close to the objects and, in Pisanello's case, even avoiding foreshortening. The internal—psychological and social—variables are restricted by the choice of an object that generates a minimum of such emotional and conventional "noise" as affection, fear, respect, or scorn.

Pisanello could have been still more objective if he had not tried to make the fox lifelike, because that required the application of style—a complex of skills and talents acquired prior to the experience of sketching the fox, which made it possible for him to consummate his extended and painstaking study giving the impression of the action of an instant. Paradoxically, a study of the corpus of the artist's drawings reveals beyond doubt that his life studies of the less sedentary animals and bird were done from dead specimens laid out on a surface in lifelike positions.[10] Dürer's *Crab* is also dead: claws are missing. The liveliness of the *Fox* is the one feature in the drawing that is not "objective" but individualized in harmony with the artist's style. This individuality is the chief clue by which connoisseurs identify drawings as being or not being the work of this artist. Indeed, the major work on Pisanello's drawings says that fig. 7.1 is not;[11] but such questions are not at issue in this book.

The reduced impact of style on naturalistic images also makes it difficult to say whether Dürer based his approach on Italian or on northern sources;[12] the *Crab* was executed during his first trip to Venice in 1495, at which time the Venetian sculptor Riccio was making bronze crabs, beetles, frogs, turtles, and the like, sometimes by

7.1 *Pisanello, Fox. Paris, Louvre, no. 2424.*

7.2 *Albrecht Dürer, Crab. Rotterdam, Boymans–van Beuningen Museum, no. M.B. 1958/T 30.*

7.3   *Albrecht Dürer, Hare. Vienna, Albertina (1502).*

simply taking casts from the actual creatures.[13] But similar naturalism can be found in earlier Netherlandish manuscripts such as the Hours of Catherine of Cleves, of about 1440.[14]

The effect of style considerations is strikingly illustrated by comparing Pisanello's animals to his depiction of figures of costumed courtiers and protagonists of religious or chivalric dramas. Such contrasts often remain unresolved in his pictures, such as the fresco depicting a scene from the life of St. George, in which such mannered figures are juxtaposed to shockingly naturalistic hanging men. The crimes of these corpses have reduced them to the level of beasts. Only lower forms of life were considered suitable objects for naturalistic treatment. In about 1390, Cennino Cennini had told the Gothic painters to whom his handbook was addressed: "I will not tell you about irrational animals because you will never discern any system of proportion in them; copy them and draw them as much as you can from nature."[15]

Later in his career, in the early 1500s, Dürer (fig. 7.3) overcame the limitations of earlier naturalistic images and was able to add to the intense observation of detail some of the richness of color, chiaroscuro, and other of those environmental effects that Renaissance artists called accidentals, without losing the precision and definition. The *Hare* is as accurate a record of its species as were the *Fox* and *Crab*, but it is shown in particular lighting conditions in a specific environment indicated by the reflection in the animal's eyes of Dürer's studio window. And clearly, though a wild species, it was depicted live. Leonardo da Vinci, in innumerable drawings covering all aspects of natural history, gained the same extraordinary mastery over the conflicting exigencies of naturalistic imagery. The botanical sketch shown here (fig. 7.4) represents the midway point in a process that proceeds from the level of taxonomy to that of sense impression. The specimens in this sketch are presented for identification and define a condition halfway between that of a general type and that of a specific, immediate experience. Though these weeds and the *Hare* of Dürer would serve a taxonomic function effectively—perhaps more effectively than most subsequent classificatory illustrations—their immediacy and particularity add information not relevant to the didactic image, and remove from them the implication of objectivity we are accustomed to demand of scientific data.

In stating that animals may be represented naturalistically because they are without proportion, Cennini implied that depictions of men (he did not include women) should conform to an ideal scheme. This arrangement of sense data to conform with predetermined principles of proportion is one of the hallmarks of early Renaissance art, and introduces my second type of image (fig. 7.5).

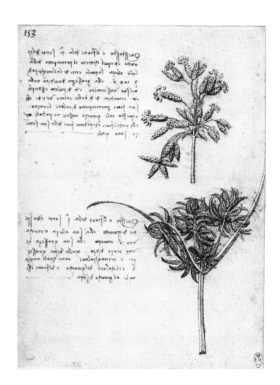

7.4   Leonardo da Vinci, botanical studies. Windsor,
Royal Library, no. 12427.

7.5   Leonardo da Vinci, anatomical study. Windsor,
Royal Library, no. 19057.

A century after Cennini, Leonardo asked in the first lines of this treatise on painting: "Is painting a science or not?" and in answering affirmatively, explained: "no human investigation can claim to be true science if it is not subjected to mathematical demonstration," adding, however, that "if you claim that the sciences that begin and finish in the mind are true this is not conceded . . . first because in such mental discourses experiment—without which nothing of itself provides certainty—does not play a part."[16] In the context of this paper, we might have expected him to have said "no investigation of humans," because he appears to have followed Cennini's dictum by attempting to apply mathematical systems almost exclusively to anatomy. I say "almost exclusively," because he also subjected the horse to proportional systems,[17] not only, I suspect, because he was commissioned to design monumental equestrian statues, but also because horses were so essential to Renaissance life that they were accorded quasi-human status.

Leonardo's approach to the astonishing series of studies of the human skull represented by figure 7.5 characterizes his early studies only.[18] Later, in his mature years, he abandoned the effort to give organic nature a mathematical structure because he had come to see that proportions change as organisms grow and move.

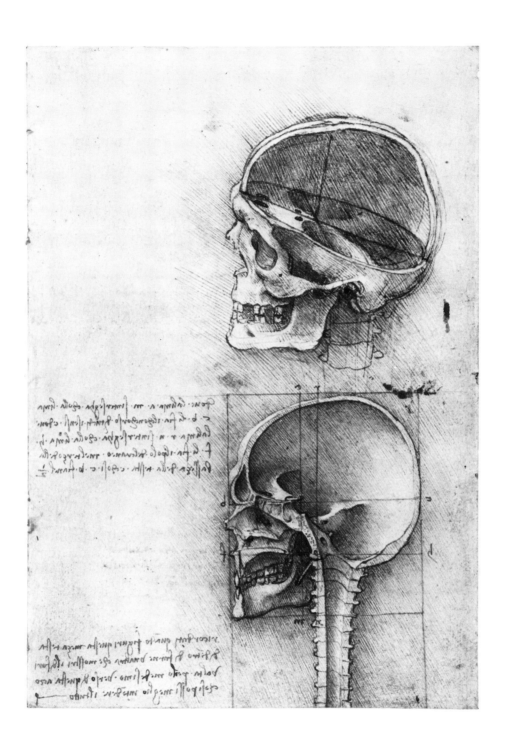

A contemporary expression of the same kind of rationalizing spirit is represented in the many studies of the human head used by Piero della Francesca to illustrate the practice of foreshortening in his book on perspective.[19] The head is divided into many horizontal and vertical sections, minutely measured, and these make it possible first to produce geometrically coordinated elevations, plans, and sections as in architectural studies, and then to produce foreshortened images from unlimited viewpoints. The culture of the late fifteenth century must have been perceived at the time as moving toward an ultimate union of art and science. Dürer, late in his life, recalled in his notes that in his youth the Venetian painter Jacopo de' Barbari had showed him drawings of a man and a woman executed according to a proportion system he would not explain, and that this fired Dürer to pursue the subject.[20] The chase took him from Nuremburg to Venice and is reflected in many drawings from the time following his first Italian trip in 1495 and in his posthumous book on human proportions of 1528.[21]

But, in the end, the effort to geometrize the human form did not bring art closer to science and rapidly lost the attention even of the artists.

The appearance of the printed book in the 1460s and '70s provided the third type of interaction between the artist and scientific material. Because illustrations cut on wooden blocks could be passed through the press together with the text at the same time, figures could be produced as fast and as inexpensively as words.[22] But just as the texts in the great majority of books published in the first decades of printing were editions of ancient and medieval authors, so early book illustrations did not represent the world as artists saw it, but were woodcut versions of the printed illuminations of surviving manuscripts. At first, the printed book was considered to be a machine-made manuscript, just as the first automobiles were modeled on horse-drawn carriages, and type fonts imitated hand script. Early woodblock illustrations were consequently more decorative than functional (fig. 7.6). The medieval models were as abstract and symbolic as medieval scientific thought, while illustrations in texts that had survived from antiquity had become so distorted by repeated reproduction—as each copyist in turn passed on errors and oversights of his predecessors and added some of his own—that the result was useless for practical purposes. But the potential of the printed image was revolutionary. It assured that every individual copy would exactly duplicate the plate approved by the author. Moreover, it not only could reinforce the author's written statement but could *itself be* the statement. In all fields of technology and descriptive science, books could be produced in which the substance was communicated primarily by images. Ultimately, in an abrupt reversal of functions, texts were partly or wholly devoted to elucidating accompanying pictures.

Renaissance readers, profoundly committed to the written word, found this development difficult to accept; it took them from 1470, when the first illustrated books appeared, until the decade 1530–1540 to shed the medieval tradition. Two editions of a fourteenth-century medical manuscript attributed to a shadowy figure named Johannes de Ketham and called *Fasciculus medicinae* were published in Venice in 1491 and 1493.[23] Its five illustrations repeat a traditional medieval set; one, called the *situs,* represents a pregnant woman in an uncomfortable hortatory position. While the cut reproduced in figure 7.6A follows its medieval predecessors in showing a tiny homunculus in a symbolic womb, the illustration in the second edition is improved both by being stylishly designed by an artist in the circle of Mantegna and by the replacement of the symbolic womb with a uterus that, while quite generalized, reflects some contact with anatomical experience (fig. 7.6B).

A similar change can be detected in the earliest printed botanical illustrations that appear in herbals, compendia of medicinal simples which were the most popular class of scientific publication in the Renaissance and were invariably illustrated.[24] Illustrators of the incunabula were satisfied to copy surviving medieval manuscripts of the Greco-Roman writer Dioscurides, and did not feel the need to refer to specimens of the plants themselves. The results were for the most part crude and conventional and gave no sense of the plants which they purportedly reproduced. One work, however, called *Herbarius* in the Latin edition of 1484 and *Gart der Gesundheit* in the vernacular edition of the following year, printed in Mainz by Peter Schöffer, the great competitor of Gutenberg, was an exception (fig. 7.7). While the majority of the large figures in the volume were copied from the manuscripts, the texts also called for the representation of plants that had not appeared in the ancient sources, and these had perforce to be reproduced from nature. Thus two figures may appear on facing pages, as in figure 7.7, one of which, on the left, is purely symbolic and the other, on the right, representational, within the limits of an emerging block-cutting technique. But the door opened by Erhard Rewich, the artist of these volumes, immediately closed again for over four decades, probably because the botanists themselves were slow to turn from traditional authority to observation.

Anatomists were still slower to commit what they had learned from dissection to images. Even a scientifically advanced text such as that of the Bolognese surgeon and anatomist Berengario da Carpi, the *Isagoge brevis . . . in anatomiae humani corporis* of 1522,[25] was illustrated with cuts that served no functional purpose and may not have been meant to; and similarly imprecise cuts were employed as late as 1545 in an elegant

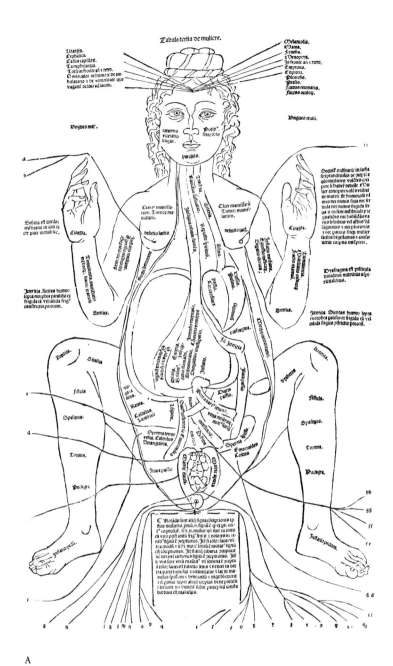

A

7.6   *Johannes de Ketham,* situs. From *Fasciculo de Medicina, editions of 1491 (A) and 1493 (B).*

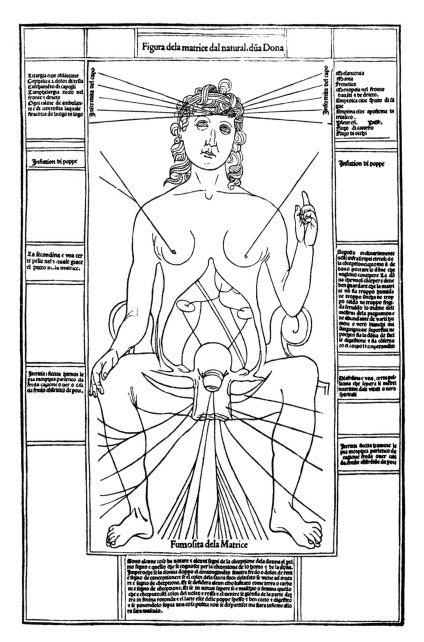

Figura dela matrice dal natural. dúa Dona

Fumosita dela Matrice

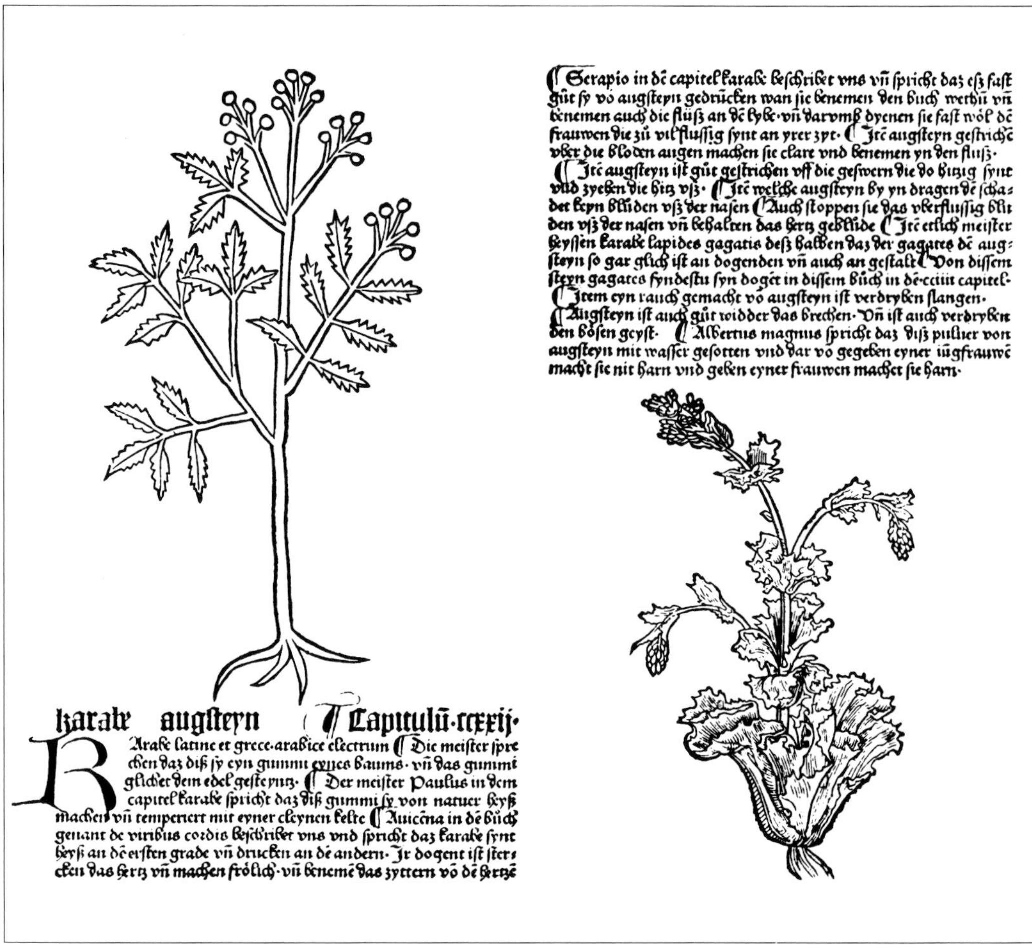

karabe augsteyn Capitulū·ccxxij·

Karabe latine et grece·arabice electrum Die meister spre
chen daz diß sy eyn gummi eynes baums· vñ das gummi
glichet dem edel gesteyntz· Der meister Paulus in dem
capitel karabe spricht daz diß gummi sy von natuer heyß
machen vñ temperiert mit eyner cleynen kelte Auicēna in dē büch
genant de viribus cordis beschribet vns vnd spricht daz karabe synt
heyß an dē ersten grade vñ drucken an dē andern· Jr dogent ist ster
cken das hertz vñ machen frölich· vñ benemē das zyttern vō dē hertzē

Serapio in dē capitel karabe beschribet vns vñ spricht daz esz fast
güt sy vō augsteyn gedrücken wan sie benemen den buch wethū vñ
benemen auch die flüsz an dē lybe·vñ darvmb dyenen sie fast wol dē
frauwen die zü vil flussig synt an yrer zyt· Itē augsteyn gestrichē
vber die bloden augen machen sie clare vnd benemen yn den flusz·
Itē augsteyn ist güt gestrichen vff die geswern die do hitzig synt
vnd zyehen die hitz vsz· Itē welche augsteyn by yn dragen dē scha
det keyn bluden vsz der nasen Auch stoppen sie das vberflussig blu
den vsz der nasen vñ behalten das hertz gebluide Itē etlich meister
heyssen karabe lapides gagatis desz halben daz der gagates dē aug
steyn so gar glich ist an dogenden vñ auch an gestalt Von dissem
steyn gagates fyndestu syn dogēt in dissem büch in dē·cciiii capitel·
Item eyn rauch gemacht vō augsteyn ist verdryben slangen·
Augsteyn ist auch güt widder das brechen· Vñ ist auch verdryben
den bösen geyst· Albertus magnus spricht daz disz pulier von
augsteyn mit wasser gesotten vnd dar vo gegeben eyner iūgfrauwē
macht sie nit harn vnd geben eyner frauwen machet sie harn·

7.7 Erhart Rewich, facing pages from Gart der Gesundheit, *1485.*

folio volume published by the humanist physician Charles Estienne in Paris, *De dissectione partium corporis humanae,* a generation after the death of Leonardo. But by this time the potential of scientific illustration had finally been fulfilled in the work of Andreas Vesalius.[26] The importance of illustration in the famous *De humani corporis fabrica,* printed in Basel in 1543, was declared in the decision to include, at enormous effort and expense, 200 plates designed in Venice by artists in the circle of Titian and laboriously transported over the Alps (fig. 7.8). These pictures brought about a revolution in anatomical imagery that Leonardo had failed to realize by not having committed his drawings to the block cutter. Perhaps the progress they represented was not so much in anatomical research as in the teaching of anatomy to university students, to literate laymen and to artists, as suggested by the frontispiece showing the author at the dissecting table with knife in hand, demonstrating to a large audience what he is finding. The equivalent plate in the volume of Ketham shows a professor reading from a work of Galen while a barber cuts up the cadaver;[27] Vesalius, like artists in the previous century, lost social status by getting his hands messy.

Many of the Vesalian plates, like figure 7.8, are presented as antique sculptural fragments; high culture entered in at the fringes. In this case, the model was the Hellenistic *Belvedere Torso* in the Vatican collections, a favorite of Michelangelo. His intestines, however, are not classicized, but greatly simplified for didactic purposes as an instructional tool. Images of this quality compare favorably with those in medical texts today; the latter are, in fact, ultimately dependent on the vision of Vesalius and his artists.

An advance comparable to that of Vesalius had been made in the herbal literature a decade earlier with the publication of Otto Brunfels's *Herbarum vivae icones* of 1530.[28] The name itself is revealing, emphasizing as it does the making of images from living specimens: that is, not copied from earlier illustrations. Brunfels's artist, in distinction from Vesalius's, is known: he was Hans Weiditz, who had inherited a tradition initiated by Albrecht Dürer of drawing plants in the field or from specimens freshly picked.[29] Dürer left several watercolors that set a new standard of precision in the imagery of flora.[30] One of Weiditz's surviving watercolors (fig. 7.9) reveals his debt to Dürer and also something of his method. He must have been given plants recently gathered in the field by the botanist Brunfels, and have reproduced them as faithfully as possible, including the broken leaves and imperfections. In the final drawing for the block cutter these idiosyncrasies would have been removed in order to produce an image that reveals as much as possible by turning the leaves toward the viewer, spread-

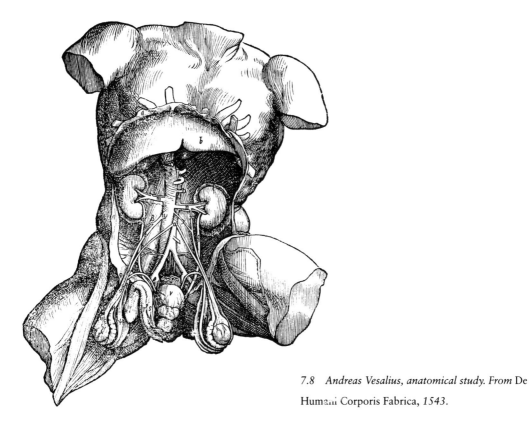

7.8   *Andreas Vesalius, anatomical study. From* De Humani Corporis Fabrica, *1543.*

ing out the roots, and so on, in a manner equivalent to Vesalius's selectivity in reproducing the human organs (fig. 7.10). Weiditz had the skill to make these changes while still preserving the vitality and grace of his models.

This publication was nearly rivaled the year before Vesalius's book by Leonhart Fuchs's *De historia stirpium*, illustrated with 512 cuts of even greater fidelity, though with slightly less elegance.[31] Some of these have been colored in by hand, a habit that recalls the original desire of publishers and customers to regard printed books as being substitute manuscripts. Fuchs was keenly aware of the power of the image and promised in this text to suppress the urge of his artists to express themselves at the cost of accuracy. In compensation, he allowed or encouraged them to include their self-portraits among the illustrations.

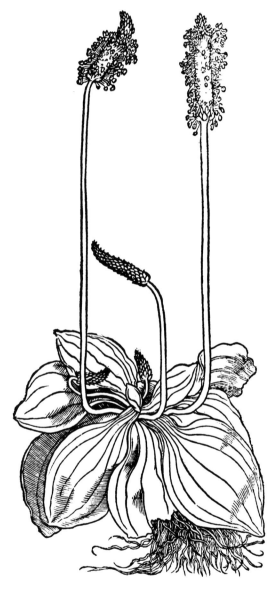

7.9   *Hans Weiditz, botanical studies. Bern, Botanical Institute Library, Felix Platter herbal.*

7.10   *Hans Weiditz,* Plantago maior. *From Otto Brunfels,* Herbarum vivae icones, *1530.*

The behavior of scientific imagery was peculiar not only in the explosive way in which it matured as if by gross mutation in 1530–1545, but also in the rapid decline that it suffered immediately thereafter. In conformity with the evolution of the image in the Middle Ages, the moment a paradigm had been attained by the confluence of imaginative scientists and devoted artists, all touched with genius, the temptation of subsequent publishers to ride on their shoulders by copying them and ultimately by copying the copyists became irresistible. Not only was it easier to reproduce a plate in the workshop than to portray anew a specimen or a cadaver, but this procedure could be carried out by the publisher's block cutters without recourse to expensive artists. Accordingly, later Renaissance herbals such as Fabio Colonna's of 1592 are cruder than those of the golden age, even though Colonna used the more sensitive technique of etching. The level of Vesalius and of Weiditz was never again attained, and modern scientific imagery is in a very depressed state.

I should have been hard put to summarize briefly the interrelationship of the scientist and the artist in the Renaissance had it not already been attempted by the botanist Leonhart Fuchs in the very volume I have discussed. Let Fuchs, then, have the last word:

Though the pictures have been prepared with great effort and sweat we do not know whether in the future they will be damned as useless and of no importance and whether someone will cite the most insipid authority of Galen to the effect that no one who wants to describe plants would try to make pictures of them. But why take up more time? Who in his right mind would condemn pictures which can communicate information much more clearly than the words of even the most eloquent men? Those things that are presented to the eyes and depicted on panels or paper become fixed more firmly in the mind than those that are described in bare words.[32]

Notes

1. Leonardo da Vinci, *Treatise on Painting* [*Codex Urbinas Latinus 1210*], facsimile and translation by A. Philip McMahon (Princeton, 1956), vol. 2, fol. 4 (the translations in the present text are mine).

2. See Erwin Panofsky, "Artist, Scientist, Genius: Notes on the 'Renaissance-Dämmerung,'" in *The Renaissance*, ed. W. K. Ferguson (New York, 1962), 121–182.

3. Eugenio Garin, *La cultura del Rinascimento* (Bari, 1973); Garin, "Gli umanisti e la scienza," *Rivista di filosofia*, 52 (1962), 259–278, and other studies; Paul O. Kristeller, "Humanism and Scholasticism in the Italian Renaissance," in his *Studies in Renaissance Thought and Letters* (Rome, 1956; first published in *Byzantion*, 12 [1944–1945]), and other studies.

4. Otto Pächt, "Early Italian Nature Studies and the Early Calendar Landscape," *Journal of the Warburg and Courtauld Institutes*, 13 (1950), 13–47.

5. I have to describe the techniques of naturalism in this oblique way because representations of nature can be called true or accurate only within a particular context agreed upon by the creator and the receiver.

6. Cf. Jan Białostocki, "The Renaissance Concept of Nature and Antiquity," *Acts of the Twentieth International Congress of the History of Art, II* (Princeton, 1963), 19–30.

7. On Giovannino de' Grassi and allied Lombard naturalists, see Pietro Toesca, *La pittura e la miniatura nella Lombardia*, 2d ed. (Turin, 1966), pp. 135ff. and figs. 242–250, 361, 380–382; A. van Schendel, *Le dessin en Lombardie jusqu'à la fin du quinzième siècle* (Brussels, 1938), 57–70. A model book of animal studies containing 31 parchment folios, one with a signature of Giovannino, in the Biblioteca Comunale of Bergamo, no. A VII, 14, is the key to all studies of this subject; it was compiled in the closing years of the fourteenth century (facsimile: Giovannino de' Grassi, *Taccuino di disegni; codice della Biblioteca Civica di Bergamo* (Bergamo, 1961).

8. See N. Fossi-Todorow, *I disegni del Pisanello e della sua cerchia* (Florence, 1966). In the discussion following the presentation of this paper, Martin Kemp keenly observed that while the refinement of naturalistic techniques made possible a high degree of verisimilitude in drawings

from nature, it also greatly improved the capacity to give credibility to fantastic creatures and to imaginary features of actual beings.

9. Cf. my study, "Dürer's Crab," *Ars Auro Prior: Studia Ioanni Białostocki Sexagenario Dicata* (Warsaw, 1981), 291–295.

10. This was called to my attention in a seminar paper by Prof. Joanna Woods-Mardsen.

11. Fossi-Todorow, *I disegni*, cat. no. 407 (Vallardi Codex, Louvre, Cabinet des Desseins, no. 2424).

12. Commenting in correspondence on my paper cited in n. 9, Svetlana Alpers remarked that Italianists have had a tendency to attribute whatever innovations they can to Italian as opposed to northern artists and that in this case northern precursors may well account for Dürer's naturalistic style. I maintain, however, that a comparison of the corpus of Pisanello drawings to those done by Dürer on his first Venetian trip demonstrates a close link.

13. Cf. Ackerman, "Dürer's Crab," 293f.

14. New York, Morgan Library, MS. 917, p. 244; cf. John Plummer, *The Book of Hours of Catherine of Cleves* (New York, 1964), p. 60, no. 119, pl. 30. The manuscript is dated (p. 24) ca. 1435.

15. Cennino d'Andrea Cennini, *Il libro dell'arte*, ed. D. V. Thompson, Jr. (New Haven, 1932), 47: "Degli animali irrazionali non ti chontero, perche nonnaparai mai nessuna misura. Ritra'ne, e disegnia piu che puoi del naturale, e proverrai in cio a buna praticha."

16. Leonardo da Vinci, *Treatise on Painting*, vol. 1, fol. 1v.

17. For example, in drawings for the Sforza and Trivulzio monuments in the Royal Library at Windsor Castle, nos. 12285–12360.

18. See the brilliant treatment of these studies by Martin Kemp, "Il concetto dell'anima in Leonardo's Early Skull Studies," *Journal of the Warburg and Courtauld Institutes*, 34 (1971), 115–134, and Kemp, *Leonardo da Vinci: The Marvellous Works of Nature and Man* (Cambridge, Mass., 1981), chap. II.

19. See Piero della Francesca, *De prospectiva pingendi*, ed. G. Nicco Fasola (Florence, 1942): illustrations in vol. 2, figs. 63–72.

20. The reference to de' Barbari appears in a draft dated 1523 of the dedication to Dürer's friend Pirckheimer of the book on proportions

(cited in n. 21). For Dürer's voyages to Italy, see Erwin Panofsky, *The Life and Works of Albrecht Dürer* (Princeton, 1945), 32ff., 37, 116ff., and on his theoretical interests, Panofsky, *Dürers Kunsttheorie, vornehmlich in ihrem Verhältnis zur Kunsttheorie der Italiener* (Berlin, 1915).

21. Albrecht Dürer, *Vier Bücher von menschlicher Proportion* (Nuremberg, 1528).

22. My interest in the subject of this study was first aroused by the stimulating work of William Ivins, *Prints and Visual Communication* (Cambridge, Mass., 1953), esp. chaps. 1–2. See also L. Febvre and H. -J. Martin, *L'apparition du livre* (Paris, 1959); E. Eisenstein, *The Printing Press as an Agent of Change*, 2 vols. (Cambridge, 1979), esp. vol. 2, section 5, pp. 463–520.

23. K. Sudhoff, *Fasciculo de medicina,* ed. and tr. Charles Singer (Florence, 1925).

24. See L. Treviranus, *Die Anwendung des Holzschnittes zur Bilddarstellung von Pflanzen* (Leipzig, 1855); W. S. Schreiber, *Die Kräuterbücher des XV und XVI Jahrhunderts* (Munich, 1924); Agnes Arber, *Herbals, Their Origin and Evolution* (Cambridge, 1938); G. Nissen, *Das botanische Buchillustration: ihre Geschichte und Bibliographie* (Stuttgart, 1966); A. G. Morton, *History of Botanical Science* (London and New York, 1980), chap. 5.

25. Renaissance anatomical illustration is reviewed in R. Herrlinger, *Geschichte der medizinischen Abbildung,* vol. 1 (Munich, 1967; English ed., London, 1970).

26. On Estienne, see P. Huard and M. A. Grmek, "L'oeuvre de Charles Estienne et l'école anatomique parisienne," preface to the facsimile of the 1546 edition of *La dissection des parties du corps humain divisée en 3 livres* (Paris, 1965). Of the vast Vesalius literature, see in particular C. O'Malley, *Andreas Vesalius of Brussels, 1514–1564* (Berkeley and Los Angeles, 1964).

27. The plate is discussed in a similar context by Panofsky, "Artist, Scientist, Genius."

28. Otto Brunfels, *Herbarum vivae eicones ad naturae imitationem, summa cum diligentia et artificio effigiate, unam cum effectibus earundem, in gratiam veteris illius, & iamiam renascentis herbariae medicinae* (Strasbourg, A. Schott, 1530).

29. See W. Rytz, *Pflanzenaquarelle des Hans Weiditz aus Jahre 1529* (Bern, 1936).

30. Dürer's watercolors of flowers are discussed by Kurt Gerstenberg, *Albrecht Dürer, Blumen und Tiere* (Berlin, 1936) and L. Kellerman, *Dürers Pflanzen- und Tierzeichnungen und ihre Bedeutung für die Naturgeschichte* [Studien zur deutschen Kunstgeschichte, 119] (Strasbourg, 1910).

31. Leonhart Fuchs, *De historia stirpium commentarii insignes . . . accessit iis succincta admodum difficilium & obscurarum passim in hoc opere occurrentium explicatio . . .* (Paris, 1543).

32. Ibid., Preface, pp. x–xi.

Postscript

This study was based on a couple of the Slade Lectures on Renaissance Art and Science that I gave at Cambridge University in 1970. While preparing the material I worked principally at the libraries of the Wellcome and the Warburg Institutes in London, and in the latter I first met the imaginative Swedish scholar Allan Ellenius, with whom I have kept in contact since that time. He later organized a symposium at the Art History Institute in Uppsala on "The Natural Sciences and the Arts," for which the text was prepared in its present form. The publisher requested that illustrations be kept to a minimum, and this restriction probably simplified the writing; but I have added one (fig. 7.6B) in order to show the impact of Renaissance artists on anatomical illustration.

I might have made more of the controversy among anatomists and herbalists over the utility of illustration in scientific books. Hoeniger (pp. 130f.) shows that Otto Brunfels did not want to have his pioneering herbal illustrated, but was compelled by his publisher to accept the splendid woodcuts of Hans Weiditz; after publication, he complained to a friend that more attention was being paid to the "dead lines" of the woodcuts than to his text. But after mid-century, Konrad Gessner was so convinced of the value of illustration that he learned to draw himself in order to do his own plates. As Karen Reeds points out (pp. 529f.; cf. also Dilg, pp. 122ff.), Galen, whose writings dominated both fields in the Renaissance, Pliny the Elder, and numerous other ancient authorities opposed illustrations because of the potential for distortion. On the other hand, a number of ancient authors favored images. A major sixteenth-century botanist, Hieronymus Bock, refused to illustrate the original edition of his herbal (Strasbourg, 1536) but, after his printer persuaded him to allow woodcuts in later editions, he sought out and quoted those ancient authors who supported illustration.

Ackerman, James S. "Dürer's Crab," *Ars Auro Prior: Studio Ioanni Białostocki Sexagenario Dicata* (Warsaw, 1981), 291–295. I propose that the *Crab*, which probably was executed in Venice in 1494, may have been influenced by Andrea Riccio's casts of actual crabs, which were made according to an antique technique of casting from nature described by Pliny the Elder.

Ackerman, James S. "The Involvement of Artists in Renaissance Science," in *Science and the Arts in the Renaissance,* ed. John W. Shirley and F. David Hoeniger (Washington, D.C., 1985), 94–129.

Ashworth, William B. "The Persistent Beast: Recurring Images in Early Zoological Illustration," *The Natural Sciences and the Arts: Aspects of Interaction from the Renaissance to the Twentieth Century (Figura,* n.s., 22; Uppsala, 1985), 46–66. Demonstrates the persistence of imaginary or grossly inaccurate representations of animals in the zoological literature through the centuries of modern science.

Dilg, Peter. "Die Pflanzenkunde im Humanismus—Der Humanismus in der Pflanzenkunde," in *Humanismus und Naturwissenschaften,* ed. R. Schmitz and Fritz Krafft (Boppard am Rhein, 1980), 113–134.

Douglas, James, and Sandra Hindman. *Pen to Press: Illustrated Mss. and Printed Books in the First Century of Printing,* exhibition catalog (Baltimore, 1977).

Edgerton, Samuel Y., Jr. "The Renaissance Artist as Quantifier," in *The Perception of Pictures,* ed. Margaret A. Hagen, 2 vols. (New York, 1980), 1:179–212. A more extended version of the following.

Edgerton, Samuel Y., Jr. "The Renaissance Development of the Scientific Illustration," in *Science and the Arts in the Renaissance,* ed. John W. Shirley and F. David Hoeniger (Washington, D.C., 1985), 168–197. The author focuses on imagery developed for the representation of newly invented machinery in the Renaissance, suggesting that the illustrators may have furthered the advances of technology. He compares the Western achievements with that of Chinese artists, whose graphic traditions did not permit them to devise usable representations, even when copying Western sources.

Florence, Galleria degli Uffizi, Gabinetto degli Stampe, *Immagini anatomiche e naturalistiche nei disegni degli Uffizi, sec. XVI, XVII,* exhibition catalog (no. 60) with essays by R. Ciardi, R. A. Bernameo, and L. Tomasi (Florence, 1984).

Grammacini, Norberto. "Das genaue Abbild der Natur—Riccios Tiere und die Theorie des Naturabgusses seit Cennino Cennini," in *Natur und die Antike in der Renaissance,* exhibition catalog (Frankfurt am Main, 1987), 198–225.

Hoeniger, F. David. "How Plants and Animals Were Studied in the Mid-Sixteenth Century," in *Science and the Arts in the Renaissance,* ed. John W. Shirley and F. David Hoeniger (Washington, 1985), 130–148.

Hulton, Paul. "Realism and Tradition in Ethnological and Natural History of the Sixteenth Century," in *The Natural Sciences and the Arts: Aspects of Interaction from the Renaissance to the Twentieth Century (Figura, n.s. 22; Uppsala, 1985)*, 18–31. This examines the power of preconceptions in the representation of primitive peoples in the old and new world, particularly among the artists accompanying the voyages of discovery.

Muraro, Michelangelo, and David Rosand. *Titian and the Venetian Woodcut* (Washington, D.C., 1976). The authors attribute the large anatomical figures of Vesalius to Titian himself, and suggest the possibility that Domenico Campagnola may have designed the landscape behind them.

Reeds, Karen M. "Renaissance Humanism and Botany," *Annals of Science*, 33 (1976), 519–542.

III

Renaissance Architecture

8

"Ars Sine Scientia Nihil Est":
Gothic Theory of Architecture at the Cathedral of Milan

Il convient de constater d'abord qu'il est impossible de séparer la forme de l'architecture du XIII siècle de sa structure; tout membre de cette architecture est la conséquence d'un besoin de la structure, comme dans le genre végétal et animal il n'est pas un phénomène, un appendice qui ne soit le produit d'un nécessité organique. . . . Cette forme n'est pas le résultat d'un caprice, puisqu'elle n'est que l'expression décorée, si vois voulez, de la structure.

E. *Viollet-le-Duc,* Entretiens sur l'architecture *(Paris, 1863), I, pp. 284, 287*

The opinion of Viollet-le-Duc, summarized in these words, typifies an approach to the interpretation of Gothic architecture which has held great appeal for the modern student. The evident harmony of this approach with the "functional" spirit of a nascent style of contemporary architecture partially explains its success. It is more significant, however, that the conflicts created in our aesthetic responses by the scientific and mechanical psyche of our age are here neatly resolved by an interpretation which is mechanistic, which explains cultural phenomena in terms of irreducible and demonstrable fact. Yet, granting that by this means Gothic architecture becomes in a sense more intelligible to the modern mind, it remains to be seen whether this intelligibility is not gained at the cost of understanding. Our problem is to determine whether a type of logic which is so distinctly tinged with the flavor of experimental science fortuitously illuminates a medieval creative process, or whether it forces us to see through a glass, darkly.

A considerable literature already exists on the subject of "Gothic Rationalism," as this view is sometimes called. In France, for example, the particular views of Viollet-le-Duc have been assaulted by Pol Abraham and others, and in turn stoutly defended.[1] Much effort has been spent in the attempt to prove, by the study of extant monuments, that certain elements believed by Viollet-le-Duc to be essential to the structural skeleton are in reality inorganic. This controversy has concentrated on the prob-

From *The Art Bulletin*, 31 (1949), 84–111; reprinted by permission of the College Art Association of America.

lem of the function of the rib in Gothic vaulting, but in spite of bringing to bear upon the question the most formidable tools of modern engineering, the arguments on both sides have remained inconclusive. The failure is largely methodological, for in their painstaking analysis of such particular elements, the adversaries of rationalism become themselves enmeshed in the web of inductive scientific technique. They have furthermore failed to appreciate that our understanding of Gothic architecture would not be substantially enriched by the destruction of a nineteenth-century interpretation. If rationalism is proven inadequate, it is the responsibility of the contemporary historian to search for data which will aid in the formation of a view better suited to both the facts and the spirit of Gothic architecture.

The problem we have posed is to discover whether or not the attempt to derive the form of Gothic architecture from its structure is justified and, if not, to suggest a more illuminating approach. The method of procedure which suggests itself is to some degree implicit in our criticism of rationalism, for if we wish to avoid the imposition of modern criteria upon the Gothic style, we are bound to seek for Gothic criteria. This involves a reconstruction of the specific intentions of the Gothic architect with respect to the form, the purpose, and structure of his building. Since the analysis of remaining monuments provides insufficient evidence for this task, we must turn, not to the works, but to the men who created them, whose aims are most concretely revealed among the textual remains of the period.[2]

It is doubtful whether a search of medieval sources will ever discover such explicit expositions of the practice of architecture as are found in the treatises produced from the mid-fifteenth century on. The claim of the architect to be placed among creative artists, his desire to formulate and spread a doctrine of architecture, is to a degree a sign of the Renaissance. Prior to the fifteenth century, writings which concern architecture are few in number and widely divergent in nature, and are for the most part of little assistance in reconstructing the concepts of the architect in relation to structure. However, evidence which bears directly on the problem of Gothic theory and practice is found in startling abundance in the late fourteenth-century records of an Italian architectural workshop: the Annals of the building of Milan Cathedral. It is surprising that a source of this nature should produce the kind of material for which we are seeking. Medieval workshop records ordinarily are concerned only with matters of supply, finance, and employment. In general, this is also the case at Milan, and the exceptions which will be considered here, representing only a small portion of the published records, are passages resulting from the unusual circumstances of the construction.[3] The constant changes of master-builders, recurrent indecisions as to procedure, and frequent errors in practice which hamper the progress of the cathedral are reflected in the records in the form of criticisms and debates which give expression to a variety of theoretical positions. Had the program of construction been better organized, we might have had fewer sources of this nature and, by way of compensation, a more admirable cathedral.

The foundation of the Cathedral of Milan in 1386 signalized Lombardy's emergence from an artistic eclipse which began at the close of the Romanesque period.[4] The political instability which had impoverished the duchy during the thirteenth and fourteenth centuries was brought to an end by Gian Galeazzo Visconti (1347–1402), whose military campaigns temporarily annexed to Lombardy a large portion of Venetian territory, most of Emilia, and a part of Tuscany. The revival of monumental architecture may be attributed both to the ambitious personality of the duke and to the increase in wealth and security which resulted from political consolidation. Within ten years of the foundation of the cathedral, three major architectural projects were undertaken in the Milan area: the reconstruction of Monza Cathedral,[5] the Certosa of Pavia (a private project of the duke),[6] and the cathedral at Como.[7]

The new architectural campaigns called for building on a scale calculated to rival the largest Gothic cathedrals of western Europe, a goal that was not destined to be achieved easily by a society which had so recently emerged from two centuries of cultural obscurity. The provincial character of the thirteenth- and fourteenth-century architectural tradition of Lombardy in itself suggests that the architects of Gian Galeazzo Visconti were poorly prepared for a renascence of monumental architecture.

A conservative Gothic church style had developed in Lombardy almost exclusively under the sponsorship of the monastic orders. The style is essentially a compromise between the Romanesque cathedrals of the region and the French Cistercian forms introduced into central Italy in the twelfth century.[8] There is no evidence of influence from contemporary developments in the architecture of western Europe. The flying buttress is rarely employed, fenestration remains limited, monumental sculpture is forsworn, and the exteriors are uniformly of unfaced brick. The style is modest to the point of poverty, and yet it developed an individuality which distinguishes it from monastic architecture elsewhere. A variety of the Cistercian plan which is typical of Lombardy is the arrangement of outer chapel rows along the side aisles, as is seen in the example in figure 9.1.[9] This produces in effect a five-aisle arrangement in the western

8.1   Milan, cathedral, façade.

arm, which has, as will appear later, an influence on the planning of Milan Cathedral. The most distinctive feature of the style is the lively decorative sense exercised in the rich brick-and-terracotta façades, and the highly coloristic bell and crossing towers. Although both these features manifest the parentage of the Lombard Romanesque style of the twelfth century, they undergo a development in the Gothic period to a point of definite individuality. On the whole, however, the imagination of the Gothic builder is channeled into the decorative aspects of his art, and there is little evidence of technical growth during the thirteenth and fourteenth centuries.

A well-preserved and typical Lombard Gothic church is the Carmine in Pavia (fig. 9.1). The chapel rows give the plan a rectangular form and produce a façade of unusual breadth. Pinnacles and terracotta ornaments enliven the façade, which contrasts to the ascetic severity of the interior, where the nave walls are relieved only by small oculi in the clerestory. The slight wall buttresses which we see on the façade are also employed to support the nave along the sides. Setting aside the ornamental features of the building, there is nothing to suggest that it belongs to the end of the fourteenth century rather than to the end of the twelfth.[10]

It proved in practice almost impossible to adopt the Lombard Gothic idiom to the structural and aesthetic requirements of the new programs sponsored by the duke. The failure of the tradition is reflected in the stylistic confusion of the Visconti monuments. Milan Cathedral leans toward the northern Gothic, Monza toward the Tuscan, Como toward the Venetian, and the Certosa of Pavia adds Romanesque revival and Florentine Renaissance elements to a fanciful Gothic core. Thus the Lombard architects of the end of the fourteenth century chose the only possible course: they borrowed their style from any and every foreign source. Tradition died hard, however, and the submission to alien forms was made unwillingly. The French and German masters who were hired to aid the architects of Milan Cathedral were bitterly received and poorly treated. The history of the cathedral is one of constant wrangling between local and foreign builders.

Evidently the inadequacy of the provincial tradition was not immediately apparent to the architects of Milan Cathedral. It seems, in fact, to have been their original intention to build without assistance from the north. The building council appointed in 1386 confidently produced its own designs, and broke ground shortly after the pope granted a charter for the construction. The essential lines of the foundations were established before the question of foreign advisers came under consideration. The first of these to be appointed was a Frenchman, Nicolas de Bonaventure, who became a privileged engineer of the cathedral in July of 1389, three years after the foundation.[11] This change in policy was evidently motivated by circumstances which forced the council or the lay deputies to admit that the self-confidence with which the project had been commenced was unwarranted. There were already faults in the foundations, and the ability to determine a pier design constituted an obstacle to progress.[12] There was a pressing need for the expert assistance of Nicolas. On the basis of this information there may be some justice in assuming that the northern Gothic character of the cathedral began to take form only after the arrival of the Frenchman, and that the initial plan was conceived in the Lombard Gothic style. We shall introduce in the course of this study certain documents in support of this assumption, although circumstantial evidence alone is persuasive. The possibility that the council began its original project in imitation of northern Gothic church architecture is rendered unlikely both by its manifest ignorance of northern art and by the nature of the cathedral plan itself. The first foreigner was hired with evident reluctance, and only when it became apparent that the problems involved in building on such a scale could not all be solved by Lombard Gothic masters. The appointment of a Frenchman was motivated not by admiration for French architecture, but by respect for French engineering. That a dose of northern stylistic concepts had to be administered with the doctoring was clearly galling to the Milanese and, like many of his successors, Nicolas was dismissed within a year.[13]

A remarkable document remains from the period of Nicolas's visit. It is a sheet of sketches which has on the recto a plan of the cathedral with the projected section of the nave, including measurements of certain elevations, and on the verso an elevation of the exterior of the sacristies. The author is Antonio di Vincenzo, a Bolognese architect who had been sent to Milan to make notes for his future work at San Petronio. The date of these drawings is 1390.[14] They constitute a primary source for the history of the cathedral, revealing in the plan the character of the foundations laid before the onset of foreign influence, as well as indicating future procedure in the section and elevation. Comparing this plan with that of the present cathedral (fig. 8.2), we find that the transept is one bay longer on either side, with flat terminations and an entrance in the northern arm.[15] Its Romanesque character, a consistent theme in Lombard Gothic, is unmistakable.[16]

Since it was evidently the problem of erecting the piers that motivated the decision to enlist the aid of a Frenchman, Antonio's sketch may help us to understand the difficulties encountered by the Milanese. The crossing piers, which the sketch and Antonio's notes represent as larger and more complex than the others, were originally the same size. This information comes from a notice of July 1390, at which time it was

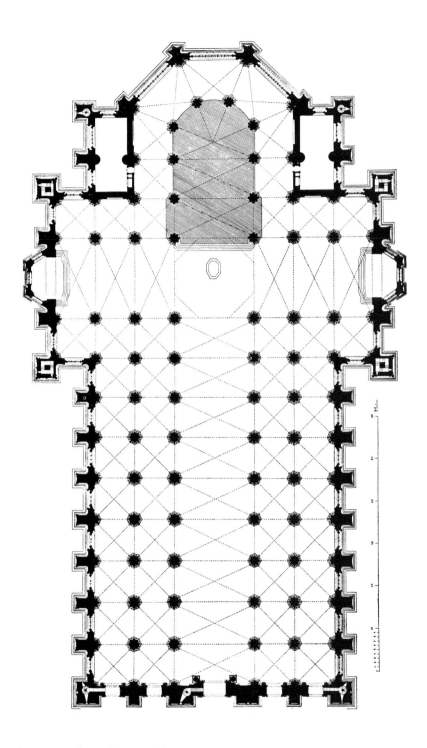

8.2   *Present plan. From Dehio and von Bezold,* Die
kirchliche Baukunst des Abendlandes.

decided to make this alteration.[17] Now, the lesser piers in Andrea's sketch are designed as a round core with four engaged shafts. A comparison with the present plan shows that this project was also altered. The pier design thus goes through three stages: first, all piers relatively thin; second, the crossing piers enlarged; third, the lesser piers enlarged. It was possibly upon the insistence of the French architect that these alterations were made. The remarkable fact is that the Milanese were guilty of this great uncertainty concerning their supports at a time when the foundations were completed, and the massing of the church established. What the rationalist would call the "skeleton" of the building was still in a state of flux! In this case, certainly, structural considerations did not determine the forms.

The proposed sacristy elevation (fig. 8.4) in Antonio's sketch shows a decorative scheme and tracery which were closely followed in subsequent work on the cathedral exterior. The distinctly northern flavor, reminding one somewhat of Strasbourg Cathedral, is in all likelihood the contribution of Nicolas de Bonaventure. That a decorative scheme of a quite different character was originally projected is clear from the present design of the lower portion of the interior wall of the north sacristy, which is executed in the style of a Lombard Gothic façade.[18]

In Antonio's delineation of the projected nave section (fig. 8.3), sufficient measurements are provided, although the drawing is not made to scale, to enable us to reconstruct the scheme with reasonable accuracy (see fig. 8.5A). The letter M (the height of the wall piers) = 30 braccia; L (height of the side-aisle piers) = 40 braccia; H (height of the capitals of both major piers) = 10 braccia; G (distance of the nave impost from the capital) = 10 braccia, or 60 braccia from the ground. No measurement is provided for the height of the nave vaults. The measurements E and F are apparently extraneous to the problem of establishing the main lines of the design. Paul Frankl, in his analysis of this project, proposes that these figures represent a very simple device on the part of the designer: the employment of a basic unit of ten braccia for the establishment of the heights of various elements.[19] Such a unit has a sound utilitarian purpose, for it is calculated to provide measurements which might be followed readily by a mason equipped only with a measuring stick (in this case, probably 5 braccia in length). Antonio's design, however, was in as tentative a state as that of the supports, because a year after the sketch was made, the archbishop was asked to call a conference to decide on the "length of the pilasters, the height of the church, of the windows, doors and other things."[20] In terms of the "rational" interpretation of Gothic construc-

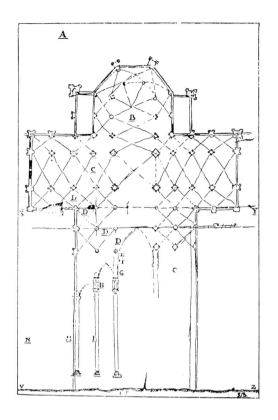

8.3   Plan and nave section, redrawn after Antonio di
Vincenzo. From Boito, Il Duomo di Milano.

8.4   Exterior elevation, redrawn after Antonio di
Vincenzo. From Boito, Il Duomo di Milano.

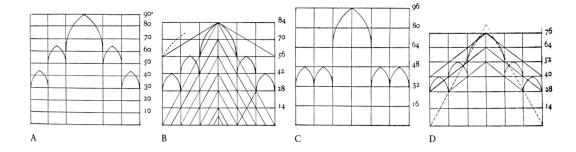

8.5 *Milan, cathedral, projects for the section to be
erected on foundations 96 braccia wide. (A) project of
1390 employing units of 10 braccia, after sketch and
notes by Antonio di Vincenzo. (B) project of 1391
employing units of 14 braccia, within framework of
equilateral triangles, after sketch by Gabriele
Stornaloco. (C) project of 1392 employing grid of
squares, reconstructed from texts. Probably proposed
by Heinrich Parler of Gmünd. (D) project accepted in
1392 employing Stornaloco's project to a height of 28
braccia (dotted lines) and continuing with units of 12
braccia within framework of Pythagorean triangles,
after specifications of cathedral council.*

tion, it is inconceivable that the height of a structure should remain undetermined after
the foundations had been completed, but this is the case at Milan. The section project
seen by Antonio was only the first of five different solutions that are known to us. This
inversion of what we would regard as logical method is not unique, and it proves to
have been standard procedure at Milan to permit the cathedral to grow haphazardly,
without an ultimate aim. In consonance with this method, the piers were redesigned in
their present form shortly after Andrea's visit, and their construction begun well before
the height of the capitals had been fixed.

As the piers grew, the problem of the nave section became, of course, increasingly pressing. The dissatisfaction with the simple but rather arbitrary scheme employing units of ten braccia may be traced to the criticisms of Annas de Firimburg, a

German architect who succeeded Nicolas de Bonaventure. Annas evidently wanted to substitute one which had a more soundly established rationale, for he proposed that the section be designed within an equilateral triangle.[21] The role of plane geometry in the building theory of the Gothic period will shortly become evident and, from the standpoint of this theory, its introduction at this point is a sign of great progress. In accepting the new scheme, however, the building council encountered a difficult problem. The height of an equilateral triangle is incommensurable, and its employment appeared to involve forgoing the advantages of simple, yardstick measurement which were secured by the earlier scheme. The solution of this dilemma was not in the province of an architect, and a mathematician named Gabriele Stornaloco was summoned from Piacenza in September 1391.[22] On his return to Piacenza he submitted his opinion in a letter accompanied by a drawing.[23] The superiority of this project lies in the fact that it not only provides a framework of equilateral triangles, but coordinates this framework with a grid as simple as that of the earlier project. Beginning with the triangle, Stornaloco solves the problem of the incommensurable height (which, figuring from the base of 96 braccia already established by the foundations, would be 83.138) by rounding off the figure to an integral 84 braccia.[24] The purpose of this compromise in measurement is immediately evident from the drawing, for it permits the section to be constructed of six equal horizontal divisions of 14 braccia each. The coordination of the triangle and the horizontal divisions provides a logical interrelation between the width of the aisles (16 br.) and the heights of the various portions. Moreover, the geometrical figures provide rational relationships among the several elements in the section itself, and a harmonic connection of the whole to its parts. Stornaloco also suggests a reference to a more abstract harmony by indicating the circle within which the triangle is inscribed, as well as the hexagon inscribed within the circle. This scheme avoids the awkwardly hunched character of the earlier project, and escapes its greatest shortcoming by providing a consistent means of determining the height of the vaults as well as the height of the imposts.[25] There is undoubtedly some significance in the fact that Stornaloco has arranged the measurement of the vaults so that the nave is just twice the height of the outer aisle.

Stornaloco's design was accepted and put into practice in the construction of the side-aisle piers and buttresses, but we shall see that it was destined to as short a life as its predecessor. Considering the inconsistent growth of the cathedral, this reduction in its total height by over 3½ meters was probably a matter of little concern to the builders. A far more important feature of the project was the introduction of a geometrical scheme into the conception.

Meanwhile, Annas de Firimburg had been dismissed, and a frantic search for a successor ensued. A ducal envoy to Cologne failed to discover a "maximus inzignerius" who was willing to accept the position, and an attractive offer to Ulrich von Ensingen, the chief engineer of Ulm Cathedral, was refused.[26] Finally, at the end of 1391, Heinrich Parler of Gmünd was appointed to the position.[27] After inspecting the cathedral, he made certain suggestions which were not readily accepted, and a great convocation of specialists was called to discuss his proposals on May 1, 1392. The full record of this conference follows.[28]

At the gathering of all the engineers named below. . . .[29]

All [of these] gathered in the building office of the Milanese church in order to remove numerous doubts which are being entertained concerning work at this church, which doubts are separately specified below, and to the doubts are added replies and statements by all these engineers, with the exception of this master Heinrich, who, although these replies are given toward [establishing] an understanding, concurs in no way with these statements.

[1.] Dubium: *Whether the portions of the rear as well as the sides and interior—namely, both the crossing and the other, lesser, piers—have sufficient strength?*
Responsio: *It was considered, replied, and stated upon their soul and conscience, that in aforesaid [portions] the strength, both of the whole and separate [parts], is sufficient to support even more [weight].*

[2.] D: *Whether this church ought to shed rain [debeat pluere] by two roofs or by more, to be constructed from either side up to the transept?[30]*
R: *It was considered that this church ought to have, and has to have, three roofs and not two, to afford greater strength and light.*

[3.] D: *Whether this church, not counting within the measurement the tower which is to be built, ought to rise according to the square or the triangle?*
R: *It was stated that it should rise up to a triangle or to the triangular figure, and not farther.*

[4.] D: *How many braccia should the piers be made which support the main nave or the middle nave?*
R: *It was stated that these piers counting bases and capitals ought to rise to 40 braccia and not farther.*

[5.] D: *How many braccia should the half-piers be which are to be made in the wall above these large piers up to the vaults or arches to be made above that point, and how many braccia ought the vaults to be made above these?*
R: *It was considered and stated that the half-piers should be twelve braccia, and the vault of this main nave should rise to the triangle, that is, twenty-four braccia.*

[6.] D: *What is thought of the design of one double portal of the transept facing the Compedum,[31] and of the entire façade of this transept?*

R: *When it had been seen and studied, it was stated that it was very beautiful, good and honorable, and that work should proceed according to this [design].*[32]

[7.] D: *Whether or not the chapels of this church ought to be divided or separated one from another, by a wall?*

R: *It was stated that since these chapels do not need any more strength, that they should remain and be made without any median, or dividing wall.*[33]

[8.] D: *Whether a room or a corridor ought to be made above the second nave, which is between the main nave and the chapels of the church?*

R: *It was said that this room is on no account to be built, since it occupies funds and adds expense.*

[9.] D: *Whether work on the exterior piers or buttresses is to proceed as it was begun or be improved in any way?*

R: *It was said that this work was pleasing to them, that there is nothing to be altered, and that, on the contrary, work is to proceed.*

[10.] D: *Whether [work] should proceed on the* guerziis *piers,*[34] *or anything be removed or changed?*

R: *It was considered that these piers, since they have their proper proportions and parts, are not to be moved, but perfected and refined.*

[11.] D: *How many braccia ought the lesser, or chapel piers, be, and the half-piers which ought to be made in the wall above them, up to the arches which cross over toward the main nave?*

R: *It was replied and stated that these lesser piers ought to be 28 braccia high, and the half-piers above them constructed up to the arches should and ought to be 12 braccia, counting bases and capitals in these measurements.*

A meeting of the following day, held to confirm the results of this conference, concludes:[35]

All the engineers gathered in yesterday's sitting confirm what is written above in all its parts, excepting Simone da Orsenigo, who agrees in general but says that the chapels of the church ought to be divided by a wall in the same manner in which they are joined beneath the ground.

The preamble to the report indicates the customary manner in which major problems are solved. The master engineers summoned to the conference vote on each problem proposed, and the solution is based on the opinion of the majority. Thus Heinrich Parler's special position as a visiting expert does not strengthen his voice in the workshop, and his opinion is equal in weight to that of the least experienced master. To this method of procedure may be attributed some of the council's difficulties in forming a definite and consistent program.

This conference of 1392 is clearly the council's first defense of its *modus operandi,* and the first direct evidence of its opposition to the north. Of the eleven problems considered here, the majority offer two alternative proposals for the future progress of the cathedral. Since the preamble informs us of Heinrich's unreserved opposition to the solutions agreed upon, we assume that he favored, in each case, those which were abandoned. In fact, a bitter debate may be inferred beneath the calm surface of this report, which, presented in terms of *Dubia* and *Responsiones,* identifies itself with a traditional scholastic disputation. In the subsequent conferences of 1400 and 1401 this method is abandoned, perhaps because it fails to represent the significant differences of opinion.

At the time of this conference the cathedral was beginning to rise above the level of the foundations, and piers and buttresses had been begun in accordance with Stornaloco's formula. The record of the conference suggests that Parler's criticisms questioned, first, the soundness of the portions already completed, and second, the desirability of continuing to carry out the project determined before his arrival.

In proceeding to the interpretation of this text, it is helpful to dispense with the rather illogical order in which the problems are submitted, and consider the items in order of their importance for the discussion.[36]

The question submitted in *Dubium* 3: "ad quadratum an ad triangulum?" has in recent times been the occasion for so much elegant geometrizing on Gothic architecture that one hesitates to explain it in simple terms. Yet this phrase refers to a problem with which we are already familiar from the drawings of Antonio di Vincenzo and Stornaloco. The importance of the geometrical figure in establishing the design of the section was obvious in Stornaloco's formula. Here it is reaffirmed, and to such an extent that the conferees are initially interested not in the question "how high shall the church be?" but "within what figure shall it be designed?" As we have just seen, a triangular system was already being used for the cathedral, and the suggestion that it be altered to a square one is probably Heinrich's.[37] What Heinrich means in proposing a square system is simply to make the height of the church equal to its width. By this suggestion, the vault summit, which Stornaloco had brought down to 84 braccia with his triangles, would have shot up to 96 braccia (see fig. 8.5C).

Parler's suggestion has certain advantages. A section based on a square would be more perfect mathematically, because it would be unnecessary to compromise the figure, as Stornaloco had to do, to achieve commensurable heights. Again, the heights of the various portions of the elevation could be established on the basis of the same

16-braccia unit upon which the ground plan itself was based. To the Italians, however, these advantages were far outweighed by the disadvantages, for the section based on a square would provide a nave so high that the entire system of piers and buttresses would be rendered inadequate (hence the criticism of the supports in *Dubia* 1, 9, and 10). Partly on this basis, the conference spurns Parler's suggestion and reaffirms the triangular section. One would naturally assume that this implies a retention of the program already in effect, but on reading the specifications in *Dubia* 4, 5, and 11, which are substantially those of the present cathedral (though reduced one-half braccio in execution), it becomes clear that here is a triangular section which is partly Stornaloco's and partly a quite new solution!

What had already been accomplished according to Stornaloco must be preserved, and thus *Responsio* 11 retains the height of the outer piers at 28 braccia. At this height, the equilateral triangle is truncated (see figs. 8.5D, 8.6). The units of 14 braccia which underlie Stornaloco's grid give way to units of 12, as indicated by the measurements determined in *Responsiones* 4 and 5.[38] These measurements establish a new geometrical system over the outer piers which proves to consist of figures as familiar as Stornaloco's: adjacent Pythagorean triangles. No mathematician was required at this point, for the short side of a Pythagorean triangle is commensurable with its base, and the height of the church could be calculated readily at 76 braccia. This peculiar alteration upsets entirely the logic of the original scheme. By employing two different geometrical systems, the chief purpose of the triangle—to provide a unified interrelation of the parts and the whole—is ignored.

To understand this capricious shift in midair, we must recall that each successive project provides a lower nave (90 br., 84 br., 76 br.), with the exception of Heinrich's, which is higher than any. For some reason, the Milanese became increasingly anxious to give the cathedral a low, broad section.[39] The Lombard Gothic tradition immediately comes to mind as a possible motivation (cf. fig. 8.1). The emphasis on breadth which is characteristic of the tradition is in violent contrast with the northern Gothic verticality introduced by Heinrich with his square section. The German is influenced by his former connections with Cologne Cathedral, where we can see to what extent a section *ad quadratum* achieves a climax of the vertical aesthetic in Gothic architecture.[40] The evolution of the section, however, cannot be explained on the basis of the aesthetic effect alone, for, after all, two earlier and taller schemes had been temporarily accepted by the council. A more compelling force behind the decision is the buttressing problem, although this is not immediately evident in the report. It will

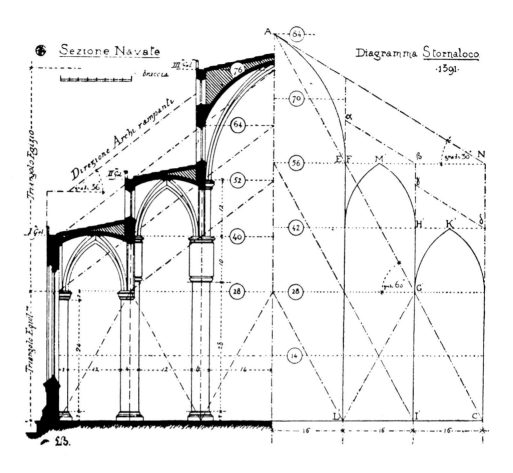

8.6 *Composite drawing of projects illustrated in figure*
8.5B, D.

gradually become apparent that the council wishes to keep the nave low enough for the two side aisles to support it without the aid of additional buttressing, and perhaps even without flying buttresses, as at the Carmine in Pavia. For this reason, the inner aisles retain in all the projects a relatively high elevation in relation to the nave. The extreme caution necessary to carry out such a tradition on an unusually large scale would explain the gradual lowering of the section. The northern builders, who probably regard the flying buttress as their most cherished tool, must have thought the Milanese fools for leaning over backward to avoid its use.

8.7 *Cologne, cathedral, nave section, from Dehio and von Bezold,* Die kirchliche Baukunst des Abendlandes.

Two of the four proposals we have examined for the section are Milanese, and two German. There is a decided difference. The Milanese are not moved by any conception of rational, causative relations among plan, section, and elevation. The upper portion of the cathedral is something entirely unrelated to the lower portion or foundations. Under German influence, geometry is employed, but so confusedly that it loses its meaning. On the other hand, the Germans propose systems which interrelate the foundations and the elevation of the cathedral. Their choice is not arbitrary and capricious, but is limited to two figures, the square and equilateral triangle: the only plausible geometrical figures all sides of which are equal to the established width of the building. Even the geometrical rationalism of the Germans, however, is not the rationalism of Viollet-le-Duc, for two vastly different forms are proposed for the same foundations. The plan must be thought of as structurally independent of the elevation.

Several of the remaining problems considered by the conference may be understood in the light of the decision reached on the various heights. The first of these, concerning the roofing of the western portion of the cathedral, is discussed in *Dubium* 2. The question of whether to construct three roofs (over the nave, inner aisle, and outer aisle) or two (nave, and two side aisles combined) depends on the relative heights of the vaults. In proposing two, Heinrich must again have had Cologne Cathedral in mind and must certainly have intended his outer aisles to be considerably lower than the nave, and of approximately equal height, as in our reconstruction of the section *ad quadratum.* The combining of the outer aisles under one roof, which is quite plausible in this project, becomes impossible when, in a later discussion, the vaults of the middle aisles are fixed at 12 braccia over those of the outer aisles (fig 8.5D). Three roofs became necessary "to afford greater *strength* and *light,*" by which the masters mean that (1) the middle aisle must be relatively high and the nave relatively low for buttressing purposes (hence, the "strength"), and (2) this being determined, a single roof could not cover both aisles without also blocking the windows of the nave (hence, the "light").

The answer given to *Dubium* 8 also is determined by the establishment of a high middle aisle. The "room or corridor" proposed by Heinrich is probably a kind of triforium gallery opening onto the nave above the main arcade, such as may be found throughout medieval architecture and, of course, at Cologne. If the section were designed *ad quadratum,* such a gallery would be desirable as a means of lightening the wall between the main arcade and the clerestory. The main arcade, however, has just been planned to reach to the very springing of the nave vaults, and there is simply no room for such a "corridor." The triforium gallery does not appear in Lombard Gothic churches, and the masters' reply indicates that they consider it a foolish luxury.

The numerous references to "chapels" in the text, and the particular concern for their design shown in *Dubium* 7, is puzzling in view of the fact that they cannot be identified on the plan. However, the references made in *Dubia* 8 and 11 make it clear that the "chapels" are the bays of the outer aisles, and if they are not identifiable as such, it is because of the decision reached in *Responsio* 7, "that they should be made without any dividing wall." Why the term "chapels" is used, once it is determined to build an uninterrupted aisle, is explained in the postscript to the report. Simone da Orsenigo, one of those responsible for the first plans of the cathedral, refers to the "manner in which they [the chapels] are joined beneath the ground," which indicates that the original plan and foundations provided for an outer chapel row such as is found in the standard plan of Lombard Gothic churches (fig. 9.1). This offers convincing evidence for our contention that the first project for the cathedral was in the Lombard tradition, and that its great breadth does not reflect the influence of northern five-aisle plans. Northern influence might appear to effect the tardy decision to change the chapel rows to aisles, but the report suggests a different cause. *Responsio* 7 indicates that the dividing walls are considered useful only if additional "strength" is required. This can only mean that such walls are, in reality, interior buttresses. They are now felt to be unnecessary because the vaults of the nave have been lowered to a point at which their thrust can be absorbed by the two outer aisles without such assistance. The masters are convinced of the stability of the new project, and are anxious to carry it out with a minimum of buttressing of any kind, as is again indicated by *Responsio* 9, where the small wall buttresses of the earliest plan are retained. Heinrich, on the other hand, must feel that the whole support system is dangerous. He is probably constrained to endorse the provincial chapel divisions of *Dubium* 7, as the only means of adequate buttressing which the council would be likely to accept, although he would normally favor an open aisle.[41]

In summary, the various questions posed in the conference, appearing at first sight to be entirely discrete considerations, prove on analysis to be intimately related. The solutions of the conference represent a single-minded aim to establish a low and broad profile with a view toward minimizing the buttressing. This aim has grown with the cathedral, which is now both lower and less buttressed than originally planned. At all points these solutions conflict with the aesthetic and practical concepts of the northern master, to whom they must appear an incomprehensible folly. Heinrich sees in the foundations a bad beginning which might somehow be made into a Cologne Cathedral, but his ideas are so basically opposed to those of the Milanese that even small compromises are impossible. A logical structural system proven by long practice is thus spurned in favor of one which, while it has vague parallels in small, provincial, brick churches, is purely experimental on this scale. Should such an experiment succeed, it would be proof either of the inventive and technical skill of men seeking to find new forms, or the sheer good luck of innocents who will try anything rather than adopt an established foreign style. From our knowledge of the wayward progress of the cathedral thus far, the latter alternative appears the more likely.

The immediate effect of the conference of May 1392 was the dismissal of Heinrich Parler under a shower of invective which he can hardly have deserved.[42] For two years the Milanese proceeded without the hindrance of northern aid, facing the walls and continuing the piers. Their indecision was again made evident in 1393, when it was questioned whether the design of the one pier capital which had been completed should be employed for the remainder.[43] When Ulrich von Ensingen was finally persuaded to come from Ulm to Milan in October 1394, he refused to execute the projected capitals or the apse windows, and left six months later without having reached any understanding with the council.[44]

During the following years, the Milanese were not disturbed by the necessity for imperative decisions, for they simply postponed the final solution of the vaulting problem until the completion of the piers forced it upon them. The appointment of three French engineers in April 1399 indicates that the accumulated weight of construction problems obliged the council to seek again for assistance from the north.[45] By December the leader of the deputation and one assistant had left the field to their persistent and belligerent associate, Jean Mignot, who lost no time in assuring the duke that the cathedral was destined to fall if certain alterations were not immediately undertaken.[46] At a hearing of January 11, 1400, the Frenchman presented his extensive criticisms to the local architects for discussion.

Mignot, like the experts who preceded him, applies standards of construction and theory which are firmly based in northern tradition, and any deviation from his norm he interprets as an error. The fifty-four criticisms which he levels against the council make no concessions to Lombard originality. Although they are partly justified, the aggressive and repetitious manner in which they are presented enrages the other conferees, who refuse to reply to more than half of the items.[47] Most of the criticisms concern details such as the form of moldings and the laying of stone, and must be passed over here. The two exchanges of opinion which we shall examine are perhaps the only ones in which questions of theory play a major role.[48] The conference opens with the most weighty problem, which brings us back again to Heinrich Parler's criticism of the system of piers and buttresses. Mignot says:[49]

First, the piers [or buttresses] which have to support and sustain the rear portions of said church between the large windows are so weak that it is necessary to make two other reinforcing piers next to them, nor will this part of the church be as strong as it should be until these two are made.

The criticism is leveled particularly at the apse of the cathedral. Here the large windows, the small wall buttresses, and the absence of chapels minimize the capacity of the outer wall to sustain the vaults and projected tower.

The masters' retort to this criticism conscientiously traces the construction of the piers from foundation to capital. They begin by asserting that both the counsel of experts and their own formal oath attest to the security of the foundations, which are sunk 14 braccia into the ground.[50] They explain that the lower levels of the foundation are composed of large blocks of stone jointed or doweled together, and that 3½ to 4 braccia are allowed in the upper portions for leveling off, while the marble dado commences in the upper half-braccio of the foundation. The piers themselves are provided with a core of finished building-stone, "and for greater strength they are doweled everywhere with spikes of leaded iron." In answer to the specific criticism of Mignot, they explain that they intend to reinforce the piers by joining one to another with large iron binding-rods to be placed above the capitals.[51] Finally, the council comes to the point which is designed to clinch the argument:

And above said capitals, they determined, as had been [previously] determined, to have pointed arches made according to the type suggested by many other good and expert engineers, who say concerning this that pointed arches do not exert a thrust on the buttresses, and for aforesaid reasons they conclude that all the buttresses are strong and adequate to carry an even greater [weight], wherefore it is not required to make [additional] buttresses in any part of the church.

Suddenly, amid a sober and painstaking analysis of technique, there is injected an explosive mechanical principle, "pointed arches do not exert a thrust on the buttresses." In a single sentence the Milanese have cast off what we consider to be the major structural problem in Gothic architecture. It would indeed be a shock to the modern historian if this view were found to be in general currency among Gothic builders, and it is with some relief that we discover in a later discussion that it is as surprising to Mignot as it is to us. The council, which to this point has appeared to be merely retarded and stubborn, begins, in its antagonism to Mignot, to fabricate strange theories to suit its ends. It becomes apparent that the fervor of its defense is a sign not of superior confidence, but exceptional ignorance.[52]

A second passage concerns a problem in design which is quite different from those we have examined previously, for it is purely aesthetic in nature. One of the unique features of Milan Cathedral is the design of the huge capitals on the piers of the nave and side aisle. Large enough to contain colossal statues of saints in niches, the capitals appear in Antonio's sketch of 1390 (fig. 8.3) and were probably conceived before the advent of northern experts. Mignot's reaction to this invention is what one would expect of a Parisian—he finds it monstrous.[53]

Moreover, that the pier capitals placed in the work above these piers are not placed according to their proper proportion, since the feet of these piers are two braccia regardless of the height, and the capitals are x braccia regardless of the height, and these capitals ought to be of the same height as the feet of these piers.

They say and reply that, according to that reasoning, if the feet or bases of the piers are two braccia, the capitals ought to be one braccia. [However,] they say that the base of the pier is called a foot [after?] the foot of a man, and it is said of the capital [that it is] the head of the pier, so by "capital" is meant the head [caput] of a man. Further, the foot is a fourth part of a man's head, and by this natural law they [the capitals] should be viii braccia, and if they were made x braccia, it is on account of the ornamentation of the piers, for the placing of figures.

The Frenchman's reaction is typically academic. He says, in effect, that a proper Gothic capital is the same height as its base, and no deviation is permissible. Here the Milanese believe that they have the best of their adversary, for they point out that if the capitals were to be truly proper in Mignot's sense, they should be half the size of the base.[54] It is not their intention, however, to observe propriety. Their attitude is epitomized in a statement made in a later controversy with Mignot, "la nostra chiesa non richiede cose vecchie ma nuove,"[55] and their answer is not only non-academic, but amazingly non-Gothic. The anthropomorphic, almost Vitruvian, terms of the defense are decidedly *cose nuove* to medieval aesthetics, and one hesitates to suggest what their source might be. While a certain classical attitude is suggested, the result is not classical proportion. The width of the pier is of no consequence, and while a plausible relationship (1:4) between "foot" and "head" is established, the "body" is not taken into consideration. Consequently, the capital measures one-fifth of the total height of only 40 braccia—an anthropomorphism which takes a sorry view of the human form.[56] The argument, it appears, is something of a fraud, and must have been concocted after the fact. It is our opinion that the actual motivation for designing capitals 8 braccia high is a geometrical reasoning which is entirely consistent with the theory we have so far considered. If the pier is 40 braccia and the capitals 8, then the shaft is 32 braccia, which is precisely the width of the nave itself. Interpreting these measurements geometrically, the height of the shaft is determined *ad quadratum,* a method which is much more likely than the one stated in the argument.[57] Finally, it is typical of the Milanese that, while they adduce a law to explain their design, they do not consider it binding. They feel that if the proportions prejudice the decorative scheme, they may justifiably be altered, and thus the capitals are enlarged by two braccia to provide ample room for the statues. The compromising of these measurements, like the compromising of the principle of triangulation, reveals an indifference to a theory which the unorthodox and illogical arguments prove to be largely beyond the comprehension of the Milanese masters.

Mignot's first conference bore no fruit, and a fortnight after the hearing in which the fifty-four criticisms were considered, a second meeting was called to reconsider his most serious allegations. The report on the proceedings, which we present in full, begins:[58]

Master Jean Mignot has stated to the council here present that he has given in writing to the said council a note computing to date all the reasons and every motive which lead him to say that aforesaid work lacks strength, and he does not wish to give other reasons.

Final statements given by aforesaid Master Jean on the 25th day of January.

Master Jean Mignot points out to you excellent lords of the workshop council of the Milanese church with respect and pure truth, that as he has demonstrated in writing elsewhere and among other matters the defects of said church, he reiterates and affirms that all the buttresses around this church are neither strong nor able to sustain the weight which rests upon them, since they ought in every case to be three times the thickness of one pier in the interior of the church.

The Masters reply:

Concerning the first statement, they say that all the buttresses of said church are strong and capable of sustaining their weight and many times more, for many reasons, since one braccio of our marble and saritium,[59] *whatever its width, is as strong as two braccia of French stone or of the French church which he gives to the aforesaid masters as an example. Therefore they say that if aforesaid buttresses are one-and-a-half times [the size]—and they are—of the piers in the interior of the church, that they are strong and correctly conceived, and if they were larger they would darken said church because of their projection, as at the church in Paris, which has buttresses of Master Jean's type, and since they can be an obstruction [there are] other reasons.*

This chauvinistic retort provides a highly entertaining insight into the council's method of reasoning, but the argument reveals more than mere prejudices. First of all, Mignot categorically states that there should be a 1:3 ratio of thickness between the piers and buttresses. It is possible that this ratio represents his final estimate of the peculiar requirements of Milan Cathedral, but it is more likely that he is applying a simple rule of thumb which is common practice among northern architects. None of Mignot's statements, either here or in the previous conference, gives any indication that he has even a crude means of arriving at a more precise estimate of the amount of buttressing required. In a sense, the terms of the ratio create a simple relationship between the mass of one member and another in the same way that the section *ad triangulum* relates their profiles. It is noteworthy that, while the Milanese propose a drastically different solution, they place particular emphasis on a similarly simple relationship of 1:1½.

It is particularly interesting that the masters' defense is based solely on the argument that the size of a buttress should be determined in inverse proportion to the *strength* of its component materials. The strength of masonry is of course a factor in computing support, but one may well be suspicious of the Italians' claim of great superiority in this respect. While they may be justified in proposing buttresses smaller than those of the "church in Paris," one feels that the real justification lies less in the greater strength of their materials than in the lesser thrust on their exterior walls. Had they been aware of thrust, the weight and mass of the buttresses would probably have concerned them more than the strength, but we know from their earlier estimate of the pointed arch that they were not conscious of the problem.

Of the two solutions offered, one is based on traditional northern practice, the other on a mixture of Lombard tradition and sheer ignorance, but neither on an accurate estimate of the requirements. It might be objected that this judgment is harsh in relation to Mignot, for his solution is founded on reasonable premises; but the evidence indicates that—in defiance of reasonability—the council's solution triumphs, and the present-day buttresses are indeed half the size demanded by the Frenchman! The empirical solutions of both parties to the dispute are, from the modern point of view, unscientific. They are not, however, irrational, for they establish a relation between members which, though irrelevant to us, is meaningful to their authors.

The remainder of the discussion follows:

Moreover, he says that four towers were begun to support the crossing tower of said church, and there are no piers nor any foundation capable of sustaining said towers, and if the church were to be made with said towers in this position it would infallibly fall. Concerning the claims, however, which were made by certain ignorant people, surely through passion, that pointed vaults are stronger and exert less thrust than round, and moreover concerning other matters, proposals were made in a fashion more willful than sound; and what is worse, it was objected that the science of geometry should not have a place in these matters, since science is one thing and art another. Said master Jean says that art without science is nothing [ars sine scientia nihil est], *and that whether the vaults are pointed or round, they are worthless unless they have a good foundation, and nevertheless, no matter how pointed they are, they have a very great thrust and weight.*

Whereupon they [the Masters] *say that the towers which they wanted to make are for many reasons and causes* [desirable]. *Namely, in the first place, to integrate aforesaid church and transept so that they correspond to a rectangle according to the demands of geometry,*[60] *but beyond this, for the strength and beauty of the crossing tower. To be sure, as if as a model of this, the Lord God is seated in Paradise in the center of the throne, and around the throne are the four Evangelists according to the Apocalypse, and these are the reasons why they were begun. And although two piers of each sacristy are not founded, but begin at ground level, the church is truly strong nevertheless for these reasons, that there are projections upon which the said piers stand, and the said projections are of large stones and joined with iron dowels as was said above with other statements, and that the weight on these three* [sic] *towers fall evenly on their square, and they will be built properly and strong, and what is vertical cannot fall; therefore they say that they are strong in themselves, and for that reason will give strength to the crossing tower, which is enclosed in the center of those towers. Therefore said church is truly strong.*

Mignot makes one specific criticism: that the four towers to be placed at the corners of the crossing tower cannot be supported. In defense of its design, the council makes four points, of which the first two purport to justify the theory underlying the towers, and the remaining two the technique of construction. The first establishes a certain relation between the towers and the crossing, "according to the demands of geometry." Again, we have the suggestion of an interrelation of part to part, in this case an element in the plan to an exterior elevation. How the four subsidiary towers effect this integration is unclear. It may be that they are intended as a symbolic emphasis to the geometrical character of the plan, but it is more likely that they were conceived for non-theoretical reasons, and that the geometrical apology is concocted on the spur of the moment in the face of Mignot's accusations. Geometry does not explain the towers, it excuses them. The second statement, which compares the design to an Apocalyptic vision, is a delightful addition to the study of the iconography of architecture. It is undoubtedly more congenial to the Milanese than the struggle with geometry, but if calculated to convince Mignot, it must fail completely, for it evidences an attitude very different from the abstract mathematical theory of the northerners. Like many of the preceding theoretical demonstrations, it rationalizes a design conceived without benefit of theory.

In defense of the construction, the first point is purely technical, claiming that the absence of foundations beneath the sacristy piers is compensated for by secure doweling. This judgment is questioned later, as we have seen in the expertise of February 1400, quoted in note 52. The final argument is as irrational as that which concerns pointed arches. It claims that the security of the project is assured, first because the weight of the towers is to be evenly distributed on their square base, and second because *"what is vertical cannot fall."* In other words, neither the size and weight of the towers, nor the number and mass of their supports (to say nothing of the stresses created) are significant, if their construction is rectilinear. Fortunately, the design under discussion was never carried out.

The meeting closes with the following exchange:

Moreover he [Mignot] recognizes that their premises are willfully conceived, nor do those who disagree wish to give in to the right and the betterment of said church and workshop, but want to win their case either for their own profit or from fear, or else from obstinacy, since they would like to continue in spite of defects. For this reason said master Jean requests that four or six or twelve of the better engineers who are expert in these matters might be brought together, either from Germany, England, or France, otherwise said work will certainly fall, which would be a great loss in every way. Further, to make the truth clear and to conserve his honor, he wishes to be allowed an audience with the illustrious lord the Lord, to explain to him in general the aforesaid things and other matters. Moreover, he indicates that it would be for the good of the church to work elsewhere in said church than over defective places, at least until such time as provisions and decisions might be clearly made concerning these defects.

Whereupon they [the masters] say and reply in the same statement, that where it says that the science of geometry should not have a place in these [matters], the above-mentioned say: if he [Mignot] invokes, as it were, the rules of geometry, Aristotle says that the movement of man in space which we call locomotion is either straight or

*circular or a mixture of the two. Likewise the same [writer] says elsewhere that every
body is perfected in three [ways], and the movement of this very church rises* ad triangulum *as has been determined by other engineers. So they say that all [the measure-
ments] are in a straight line, or an arch,*[61] *therefore it is concluded that what has been
done, has been done according to geometry and to practice, and he [Mignot] has said
that science without art is nothing; concerning art, however, replies have been made
already in other statements.*

Considering the conference as a whole, it becomes abundantly clear that the
attack with which Mignot opens the meeting is justified. We see that he ascribes the
council's position on the pointed arch to "ignorance" and "passion." His main objection, however, is to the council's contention that "the science of geometry should not
have a place in these matters since science is one thing and art another." This exposes
the crucial difference between the two schools of thought which we have repeatedly
emphasized. For "science" we may read "theory"—the higher learning in architecture.
Mignot goes on to imply that it is through ignorance of this "science" that the council
is unaware of the "very great thrust and weight" of a pointed arch, or vault. Without
this science, he says, art is nothing. He is not, of course, talking of "art" in the modern
sense, but in the sense of craft; in this case the craft of the mason. His statement may
be paraphrased to read, "technical proficiency in building is worthless if the higher
geometrical principles are not employed." There is no question that the implied criticism is warranted. The axiom "what is vertical cannot fall," which we have just considered, is an excellent example of thinking in terms of "art without science," for it
suggests that the soundness of the scheme depends solely on good technique. In retrospect, a large part of the entire Milanese defense champions "art," as we are reminded
by the closing statement of the meeting. In defending the apse supports, they tirelessly
describe the foundations; in defending the buttresses they affirm the superiority of their
masonry, and so forth. The pride which they display in their technique is understandable, since the Lombards are famed for their masonry from the early Middle Ages
through the Renaissance.

The partiality which the Milanese manifest for "art" in contrast to "science"
is explained by a familiarity with the former (which is probably greater than Mignot's),
and an almost complete ignorance of the latter. We cannot ignore, however, their occasional flights into the realms of geometry. In such cases, one has the impression that,
while they are quite discomforted by a science in which they have so little proficiency,
they are constrained to pay it lip-service. The history of the triangular section, for
example, proves that foreign influences were the cause of this constraint, for the section

projected before the advent of northerners was designed without the aid of geometry. Similarly, in the closing argument of the present conference, the Milanese are shamed by Mignot into a scientific discourse which it is far beyond their capacity to carry off. In attempting to hide their deficiencies, the masters have taken cover behind irrelevant quotations from Aristotle, intending the mere reference to lend authority to their claims. The first of their "geometrical" proofs is borrowed from a passage in the *Physics* which concerns infinite motion.[62] Chosen for the reason that it refers to straight and circular lines, it is perverted into a rationalization of the straight lines and arches of the cathedral. It may readily be seen that this argument is invalid; not only because it implicitly claims that the cathedral is correctly designed simply because it has piers and arches, but also because it applies a law of locomotion to a problem which is specifically claimed to be geometrical. The second proof is more to the point, for in defending the triangular section, the council is actually demonstrating an example of its deference to geometry. The attempt to adduce the support of Aristotle, however, is again abortive. The statement "every body is perfected in three ways" is adapted from certain passages of Aristotle which refer not to extension but to dimension (the "three ways" are height, breadth, and depth), and its application to the triangle (which has three sides but only two dimensions) completely perverts the original meaning.[63] The entire passage shows that the question of "science" has caught the council unawares. The masters are in such a hurry to appear scientific that they choose the wrong passages, if not the wrong authority, for a *post facto* rationalization of their work. Having grossly misused Aristotle, they apply the same treatment to Mignot, and, reversing his statement to suit their own philosophy, they conclude with the misquotation "science without art is nothing."

As might be expected, the meeting ends in the same spirit of antagonism in which it begins. The discussion bears fruit in one respect, however, for Mignot apparently wins the support of the duke. Foreign experts are shortly invited to pass judgment, and over a year later, the Frenchman is still in good graces, as indicated by a letter of July 25, 1401, from the ducal secretary to the deputies of the cathedral.[64] Further evidence of Mignot's influence is provided in the final conference held under his leadership, on May 15, 1401.[65] Here the word-for-word transcription of the proceedings permits us to see that a majority of the masters take his part, but this reversal of the council's policy is probably due more to a change of personnel than to a change of heart.

This conference, not attended by Mignot, deals principally with his designs for the vaulting of the cathedral. The debate is peculiarly bitter for, as one of the discussions proves, twelve to sixteen stones have already been laid, and sixty to seventy cut, for one or more vaults to be completed according to the original design.[66] Here the procedure is even more irregular than before, for a major change is considered for a portion already under construction. It is not possible to examine here the full text of this lengthy conference, nor is it necessary, for the many pages of heated argument serve to prove but one point: that neither the partisans nor the opponents of Mignot have the means of determining whether the proposed vaults are sounder or more desirable than those under construction. There is simply no common ground upon which varying attitudes may be discussed. The masters disagree on whether the new project is more solid; whether it is more "beautiful and raiseworthy"; whether it will cost more, and if so, how much; and whether the stones used must be larger or smaller than in the earlier project. The one problem which the "science of geometry" might be expected to solve without question is the last to be considered, and is stated, "VII Question: If, following the form of the second project, the work would be changed only with respect to the former dispositions concerning the maximum height or width of the church, or would its essential form be somehow changed?"[67] To our amazement, the question discloses that Mignot's project might involve a change in the proportions of the church itself—that here, at the last moment, the scheme of triangulation formulated nine years before is still open to revision. This question would seem to be formulated in a way that leaves no room for controversy, but the answers show the widest possible divergence of opinion concerning the effect of the project on the form of the church, as is evidenced by the following excerpts from the report.

Paderno: I reply that since the design presented by master Giovanni does not contain any indication as to the height of all the arches, as had been done by other engineers, I cannot reply concerning the height of the vault, only because he makes no sign of it on his design.

Serina: Replies that the main, center nave would become 8 braccia higher than that which was first arranged, after the design and the measurements given by master Giovanni, by whom a miracle must be in the making, since this same master Giovanni has said at other times that the whole edifice was not solid, and now, being even higher, it must needs be even less solid.

Calco: Replies that, following the form of the new project, one would not change the disposition already given relative to the maximum height and width, or relative to any substantial form, but only with respect to the maximum mass [grossezza] of the body of the church.

Della Croce: Following the form of the second project, one would change the false system already in place and respect the proper system of the triangle, which cannot be abandoned without error, as master Enrico and a certain German master Annex, before him, preached in former times with a high and faithful voice into the ears of deaf fools.

The remaining masters, with one exception, agree that certain changes in proportion are implicit in the project, but fail to specify what they may be. It is strange that the drawing which Mignot has presented for discussion gives no indication concerning the measurement of the vaults. Lacking any definite figures, let us tentatively assume that Serina's estimate of an 8-braccia alteration in the nave is correct. This is highly probable, for the previously established height of 76 braccia would thus become 84 braccia, which is, of course, just the height proposed by Stornaloco in 1391. In other words, Mignot has made an eleventh-hour attempt to restore the equilateral triangle. This interpretation fortunately helps us to explain the otherwise unclear statement of Della Croce, in which he pointedly favors the abandonment of the existing system of triangulation, and yet praises the new project because it "rispetta il retto ordine del triangolo." How can he be opposed to the triangle and yet support it? Obviously he makes a distinction between kinds of triangles: the *retto ordine* is the equilateral form, and the *falso ordine,* the Pythagorean compromise of 1392.

If Mignot's proposal actually restores the height of Stornaloco's design, it does so merely by raising the vaults themselves, and thus involves an even greater compromise than the 1392 solution, for these vaults must spring from capitals already constructed according to the earlier scheme. The result would be, so to speak, a Pythagorean sandwich on equilateral bread.[68] Mignot's supporters excuse this inconsistency by pointing out that he had no opportunity to reconstruct the church as it should be. This fifth and last in the series of solutions for the section is not employed. As has been indicated, the present cathedral follows the scheme of 1392. Following this failure, we hear of Mignot only in connection with the accusations leveled at him, and the defense made in his behalf by his Milanese supporters. His dismissal on October 22, 1401, becomes a subject of controversy which continues well into the following year.[69]

In retrospect, the history of foreign intervention which Mignot's departure brings to a temporary close seems distinguished more by the failures than the successes of the visiting experts. Time and again northern masters expose the inadequacy of the entire structural system, attribute to it faults of the greatest magnitude, and leave, convinced that the work is destined to ruin. The Milanese plod stubbornly along, borrowing from the visitors here a superficial decorative device and there a geometrical phrase, but on the whole determined to accept no foreign solutions to the major problems in construction. While the piers may originally have been redesigned by Nicolas de Bonaventure, they are not altered to suit the demands of Parler and Mignot. The original foundations and buttresses remain unchanged despite criticism from both Italian and northern engineers, and the elevation of the cathedral remains too low to satisfy anyone but a Lombard.

The fact that the contentions of the northerners appear sound, and that they are repeatedly voiced by numerous critics over a ten-year period, in itself prejudices us against the Milanese. Any doubts that remain are dispelled by a defense which is alternately absurd and unwise. Only one argument, and an incontrovertible one, speaks in favor of the Milanese: the cathedral was built entirely according to their designs, and it stands. The poor foundations, weak piers, inadequate buttresses, undivided chapels, the *falso ordine* of triangulation, and vaults which "do not exert a thrust on the buttresses," have successfully survived five and a half centuries. Moreover, the present flying buttresses, which would appear to be the unique concession to northern criticism, are in fact an addition of the late eighteenth and early nineteenth centuries.[70] In the mid-eighteenth-century print reproduced in figure 8.8, we see the upper portion of the cathedral buttressed only by a low wedge of masonry. This is the crowning success of the Lombard Gothic system. Consequently, for all the learning of the northerners and the shocking and amusing ignorance of the Milanese, the cathedral itself is evidence to the fact that the former were in error and the latter triumphantly justified. Their achievements rather than their words demonstrate that "science without art is nothing."

It is our great good fortune that we have in hand not only evidence of the singular philosophy of medieval building which explains the late, provincial style of Milan Cathedral itself, but also a rich fund of information on the Gothic theory which undoubtedly prevailed throughout western Europe. In examining this theory, or rather, *scientia,* we are first struck by the fact that it does not approach structural problems in a manner which we would regard as scientific. Mignot, for example, while recognizing the thrust exerted by a rib vault, is unable to make even a vague estimate of its force, and demands buttresses of twice the necessary size. Moreover, having declared the structure inadequate to carry the vaults projected by the council, he proceeds to design

8.8 *Milan, cathedral, anonymous eighteenth-century*
drawing. From Boito, Il Duomo di Milano.

vaults of his own which would have further increased the stresses. At no point in the various controversies over structure is either party to the debate able to provide reasons for believing that a given member will or will not serve its purpose. The northern experts simply draw upon their experience and on Gothic tradition, and attempt to reproduce northern forms at Milan, without consideration or understanding of the peculiar structural requirements of the cathedral.

Such shortcomings suggest that to approach this *scientia,* it is necessary to put aside the predominantly mechanical or structural implications which the term "science" suggests to the modern mind. The *scientia* is not that of the modern engineer, but, to our way of thinking, a discipline larger in scope, if less effective in practice. In essence, it is based on the adoption of certain *a priori* formulae to which the entire structural *and* aesthetic character of a building must conform. The geometrical projects for the design of the section of Milan Cathedral immediately come to mind as the most striking example of the use of such formulae. Generally considered by scholars out of their proper context, they have been frequently misinterpreted.

The principal function of the geometrical formulae has already been suggested. They establish ideal figures for the whole which are reflected in consistent relationships throughout the parts of the cathedral. Within certain limits the figures, and consequently the relationships, may be altered, as is demonstrated by the choice between the triangle and the square. Certain similarities between this approach and antique and Renaissance canons of proportion are evident, but it is of utmost importance for the understanding of our theory that we be aware of the differences. The classical system of proportions is what might be called organic. That is, a particular element such as a column is proportionately taller and wider in a large building than in a small one. The Gothic approach is what might be called abstract, and is comparatively unconcerned with proportions. Here the height and breadth of a particular element are determined only by a simple mathematical relationship to the whole scheme, and given this, the element may be relatively tall or short, wide or thin, according to the circumstances in which it is used. In essence, the difference is that a given element has no autonomous existence, but gains its form only by virtue of its logical association to the whole. Our *scientia* may thus be called a theory of consistent relationships. The tests to which it is put at Milan prove that, while it does not demand a particular proportion between the given width and the height of the cathedral or its parts, it is highly critical of the mixture of triangular figures which disrupts the consistency of the relationships. Furthermore, it may be assumed that the interrelation of parts provided by geometrical formulae compensates for the Gothic engineer's ignorance of the laws of mechanics. In a sense, this interrelation is a symbol of structural stability. This function of geometry is emphasized by Mignot in the speech in which he emphasizes the importance of *scientia*, for he speaks of the "scientia geometriae" only in connection with structural problems: the support of the crossing tower, and the thrust of a pointed arch. It is obvious that whatever knowledge Mignot has of stresses and thrusts is attributed to geometry. He consequently feels that a structure which does not conform to a simple geometrical figure is unsound. His late design for the vaulting, which actually increases the thrust by raising the arches, is judged sounder than the earlier solution for the specific reason that it restores the equilateral triangle.

The contrast between the organic character of classical proportions and the abstract relationships of this *scientia* may be carried farther. Given the plan of an antique temple, one is able to reconstruct the elevation with fair accuracy. In contrast, given the plan of Milan Cathedral, even its architects are unable to agree upon an elevation. This may be partially attributed to inexperience, but is due principally to the limitations of an abstract theory. For the reason that no member of a Gothic structure has an autonomous existence, there is no established connection between plan and elevation or plan and section. It is this disconnection which makes a triangular and square section equally plausible for Milan's predetermined plan. For the same reason, once the position of a given member is established there remains the problem of determining its extension. This is not a geometrical problem. The section *ad triangulum,* for example, represents a pier by a line, and a plan designed geometrically would represent it as a dot. We have already had an indication of the next step in the design. The *scientia* employs arithmetical formulae in much the same fashion as geometrical. Thus the thickness of the buttress is discussed in terms of a simple numerical relationship with the thickness of the piers, Mignot's 3:1 formula being opposed by the council's 1½:1. By this means, two elements which are interrelated in elevation through the triangular formula are also interrelated in section through the numerical. How the breadth of the piers themselves was originally established is not discussed in the texts, but the answer may be found in the left-hand portion of figure 8.6. The piers are 4 braccia wide and hence stand in a relation of 1:3 to the intercolumnar space of 12 braccia. While it appears irrational in terms of modern mechanics that the thickness of a buttress should be established in terms of the thickness of the piers, it is quite logical in terms of the theory we are examining, for this theory is built not on forces, but on relationships.

These arithmetical formulae may also be employed for the establishment of relationships within a given member, as we have seen in the controversy over the pier capitals. We recall that Mignot and the Milanese disagree over the orthodox ratio between the base and capital (they argue 1:1 and 2:1 respectively), and that finally the unusual proportion of 1:4 is accepted. Now this controversy takes place after the piers have been raised. The 2-braccia height of the base has already been established, not in accordance with the height of the piers (which had not been determined when the bases were designed), but in accordance with their width of 4 braccia, to which its ratio is 1:2. Furthermore, the height of the shaft is established *ad quadratum,* in accordance with the width of the nave. Finally, when the capitals are discussed, they are related, not to the pier as a whole, but only to the bases. This rather confusing procedure is a consequence of a theory of interrelationships as against one of organic proportions. The form of the pier is determined by a series of discrete ratios.[71]

In summary, the *scientia* which we are examining is based on the employment of simple geometrical and arithmetical formulae, the purpose of which is to establish a complex of abstract relationships connecting the parts of a building to the whole, and interconnecting the parts. The theory is extremely sophisticated, but has one shortcoming which may be readily appreciated: given a problem which may be solved by two reasonable formulae of equal simplicity, there is no provision for determining which is preferable. Thus the problem of choosing a square or triangular section, or a 3:1 or 1½:1 ratio of buttress to pier, may be solved only by considerations exterior to the *scientia.* It is here that the medieval builder calls upon *ars.* Questions which the theory is too abstract to answer are referred to traditional practice and to the mason's skill. *Scientia* and *ars* are the handmaidens of medieval building, and each plays its decisive role in the creative process. It is irrelevant to question which of the two is preeminent, and the controversy on this subject at Milan is evidence only of the "artistic" deficiencies of the northerners, and the "scientific" deficiencies of the Milanese.

Our consideration of this theory cannot be closed without reference to its strikingly apparent Platonic character. The actual cathedral, being a compromise between *scientia* and *ars,* becomes in a sense an imperfect imitation of the ideal cathedral envisaged by *scientia.* A more obvious and direct influence of Platonic concepts is observable in the choice of geometrical formulae. As Dr. Frankl has pointed out, "Plato sanctified the equilateral triangle and the square,"[72] and it is partially for this reason that the northern experts at Milan prefer these two figures as the basis for solving the problem of the section. By Platonic standards, the inconsistent triangulation of the present cathedral is not only "falso," but ugly.[73] It is particularly interesting that, in view of the Platonic character of the theory, the Milanese should choose to employ Aristotelian quotations in their defense. As it happens, their confusion is such that they attempt to justify geometrical figures by physical and astronomical laws, but in more capable hands, the readjustment of Gothic *scientia* along Aristotelian lines might have had far-reaching consequences. By 1400, the Platonic theory of the northern architects had become academic, and tended to stifle the investigation of new possibilities in their art. It is only by virtue of ignoring this theory that certain successful experiments were made by the Milanese, though their lack of erudition prevented them from formulating a new *scientia* from their practice. Though it never came to fruition, it is exciting to speculate what an Aristotelian theory of architecture might have been.

In conclusion, let us return to our consideration of the position of the Gothic rationalists, to determine whether, on the basis of the material we have examined, it may be said that "tout membre de cette architecture est la conséquence d'un besoin de la structure." First of all, we have seen that, regardless of the intentions of the architects of Milan Cathedral, the method of construction made it impossible for structural considerations to determine the forms of members. As we have consistently shown, almost every member was designed before its structural purpose had been determined. The entire plan was conceived for a cathedral considerably different from that which was erected; buttresses and piers rose toward an unknown objective, and finally the primary and basic structural problem, that of the vaults, was the last to be solved. At Milan, however, construction was carried on, to use Mignot's phrase, "in a fashion more willful than sound." It remains to be seen whether structural considerations would have been preeminent in determining the form of any other Gothic cathedral. If our northern *scientia* is any indication, it would appear that structure plays a secondary role in the process of creation. The overall character of the Gothic cathedral is determined on the basis of geometrical grids of lines and dots in which the specific problems of form and structure play no part. Within this embracing pattern, the actual elements of the cathedral thereafter take shape by virtue of a compromise of ideal formulae and practical know-how. The medieval builder is evidently concerned with the problem of balancing theory (or *scientia*) and practice (or *ars*). In no sense is this equivalent to the distinction between structure and form. Structure and form are intimately related and interconnected in every step of the creative process.[74]

In consequence, to impute to Gothic architecture a theory of "form follows function" is to make not only an error in interpretation but an error in method, for the dichotomy of form and structure so cherished by recent criticisms simply does not exist for the Gothic architect. The formulae of Gothic theory establish generalities of form and structure as one, while the methods of Gothic "art" particularize them. The modern argument of form versus structure is as meaningless as the medieval argument of *ars* versus *scientia,* for it likewise disrupts a partnership which can function only in happy union.

Appendix

I. 1392. Mercoledi, 1° Maggio

Coll'intervento di tutti gli ingegneri sottonominati—maestri, Giovanni da Ferrara, Zanello da Binasco, Stefano Magatto, Bernardo da Venezia, Giovannino de' Grassi, Giacomo da Campione, Simone da Orsenigo, Pietro de' Villa, Enrico da Gamondia (qui non consensit), Lorenzo degli Spazii, Guarnerio da Sirtori, Ambrogio da Melzo, Pietro da Cremona, Paolo degli Osnago.

Omnes congregati in camera fabricae ecclesiae mediolanensis pro tollendis pluribus dubiis quae moventur super fabrica ipsius ecclesiae, quae dubia inferius distincte specificantur, et juxta dubia factea sunt responsiones et declarationes per omnes ipsos inzignerios, excepto ipso magistro Henricho, qui quamvis responsiones ipsae siti datae ad intelligendum, ipsis declarationibus nullatenus consensit.

Dubium.—Utrum partes ecclesiae tam posteriores quam collaterales et interiores, scilicet pilloni tam tiburii quam alii minores habeant fortitudinem suffitientem?

Responsio.—Deliberaverunt, responderunt et declaraverunt super eorum animabus et conscientiis quod in praedictis omnibus et singulis est fortitudo suffitiens etiam ad majora sustinenda.

D. Utrum ipsa ecclesia debeat pluere in duobus tectis an in pluribus, proportionabiliter fiendis ab utraque parte usque ad croxeriam?

R. Deliberaverunt quod ipsa ecclesia debet et habet pluere pro majori fortitudine et claritate in tribus tectis et non in duobus.

D. Utrum ecclesia ipsa non computando in mensura tiburium fiendum debeat ascendere ad quadratum an ad triangulum?

R. Declaraverunt quod ipsa posset ascendere usque ad triangulum sive usque ad figuram triangularem et non ultra.

D. Quot brachia debent fieri pilloni servientes navi majori sive navi de medio?

R. Declaraverunt quod ipsi pilloni computando bases et capitellos debent ascendere brachia quadraginta et non ultra.

D. Quot brachia debent ascendere medii pilloni qui in muro fient super ipsis pillonis magnis usque ad volturas sive arcus super inde fiendos, et quot brachiorum debent esse volturae super ipsis fiendae?

R. Deliberaverunt et declaraverunt quod medii pilloni sint brachiorum duodecim, et voltura ipsius majoris navis ascendat ad triangulum, videlicet brachia vigintiquatuor.

D. Quid sibi videatur de designamento unius portae gemellae croxeriae versus Compedum cum tota facie ipsius croxeriae?

R. Ea visa et perspecta declaraverunt quod ipsa est valde pulchra et bona ac honorabilis, et quod super ea procedatur.

D. Utrum debeant mediari sive intramezari capellae ipsius ecclesiae muro, una ab altera, nec ne?

R. Declaraverunt, quia non egent ipsae capellae aliqua alia fortitudine, quod remaneant et fiant sine alio medio, seu sine muro mediano.

D. Utrum debeat fieri una sala sive unus corrator supra secunda navi, quae est inter navim magnam et capellas ecclesiae?

R. Dixerunt quod ipsa sala nullatenus est fienda quia occupat aerem et adducit expensas.

D. Utrum sit procedendum ad laborandum pillonos sive contrafortes exteriores prout est incoeptum, an aliquid innovari?

R. Dixerunt quod id opus sibi placet, et quod non est aliquid mutandum, ymo est procedendum ad laborandum.

D. Utrum debeat procedi super pillonis guerziis an aliquid de eis dimoveri vel commutari?

R. Deliberaverunt quod ipsi pilloni, quia suas debitas proportiones et membra habent, non sunt movendi, ymo perfitienti et affinandi.

D. Quot brachia debent ascendere pilloni minores sive pilloni capellarum et medii pilloni, qui cum muro super eis fieri debent usque ad archus respondentes versus navem magnam?

R. Responderunt et declaraverunt quod illi minores pilloni debent esse alti brachia 28, et medii piloni super eis construendi usque ad archus sint et esse debeant brachiorum 12, computatis in ipsis mensuris bases et capitellos.

(*Annali,* 1, 68, 69)

Ia. 1392. Giovedì, 2 maggio

Tutti gli ingegneri intervenuti nella seduta di jeri confermano in ogni sua parte quello che è scritto più sopra, eccettuato Simone da Orsenigo il quale vi consente in massima, fourchè dice doversi le cappelle della chiesa tramezzare con muro nello stesso modo con cui sono state collegate sotto terra.

(*Annali*, 1, 69)

II. 1400. Domenica, 11 gennaio

Deliberarono pagarsi i notaj, che scrivono i difetti e rimedii necessarii per la fabbrica dietro la requisizione dell'ingegnere Giovanni Mignoto di Parigi. Le dette note sono come segue:

1. Dubbii elevati dal Mignoto, e risposte degli ingegneri della fabbrica:

Item piloni qui habent manutenere et sustinere dictam ecclesiam a parte posteriori inter magnas fenestras sunt debiles per modum quod expedit duos alias pilones remediabiles apud illos facere, nec adhuc ipsis duobus factis et ea pars ipsa ipsius ecclesiae erit fortis sicut deberet esse.

Respondunt ipsi magistri quod habita informatione et deliberatione cum pluribus et discretis personis, qui interfuerunt fundamentis dictae ecclesiae, et qui per sacramentum eis delatum in manibus dominorum vicarii provisionum et multorum aliorum sapientium fabricae praedictae, et qui laboraverunt ad faciendum fundamenta ecclesiae a parte posteriori et in aliis partibus, et qui per suum sacramentum dixerunt praedictum opus est bene fundatum cum sit profundatum per br. XIV [*sic*] usque ad anixium, et quod in primo cursu positi sunt lapides magni sarrizii et sunt retracti in dicto fundamento, et in multis aliis partibus sunt inclavati magnis lapidibus sarrizii, et quod super dicto fundamento ex dictis brachiis XIV vel id circa sunt brachia tria cum dimidio et quator pro adequato sarrizii computata bancha et retracta banchae usque ad marmorem est brachium medium vel id circa. Item retracta cornixiarum marmoris est quartarum trium cum dimidia usque ad murum rectum et murus contrafortum et pilonorum simul se tenentium cum aliis est de lapidibus marmoreis intus ecclesiam et extra, et in medio piloni sunt lapides sarizii bene splanati et bene clavati, et ad majorem fortitudinem sunt clavati cum clavelis ferri pomblatis ubique. Et praedicta omnia patent. Et ulterius praedicti magistri volunt super capitellis ponere ferros seu strictores ferri magnos qui inclavent unum pilonem cum altero et ita fiat ubique per totam ecclesiam. Et super dictis capitellis deliberaverunt prout deliberatum est fiere facere archus spigutos secundum ordinem datum per multos alios inzignerios bonos et expertos, inde dicunt quod archi spiguti non dant impulzam contrafortibus, et rationibus praedictis concludunt omnes contrafortes esse fortes et sufficientes ad majus onus, quapropter non indigent facere contrafortes ecclesiae in nulla parte.

(*Annali,* 1, 202, 203)

IIa.

    8.   Item quod ex illis pilonis viginti duobus qui sunt infra crucem et navem dictae ecclesiae adsunt piloni decem et octo, qui non respondent prout correspondere debent ad suam rationem debitam, alii vero quatuor piloni qui sunt posteriores bene se respondent.

    Dicunt et respondent quod piloni quos ipse magister Johannes asserit esse XXII et non sunt nisi XXI qui appareant, inter quos adsunt quindecim qui respondent ad suum quadrum bene ordinatum, alii vero sex correspondent ad retondum secundum suum ordinem.

(*Annali,* 1, 203)

IIb.

    9.   Item quod capitelli pilonorum positi in opera supra ipsis pilonis non sunt positi ad rationem suam, quia pedes ipsorum pilonorum sunt brachiorum duorum pro quolibet in longitudine, et capitelli sunt br. X pro quolibet ipsorum in longitudine, debent esse ipsi capitelli tantae longitudinis quantae sunt pedes ipsorum pilonorum.

    Dicunt et respondent quod pedes sive bassae pironorum si sunt brachiorum II capitelli debent esse brachium unum, ipsis rationibus dicunt bassam pironorum et pes dicitur pes hominis et capitellum dicitur caput piloni, ita caput hominis dicitur a capitello. Ita quod pes est quarta pars capitis hominis et per istam rationem naturalem deberent esse brachia VIII et si essent facti de br. X essent propter ad ornamentum pironorum pro ponendo figuras.

(*Annali,* 1, 203, 204)

III. 1400. Domenica, 25 gennaio

    Magister Johannes Mignotius de Parisiis dixit in consilio praesenti dedisse in scriptis usque nunc computata caedula per eum data in consilio praedicto omnes rationes et omnia motiva per quae vult dicere praedicta opera non habere fortitudinem et alias rationes non velle dicere.

    Capitula ultimata data per suprascriptum magistrum Johannem de die 25 januarii.

1. Vobis egregiis dominis de consilio fabricae ecclesiae Mediolani cum reverentia et pura veritate significat magister Johannes Mignotius quod, sicut alias et inter alios defectos dictae ecclesiae exhibuit in scriptis, iterato dicit et proponit quod omnes contrafortes circum circha dictam ecclesiam non sunt fortes nec habiles ad sustinendum onus quod eis incumbet quia debent esse tribus vicibus pro quolibet grossis quantum est grossus unus pilonus de intus ecclesiam.

Magistri respondent:

Supra primo capitulo dicunt quod omnes contrafortes dictae ecclesiae sunt fortes et habiles ad sustinendum suum onus et plus multis rationibus quia unus brachius nostri marmoris et sarizii in quolibet latere est tam fortis sicut brachia duo lapidum Franziae vel ecclesiae Franziae quam dat in exemplum suprascriptis magistris. Qui inde dicunt quod si sunt et sunt totidem et medium quotidem sunt piloni intus ecclesiam praedictos contrafortes esse fortes et esse ad suam rationem, et si fuissent majores obscurassent ecclesiam praedictam obstante, videlicet ecclesia Parisiis, et quae habet contrafortes ad modum magistri Johannis et aliae rationes quia nocuisse possunt.

2. Item dicit quod quatuor turres sunt incoeptae pro sustinendo tiburium dictae ecclesiae et non adsunt piloni nec aliud fundamentum habiles pro sustinendo dictas turres, imo si ecclesia esset facta in toto illico cum dictis turribus infalibiliter rueret, super iis vero quod certe per passiones factae sunt per aliquos ygnorantes allegantes quod voltae acutae sunt plus fortes et cum minori onere quam voltae retondae, et plus super aliis propositum est ad voluntatem quam per viam virtutis; et quod est deterius oppositum est quod scientia geometriae non debet in iis locum habere eo quia scientia est unum et ars est aliud. Dictus magister Johannes dicit quod ars sine scientia nihil est, et quod sive voltae sint acutae sive retondae non habendo fundamentum bonum nihil sunt, et nihilominus quamvis sint acutae habent maximum onus et pondus.

Item dicunt quod turres quos dixerunt sibi velle facere dicunt pluribus rationibus et causis, videlicet, primo pro retificando praedictam ecclesiam et croxeriam quod respondent ad quatrangulum secundum ordinem geometriae; alia vero pro fortitudine et pulchritudine tiborii, videlicet quasi per istum exemplum in paradixo Dominus Deus sedet in medio troni, circha tronum sunt quatuor evangelistae secundum Apocalissim, et istae sunt rationes quare sunt incoeptae. Et quamvis non sint fundati duo piloni pro qualibet sacrastia incipiendo super terram, ecclesia est tamen fortis bene istis rationibus, quia reprexae super quibus dicti duo piloni et praedictae reprexae sunt de magnis lapidibus et inclavatis cum clavibus ferri sicut dictum est supra cum aliis capitulis, et quod pondus dictis tribus turribus ponderat ubique super suum quadrum, et erunt aedificata recte et fortiter, sed rectum non potest cadere; unde dicunt quod sunt fortes per se et ergo dabunt fortitudinem tiborio, quia clausus est in medio illarum turrium unde dicta ecclesia bene fortis est.

3.   Item cognoscit quod voluntarie agitur in praemissis nec contradicentes volunt condescendere juri et meliori dictae ecclesiae et fabricae, sed volunt aut per eorum lucro aut timore, quia voluerunt consequi fabricam super defectibus, aut obstinatione vincere causam, et pro tanto petit dictus magister Johannes committi debere IV vel VI vel XII ex melioribus inzigneriis expertis in talibus, sive de Alamania, sive de Anglia, sive de Franzia, cum aliter dicta fabrica ruet pro certo, quod erit magnum damnum universimodo. Ulterius pro veritate evidenti et sui honoris conservatione accedere vult ad presentiam illustrissimi domini Domini et eidem praedicta et alia latius explicare—Item significat quod pro bono ecclesiae foret bonum alibi laborare in dicta ecclesia quam super locis defectuosis saltem usquequo fuerit clare provisum et decisum super istis defectibus.

Item dicunt et respondent in eodem capitulo quod ubi dicit quod scientia geometrica non debet in iis locum habere, dicunt suprascripti quod si hoc testante videlicet per regulam geometriae Aristotulus dixit hominis autem motus secundum locum quem vocamus lationem, aut reclusus aut circularis aut ex eis mixtus. Item idem dixit alibi omne corpus perfectum est in tribus et motus ipsius et dictae ecclesiae ascendit ad triangulum ut jam declaratum fuit per alios inzignerios, unde dicunt quod omnia sunt per rectam lineam, aut per sextum, ergo concluditer quod quae facta sunt, sunt facta per geometriam et per praticam, quia ipse dixit quod scientia sine arte nihil est; de arte autem jam responsum est in aliis capitulis.

(*Annali*, 1, 209, 210)

IV. 1400. Addi 21 febbraio

In nomine Domini 1400 die 21 februarii.

Fuerunt in domo reverendissimi in Christo patris domini Archiepiscopi Mediolani in ipsius praesentia et plures ex deputatis et consilium fabricae ecclesiae majoris Mediolani fuerunt interrogati Simonetus Nigrus, Johannes Sanomerius, et Mermetus de Sabaudia, omnes tres inzignerii francischi, in et super infrascriptis quaestionibus et artichulis infra nominatis, quod debeant dicere et determinare pro suo sacramento et pro viagio quod faciunt eundo Romam.

Imprimis interrogaverunt super istam quaestionem suprascriptos dominos si ipsis videbatur quod dicta ecclesia esset suffitienter fundata pro sustinendo et portando onus pertinens dictae ecclesiae.

Nos supradicti inzignerii et operarii massonariae discimus quod nos visa et revisitata tota dicta ecclesia, et spetialiter vidimus discopertum fundamenta duorum pilonorum, qui duo piloni debent sustinere et butare contra culatam ipsius ecclesiae, qui sunt parviter et male fundati, et ad falsum unus talis est interius operis plus de uno pede, et de mala materia, et quod omnes piloni dictae ecclesiae intus et extra sint revisitati usque ad minimum fundum et omnes qui erunt male fundati ut suprascripti sunt sint refundati de magnis quarteribus lapidum bene jacentium et lectus sit bene drizatus et planatus et bene jungeneos et butatis per apalattas intus aliis fundamentis bene intus et massonatis ad bagnum de morterio, et dicti fundamenti fiant de duobus brachiis vel plus ultra plumbatis bassarum pilonorum veniendo per reotractam in superficie ad unum brachium.

Item interrogaverunt et fecerunt quaestionem si suprascripti duo piloni extra culatam dictae ecclesiae sunt satis fortes pro sustinendo et butando contra totum suum onus.

Nos dicisimus quod qui funderet duos pilonos pro portando duos archos butantes quod ecclesia redderetur fortiorem sed pro minori impedimento discimus quod refundaret de novo ad unum pondum de magnis quarteriis lapidum bene, et goger, et gont, idest bene quadras et junctas et assisas ad bagnum de morterio de quatuor brachiis butatis totum ac longum usque ad superficiem terrae, et dictae lapides sint butatae de subtu aliud fundamentum per apalattam, et de sumitate terrae in sursum allungando seu alargando dicti duo piloni de brachiis duobus usque ad ipsorum altitudinem et sint inclavatae novae lapides cum veteribus, et isto modo nos putamus quod possint portare suum onus.

Item interrogaverunt et fecerunt quaestionem si omnes alii piloni dictae ecclesiae nobis videntur esse boni.

Nos discimus quod si essent adhuc fiendi possent fieri meliores.

Item interrogaverunt si omnes supradicti piloni possunt portare et passare suum onus sicut sunt.

Respondimus quod nobis videtur quod sic unum habeant unum bonum magistrum operarium massoneriae qui fiat cambiare moluras et carichas de super capitella, et faciendo ipsa molura bona et levia pro causa, quod aliqui dictorum pilonorum non sunt bene aligniati et hoc est pro ponendo ipsas ad suam rationem taliter quod non perpendatur de eorum mala facione et pro minus charichando.

Item discimus quod naufrati sunt et forati de foraminis retondis piloni cornerii sacrastiarum dictae ecclesiae pro portando foris aquas pluvianas descendentes de copertura sacrastiarum et cappellarum, et est contra rationem, et oportet quod claudentur et massonentur et fiant alias novas gargolas quae portabunt suas pancas et noves, et brodes, pro recipiendo dictas aquas et facient subbassamentum pro corotoro factum ad claritatem. Symonetus Nigrus, Johannes Sanomerius, et Mermetus de Sabaudia.

(*Annali*, 1, 211)

V. 1400. Addi 8 maggio

Al nome de Deo e dela Vergine Madona Santa Maria de l'anno del mille quatrocento adi 8 di Mazo. Io Bertholino da Novara el qualle sono stato mandato per lo illustro et excelso principo segniore messere lo duca per certe openione e differentie mossi per alchuni maestri in la fabrica e maiesterio dela giesia de Madona Santa Maria, le qualle differentie et openione li deputati dela dicta fabrica a mi hanno dato per scripto, le quale ho veduto, e examinato, e oltra questo sono stato cum li magistri e inzignieri, li quali sono al presente in la dicta fabrica, a vedere a ochio de sotto, e de sopra le deferentie de la dicta giesia. Et oltra quello vedere ho facto cavare in certi lochi li fondamenti de la dicta giesia per vedere li dicti fondamenti per essere più giaro deli dicti dubii mosi ala dicta fabrica; in breve respondendo digo che la giesia potrave aver habiudo in tre li fondamenti, e in alchuni altri lochi supra terra più debita proportione. Ma per questo non se po biassimare, anche se de lodare per uno belentissimo edifitio e grande, ma secundo el mio parere serave de bisognio per eterna fortificatione fare questa adgionta overo additione zoè:

In prima perchè li contraforti del corpo dela giesia non hanno tuta quella grandeza che sareve de bisognio, conscidirando la largheza e l'alteza dela dicta giesia, vorave se reduze la prima nave in forma de capelle cum le mezature tra l'una capella e l'altra cum alchuni strafori, per li quali se porave vedere el corpo de Cristo da l'uno con l'altro de la giesia, e fazendo così vegniarevese a dare grandissima forteza ale altre tre nave per quilli archi butanti avereve più fermo el suo principio e el corpo dela giesia parerave più bello, e più con sova rexone per che el seguireve la grandeza de la cruxe.

Item serave de besognio fare una capella in la culaza de la giesia verso el campo santo, la quale capella se acostaze a quelli dui contraforti da el lado de drecto fazando la menore che se possesse. e non guastando alchuna cossa de quello chi è facto, e per questa capella seguirave più forteza, e in questa capella porave se redure quella archa, che se dixe che vole fare fare lo el signiore messere lo duca, e siando reducta l'archa in lo dicto locho poravese ponere più in drecto, cel cor vegniarave a essere più grande.

Item digo che per queste additione o sia zonte non starava de fare lavorare e livrare le parte principale, e seguire la maynera principiada e comenzada. Magistro Bernardo da Vanezia, magistro Bertholino da Novara.

(*Annali,* 1, 213)

VI. 1401. Domenica, 15 maggio

VII. Domanda: Se seguendo la forma del secondo progetto si muterebbero soltanto per questa opera le precedenti disposizioni circa la maggiore altezza o larghezza della chiesa, od in qualche sua forma sostanziale?

Carona: La riposta è che si varierebbe l'ordine stabilito dagli altri ingegneri, secondo il già principiato.

Paderno: Rispondo che siccome il disegno presentato da maestro Giovanni non contiene alcuna dimostrazione circa all'altezza di tutti gli archi, come era stato fatto dagli altri ingegneri, così non posso rispondere intorno all'altezza della crociera, se non che esso non ne fece cenno nel suo disegno.

Serina: Risponde che la navate principale di mezzo andrebbe ad essere di 8 braccia più alta di quello che era stato disposto prima, giusta il disegno e la misura datine da maestro Giovanni, per cui deve far meraviglia se altre volte lo stesso maestro Giovanni disse che non era solido tutto l'edificio, che ora essendo ancora più alto dovrebbe essere meno solido.

Calco: Risponde che seguendo la forma del nuovo progetto non si varierebbe la disposizione già data relativamente a qualche forma sostanziale, ma solamente quanto alla maggior grosezza del corpo dell'edificio.

Donato: In confronto di quella prima ordinata si fa qualche variazione all'altezza compiendo il progetto Mignoto, ma questa variazione è lodevole perchè segue la ragione geometrica del triangolo.

Alcherio: Se non erro, col progetto Mignoto si fa qualche variazione nell'altezza, ma qualunque variazione succeda per lo stesso, sarà un miglioramento della solidità, della congruità, della bellezza, e della celerità di costruzione della fabbrica, e ciò riescirà un gravissimo documento contro i ciechi che fingono di essere geometri.

Della Croce: Seguendo la forma del secondo progetto si muta il falso ordine già disposto, e si rispetta il retto ordine del triangolo, che non può essere abbandonato senza errore, come altre volte maestro Enrico, e certo maestro Annex tedesco, prima di lui, predicarono con alta e fedele voce nelle orecchie dei falsi sordi.

Scrosato: Rispondo che se si varia qualche disposizione precedente, la si varia in meglio, in più bello e più lodevole modo, secondo la geometria triangolare.

Galleto: Dico che seguendo il nuovo progetto si muterebbe la disposizione precedente, ma questo non si allontana dalla forma triangolare, dalla quale nessun geometra perito non può ne deve recedere, cosicchè anche con qualche variazione non si abbandona la suddetta forma triangolare, ciò che vidi fatto anche da altri maestri periti in simili cose.

Cavagnera: Dicho che otegniando lo modo di magistro Johanne, zoè per li archi e croxere tanto che la nostra gexia non andava ni più bassa ni più alta, nè si difformava a nessuna provvisione data in fata.

(*Annali,* 1, 227)

Notes

This study is based on a paper delivered at the thirty-sixth annual meeting of the College Art Association in January 1948. I wish to express my gratitude to Professor Richard Krautheimer for his generous assistance and criticism, and to Dr. Erwin Panofsky, who directed me to the Milan texts, for clarifying some difficult passages.

1. The most comprehensive criticism of Viollet-le-Duc is made in Pol Abraham, *Viollet-le-Duc et le rationalisme médiéval* (Paris, 1934), and a digest bearing the same title in *Bulletin Monumental,* 93 (1934), 69–88.

2. The validity of the textual approach to the problem of rationalism has been ably proved by George Kubler in "A Late Gothic Computation of Rib Vault Thrusts," *Gazette des Beaux-Arts,* 26 (1944) (Mélanges Henri Focillon), 135–148 (which includes a valuable digest of the rationalist controversy). This study of a tract on structural problems by the sixteenth-century Spanish architect Rodrigo Gil de Hontañon reveals a theory of vault construction which is different from those of both Viollet-le-Duc and his opposition. The mathematical systems employed by Rodrigo in the calculation of thrusts are perhaps too advanced to be regarded as part of the medieval tradition, but his testimony is none the less valuable as an essential link in the reconstruction of Gothic theory of architecture.

3. The eight-volume edition of the records of the cathedral, published by its administration under the title *Annali della fabbrica del Duomo di Milano dall' origine fino al presente* (Milan, 1877–85), makes available a wealth of material which is almost unique in medieval architectural studies. Comparison with the earlier publication of Ambrogio Nava, *Memorie e documenti storici intorno all' origine, alle vicende ed ai riti del Duomo di Milano* (Milan, 1854), indicates that the *Annali* are not complete or consistently accurate, but it may be assumed that they include the great majority of remaining documents.

4. For the history and a critical bibliography of the cathedral, see Camillo Boito, *Il Duomo di Milano e i disegni per la sua facciata* (Milan, 1889). Stylistic criticism and interpretation of textual sources is found in Luca Beltrami, *Per la facciata del Duomo di Milano* (Milan, 1887).

5. See A. G. Meyer, *Lombardische Denkmäler des vierzehnten Jahrhunderts* (1893), 112ff. An inscription on the cornerstone dates the completion of the façade in 1396, and names the master Matheus de Camplione.

6. The Certosa was ceremoniously founded by Gian Galeazzo Visconti and his sons on August 27, 1396 (see Luca Beltrami, *Storia documentata della Certosa di Pavia* [Milan, 1869], 62f., 140).

Only the foundations of the church were completed before the second half of the fifteenth century.

7. The rebuilding of an older Como Cathedral was probably started in 1396, but no building records remain from the fourteenth century (see D. S. Monti, *La Cattedrale di Como* [Como, 1897], 27–32). As at the Certosa, progress on the building was virtually halted between the death of Gian Galeazzo and the commencement of the Sforza rule in 1450.

8. Although this "Lombard Gothic" style has numerous features which differentiate it from contemporaneous architecture in northern Italy, its individuality has not been recognized. Perhaps because of the provincial character and dilapidated condition of the few remaining examples of the style, it has been bypassed by recent scholarship. There was, however, a flurry of interest in this field during the nineteenth century, which, rising and fading with the Gothic Revival movement, maintained a uniformly superficial approach. Some consideration of Lombard Gothic architecture may be found in the following: Thomas Hope, *An Historical Essay on Architecture* (London, 1835); R. Willis, *Remarks on the Architecture of the Middle Ages, Especially of Italy* (Cambridge, 1835); Amico Ricci, *Storia dell'architettura in Italia* (Modena, 1857–59); Franz Kugler, *Geschichte der Baukunst* (Stuttgart, 1856–59); W. Lübke, "Reisenotizen über die mittelalterlichen Kunstwerke in Italien," *Mitth. der Kaiserl. Königl. Centralcommission,* 5 (1860), 112–120, 134–140, 160–173; Max Nohl, *Tagebuch einer italienischen Reise* (Stuttgart, 1866); L. Gruner and F. Lose, *The Terra-Cotta Architecture of North Italy* (London, 1867); George E. Street, *Brick and Marble in the Middle Ages* (London, 1855, 2d ed. 1874); Carl Schnaase, *Geschichte der bildenden Künste,* vol. 5 (Düsseldorf, 1876); Oscar Mothes, *Die Baukunst des Mittelalters in Italien* (Jena, 1884); L. Runge, *Beiträge zur Kenntniss der Backstein-Architektur Italiens* (Berlin, 1885); Heinrich Strack, *Ziegelbauwerke des Mittelalters und der Renaissance in Italien* (Berlin, 1889). A. Kingsley Porter's *Lombard Architecture* (New Haven, 1917), treats a few Gothic monuments which originated in the Romanesque period.

The area of the style spreads westward from Milan to Brescia and Mantua, and is bordered by the Alps to the north and Piacenza to the south. Genoa, Bologna, and Venice are centers of styles clearly separable from that of Lombardy. The chronological limits, however, are more difficult to determine, and the paucity of reliable dates makes even the tracing of a stylistic development impossible. All but a few of the remaining monuments appear to have originated in the century 1280–1380, while the course of the preceding century remains uncharted.

The monastic plan type of the Lombard Gothic church is evidently imported from Tuscany, while the façades reflect the local Romanesque style of San Michele in Pavia, Modena, Piacenza, etc. The cubic Romanesque bell tower of northern Italy is transformed into a delicate and open form capitalizing on terracotta ornament, as seen at the "Torazzo" of Cremona Cathedral, of 1284, and the mid-fourteenth-century tower of San Gottardo in Milan. At Chiaravalle Milanese this type is employed over the crossing of an earlier church (fig. 9.18). The Gothic forms of central France imported into north Italy at San Andrea in Vercelli in 1219 (flying buttress, two-tower façade, etc.) apparently had little influence on the architecture of the region.

Besides Santa Maria del Carmine in Pavia (figs. 9.1, 9.2), the Lombard Gothic type is well represented in San Agostino and San Luca in Cremona; San Bassiano and San Francesco in Lodi; San Francesco in Pavia; Santa Maria del Carmine, San Francesco, and San Antonio in Piacenza (the latter with a unique western porch); San Francesco in Vercelli; and numerous village churches. Remaining examples in the Milan area—among them San Giovanni in Conca, San Marco, and Santa Maria in Strada in Monza—are largely defaced by nineteenth-century reconstruction.

9. Although this plan is peculiarly Lombard, it occasionally appears elsewhere, as at San Fortunato in Todi, a Tuscan church of the early fourteenth century (see W. Krönig, "Hallenkirchen in Mittelitalien," *Kunstgesch. Jahrbuch der Bibl. Herziana,* 2 [1938], 78ff.).

10. The church has been traditionally assigned a date of 1373 (see A. Ricci, *Storia,* 2:397; Willis, *Remarks,* 165). Lübke's suggestion of 1325 ("Reisenotizen," 161ff.) is unsupported. The decorative style of the façade gives more credence to the later date.

11. *Annali,* 1:25 (6 July).

12. Certain features of the foundation were criticized in a conference in March 1388 (ibid., l:19). The design for the piers which was hurriedly adopted (see Boito, *Il Duomo,* 99) had to be abandoned in the following two years.

13. *Annali,* 1:36 (31 July): "che si cassi maestro Nicola de' Bonaventuri, ingegnere della fabbrica, dal salario che gli si corresponde, e lo si tolga intieramente dalle opere della stessa fabbrica."

14. The text accompanying the sketches reads:

A: Nota che le nave pezole sieno larghe piedi XXV e unze octo commentzando da mezo del pilastro al altro mezo e così sono posti tutti li pilastri per quadro. Note chè li quatro pilastri grosi che sono in mezo la croxeria zoè la truna sono grosi piedi sette onze otto piliando tute le tetaze. Tutto al resto di li pilastri sono grosi piedi sette onze una.

B: da mezo questo pilastro al altro mezo siè piedi LI onze IIII.

C: Piedi LI onze IIII.

D: Piedi XXV once VIII.

E: braza VI.

F: braza III.

G: braza X.

L: braza XXXX per fino sotto el capitelo.

M: braza XXX milanese piliando el capitelo.

N: va alta la cupola dal mezo braza CXIII.

A Milanese braccio of this period measures about .595 meters. Since we know that the aisle bays measure 16 braccia and the nave bays 32 braccia, we are able to transpose Antonio's Bolognese foot to roughly .369 meters. The "unze" or "onze" is analogous to our inch.

The text and the plates which accompany it have been taken from Boito, *Il Duomo,* 106, 108. Both were copied by Luca Beltrami in the archives of San Petronio in Bologna and published in *Raccolta milanese,* December 1887, a periodical which I have been unable to find. Beltrami bases the dating of the sketch on a notice in the records of San Petronio, according to which Antonio left Bologna for Milan in February 1390.

15. Boito's suggestion (*Il Duomo,* 107) that Antonio was confused by scaffolding and rubble into adding two bays onto the transept is difficult to accept. The plan is executed with some care, and lacking further evidence on the early project, we can assume only that the additional bays were either in existence or under consideration in 1390. Antonio's omission of piers in the western portion of the nave is also intentional, for the erection of the bays nearest the entrance awaited the demolition of the façade of the ancient cathedral (see Giulio Carotti, "Vicende del Duomo di Milano e della sua facciata," *Archivio storico dell' arte,* 2 [1889], 118 and fig. 2).

16. I refer particularly to the cathedral of Piacenza, where the relationships in plan of the principal portions of the building are strikingly similar to those in this sketch.

17. *Annali,* 1:36 (19 July): "Super sala reverendi domini archiepiscopi deliberaverunt quod illi quattuor pironi tiburii fabricae augmententur in grossitudine se ingrossentur per quartas tres in quadro, taliter quod sint in circitu quartas I 112 [sic—1½?] plus aliis pironis." Although it is not specifically stated, it is reasonable to assume that at the time of this decision, the crossing piers were of the same thickness as the lesser piers. The precise character of this change is unclear. The term "quarta" is frequently employed in the records as a unit of measurement, and may be equivalent to ¼ braccio. Whatever its value, it is difficult to see how the increase in the circumference of the pier (if it is 1½ quartas) can be exactly half of the increase in the "square" (3 quartas).

18. See Boito, *Il Duomo,* plate 29, and Beltrami, *Per la facciata,* 1:29.

19. Paul Frankl, "The Secret of the Mediaevel Masons," *Art Bulletin,* 27 (1945), 51f. For a more detailed consideration of Antonio's design, and the subsequent solutions which are briefly considered here, I refer the reader to Dr. Frankl's excellent study, to which I have been greatly indebted.

20. *Annali,* 1:53 (24 August 1391).

21. The architect Annas (or Giovanni) de Firimburg (Freiburg) is not to be confused with the sculptor Anna de Fernach, who was also active at the cathedral (see Thieme-Becker, 11:406 and 14:118). This architect was apparently appointed early in 1391, presented his criticisms in writing on March 12 of that year, and was dismissed in June (*Annali,* 1:45, 48). His role as the first foreigner to introduce a geometrical scheme for the section may be reconstructed from a statement by a Milanese architect in a conference of 1401. The latter, speaking of a later scheme for the section, says that it respects "il retto ordine del triangolo, che non può essere abbandonato senza errore, come altre volte maestro Enrico, *e certo maestro Annex tedesco,* primo di lui, predicarono con alta e fedele voce nelle orecchie dei falsi sordi." In a consideration of this conference below, I shall attempt to prove that the "retto ordine del triangolo" specifically refers to the equilateral.

22. *Annali,* 1:55 (13 October 1391): "Deliberaverunt quod discreto viro Gabrieli Stornalocho de Placentia experto in arte geometriae, pro quo missum fuit parte deputatorum dictae fabricae juxta deliberationem in consilio dictae fabricae factam die 24 septembris p.p. et Mediolanum venit . . . causa discutendi cum inzigneriis dictae fabricae de dubiis altitudinis et aliorum de quibus dubium erat inter dictos inzignerios . . . dentur . . . dono pro recognitione et recumpensatione expensarum per eum factarum veniendo. . . ."

23. A copy of Stornaloco's sketch and the letter which accompanies it are reproduced in Beltrami, *Per la facciata*, 3:12–15, and Frankl, "Secret of the Mediaeval Masons," 53–55.

24. The mathematics employed by Stornaloco in calculating the incommensurable heights are interpreted by Erwin Panofsky in a postscript to Frankl's article ("An Explanation of Stornaloco's Formula," *Art Bulletin*, 27 [1945], 61–64).

25. The grid employed in the first project made it impossible to determine the height of the summits of the lesser vaults according to the basic unit of 10 braccia. While the height of the nave vault was probably 90 braccia, and hence consistent with the system, it is significant that Antonio did not record this measurement, and it is possible that the masters were interested in fixing only the heights of the imposts.

26. *Annali*, 1:45 (12 March 1391) and 51 (15 July 1391). The mission of March 12 was sent prior to the dismissal of Annas.

27. Ibid., 57 (11 December 1391). The appointment was made for only three months, and was extended on the following March (ibid., 66).

28. Ibid., 68ff. (1 May). This and subsequent passages which appear in translation are reproduced in the original in the Appendix.

29. A list of fourteen masters is given. After Parler's name is the note, "(who does not concur)."

30. On the basis of the context in *Dubium 6*, "croxeria" is translated as "transept" in this text, although the term occasionally is used elsewhere to mean "vault."

31. The reference is to the Strada del Cómpito, which ran along the north side of the cathedral. See the map published by Carotti ("Vicende del Duomo di Milano," p. 116, fig. 2, or the same author's *Il Duomo di Milano e la sua facciata* [Milan, 1888], fig. 2).

32. The northern transept façade was not built as planned here. In Cesariano's ground plan of the cathedral (*Di Lucio Vitruvio Pollione De architectura* [Como, 1521], pl. XIII), there is a single portal on each transept arm, which was closed off by the present chapels in 1614 (see Boito, *Il Duomo*, 244–247).

33. The solution of this problem was intentionally delayed until the arrival of a foreign expert. A record of March 19, 1391, which does not appear in the *Annali*, is quoted in Nava, *Memorie*, 22. At a conference of masters it is decided "Quod differatur ad deliberandum supra facto intramezatarum fiendarum in Eccl. ne usque ad eventum inzig. teutonici quem Anes Fernach ire debet ad accipiendum et ducendum, et sic etiam super facto pillonorum ad dictas capellas fiendorum."

34. I have left untranslated the term "pilloni guerziis" for lack of a convincing interpretation. Cf. its appearance in 1401 (*Annali*, 1:223), ". . . debba . . . riadattari ed abbassare il capitello che esso fece fare sopra uno dei piloni (guerziis)." It is possibly a cognate of the Italian "quercia," in which case it may refer to the wooden models of the piers which are mentioned in n. 43.

35. Ibid, 69 (2 May). See Appendix Ia.

36. The most important decisions made, concerning the height of the church and of the various supports and vaults, appear in *Responsiones* 3, 4, 5, and 11. Two problems which should properly be contingent upon these decisions—namely, the adequacy of the piers and the design of the roofing—are considered beforehand (*Dubia* 1 and 2). Either the text fails to reproduce the original order in which the problems were discussed or, what is more likely, the Milanese are so hard-headed that they believe their piers to be sound, and their roofs correct, regardless of what decisions are made later on concerning the heights of the several portions.

37. The passage quoted in n. 21 informs us that Parler ("maestro Enrico") favored the equilateral triangle. This does not necessarily militate against the suggestion that the square section was also his proposal. I offer that after it had been finally determined to employ the triangle, Parler insisted that it be equilateral, in opposition to the Milanese proposal which we are about to examine.

38. In *Responsio* 4 the piers are lowered from Stornaloco's 42 braccia to 40 braccia. In *Responsio* 5 the engaged columns which rise above the main capitals to the springing of the vaults are lowered from 14 braccia to 12 braccia, and the main vaults lowered from 28 to 24 braccia. The total diminution in height is thus 8 braccia.

39. I believe that the phrase "and not farther" used in both *Responsiones* 3 and 4 emphasizes merely the wish for a low section. Frankl, on the other hand ("Secret of the Mediaeval Masons," 56), suggesting that *Responsio* 3 be paraphrased

"up to the Pythagorean triangle or up to the equilateral triangle and not above," proceeds: "If this is right, the words 'et non ultra' mean that one should not enlarge the height of 27.71 . . . to 28 as Stornaloco did, but reduce it to 27½ braccia. This explains the lowering [of the measurements of the present cathedral] by half a braccio or one foot." This explanation unfortunately does not work. If the outer piers were intended to be 27½ braccia, the main piers (in order to keep within the Pythagorean triangle) would have to be 39½ braccia. *Responsio* 4, however, fixes them at precisely 40. Hence, the reduction of ½ braccio must have been decided upon after this conference of 1392.

40. My hypothesis that Cologne Cathedral is constructed *ad quadratum* is based on Dehio's section reproduced in figure 8.7, where the height of the nave keystone is equal to the breadth of the building measured from the inner surface of the walls. Paradoxically, Dehio himself lists Cologne as an example of construction *ad triangulum* (*Die kirchliche Baukunst des Abendlandes* [Stuttgart, 1901], 2:567, and *Ein Proportionsgesetz der antiken Baukunst* [Strasbourg, 1895], 21, 23). He claims that the height of the vault is established by superimposing small equilateral triangles. As in all questions of this kind, the answer must await accurately measured drawings.

41. The decision concerning the chapel divisions was perhaps the most controversial one of the conference. As time went on, several of the local masters joined the northern experts in the conviction that these divisions were necessary to the stability of the cathedral. Nine years later the controversy still was a major issue, and the duke ordered Bertolino da Novara, and his court architect Bernardo da Venezia (who had subscribed to the original decision to abandon the divisions), to give their opinion on the matter. Their report, dated May 8, 1400 (Appendix V), includes the suggestion: "First because the buttresses of the body of the church do not have all the mass that they need, considering the breadth and height of said church, the first nave should be reduced to the form of chapels with the division between one chapel and another, with several perforations through which one could see the Host from either side of the church. Such a construction would succeed in giving the greatest strength to the other three naves, and through these flying buttresses, as it were, its base would be stronger, and the body of the church would look more beautiful, and more in proportion, and would follow the grandeur of the

transept [? *cruxe*]." The advice of the two experts was of course ignored, as was virtually all outside opinion.

It is worth noting that the chapel system had lost its liturgical function to such an extent that the dividing walls were considered a hindrance to the congregation which must be alleviated by "several perforations."

42. *Annali*, 1:71 (7 July 1392). The cathedral deputies say that Heinrich ". . . male servierit ipsi fabricae, ymo dedit magnum damnum et detrimentum ipsi fabricae pro suis malegestis. . . ."

43. Ibid., 105 (14 December 1393): "Quod si videatur alios capitelos posse meliorari referant, et fieri faciant de formis hujusmodi capitelorum fiendorum in futurum de ligno aut gesso, ut determinari possit circa alios capitelos fiendos pro utiliori fabricae."

44. For Ulrich's arrival see ibid., 120 (15 November 1394), and departure, 134 (28 March 1395). From the latter: "dixit non velle facere ipsam fenestram secundum mensuras ordinatas, quia volebat mutare altitudinem et modum ipsius fenestrae; et ulterius si volebat facere de capitelis pilonorum, similiter dixit quod non volebat facere de capitelis pilonorum in illa mensura qua finitus est primus capitelus. . . ."

45. Ibid., 1:194 (13 April 1399).

46. Ibid., 1:199 (14 December 1399): "Avendo l'ingegnere Giovanni Mignoto riferito al Duca che la fabbrica corre pericolo di ruina, gli ordinarono di farne relazione scritta, ed intervenire in seduta per le necessarie deliberazioni."

47. Twenty-five criticisms are answered by the masters. The postscript to the report explains their silence in the second half of the conference: "No response is given to all these statements by abovementioned Jean Mignot, since they contain neither substance nor weight, and especially since, if they [the masters] should reply to aforesaid statements, and others which he might give in writing in the future, the negotiations would never end, but the work on aforesaid church would be held back to the great shame and scandal of men, not only in the city, but in the whole realm of the illustrious lord, our Lord, and consequently would never be finished" (ibid., 208).

48. A third criticism of which the content may be significant from a theoretical standpoint I have been unable to interpret for lack of evidence on the precise state of the cathedral in 1400. Because of its geometrical allusions it has been included in

Appendix IIa. The square and circle referred to may describe either the section of the pier or the arrangement of the piers in the plan.

49. *Annali,* 1:202 (11 January 1400), Item I. (See Appendix II.)

50. The same passage quoted in Nava, *Memorie,* 86, gives the depth of the foundations as 9 braccia, which seems more likely than 14. By way of comparison, the records of Florence Cathedral of June 1357 provide "che il fondamento delle cholonne dallo spazio in giù si faccia br. vij per ogni verso" (Cesare Guasti, *Santa Maria del Fiore; la costruzione della chiesa e del campanile secondo i documenti* [Florence, 1887], 94). The Florentine braccio is only about one centimeter less than the Milanese (see *Enciclopedia italiana,* 7:649).

51. The use of binding rods between the capitals to reinforce the arches was common practice in Italy, and probably less frowned upon than in the north. See again the records of Florence Cathedral for August 3, 1366: "... chonsigliano che al presente si facciano due stanghe di ferro grandi di buono ferro e bene salde, e mettansi negli archi de le volte grandi, cioè una in ciascuno archo ..." (Guasti, *Santa Maria del Fiore,* 173).

52. Mignot evidently feels that it is hopeless to attempt to make his point against such opposition. In a second hearing which he is granted a few days later, and which we shall shortly consider, he asks that experts from any northern country be called in to testify whether or not his criticisms are justified. Consequently, a month later, on February 21, 1400, a deputation of three "inzignerii francischi" en route to Rome is asked to pass judgment on the apse supports. The report reads: "First it was asked on this question by the above-mentioned lords if it seemed to them that this church were sufficiently founded to sustain and carry the weight belonging to said church.

"We the aforesaid engineers and masons say that we have seen and reviewed all of said church, and especially we have seen the foundations of two piers exposed, which two piers should sustain and abut the apse of said church, and are inadequately and poorly founded. And one of these is more than a foot at fault inside the work, and of poor material. All the piers of said church both inside and outside are to be reviewed down to the lowest base and all of those which were badly founded as are the aforementioned, are to be refounded of large blocks of well-laid stone, and their bedding should be well leveled and planed and joined and buttressed by dovetailing into the

other foundations well inside, and built in with a mortar bath. These foundations should be made two braccia or more beyond the plumb line of the bases of the piers, coming to one braccio at the surface by a setback.

"Furthermore, it was asked and the question was put if the aforementioned two piers outside the apse of said church are strong enough to sustain and buttress against all its weight.

"We state that if one founded two piers for carrying two flying buttresses, that the church would be made stronger, but to avoid impediment, we state that it should be refounded of one weight of large blocks of good stone, and mortared [? *goger*] and joined [? *gont*], that is, well squared and set in a bath of mortar of four braccia abutting along the whole length up to the level of the earth. And said stones should be buttressed by dovetailing below the other foundation, and from ground level up, by lengthening or widening said two piers by two braccia all the way up. And the new stones should be doweled with the old ones, and in this fashion we think they can carry their weight.

"Furthermore, it was asked and the question was put if all the other piers of said church seemed to us to be good.

"We state that if they were to be made now they could be made better ..." (*Annali,* 1:211; Appendix IV).

Thus the judgment of the deputation bears out Mignot's opinion, suggesting not only that the wall piers be reinforced, but that they carry flying buttresses. The criticism of the foundations suggests that the foreigners believe the Milanese to be quite as deficient in practice as they are in theory.

53. *Annali,* 1:203f., Item 9; Appendix IIb. The reader is advised to refer to the original, as the phrasing of the reply eludes adequate translation.

54. In a sense, the Milanese are more up-to-date in their argument than Mignot, for the capital-base ratio averages about 1:1 in early Gothic architecture, while later the capital tends to shrink and the base to grow, although not according to fixed ratios.

55. *Annali,* 1:224 (15 May 1401).

56. In Vitruvius, for example, the proportion of head to body is 1:8. See *De architectura,* III, c. 1, 2.

57. Beltrami (*Per la facciata,* 3:18) draws essentially the same conclusion from the piers as executed. He demonstrates that a base of 2 braccia and a capital of 10 braccia leave between them a

shaft of 28 braccia, which is equal to the width of the nave measuring from the exterior of the columns rather than the center.

58. *Annali,* 1:209f. (25 January 1400); Appendix III.

59. A local building stone, employed in the foundations and under the marble facing.

60. Aside from the reappearance of the elusive term "croxeria," it is difficult to determine with any precision what the masters have in mind in this sentence, which reads, "pro rectificando praedictam ecclesiam et croxeriam quod respondent ad quatrangulum etc."

61. "per rectam lineam aut per *sextum.*" Cf. the Italian *sesto acuto.*

62. The statement "hominis autem motus secundum locum quem vocamus lationem, aut rectus, aut circularis aut ex eis mixtus" obviously derives from a passage in *Physics,* VIII, 261b, 27, which is translated: "We are now to show that there actually is in nature, a motion ever-enduring, uniform and uninterrupted; and that its nature is that of rotation. All local motion is circular or rectilinear or a combination of the two, so that if either of these cannot be continuous, neither can any combination of them be so" (Loeb Classical Library, *The Physics,* tr. Wicksteed and Cornford [London and New York, 1929]). A passage in *De caelo* (I, 270b, 25) states a similar principle, without considering the combination of the two. The manner in which these passages are applied to the design of the cathedral indicates that they were either misunderstood or purposefully misused.

The word "rectus," which appears in this passage, is wrongly transcribed as "reclusus" in the *Annali.* Nava, *Memorie,* 96, provides the correct version.

63. The second reference to Aristotle is stated, "idem dixit alibi omne corpus perfectum est in tribus." The reference is evidently to *De caelo,* I, 268a, 20, which is translated: "In this sense, therefore, body is the only complete magnitude, since it is the only one which is defined by extension in three directions, that is, which is an 'all.'" To clarify Aristotle's intention in this passage, one may refer to ibid., 268a, 7: "Magnitude divisible in one direction is a line, in two directions a surface, in three directions a body. There is no magnitude not included in these; for three are all, and 'in three ways' is the same as 'in all ways'" (Loeb Classical Library, *On the Heavens,* tr. Guthrie [Cambridge, Mass., 1939]). Reference to this principle is made also in the *Metaphysics,* V, 1066b, 32, and VI,

1016b, 28. In referring to these passages the council has not only misused the source, but misunderstood it.

64. The letter is worth quoting as an impartial judgment of the controversies raging over the cathedral: "ad ipsius excellentissimi Domini nostri notitiam pervenisse displicenter quandam controversiam et discordiam jam diu versam inter suas cives Mediolani, occasione tam solemnis fabricae ecclesiae Mediolani, iterato renovari, videlicet per nonnulos allegari prefatam ecclesiam suam non habere rationem et mensuram nec fortitudinem respectu sequendorum in dicta ecclesia . . . per aliquos e contrario allegatur ipsam ecclesiam debitam rationem habere et mensuram ac proportionem et fortitudinem praedictorum omnium respectuum. . . . Considerantes altercationem et differentiam majorem solito oriri magis et procedere ex ignorantia inzigneriorum non expertorum nec se intelligentium circa necessaria fabricae, quam obstinatione suorum civium . . . deposuit, vult et mandat antelatus noster Dominus quod vos domini procuretis habere magistrum teutonicum de dicta fabricatione jam informatum, ac altios peritos et expertos inzignerios, qui cum Johanne Mignoto, perito et experto, ac aliis inzigneriis ipsius fabricae se intelligant et taliter ordinent quod dicta ecclesia debito et suo jure et ordine procedat, defectus corrigendo quam melius fieri potest . . ." (*Annali,* 1:230f.).

65. Ibid., 224–229 (15 May 1401).

66. Ibid., 226. In answer to the question "Qual numero di pietre poste in opera giusta il progetto già incominciato se dovrebbe rimuovere faciendo il secondo?," one of the masters replies: "Sono circa 12 le pietre che bisogna rimuovere, e le altre già lavorate sono circa 60 o 70. . . ."

67. Ibid., 226, 227; Appendix VI. The text as given in the *Annali* is largely in modern Italian, probably translated from the Latin, although no indication of this is given.

68. To increase the confusion, the 8-braccia alteration would change the vaults from 24 to 32 braccia in height, so it may also be said that the vaults, taken alone, are designed *ad quadratum.*

69. The week beginning October 15, 1401, is given over to vilifying Mignot. No other business appears in the records (*Annali,* 1:236–238). That there is some question as to the justice of his dismissal is apparent in a notice of November 27 (ibid., 240), and a letter which warmly defends him is sent to the duke on December 20 (ibid., xvi f. of Preface, dated February 1402, by Nava, *Memorie,* 130).

70. As I have indicated above, I believe that it was the intention of the designers of the Pythagorean section to dispense with flying buttresses, in accordance with Lombard tradition. The expertise translated in n. 52 may be interpreted to suggest that they had not been projected before 1400. However, in 1410, they were definitely under consideration, as evidenced by the specification given in a report of September 16 (*Annali,* 1:304).

71. The reader will recall a further example of the numerical ratio in Stornaloco's sketch (fig. 8.1B), where the height of the outer aisle is just half that of the nave.

72. "Secret of the Mediaeval Masons," 58.

73. Given sufficient evidence, it would undoubtedly prove that the choice of numerical formulae was similarly subject to aesthetic concepts of antique origin.

74. The discussions at Milan demonstrate the inseparability of form and structure within the theory. Precisely the same arithmetical ratios are used in solving what might be called the purely formal problem of proportioning the pier capitals and bases as are used in solving the predominantly structural problem of the mass of the buttresses.

Postscript

Though this article, based on a paper written for a course by Erwin Panofsky on the evolution of Gothic art, was completed before I began my dissertation, it has enjoyed a greater fame and has been more frequently cited than any I have written as a certified professional. Could this imply anything about the value of the Ph.D.? Its impact should be credited partly to Panofsky, who grasped the potential of the texts on which it is based and directed me to the publication in which they are reproduced. In the ensuing forty years a large literature has come forth on the geometrical systems employed in Gothic architecture and on the surviving theoretical and working drawings of the late Middle Ages. What remains valid in my article is the exposition of the opposing theoretical schemes and the analysis of the texts. But much has changed—due to research on the history of the Milan Cathedral by Angiola Romanini and her associate Antonio Cadei—with respect to the interpretation of the milieu in which these schemes were proposed.

In the long section on architecture in the lavish 1973 volume on the cathedral, Romanini demonstrated (Ferrari da Passano, Romanini, et al., pp. 102ff., 168ff.) that the original project for the cathedral, starting in 1386, was in the latest northern Gothic style (known in central Europe as *Sondergotik*), as represented by Peter Parler and others in his family. She cites as instances Parler's Prague Cathedral, the Chartreuse de Champmol, Heilige Kreuz in Schwäbisch-Gmünd, the Communal Palace at Bruges, and Ulm Cathedral. The hypothesis is convincing, and supersedes my proposal that "the northern Gothic character of the cathedral began to take form only after the arrival of the Frenchman [Nicolas de Bonaventure, in July 1389], and that the initial plan was conceived in the Lombard Gothic style."

Thus the original project, indicated in the drawings of Antonio di Vincenzo of Bologna (figs. 8.3, 8.4, 8.5A), was in the northern style, except that it lacked a geometrical scheme. Cadei (in press) reinforces my point that the underlying opposition in the theoretical arguments was between the northern commitment to geometry and the more practical Milanese preference for whole figures, which is what caused them to summon Stornaloco to make a compromise between the two. Antonio's drawings (figs. 8.3, 8.4) show that the earliest project proposed a simple modular system; his plan records a grid of 16 Milanese braccia and his elevation one of 10 braccia, which could not be combined in a geometrical system (Cadei interprets Andrea's employment of Milanese measurements rather than those of his native Bologna as indicating that he took them from the original drawings rather than from his own measurements).

The evidence for the northern character of the first project is in the similarity of plan elements (e.g., the side chapels with dividing walls, intended as internal buttresses, that were built into the foundations and later eliminated—features of Parler's Prague Cathedral) and of the decorative schemes of the exterior, most notably the apsidal windows. The hypothesis explains more satisfactorily the different opinions offered by visiting experts, some of whom, like Heinrich Parler, defended the original scheme, and others of whom, especially those from France, had in mind other, more classic models like Cologne and Strasbourg.

In spite of strong differences of opinion, the original design was retained from the presentation of pier models in 1388 to 1392 (Cadei, *in litteris*), though in 1391 a major feature of the original program was challenged: the walls that were to have separated the outer aisles into rows of chapels and also to have served as internal buttresses.

As I wrote, the years 1391–92 were crucial to the evolution of the design. Many experts were called, including Stornaloco. The duke, reluctantly brought in to arbitrate, sought the advice of his court architect in Pavia, Bernardo da Venezia. Ultimately, the chief architect of Ulm Cathedral, Heinrich Parler, was summoned, and the crucial meeting of May 1, 1392, sealed the fate of the original Parlerian design and led to the adoption of the scheme with a Pythagorean triangle superimposed on a truncated equilateral triangle (fig. 8.5D). In the light of the new interpretations, I would emend my assumption that the questions debated in 1392 were posed by Parler. Rather, they were issues that had been brought forward by a number of different parties. Thus on the question (*Dubium* 3) of whether the section should be built *ad quadratum* or *ad triangulum* (fig. 8.5C) there is no evidence to demonstrate that Parler favored the latter (we don't know who the proponent may have been); given the advanced state of construction Parler probably would have accepted the original section represented in figure 8.5A, though its nongeometrical basis must have distressed him.

Romanini suggests (Ferrari da Passano, Romanini, et al., p. 176) that it was Giovannino de' Grassi who was one of those who put forward the superimposed-triangle solution and put it into practice in 1392–98, when he was in charge of the *fabrica*. Though Giovannino, known primarily as a painter of the international style, was Italian, he was not one of the Lombard masons who continued to constitute the intransigent party. He belonged to the international milieu of the courts, and the design he executed and perhaps initiated was a compromise in the sense that it accepted a low Lombard profile but insisted on a geometrical justification. Such a compromise later proved to be unacceptable to Jean Mignot, the French expert who arrived in 1399, following the deaths of Giovannino and his associate Giacomo da Campione; Romanini's account of the import of his visit does not differ significantly from mine.

Romanini also brings to bear her knowledge of medieval Lombard architecture to give a clearer idea of the sources for the design concepts of the Milanese masters, citing a large group of hall churches of the later fourteenth century (ibid., pp. 105f.), for example, San Giacomo a Pontida, which provided a model for the cathedral piers. She suggests (108ff.) that Gian Galeazzo Visconti, who did not choose to become deeply involved in the cathedral design and who, in his patronage elsewhere, was committed to the Lombard architectural traditions, would have promoted the latest northern aristocratic style for the cathedral in order to avoid the appearance of provincialism.

That the summoning of experts to examine and give advice on the construction of provincial cathedrals was common practice in the fourteenth century is demonstrated by records of Troyes Cathedral recently published by Stephen Murray. The earliest of the visitations is recorded in 1362 (Murray, pp. 30ff., 120ff.). The report is relatively detailed and extensive and recommends dismantling the upper flyers of the buttresses in order to reconstruct them at a lower level, but there is no indication of how the advice was arrived at. A 1401 document mentions "other expense made at the orders of my lords to go to Paris and elsewhere to seek masons and other workers to visit the church. And first, for the expenses of my lord Jehan Gaillart who was sent by my said lords to Paris to talk with Master Remond, master of the king's works, and to find out from him if he could come here to visit the church. [Master Remond] excused himself in the presence of my lord of Auxerre and offered to the said lord Jehan Gaillart [the services of] Master Jehan Aubelet and Master Jehan Prevost, his nephew, for the said visit." (Ibid., p. 137f.) In 1407–08 Master Jehan de Dixon, "master mason of the church at Reims," visited and gave advice that proved to conflict with that of Jehan Aubelet (p. 139). Visitations continued into the sixteenth century.

So far as I know, only one further text relating to the use of geometry as a foundation for engineering (that of Rodrigo Gil de Hontañon, discussed by Kubler) has come to light. Rodrigo's text, dated by Kubler to ca. 1538, proposed a means of assessing the thrust of vaults and the consequent mass of the buttresses by calculating from the cumulative lengths of the vault ribs in each bay, plus the height of the intended buttress. But Rodrigo recognized that his calculations had no real scientific foundation and concludes rather sheepishly, "I have often attempted to rationalize the buttress needed for any bay, and have never found a rule adequate for me. I have also pursued the inquiry among Spanish and foreign architects, and none appears to have established a rule verified by other than his own judgment. Upon asking how we shall know whether such and such a buttress is enough, we are told that it is needed, but not for what reason. Some take the fourth [of the span], and others arrive [at an estimate] by certain orthogonals, and dare to have confidence. . ." (Kubler, p. 146). Another text, perceptively interpreted by Franklin Toker, provides insight into the use of geometry in establishing proportions in domestic façades of the Tuscan type, and is almost Renaissance in outlook.

Jacques Heyman's article on vaulting points out that regardless of the accuracy of one's estimate of the stresses and buttressing requirements of Gothic stone vaulting, the modern engineer would calculate them in terms of proportions, as was done in the Milan workshop. But the solutions so confidently proposed by Jacques Mignot were, he suggests, no more than pedantic repetitions of tired workshop dogma, far removed from the experimental and imaginative solutions reached in the late twelfth and thirteenth centuries.

That the arguments over theory and practice in geometrical matters were based on distinctions familiar to medieval writers has been shown by Lon Shelby, who cites (p. 401) the *Practica geometrica* by the twelfth-century philosopher Hugh of St. Victor: "Omnis geometrica disciplina aut theorica est, id est speculatium, aut practica, id est activa. Theorica siquidem est que spacia et intervalla dimensionum rationabilum sola rationis speculatione vestigat, practica vero est que quibusdam instrumentis agitur et ex aliis alia proportionaliter coniciendo diiudicat." Dominicus Gundissalinus, in another twelfth-century treatise, *De divisione philosophiae,* makes a parallel distinction: "Finis enim theorice est aliquid docere; finis vero practice est aliquid agere."

Beaujouan, G. "Calcul d'expert en 1391 sur le chantier du Dome de Milan," *Le Moyen-age: Livre jubilaire,* 1963.

Beaujouan, G. "Réflexions sur les rapports entre théorie et pratique au Moyen Age," *The Cultural Context of Medieval Learning,* ed. J. Murdoch (Dordrecht and Boston, 1975), 449–463.

Booz, P. *Der Baumeister der Gotik* (Munich, 1956).

Bucher, François. "Design in Gothic Architecture: A Preliminary Assessment," *Journal of the Society of Architectural Historians,* 27 (1968), 49–71.

Bucher, François. "Medieval Architectural Design Methods," *Gesta,* 11 (1972), 37–51.

Cadei, Antonio. *La costruzione del Duomo di Milano dalle origini a Giovannino de' Grassi,* tesi di laurea, Univ. of Pavia, 1967.

Cadei, Antonio. "Cultura artistica delle cattedrali: due esempi a Milano," *Atti del Convegno per il VI Centenario della fondazoine del Duomo di Milano* (1987), in press.

Ferrari da Passano, Carlo, A. M. Romanini, et al. *Il duomo di Milano,* 2 vols. (Milan, 1973). Romanini's contribution to this work, the most thorough modern study of the cathedral, supersedes the portions devoted to the cathedral in her earlier book, *L'architettura gotica in Lombardia,* 2 vols. (Milan, 1964).

Friedman, David. "Geometry," in *Florentine New Towns: Urban Design in the Late Middle Ages* (Cambridge, Mass., 1988), 118–148.

Heyman, J. "On the Rubber Vaults of the Middle Ages," *Gazette des Beaux-Arts,* 71 (1968), 177–188.

Kubler, George. "A Late Gothic Computation of Rib Vault Thrusts," *Gazette des Beaux-Arts* (1944), 135–148.

Lyman, Thomas W. "Opus ad Triangulum vs. Opus ad Quadratum in Medieval Five-Aisled Churches," in *Artistes, artisans et production artistique au Moyen-Age,* 2 (1988), 202–219. Lyman's study, which grew out of his work on San Sernin in Toulouse, demonstrates that the triangulation of the section of Gothic churches, as proposed in the drawing of Stornaloco, was frequently employed in northern Europe as well. But the rationale was symbolic rather than practical because of the difficulty of applying angular and nonmodular measurements in actual construction.

Murray, Stephen. *Building Troyes Cathedral: The Late Gothic Campaigns* (Bloomington, 1986).

Scholfield, P. H. *The Theory of Proportion in Architecture* (Cambridge, 1958).

Shelby, L. R. "The Geometrical Knowledge of Medieval Master Masons," *Speculum,* 47 (1972), 395–421 (summarized in *Studies in Medieval Culture,* 5 [1975], 133–144).

Toker, Franklin. "Gothic Architecture by Remote Control: An Illustrated Building Contract of 1340," *The Art Bulletin,* 67 (1985), 69–95.

Velte, Maria. *Die Anwendung der Triangulatur und Quadratur bei der Grund- und Aufrissgestaltung der gotischen Kirchen* (Basel, 1951). This doctoral dissertation, written without knowledge of my article, examines some of the same Milanese texts and gives a clear interpretation of the use of geometric figures to form the plan as well as the section of medieval churches.

Wittkower, Rudolf. *Gothic vs. Classic: Architectural Projects in Seventeenth-Century Italy* (New York, 1974).

9

The Certosa of Pavia
and the Renaissance in Milan

The writer who undertakes to treat Renaissance architecture in Milan before Bramante must inevitably start out on the defensive. He cannot hope to bring to light undiscovered masterpieces, nor can he hope to uncover fully the roots of the extraordinary intellectual revival of the end of the fifteenth century at the court of Ludovico Sforza. Yet the early Lombard Renaissance is far from being an artistic desert. It is rather a botanical garden where indigenous and imported plants are variously crossbred. While there is, properly speaking, no early Renaissance style of architecture in Milan, there is a search among all available sources for a distinctively Lombard mode of expression. In this respect, the architecture we are considering is perhaps more typical of quattrocento Italy than the Florentine development to which our attention is naturally drawn. For throughout northern Italy in particular, the early Renaissance has the flavor of nationalism in its attempt to express a new spirit in terms of local tradition from both the immediate and far distant past.

For this reason a careful study of such commune-capitals as Milan, Venice, Genoa, and Bologna promises to reveal aspects of the Renaissance which were scarcely evident in the rarified atmosphere of Tuscany. If we uncover an unsure and conservative art, it is because insecurity and conservatism are significant characteristics without which the period cannot fully be understood.

From *Marsyas*, 5 (1947–49), 23–27.

The Renaissance in Lombardy has perhaps a closer connection with political events than elsewhere in Italy, for the rapidly changing fortunes of the state make artistic expression in turn inevitable and impossible. The centralization of economy and government made it possible for the two dukes who were chiefly responsible for the unification and expansion of Lombardy to establish their palaces in Pavia and Milan as virtually the sole fountainheads of Lombard art. They were Gian Galeazzo Visconti, who ruled from 1378 to 1402, and Francesco Sforza, who succeeded the Visconti regime from 1450 to 1466. It may seem odd to link the first of these—a trecento ruler—with the Renaissance, for the monuments initiated by him are all quite Gothic. But in fostering an extraordinary awakening of artistic activity he revived a creative spirit which had been dormant since the twelfth century, and brought Lombardy into contact with the outside world. The last quarter of the fourteenth century marks a kind of premature Renaissance.

To appreciate the importance of the Visconti revival we must for a moment look back to the provincial Gothic ecclesiastical style which persisted virtually unchanged throughout the thirteenth and fourteenth centuries.[1] The adverse political fortunes and uncertain economy of the area left building activity exclusively in the hands of the monastic orders. The abbeys and parish churches of this period were not only typically modest, but extremely conservative. In plan and elevation they repeated a pattern imported from Cistercian France of the twelfth century, adapting to it certain reminiscences of the local Romanesque style. There is no evidence of influence from contemporary developments in the architecture of western Europe. The flying buttress is rarely employed, fenestration remains limited, tracery, moldings, and profiles are of a twelfth-century style, and the exteriors are uniformly of unfaced brick. Yet the style is not merely degenerate, for it develops an individuality which distinguishes it from monastic architecture elsewhere. A variety of the Cistercian plan which is typical of Lombardy is the arrangement of outer chapel rows along the side aisles, a buttressing device which strongly influenced later construction. The most distinctive feature of the style is the lively decorative sense exercised in the rich brick and terracotta façades and the highly coloristic bell and crossing towers.

The uniformity of this style makes it permissible for present purposes to take a single church as representative. The Carmine in Pavia, a mid-fourteenth-century example, has the typical rectangular plan with chapel rows and side aisles flanking square quadripartite nave bays (figs. 9.1, 9.2).[2] The plan demands an unusually broad façade in which the verticality of northern Gothic scarcely has an opportunity for expression.

The lively pinnacles and terracotta ornament of the façade contrast with the ascetic severity of the interior, where the nave walls are relieved only by small oculi in the clerestory. The wall buttresses of the façade are repeated along the sides. The chief characteristics which are of significance for the Renaissance are first, that this Lombard Gothic has ignored thirteenth- and fourteenth-century developments elsewhere, and second, that it is nonetheless truly Gothic, and not a sub-Romanesque vestige.

Against such a background the Visconti "pre-Renaissance" makes its unheralded appearance. In the short space of ten years construction is begun on the Cathedral of Milan, the façade of Monza Cathedral, the Certosa of Pavia, the Cathedral of Como, and we may even add San Petronio in Bologna, which was momentarily in the Visconti sphere. The mere list is revealing. These are no longer parish establishments, but cathedrals and monumental projects backed by the financial power of a consolidated state and court. Moreover, it was the expressed intention of Gian Galeazzo to rival in size and richness the greatest monuments of the Middle Ages. Today, Milan Cathedral remains the second largest in Europe.

Now it may easily be appreciated that those entrusted with this monumental revival found themselves on the horns of a dilemma, for the structural and decorative forms of the monastic tradition were poorly suited to the grandiose projects of the duke. It became necessary to look abroad for suitable technical means and formal expression, and the search for a style produced surprisingly heterogeneous results. The five monuments mentioned eventually took on wholly different aspects, borrowing from every available source. For example, Milan Cathedral has a strong German Gothic tinge, and Monza a Tuscan flavor.

The departure from local traditions, however, was made only with the greatest reluctance on the part of the designers. Milan Cathedral is a case in point. Although it is a familiar fact that the structure was directed by engineers invited from France and Germany, it is not generally recalled that Milanese architects laid the entire foundations up to the base of the piers in the three years previous to the calling of the first French expert in 1389. I believe that there is sufficient evidence in the cathedral records to demonstrate that this early plan was conceived within the orthodox monastic system, and that the summoning of foreigners was forced upon the local masters only when they failed to convince the duke and civil authorities that this system was capable of sustaining the huge edifice projected. [But see now the postscript to the preceding essay in this volume.] The unwillingness of the Milanese to submit to foreign intervention is attested by the uncontrolled and uninterrupted maltreatment accorded to the visitors

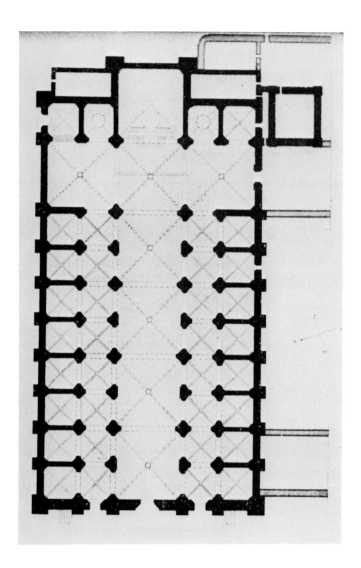

9.1 Pavia, Santa Maria del Carmine, plan.

9.2 *Façade.*

throughout the period of construction. Every meeting of the cathedral council becomes the occasion for a chauvinistic fracas which serves only to emphasize the quite inadequate technical equipment of the Milanese. In this fashion the distaste for northern Gothic which is common to all of fifteenth-century Italy is heightened by bitter firsthand experience.[3]

Something of the character of the earliest plan of the cathedral is indicated by a rough sketch of 1390 made, interestingly enough, by the future architect of San Petronio in Bologna (fig. 8.3).[4] It differs from the final solution (fig. 8.2) chiefly in the greater length of the transept—a feature which probably was developed from the Romanesque transepts of Piacenza and Cremona. That this plan already shows an alteration of the original is evident from records which indicate that the outer aisles were planned not as aisles but as the chapel rows of the Lombard Gothic style. A conference of 1392 studies, among other considerations, "whether or not the chapels of this church ought to be divided or separted one from another by a wall." The decision is in the negative, which causes one of the original architects to register his objection "that the chapels ought to be divided in the same manner in which they are joined beneath the ground," in other words, in the original foundations.[5] Further evidence of the provincial nature of the early work is offered in a vestige of the early decoration remaining in the north sacristy—a terracotta facing executed in the same technique as the façade decorations of churches and civil monuments of the preceding century.[6]

In the 1390s many of these Lombard traits are eradicated from the cathedral, but the local masters gain one highly significant point—they establish a nave section of the low and broad dimensions of their tradition, dispensing with flying buttresses.[7]

As the first and major monument of the Visconti era, the cathedral became the school for every young architect of the duchy for almost one hundred years. That it is nonetheless the only building in rayonnant style in Lombardy proves further the failure of the effort to transplant an exotic growth.

The Certosa of Pavia provides a much more satisfactory record of Lombard activity. It was, to begin with, a private project of the duke, and its extraordinary richness was quite frankly calculated to increase his personal prestige.[8] The seat of government under the Visconti was still at Pavia, and the monastery was significantly placed at the border of the ducal hunting preserve.[9] Already in the early 1390s, tithes from many neighboring parishes were channeled into the Carthusian treasury, and when the cloisters were begun in 1396 it was possible to provide each monk with a regal setting.[10] The cells are two-story cottages with loggie and private gardens.

The complex was planned by Gian Galeazzo's private architect, Bernardo da Venezia, and a score of Milanese assistants, many from the cathedral workshops. It is particularly noteworthy that, at a time when German and French architects were considered essential for the successful continuation of work at the cathedral, not one foreigner appeared at the Certosa. The duke, a consistent patron of foreign architects in Milan, undoubtedly wished his monastery to be a purely Lombard creation. The architects at the Certosa could profit by the technical experiences at Milan without contaminating their design.

The contrast of the cathedral and Certosa reaches beyond merely national characteristics, for, while the program for the cathedral was entirely fixed during the fourteenth century, the Certosa remained skeletal enough to submit to Renaissance variations under the second great patron, Francesco Sforza. The Certosa thus becomes the only monument which provides a link between two eras.

From 1396 to the death of Gian Galeazzo in 1402, building efforts were devoted to the cloisters. The church itself, on which our attention is concentrated, would hardly be worth investigating in this period were it not for a carefully inventoried description of the whole complex made by an engineer summoned for the purpose in 1402.[11] The detailed measurements make it clear that the major and minor cloisters were partly complete in substantially their present form. The church, however, was constructed only "ad superficiem terram," in other words, only the foundations were in place.[12] Its form and dimensions are unfortunately not recorded, but a note on the measurements of the minor cloister adjacent to it reveals a surprising fact. The chapter house and sacristy which continue along the axis of the south transept of the present church (fig. 9.3A) extended at that time some twenty braccia farther to the north (fig. 9.3B), completing the square of the cloister and invading the area of the present transept.[13] The only possible conclusion is that the original project for the church had no salient transept, and that the wall of the outer aisle simply continued without break across this area. It is perhaps not too rash to proceed to the assumption that the choir was similarly shorter by one bay, and terminated in a flat wall. The likelihood of this reconstruction is heightened by the appearance of the church plan without these outer bays. It proves to be the very essence of the Lombard Gothic system, varying only in detail from a number of fourteenth-century churches (fig. 9.1). Thus, like the cathedral, it hides beneath a novel style the provincial core which so powerfully resisted novelty.

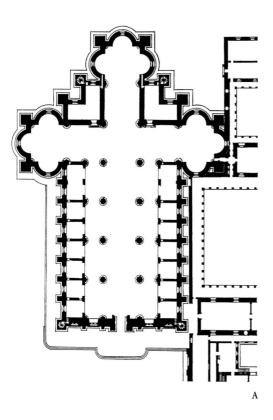

A

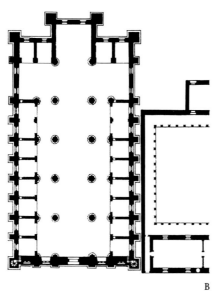

B

9.3 Pavia, Certosa: (A) *existing plan,* (B)
reconstruction of plan in 1402. Drawing by Henry
Fernandez.

Our consideration of the Certosa may well be interrupted here, for with the death of Gian Galeazzo in 1402, the political conditions which made possible his ambitious patronage suddenly worked in reverse. His weak son quickly lost control of the rapidly expanded state and the revenues which made patronage possible. For fifty years no building was initiated in the Milan area, and progress on those already started was practically brought to a halt. It is this dark age and its spectacular conclusion which makes the Milanese Renaissance unique. In 1448 the Visconti were overthrown by a people's republic, but despotism was necessary to a state threatened on three sides, and particularly by the French monarchy. Two years later Francesco Sforza, a *condottiere* who had fought with equal success for and against Milan, and who had married the daughter of the last Visconti, was invited to enter the city as Lord of Lombardy.

Francesco's close friendship with the Medici was of itself enough to restore order if not peace, and he immediately set to work to, so to speak, provide a Renaissance. While in Florence the art of the Renaissance gradually evolved in a congenial atmosphere, here it was virtually decreed. To Milan the Renaissance was not a state of culture, but a style—as foreign to Lombard soil as the northern Gothic had been, and like northern Gothic it was imposed from above. The introduction to Florentine art was not immediately destined to produce an imitative architecture. The result was rather a new tension, a new impetus on the part of the resentful local artist to evolve a distinctly Lombard expression.

It is interesting that an oratory of the Brunelleschi school built in the 1440s on Lombard soil, at Castiglione d'Olona, attracted no attention among northern Italian architects.[14] The Renaissance, in fact, came to Milan in the persons of two of its least classical practitioners: Filarete, the most fantastic of fifteenth-century architects, and Michelozzo, whose early work, as Heydenreich has shown, was unmistakably Gothic in origin.[15] It is amusing to note that these architects, who came to the north as champions of the Florentine Renaissance, were to become in many respects the students rather than the teachers of their hosts.

Francesco Sforza turned his attention to the cultivation of the arts as soon as he had become established in Milan, and immediately invited Filarete to the city to execute the sculptural decorations of part of the newly commenced Castello Sforzesco.[16] This fortress, like the prince who built it, was to become entirely medieval in character with a veneer of sophisticated decoration.

Filarete was occupied from 1451 to 1453 with the designs for the bridge and central tower, which were unfortunately leveled by lightning in the following century. During this period he was constantly frustrated by the Milanese architects. The opposition to him was so great that even the constant disciplinary orders from Francesco failed to stop interference with his work. In May 1452 one of the architects, whom Filarete scornfully refers to as a *muratore,* writes to Francesco that Filarete's projected garlands are holding up construction, that they are not weatherproof and are too expensive. He asks permission to leave them off, and being categorically ordered to retain them, somehow or other manages to have his own way.[17] The remainder of Filarete's work is hopelessly retarded for lack of materials. During this period he writes of his hardships to Pietro de' Medici, praising his patron and announcing that Francesco intends to make him *Capomagistro* at the cathedral, but he adds: "The fact is that because I am a foreigner they are incensed about it. I believe, though, that they will carry out the Lord's wishes."[18]

Filarete's estimate was quite correct. In 1452 he was nominated to the post at the cathedral as co-director with Giovanni Solari. His partner Giovanni was holding the same post at the Certosa, but progress there was still limited to purchasing materials for the church. The cathedral deputies immediately appointed their countryman, but delayed Filarete's appointment for so long that the duke was forced to write a severe letter in which he pointed out that there was no cause for complaint, since he was providing two masters for the price of one. Two years later the deputies apparently had had enough of such bargains and dismissed the Florentine, explaining to the duke that he was superfluous, since the *fabbrica* had an adequate engineer.[19]

Filarete did not remain idle for long, since in 1451 the decision had been reached to build a central hospital for the city to supplant the twenty-nine scattered establishments which then existed.[20] The architect was sent in 1456 to Florence to study the renowned hospitals there, and returned in the following year to start clearing ground. His work at the Ospedale Maggiore continued for seven years. Although he accomplished a considerable part of his huge project, he did so under as persistent opposition as he had previously encountered. This time it took the form of withholding his salary. The deputies felt that his inordinately large pay was wasteful and insulting to local masters, and continually petitioned to have it lowered. Even after succeeding in this aim, they were 387 lire in debt to Filarete when he resigned in 1465.[21] We can appreciate his position when we recall that his salary in 1453 was 12 lire monthly.

9.4 Milan, Ospedale Maggiore, perspective, from
Filarete's Trattato.

The Ospedale (fig. 9.4) is Filarete's only extant architectural work. It was an extraordinarily ambitious project involving a great central court with a chapel in the center and cruciform wards on either side marking off another eight courts. A canal at the rear was to be employed for sanitation. While it was a remarkably functional building for its time, it evidences that love for geometrical shapes per se which makes the ideal city of Filarete's *Trattato* seem so uncomfortable.[22] Only part of the extreme right wing was completed under the author of the plan. What has survived shows Filarete to be a rather pedestrian student of the first generation of Florentine architects. The forms are heavy and the ensemble monotonous. Unfortunately, later remodeling has removed a distinctive device which is strongly favored throughout the pages of the *Trattato*: the facade loggia, which at the Ospedale opened the second story to a depth of one bay. The device is clearly dependent on Brunelleschi's hospital in Florence.

The upper story of the Ospedale is a strange mixture of classic decorative detail and pure Gothic forms. This is in contrast to the author's designs for the building and to his ardent championing of the antique as against the Gothic style.[23] The unexpected inclusion of Gothic detail represents a betrayal of the original concept which cannot be assigned to Filarete. On his resignation in 1465 he was supplanted by Guiniforte Solari, the son of his former partner and at this time the leading architect in

9.5 Bergamo, cathedral, interior elevation, from
Filarete's Trattato.

9.6 Pavia, San Michele, section.

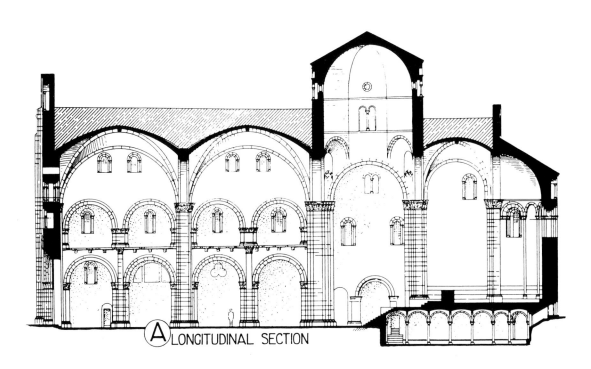

Ⓐ LONGITUDINAL SECTION

Milan. On stylistic bases it is quite plausible to assign the Gothic portions to the local architect, who in thus altering Filarete's intention delivered the crowning insult of a stormy career to the unpopular Florentine.

The discussion of Filarete began with the suggestion that he took from Milan more than he gave to it. So far, we have certainly seen no evidence of exchange in either direction, but ultimately the master appears to have absorbed from his environment a certain Lombard quality which appears in his last work. The Cathedral of Bergamo was designed shortly after the founding of the Ospedale.[24] Only the drawings in the *Trattato* remain for, as if to perpetuate the feud against Florence, the building was entirely remodeled by Carlo Fontana in the seventeenth century. The plan is a Latin cross with chapels opening onto the single nave—a scheme which may or may not reflect the Gothic tradition. The interior elevation (fig. 9.5) is more revealing. Here the main arcade is carried by inordinately heavy cubic piers. Between the arcade and the small clerestory windows a gallery is placed behind a second arcade on cubic piers. One cannot escape the parallels with certain Lombard Romanesque elevations. The main arcade, galleries, and unadorned clerestory windows are strikingly close to the Romanesque church of San Michele in Pavia (fig. 9.6). The suggested alternation of supports, which arranges two bays of the aisles to one of the nave, and the massive, wall-like quality of the supports is purely Romanesque in spirit. The ambiguous articulation, which confuses the relation of the main arcade to the gallery openings, results in a kind of Romanesque mannerism. We shall shortly see the great extent to which the Romanesque style figures as an element in the early Lombard Renaissance.

Passing on to Michelozzo, we find an agent of the Renaissance who was much more inclined to submit to the Milanese penchant for the Gothic. As the family architect of the Medici his work was restricted to two buildings for their agent in northern Italy, Pigello Portinari. His position in this respect differed significantly from that of Filarete, for he could not be accused of usurping the position of Lombard masters. His first work was the remodeling and extension of a palace given to the Medici in 1456 by Francesco, which became known as the Banco Mediceo. Since destroyed, it remains in a drawing from Filarete's *Trattato* (fig. 9.7).[25]

One immediately feels the Gothic quality of the design, and the adaptation of north Italian terracotta technique in the decorative devices. The arches of the upper windows are pointed and ornamented with crockets. In contrast to this, the heavy cornice on volute brackets and the arrangement of the lower story are much closer to the Florentine Renaissance. The result is a palpable compromise which must have been eminently satisfactory both to the patrons and the Milanese public.

9.7   *Milan, Banco Mediceo, façade, from Filarete's*
Trattato.

In 1462 Michelozzo began his second Medici commission in Milan—the Portinari Chapel, adjoining the Romanesque church of San Eustorgio.[26] Here the architect
shows himself a past master of compromise. In plan and conception the chapel reflects
the early work of Brunelleschi (fig. 9.8). The drum with oculi which rises from the
cubic mass of the building interprets Brunelleschian color contrasts and thin membering in the familiar brick of north Italy. The lantern reminds us of the Pazzi Chapel. The
pinnacles at the four corners, on the other hand, are simply reinterpretations of the
buttress spires of Lombard Gothic churches. One Romanesque feature finds its way
into the interior, where the drum is decorated with a painted gallery on colonnettes
reflecting a similar device at Piacenza and other Lombard cathedrals. In sum, the Michelozzo building is a quite harmonious counterpart to San Eustorgio, its twelfth-
century neighbor.

　　This rapid survey has revealed the full extent of the Florentine invasion of
Milan in the third quarter of the century. It demonstrates that whatever was uncom-
promisingly Renaissance in spirit met the most stubborn resistance. It was precisely the
same resistance as that encountered half a century before by the apologists of northern
Gothic art. The ultimate effect of the importations from the north and south was nothing more than an intensification of the opposition to all foreign modes of expression.
The architects of Francesco Sforza were by this token partly committed to a merely

9.8   *Milan, San Eustorgio, exterior of Portinari*
Chapel.

negative position. The reverse of this coin was their devotion to local tradition. Considering the limitations of the tradition, it is no wonder that the result was for the most part an undistinguished school of Lombard Gothic building. But the tradition proved not to be wholly confining. It was occasionally employed with a fantastic genius in the creation of something quite unique.

It is extremely difficult to discover whom we may credit with the conception of the more interesting monuments of the period. Paradoxically, while we are richly supplied with the histories of both the buildings and the architects, we have no means of coordinating the two. The anonymity that blankets building activity is in itself a mark of a pre-Renaissance point of view. The documentation on Guiniforte Solari is a case in point.[27] He was born in 1429, at which time his father Giovanni was employed at the cloisters of the Certosa. In 1459 he appears in the register of the cathedral and is employed at about the same time at the Certosa, where he works as *Capomagistro* from 1462 to 1480. During the same period he is occupied in constructing the church of Santa Maria delle Grazie. As we have seen, 1465 marks his succession to Filarete at the Ospedale. In 1471 he succeeds his father as chief architect to the second Sforza duke, carrying out numerous projects which have since disappeared. Tradition assigns to him the Benedictine church of San Pietro in Gessate. In spite of a considerable array of data, it is only on circumstantial evidence that Guiniforte may be assigned the actual design of any of these works, but convenience demands that we tentatively accept the attributions.

A necessary introduction to the consideration of the Certosa is the contemporary Santa Maria delle Grazie, a church renowned for Bramante's choir and Leonardo's *Last Supper*.[28] It is chosen arbitrarily as a representative of that large conservative school of ecclesiastical architecture which formed in reaction to the foreign invasions. The monastery that adjoins it was founded in 1464, and the church itself was in construction during the 1470s. A seventeenth-century history of the monastery records an event of considerable importance to the design. A difference of opinion concerning the form of the church arose between the Dominican monks and Count Gasparo Vimercanti, the patron of the monastery.[29] The latter demanded a large vaulted edifice, while the brothers held out for a small, flat-ceilinged construction. In the compromise which was reached after considerable delay, the count gave ground with respect to size, and the monks accepted stone vaulting. The story could be apocryphal, but it accords too well with what we have already seen of the artistic climate to be without foundation. The nobility again attempts to break through the bounds of conservatism, and meets formidable resistance. This time it is not from the architects but from the clergy, and it is one of numerous similar events which indicate that the role of the orders in Renaissance architecture bears careful study.

On first sight the building shows no signs of its fifteenth-century origin. It has most of the earmarks of the Lombard Gothic style (fig. 9.9). The plan has chapel rows flanking its three aisles. The broad profile of the brick façade is familiar, as are the central rose and the decorative oculi, while the windows, though round-arched, retain a Gothic verticality. On the other hand, a certain ordered rhythm in the fenestration gives some evidence of a new outlook, as does the absence of spires over the buttresses. On entering the nave we are surprised to find that the structural system employed is not merely outmoded, but the most primitive available in the Gothic vocabulary. The low vaults preclude a clerestory. They are articulated by ribs of a torus profile that characterize the earliest rib vaulting of Lombardy. The transverse arches are carried by primitive rectangular shafts which fall awkwardly, not onto the typical Gothic compound pier but onto columns, whose capitals might well be Romanesque. Virtually all of these elements are found in one of Lombardy's most ancient ribbed structures, the Romanesque abbey of Viboldone (fig. 9.10), founded in 1176 and vaulted possibly in the following century.[30]

It is amply evident that, whether or not the architect was consciously concerned with the employment of Romanesque forms, he was certainly intent on reaching back to a far-distant past. It is impossible to see this nave as a mere continuation of the style which was interrupted by Gian Galeazzo, for the fourteenth century is clearly brushed aside in a search for the ultimate roots of the Gothic style. Authority is sought in the unchallengeable antiquity of the vocabulary. It must be admitted that this interpretation of the Grazie is the result of working backward, for the easily overlooked revival character of this church is only a confirmation of what is unmistakably evident at the Certosa. Guiniforte Solari is presumably the author of both designs, and we can imagine that the great wealth and aristocratic orientation of the Carthusians allowed a far greater freedom to the architects. In point of fact, the Carthusians were so far from imposing any ascetic restrictions upon their artists that they poured money into the monastery for fear of having to meet a contractual obligation to give the surplus to the poor.[31]

In the years which preceded the accession of Francesco Sforza, progress at the Certosa was limited to the completion of the two cloisters, save for the decorative arcade of the smaller one.[32] The new duke immediately provided for resumption of activity at the church, and Giovanni Solari was occupied on this project from 1452 to 1454. This is the last appearance of the elder Solari at the Certosa, and the sparsity of records in the late fifties indicates that work was again interrupted.[33] After 1459, under Guiniforte's direction, rapid progress was made. In 1462–63 vaulting stones and capitals were being cut, and in the following year vault decorations were ordered.[34] By 1473 the roof was leaded, and two portrayals of the consecration of May 1497 show the church complete except for the upper portion of the façade.[35]

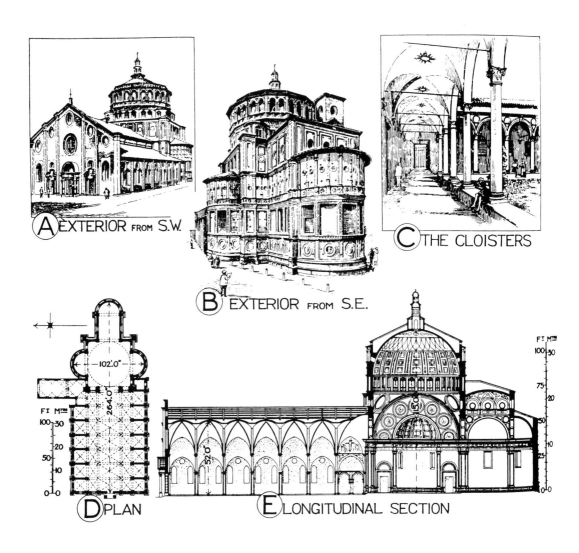

(A) EXTERIOR FROM S.W.

(B) EXTERIOR FROM S.E.

(C) THE CLOISTERS

(D) PLAN

(E) LONGITUDINAL SECTION

9.9   Milan, Santa Maria delle Grazie.

9.10   Viboldone, abbey church, nave.

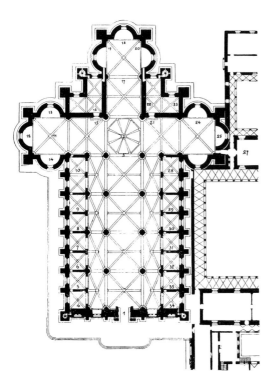

9.11 *Pavia, Certosa, plan. From Chierici*, Guida della Certosa di Pavia.

9.12 *Pavia, Certosa, interior.*

Recalling the foundation left by Bernardo da Venezia in 1402, we see that the problem faced in the 1450s was whether to complete the purely Lombard Gothic project of the previous century or to employ the old foundations as a starting point for a modern scheme. The latter alternative was chosen. The original plan was largely retained in the nave, but the eastern portion was wholly remodeled (fig. 9.11).

As we enter the church we are not made particularly conscious of its fourteenth-century heritage (fig. 9.12). In fact, its most striking characteristic is its total unfamiliarity. The forms are basically Gothic but there is an accent on horizontality and a lateral expansion of space which goes beyond even the Tuscan Gothic. Closer inspection reveals a quite unashamed mixture of vocabulary. Round as well as pointed arches are employed without regard to structural requirements. The square bays of the nave have pointed transverse arches, while those on the axis are round. The round arches of the side aisles are a positive hindrance structurally, and must be converted to a pointed form by a diaphragm. The vaulting system is even more eclectic. The square vaults of the nave are carried on sexpartite ribbing, which is plausible only in the early

Gothic alternating system, where small square bays in the side aisles provide a support for the transverse rib. Here it is carried only by a corbel, at some risk to stability. This fantastic revival is reflected in the side aisles, where the rib must be cut off at the center, due to the impossibility of providing support toward the nave. The result is a rectangular quinquepartite vault, which appears only at rare intervals in late Gothic architecture.

The most likely model for the use of the sexpartite vault is the only great Romanesque monument employing this system, the Cathedral of Piacenza, begun in 1122 and possibly vaulted before 1215.[36] The choice of this cathedral, in the Romanesque center closest to Pavia, is borne out by other similarities (fig. 9.13): the combination of pointed and round arches with a connecting diaphragm, and the employment of a dome on squinches with an interior dwarf gallery. There are grounds here for suspecting the conscious Romanesque revival which becomes unmistakable in the exterior elevations. We need not be put off by the realization that the vaulting of Piacenza was influenced by the early Gothic of the Ile de France. If it is not thoroughly Romanesque, it must at any rate have appeared so to the fifteenth century when sensitivity to style was notoriously vague.

If our hypothesis based on the survey of 1402 is correct, the eastern complex was entirely altered under the Solari. The arms of the transept were extended by the addition of similar bays, each with three circular chapels. The consequent alteration in massing is characteristically Romanesque. We have only to refer to a second twelfth-century cathedral, at Parma, for the source of the plan (fig. 9.14). The Certosa is essentially a rationalization of the potentialities of its forerunner.

The exterior is primarily notable for its lavish use of the dwarf gallery (figs. 9.15, 9.16). It is important to note that this Romanesque device was rarely employed in the fourteenth century, and its appearance here can decidedly be characterized as a revival. It is employed in such a way that any gothicisms remaining in the nave interior are here obliterated. The sole reminders of the Gothic past are the delicately carved pinnacles surmounting the heavy corner buttresses and stair towers. With this exception there is not a pointed arch or sign of tracery in evidence. Faithful to the fourteenth-century plan, piers rise along the outer walls as if they expected to become flying buttresses, only to become the supports for richly carved pinnacles of purely Renaissance detail.

The handling of the chapels on the exterior, with their low conical roofs, dwarf galleries, and high windows, is so strikingly similar to Romanesque prototypes that the comparison to similar chapels at Santa Maria Maggiore in Bergamo (fig. 9.17)

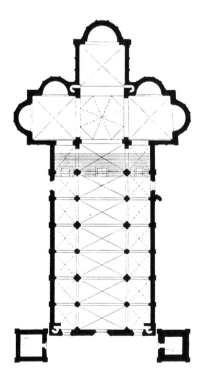

9.13 Piacenza, cathedral, crossing.

9.14 Parma, cathedral, plan. From Dehio and von Bezold, Die kirchliche Baukunst des Abendlandes.

9.15   *Pavia, Certosa, view from northeast.*

9.16   *View from small cloister.*

needs no elucidation. A closer view of the Certosa chapels reveals an exclusively classic decoration. This is perhaps a second example of the acceptance of Florentine Renaissance forms, but recalling the dentil frieze at Bergamo, we realize that antique elements may also be reached through the Romanesque.

Finally there is the question of the crossing tower. The employment of a monumental octagonal lantern over the crossing is one of the distinctive marks of the Lombard Romanesque. It remains only to demonstrate that its interpretation here is in the spirit of a revival, and not simply an example of the persistent survival of a characteristic form. Almost every commentator on the Certosa has emphasized the parallel between the Certosa and the magnificent Gothic tower of Chiaravalle Milanese of the mid-fourteenth century (fig. 9.18).[37] Yet, in comparing the two, the Certosa seems to return to the squat profile of Romanesque towers. The strongest vertical accent is provided by the tall uppermost story, which, in its Bramantesque detail, betrays a late alteration of the original project. Moreover, it is only in the Romanesque period that colonnettes are employed to support an entablature rather than arches.

In sum, lest the impression of the Romanesque character of the Certosa become overwhelming, let us recall the strictly Gothic character of the nave, the purely Renaissance form of the buttress pinnacles, and finally glance at the subversive entry of flamboyant tracery in one of the windows of the sacristy tribunes. This is apparently the only element that the Cathedral of Milan contributed to its country sister.

This polyglot collection of styles which characterizes the early Renaissance in Milan hangs on to the end of the century, and tends here and there to evolve into the fantastic goldsmith type of architecture represented by the façade of the Certosa, an anonymous work of the 1490s.[38] It represents a new stage, in which the antique heritage is accepted as the source of the vocabulary. Though the principles of the Renaissance finally take hold in the Milan of Bramante and Leonardo, the Lombard heritage is never abandoned and continues to affect foreign visitors as strongly as it is affected by them.

In conclusion we are bound to seek an explanation for the strange phenomenon of the Romanesque revival, proposed here as the leitmotif of the Milanese Renaissance. I have tried to demonstrate that a primary cause is the tension brought about by the sudden contact of a backward region with more highly developed cultures. The Gothic of the north and Renaissance of the south combined to intensify the regionalism of Lombard architects. Furthermore, the tendency of the nobility to foster the imported styles in a high-handed fashion undoubtedly made them even less palatable to the artists, the lesser clergy, and the people at large.

9.17   *Bergamo, Santa Maria Maggiore, apsidal chapel.*

9.18   *Chiaravalle Milanese, view from south.*

Why the stylistic regionalism should have taken the form of a specifically Romanesque revival is another question. It might just as well have expressed itself, as it did in minor monuments, as a perpetuation of the style of the fourteenth century. The answer lies partially in the fact that the Lombard Gothic style proved inadequate to the structural and aesthetic problems posed by the Renaissance. The monumental Romanesque cathedrals, on the other hand, provided the impressive effects of massing and interior space and the variety of technical solutions which were required.

But aside from matters of convenience, the Romanesque revival partook of the Renaissance just by being non-Gothic. To claim that the architecture of the twelfth century was more "modern" than that of the fourteenth is no paradox at this period. The Romanesque was, in fact, the stepping stone to Rome, and as such enjoyed a high repute. We have only to recall the conviction of the fifteenth century that the Romanesque baptistery in Florence was an ancient Temple of Mars to realize the position of the style. As against the Gothic, imported from the barbarian north, the Romanesque seemed not only to belong to the antique tradition, but to belong to the people and region which created it. By reviving the Romanesque the Milanese thus expressed at one time the Lombard tradition and the Renaissance spirit.

An investigation of Romanesque revival elements in Lombardy serves only to scratch the surface of a fascinating problem in Renaissance studies, for Lombardy is not an exception in the fifteenth-century world. I feel that the formula of revival is evident at an earlier date in Florence, with certain works of Brunelleschi and Alberti, and contemporaneously at Venice in the architectural fantasies of Jacopo Bellini, and in church architecture as well. The phenomenon has been richly documented by Baltrušaitis for late Gothic France,[39] and may be connected with the appearance of Romanesque settings in the panels of Jan van Eyck and his Flemish contemporaries. In each case the regional revival appears as a transition to the revival of classical antiquity. The classical heritage, common to Europe as a whole, gradually overcomes regional determinism. As a result of what might be called a law of cultural primacy, the restricted revival must ultimately give way to the broad and general.

Notes

1. In spite of the fact that the "Lombard Gothic" style of the late thirteenth and fourteenth centuries is clearly distinguishable from Gothic ecclesiastical architecture elsewhere in Italy, it has yet to be seriously studied. The great interest in this style, which arose during the Gothic Revival period of the nineteenth century, produced a wealth of superficial studies which rapidly declined with a change in art-historical fashions in the 1880s. [See n. 8 of the preceding essay for a selection of studies on the subject; these are cited by short title in following notes of this essay.]

2. The church is described in Lübke, "Reisenotizen," 161ff. The foundation date remains a problem. Lübke proposes 1325, while Ricci (*Storia*, 2:397) repeats an earlier tradition assigning it to 1373. On the basis of style the latter date—or 1390, which appears in the C. T. I. guide, p. 720—seems more plausible.

3. The early history of Milan Cathedral is richly documented in the exhaustive edition of the cathedral records: *Annali della fabbrica del Duomo di Milano dall'origine fino al presente*, 8 vols. (Milan, 1877–1885). See also Camille Boito, *Il Duomo di Milano e i disegni per la sua facciata* (Milan, 1889), 12–97. The problem of the early project will be studied in the author's forthcoming article, "Ars Sine Scientia Nihil Est" [reprinted in this volume].

4. The sketch was made while Antonio di Vincenzo was in Milan, presumably to pick up ideas for his San Petronio project, which was commenced later in the same year, 1390. It is accompanied by notes which record the measurements of the plan and section. The tracing which appears here was first published by Luca Beltrami in *Raccolta milanese*, December 1887. The original remains unpublished.

5. *Annali*, 1:68ff.

6. Cf. Luca Beltrami, *Per la facciata del Duomo di Milano* (Milan, 1887), 1:29, and Boito, *Il Duomo*, plate 29.

7. The flying buttresses employed along the nave walls are unnecessary additions of the eighteenth and nineteenth centuries. Their construction postdates the early eighteenth-century engravings of the cathedral published by Giulio Carotti, "Vicende del Duomo di Milano e della sua Facciata," *Archivio storico dell'arte*, 2 (1889), 113ff.; Paolo Arrigoni, *Milano settecentesca dall'album dell'incisore Marc'Antonio Dal Re* (Milan, n.d.).

8. In a letter of November 20, 1394, the duke states his intention to erect "unum Carthusiense monasterium propre hanc nostram civitatem papiae ob devotionem dicti ordinis quam solempnius et magis notabile poterimus" (Carlo Magenta, *La Certosa di Pavia* [Milan, 1897], 87). The placing of the cornerstone in August 1396 is the occasion for a courtly display in which the duke pointedly shares the honors with his three sons. A contemporary description of the ceremony is published in Luca Beltrami, *Storia documentata della Certosa di Pavia* (Milan, 1869), 62f.

9. The preserve, known as *Il Barco* (*sic*) has now disappeared, but is recorded in sixteenth-century maps discovered by Beltrami (*Storia*, 21–27).

10. Gian Galeazzo's will of 1397 confirms earlier grants and instructs his son to provide the monastery with an annual income of 10,000 florins. Cf. Magenta, *La Certosa di Pavia*, 85; Beltrami, *Storia*, 36f.

11. Published in Beltrami, *Storia*, 208–215.

12. Ibid., 212: "Item paries a sero parte qui facit refitoria monachorum et conversorum est long. circha brachia sexaginta quinque, gross. de testis novem alta a contrafortibus ecclesie super quibus pars ipsius parietis fundata supra curs. viginti novem, qui contrafortes sunt ad superficiem terrae." That is, the outer west wall of the cloister, where the two refectories stand, is 65 braccia long and 29 high. The height is measured from the buttresses (actually the foundations for the buttresses) of the church, which serve as a common base for the north wall of the refectories and the church and are at this time level with the ground.

13. The chapter house–sacristy is on the east side of the cloister, directly opposite the refectories. The survey (p. 112) informs us that it faced the cloister along the entire side—a distance of 54½ braccia (the present building is only about 36 braccia in length). This is approximately equal to the cloister frontage of the refectories. These specifications indicate that part of the chapter house–sacristy was constructed on the area now occupied by the transept. This impression is reinforced by the statement that the north wall of the building is founded upon the "contrafortibus ecclesie suprascriptis," referring to the buttresses mentioned in the passage quoted in n. 12. [As published in this volume, figure 9.3B represents a partial revision of this analysis, based on research by JoAnne Bernstein cited in the postscript to this essay.]

14. The problem of Brunelleschian influences in the Milan area is discussed by Agnoldomenico Pica, "Il Brunellesco e le origini del Rinascimento Lombardo," *Atti del Primo Congresso Nazionale di Storia dell'Architettura* (Florence, 1938). I came upon this volume only recently and was gratified to discover that Pica's suggestion for an interpretation of the Milanese Renaissance, and in particular the phenomenon of the Romanesque revival, are substantially the same as those which appear here.

15. "Gedanken über Michelozzo di Bartolomeo," *Festschrift Wilhelm Pinder* (Lepizig, 1938), 264ff.

16. Cf. M. Lazzaroni and U. Munoz, *Filarete: scultore e architetto del secolo XV* (Rome, 1908), 163.

17. Ibid., 166f.

18. Ibid., 164. Letter of December 20, 1451: "Io o isperanzia di qua mediante la gratia di dio farvi honore a voi e a me dico a voi perche voi e per vostra reccomandatione il signore mi mostra assai amore. Avisandove chellui vuole che sia capomaestro nel Duomo ben a vero che perche sono forestiere loro ci fano ripulsa, credo pure faranno la volunta del Signore etc. Bene valete e vester sum. Antonius ischultor."

19. *Annali della fabbrica del Duomo*, 2:155, entry for Jan. 7, 1455: "considerando che detto maestro Antonio e superfluo, perche la fabbrica ha gia un ingegnere sufficiente, fu deliberato di non doversi accetare."

20. Lazzaroni and Munoz, *Filarete*, 185ff.

21. Ibid., 204.

22. Cf. the W. Oettingen edition of the *Trattato*, *Quellenschrifte für Kunstgeschichte*, n.s. 3 (1890).

23. In the *Trattato*, which takes the form of a hypothetical dialogue between the architect and his patron, Filarete takes pains to explain to an eager duke that the current Gothic architecture is unworthy of patronage. It is a noteworthy sign of the artistic climate in Milan that the architect refers to the Gothic as "stile moderno," and to the Renaissance as "stile antico." In accordance with contemporary Florentine theory, the "barbarians" are held responsible for introducing Gothic architecture to Italy. See especially the passage in the Oettingen edition, 272–274.

24. Lazzaroni and Munoz, *Filarete*, 219–224. At the request of the archbishop of Bergamo, Filarete left his work on the Ospedale in April 1457 to initiate the project for the new cathedral.

25. An elaborate description of the building is provided in the *Trattato* (Oettingen ed., 697ff.), but without any reference to Michelozzo. Cf. also A. G. Meyer, *Oberitalienische Frührenaissance* (Berlin, 1897), 1:99ff.

26. Meyer, *Oberitalienische Frührenaissance*, 1:110ff.

27. Malaguzzi-Valeri, "I Solari, Architetti e Scultori Lombardi del XV secolo," *Italienische Forschungen vom Kunsthistorischen Institut in Florenz*, 1 (1906), 76–91.

28. Two recent publications on the Grazie include an extensive bibliography: *I monumenti italiani*, Fasc. X (Rome, 1937), and A. Pica and P. Portaluppi, *Le Grazie* (Rome, 1938).

29. Cf. Malaguzzi-Valeri, "I Solari," 84.

30. A. Kingsley Porter, *Lombard Architecture* (New Haven, 1917), 1:167, 3:549f.

31. Cf. Beltrami, *Storia*, 32; Magenta, *La Certosa di Pavia*, 87.

32. Magenta, *La Certosa di Pavia*, 105–109.

33. The *Registro* for these years includes the entry: "Item pro expensis factis per unum famulum nostrum qui associavit magistrum Johannem de Solario, qui venit ad considerandum edificium ecclesie fiende." (L. Beltrami, *La Certosa di Pavia* [Milan, 1895], 53).

34. Ibid., 57.

35. Illustrated in ibid., 82–83.

36. Kingsley Porter, *Lombard Architecture*, 3:241–245.

37. Ibid., 2:295–300; Michele Caffi, *Dell'Abbazia di Chiaravalle in Lombardia* (Milan, 1842). The monastery is Romanesque but the tower was raised over two centuries after the foundation. It may be dated by its stylistic similarities to the bell tower of San Gottardo in Milan, erected after 1336 (Mongeri, *L'arte in Milano* [Milan, 1872], 172).

38. In the early seventies, a façade project, probably by Guiniforte Solari, was begun and shortly thereafter abandoned. The present work was commenced only in the late nineties. There are no records concerning the construction or individuals concerned.

39. Lecture at New York University Institute of Fine Arts, Fall 1948, constituting a portion of a book now in press. I am indebted to Dr. Baltrušaitis for the use of his notes on Romanesque revival elements in France.

Postscript

My interest in the Milanese Renaissance, which was the subject of my master's thesis, goes back to the spring of 1945, immediately after the surrender of the German and Italian forces in Italy. My company was awaiting reassignment and I volunteered for temporary service with the Monuments and Fine Arts Commission. I was assigned to make daily trips from Milan to the Certosa of Pavia to supervise the return of archival material that had been removed there from the Royal Palace in Milan for safe-keeping during the war and, while packets were being loaded onto trucks, I would wander in and around the church. A few weeks later, after the company was rushed back to the United States to be retrained for the Asian theater, the war in the Pacific also had come to an end and the army suddenly discharged the company. I went directly from the barracks in New Jersey to the Institute of Fine Arts of NYU in time to register for the fall semester. After apologizing to Karl Lehmann for abandoning the thesis on "Greek Grave Stele with a Sitting and Standing Figure" which I had begun in 1942, I sought out Richard Krautheimer's guidance for this new subject.

The principal achievement of this study was the definition of the Romanesque revival as an aspect of the Lombard Renaissance, and its relation to Gothic survival. The phenomenon has been briefly discussed by some exceptional scholars, primarily in its manifestation in painting: it was first observed by Hans Tietze, taken up by Erwin Panofsky in his discussion of certain paintings of Jan van Eyck, and later expanded by him to more general but brief observations in *Renaissance and Renascences;* more recently Federico Zeri alluded to it in his discussion of the "Pseudorenaissance." I returned to it in my paper on quattrocento churches in Florence and Venice, which develops a similar hypothesis about the use of Byzantine forms in Venice. But it calls for focused attention.

Two corrections are in order. First, Bernardo da Venezia, the architect of the Certosa in 1396, was also the designer of the Carmine in Pavia (figs 9.1, 9.2), and the duke had also asked him to consult on the construction of the cathedral in Milan (see the reviews of the documentation by Albertini Ottolenghi and Morscheck).

Second, one of the reasons for reconstructing the fourteenth-century plan of the Certosa without a projecting transept was that the buildings of the smaller cloister would have taken up the space required for the projection. I had assumed, following Beltrami (and followed by Romanini and Albertini Ottolenghi), that the structures around the smaller cloister as described in the building survey of 1402 completely surrounded the cloister portico and thus preempted the required space. JoAnne Bernstein's close analysis of the measurements in the survey suggests that there could have been enough unoccupied space on the east side of the cloister to permit the transept to project into the northeast corner of the cloister behind the portico (figure 9.3B, my reconstruction of the original plan, has been redrawn to reflect this change). I do not believe, however, that this makes my reconstruction less credible. Regardless of the condition of the site, the plan is more likely to have followed the model of the Carmine (fig. 9.1), particularly if the same architect was responsible for both, than to have departed from the common practice of Lombard monastic architecture.

The existing church at the Certosa must have been barely started in 1462 when Guiniforte Solari was assigned to complete it (Morscheck 1977, p. 6, with new documents contradicting my assumption and that of earlier and later writers that the piers were largely complete and construction of the vaults under way). It was substantially complete by 1473.

The attribution of the Banco Mediceo (founded before 1459) and the Portinari Chapel (1462–68) to Michelozzo originated with Vasari but was first questioned by Costantino Baroni on grounds of style and technique, in his article of 1939 of which I was originally unaware. Now Ferrara and Quintero, in the first thorough work on Michelozzo's architecture, and Luciano Patetta raise further doubts. Filarete appears in documents on the Banco as an adviser to the patron, Pigello Portinari, and the drawing of it in his *Trattato* (fig. 9.7) is accompanied by a long description detailed enough to provide Patetta (p. 267) with the basis for a reconstruction of the plan. That does not prove that he had a role in designing it, but his long description of it makes it seem a twin of his Ospedale Maggiore. Patetta proposes Guiniforte Solari as plausible alternative to Filarete as the designer of the Portinari Chapel. I agree that our understanding of Florentine and Milanese quattrocento architecture is not improved by maintaining the traditional attributions.

Ackerman, James S. "Observations on Renaissance Church Planning in Venice and Florence," in *Florence and Venice, Comparisons and Relations* (Florence, 1980), 2:287–308.

Albertini Ottolenghi, Maria Grazia, et al. *La Certosa di Pavia* (Milan, 1968).

Averlino, Antonio, called Filarete. *Treatise on Architecture*, ed. John Spencer, 2 vols. (New Haven, 1965).

Baltrušaitis, Jurgis. *Reveils et prodiges: le gothique fantastique* (Paris, 1960).

Baroni, Costantino. "Il problema di Michelozzo a Milano," *Atti del IV Convegno internazionale di storia dell'architettura* (Milan, 1939), 123–127.

Bernstein, JoAnne. "The Architectural Sculpture of the Cloisters of the Certosa of Pavia," Ph.D. diss., New York University, 1972.

Borlini, G. "The Facade of the Certosa of Pavia," *The Art Bulletin*, 25 (1963).

Caroselli, S. "The Casa Marliani and Palace Building in Late Quattrocento Lombardy," Ph.D. diss., Johns Hopkins University, 1980.

Ferrara, Miranda, and Francesco Quintero. *Michelozzo di Bartolomeo* (Florence, 1984).

Morscheck, Charles R., Jr. *Relief Sculpture for the Facade of the Certosa di Pavia, 1473–1499* (New York, 1977).

Morscheck, Charles R., Jr. "The Profession of Architect in Milan before Bramante," *Arte Lombarda*, 78 (1986), 94–100.

Panofsky, Erwin. *Renaissance and Renascences in Western Art* (Stockholm, 1965).

Patetta, Luciano. *L'architettura del Quattrocento a Milano* (Milan, 1987).

Peroni, Adriano, et al. *Pavia, architetture dell'età sforzesca* (Turin, 1978).

Romanini, Angiola M. "L'architettura milanese nella seconda metà del quattrocento," *Storia di Milano* (Milan, 1956), 7:601–667.

Romanini, Angiola M. *L'architettura gotica in Lombardia*, 2 vols. (Milan, 1964).

Salmi, Mario. "Antonio Averlino detto il Filarete e l'architettura lombarda del primo rinascimento," *Atti del primo Congresso Nazionale di Storia dell'Architettura* (Florence, 1938), 185–196.

Tietze, Hans. "Romanische Kunst und Renaissance," *Vorträge der Bibliothek Warburg* (1926–27), 43ff.

Vaccari, Pietro. "Ancora uno sguardo alla genesi della Certosa di Pavia," *Studi in memoria di Gino Chierici* (Rome, 1965), 67–69.

Zeri, Federico. "Rinascimento e Pseudorinascimento," in *Storia dell'arte italiana*, II, 1 (Turin, 1983), 545–572.

IO

Sources of the Renaissance Villa

When we discuss antiquity and the Renaissance, the villa poses a peculiar problem,[1] because Early Renaissance architects did not know what an ancient villa looked like. Villa plans do not appear among fifteenth-century drawings after the antique, and there is no sign that Hellenistic landscape paintings with villa views were discovered before 1500. The only available source of knowledge was Roman literature; actually there were more surviving treatises on rustic life than on other themes relating to architecture. But while Cato, Varro, Palladio, Columella, and others wrote extensively about the villa, they were interested in it almost exclusively as an economic unit; they gave more information about the housing of grain, wine, and birds than of people. Furthermore, with proud republican austerity, they scorned rural luxury as represented by elegant dwellings, and praised the rustic life as the antithesis of sinful urban splendor. Vitruvius, who struck the spark for so many Renaissance inventions, slighted villas; they appear in his book only as displaced city houses in which the atrium is moved from the front to the rear.[2] Pliny the Younger provided the only specific descriptions of villas, but his letters pictured lavish and extensive architectural complexes that suited neither the finances nor the taste of quattrocento patrons.[3] Pliny's influence cannot be detected before the time of Bramante's Belvedere and the Villa Madama, when Early Renaissance reserve gave way to neo-imperial splendor.[4]

From *Studies in Western Art: Acts of the Twentieth International Congress of the History of Art,* edited by Millard Meiss, 2 vols. (Princeton: Princeton University Press, 1963), 2:6–18.

Ignorance of antique precedent is reflected in the failure of Renaissance architectural theorists to contribute to the development of a villa style. Some, like Filarete, ignored villa architecture and concentrated on garden design; others discussed it in vague and impractical terms. Palladio, whose career was devoted largely to villa design, wrote merely a gloss on Vitruvius that conforms neither to his own practice nor to that of the ancients.[5] Alberti was the most informative, but his villa is neither architecturally nor historically plausible.[6] It is Hellenistic in being of one story with many cubicles clustered around interior courts,[7] but it is medieval in being enclosed within high walls; one enters the principal court directly through an imposing gateway, as in a trecento castle or the villa described in the agricultural treatise of Piero de' Crescenzi, a contemporary of Dante.[8] It seems as if the walls would screen the low buildings from both sun and view, which Alberti regards as the major rewards of rural life.[9]

When the sixteenth-century theorist Pietro Cattaneo came to illustrate the villa in the sketchbook now in the Uffizi,[10] the curiously unclassical structure which appears among reconstructions of Greek architecture proves to be an illustration of the buildings described in Crescenzi's thirteenth-century text. As if to emphasize the confusion of the theorists, the plan of an ancient bath drawn on the same sheet resembles that of the Villa Giulia in Rome.

In practice as in theory, ignorance of ancient precedent promoted the survival of medieval forms. The villas of the Medici, who were patrons of radical church and palace architecture, were modifications of the fortified rural castles of fourteenth-century Tuscany.[11] Michelozzo's design of Cafaggiuolo may have been affected by the form of a medieval predecessor on the site that Cosimo purchased in 1427; but even villas newly erected in mid-century, such as Careggi, have the same Gothic vocabulary, enclosed form, and irregular plan. At Careggi, the towers have disappeared and two graceful Renaissance loggias have been applied to the rear in a strangely asymmetrical and inorganic way to form a small protected court; but such changes are superficial. Yet, the fact that it was practical to build such light and airy appendages proves that defense was no longer a significant function of the villa; if Careggi looks like a castle, it is not because it had to, but because the taste for traditional architecture was stronger than the aspiration to invent plausible reconstructions of Roman villas. We know from painted panoramas of the time, such as Gozzoli's frescoes in the Medici palace,[12] that the mid-fifteenth-century Tuscan and north Italian landscape was covered with such castle-villas.

The second generation of Renaissance patrons and architects, in the seventies and eighties, first attempted radical departures from tradition in villa architecture. The same generation abandoned medieval traditions in villa decoration, as represented by Uccello's battle scenes or Castagno's portraits of past heroes, in favor of antique themes such as Botticelli's mythologies or Pinturicchio's city-landscapes at the Belvedere of Innocent VIII.[13]

We would get a clearer image of Early Renaissance architecture by recognizing that, while the archetypes of the palace and church were formed in the second quarter of the fifteenth century, villa design took shape in the last quarter. No one has studied the problem since Patzak, whose excellent work of half a century ago failed to distinguish the late quattrocento contribution; it was only about Tuscany, where a premature start burdened architects with a semi-medieval style that retarded later experiment. The character of the new style can be defined only on a pan-Italian scale.

The essential features of this new style are symmetrical massing and a change from closed to open planning, so that the building is freed from encircling walls and turns outward to the landscape rather than inward toward a court. Within this general scheme there are many solutions, but one is dominant and symptomatic; its classical statements may be found in the Belvedere of Innocent VIII at the Vatican (fig. 10.1) of 1484–87,[14] the earliest surviving model; in the Villa Farnesina in Rome, of 1509; and later in Sanmicheli and early Palladio.

Common to all examples is a façade of two stories composed of three parts: a central block with an arcaded ground-floor loggia-hall, and two closed lateral blocks which often project forward from the plane of the loggia—slightly, in the form of towers, or boldly, in the form of wings of one or two bays—forming a U-shaped plan. At the Belvedere, the precipitous cliff prevented strict regularity: the left wing is slightly shorter than the right, but the tripartite scheme is calculated to promote symmetry in elevation. Not, however, in plan (fig. 10.2) because it is non-axial; the central axis is unaccented, there is no portal, and the internal disposition has to be a somewhat irregular grouping about the loggia-hall. Vasari's statement that the Belvedere was designed by Pollaiuolo, who came to Rome in 1484, has been questioned on the grounds that the documents mention only the Roman architect Jacopo da Pietrasanta. But a Tuscan source is possible, in spite of the castle tradition. A fresco by Benozzo Gozzoli in the Campo Santo at Pisa, dated 1478,[15] suggests that the form had been conceived, if not actually built, before the Belvedere. It was anticipated around 1460 in the garden façade of the Badia of Fiesole, a two-story loggia between projecting blocks.[16]

10.1   Vatican, Belvedere of Innocent VIII, 1484–87,
reconstruction by Redig de Campos.

10.2   Vatican, Belvedere of Innocent VIII, plan.

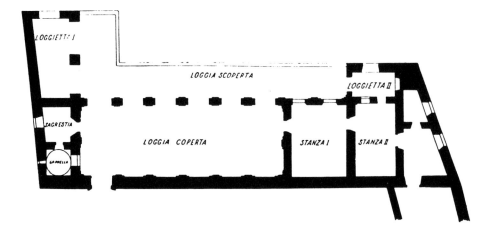

The type also appeared in the Veneto as soon as it became practical to build unfortified villas on the Terraferma. The best preserved example is the Villa Porto Colleoni at Thiene near Vicenza (fig. 10.3),[17] which obviously stems from late medieval palace architecture in Venice. The tile roof is modern; originally it was flat with a crenellated silhouette remarkably like the Belvedere. The Ca' Brusà, also near Vicenza, of about 1475–90, is interesting because it is so close to the earliest works of Palladio.[18]

The Farnesina owes less to the Belvedere than to the more developed Villa alle Volte near Siena (fig. 10.4).[19] It was built ca. 1500–1505, possibly as the first work of the Farnesina designer Baldassarre Peruzzi, for Sigismondo Chigi, brother of the owner of the Roman villa. The high stories, the design of the windows, and the attic motif bring the two villas into a relationship as close as that of their owners.

For more grandiose palace-villas the system could be extended beyond the principal façade and combined with interior courts.[20] The most palatial villa of the period was Poggio Reale (fig. 10.5), designed in 1487 by the Florentine Giuliano da Maiano for the king of Naples.[21] It was destroyed, but appears in a woodcut after Serlio with open loggias on four sides surrounding a great theater court, and corner towers providing the living accommodations.[22] We know from a sketch by Peruzzi that Serlio distorted the form from a rectangle of five by seven bays in order to make a square.[23] Poggio owes something to the four-towered medieval castle of the French *manoir* type, but it repaid the debt by returning to France, as Schreiber showed, to make an imprint on the Château Madrid, of 1528, and on Ancy-le-Franc, St.-Maur, and the Tuileries.[24]

The design must have been exported to France by Florentine architects, whose imagination was restrained by conservative patrons at home but encouraged by patrons abroad. Giuliano da Sangallo made a palace model for Charles VIII, now lost, which may have been close in style to Poggio Reale, and Poggio influenced another royal project by Giuliano, for King Ferdinand of Naples, dated 1488.[25] Leonardo's grandiose drawings for a towered French château, identified by Heydenreich with Romorantin, echo the familiar scheme with perhaps a dash of Venetian flavoring.[26] Leonardo's earlier projects follow both the Belvedere U and the Poggio four-towered scheme. The Belvedere, by the way, is the only actual villa that Leonardo recorded in his sketchbooks.[27]

Giuliano's villa masterpiece at Poggio a Caiano (fig. 10.6), designed for Lorenzo the Magnificent about 1480, is unique, but it conforms to the type rather more than meets the eye.[28] Not only is there a central loggia, but the windows are rhythmically disposed so as to isolate those at the ends. There is no Tuscan precedent for this

10.3   *Thiene, Villa Porto Colleoni, ca. 1447.*

10.4   Siena, env., Villa alle Volte, by Baldassarre
Peruzzi, ca. 1500–05.

10.5   Naples, villa of Poggio Reale. After Serlio.

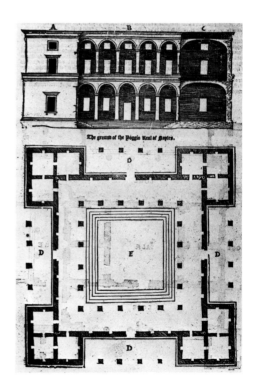

10.6 *Poggio a Caiano, Medici Villa, 1485.*

10.7 *Venice, Palazzo Loredan.*

motive; it is a Venetian habit, and it originated in the tripartite façade with an arcaded central tract flanked by closed towerlike blocks at the sides, as in the twelfth- or thirteenth-century Palazzo Loredan (fig. 10.7). The central dormer above the eaves, now replaced by Buontalenti's more massive substitute, is also characteristically Venetian.[29]

My motive in returning to Venice is to find a source for our ubiquitous late quattrocento villa type. If the Renaissance knew no ancient loggia-villa with corner towers, the tradition must be traced to medieval architecture, and Venice had the only medieval buildings that could have provided inspiration.[30] Its palaces of the Loredan type reveal the connection in plan as well as in elevation. Here only the façade portion is relevant, but this itself is significant; it reminds us that only one façade is emphasized

in villas of the Belvedere type. Though they are isolated on a height in the open countryside, their plan does not radiate outward toward the view on all sides but is strictly oriented in a single direction. The favoring of one of the four sides of the villa suggests a background in urban architecture, where—especially in Venice—only one façade *can* be accentuated. These similarities might seem fortuitous if they were not seen in the light of another major building of medieval Venice, the Fondaco dei Turchi, where both plan and elevation demonstrate an unmistakable bond with the fifteenth-century villa (figs. 10.8, 10.9).[31] Similarities to the Belvedere, for example, are too obvious to recite. The decorative crenellations above the Belvedere cornice may not come straight from Venice, but they do justify my assumption that these villas have medieval roots. The tripartite façade with central loggias and corner towers is the source of all later Venetian palace forms, so the influence may have come either directly from the Fondaco or indirectly from its descendants.[32] Whether the rare instances of the type in medieval Tuscany, such as the Palagio ai Torri near Compiobbi,[33] or the villa in a fresco by Antonio Veneziano of the 1380s in Pisa,[34] are earlier instances of Venetian influence, I cannot say.

But that problem is irrelevant, since Venice itself was not the creator but the purveyor of a villa type originating in imperial Rome, a type which Swoboda has defined as the *Portikusvilla mit Eckrisaliten*.[35] This form dominated the design of small villas in the late western Empire as it did those of the late fifteenth century.[36] The Rhineland villa at Mayen, founded as early as the first century, already has the characteristic plan appearing again at Mungersdorf near Cologne, in a villa which was occupied continuously from the first to the fourth centuries.[37] Mansfield Woodhouse (fig. 10.10) may serve as an example of the many rural structures of the type excavated in Britain.[38] More luxurious villas, such as Diocletian's palace at Spalato, often have porticoes and corner towers as façade elements in a complex plan with interior courts.[39]

The elevations of these villas, often difficult to determine from the excavations, are well illustrated in a group of African mosaics of the third and fourth centuries. In one of the best known, from Tabarca (fig. 10.11), the familiar loggia happens to be on the upper story, but there are less precise and appealing ones of the familiar form.[40]

The fact that all the examples are provincial does not prove an absence of the type in Italy. Pliny's Laurentinum had porticoes and corner blocks,[41] and excavations in nearby Istria and Dalmatia—the villas recently published by Ejnar Dyggve, as well as Diocletian's[42]—suggest that Italian practice did not differ from that of the outlying regions. I suspect that if Italian excavators did not have more urgent assignments, they might find as many small portico-villas as their northern colleagues.

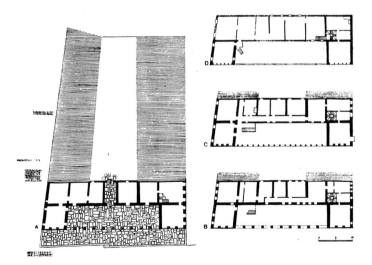

10.8   *Venice, Fondaco dei Turchi.*

10.9   *Venice, Fondaco dei Turchi, plan. From Chiolini,*
I caratteri distributivi degli antichi edifici.

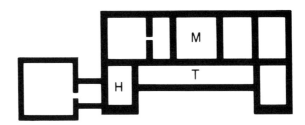

10.10 *Mansfield Woodhouse, Roman villa, plan.*
From Haverfield, The Roman Occupation of Britain.

10.11 *A villa. Roman mosaic from Tabarca, North*
Africa, early fourth century. From Inventaire des
Mosaïques de la Gaule et de l'Afrique.

10.12   *Galeata (near Forlì), palace of Theodoric, ca.*
500, reconstruction. After Krischen.

Recently Fiocco[43] and Swoboda[44] have closed the considerable gap between late antique villas and the Fondaco dei Turchi which Patzak had tried to fill with diffuse Oriental and Germanic influences.[45] They discovered in Ravenna the crucial link that confirms an unbroken descent of forms of domestic architecture on Italian soil from Hellenistic times to medieval Venice. We now recognize Ravenna as the center of an indigenous style independent of Constantinople, though of course related to the East by common origins and by direct influence. The façade and plan of Theodoric's palace at Galeata near Forlì (fig. 10.12) is proof of the Italian ancestry of the Fondaco which may be added to Ravennate decorative contributions adduced by Fiocco.[46]

   Venice's role as a conveyor of the villa tradition may be attributed to a geographical situation that assured security without the aid of enclosed, fortified architecture. Venice was the only medieval Italian city that could sustain an elegant, open domestic style, and this contributed to the development of a Venetian taste for the concourse between the architectural and the natural environment effected by opening buildings outward rather than inward. So, as the Renaissance countryside gained security, Venice was better prepared by tradition and by inclination to enjoy the delights of *villeggiatura* than was Florence, where the walled castle and enclosed garden long protected humanists from the discomforts of rusticity.

The possibility of an uninterrupted lineage from Rome to the Renaissance villa did not occur to me as I began this study. I was prompted only by curiosity to know how Renaissance artists proceeded when they knew too little to produce a convincing revival of antiquity. Our image of the Renaissance as an age of conscious *re*vival is established so firmly that we tend to underrate evidence of unconscious *sur*vival in which the forms of art are handed down from generation to generation like myths, without evidence of their original sources. It is symptomatic of this prejudice that Renaissance scholars have recognized the relevance of the Fondaco dei Turchi but have ignored the medievalists for whom that building was the terminus of a sequence that had started in antiquity.[47]

Renaissance studies are subject to another prejudice, that new quattrocento forms tend to originate in and emanate from Florence. So long as the villa style had to be traced to Michelozzo and Giuliano da Sangallo, it was impossible even to distinguish its dominant patterns; the possibility that supposedly Byzantine Venice should have been a seminal point was mentioned only to be brushed aside.

The basis for both biases is the same: rigidity in defining historical barriers dividing one so-called period from another, combined with the implication that there is something inherently more praiseworthy in innovation than in tradition. If this study is correct in its conclusions, it suggests the hazards of taking the term Renaissance too literally. The ancient villa was not reborn, because it never died; and its medieval descendants could provide the quattrocento with a more vital inspiration than the ruins of Rome.[48]

Notes

1. After the conclusion of the Congress I received Christoph Frommel's important monograph, *Die Farnesina und Peruzzis architektonishes Frühwerk* (Neue münchner Beiträge zur Kunstgeschichte, I, Berlin, 1961). Chapter VII in Frommel's book, a substantially more intensive study of the villa type I am considering here, generally anticipates my conclusions, though it does not examine the nature and significance of the medieval Venetian contribution beyond allowing that there was such a contribution (p. 116).

2. *De architectura,* 6, 5.

3. Pliny the Younger, *Letters,* 2, 17; 5, 6.

4. On the High Renaissance use of Pliny and other Roman sources, see J. Ackerman, *The Cortile del Belvedere* (Vatican City, 1954), 125–138.

5. *Quattro libri sull'architettura* (Venice, 1570), II, 69.

6. *De re aedificatoria,* V, 17. Alberti's essay of about 1438 on the villa (published by C. Grayson, *Rinascimento,* 4 [1953], 43–53, and in *Opere volgari* [Bari, 1960], 1:359–362) is in the tradition of rustic literature and does not deal with architecture.

7. An error in the Italian and English translations should be corrected, since it has led to misinterpretations of Alberti's plan. Among the open areas recommended for the relaxation of older members of the family are *emicycli,* which Bartoli rendered "alcuni in *cerchio*" (italics mine).

8. *De agricultura,* I, 7 (I use the editions of Venice, 1519, and Milan [Classici italiani], 1805). See D. Zucchini, "Precetti di architettura rurale," in *Società agraria di Bologna, Pier de' Crescenzi 1233–1321, Studi e documenti* (Bologna, 1933), 231ff.

9. But these comments apply specifically to Alberti's real country villa. The smaller suburban villa of the busy merchant (*De re aedificatoria,* IX, 2) also is one-storied, but has no encircling wall. It is characterized by its variety of room shapes: one proceeds "ex quadrangulis areis rotundas; ex rotundis rursus angulares; ex his in eas progressus detur quem neque totem rotundem neque lineis omnibus rectis concludantur." This type appears in the quattrocento only in ideal plans (e.g., Francesco di Giorgio) and has no relation to the form I shall be discussing here. Alberti's dissatisfaction with contemporary villa design is reflected in his scathing comment (IX, 4) on villas with towers and battlements.

10. Uffizi, Arch. 3294. I do not know the grounds for the attribution of this sketchbook, which I have not examined in the original.

11. Bernhard Patzak, *Palast und Villa in Toscana* (Leipzig, 1912–13), 2:68ff.; Ottavio Morisani, *Michelozzo architetto* (Turin, 1951), passim.

12. Details of the frescoes with villa views are reproduced by Patzak, *Palast und Villa,* vol. 2, pl. XLIX.

13. On the iconographical innovations in villa decoration in the second half of the century, see A. Chastel, *Art et humanisme à Florence au temps de Laurent le Magnifique* (Paris, 1959), 168ff. The significance of Pinturicchio's frescoes at the Belvedere is discussed in two important recent studies: S. Sandström, "The Programme for the Decoration of the Belvedere of Innocent VIII," *Kunsthistorisk Tidskrift,* 29 (1960), 35ff.; and J. Schulz, "Pinturicchio and the Revival of Antiquity," *Journal of the Warburg and Courtauld Institutes,* 15 (1962), 35–55.

14. See D. Redig de Campos, "Il Belvedere di Innocenzio VIII," *Triplice omaggio a Sua Stà. Pio XII* (Vatican City, 1958), 2: 289–304, with earlier bibliography.

15. *The Infancy and Youth of Moses;* see M. Bucci, *Camposanto monumentale di Pisa* (Pisa, 1960), fig. 122 and pp. 111, 136ff.

16. Of the late 1450s or early 1460s; see Patzak, *Palast und Villa,* 2: 84ff.; C. von Fabriczy, *Filippo Brunelleschi* (Stuttgart, 1892), 266ff., 584ff. The plan (Stegmann-Geymüller, *Die Architektur der Renaissance in Toscana* [Munich, 1885–1908], 1:49, fig. 1; 1:54, fig. 10), which has been altered, suggests that the loggia originally may have been flanked by towerlike blocks rather than the long tracts of the modern monastery. Frommel, *Die Farnesina,* 100 and fig. 18, cites another monastic contribution to the villa type: the convent of Sta. Chiara at Urbino, of 1478–1482, by Francesco di Giorgio.

17. *Le ville venete,* ed. Giuseppe Mazzotti (Treviso, 1954), 331f.

18. Ibid., p. 252, in the village of Lovolo. For other fifteenth-century villas in the Veneto, see also G. Mazzotti, *Palladian and Other Venetian Villas* (London, 1958), esp. 33–85.

19. Patzak, *Palast und Villa,* 2:143ff., figs. 180–182, 186–187; Stegmann-Geymüller, *Architektur der Renaissance in Toscana,* 10:9f., figs. 1, 2, and pl. X; Frommel, *Die Farnesina,* 106–109, 122–

124, figs. 20–21, pls. XIV a-f, XV a, b, d, XVI a. Here the main building program is dated ca. 1500–1505 and the attribution is made to the young Peruzzi rather than to Patzak's candidate, Giacomo Cozzarelli.

20. Michelangelo Muraro ("Tipi e architetture delle ville venete," Le ville venete [Treviso, 1954], 62ff.) discovered a manuscript of Anton Doni describing various types of villas classed according to social and economic levels. The "villa civile da re, da duca e da signore" requires a "stupenda loggia colonnata" on the main façade and another of the same design at the rear.

21. Fritz Schreiber, "Die französische Renaissance-Architektur und die Poggio Reale-Variationen des Sebastiano Serlio," dissertation, Halle, 1938, pp. 5ff.; Stegmann-Geymüller, Architektur der Renaissance in Toscana, 4:16, figs. 39, 40. Frommel (Die Farnesina, 90–96, fig. 16 and pl. XIII c-f) reconstructs the palace and garden plan by reinterpreting the sources; his conclusions make the earlier studies obsolete.

22. Sebastiano Serlio, Il terzo libro (Venice, 1584), fol. 122.

23. Schreiber, Die französische Renaissance-Architektur, fig. 1; Stegmann-Geymüller, Architektur der Renaissance in Toscana, vol. 4, fig. 40; and see Frommel.

24. Schreiber, Die französische Renaissance-Architektur, 17–62. The destroyed Bolognese Villa Foggianova (near Marano), built for Giovanni II Bentivoglio, was a primitive version of the Poggio Reale type, more obviously derived from the manoir. It had round towers at the four corners of a rectangular mass, and a two-story loggia only on the principal façade (U. Beseghi, Castelli e ville bolognese [Bologna, 1957], 281 and figure on 282, from an old print). Serlio (Il terzo libro, fol. 122) speaks of a Bolognese villa of the Poggio Reale type in his time. Giovanni II also built a loggia-villa on the U-plan at Poledrano in 1480 (Beseghi, 19ff., figure on 21).

25. On the two designs, see G. Vasari, Le vite . . . , ed. G. Milanesi (1879), 4:280, 272. The Naples plan is included in Giuliano's Barberini Codex (cf. Il libro di Giuliano da Sangallo Codex Vat. Barb. Lat. 4424, ed. C. Huelsen [Leipzig, 1910], fols. 8v, 39).

26. L. H. Heydenreich, "Leonardo da Vinci, Architect of Francis I," Burlington Magazine, 94 (1952), 277–285. Schreiber unaccountably ignored Leonardo in his account of Italian influences on Early Renaissance design in France.

27. Codex Atlanticus, fol. 78v (Accademia dei Lincei, Il Codice Atlantico di Leonardo da Vinci, vol. 1 [Milan, 1894], 180f., pl. CCXXXIV).

28. On the history of the villa, see A. Chastel, Art et humanisme, 148ff.

29. The contemporary Palazzo Corner-Spinelli (Mauro Coducci? 1480?) has a pedimented dormer with pendant volutes remarkably close to the original one at Poggio, though it has windows, not bells. P. Hamberg ("The Villa of Lorenzo il Magnifico at Poggio a Caiano and the Origin of Palladianism," Idea and Form [Figura, n.s. 1, Stockholm, 1950], 76ff.) associates Poggio with Alberti's chapters on the villa, and attempts to demonstrate its influence on Palladio without considering the achievements of a century of Venetian architecture before Palladio. I believe, however, that he correctly emphasizes the influence of Giuliano's use of the temple porch and pediment as the central façade motif; the device legitimized the medieval lobia (Patzak, Palast und Villa, 1:12, 41, passim) by clothing it in ancient dress. It appeared in Venice long before Palladio's time at the Palazzo Contarini delle Figure (ca. 1504–46), attributed to Antonio Abbondi (cf. Luigi Angellini, Le opere in Venezia di Mauro Codussi [Milan, 1945], 105ff., fig. 106).

30. See P. Chiolini, I caratteri distributivi degli antichi edifici (Milan, 1959), 321ff. As this paper went to press, I received a fundamental contribution to the history of medieval architecture: Paolo Maretto, L'edilizia gotica veneziana (Studi per una operante storia urbana di Venezia, II, Rome, 1960; published also in Palladio, 10 [1960]).

31. Patzak (Palast und Villa, 2:91ff.) first suggested Venetian influence in connection with the Medici villa in Fiesole by Michelozzo, who visited Venice ca. 1433–34. But he defined the contribution as being restricted to the front-to-rear communication corridor, and discounted the influence of the façade design and loggias. Furthermore, the villa in question is atypical and was entirely remodeled in the late Renaissance. It was Fritz Schreiber (Die französische Renaissance-Architektur, 24ff.) who correctly defined the significance of the Fondaco dei Turchi and its connection both with the ancient villa tradition discussed below and with the Renaissance villa (see below, n. 47).

32. For example, in the contract of the sale of the "Cà del Duca" in 1460, to Duke Francesco Sforza of Milan, Marco Cornaro, the owner, described the palace: "Item la dicta fazada a do torre da

lado, como a la caxa del Marchixo da Farara, le qualle torre sono de marmoro a diamante, e la riva fra le do torre con colone grossissime de marmoro" (Luca Beltrami, *La "Cà del Duca" sul Canal Grande* [Milan, 1900], 55; Professor Schulz called my attention to this text). Today only the basement and one story of one tower are preserved.

33. Thirteenth century; Patzak, *Palast und Villa,* 1:78, pl. XLI.

34. *The Funeral of S. Ranieri* in the Campo Santo. See Bucci, *Camposanto,* 69ff., fig. 72 (dated 1384–86). Antonio, a student of Taddeo Gaddi, did not necessarily turn to Venice for architectural inspiration; the crenellated wall suggests Tuscan models.

35. Karl M. Swoboda, *Römische und romanische Paläste,* 2d ed. (Vienna, 1924), 77–132 (chap. IV). See also his "Palazzi antichi e mediovali," *Bollettino del Centro di Studi per la Storia dell' Architettura,* 2 (1957), 3–32, and "The Problem of the Iconography of Late Antique and Early Mediaeval Palaces," *Journal of the Society of Architectural Historians,* 20 (1961), 78–89.

36. See R. Paribeni, "Le dimore dei potentiores nel basso impero," *Römische Mitteilungen,* 55 (1940), 132–148; Guido Mansuelli, *Le ville nel mondo romano* (Milan, 1958).

37. F. Oelmann, "Ein gallorömischer Bauernhof bei Mayen," *Bonner Jbh.,* 133 (1928), 51–152, pls. 1–13; F. Fremersdorf, *Der römische Gutshof Köln-Müngersdorf* (Römisch-germanische Kommission des Deutschen Archäologischen Instituts zu Frankfurt a. M., *Römisch-germanische Forschungen,* 6; Berlin and Leipzig, 1933), 12ff., 108ff., pls. 4–6, 14, 15. For other examples, see Oelmann, "Die Villa rustica bei Stahl und Verwandtes," *Germania,* 5 (1921), 64–73. The villa in Gaul is surveyed in A. Grénier, *Archéologie gallo-romaine (Manuel d'archéologie,* ed. J. Déchelette, VI, 2; Paris, 1934), 782–883.

38. For Mansfield Woodhouse, see H. Rooke, *Archaeologia,* 8 (1788), 363ff., pl. 22; F. Haverfield, *The Roman Occupation of Britain* (Oxford, 1924), 229f., fig. 57. For British villa types, see R. G. Collingwood, *The Archaeology of Roman Britain* (London and New York, 1930), 113ff., figs. 28, 30; and J. Ward, *Romano-British Buildings and Earthworks* (London, 1911), 156ff.

39. Swoboda, *Römische und romanische Paläste,* 148ff., and H. Mylius, "Die Rekonstruktion der römischen Villen von Nennig und Fliessem," *Bonner Jbh.,* 129 (1924), 109–128, pls. IV–VI

(Mylius's reconstructions of the German villas arouse the suspicion that he may be rather more of a Palladian than the Romans). The luxury villas, which do not affect the Early Renaissance style, deserve study in relation to sixteenth-century architecture. Apart from the effect on Bramante, Raphael, and later Italians, there appears to have been an independent tradition that survived in the Roman provinces, as suggested by similarities between the British type with a large court (e.g., Spoonley Wood, Woodchester, in Ward, *Romano-British Buildings,* figs. 46, 47) and Elizabethan country houses.

40. M. Rostovstzeff, "Pompeiianische Landschaften und römische Villen," *Jahrbuch des Deutschen Archäologischen Instituts,* 29 (1904), 124ff.; Swoboda, *Römische und romanische Paläste,* 142ff.; *Inventaire des mosaïques de la Gaule et de l'Afrique,* II (*Afrique proconsulaire*) (Paris, 1910–14), pls. 92, 93, 126, 646, 940b, 940d.

41. Swoboda, *Römische und romanische Paläste,* 77ff.

42. E. Dyggve, "Drei Paläste vom gleichen Fassadentypus aus dem jugoslawischen Küstenland," *Festschrift Swoboda* (Vienna, 1959), 83–90; Mogorilo is a fourth-century palace of the type of Diocletian's; Bilice is the small U-type of Gaul and Britain. See also the villa in Val Catena (A. Gnirs, "Forschungen über antiken Villenbau in Sudistrien," *Jahreshefte des Österr. Arch. Inst. in Wien,* 18 (1915), cols. 99–144.

43. G. Fiocco, "La casa veneziana antica," *Atti della Accademia nazionale dei Lincei. Rendiconti,* 346 (1940), 38ff. Fiocco particularly emphasized the Ravennate character of the medieval vocabulary and veneers.

44. Swoboda, "The Problem of the Iconography," 81ff.

45. Patzak was greatly influenced by Strzygowski's theories and devoted his study to proving the non-Mediterranean origins of medieval and Renaissance domestic architecture; see his italicized statement (*Palast und Villa,* 1:36): "Auf echt germanischen Siedlungsbrauch und auf seinen aus den orientalischen Saalhause entwickelten Pfalzenbau, nicht etwa, wie man schon so oft behauptet hat, auf die aus dem städtischen Wohnwesen abgeleitete Planung der hellenistisch-römischen Villa, geht in der Hauptsache die Anlage der toscanischen Renaissancevilla zurück." The more balanced position of recent scholarship, admitting both Oriental and Hellenistic contributions, is represented in A. Boëthius, *The Golden House of Nero* (Ann Arbor, 1960).

46. F. Krischen, "Sitzung am 3 November 1942," *Jbh. d. Deutsch. Arch. Inst., Arch. Anzeiger,* 58 (1943), 459 and figs. 2, 3; quoted by Swoboda, "The Problem of the Iconography," 83.

47. Excepting Schreiber (*Die französische Renaissance-Architektur*), who realized the significance of Swoboda's research for the design of Poggio Reale and anticipated the thesis presented here. He was not aware, however, that Poggio Reale was an example of a cohesive late quattrocento style; since he represented it as a unique innovation, his important discovery failed to make an impression on criticism of the period as a whole. It is revealing that another instance of survival rather than revival—in medieval and Renaissance palace design—has been brought out only in the last few years, by Boëthius (*The Golden House of Nero,* 129ff.), and W. Paatz, "Ein antikischer Stadthaustypus im mittelalterlichen Italien," *Römisches Jahrbuch,* 3 (1939), 129–140.

48. In the discussion meeting following the presentation of this paper, Phyllis Bober suggested that a study of Roman villas in the Campagna might provide further antique prototypes. D. Redig de Campos pointed out that the "Villa" of Innocent VIII was planned originally only as a *belvedere,* and was transformed into a habitable villa later. Richard Krautheimer suggested that in my attempt to demonstrate a native Italian ancestry for the Venetian palace and the quattrocento villa, I had slighted Constantinopolitan-Byzantine monuments that may have reinforced the Ravennate contribution.

Postscript

This study was written for presentation at the first meeting of the International Congress of the History of Art to be held in America, in 1960. It is particularly memorable to me because I arrived in New York without my manuscript and spent the night before the presentation reconstructing my argument in notes. This lent an air of informality to the delivery that seems to have awakened the audience from the customary conference torpor.

My argument focused on a single early Renaissance villa type, the portico-villa with projecting wings or towers, suggesting that it may have spread out from the Veneto. There were other types but, at the time I wrote, this one seemed paradigmatic, in central Italy as well as in the north. Shortly after the meeting at which my paper was delivered, and before its publication, an exhaustive study of the type was published independently by Frommel in his monograph on the Villa Farnesina in Rome. Since the early 1960s, intense investigation of the villas of the Venetian terraferma, particularly those of the fifteenth century and of Palladio, has provided a much clearer grasp of the typology, the economic base, and the patronage. More examples of this type discussed in my article have emerged, but it has become clear, particularly in the studies of Rupprecht, Rosci, Prinz, Heydenreich, Forster, and in the exhaustive catalogs of Cevese and Kubelik, that even in the Veneto other competing types were widespread, some involving variations on Venetian palace façades and others attributable to the vernacular tradition in its varied forms (Carunchio's small book, which bears the same title as my article, gives an adequate overview of central Italian villas but incomprehensibly excludes consideration of the Veneto).

If I were revising this study now, I should try to lessen the implication that the portico-villa with projecting wings was the dominant type. It was, however, the type that attracted the most attention from the patrons and designers of luxury villas in the late fifteenth and early sixteenth centuries, and, as Frommel has pointed out in his fine study of Roman villas, it had the most resonance in the later examples in Rome and Frascati (Medici, Borghese, Mondragone). In addition to the instances that I cited, Rosci and Forster called attention to the villa projects for rich peasants drawn by Sebastiano Serlio in his unpublished Sixth Book on domestic dwellings, which are pure examples of this type. Frommel has added other unexecuted projects by Francesco di Giorgio Martini and Baldassarre Peruzzi in which the central loggia is flanked by towers that were to serve also as fortified bastions.

A new date in the 1440s for the Villa Colleoni Porto in Thiene (fig. 10.3), which I cited as one of the earliest surviving examples of the type, has been proposed in the recent monograph of Morresi on the basis of a deposition in a sixteenth-century trial. While this is not conclusive, it accords better with the evidence of style than the recent proposal, based primarily on examination of the bricks by thermoluminescence, of 1520–25 (Goedicke et al.).

Claudia Lazzaro has demonstrated the widespread use of another villa type in Rome and Florence and their environs from the mid-sixteenth century on: a cubic block with a roof crowned by a smaller cube on a tripartite plan, as built by Vignola for the Villa Tusculana at Tivoli, Villa Lante at Bagnaia, and the hunting lodge at Caprarola. She proposes that the design was typical of a class of rustic farmhouse, and that in the course of time some of these became villas and some villas reverted to their agricultural origins.

In my book on the villa I discuss (pp. 85ff.) one other type that may be of ancient ancestry: the platform villa (the importance of which was first pointed out by Bierman) built on a high blocky base that extends beyond the walls of the building proper and elevates it from the surrounding landscape. Important early Renaissance examples are found at the Medici villas at Fiesole and Poggio a Caiano outside Florence (fig. 10.6) and, in Venetian territory, the Villa dei Vescovi at Luvigliano, near Padua. It was widely used on the Italian peninsula from the first century BC to the second AD. One ancient example of the type, at Settefinestre, was known, and details of it were sketched by a fifteenth-century draftsman, which would make its transmission into the Renaissance less mysterious than that of the portico-villa.

Ackerman, James. *Palladio* (Harmondsworth, 1966; 2d ed. 1976).

Ackerman, James. *Palladio's Villas* (Locust Valley, 1967).

Ackerman, James. *The Villa: Form and Ideology of Country Houses* (London and Princeton, 1990).

Bierman, H. "Lo sviluppo della villa toscana sotto l'influenza umanistica della corte di Lorenzo il Magnifico," *Bollettino del Centro Internazionale di Studi di Architettura*, 11 (1969), 36–46.

Bierman, H. "Das Palastmodell Giuliano da Sangallos für Ferdinand I, König von Neapel," *Wiener Jahrbuch für Kunstgeschichte*, 23 (1970), 154–195.

Carunchio, Tancredi. *Origini della villa rinascimentale* (Rome, 1974).

Cevese, Renato. *Ville della provincia di Vicenza . . .* , 2 vols. (Milan, 1971).

Coffin, David. *The Villa in the Life of Renaissance Rome* (Princeton, 1975).

Forster, Kurt, and Richard Tuttle. "Back to the Farm: Vernacular Architecture and the Development of the Renaissance Villa," *Architectura*, 1 (1974), 1–12.

Frommel, C. L. *Die Farnesina und Peruzzis architektonisches Frühwerk* (Berlin, 1961), 85–119.

Frommel, C. L. "La villa Madama e la tipologia della villa romana nel Rinascimento," *Bollettino del Centro Internazionale di Studi di Architettura*, 11 (1969), 47–64.

Goedicke, C., M. Kubelik, and K. Slsallek. "La datazione scientifica della Rotonda di Palladio e della villa da Porto-Colleoni-Thiene a Thiene," *Ateneo veneto*, n.s. 24 (1986), 1–26.

Heydenriech, L. H. "La villa: genesi e sviluppo fino al Palladio," *Bollettino del Centro Internazionale di Studi di Architettura*, 11 (1969), 11–22.

Hofer, P. *Palladios Erstling: die Villa Godi Valmarana in Lonedo bei Vicenza . . .* (Basel and Stuttgart, 1969).

Kubelik, Martin. *Die Villa im Veneto—zur typologischen Entwicklung im Quattrocento* (Munich, 1977).

Lazzaro, Claudia. "Rustic Country House to Refined Farmhouse: The Evolution and Migration of an Architectural Form," *Journal of the Society of Architectural Historians*, 44 (1985), 346–367.

Monneret de Villard, U. "Sul palazzo di Theodorico a Galeata," *Accademia dei Lincei, Classe morali. . . . , Rendiconti*, 8th ser., 7, nos. 1–2 (1952), 26–32. Proposes the origins of the type in Anatolian/Mesopotamian palace types of the eighth and seventh centuries BC, but without linking it persuasively with the West.

Morresi, Manuela. *La villa Porto Colleoni a Thiene* (Milan, 1988).

Muraro, Michelangelo. *Civiltà delle ville venete* (Udine, 1986).

Prinz, Wolfram, et al. "Studien zu dem Anfängen des oberitalienischen Villenbaues," *Kunst in Hessen und am Mittelrhein*, 13 (1973), 7–45.

Puppi, Lionello. "Funzioni e originalità tipologica delle ville veronesi," in F. F. Vivinai, ed., *La villa nel veronese* (Verona, 1974).

Rosci, Marco. "Forme e funzioni delle ville venete prepalladiane," *L'Arte,* 2 (1968), 27–54.

Rosci, Marco. "Ville rustiche del Quattrocento veneto," *Bollettino del Centro Internazionale di Studi di Architettura,* 11 (1969), 78–82.

Rupprecht, Bernhard. "Ville venete del '400 e del primo '500," *Bollettino del Centro Internazionale di Studi di Architettura,* 6 (1964), 239–250.

Stopani, R. *Medievale 'case da signore' nella campagna fiorentina* (Florence, 1981).

Viviani, G. F., ed. *La villa nel veronese* (Verona, 1974), with catalog.

Wolters, Wolfgang. "Sebastiano Serlio e il suo contributo alla villa veneziana prima del Palladio," *Bollettino del Centro Internazionale di Studi di Architettura,* 11 (1969), 83–94.

11

The Belvedere as a Classical Villa

A fresco of extraordinary interest for both its subject and its style has been hanging in the Castel Sant'Angelo in Rome since its transference to canvas, probably at the end of the last century. Perhaps because it is so often seen, it has never attracted notice, and the only published indication of its existence is a photograph in a monograph on the Castel in which it appears hanging in the dim background of the second Camera di Clemente VII.[1]

Together with a second fresco fragment on canvas from the same room, it has recently been removed to the corridor of a small site known as the Appartamento del Castellano. The origin of the second is established by a label reading: "Affresco attribuito a Vasari [doubtful] proveniente dal Palazzo Altoviti."[2] With no evidence other than the recent physical proximity of the two frescoes, this indication of provenance has come to be applied as well to the first.[3] But given the marked dissimilarity of both the style and the purpose of the two fragments, it is certainly permissible to set aside the tradition which associates them, and to investigate the one as an autonomous work.

The fresco we are to consider here is clearly part of an architectural composition which originally formed the decorative frieze of a *sala* of considerable size.[4] It is framed below by a painted entablature and above by a cornice, while at either end the original composition apparently continued with further scenes and figures. The portion which remains is divided into two parts by a fantastic volute, around and within which

From *Journal of the Warburg and Courtauld Institutes*, 14 (1951), 70–91.

masks, a parrot, garlands of fruits and vegetables, and draperies are arranged. The projection of the entablature above and below the volute suggests that in its original position it either surmounted or "carried" an architectural element such as a pilaster or beam. To the right of the volute a female allegorical figure reclines on a varicolored *rinceau*. The yellow drapery which covers her left leg billows behind her head, while she rests her left arm on the back of a unicorn posed in an undisguised heraldic position.

While the decorative figures to the right are conceived in more or less the same relief plane as the architectural elements, the scene to the left abandons this tectonic metaphor to reveal a sweeping landscape composition seen as if through an aperture in the frieze (fig. 11.1). That this portion of the composition is intended to imply a sort of window is evident from the dark band which frames it above and on the sides, suggesting the inner surface of the masonry. What we see beyond is a majestic complex of buildings, partly in decay, constructed on a steep rise at the foot of which is a lake artificially dammed by the building on the lower right. At the upper left a well-cultivated hedge crowns an area of dense natural foliage in the midst of which appears a masonry enclosure. Craggy mountains rise in the background to the right above another group of buildings.

The impression that this composition is simply an architectural fantasy modeled on the decorative landscapes of antique wall painting is reinforced by the evident lack of narrative purpose. To be sure, the barques in the foreground are engaged in a martial skirmish which a group of classically robed figures to the right is unconcernedly observing; but whatever the implication of this action, it is subordinated to the exposition of the architectural complex. The principal subject of the composition is, then, the architecture itself; but that this architecture is not simply a fantasy of the painter becomes evident on closer inspection.

The primary clue to the identity of the buildings is virtually self-evident, for a careful rechecking of the edifices in the distance to the right proves that they are nothing less obvious than the Castel and Ponte Sant'Angelo with their fortifications. The cylindrical body of Hadrian's tomb, surmounted by the cubical palace erected gradually during the first half of the sixteenth century, is unmistakable. In addition, both the monumental gateway familiar from sixteenth-century views and the bridge with its balustrade are accurately portrayed.[5]

11.1 Pierino del Vaga(?), The Belvedere as a Classical
Ruin, *ca. 1545. Detail of a fresco in the Castel
Sant'Angelo, Rome.*

11.2   *The Belvedere from the Vatican Palace. Musei Vaticani.*

The point of vantage from which this group may be seen at this particular angle is the roof of the Vatican Palace; but the author of the fresco has clearly carried it off to another site behind a high hill. His sense of topography will perhaps seem less licentious if we proceed on the hypothesis that he has merely contracted the broad panorama visible from his elevated perch, and that the castle before him has to this end been brought behind the Mons Vaticanus on his left. This hypothesis is justified by the appearance of a faintly indicated structure at the crown of the hill, with its medieval crenellations silhouetted against the sky. The building exists today, though in great part hidden from view by subsequent construction. It is the Belvedere of Innocent VIII, built as a summer retreat at the summit of the northeastern slope of the Vatican hill. It may be recognized not only by the crenellations, but by one of its two towers which appears on the right, and a short lower extension at the left.[6]

The terraced hillside is now readily identifiable as the site of the Cortile del Belvedere, the connecting link between the Vatican Palace and the museum which since the early sixteenth century has grown up around the garden of Innocent's villa. Yet the Cortile appears here in a form so different from the present crowded complex of courts and high buildings (fig. 11.2) that the fresco would seem to represent a purely imaginative project. The villa is now obscured by a two-story palace. At the center of this palace, where the fresco depicts a low exedra accessible by a stairway of circular plan, there now rises the great three-story "nicchione," with a triangular stair at its base. Where we see a broad stairway leading to a lower, semi-domed exedra and a ramp, the court is now divided respectively by the high library building and the lower Braccio Nuovo of the museums. The lowest level is the site of a large courtyard flanked on both left and right by four-to-five-story corridors and suites. The impression that the fresco is a fanciful remodeling of the dreary enclosure is supported by the poetic ruins of the western corridors and the impossible lake in the foreground. But that such a structure actually existed in the early sixteenth century and that it is here delineated with considerable accuracy is beyond question, and may be demonstrated from documents of the time.

Vasari records as the first activity of Donato Bramante after the election of Julius II in 1503 the systematization of "that area which was between the Belvedere and the palace, which he wished to have in the form of a rectangular *teatro* [!], enclosing a small valley which was between the ancient papal palace and the building which Innocent VIII had newly made as a papal habitation; and furthermore by two corridors in this valley one might pass from the Belvedere to the Palace along *loggie;* . . . and also from the valley one might ascend to the level of the Belvedere by a system of stairways of different sorts."[7] Vasari continues to describe Bramante's project as comprising two passages of two superimposed orders in the lower court, rising to the ground level of Innocent's villa, carrying as a third story a loggia 400 paces in length running the entire distance from the Vatican Palace to the villa. In the lower court, the ground was to be leveled and a fountain erected between the passages. Vasari proceeds: "Of this design Bramante finished the first corridor which leads from the palace to the Belvedere on the side toward Rome [to the right in the fresco], excepting the last loggia which was to go on top; but the part toward the woods opposite [left in the fresco] was well founded, but impossible to finish, as the death of Julius [1513] and then of Bramante [1514] intervened." Vasari says that Bramante was also able to complete the statue court around the garden of the villa, but that the corridor toward the woods was left undone until the time of Pius IV (1559–65). He further adds that the inordinate speed demanded of the architect by the pope ("che aveva voglia che tali fabbriche non se murassero, ma nascessero") resulted in faulty construction, and that a portion 80 braccia in length crumbled in the time of Clement VII (1523–34) and had to be reconstructed and buttressed under Paul III (1534–49).

Vasari's accuracy in this instance is fully attested by contemporary documents. That construction was begun immediately on the election of Julius II is indicated by an inscription, now lost, which recorded the removal in 1504 of the great basin from the baths of Titus to the site of the projected museum.[8] Documents from 1505–13 indicate continuous activity in various portions of the Cortile, corridors, and loggie.[9] One of these, which records the leveling of the lower court in preparation for a bullfight, suggests a likely explanation for the term "teatro" used by Vasari and other contemporaries in reference to this portion of the complex.[10] Consistent with Vasari's account of the interruption of the program, no records of new building exist from the pontificate of Leo X (1513–21). The report of the fall of a considerable portion of the structure is supported by various contemporary accounts which vary considerably in their estimate of the extent of the damage. It took place on January 7, 1531, and the pope was very nearly involved in the disaster.[11] Evidence of 1534–36 demonstrates that in that period it had not yet been repaired;[12] but reconstruction was begun by Baldassarre Peruzzi, who died early in 1536, and completed with new additions by Antonio da Sangallo the Younger from 1541 until his death in 1546.[13] The buttressing which Vasari says was made necessary took the form of shoring arches constructed in brick inside the original arches of the ground-floor corridor, and is still visible today. Finally, the most energetic phase of building, which quite changed the aspect of the site, took place during the pontificate of Pius IV under the direction of Pirro Ligorio. At that time the Nicchione was raised over the building at the head of the court (which had been heightened to two stories in the fifties), and a greater part of the eastern or left-hand corridor mentioned by Vasari was completed.[14]

What Vasari failed to mention, however, is that the open loggia on the third story of the lower court, joining with the corridor visible in the upper court in the fresco, was actually carried out by Antonio da Sangallo, who was an assistant of Bramante until the master's death. In a drawing by Antonio in the Uffizi Gallery, a carefully delineated Ionic capital is identified by the architect: "pilastro palmi 3 nel vivo del terzo ordine del corritoro de belvedere di peperigno terminato per me ant⁰ sangallo per che Bramante lo lasso imperfetto." A guide to St. Peter's composed later in the century assigns the completion of the loggia to the pontificate of Leo X, which would suggest that Antonio carried on without interruption after Bramante's death.[15]

The historical plausibility of the fresco representation once determined, it remains to consider the extent of its descriptive accuracy. Until now, our conception of Bramante's project has been formed from a number of early sixteenth-century sketches varying in precision and conflicting in data. The present fresco, as the only complete perspective of the complex before alterations changed its character, on the one hand clarifies the interpretation of this data and on the other is amply supported by it.

The chief comparative document is a plan drawn by an anonymous follower of Bramante, which appears in a sketchbook in the Soane Museum (fig. 11.3).[16] It is obviously copied from Bramante's master plan rather than from the building itself, since it shows the left as well as the right-hand corridor; the two joined by a terminating wall in the lower court which ultimately was built according to another plan.[17] We immediately see that the building in the fresco carries out the essential elements of this plan: the northern terminus with its niche and round staircase ("B" in the plan); the ramp rising above a sort of nymphaeum ("C" in the plan); and the monumental stairway below, with its central passageway flanked by colossal steps, presumably the seats of the "teatro." The principal difference is that the fresco fails to represent the open arcades and membering of the corridor in the lower court. The reason for this is obvious: that the painter had to be rather offhand with the architecture in order to make his sea battle plausible. Finally, though it is difficult to recognize in a photograph, the ruinous arcade of the topmost corridor to the right is properly represented by the painter as a series of arches carried on piers with coupled pilasters ("E" in the plan).

A second drawing, attributed to Giovanni Antonio Dosio (1533–after 1609), and probably executed in 1558–60,[18] makes an even more striking comparison with the fresco, as the court is here seen from the identical point of vantage (fig. 11.4).[19] In the sketch, however, Bramante has already begun to disappear, as the northern wall has now become a two-story palace, and the ingenious circular staircase of the exedra a smaller echo of the central ramp. The change was made in 1551 on Michelangelo's designs, and if we refer again to the plan we will see how it came about.[20] With the decision to construct suites of rooms at the head of the court, Bramante's exedra became rather a nuisance, as it would have cut off those on the right from those on the left. As the court behind forestalled the construction of a rear passageway joining the wings, the exedra had either to be destroyed entirely or made itself into a passageway. The latter alternative was easily achieved by enclosing it within an outer wall that was raised along the topmost of the concave steps, thus creating a semicircular corridor. So the exedra seen by Dosio, while it echoes Bramante's idea, is formed by the new wall, and is articulated not by niches but by the windows which light the corridor behind. With this remodeling, Bramante's stairway became obsolete, leading only to a masonry barrier. By designing a stair in front of the building, Michelangelo masked the now awkward inequality of levels and gave access to a small semicircular podium, suitable for dining or relaxation in the open air.[21]

The corridor at the right of the upper court is essentially the same as the one represented in the fresco, as is the garden wall with its gate, visible at the upper left in both. The three stories of the lower court are precisely represented by Dosio, but have already lost their Bramantesque quality.[22] The ground-floor arcade is fortified with the shoring arches mentioned above, while the upper loggia, which was once open to the winds, is now walled in except for the three arched windows in each bay.

In further comparing the fresco with the two drawings, we see that the former errs in omitting the foundations that flank both the colossal steps leading to the lower court and the central ramps. These were evidently conceived as towers reaching to, or perhaps slightly above, the cornice of the loggie. I believe that the main purpose of these was aesthetic, as Bramante was devoted to the device of revealing unexpected space behind mass. The same device is used (see detail "B" of the plan) to mask the sides of the northern niche from the distant observer. Finally, it should be noted that the colossal steps which appear in the plan and fresco are missing from Dosio's perspective. They were in fact built only in the pontificate of Pius IV to provide seats for the great tournament of 1565: the most elegant and the last theatrical celebration in the court previous to the wave of sobering influence of the Counter-Reformation.[23]

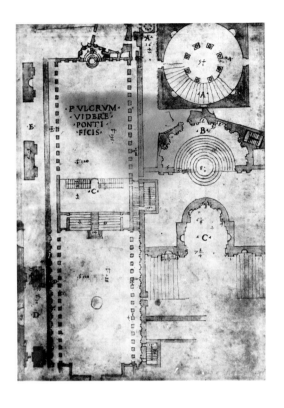

11.3 *Bernardo della Volpaia, plan of the Belvedere after Bramante, second decade of the sixteenth century. London, Soane Museum.*

11.4 *Giovanni Antonio Dosio, view of the Belvedere from the Vatican Palace, 1558–60. Florence, Galleria degli Uffizi.*

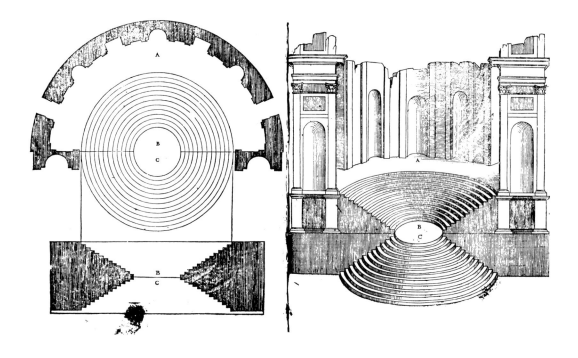

11.5   *Sebastiano Serlio, plan and perspective of the*
upper exedra of the Belvedere. From Libro terzo delle
antichità, *1566.*

Here, then, the fresco represents Bramante's project rather than the fact; and probably only from hearsay, since it gratuitously supplies a flight of podia at the point where the colossal steps meet the smaller ones at the center. The rectangular stepped platform at the foot of the central stairs has, like the corridors, been sacrificed to nautical fancy.

The preceding observations help to establish the fact that at least from the level of the ramps northward, Bramante's project is correctly portrayed. In this lies the peculiar importance of the representation, because while a number of elevation drawings and plans of the lower court have made its history relatively clear, the elevation intended by Bramante for the upper court has remained a mystery. The cause of the mystery has been first an unwillingness in modern times to give up the tradition that Bramante designed the present majestic Nicchione, and second the persuasive evidence that he planned at least the second story.[24] The principal source of this conviction is Serlio's engraving of the niche (fig. 11.5).[25] Serlio obviously made his preparatory sketch while construction was still in progress, as the strangely chewed appearance of the upper portion is intended to signify. Over the entablature on either side there rises what appears to be the rudiments of a second story. I think that comparison with the fresco makes obvious the conclusion that what Serlio saw were merely low rectangular panels which would have been framed by a slight cornice just above the portion which he sketched. From the fresco we can see that such an attic would have had to be provided in order to bring the cornice of the front wall up to the level of the cornice of the exedra, the bases, and hence the capitals, of the exedra pilasters being so much higher than those of the wall. It is moreover structurally improbable that a mere wall such as is indicated in the plan would have been erected to a height of two stories.[26]

I have so far left unexplained the incomplete condition of the western gallery, since it is here that the painting apparently ceases to be documentary. But before putting down this portion to the workings of the romantic imagination, I would like to consider whether at some time during the sixteenth century the corridors could in fact have been abandoned in mid-passage. There are two distinct possibilities: first, that the perspective was drawn during a halt in the early stages of construction, or second, that it describes, however inexactly, the condition after the accident of 1531.[27] The first alternative implies that the fresco was conceived before the death of Bramante, who finished the second story, and poses the problem of explaining why a third story should have begun at this point, and further, how a painting executed well before 1514 could have so many features of the late style of Raphael and his workshop. Certainly only the latter alternative is acceptable, because it explains the really ruinous state of the corridors, which were untouched during the years 1531–1535, and after Peruzzi's death again left, as we see them, to the creativity of nature. Accordingly, we can prove not only the reliability of the painter, but, in a general way, the date of his work; for a sketch must have been made after the accident and before the reconstruction. As the records show the reconstruction to have been well advanced by the end of 1541, we may assign the view to the decade 1531–41.

In searching for a more exact date, it occurred to me that there might be some evidence in the scene of some building executed during the decade established. Having associated all of the architecture of the Cortile with Bramante's program, there remained only the possibility of identifying the rectangular enclosure in the woods to the left. It proved that this enclosure is readily recognizable in the perspective of the Belvedere engraved by Mario Cartaro in 1574, where it is identified as "giardino secreto di Papa Paulo III."[28] Fortunately, the creation of a garden in the woods by the Belvedere in the early years of the pontificate of this pope is fully documented in the payments of the Tesoreria Segreta.[29] Excavations started in November 1535 and continued through 1536. It is probable that the walls were erected in the course of the following year, and a payment for finishing the last parterre of the garden was made on November 2, 1538. With this identification, the period in which the Cortile could have been seen as it is in the fresco is narrowed to at most the four years 1537–41. The date of the actual execution of the fresco I shall consider in discussing the identity of the artist.

In attempting to establish the documentary significance of the fresco, I have not intended to minimize its intrinsic interest as a work of art; for it is the extraordinary conception of the painting that first attracted my notice. Actually it is unique among the *vedute* of sixteenth-century Rome in that its subject is not merely presented, but, so to speak, criticized. Interwoven with an objective description of the scene is a historical commentary, emphasized by the revival of a historical vocabulary, expressed in such a way that we are led to consider not so much the iconography of the painting as the iconography of the architecture which it depicts.

It is immediately apparent that the overall conception of the scene is uncommonly close to the architectural landscapes of Roman painting.[30] Careful analysis proves the similarity to be the result of studied imitation. To begin with, the very conception of a landscape seen through the framework of an architectural frieze originates in Roman decorative frescoes. To take one of the many surviving examples, a fragment from Pompeii in the Naples Museum employs in a remarkably similar fashion the two characteristic architectural devices of our frieze: the entablature above and below the scene with its painterly profusion of moldings, and the dark neutral band bordering the landscape itself.[31] Within the Belvedere landscape we immediately recognize a familiar juxtaposition of nature and architecture: uncultivated woods and a foreground body of water with boats are the stock accoutrements of the ancient formula. The symbolizing of natural herbage by a single gracefully delineated tree is here adopted (at the left) without concern for its fantastically disproportionate size; while in the background the craggy mountains which impetuously rise from the plain are tardy importations from the hellenistic East. The elements of landscape, moreover, are rendered in such a way that the transitions from the space of the foreground to that of the rear are, as in most antique landscapes, vague and figurative rather than descriptive. Miniscule figures and beasts of burden are casually deployed about the buildings in the Roman manner, which they follow also in their puppet-like articulation, emphasizing action rather than form. This imitation is carried on in the type of movement and gesture, and finally in the costume of the armored boatmen (not to mention the barques themselves) and incidental observers.

This typological similarity to Roman landscape is presented in technical terms which substantially reinforce the reference. The palette, with its predominately neutralized pastel tones, and juxtaposition of cold gray-blue and lifeless greens to yellow ochres and earthy reds, while betraying an occasional subdued sign of the Renaissance scale, demonstrates an intended imitation of the antique. By comparison with the clear and brilliant color so popular among the followers of Raphael and Michelangelo, the restriction of range and avoidance of intensity here indicates a self-conscious adjustment to an antique scheme foreign to the painter, as is evident in the contrast with the livelier color of the decorative portions of the fresco.

It is perhaps improper to persist in referring to the landscape as a fresco, for the reconstruction is faithful to the extent of reproducing the antique *secco* technique. The paint apparently has a limelike binder which tends to give a pastel effect to its tone, and here and there the heavy mixture remains well above the surface of the plaster. The frequent employment of a rapidly applied *impasto* for the highlights, which effects the delineation of figures in action with an extreme economy of strokes, is strikingly close to the impressionistic technique of the majority of Roman paintings in which landscape plays a predominant part. The figures in violent action are rendered in a fluid style, the most expressive portions of their bodies heavily splashed on in a fluid and thick whitened paste, without concern for detail. Figures at rest are delineated with varying precision in overlaid vertical strokes which emphasize their elongated proportions. Wooded landscape is hastily characterized by suggested foliage sketched onto an undifferentiated green ground; while bushes, such as those spraying forth from the ruins, are thinly sketched in earthy colors.

For all of these technical devices ample comparative material is available from examples of ancient painting that survive today. It is unlikely, however, that any amount of diligence would bring to light the specific models employed, considering the number of Roman frescoes lost since the sixteenth century. Probably the landscapes and figure compositions from Nero's Golden House were influential, as they constituted the largest fund of Roman decoration known to the Renaissance, but the decayed state of the remaining decoration renders it virtually useless in this connection.[32] For the sake of a rapid comparison I turn to a Roman landscape cycle in excellent condition which, though discovered only a century ago, suggests itself for its stylistic similarities as well as its availability: the Odyssey landscapes in the Vatican Museum.[33] Here the color, though brilliant in the architectural framework bordering the scenes, is reserved in range and subdued in intensity. Except for the not uncommon predominance of green in the sky and water, and the violet atmosphere of the middle ground, the palette is remarkably close to that of the Belvedere fresco, particularly in the earthiness of the colors employed in the landscape and architectural elements. The greens of the foliage are similarly toned down with an admixture of red-browns. More striking similarities appear in details: the underpainting of the architectural elements with a thin yellow ochre; the symbolic rendering of water with long horizontal strokes of a light neutral color on a dark base; the cursive indication of foliage, and in particular those isolated clumps of bushes which spray out from their roots fountain-like; the representation of shadows in reds and browns. The relationship is perhaps closest in the painting of figures: their elongated proportions; their gestures, exaggerated in action and languid at rest; a strong contrast of light and dark, and the sharp shadows which they throw. In the rendition of draped figures painted in light and varied pastel tones, the likeness carries into the long elliptical strokes which make the body and its elements into attenuated ovals. A comparison particularly revealing in this connection may be made between the group of figures in the lower corridor and a similarly posed group which receives Ulysses into the underworld (figs. 11.6, 11.7). The parallel carries further into the shorthand delineation of the ghostly figures in the rear.

This comparison is valid only to a certain point, in all likelihood because the Castel fresco is a pastiche of ancient impressionist landscapes, and not an interpretation of a particular style. Whatever comparative material is chosen, traces of the Renaissance painter's technique and observation will betray the contrasts; as particularly his precision of line and consideration of detail, not to speak of the meticulously rationalized perspective.

Of the many elements of iconography, style, and composition borrowed from antique wall painting, the only one that definitely inhabits the proper representation of the sixteenth-century scene is the artificial body of water in the foreground. That a lake of this kind could not have been even temporarily provided is evident not only from the actual architecture of the eastern corridor, but from the topography of the Vatican hill, which slopes off toward the west in such a way that considerable constructions would have been necessary to dam the court on that side. Clearly this lake is a fiction

11.6 *Roman first-century fresco,* Visit to the
Underworld, *from the* Odyssey Landscapes. *Musei
Vaticani.*

11.7 *Figures in the antique style, detail of figure 11.1.*

intended to make the reference to ancient villa landscapes inescapable. But the intention is evidently more complex than it first appears, because while the association of water, barques, and rural architecture is perfectly consistent with Roman models, the armed conflict in which some of the boatmen are engaged is not, strictly speaking, a proper element of the villa scene.[34] It is moreover foreign even to the atmosphere of this fresco itself, given the casual deportment of the figures in the corridor, and stranger yet, the peaceful attire and pursuits of the boatmen at the left. In short, this battle, whether mock or serious, is brought into the composition at considerable cost to the accuracy, credibility, and even consistency of the representation, leaving us with the impression that it must be explained by something other than a taste for the bizarre.

The explanation proves to be one which, though not likely to occur to the modern observer, would have been quite obvious in the sixteenth century. We find the key in Renaissance topographical studies of ancient Rome. The first of these, Flavio Biondo's *Roma instaurata*,[35] devotes considerable discussion to the Vatican. In a passage describing the ancient topography of the area he writes: "Cornelius Tacitus, who treats particularly of the deeds of Nero, states that he enclosed a space in the Vatican valley in which he might maneuver the horses without having a public spectacle, and adds a little farther on that he constructed trysting places and inns by the woods which he placed around an artificial pond.[36] There was a temple of the God Vaticanus on this hill, of which we have given a description above from Bugellius; but the artificial pond, or, as it is called in Greek, the Naumachia, was just off this hill at the foot of Mount Aureus [Montorio], where one goes to the Porta Pertusa, and where, since the drying of the mud, we have recently seen a garden begun. Thus in many church writers we see a great part of the Vatican called the Naumachia, and in the life of St. Peter of which we have spoken, it is said that the church of St. Peter was built by the Naumachia; and similarly, the hospital which Pope Leo III built; and the area of the church of St. Andrea dedicated by Pope Symmachus; and St. Petronilla, which is situated at the Temple of Apollo at the obelisk, are called after the Naumachia."[37]

The Naumachia or *navale stagnum* in question was one of the amphitheaters built in imperial Rome for the staging of naval battles, and is now believed to be identifiable in ruins near the Castel Sant'Angelo. References to the Vatican area as the Naumachia are found in unbroken succession from the Constantinian list of Regions throughout the Middle Ages. Furthermore, the small church which stands just behind S. Anna dei Palafrenieri in the shadow of the walls of the lower court of the Belvedere was known in the sixteenth century as S. Pellegrino "ad Naumachiam."[38]

There is a certain vagueness in the sources concerning the exact location of the Naumachia, but Biondo dispenses with caution to nail the position down firmly. By placing the Naumachia alongside St. Peter's on the lower slope of the hill which rises to the Porta Pertusa (the western gate of the Leonine city), Biondo specifies the general area of the Vatican palace. The further indication that it was on the site of a recently founded garden narrows the area down to either the "giardino segreto" which was later supplanted by the Cortile di San Damaso, or the "vigna" below the Borgia apartments, referred to in the diary of Burchardo.[39] As the two were almost contiguous it is not necessary to choose between them, but I cannot resist singling out the latter, as it places the Naumachia precisely at the foot of the Cortile del Belvedere, where the lake appears in the fresco![40]

This evidence leads inevitably to the conclusion that the painter has altered the view of the Belvedere with the object of reconstructing the ancient naval amphitheater. In so doing he at once completes his imitation of the antique architectural landscape with the familiar body of water, refers to the ancient topography of the Vatican in its relation to the modern, and emphasizes the architectural conception of the lower court as a "teatro."[41]

When I said a few pages back that this fresco is unique among contemporary works of its kind, I did not mean to imply that a return to antique models at that time was anything out of the ordinary. What strikes me, rather, is the painstaking thoroughness of this revival—in composition, style, technique, and subject matter—to the extent that the personality of the artist himself is almost effaced. This kind of studious reconstruction is familiar enough in purely ornamental frescoes and stucchi of the mid-sixteenth century, but is ordinarily far less in evidence in larger landscape and figure compositions of this type.[42] It is quite obvious to me that something more than a demonstration of skill is implied in this rare immersion in the past, and that one ought to seek an explanation why it should have occurred just in this scene, and not elsewhere.

That the Cortile del Belvedere should be the one monument of a rapidly expanding Rome chosen for representation in ancient dress is not mere chance. It was not only the first truly monumental construction to rise out of the medieval city, but one in which for the first time an ancient sense of scale and spatial composition was revivified in a vocabulary of details studiously gathered among the ruins. Bramante's contemporaries must have been overwhelmed by his control of a vast area of seemingly unmanageable terrain within a rational tectonic scheme; an impression heightened by the unavoidable comparison to the fifteenth-century villa concept embodied in Innocent's lonely crenellated box which rose behind it. In fact, no contemporary church, palace, or villa was so completely free of the impediments of tradition and habit, for here a form of architecture which had been extinct since imperial times was suddenly brought to life. It is the architectural garden, which at the same time takes its form from the contours of the site and re-forms its natural environment.

I cannot believe that the similarities in general concept between Bramante's project and the ancient villa are circumstantial. I am convinced, rather, that Julius II specifically commissioned his architect to compose in the Roman style, and that the plans were the result of considerable archaeological research. If Bramante was constricted by the poverty of information then available on the Roman villa, he showed remarkable ingenuity in compensation for his ignorance. Perhaps the primary motivation was provided by ancient literary remains describing the palatial villa. A particularly suggestive source of inspiration could be found in the descriptions of Nero's Domus Aurea, a city-villa which extended over a vast tract of land, significantly embracing a valley, between the Palatine and Esquiline hills.[43] The imperial palace, so similar to the Vatican in site, was, according to Tacitus: "a palace the marvels of which were to consist not so much in gems and gold, as in fields and lakes and the air of solitude given by wooded ground alternating with clear tracts and open landscapes. The architects . . . had the ingenuity and courage to try the force of art even against the veto of nature. . . ." In a more extended passage, Suetonius describes as a "porticus triplices" the mile-long colonnade linking its various parts. The possibility that Bramante considered this passage in composing his extensive three-story arcade is suggested not only by the similarity in size and purpose, but by what the sixteenth century evidently regarded as a similarity in form. This is persuasively indicated by a reference to the arcade in the guide book mentioned above as a "triplices porticus."[44]

Striking parallels are found in the most specific of the ancient villa descriptions: the letter of Pliny the Younger on his Tuscan villa.[45] On the orientation of the villa he writes: "The exposure of the main part of the house is full south [as is the short wall of the Belvedere]; thus it seems to invite the sun . . . into a wide and proportionately long portico, containing many divisions, one of which is an atrium, built after the manner of the ancients. In front of the portico is a terrace divided into a great number of geometrical figures, and bounded by a box hedge [the bird's-eye views of the Belvedere show the upper court and gardens flanking it laid out in geometrical parterres flanked by box hedges].[46] The descent from the terrace is a sloping bank, adorned with a double row of box trees, but in the shape of animals." He further describes an elevated gallery with large open windows, which connects the main part of the villa with another suite of rooms alongside a hippodrome, a concept functionally and possibly formally similar to the linking of the Vatican with the museum. The hippodrome itself, though described by Pliny rather as a garden than an architectural composition, suggests in the following words the generic form of the Cortile: "the raised path around the hippodrome, which here runs straight, bends at the farther end into a hemicycle[47] and takes on a new aspect, being embowered in cypress trees and obscured by their denser and more gloomy shade." The cypresses imported onto the Vatican hill can only have had the purpose of bringing to life the ancient tradition associating this tree with the garden-hippodrome.

For all its detail, Pliny's description is not precise enough to make an accurate reconstruction, as modern attempts have shown.[48] Adding to it similar literary accounts, Bramante can have collected only a number of ideas and forms, the visualization of which would have had to depend on the ruins at hand, whatever their character. It is for this reason that, in attempting to realize a Roman villa, he was forced to use as a basic source a religious structure. In the Temple of Fortuna at Praeneste (Palestrina) he found the best-preserved and most comprehensible answer to the problem of a monumental construction on sharply rising ground.[49] The choice was not as strange as it may seem, for the size and complexity of this architecture, as well as its site, brings it closer in concept to the villas than to the temples of its period.

The similarity of Bramante's court to Palestrina is now more evident than ever, as the bomb damage of the last war brought about the removal of the many buildings of the modern town which had covered the main lines of the temple (fig. 11.8).[50] From the plain below a steep hill, the dominant feature of Palestrina is now the triangular ramp, the two sides of which rise in a gentle slope to the central axis of the composition. Bramante not only adopted this device as the major link between the courts, but acknowledged his debt by taking as well the characteristic central niche carved under the apex of the triangle, which provides a deep shaded contrast to the flat wall of the ramp, accentuating the axis.[51] A parallel may similarly be drawn to the great temple square at Palestrina (still the main piazza of the town) and the lower court of the Belvedere: both establishing the axis which is carried through the whole complex. Finally, the Temple of Fortune itself is placed at the highest point as a crowning element to the whole, reached by a broad flight of stairs arranged theater-like in a concave semicircle. That this provided Bramante with his inspiration for the circular stairs of the upper exedra is virtually certain. The convex stairs with which he leads to the theatral form are his own reconstruction, as the original front stairway had disappeared with the building of medieval and Renaissance palaces on the site. In reconstructing Palestrina fifty years later, Pirro Ligorio demonstrated the connection between the buildings by drawing the entire stairway in a form identical with that of the Belvedere, and since Pirro's sketches were for a long time the only Renaissance records of Palestrina known, his interpretation had a considerable vogue among archaeologists.[52] In this way, the Palestrina which came to be known to the scholars of the last century was at least in part a copy of the Belvedere, and the circle was completed figuratively as well as formally. Excavations carried out only a few weeks before this writing have demonstrated for the first time that the original stair was narrow, straight, and on axis, thus indirectly adding another document to Bramante's inventiveness. In all, the elements borrowed from Palestrina were such that the religious character of the source did not obtrude into the design, and the quality of a villa could be fully retained.

The Palestrina solution for the building of an open terraced structure answered only the problem of elevation for Bramante. Adapting this to a plan which had to serve the functions of a corridor and a *teatro* required suggestions from ancient remains of a quite different sort. To follow this step we have only to turn back to the passage from Pliny. In Pliny's hippodrome, or garden-circus, could be found the required concentration of building around a limited area which was conspicuously absent in the broad lateral extension of Palestrina. Thus the main lines of the plan of the Belvedere—a rectangle in the proportion of 3:1—reproduces the circus-like plan preserved in a number of Roman structures associated with villas or palaces.[53]

Among examples in Rome and the Campagna, the "Stadium" on the Palatine provides perhaps the most convincing comparison (fig. 11.9).[54] It is only slightly longer in proportion than the Belvedere: closed at both extremities, with a flat wall at the northeast, and a segmental one at the southwest. The most remarkable feature of the comparison is the arcade carried on piers with an applied order (half-columns rather than the pilasters of the Belvedere) which forms corridors on four sides. Traces of the construction along the rear walls show that the arcade was at least two stories in elevation, and the reconstruction of a third would not be unreasonable. This arcade was a late addition to the Stadium, but was certainly not recognized as such in the Renaissance. Although the Stadium is excavated into the hillside rather than following its level like the Belvedere, the similarity of site is suggestive. I doubt, however, that the longitudinal division into three parts is directly related to Bramante's conception, as the low walls separating the areas were first excavated in 1877.

11.8   *Palestrina, Precinct of Fortune, first century* BC.

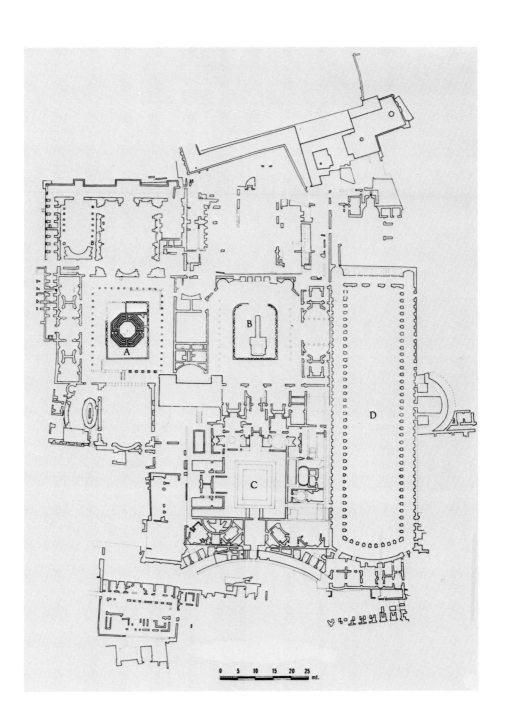

11.9   Rome, Palatine Hill, plan of the Augustan and Flavian palace, with garden hippodrome.

That the Palatine hippodrome need not have been the principal source for these conceptions is indicated in a reconstruction of the Horti Sallustiani preserved in a drawing of the first half of the sixteenth century, probably by Aristotile da Sangallo.[55] The central element of the area is reconstructed here as a hippodrome close in form to that on the Palatine, and ringed with arcades. Although these arcades are in part discontinuous, being interrupted on the long sides by heavy buttresses in every fourth bay, the lower court of the Belvedere is brought to mind by the niches carved into the rear wall of the passages at the center of each bay.[56] The Circus of Maxentius on the Appian Way, known to the Renaissance as "Circo di Caracalla," attracted a good deal of attention in the sixteenth century. Though closer to the functioning racetracks of the Circus Maximus type, it resembles the hippodromes in its close association with a villa. It suggests the Belvedere, however, only in the emphasis on the central axis, effected by monumental arches on the short sides.[57]

In considering these relationships, I have the impression that the Roman hippodrome influenced the conception of the Belvedere in a still more fundamental way. Considering that all the examples of this form known to us are closely incorporated into the plan of a palace or villa, it seems likely that Julius would have had this association in mind when commissioning an addition to the Vatican Palace. His political efforts for the reunification of Italy, which he caused to be celebrated in the Stanze of Raphael, might contemporaneously be celebrated in even subtler fashion in architectural form. I think the Renaissance mind would have been quick to appreciate the connection between the hippodrome of the Palatine and the hippodrome of the Vatican. The Vatican, with the majestic façade of the Cortile San Damaso rising as a new *Septizonium* to mask its medieval form, began at the same time to reach out over the Mons Vaticanus as the Domus Augustiana had extended over the Mons Palatinus. The fabled splendor of the Domus Aurea was reflected in the embracing of hills and valleys. The choice of similar architectural forms associating the new city on one side of the Tiber with the ruins on the other certainly added to the image of Julius as the new Caesar, restoring the Rome of the Church to the status of the Rome of the Emperors.

I return again to the fresco only to propose that its antique references and style serve to demonstrate the validity of this argument on the ancient sources of the conception of the Cortile. It is, in fact, so conceived as to force us to recognize what I have called the iconography of the architecture. Throughout the first half of the sixteenth century, Bramante's project was seen as he meant it to be seen: a reembodiment of the Roman villa- or palace-garden. The destruction of this conception from mid-century onward I see as the result, not so much of an inability to understand the original intention, as of a change in the attitude toward antiquity and its significance for the present. By 1550 the age of humanism was in decline, and to Pirro Ligorio and his followers the antique, and Bramante as well, served as a springboard for fanciful flights.[58]

In conclusion I want to consider the problem of the authorship of the fresco, which has remained unsolved largely from disinterest. To begin with, the tradition ascribing it to the Casa Altoviti is undocumented, and is neither confirmed nor denied by what we know of the decorations there. Vasari gives us a clear account of his own activity in the palace, which involved the painting of a loggia and the ceiling of a salone, the latter with figures of the Seasons in oils.[59] This was accomplished rapidly in the autumn of 1553; in other words, at least twelve years after the date I have suggested for the planning of the Castel fresco.[60] In any case, the style of the fresco makes it extremely unlikely that it fitted into a Vasari program. That Vasari was not the only painter employed in the palace is evident from the remains of one of its rooms transported to the Palazzo Venezia, with frescoes attributed to Giovanni da Udine or Pierino del Vaga.[61] However, its scheme of delicate grotesques and medallions forestalls any useful comparison with the imposing composition we are attempting to place.

On the other hand, evidence in the fresco itself offers considerable ground for opposing the word-of-mouth tradition. The appearance of a unicorn in heraldic pose, in a portion of the composition which cannot have other than a heraldic implication, strongly suggests that the work was commissioned by a member of the Farnese family.[62] As a symbol for this family the unicorn appears almost as frequently as the fleur-de-lis of their coat-of-arms. In fact, a countless number of nude ladies solacing unicorns appear in the decoration ordered by Paul III (Farnese) for the Castel Sant'Angelo. This consideration, added to the fact that the Castel is drawn into the view of the Belvedere at considerable cost to topographical accuracy, led me to consider the possibility that the fresco was conceived for the Castel itself, and has always remained there. Stylistic comparison with other decorations in the Castel makes this hypothesis not only credible but virtually inescapable. The attractive architectural metaphor of the fresco, while still a relatively rare device by the mid-sixteenth century, emerges in various forms in a number of rooms at the Castel. Furthermore, standard usage in this decorative program is the separation of perspective vistas by allegorical figures, decorative garlands, and architectural members. A close analysis of the decorative elements of our fragment makes evident its affinities with other frescoes in the Castel. The scroll supporting the figures to the right, which unexpectedly changes violently in color from branch to branch, its leaves sharply and crudely delineated in a dull neutral tone, is an exact repetition of those bearing the putti of the frieze in the Camera dei Festoni.[63] The garlands of fruit are conceived and executed in the same fashion as those of the Sala Paolina.[64] The Belvedere scene, however, is quite different from and considerably superior to the landscapes associated with the decoration I have mentioned, but may also be paralleled in still another room.

The technical assurance (both in the painting and in the imitation of the antique) evidenced in the landscape permits comparison only with the fresco frieze in the Camera del Perseo.[65] Here I see a decided similarity in the sense of limitless space, the articulation and proportion of figures, the painting of sky and water, and the reserved, classic balance of composition which contrasts so strongly with the mannerist designs of other rooms. If the fluid chiaroscuro—especially in the distant architecture—and the areas of brilliant color in the Perseus scenes constitute marked disparities with our piece, may they not be ascribed to the fact that these scenes are not specifically intended as revivals of the antique, and on this account evidence a more personal style? In any case, the iconographic and stylistic evidence combine to produce a rather convincing demonstration of the provenance of the frieze. The Castel has surely been repaired and altered frequently enough since the time of Paul III to explain the destruction of the decoration of a large salone, as the number of recently whitewashed walls will attest.

If this conclusion be granted, the final step is to find the author. This is fortunately simplified by the ample documentation of the program of Paul III. In the early 1540s the apartments which Paul commissioned for his living quarters were being constructed under Antonio da Sangallo the Younger.[66] It is clear then, that the documents recording the decoration of these rooms from 1545 to 1548 are, if not complete, at any rate indicative of the earliest activity.[67] The death of Paul in 1549 establishes the other terminus for decorations with the Farnese insignia. These documents mention only two master painters, Pierino del Vaga and Luzio Luzi, both with a number of assistants.[68] I think the consideration of the rather shadowy figure of Luzio may be eliminated by the fact that the fresco is so clearly in the tradition of the Raphael circle, and, in the setting of the Castel Sant'Angelo, is already old-fashioned in the sense of pre-mannerist. In weighing the attribution of Pierino I find it more helpful than upsetting that a fresco executed in 1545 or after should utilize a sketch of the Belvedere made four or five years before, as Pierino was working almost steadily in various parts of the Vatican in the early 1540s. It is possible that the Belvedere scene was executed by an assistant, but

I take its superiority to the decorative portions to be a sign that the master executed it himself, leaving the rest to the painter of the Camera dei Festoni. In addition, the similarity to the Perseus scenes, universally accepted as Pierino's, points in the same direction. I feel that the fascination and familiarity with antiquity which this fresco exhibits is not only equal to, but of the same quality as the architecture it represents, and that it is similarly a typical document of what we call the High Renaissance. It is even questionable whether anyone other than Pierino, the last Raphael student in mid-century Rome, would have been up to the task of such a reconstruction and interpretation.

Notes

My thanks to the American Academy in Rome, which has provided the requisite leisure and setting for the writing of this article, and to Professors Frank Brown and Otto Brendel for their generous assistance.

1. M. Borgatti, *Castel Sant'Angelo in Roma* (Rome, 1931), fig. 275.

2. This palace, which formerly stood at the opposite terminus of the Ponte Sant'Angelo directly across the Tiber from the Castel, was destroyed, and its decorations dispersed, during the reconstruction of the river embankment in 1887–88.

3. In his brief description of the Clement VII rooms, Borgatti (*Castel Sant'Angelo*, 570) assigns both frescoes to the Palazzo Altoviti.

4. Measurements inside the frame: 1.42 × 3.90 meters.

5. The gateway here shown was known as the Porta Collina or Port Aenea, and was constructed by Alexander VI in 1500. In a Lafréry engraving of 1556–57 it appears partly demolished. It was completely razed by Urban VII. Cf. Borgatti, *Castel Sant'Angelo*, 237, 379.

6. Most of the north façade of the original Belvedere is still visible today in somewhat altered form, while the south façade seen in the fresco is hidden under later construction. For sketches of the building in its original state, see Hermann Egger, *Codex Escurialensis* (Vienna, 1906), 1:63, 2:8; and the three views of Heemskerk in C. Huel-

sen, *Die römischen Skizzenbücher von Marten van Heemskerk* (Berlin, 1913–16), 2:24, 31f., 68ff., plates 42, 67, and 130.

7. *Vite* (ed. Milanesi), IV, 155ff.

8. IULIUS II PONT. MAX. LABRUM. LAT. PED. XXIII S. AB TITI VESPASIANI THERMIS IN CARINIS TEMPORUM/ INIURIA CONFRACTUM IN VATICANOS HORTOS ADVEXIT. PRIMAMQ. IN FORMAM RESTITUIT ORNAVITQ.PONT.SUI AN. PRIMO MDIIII. (V. Forcella, *Iscrizione delle chiese e d'altri edificii di Roma*, vol. 6 [Rome, 1875], 55, paragraph 122.

9. Karl Frey, "Zur Baugeschichte des St. Peter, *Jhb. d. Preuss. Kunstsamml.; Beiheft* to vol. 31 (1911), pp. 11, 18, 19, and 23; documents 21–22, 85–86, 97.

10. G. I. Hoogewerf, "Documenti ... che riguardano Rafaello ed altri Artisti contemporanei," *Atti della Pont. Accad. Romana di Archeologia*, Ser. 3, *Rendiconti* 21 (1945–46), p. 263, document 13.

11. Cf. L. Pastor, *Storia dei Papi* (Rome, 1923 ff.), IV², 739f., documents 133–134. The first of these, a letter from Girolamo Cattaneo to the duke of Milan, dated Jan. 7, 1531, reads: "Hoggi ad hore 17 vel circa al medesimo solito che S. Stà. va in Belvedere è caduto el muro dil corridore che va a Belvedere da la zima sino al fondamento et sonno 3 volte una sopra de l'altra perchè sonno ancora tre gli corridori. La longhezza del muro fracto ponno passar 20 canne al usanza Romana.

La causa è stata che mai fu coperto dipo che lo fece fare papa Julio. . . ." The estimate of damage at 20 canne (44.6 meters) is close to Vasari's 80 braccia (47.60 meters); but Baldassarre Peruzzi in a working drawing for the restoration (Uffizi, Arch. 569) notes in the lower corridor: "rotto can. 15" (33.75 meters).

12. The corridors were still in a ruinous state when seen by a German traveler, Johannes Fichard, in 1536 ("Observationes antiquitatium et aliarum rerum . . . quae Romae videntur collectae per me Johannem Fichardum J. C. in eadem urbe Mense VIIbri et VIIIbri anno MDXXXVI," *Frankfürtisches Archiv*, 3 [1815], 50), and by Marten van Heemskerk, whose sketches of 1534–36 are cited in n. 6.

13. On his engraving of the Cortile del Belvedere celebrating the tournament held there in 1565, Antonio Lafréry appended a short history of the buildings, reading in part: "Minacciando poi rovina detto edifitio, et mancandogli alcune cose fu dalle bon. me. di Clemente 7° et Paulo 3° sotto la cura di M. Baldassare Peruzo et dalla fe. re. di Giulio 3° per ingegno d'Antonio da Sangallo instaurato." The personalities are correctly given, as attested by a number of working drawings by the two architects in the Uffizi Gallery. The chronology, however, is quite inaccurate. Some makeshift repairs may have been carried out by Clement VII, but the major work was done under Paul III. Peruzzi's activity falls between his return from Siena in the winter of 1534–35 and his death in January 1536. That of Antonio da Sangallo is recorded in documents on the reconstruction starting in September 1541 (Archivio di Stato, Rome, Camerale I: Fabbriche, section 1509, fols. 30ff.). It is unlikely that the reconstruction was still in progress after Antonio's death in October 1546, much less that it dragged on into the pontificate of Julius III (1550–55).

14. Cf. R. Lanciani, *Storia degli scavi di Roma* (Rome, 1902–1907), 3:213ff., for some indications of the activity of Pius IV. The majority of pertinent documents on the chronology of the Belvedere after the death of Bramante are unpublished—a gap in our knowledge of the sixteenth century which I hope to fill shortly. The gradual destruction of the original concept beginning with the bisection of the court by the library building in 1587–90 is reviewed by J. Hess: "La Biblioteca Vaticana," *L'Illustrazione vaticana*, 9 (1938), 233ff.

15. Onophrius Panvinius, "De Rebus . . . Basilicae sancti Petri Libri Septum" (Vat. lat. 6115, 6237, 6780, 7010), in A. Mai, *Spicilegium romanum* (Rome, 1839–44), 9:376: "Iulius II atrium quo villam palatio coniungerent, incohavit; Leo X perfecit triplices porticus, et cubicula struxit." The cubicula are probably the rooms at the right of the exedra in the upper court, shown in the plan.

The drawing, Uffizi, Arch. 303, is illustrated by Dagobert Frey: *Michelangelo-Studien* (Vienna, 1920), fig. 18 and p. 52.

16. T. Ashby, Jr., "Sixteenth-Century Drawings of Roman Buildings Attributed to Andreas Coner," *Papers of the British School at Rome*, 2 (1904), 23ff., pl. 25; and "Addenda," ibid., 6 (1913), 184ff. Here a number of sixteenth-century sketches relating Bramante's project are cited and illustrated, and the tradition of Bramante's authorship of the Nicchione convincingly destroyed. [For the authorship and dating, see the postscript to this essay.]

17. The execution of Bramante's project was assigned to, and even begun by, Giuliano da Sangallo in 1513. Records exist for the laying of foundations (K. Frey, *Jhb. d. Preuss. Kunstsamml.; Beiheft* 31 [1911], p. 20, document 90), and an elevation drawing of the portion before the Torre Borgia is in the Uffizi collection (Arch. 134; cf. G. Marchini, *Giuliano da Sangallo* [Florence, 1942], 99 and pl. XIXb). This was interrupted by the death of Julius, and the area left untouched until the pontificate of Pius IV, when Pirro Ligorio designed and executed a theater hemicycle. The plans for this project have been published by Adriana Modigliani: "Disegni inediti di Pirro Ligorio," *Rivista del R. Ist. d'Archeologia e Storia dell'Arte*, 4 (1932–33), 211–226. The present hemicycle, a substitution of Benedict XIV (1740–58), retains only the plan of the Ligorio project.

18. Uffizi, Arch. 2559. P. G. Hübner, "Der Autor des Berolinensis," *Monatshefte für Kunstwissenschaft*, 4 (1911), 367, n. 19, makes the quite ingenious observation that the building materials and footpath sketched by Dosio in the lower court give evidence of the construction of the Casino of Pius IV, which is situated just behind the aperture in the west wall. The Casino was begun in 1558 (W. Friedländer, *Das Kasino Pius des Vierten, Kunstgeschichtliche Forschungen*, vol. 3 [Leipzig, 1912], 3, 123) and by 1561 the west corridors of the Cortile were already under construction (the

cornerstone was laid by the pope on August 1, 1561; cf. *Concilii Tridentini Diariorum,* ed. Merkle, vol. 2 [Freiburg, 1912], 542); thus the drawing may be dated with relative accuracy. The attribution of this perspective to Girolamo da Carpi (Alberto Serafini, *Girolamo da Carpi* [Rome, 1915], 60) is irresponsibly made on the unsupported supposition that Girolamo designed the second story at the northern end of the court, and that this typical veduta is his working drawing.

A drawing remarkably similar to the well-known Dosio perspective has recently been published by Mongan and Sachs: *Drawings in the Fogg Museum of Art* (Cambridge, 1946), 1:44f., 2: figs. 45–46. This sketch, attributed tentatively to Ammanati, shows the roof of the second story in construction. I believe that it may be assigned to the years 1552–53, on the basis of documents on the program of Julius III.

19. I.e., in the Vatican Palace, most probably at the window of the Stanza dell'Incendio, which is roughly on the central axis of the Cortile.

20. Vasari, *Vite,* VII, 228: "in Belvedere . . . si rifece la scala che v'è ora in cambio della mezza tonda che veniva innanzi, saliva otto scaglioni, ed altri otto in giro entrava in dentro, fatta già da Bramante, che era posta nella maggior nicchia in mezzo Belvedere; Michelangelo vi disegnò e fe fare quella quadra coi balaustri di peperigno, che vi è ora, molto bella. Aveva il Vasari quell'anno finito da stampare l'opera delle Vite." The reference at the end of the passage is to the first edition of the *Lives,* 1550 (n.s., 1551).

21. For a detailed study of the alteration differing in part from that above, see D. Frey, *Michelangelo-Studien,* 18–22. Frey's assumption that the conception of the stairs presupposes the construction of the Nicchione, which would then be attributed to Michelangelo (p. 24), is rendered unlikely by the evidence of the Dosio sketch. As the exedra is there roofed, with every indication of an intended permanence, the notion of the Nicchione evidently developed well after the construction of the stairs. The assumption has also been attacked on aesthetic grounds (E. Panofsky, "Bemerkungen zu D. Freys 'Michelangelo-Studien,'" *Wasmuths Monatshefte,* 5 [1920–21], *Archiv,* p. 35).

22. Dosio's efforts to provide an exact description of the building extended to distorting the perspective of the lower court to permit a clear exposition of its articulation.

23. An engraving of this tournament from the shop of Dupérac and Lafréry shows the steps completed. Cf. Th. Hoffmann, *Raffael als Architekt* (Leipzig, 1908–11), vol. 4, pl. XII, 1. Hoffmann's volume contains the most complete collection of visual documents on the history of the Belvedere and Vatican Palace.

24. D. Frey (*Michelangelo-Studien,* 24ff.), discussing the pertinent material from the early sixteenth century, concludes that a one-story elevation was intended. His solution, however, fails to embrace all of the seemingly contrary evidence, and the reconstruction which he offers does considerable violence to the data given in Serlio's engraving of the exedra.

25. *Libro terzo delle antichità,* Book III (Venice, 1566), fols. 119/120. Serlio's drawing is by no means the only document illustrating Bramante's exedra in elevation, but I have chosen it as the only one of the group which is both clear and objective. For comparison, cf. the fantasy based on the exedra design (a two-story loggia) by Giulio Romano (?), inscribed 1524, in the window jambs of the Vatican Sala di Constantino (unpublished); the so-called du Cerceau drawing, Windsor Castle, no. 10496 (T. Ashby, *British School Papers,* 2:87, 6:197ff. and fig. 6; D. Frey, *Michelangelo-Studien,* 20 and fig. 5; A. Blunt, *French Drawings at Windsor Castle* [London, 1945], 15; I understand that Mr. Blunt has recently withdrawn the attribution to du Cerceau, originally made by Geymüller, *Les du Cerceau* [Paris, 1887], 13f.); the sketch of Amico Aspertini, Brit. Mus., Codex 1862-7-12-394, fol. 29^r (Ashby, *British School Papers,* 6:200 and pl. 39; D. Frey, *Michelangelo-Studien,* 24 and fig. 6, and others); Francesco de Hollanda's fantasy on the exedra (Ashby, 2:24 and fig. 2; E. Tormo, *Os disenhos das antigualhas que vio Francisco d'Ollanda* [Madrid, 1940], 89ff. and pl. 19v); and the last of the series, an inaccurate sketch by Battista da Sangallo in the Lille sketchbook, Musée Wicar, paragraph 731 (H. Pluchart, *Musée Wicar: notice des dessins* [Lille, 1889], 161f.; K. Tolnay, "Beiträge zu den späten architektonischen Projekten Michelangelos," *Jhb. d. Preuss. Kunstsamml.,* 51 [1930], 29 n. 1 and fig. 18).

26. The photograph may yet cause a certain confusion about this matter of a second story, because a building rises over the right half of the northern wall which gives the appearance of an attic story. In the original it clearly recedes to a point just behind the wall, as it is painted in a dull earth-red, while the wall itself is blue-gray.

27. The Heemskerk sketches cited in n. 6 indicate that the extent of destruction was not by any means as great as the fresco implies, and that in fact a considerable portion of the third-story loggia remained intact.

28. The engraving is reproduced in D. Frey, *Michelangelo-Studien,* fig. 14; W. Friedländer, *Kasino,* fig. 1. A copy of it made by Claudio Duchet in 1579 may be seen in Th. Hoffmann, *Raffael,* vol. 4, pl. XI, 1.

29. The records appear in two volumes of the *Tesoreria Segreta* which escaped their proper habitat in the Rome archives and are in a private collection in Paris. They have been published in their entirety by L. Dorez: *Le cour du pape Paul III* (Paris, 1932). For the discussion of the garden of Paul III, cf. 1:14f., and for documents vol. 2 passim.

30. Cf. M. Rostovstzeff, "Die hellenistisch-römische Architekturlandschaft," *Mitt. des Deutschen Arch. Inst. (Röm. Abt.),* 26 (1911); C. Dawson, "Romano-Campanian Mythological Landscape Painting," *Yale Classical Studies,* 9 (1944).

31. Paul Herrmann, *Denkmäler der Malerei des Altertums* (Munich, 1904–31), ser. I, pl. 170. Note also the frieze motive in frescoes in the Casa della Piccola Fontana, Pompeii (pl. 169), and in the Naples Museum, from Herculaneum (pl. 171). The frieze composition is generally discussed by Rostovstzeff "Die hellenistisch-römische Architekturlandschaft," 11ff., 121f.

32. F. Weege, "Das goldene Haus des Nero," *Jhb. d. D. Arch. Insts.,* 28 (1913), 127ff., combines a study of the palace and its decoration with an account of its history during the Renaissance.

33. Cf. B. Nogara, *Le Nozze Aldobrandini, I paesaggi con scene dell'Odissea, etc.* (Milan, 1907), 37ff.

34. While the sea battles of Roman wall paintings are sometimes represented against a vague architectural background *(Monumenti della pittura antica scoperti in Italia: Pompeii, III-IV (Tempio di Iside)* [Rome, 1941], pls. III, IV) and conversely, a villa landscape may include warships (Rostovstzeff, "Die hellenistisch-römische Architekturlandschaft," fig. 58 and p. 92), it is understandable that the pastoral and the martial remain separate.

35. Written in 1446; published Verona, 1481; Venice, 1503, 1510, 1542, 1543, 1549; Turin, 1527; Basel, 1531; various later editions. Cf. L. Schudt, *Le guide di Roma* (Vienna, 1930), 139f., 362ff., 507ff.; J. Schlosser, *Die Kunstliteratur* (Vienna, 1924), 194.

36. Tacitus, *Annals,* XIV, 14–15.

37. Flavio Biondo, *De Roma instaurata,* xliii-xliiii (ed. Venice, n.d. [1510], fol. 6): "Cornelius Taci. apud quem Neronis gesta particulari narrationem habentur dicit illum clausisse in valle Vaticani spacium in quo equos regeret haud promiscuo spectaculo: & paulo infra addit eundem apud nemus quod navali stagno circumposuit extruxisse conventicula & cauponas: Fuit ergo in monte illo Vaticani dei templum: quod supra ab Bugellio descriptum ostendimus [? oñdimus]. Navale aut stagnum sive ut graeco vocabulo apellant Naumachiam fuit secus ipsum montem sub aurei montis radicibus qua [? quã] ad porram [sic] Pertusam itur: & ubi nuper hortos exicato limo vidimus incohatos. Una in multis quae [? q] legimus apocrisis magna Vaticani pars Naumachia appellatur: & in vita beati Petri de qua [?q] diximus etiam habetur ecclesiam sancti petri extructam fuisse apud Naumachiam pariterque hospitale quod Leo pa. iii. aedificavit e regionem ecclesiae. s. andreae a Simacho. i. pa. dedicata: & sce Petronile quae templum appollinis in obeliscum vergit ad naumachiam appellatum est."

38. C. Huelsen, "Il Gaianum e la Naumachia Vaticana," *Diss. della Pont. Accad. Romana di Archeologia,* ser. II, 8 (1903), 355ff. The tradition of the Naumachia in the Middle Ages is here traced in some detail with citations from the sixth century through the sixteenth (pp. 368–379). See also the earlier study of L. Duchesne, "Vaticana: notes sur la topographie de Rome au Moyen Age," *École Fr. de Rome: Mélanges,* 22 (1902), 3ff. On the church of S. Pellegrino (now known as "de Svizzeri"): Armellini and Cecchelli, *Le chiese di Roma* (Rome, 1942), 2:971, 1409.

39. Under the year 1488, Burchardo's diary refers to the second room from the eastern end of the Borgia apartments as the "Sala sopra la *vigna* subito dopo la sala dei Pontifici." The vigna referred to is identified by Ehrle and Stevenson as being in the lower court of the Belvedere (*Gli affreschi del Pinturicchio nell'appartamento Borgia* [Rome, 1897], 19f.). It appears there is a bird's-eye view of the Vatican in oil by Hendrik van Cleve reproduced in H. Egger, *Römische Veduten,* vol. 1 (Vienna and Leipzig, 1911), pl. 42, though not in this engraving of the same scene.

40. Hence the likelihood that an edition of Biondo is the source of the reference, rather than the later work of Marliani, *Urbis Romae topographia* (Rome, 1534), which is less precise.

41. It is interesting that among the very scarce visual records of ancient naval amphitheaters, two representations on Greek coins should have been drawn by Pirro Ligorio, the later architect of the Belvedere. Copies of his drawing are in the Vatican Library, Vat. lat. 3439, fol. 168v, identified "Nel Libro di M. Pyrrho delle medaglie Greche a fogli 406."

42. The closest parallel, perhaps, is to be found in the two remarkable landscapes of Polidoro da Caravaggio in the church of San Silvestro al Quirinale in Rome (H. Voss, *Malerei der Spätrenaissance in Rom u. Florenz* [Berlin, 1920], 1:80ff.); which, however, are better described as reinterpretations than as imitations of antique landscape.

43. Tacitus, *Annals,* XV, 42; Suetonius, *De vita Caesarum, Nero,* 31.

44. Cf. the quotation in n. 15.

45. *Letters,* V, 6. I chose this particular source because, as far as I know, it is the only villa description which is both pertinent to the Belvedere and detailed enough to awaken the reconstructive urge. The architecture is discussed by H. Winnefeld: "Tusci und Laurentinum des jüngeren Plinius," *Jhb. d. D. Arch. Inst.,* 6 (1891), 201ff. See also Pliny's description of the Villa Laurentinum, *Letters,* II, 17; O. E. Schmidt, "Ciceros Villen," *Neue Jahrbücher,* 2 (1899), 328ff.; 466ff.; A. Van Buren and R. M. Kennedy, "Varro's Aviary at Casinum," *J.R.S.,* 9 (1919), 55ff.

46. Cf. particularly the Cartaro engraving cited in n. 28 and the painting of Hendrik van Cleve (Egger, *Römische Veduten,* pl. 36—left half).

47. It is worth noting that the term invariably used in the building records to describe the exedra of the upper court is *hemiciclo,* and not the post-Ligorian *nicchione.*

48. Helen Tanzer (*The Villas of Pliny the Younger* [New York, 1924]) has collected and added to the reconstructions of the past three centuries, which are remarkable as documents of changing tastes in archaeology.

49. The importance of Palestrina for Bramante's design was first noticed by B. Patzak, *Die Villa imperiale in Pesaro* (Leipzig, 1908), 138; expanded by D. Frey, *Michelangelo-Studien,* 36, and further by C. Huelsen ("Bramante und Palestrina," *Egger Festschrift* [Graz, 1933], 57ff.) without knowledge of the previous comments. Huelsen further attributed to Bramante an anonymous plan (Peruzzi's?) for the remodeling of the tower of Nicholas V, similar in form to a tomb near Palestrina. The attribution is the result of a confusion of towers, as

Bramante designed a cupola for the Torre Borgia, executed in 1511 by Antonio da Sangallo the Younger and destroyed by fire in 1523. Cf. the Giuliano da Sangallo sketch for the Torre Borgia cited in n. 17. Details of the cupola were drawn by Peruzzi (Uffizi, Arch. 130), and identified: "Questa brucio di Luglio 1523/ tempore Adrianj vi/ Tore di borgia in palazzo di papa in roma."

50. Cf. the brief preliminary report in *Bollettino d'arte,* 33 (1948), 346ff., and the excellent recent photographs and revised reconstruction in the new publication *Spazio,* 1 (1950) (F. Fasolo, "Il Tempio della Fortuna Prenestina," pp. 17ff.).

51. Bramante interprets this central element as a kind of nymphaeum (see plan, "C"), provided with niches for statues. This is the first use of a garden grotto, which became standard in the generation after Bramante (Giovanni da Udine in Villa Madama; Peruzzi in Palazzo Massimo; Vignola in the Orti Farnesiani; Ligorio in Villa d'Este; etc.), and had thereafter a long history in garden design. Heemskerk singled it out as the only element of the Vatican City which he saw fit to sketch in plan (Huelsen, *Skizzenbücher,* 2:7, pl. 8, with the identification, "Kirchengrundriss(?)"). It is possible that the articulation was inspired by the niched absidal grottoes of the two temples on the lower level of Palestrina.

The lower level of the ramp, which returns again to the axis, is now visible on the left side of the complex. Its precise form is still uncertain, and must have been even more so in the sixteenth century.

52. For example, H. C. Bradshaw, "Praeneste: A Study for its Restoration," *British School Papers,* 9 (1920), 233ff. If Ligorio's original reconstruction exists at Turin, as Bradshaw states, it has not to my knowledge been published. Copies have been noted in the Hofbibliothek in Vienna (Bradshaw, fig. 4) and in the Vatican Library (Ottob. lat. 3373; Vat. lat. 3439; cf. Egger, *Krit. Verzeichnis der Samml. Architekt. Handzeichnungen der KK Hofbibliothek in Wien* [Vienna, 1903], reproductions of the Vatican 3439 drawings, fig. 20 and pl. 5, here attributed to Girolamo Rinaldi [p. 69]). The continuation of the Ligorian tradition in reconstructions of the seventeenth century has been studied by R. Wittkower, "Pietro da Cortonas Ergänzungsprojekt des Tempels in Palestrina," *Goldschmidt Festschrift* (Berlin, 1935), 137f.

Less notice had been given to the more accurate reconstructions of Palladio (F. Burger, "Neue Rekonstruktionsentwürfe des Tempels in Präneste aus der Renaissance," *Zeitschr. für Geschichte d. Architektur,* 2 [1909], 203ff.). Palladio correctly interprets the great central ramp, which is broken into small staircases by Ligorio. He connects the upper hemicycle to the space below it by two small flanking stairways, rather than completing the circle in the Bramante-Ligorio fashion. The drawings are in the Burlington-Devonshire Collection of the Royal Institute of British Architects.

An unpublished drawing of the Anonymous Destailleur is the earliest known reconstruction of Palestrina. It appears on fol. 115 of Volume B of the collection formerly owned by M. Hyppolyte Destailleur (cf. H. von Geymüller, "Trois albums de dessins de Fra Giocondo," *École Fr. de Rome: Mélanges,* 11 [1891], 133ff., where this drawing is not specifically mentioned). The collection was sold to St. Petersburg after having been photographed in large part by Geymüller. The films came to the German Archaeological Institute in Rome in 1942 in the bequest of Hermann Egger, with an explanatory note stating that the original drawings were lost in the Russian Revolution. The reconstruction concerns only selected details from the upper levels of the Temple, and probably was associated with another drawing not photographed by Geymüller. The representation of the exedra is strikingly similar to the Soane plan of the Belvedere, except that the staircase, like Palladio's, is shown as a hemicycle. Unlike the Palladio stair, it has no link whatsoever to the ground level. A staircase of circular plan is represented in another portion of the folio, but the confused order of the details presented and the defective quality of the film make it difficult to interpret the author's intentions.

53. Dagobert Frey, in his perceptive commentary (*Michelangelo-Studien,* 36ff.), was the first to note the complex relationships of the Cortile to antique forms, and in particular, the hippodrome, which, as he demonstrated, was reused shortly afterward at the Villa Madama. For a general discussion and bibliography of the ancient hippodrome, cf. P. Grimal, *Les jardins romains . . .* (Paris, 1943), 265ff. Here the form is derived from the ancient gymnasium.

54. Cf. F. Marx, "Das sogenannte Stadium auf dem Palatin," *Jhb. d. D. Arch. Insts.,* 10 (1895), 129ff.; Jordan and Huelsen, *Topographie der Stadt Rom,* I, 3 (Berlin, 1907), 94ff.

55. Published by Lanciani and Geymüller, "Quatre dessins inédits de la Collection Destailleur," *École Fr. de Rome: Mélanges,* 11 (1891), 159ff. and pl. II. The drawings are attributed there (p. 161) to Francesco da Sangallo, but the handwriting is identical with that found on drawings of his cousin Aristotile.

A similar reconstruction of a hippodrome, unidentified by the author, is found among the drawings of Sallustio Peruzzi. Cf. A. Bartoli, *I monumenti antichi di Roma nei disegni degli Uffizi . . .* (Rome, 1914), pl. 372, dis. Arch. 687. Bartoli (text, p. 115) inexplicably identifies the subject as the Forum of Trajan.

56. Although the drawing is a fanciful reconstruction, a hippodrome was without doubt the central feature of the gardens; hence the Renaissance references to the ruins as "Circus Sallustii" or "Circus Florae." Cf. Jordan and Huelsen, *Topographie der Stadt Rom,* 433f. For the relation of the hippodrome to the general plan: Lehmann, Hartleben, and Lindros, "Il Palazzo degli Orti Sallustiani," *Skrifter av Svenska Inst. i Rom,* 4 (*Opuscula,* I) (1934), 219f.

57. Cf. G. L. Bianconi, *Descrizione dei circhi, particolarmente di quello di Caracalla* (Rome, 1789); and the notes of G. Lugli, "Studi topografici intorno agli antiche ville suburbane," *Boll. arch. comunale di Roma,* 52 (1925), 127ff.

Other villa-hippodromes may be found in the vicinity of Rome, at the Villa of the Quintili on Via Appia, and Sette Bassi (cf. N. Lupu, "La Villa di Sette Bassi sulla Via Latina," *Ephemeris dacoromana,* 7 [1937], esp. 165f.).

58. The problem of the antique revivals studied here, as well as Ligorio's interpretation of antiquity in his designs for the Vatican, has been considered in a stimulating pamphlet which reached me only after the preparation of proofs: C. Elling, *Villa Pia in Vaticano: et Renaissance-anlaeg og dets Forhold til Antiken* (Copenhagen, 1947). The author relates Ligorio's designs for the Casino and the Nicchione to Renaissance reconstructions of the Roman Naumachia, a discovery eminently suited to the argument presented above.

59. *Vite,* VII, 695.

60. W. Kallab, *Vasaristudien (Quellenschriften f. Kunstgeschichte)* (Vienna and Leipzig, 1908), 91, paragraph 200: quotations from Vasari's letters of October–November 1553.

61. D. Gnoli, "Le demolizione in Roma: Il Palazzo Altoviti," *Archivio stor. dell'arte,* 1 (1888), 206, with the attribution to Perino, citing the tradition of Giovanni da Udine. Followed by A. Venturi, *Storia,* 9, 2 (1926), 413ff.

62. I am indebted to Dr. Jacob Hess for bringing this to my attention.

63. Borgatti, *Castel Sant'Angelo,* 580, fig. 281.

64. Ibid., 343, fig. 139.

65. Ibid., 346, figs. 142–143; 577, fig. 278.

66. Cf. Vasari, *Vite,* V, 628f. for a description of Paul's program. The building is dated by an inscription at the entrance to the papal apartments: PAULUS III PONT. MAX. CUM MULTA AD FIRMITATEM AMPLISS. HUIUS ARCIS ADDIDISSET HUNC ETIAM LOCUM ANIMI CAUSA EXTRUENDUM ORNANDUMQ. MANDAVIT MDXXXXIII TIBERIO CRISPO PRAEFECTO (V. Forcella, *Iscrizione,* vol. 13 [Rome, 1879], 144, paragraph 252).

67. The documents are published by A. Bertolotti, "Speserie segrete e publiche di papa Paolo III," *Atti e memorie delle R. Deput. per le provincie dell'Emilia,* n.s. 3, 1 (1878), 250ff.; and in part by E. Rodocanachi, *Le chateau St. Ange* (Paris, 1909), 146–148.

68. Among whom, Marco da Siena and Pellegrino Tibaldi. Cf. G. Briganti, *Il manierismo e Pellegrino Tibaldi* (Rome, 1945), 72ff.

Postscript

This essay was prepared while I was working on my dissertation on the Cortile del Belvedere. I had not chosen this subject, but when I arrived in Italy with a fellowship to the American Academy in Rome, I decided to begin searching for a topic among the architectural designs of the High Renaissance in the drawing cabinet of the Uffizi. This turned up a number of instances of projects by Antonio da Sangallo the Younger and Baldassarre Peruzzi for the same Roman buildings, and I planned to make these the basis of the dissertation. On returning to Rome, I showed the drawings related to the Vatican and Belvedere to Filippo Magi, the director of the Musei Vaticani, and he proposed, without really investigating my qualifications, that I turn these into a monograph, which the Vatican Press would publish, for their series on the history of the Palace that had been interrupted by the war. A few months into this project, I was wandering through the Castel Sant'Angelo and passed, on the wall of a dark back stairway, the detached fresco fragment of figure 11.1. I went by, registering only another decoration *all'antica* typical of the Castel, when it suddenly struck me, with the greatest excitement, that this was the only surviving view of Bramante's Belvedere. It had never been identified for the apparent reason that no one familiar with the early projects and *vedute* had chanced upon that particular stairway.

A catalog essay by Uwe Geese has deciphered the symbolism underlying the acquisition and installation of the ancient sculpture collected by Julius II for display in the statue court built by Bramante. The court was created between the exedra at the head of the Belvedere court and the villa of Innocent VIII. Contemporary sources reveal Julius's intention to represent himself as a descendant and reincarnation of Julius Caesar: among them a coin of 1506 inscribed JULIUS. CAESAR. PONTIFEX II, and an inscription on a triumphal arch erected for Julius's return from his victory at Bologna in 1507 reading "Virtuti et Gloria Sancti Pontificis/ auctoris paces libertatisque: veni, vidi, vici." The newly discovered statue group of Laocoon and his sons, which was given a place of honor in the court ("as in a chapel," in the words of Cesare Trivulzio), was the subject of a poem by Jacopo Sadoleto, who represented its rediscovery by the city walls as symbolic of a renewal of the city's ancient glory, a second Golden Age. The recumbent statue then known as Cleopatra, which was placed in a corner niche over a fountain in the corner of the sculpture court, was referred to in 1513 by a Roman poet (perhaps Evangelista Maddaleni de' Capodiferro) in an epigram: "Julius Caesar burned with love for me while I lived; the second Julius loves me now that I have turned to stone and I must serve him as nymph of the fountain." The sculpture court was planted as a garden with fruit trees in emulation of the garden of the Hesperides, the abode of Apollo (the Apollo Belvedere was assigned a niche nearby the Laocoon) and the muses—a literal reconstruction of the Parnassus depicted for Julius II by Raphael in the papal chambers at the base of the Belvedere court.

In his exhaustive monograph on Bramante, Arnaldo Bruschi amplifies upon my study, but does not essentially alter the interpretation of the meaning of the Belvedere. He adds an important graphic document, a drawing from the architectural treatise of Filarete of the Circus of Maxentius at the emperor's villa off the Via Appia, which shows the building with (one-story) lateral arcades terminating at a niche at the curved end. Bruschi also provides a drawing (fig. 214) illustrating my hypothesis (1954, pp. 122ff.) that Bramante intended to create a three-dimensional perspective construction with a viewing point at a window in the papal apartments.

The author of the drawing in figure 11.3 showing the plan and details of Bramante's project was identified by Buddensieg as Bernardo della Volpaia, who worked for the Sangallo family from the 1490s on. Buddensieg dates his codex in the Soane Museum, London, between 1495 and 1515.

Brummer published (pp. 25f., fig. 10) a drawing from the so-called Marten de Vos sketch-book in the Rijksmuseum, Amsterdam (inv. 1935, fol. 9v), with a view of the Belvedere from the papal apartments evidently copied from a lost drawing from Marten van Heemskerk of 1532–33. This provides the only representation of the interior of the court executed prior to the fresco in figure 11.1. It gives substantially the same information as the fresco except that the construction on either side of the terminal exedra is still incomplete and the right-hand loggias of the lower court are finished to a height of three stories: there is no indi-cation of the structural failure at that point. Like the Dosio drawing in figure 11.4, it dem-onstrates that the large lateral stair/theater seats had not actually been constructed at the time of the execution of the fresco, but were based on Bramante's project.

I published in my book on the Belvedere (p. 216, fig. 25) a view in the Fogg Museum, Harvard University, of the court from a position in the papal apartments farther to the left than those in figures 11.1 and 11.4. Executed in 1552–53, it postdates the fresco but pre-cedes the Dosio drawing. At the time of my publication the drawing was attributed tenta-tively to Ammanati, and is presently assigned to Battista Naldini. In his review of my book, Wolfgang Lotz published a drawing of about 1560 (his fig. 1) from the same viewpoint as Dosio's (subsequently sold to an American collection), which he attributed to Sallustio Peruzzi. Both drawings add and confirm information on the building history but neither materially affects my argument.

A plan of the lower court of the Belvedere with a huge conclave hall outside the entrance gate, which I attributed to Peruzzi (1954, cat. no. 11), is now tentatively assigned by Frommel to Bramante (p. 360). Although the design does not bear directly on the present study other than being derived from Roman monumental structures, I mention it because Frommel's commentary adds significantly to our understanding of Bramante's contribution to the Vatican Palace.

Ackerman, James S. *The Cortile del Belvedere* (Studi e documenti per la storia del Palazzo Apostolico Vaticano, III, Vatican City, 1954) (cf. the review by Wolfgang Lotz, *Kunstchronik,* 11 [1958], 96–100).

Brummer, Hans. *The Statue Court in the Vatican Belvedere* (Stockholm Studies in History of Art no. 20, Stockholm, 1970).

Bruschi, Arnaldo. *Bramante architetto* (Bari, 1969), 291–434, 865–82; English ed., *Bramante* (London, 1977), 87–11.

Buddensieg, Tilmann. "Bernardo della Volpaia und Giovanni Francesco da Sangallo," *Römisches Jahrbuch für Kunstgeschichte,* 15 (1975), 89–108.

Frommel, Christof. Catalog No. 2.17.1 in C. L. Frommel, S. Ray, and M. Tafuri, *Rafaello architetto* (Milan, 1984), 60ff.

Geese, Uwe. "Antike als Programm—Der Statuenhof des Belvedere im Vatikan," *Natur und Antike in der Renaissance* (Frankfurt, Liebieghaus Museum, 1985), 24–50.

Grisebach, L. "Baugeschichtliche Notiz zum Statuenhof Julius' II im vatikanische Belvedere," *Zeitschrift für Kunstgeschichte,* 39 (1976), 209–20.

12

Architectural Practice in the Italian Renaissance

In this paper I have chosen to concentrate on the High, or as I prefer to call it, the Roman Renaissance of the first half of the sixteenth century only because I am more familiar with the sources of this period than of those that precede and follow. But I think that a proper study of Italian Renaissance practice ought to divide the field into at least three parts: first, the generation of Brunelleschi and Alberti which is documented by archival material, theoretical writing on architecture, and biography. Here one might trace the emergence of practice from the medieval guild system into the sphere of humanism. Second, the period I shall discuss, which is not strong in theory, but which compensates by providing richer biographies, more letters and archival records, and above all, large collections of drawings—sources which are almost nonexistent for the first period. This is an age of rugged individualism in architectural practice. Finally, something should be said about the later sixteenth century when, along with the foundations of the first academies, architects begin to write about practice, while they tend to stabilize theory into law. Here architecture begins to take shape as a distinct profession, perhaps for the first time since antiquity.

Leaving this more ambitious scheme to future students, my present intention is to draw from the sources at hand certain generalizations concerning the apprenticeship and training of the architect, the practice of the profession, and the process of design during the period bounded by Bramante's arrival in Rome in about 1500 and

From *Journal of the Society of Architectural Historians*, 13, no. 3 (October 1954), 3–11.

Antonio da Sangallo's death in 1546. Antonio will get more attention than his distinguished contemporaries because we know more about him and also because he deserves distinction for being one of the few architects of his time who never wanted to be anything else.

Italian architects in the fifteenth and sixteenth centuries ordinarily turned to building at an advanced age. They apprenticed in the studio of a painter or sculptor and practiced one or both of these arts until the requirements of some patron turned them to architecture. There was no guild to harbor architects and no means of serving an apprenticeship in the profession. The title of master architect, rather than being a prerequisite of employment, was normally granted to a master craftsman in another field in consequence of his receiving his first building commission. Because in this system architecture perforce involved more taste than technique, the social position of the architect was high, and if a man was not a gentleman before practicing architecture, he became one after. Antonio Sangallo rose to eminence by another path, which appears to have been a risky and unpromising one. He apprenticed in carpentry.[1] By virtue of excellent family connections and good fortune of working under Bramante at the Vatican, he was able to overcome this stigma and to gain the title "architect," but only at the age of 32, when he was appointed to assist Raphael at St. Peter's.[2] He was the only important Roman Renaissance architect who rose from the building trades, though a generation later Palladio did the same with the help of equally distinguished patronage.

The practical knowledge that the young Antonio gained working in the *fabbriche* of St. Peter's, the Vatican Palace, and the Castle of Ostia, combined with design training as a draughtsman for the aging Bramante, appears today to be an excellent background for the practice of architecture. But the sixteenth-century attitude is typified by Benvenuto Cellini, who wrote after Antonio's death that his inferiority to Michelangelo must be ascribed to the fact that he was neither a sculptor nor a painter.[3] The reason for this attitude is best explained by Michelangelo, who once wrote, "there is no question but that architectural members reflect the members of Man, and whoever has not been or is not a good master of the [human] figure and likewise of anatomy cannot understand [anything of them]."[4]

Those sixteenth-century sculptors and painters who undertook the designing of buildings cannot have brought to their first attempts much more than a trained eye and an admiration for antiquity. Even Michelangelo complained that he was forced to build though he was not an architect.[5] Generally the solution of structural problems had to be left to masons and carpenters who had been accustomed for centuries to inventing means to achieve a given end. Bramante, in spite of some 30 years in the practice of architecture, never did gain much competence in technical matters, and after his death Antonio was kept busy patching up his errors. The Vatican *loggie* had to be reinforced from below, the Belvedere corridors crashed to the ground, nearly killing a pope, and the St. Peter's crossing piers had to be fattened, much to the detriment of their handsome profile.[6] This lack of technical discipline may explain in part why the High Renaissance is one of the few great eras in architectural history in which a new style emerges without the assistance of any remarkable structural innovation.

Aside from training in one or another of the plastic arts, which provided a foundation in mathematics and perspective, the essential prerequisite for the practice of architecture was a knowledge of Roman remains. This was gained at first hand wherever possible, not only in Rome itself, but throughout Italy and Provence. Most of the major architects, and many whom we know only through their sketches after the antique, filled volumes of notebooks with measured drawings of plans and details, or with impressions in perspective.[7] They became familiar with monuments beyond their reach through the sketchbooks of their contemporaries, which had a wide currency and constituted the textbooks for architectural training.[8] In present-day collections of Renaissance architectural drawings these sketches far outnumber the studies for contemporary buildings. Fanciful reconstructions of Roman remains, which were a passion with late fifteenth-century architects such as Cronaca and Bramantino, were out of fashion after the turn of the century, when the accent turned from a romantic to a practical and archaeological approach.[9]

A knowledge of Vitruvius was equally important and for the same reasons. Vitruvius was significant not because he was a theorist, but because his subject was Roman architecture. If theory in itself had been valued, High Renaissance architects would have studied the writings of Alberti, Francesco di Giorgio, and perhaps Filarete, which they manifestly did not do. Nor did they trouble to theorize themselves; they left writing to their disciples, of whom Serlio is the best known, and his volumes are significantly visual compendia rather than philosophical treatises—best to be described as printed sketchbooks.

The schooling of the architect dispensed not only with the theories of the fifteenth century but with the monuments as well. It is curious that while Bramante's Roman work was measured and drawn by innumerable architects through the sixteenth century, his Milanese buildings were never examined. His predecessors virtually were relegated to the Middle Ages. I know only three Renaissance drawings after Alberti, and all are copies of one plan for S. Sebastiano in Mantua.[10] The late Brunelleschi interested one or two architects, who sketched the lantern (not the dome!) of Florence Cathedral, and the plan of Santa Maria degli Angeli, presumably because they were adequately Roman.[11] On the other hand, certain buildings constructed or projected after 1500 took their place beside ancient remains, and the younger architects devoted a portion of their sketches to Bramante, or occasionally to Peruzzi, Antonio Sangallo, and Michelangelo.

To this preparation for the practice of architecture—at best a haphazard one—was added a kind of schooling that the grandiose projects of the period made available to most of the potential architects in the urban centers. Projects such as the construction of St. Peter's and the Vatican Palace brought innumerable artists and artisans into close contact with an architectural workshop, and I can readily believe that the practical precepts of the profession were learned by Raphael, Peruzzi, and even by Michelangelo, from observing what went on in Bramante's Vatican studio, whether or not these men originally were given any architectural assignments there.

So much for training. Once launched as an architect, the early sixteenth-century aspirant established himself by doing well on an initial commission, and his practice grew much in the same fashion as that of the modern architect. Sangallo's earliest commissions are typical. Santa Maria di Loreto he probably inherited from one of the architects of Julius II.[12] The church of the Hospital of San Giacomo, as we shall see shortly, was designed for a competition, one in which Antonio had the advantage of being a tenant and neighbor of the institution.[13] The monks of Santa Maria della Quercia in Viterbo employed him because they said they wanted a ceiling as elegant as the one he had built for the pope in the Vatican consistory.[14] The Farnese Palace is only the first of innumerable commissions for Cardinal Alessandro Farnese (later Pope Paul III) and his sons, euphemistically called nephews. The alliance of an architect with a distinguished family was a common occurrence: Bramante supplanted Giuliano Sangallo as the architect of Julius II, Raphael was the favorite of the Medici popes, Peruzzi worked for his Sienese compatriots, the Chigi, and so forth. But the arrangement entailed no obligation on either part; clients changed architects and vice versa. Clients, in fact, often resorted to competitions in selecting architects for important commissions. One of the best-known examples of this is the competition for the design of S. Giovanni dei Fiorentini, to which Leo X called Sangallo, Jacopo Sansovino, Raphael, and Peruzzi.[15] Sansovino got the job, but was replaced by Sangallo (it is hard to tell whether an injury or incompetence precipitated this), and after the church was nearly finished

Michelangelo was called in to design a new one. Other competitions were held for completing earlier churches such as San Lorenzo in Florence, San Petronio in Bologna, and Milan Cathedral. Sangallo and Peruzzi competed on other occasions; for the S. Giacomo degli Incurabili commission and I believe also for Santo Spirito in Sassia.[16] Several of their designs for the former are preserved, and a comparison of two of them (figs. 12.1, 12.2) shows that both men were working for the same general type of solution: placing the wards along the longer sides of the plot, courts on the interior, and providing churches with access to the street. The absorption with centrally planned churches is symptomatic of the period.

The greatest setback of Sangallo's career was the competition for the cornice of the Farnese Palace. In the last year of his life, as he was completing the chief master-piece of his long service for Paul III, Antonio was forced to submit to a reconsideration of his cornice design and four other architects and painters were invited to submit drawings.[17] As everyone knows, Michelangelo triumphed, and Antonio was to have carried out his project, but he shortly died, as the Romantic historian would put it, from shame. I imagine that this affair may be attributed to court intrigues.

As in the preceding century, the duties of the architect reached far beyond the building of palaces and churches. Sangallo, who was fortunate in reaching the peak of his career at the same time as his patron, spent most of his later years fortifying Rome and the Papal States, building entire towns, such as Castro, in the new duchies carved out for the *nipoti,* restoring the Vatican, and designing settings for sundry celebrations. He even built a monumental well for the town of Orvieto.[18]

Financial relations between clients and architects are a mystery. Where private building accounts are preserved, the name of the architect rarely appears, and almost never as the recipient of a fee. Perhaps he was paid by grants of property or by casual sums from the pocket of the head of a family or the trustee of an institution or confraternity. Papal commissions, however, were rewarded in a more orderly manner. A monthly stipend attended each supervisory job. In 1536 Sangallo was receiving 25 scudi monthly as *capomaestro* of St. Peter's, the same for fortifying Ancona, and 10 scudi for the *Santa Casa* in Loreto; two years later another 25 was added for the forti-fication of Rome.[19] It was understood that any other jobs for the Holy See would be done without further remuneration. But there were exceptions to this arrangement; Michelangelo wrote in 1555 that he had been forced to work on St. Peter's for 8 years without pay.[20]

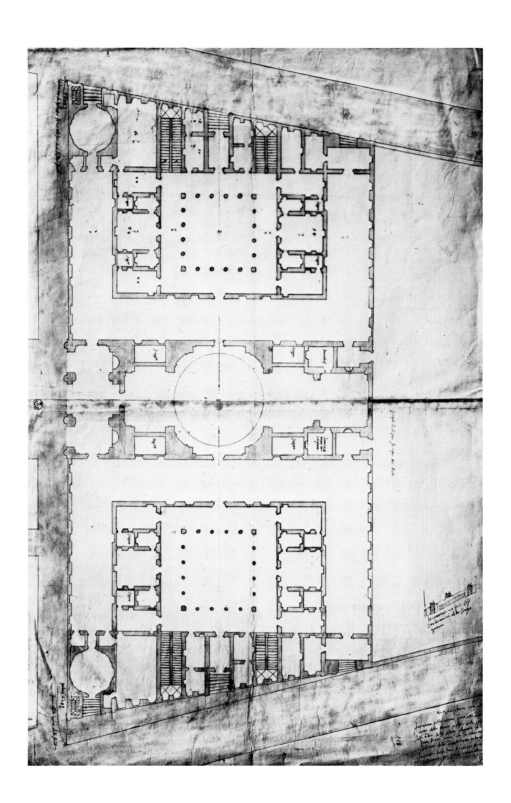

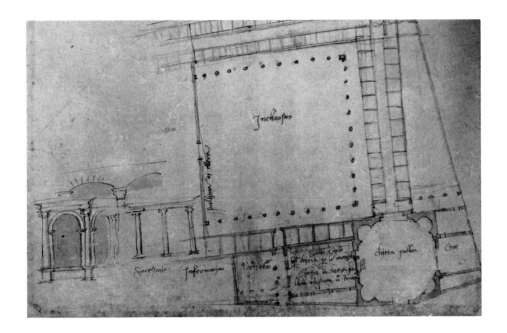

12.1   *Antonio da Sangallo the Younger, plan project*
for the Church and Hospital of San Giacomo degli
Incurabili, Rome, after 1538? Florence, Uffizi, A. 870.

12.2   *Baldassarre Peruzzi, plan project and elevations*
for the Church and Hospital of San Giacomo degli
Incurabili, Rome, ca. 1534–36? Florence, Uffizi, A.
558.

In the largest building programs, an architect could devote most of his time to design and supervision because other duties were carried out by a large staff. At St. Peter's, for instance, there was a hierarchy that became more complex as the building grew.[21] In the 1520s and '30s it apparently was organized with an architect (Sangallo) at the head along with a co-architect (Peruzzi). The execution was in charge of a *curatore* (Giuliano Leno) and a *computista* (Francesco Megalotti; later Jacopo Meleghino) immediately below him, if not on a par, who served as paymaster, and for this reason was a member of a board of three who measured and priced completed work; the *mensuratori* (Giov. Francesco da Sangallo and Rainieri da Pisa). The funds allotted by the Camera were distributed by two *depositari* or treasurers (Simone Ricasoli, Leonardo Bini). This staff had its *segretario,* whose hand is found in the records alongside that of the *computista.* On the job there was a group of 5 to 10 *soprastanti,* who might also be *mensuratori,* indicating that this position was higher than what we would call "foreman." It was probably comparable to a junior partner in an architectural or engineering firm. Next there were the *sotto soprastanti,* who were foremen and occasionally specialists, as: *sotto soprastante sopra i legnami* (carpenters). At the bottom of the official hierarchy came the *capomaestri* directing crews in their special crafts: carpentry, masonry, carving, ironwork, etc.

In this scheme the Renaissance architect played a role similar to his modern counterpart. But an organized *fabbrica* was exceptional. As a rule the architect assumed many of the duties described above. He was the chief estimator, determining the sum to be paid for a given construction job; he was often the paymaster, and he might be called on to supply mortar or materials for large sums that only later would be reimbursed by the client's treasurer. In doing this he assumed some of the duties that nowadays are assigned to the contractor. However there were contractors, and they served almost the same function as they have served in later times. For example, when the rebuilding of the Farnese Palace in Rome was started in 1541, the agents of Pierluigi Farnese signed a contract with the impresario Bartolomeo Baronio for its construction. It itemizes in detail the responsibilities of both parties.[22] The duke is to supply the mortar ready mixed, while the stone and brick are to come from the contractor, its quality subject to review by Sangallo and his associate Meleghino. The price of construction on walls and vaults is set by the *canna,* the measurement being assigned to two technicians: one appointed by the duke and one by Baronio. Certain prices, related to roofing and moldings, are left to the architects' judgment. The document closes: "and in the event that the said masters should make some omission that causes damages to the said structure by not working honestly as they ought to do, it shall be in the power and judgment of the said master Antonio Sangallo and Giacomo Meleghino to deprive them of the work and to give the structure to other masters."

Antonio's association with Meleghino on this job was not at all to his taste, and it illuminates a curious custom that permitted clients to create partnerships among architects who were unsympathetic to one another. Meleghino was the pope's toady and not much of an architect, which is sufficient explanation for the animosity.[23] Since Antonio's many commissions kept him away from Rome for long periods, he did his best to keep in touch with Meleghino's activities as well as with the progress of the construction. An amusing letter is preserved in which a faithful workman writing from Rome to Antonio in Rieti discusses the design of two windows which are sketched on the same page and proceeds to report: "You ought to know, Sir, that Master Jacopo Menichino (sic) has been here at the palace and has given me a message from the Pope that I should make the architraves that go over the pilasters of the entrance toward Santo Gerolamo [i.e., south] and that I should make the cornice there separately [? istachata] because there is no stone for it. Now, Sir, advise me if I should do it, and Vincenzo and I reverently send our best wishes. Written on the 9th day of January 1546. Obediently yours. Nardo di rafaello de rossi, carver."[24]

As a rule, the leading architects were assisted by subordinates who could be relied on not to meddle in the design. Antonio had Aristotile and Giovanni Battista Sangallo, for instance, who consistently helped him to keep an eye on far-flung projects, and his notes and theirs are often found together on preparatory sketches. Along with other adherents, these men formed what Vasari disdainfully called the *Setta Sangallesca,* or "Sangallo Clique," but it is hard to see in the group what we should call an architectural firm.[25] Even in the rare cases when a lesser architect executed drawings or made surveys for a more distinguished one, the relationship seems to have been informal. In fact, closer parallels to the modern office are found among painters than among architects in the Renaissance. Painters had to have a shop that was stylistically cohesive, while architects did not, as evidenced by the building of St. Peter's, which brought together some unlikely partners: Bramante and Giuliano Sangallo, Raphael and Fra Giocondo, Antonio and Peruzzi, and Vignola and Ligorio.

The High Renaissance architect managed without a firm and usually without even an office because he did so little detailed designing. It is in the process of design that his methods are most at variance with those of later periods, a fact that is amply documented by the many surviving early sixteenth-century drawings. In examining a collection of these drawings one's first impression is that very few of them were intended to be used in constructing a building or to be seen by anyone other than the architect. They are nearly all rapidly sketched studies of tentative ideas, sometimes for specific buildings, and sometimes for ideal structures. The few that are finished may be classed in two categories: first, the large, carefully drawn and attractively rendered projects that were made for the client. These are called presentation drawings; they are rare and they cannot have been much use for construction because they almost never include measurements or a scale. Moreover, they typically show the building that was to have been built rather than the one that was built. A good example is figure 12.3, Antonio's final plan for the Farnese Palace. It is a large sheet, without the usual scribblings and measurements, and without indication of scale, though it is identified, "Palace of the Duke of Castro." The wing facing the square appears as executed (though changes were made in partition walls) while the garden front drawn here does not at all resemble what ultimately was built. Figure 12.1 is, of course, the same sort, though it contains a few measurements, and another well-known example is Bramante's parchment half-plan of St. Peter's in the Uffizi. The second type of finished drawing was intended for use in construction, but it is limited to details—a window, an entablature—and was intended only to guide masons and carvers. Here again one of the Farnese series is a handy example (fig. 12.4), in which Antonio has drawn meticulously the profiles of window moldings for the use of the stonecarvers. They are identified as belonging to windows in the arcade as: "Molding for the capital of the pilaster [*stipite*] of said Farnese Windows." The tradition of verbal communication between architect and craftsman typically comes to the fore as the architect fills the left side of the sheet with instructions in longhand that might readily have been graphically presented. They deal mostly with linear measurements.

All other drawings fall into the category of preliminary sketches, and anyone who has tried to straighten out the history of a sixteenth-century building from drawings will know what a mêlée of undigested ideas they create. A sheet by the elder Antonio Sangallo presents a familiar confusion (fig. 12.5). Here the arches and the campanile of San Biagio in Montepulciano appear together with unidentified door brackets, balusters, and the plan of a domestic (?) structure, one piled on top of another. His nephew does the same thing (fig. 12.7), though he sticks to one project and is spendthrift enough to fill up the whole page with it.

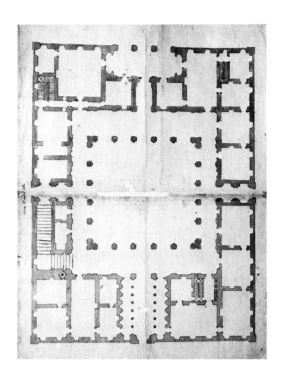

12.3   *Antonio da Sangallo the Younger, presentation plan of the Farnese Palace, Rome, 1541–46. Florence, Uffizi, A. 298.*

12.4   *Antonio da Sangallo the Younger, profiles for the Farnese Palace, Rome, 1541–46. Florence, Uffizi, A. 1007v.*

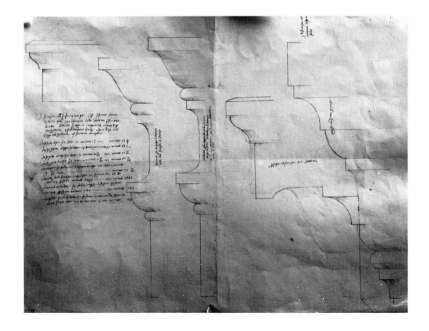

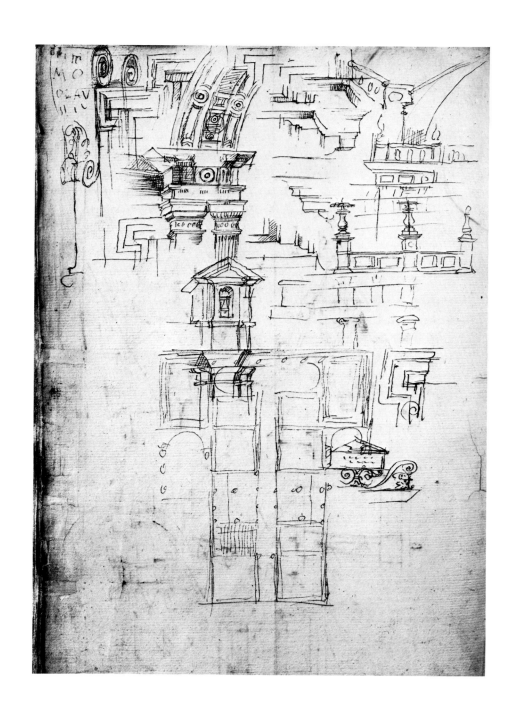

12.5   *Antonio da Sangallo the Elder, studies for S. Biagio, Montepulciano, ca. 1518. Florence, Uffizi, A. 7836.*

I can conclude from this evidence only that drawings were not the chief means of communication between architects and builders. The enormous expense and effort devoted to the construction of models for the larger projects suggests that much of the designing went on in plastic form at this stage.[26] Builders, rather than work with detailed specifications, got the gist of the design from the model, and when they encountered problems, they simply got the answer from the architect or supervisor by word of mouth. But the importance of models should not be overestimated: like the presentation drawings they rarely represent the structure that ultimately was built, and in any case they were made only for the most grandiose structures. I think that the average palace or church was built from rough plans and a batch of details.

What is curious about High Renaissance drawings is not that they are so frequently plans and details but that they are so seldom anything else. Sections appear where there is a vaulting problem, but what I find most surprising is the rarity of elevation drawings, and particularly of façades. A fear of façades is an Italian phobia of long standing that blighted most of the great Gothic structures: Milan Cathedral; San Petronio in Bologna; in Florence, the cathedral, Santa Croce, Santa Maria Novella, Santa Trinita; Santa Maria sopra Minerva in Rome; and others. The loss of many Renaissance drawings does not quite explain away this phenomenon, because it is clear from the surviving ones that the plan dominated architecture as never before or since. In the development of a design we frequently find plan studies in which the exterior of a building is not even indicated, as is effectively illustrated in Antonio's study for San Giovanni dei Fiorentini (fig. 12.6). In churches the great trend toward the central plan was accompanied by a method of design that can be described only as centrifugal. The architect starts drawing in the center and works outward, and it is not until he has reached a final solution that he begins to consider what the outer face shall be. I have chosen two examples of this procedure (figs. 12.7, 12.8) because it seems to me so revealing of the aesthetic of the period. In the first, which contains further studies by Antonio for San Giovanni in Rome, the only sure thing is the void—a given volume of space—in the middle. Around this, architectural elements appear to explode outward in all directions: a central plan, a longitudinal plan (related to fig. 12.6), both with variants. The sense of centrifugal force is heightened by the virtual absence of exterior walls. Peruzzi's study for the crossing of St. Peter's (fig. 12.8) is more definite because the piers were already there when he started. But the outward movement is just as strong, and it is emphasized by the fact that elements lose definition in direct ratio to their distance from the center. The cross section, furthermore, is not drawn as the central portion of a great church, nor even as an isolated chapel, as it seems on first

12.6   *Antonio da Sangallo the Younger, plan project for San Giovanni dei Fiorentini, Rome, ca. 1520–25? Florence, Uffizi, A. 861.*

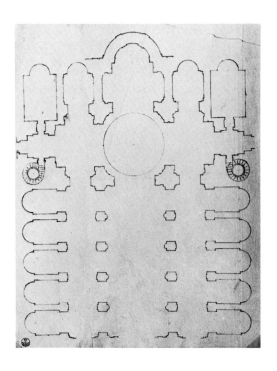

12.7   *Antonio da Sangallo the Younger, plan projects and elevations for San Giovanni dei Fiorentini, Rome, ca. 1520–25? Florence, Uffizi, A. 1292.*

12.8   *Baldassarre Peruzzi, plan project for the crossing of St. Peter's, Vatican, ca. 1530. Florence, Uffizi, A. 107.*

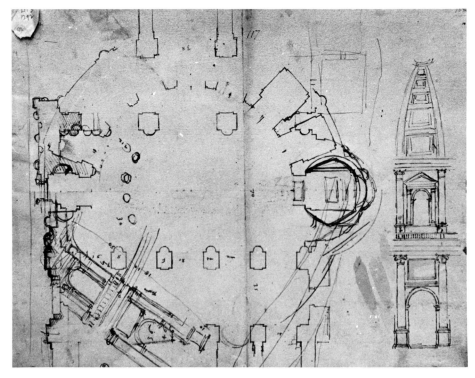

sight, but as a scene such as one would view when standing in the center of the space: a painter's concept of architecture. My impression is that the centrifugal character all comes from the tendency of these architects to visualize themselves in the center of a given space, looking outward. This is why they were so attached to the central plan and, to go a step further, to *scenografia:* two ways of making it possible to view the whole environment from a single point.

Even when the architect finally applies himself to the problem of designing the façades he seldom undertakes to make a scale drawing of an exterior elevation. He proceeds from the perfected plan to entrance portals, windows, and entablatures (fig. 12.9). The significance of this procedure is that the architect thinks of the elevation as a neutral field into which plastic incidents are set at intervals: often, rather than draw up an elevation, he will explain it verbally in his plan.[27] As a consequence it often happened that the High Renaissance façade could be expanded or contracted at will, and Raphael's work provides a good example of this. The Vidoni-Caffarelli Palace in Rome was almost doubled in length, the façade of the Vatican Palace was tripled in size and twisted into a court (the Cortile di San Damaso), and a large part of the design for the Pandolfini Palace in Florence was left out. I believe that none of the designs suffers much from this treatment. It is important by way of contrast to recall Alberti's demand that the façade be developed as an intricate system of interrelating proportions, giving the wall a vitality in plane; the failure of this principle in the early cinquecento is another example of the strange eclipse of the fifteenth century.[28] Perhaps proportions of this sort were too abstract for the anti-theoretical High Renaissance and had to wait for another humanist, Palladio, to rediscover their place in architecture. With Palladio, elevations and façades take on a role that they never again lost. I wonder if the absorption of the High Renaissance in Roman ruins does not explain this in part. Architects' drawings after antiquity were almost all plans and details—of necessity, since so few ancient elevations remained elevated. In addition, the study of Vitruvius encouraged the dominance of the plan, since the Hellenistic module is an arithmetic one found in the plan of the column, in contradistinction to Alberti's geometric harmony that integrates plan and elevation in one musical system.

Perhaps the character of Renaissance architecture owes much to the fact that its monuments started, not from a complete idea, fixed in the symbolism of the blueprint, but from flexible impressions constantly susceptible to change. The ultimate statement, like that of the sculptor, evolved in the process of creating the mass itself. This way of conceiving architecture explains also the peculiarly biological character of

12.9   *Michelangelo Buonarroti, window(?) and niche*
studies. Florence, Uffizi, A. 96.

Italian Renaissance building. The large monuments that took more than a decade to complete seldom followed an original conception, but evolved like a living organism in their growth. The successive architects at St. Peter's, while they held Bramante in reverence, never made the least attempt to carry out what he would have wanted. They took what was there as an inspiration for new ideas, and this habit of working with and in the building itself brought the efforts of many generations to a cohesive conclusion. How different this is from Renaissance France, where at Fontainebleau, Blois, the Louvre, each successive portion of the structure is methodically isolated from its predecessor! It is not chance that Renaissance Italy had no du Cerceau to preserve its projects the moment they had taken form.[29]

When I began to write this paper I expected to finish with a picture of an architect more like today's. But now he appears to be of quite a different species. What I have called his rugged individualism is illustrated first in his unwillingness to be bound by those abstractions we call plans and elevations; second in his refusal to establish a permanent office staff or even a studio for his own work; and third in his suspicion of theoretical principles and his avoidance of the written word, whether it be his or another's. We are accustomed to caricatures of the bohemian painter and sculptor in the proverbial garret, and the businesslike architect with offices in the commercial district, but in this segment of the Renaissance these roles, in a sense, were reversed. The Roman Renaissance architect was less trained in the technique and less organized in the practice of his calling than any of his contemporaries in the arts. But paradoxically this was a step toward establishing architecture as a respected profession, because it represented, far more than the procedures of painters or sculptors, a liberation from the bonds of the medieval shop system. At this stage the development of the architect's freedom and social stature was more important than the establishment of standards of workmanship.

1.   Antonio appears first in Rome in 1504 as a *falegname* at Castel Sant'Angelo (G. Clausse, *Les San Gallo* [Paris, 1901], 2:45) and in documents of 1510–11 as an assistant to Bramante with the title *faber lignarius* or *carpentarius* (Ackerman, "Bramante and the Torre Borgia," *Rendiconti della Pontificia Accademia di archeologia, 25–26* [1949–51], 251ff.). He held the same position in 1513–14.

2.   The papal Breve, in which Antonio is appointed at half the salary of Raphael, is reproduced by V. Golzio, *Raffaello* (Vatican City, 1936), 50f.

3.   Benvenuto Cellini, "Discorso dell'architettura," *Opere* (Milan, 1811), 3:249. He says of Antonio: "But because he had been neither a sculptor nor a painter, but rather a master of carpentry only; for this reason one never sees a sign in his work of that certain noble Character [*virtù*] such as is seen in our true Third [the first and second being Bramante and Sangallo], whom we may place first of all, Michelangelo Buonarroti." This was probably written before Michelangelo's death, but remained unpublished until the late eighteenth century.

4.   Letter of 1560 or thereabouts, supposedly to the Cardinal Rodolfo Pio de Carpi. Milanesi (*Le lettere di Michelangelo Buonarroti* [Florence, 1875], 554) transcribes it from an original in the Archivio Buonarroti, while Schiavo (*Michelangelo architetto* [Rome, 1949], fig. 96) reproduces the same text photographically as a leaf from a Vatican codex *3211* (which collection?), fol. XCVII.

5.   For example, in the draft of a letter on a drawing of about 1546 in the British Museum, he says: "I lack the spirit for it because I am not an architect." Wilde, in his recent publication (*Italian Drawings in the British Museum: Michelangelo and His Studio* [London, 1953], no. 70, pp. 108ff.), associates this complaint with the commission for the Farnese Palace; but the St. Peter's commission is a more likely cause, since Vasari (*Vite*, ed. Milanesi, VII, 218) reports a similar statement in that connection. Wilde notes that Michelangelo objected for the same reason to his first architectural assignment (Milanesi, *Le lettere*, p. 431).

6.   Vasari (*Vite*, IV, 157f.) blames the state of Bramante's structures on the fact that Julius II demanded inordinate haste in construction—"he wanted buildings not to be built but to be born"—but nevertheless adds: "a carelessness which was the reason why his [Bramante's] works are all cracking and stand in danger of ruin."

7.   A huge collection of these drawings is preserved in the Uffizi Gallery and many are published in the six-volume work of A. Bartoli, *I monumenti antichi di Roma nei disegni degli Uffizi di Firenze* (Rome, 1914–22). See also H. Egger, *Kritisches Verzeichnis der Sammlung architektonischer Handzeichnungen der K. K. Hofbibliothek in Wien* (Vienna, 1903), vol. 1.

8.   For example, Huelsen's study of the sketchbook of Giuliano da Sangallo, *Il libro di Giuliano da Sangallo; Codice Vaticano Barberiniano Latino 4424* (Leipzig, 1910), xxxvi ff., shows that copies were made from that source by Antonio da Sangallo the Younger, Giambattista Sangallo, the anonymous author of the Soane Museum "Coner" Sketchbook, the Anonymous Destailleur, Vasari the younger, Cassiano del Pozzo, and many others.

9.   Some of Cronaca's drawings are reproduced by Bartoli, *I monumenti*, vol. 1, pl. XVI, fig. 33 to pl. XX, fig. 42. Bramantino's notebook is published in facsimile, *Le rovine di Roma* (ed. Mongeri, Milan, 1875).

10.   One by Antonio Labacco is in the Uffizi (Manetti, *Vita di Leon Battista Alberti* [2d ed.; Florence, 1911], 396). A second is in the sketchbook of about 1535–40 attributed to Aristotile and Giovanni Battista Sangallo in the Palais des Beaux-Arts in Lille (Fonds Wicar, fol. 840) and a third, copied from the second, is in a sketchbook of about 1580 by Oreste Vannocci in the Biblioteca Comunale of Siena (S. IV. 1., fol. 140). The measurements given on these plans are the roughest approximations of the actual dimensions of the building and helped to hide from the sixteenth century the intricate system of proportions employed by Alberti.

11.   Brunelleschi's lantern appears in the Lille MS mentioned above (fol. 726) and in the Siena MS (fol. 139), where it is compared to Michelangelo's lantern of the Medici chapel in Florence. The plan of Santa Maria degli Angeli appears in fol. 15v of Giuliano Sangallo's sketchbook (Huelsen, *Il libro di Giuliano Sangallo*, 27), on a drawing attributed to Jacopo Sansovino (Uffizi, Arch. 1949), and in many other sixteenth-century drawings.

12.   This church generally is said to have been built by Sangallo in 1507. This is clearly an error, as he was not an architect at that time (see n. 1). His activity there dates from the 1520s and no ear-

lier construction is visible in the present church (see my *The Cortile del Belvedere* [Vatican City, 1954], p. 48, n. 2). But Julius II must have founded the church, since it is mentioned among the pope's contributions to Rome by Francesco Albertini, *Opusculum de mirabilibus novae et veteris Urbis Romae* (Rome, 1510).

13. The hospital owned property all along the Via di Ripetta in an area that has always been the artists' quarter of Rome. Antonio rented "property . . . in the new Via del Popolo" from the Trustees as early as 1512 and remained a lessee until his death (Archivio di Stato, Rome, Archive of the Ospedale di San Giacomo degli Incurabili, Libri di entrata e uscita, no. 1142, fol. 15v, to no. 1198). At a later date, Peruzzi became a tenant as well, and painted for the trustees.

14. According to a document in the archives of Viterbo dated December 8, 1518, Antonio was hired "ad faciendum palcum subtus tectum Ecclesiae Sanctae Marie in Quercie . . . che detto palco habia essere de quella richeza che è quello de camera de Papa Leone in palazo di Papa in Roma, dove se fa concistorio; et uno palmo più sfondado . . ." (from C. Pinzi, "Memorie e documenti inediti sulla Basilica di Santa Maria della Quercia in Viterbo," *Archivio storico dell'arte*, 3 [1890], 322).

15. This competition is reported by Vasari (*Vite*, VII, 498) and by Temanza (*Vite dei più celebre architetti e scultori veneziani* . . . [Venice, 1778], 212f.) in their Lives of Jacopo Sansovino, and it is mentioned in a letter from Pietro Aretino to Sansovino (reproduced by Giovannoni in *Saggi sull' architettura del Rinascimento* [Milan, 1935], 123ff.). Modern studies on the early history of the church include two by A. Nava, in the *Archivio della r. deput. romana di storia patria*, 59 (1936), 337 ff., and *Critica d'arte* 1 (1935), 102ff.; and an unpublished master's thesis by Ruth Olitsky, "San Giovanni dei Fiorentini," Institute of Fine Arts of New York University, 1951.

16. There is no literature on the competition for San Giacomo, but competing designs for the complex were discovered in the Uffizi by Wolfgang Lotz and published in a short notice in the *Mitteilungen des Kunsthistorischen Insts. in Florenz, 5* (1940), 441ff., figs. 1–3. The only remaining evidence of Sangallo's winning plan is the small church of Santa Maria in Porta Paradisi on the Via Ripetta (fig. 7, upper left-hand corner), built in 1519–26. The Santo Spirito competition is a hypothesis of mine; I have discovered a plan by Peruzzi (Uffizi, Arch. 558) for an unidentified church with an adjoining cloister or court to be built on a plot identical in proportion to the oddly shaped plot of the present church and court.

17. The competition, which involved Sangallo, Michelangelo, and the painters Perino del Vaga, Sebastiano del Piombo, and Vasari, is recorded by the latter in his Life of Sangallo (*Vite*, V, 470ff.; the account in VII, 223 conflicts with this), and also in letters published by Gotti, *Vita di Michelangelo Buonarroti* (Florence, 1875), 1:292ff. The sources are discussed by Meller, "Zur Entstehungsgeschichte des Kranzgesims am Palazzo Farnese," *Jbh. d. Pr. Kunsts.*, 30 (1909), 1ff. In discussing the competition, Tolnay ("Beiträge zu den späten architektonischen Projekten Michelangelos," *Jbh. d. Pr. Kunsts.*, 51 [1930], 33ff.) published an unknown design from the Munich Graphische Sammlung which he attributes to Sangallo. It shows a fourth story or high attic. I believe the attribution is groundless because both the draftsmanship and the architecture are far too feeble to be assigned to the mature Sangallo and because the solution bears no relation to his preserved studies, of which there are several in the Uffizi.

18. Antonio's career is outlined by G. Clausse, *Les San Gallo* (Paris, 1901), vol. II. The book is obsolete but no other general study exists.

19. Papal Breve of May 28, 1536, reproduced by Pastor, *Storia dei Papi* (1st Italian ed.; Rome, 1924), 5:792, doc. 20; Breve of January 14, 1538, ibid., 5:796ff., and several other authors.

20. Letter of May 11, 1555, to Vasari (*Lettere*, ed. Milanesi, 537, from the Archivio Buonarroti): "Io fu messo a forza ne la fabrica di Santo Pietro, e ò servito circa otto anni non solamente in dono, ma con grandissimo mie danno e dispiacere."

21. The following data were culled from the nearly 1,000 documents on the construction of St. Peter's during this period published by Karl Frey ("Zur Baugeschichte des St. Peter: Mitteilungen aus der R. da Fabbrica di San Pietro," *Jbh. d. Pr. Kunsts.*, Beiheft to 31 [1911], 1ff.; Beiheft to 32 [1913], 1ff.).

22. The exact source of this document is unknown. It was published by Umberto Gnoli, "Le Palais Farnese (Notes et Documents)," *Mélanges de l'Ecole Française de Rome*, 54 (1937), 209ff., from the transcripts that his father, Domenico, had made in the Archivio di Stato, Rome.

23. On Meleghino's career, see K. Frey, "Studien zu Michelangelo Buonarroti u. der Kunst seiner Zeit," Part III, *Jbh. d. Pr. Kunsts.*, Beiheft to 30 (1909), 138f.

24. This letter and the two accompanying drawings are in the Uffizi drawing collection, Arch. 302. The text is reproduced by Milanesi in his edition of Vasari's *Vite,* V, 487.

25. The term is used in the *Vite,* VII, 218. The Sangallo group must have included Antonio's brother Giovanni Battista (il Gobbo), his cousins Aristotile and Francesco, Nanni di Baccio Bigio, and Antonio Labacco, among others. The cohesiveness probably was due to the fact that most of them owed their jobs to Antonio and that after his death they were not imaginative enough to continue ahead with Michelangelo. Vasari repeats a story that shortly after Antonio's death the "clique" confronted Michelangelo with the sententious statement that Antonio's model for St. Peter's was "a field that will never cease to be a pasture." "You are quite right," Michelangelo reportedly answered, "if you are talking of sheep and cows, who do not understand art."

26. Antonio's model for St. Peter's, which still exists, was built for him by Antonio Labacco. It took from 1539 to 1546 to complete, and Frey estimated the cost at between 5,500 and 6,000 ducats. To judge from the salary paid to the chief architect of the Holy See (see above, at n. 19) a ducat ought to be over $10 in today's exchange. Michelangelo's model for the dome of the Basilica cost about 600 ducats. Cf. K. Frey, "Studien zu Michelangelo Buonarroti," *Jbh. d. Pr. Kunsts., Beiheft* to 30 (1909), 167ff., 171ff.; Frey, "Zur Baugeschichte des St. Peter," *Jbh. d. Pr. Kunsts., Beiheft* to 33 (1913), 21 ff.; *Beiheft* to 37 (1916), 81ff.

27. Interesting examples of this are Peruzzi's early study for the Palazzo Massimi in Rome and a church plan by Antonio Sangallo. The first (Uffizi, Arch. 368, reproduced by L. Venturi, *Storia dell'arte italiana* [Milan, 1938], XI, 1, p. 417, fig. 387) is a plan of the palace accompanied by a text explaining the façade: "In front of the portico metopes XX and triglyphs XXI height of the columns with base and capital palmi XX and thickness palmi two and one half that is II ½." In Sangallo's sketch (Uffizi, Arch. 168, reproduced by Gab. Fot. della Sopraintendenza alle Gallerie, Florence, no. 14389), the plan of a centralized church (study for S. M. in Monserrato?) is accompanied by the text: "This may be vaulted in two ways. The first, or cheaper, is this: the curve [*sexto*] of the cupola is begun at the same level as the impost of the great arches and the dome is built as a cloister vault [*vela*]. The second way is

to make a cornice at the top of the arches constructed to a perfect circle and above this to go on straight so that you may cut in apertures of any kind you want or windows or even roundels. And over the said apertures make another round cornice from which you may begin to spring the cupola; but first keep it straight [i.e., "continue vertically"] for a distance of 2½ times the projection of the cornice [an optical correction to make visible a full hemisphere]."

28. On Alberti's principles of design, see R. Wittkower, *Architectural Principles in the Age of Humanism* (London, 1949), 40f., 94ff.

29. But it may be coincidence that we know Michelangelo's designs mostly through the engravings of Frenchmen: Beatrizet, Dupérac, Le Mercier.

Postscript

In the course of three years of preparation for my dissertation (on the Cortile del Belvedere in the Vatican) at the American Academy in Rome, from 1949 to 1952, I saw a great number of drawings and documents that related to architectural practice in the Italian Renaissance, and this prepared me to speak on the subject at a session on practice at the annual meeting of the Society of Architectural Historians in 1954. Not much has been written specifically on the subject since that time, but excellent work has been done by Goldthwaite and Toker on the fifteenth century in Florence showing that the concept of the architect gelled slowly in the course of the century. The term "architect" was rarely employed and, apart from its appearance in theoretical works like those of Alberti and Francesco di Giorgio, which sought to revive the Vitruvian image of the architect as a design professional (Toker, 1985, suggests that the Gothic master realized this goal better than the Renaissance architect), it most frequently applied to experts in the building trades who supervised construction or advised or served on building committees. No one was trained as an architect: competition designs would be submitted by masons, intellectuals, and citizens with experience serving on building committees, as well as by sculptors, metalsmiths, and painters, who were presumably the most qualified. Most of the time, the design of a major new structure would be attributed to the patron—often on good grounds, as in the building programs of Lorenzo de' Medici.

Considering that this study accounts only for architectural practice in Rome during the first half of the sixteenth century, its title is misleading. Were I writing on the subject today, I would compare the situation in Rome with that of Venice in the same period and Florence in the previous century. In Venice, the office of *Proto*, an architect employed as overseer of state projects, possessed greater power and greater control over major commissions than designers elsewhere; in contrast, master masons were more likely to become designers than in central Italy (Boucher, Tafuri).

My assumption that the designs of Antonio da Sangallo the Younger and Baldassarre Peruzzi for the Ospedale and the church of San Giacomo degli Incurabili (figs. 12.1, 12.2) were prepared for a competition at the time the new complex was founded in 1518–19 requires revision in the light of the study by Heinz. At that date, Sangallo apparently designed only the chapel of Santa Maria in Porta Paradisi, which still survives on Via Ripetta, and perhaps the hospital ward behind it, the construction of which continued until 1526.

But he and Peruzzi did not participate in a competition in the literal sense. Peruzzi was commissioned by the hospital to design a tomb in 1526 and, after a long halt in construction, to prepare, in 1534–36 (the last two years of his life), a master plan for the Hospital and the church of S. Giacomo. Sangallo was rehired in 1538–46 to prepare and oversee a new master plan, and it is in that period that the drawing in figure 12.1 was executed. In the original publication, I illustrated in figure 2 a drawing identified as Peruzzi's which was in fact from the Sangallo workshop; the new figure 12.2 is legitimate Peruzzi.

Boucher, Bruce. "Il Sansovino e i Procuratori di San Marco," *Ateneo veneto,* n.s., 24 (1986), 59–74.

Frommel, Christof. *Der römische Palastbau der Hochrenaissance,* 3 vols. (Tübingen, 1973).

Giovannoni, Gustavo. *Antonio da Sangallo il giovane,* 2 vols. (Rome, 1959?).

Goldthwaite, Richard. *The Building of Renaissance Florence* (Baltimore, 1980), 351–396.

Günther, Hubertus. "Studien zum venezianischen Aufenthalt des Sebastiano Serlio," *Münchner Jahrbuch der bildenden Kunst,* 3d ser., 32 (1981), 43–94.

Günther, Hubertus. "Werke Bramantes im Spiegel einer Grupper von Zeichnungen der Uffizien in Florenz," *Münchner Jahrbuch der bildenden Kunst,* 3d ser., 33 (1982), 77–109.

Heinz, Marianne. "Das Hospital S. Giacomo in Augusta in Rom, Peruzzi u. Antonio da Sangallo il G.: Zum Hospitalbau der Hochrenaissance," *Storia dell'arte,* 41 (1981), 31–49.

Hollingsworth, Mary. "The Architect in Sixteenth-Century Florence," *Art History,* 7 (1984), 385–410.

Lewine, Milton. "Roman Architectural Practice During Michelangelo's Maturity," *Stil und Überlieferung in der Kunst des Abendlandes* (Acts of the 21st International Congress for the History of Art, 1964; Berlin, 1967), 20ff.

Morscheck, Charles R., Jr. "The Profession of Architect in Milan before Bramante," *Arte lombarda,* 78 (1986), 94–100.

Saalman, Howard. "Early Renaissance Theory and Practice in Antonio Filarete's *Trattato di architettura,*" *The Art Bulletin,* 41 (1959), 102–106.

Tafuri, Manfredo. *Venezia e il Rinascimento* (Turin, 1985).

Toker, Franklin. "Alberti's Ideal Architect: Renaissance or Gothic?," *Renaissance Studies in Honor of Craig Hugh Smyth* (Florence, 1985), 1:667–674.

Toker, Franklin. "Gothic Architecture by Remote Control: An Illustrated Building Contract of 1340," *The Art Bulletin,* 67 (1985), 69–95.

Wurm, Heinrich. *Baldassarre Peruzzi: Architekturzeichnungen,* I, Tafelband (all published) (Tübingen, 1984). Wurm does not identify my figure 12.2 with S. Giacomo degli Incurabili.

13

The Capitoline Hill

Medieval Rome had no center. Other Italian towns that had been smaller in antiquity grew in clusters about their ancient squares, while Rome gradually shrank until its fora and major churches were on the outskirts, and the remnants of a metropolis settled in compressed disorder along the banks of the Tiber. When the city government decided to raise a communal palace in the twelfth century, it chose the deserted site of the Tabularium on the slope of the Capitoline hill overlooking the republican Forum. The decision must have been dictated by the dream of *renovatio*—the restoration of ancient glory—as the hill had been the site of the *Arx* of the earliest settlers and of the major temples of imperial Rome.[1] Isolated from the everyday life of the city on a summit without paved accesses, the Capitol, or Campidoglio as the Romans called it, failed until the sixteenth century to arouse sufficient civic pride to foster the construction of a monumental communal piazza such as nearly every major Italian city had produced in the Middle Ages. We owe to this delay one of the most imposing architectural compositions of all time; nowhere but in Rome had a Renaissance architect been given the opportunity to create a grandiose environment for the political life of a great city.

It was lack of opportunity rather than of desire that deterred early Renaissance designers from executing ambitious civic schemes. Every architectural theorist of the Renaissance was a philosopher of urbanism; Alberti and Leonardo thought primarily of improving the appearance and convenience of existing towns; Filarete and Francesco

From James S. Ackerman, *The Architecture of Michelangelo,* second edition (Chicago: University of Chicago Press, and Harmondsworth: Penguin Books, 1986), 136–170.

di Giorgio drew ideal, geometrically perfect projects to be raised anew. But their schemes remained on paper, and only in occasional provincial villages, such as Pienza, Cortemaggiore, or Vigevano, or in the refurbishing of existing squares, could modern ideas be tested. Unfortunately, the largest planning project of the sixteenth century was totally destroyed: the town of Castro, redesigned by Antonio da Sangallo the Younger for Pope Paul III as the capital of a duchy fabricated for the Pope's son.[2]

The square at Pienza, of 1456/8–64 (fig. 13.1), is the only quattrocento scheme comparable to the Campidoglio. Built for Pope Pius II by Alberti's follower Bernardo Rossellino, it was the core of the town's life, containing the cathedral at the center and, on three sides, the palaces of the bishop, the Piccolomini family, and the commune.[3] By chance, the plan is trapezoidal, like Michelangelo's (fig. 13.7), because of the axes of the preexisting streets on either side, and because the expansion in width opened prospects past the cathedral transepts over a panorama of Tuscan valleys and hills. Though the major street runs through the base of the trapezoid, a lesser one enters, like the Capitoline *cordonata*, on the principal axis. Rossellino divided the piazza into rectangles by horizontal and vertical bands which help to draw together the façades and lead the eye toward the cathedral. The projects of Rossellino and Michelangelo have similar devices: the regular plan, symmetrically organized about the entrance axis of the central building; the systematization of the entrance ways into the piazza; and the pavement pattern calculated to integrate the several buildings. But the effect is quite different; the Pienza buildings are diverse in size and scale, and above all, in style; the sole monument within the square—a wellhead—is eccentrically placed on the right edge. The harmonious relationship among independent units, characteristic of the quattrocento, focused attention on the individual buildings, and spatial effects were a by-product of the design of the enframing masses. Only in the last generation of the fifteenth century did architects begin to think of single elements as a function of the whole—to regard a given environment not merely as a neutral repository for a work of art, but as something that might be formed and controlled by the manipulation of voids and the coordination of masses. The difference in approach is illuminated by a similar change in the music of this generation; the polyphonic structure which produced harmonies through the superposition of independent melodies began to give way to homophonic forms in which the several lines were subordinate to harmonies constructed vertically to produce sequences of chords; a concordance of voices became primary.[4]

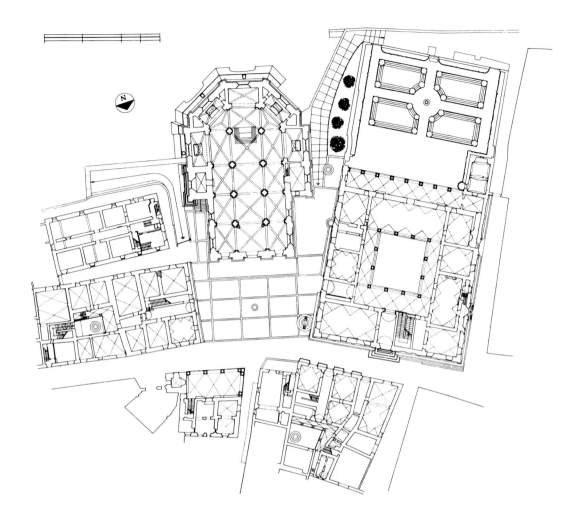

13.1   *Pienza, cathedral square. After Cataldi.*

13.2   *Rome, Capitoline Hill, view.*

The new spirit, foreseen in certain sketches of Francesco di Giorgio, appeared in the planning schemes of Leonardo and Giuliano da Sangallo, but was first applied in practice by Bramante. In his plan of 1502 for the precinct of the Tempietto of San Pietro in Montorio, the central building was not intended to stand isolated in a neutral space as it does today, but to be the nucleus of a scheme which controlled the total environment, which formed palpable spatial volumes as well as architectural bodies, in such a way that the observer would be entirely enveloped in a composition that he could grasp only as a whole. Two years later Bramante applied the principles of environmental control to the most monumental program of the age, the Cortile del Belvedere (fig. 11.1). Here his raw material was an entire mountainside; his design had to impose the authority of intellect upon nature. Inspired by antique precedents, he devised a sequence of rectangular courts on ascending levels, bound by stairways and ramps of varying form and framed by loggias. His principles of organization were: first, emphasis on the central axis (marked by a centralized monumental fountain in the lowest court, a central stairway and niche in the central court, and a focal one-story exedra in the garden at the upper level, the last already destroyed by Michelangelo in figure 11.4); second, the symmetrical design of the lateral façades; and third, a perspective construction in three dimensions devised for an observer in a fixed position within the papal *stanze,* and reinforced by the diminishing heights of the loggias as they recede toward the "vanishing point" at the rear.[5]

Michelangelo must have borrowed certain elements of his composition from the Belvedere; the fact that he used a replica of the Senatore staircase in remodeling Bramante's exedra in 1551 (figs. 13.2, 11.4) indicates his awareness of the similarity of the two plans. Both required the regularization of rolling hillsides, the integration of preexisting buildings, and covered porticoes on either side. Several of Bramante's devices were applicable to the Campidoglio, particularly the central monument and stairway used for axial emphasis and the niche centered in a triangular plane formed by ramps. Bramante's static perspective construction was unsuitable to the Capitoline topography and was anyhow uncongenial to Michelangelo's interest in movement through space; but the Campidoglio plan does fix the observer's viewpoint momentarily by forcing him to enter the piazza on the central axis at the only point from which the composition can be viewed as a whole.

The common feature of the two plans is a unity achieved by the organization more than by the character of the component parts, a unity imposed by general principles—axis, asymmetry, convergence—which command the voids as well as the architectural bodies. The actual form of certain elements might be changed without disturbing the organization—for example, the Marcus Aurelius monument could be a fountain; and this illuminates what Michelangelo meant when he said in speaking of axial compositions: "the *means* are unrestricted and may be chosen at will." What distinguishes Michelangelo from his predecessor is that his choice of means more effectively reinforces the principles of organization and binds the Campidoglio into a coherent unity. His individuality emerges in dynamic composition; the elements in the Campidoglio do not produce the restful progression of the Belvedere, but are directed toward a dramatic climax at the portal of the Senators' palace. Internal tensions built up by contrasts of equally potent forms—horizontals and verticals in the façades; oval and trapezoid in the pavement—offer diversions and ambiguities that only amplify the ultimate confluence toward the goal. This crescendo of forms was destined to become archetypal in civic planning; though the vigor and ingenuity of the Campidoglio have rarely been equalled, the U-shaped plan, the convergence of low wings toward a dominant central accent, the double-ramped stairway, and the centralized monument were to become characteristic components of urban and villa design in the following centuries.

On December 10, 1537, "Master Michelangelo, sculptor" appeared on a list of foreigners awarded Roman citizenship in a ceremony at the Capitol;[6] in the same month, he probably started designing for the statue of Marcus Aurelius—which Pope Paul III had brought to the hill against his advice—a pedestal, the shape and orientation of which implies the conception of the entire plan. No more is known of the circumstances leading to his project for the Piazza; but certain conditions of the commission may be deduced from knowledge of the site in these years. The statue had been placed in an uneven plateau in the saddle of the hill between the northern peak occupied by the church of Santa Maria in Aracoeli and the southern rise toward the Tarpeian Rock (fig. 13.3). Two structures bordered the plateau: the medieval Senators' palace on the east, and the quattrocento Conservators' palace on the south. The only paved access was a stairway descending from the transept of the Aracoeli; toward the city the slope of the hill, creased by muddy footpaths (fig. 13.6), fell sharply off to the west. Michelangelo must have been asked to submit proposals, first, for an entrance from the city, second, for the conversion of the plateau into a level paved area, and third, for a modest restoration of the dilapidated palaces.

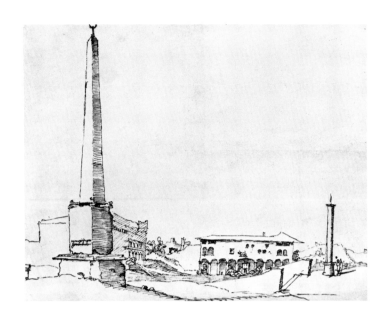

13.3 *Marten van Heemskerk, view, ca. 1535–36.*
After Egger, Römische Veduten.

13.4 *H. Cock, view, ca. 1547. From* Operum
antiquorum . . . romanorum . . . reliquiae *(Antwerp,
1562).*

13.5 *Anonymous, view, ca. 1554–60. Brunswick,*
Kupferstichkabinett. After Thies.

13.6 *Anonymous, view, ca. 1554–60. Louvre,*
Collection d'Italie, no. 11208. After Egger, Römische
Veduten.

The plan that transformed the disorderly complex into a symmetrical composition unifying five entrances, a piazza, and three palace fronts (figs. 13.7–13.9) was too extraordinary to have been foreseen by lay administrators; Michelangelo must have found in their mundane program an inspiration for a design the grandiose character of which persuaded them to raise their goals. The Conservators may not have assented easily: their budget was restricted throughout the sixteenth century, and they cannot have anticipated proposals to build a new campanile simply to emphasize the axis, and to raise a third palace along the left side of the square the function of which was to be purely aesthetic. Yet without the "Palazzo Nuovo" (the name indicates the absence of a practical purpose), no order could be imposed on the scheme; it achieved precisely the goal that Michelangelo so vigorously defined in a letter in which, suggesting the principles of his architecture, he affirmed the relationship of architecture to the human body, in the sense that necessary similarity of the eyes and uniqueness of the nose implies that architectural elements to the left of a central axis must be mirrored by those on the right, while the central element must be unique.[7] Aside from the gratuitous addition of a palace front, economy was a major determinant in Michelangelo's solution; he accepted the condition that the existing palaces were to be retained intact and merely to be covered with new façades. This gave his patrons the freedom to execute the project in stages, according to their means; the Senators' stairway could be finished fifty years before the façade, and the Conservators' façade be built in one-bay sections without demolishing the earlier façade or interrupting the normal functions of the offices inside.

In accepting the existing conditions, Michelangelo had to rationalize the accidental orientation of the two palaces, the axes of which formed an 80° angle. An irregularity that might have defeated a less imaginative designer became the catalyst that led Michelangelo to use a trapezoidal plan and to develop from this figure other features of his scheme; he so masterfully controlled this potential disadvantage that it appears quite purposeful.

In the engraved plan and perspectives after Michelangelo's design (figs. 13.7, 13.8) only those elements are specified that may be seen by an observer within the square: of the five access stairways only the first steps are indicated, and nothing is shown of the palaces except the façades and porticoes. Obviously the project was not envisaged as a complex of individual building blocks, but as an outdoor room with three walls. This is a response to topographical conditions that are falsified by engravings and modern photographs (fig. 13.2) where the observer is artificially suspended in

AREAE·CAPITOLINAE·ET·ADIACENTIVM·PORTICVVM·SCALARVM·TRIBVNALIVM·EX·
MICHAELIS·ANGELI·BONAROTI·ARCHITECTVRA·ICHNOGRAPHIA
ROMAE·ANNO·∞·Ð·LXVII

13.7   *Plan project, after Michelangelo. Engraving
published by B. Faleti, 1567. Reproduced from copy
cropped on the right side.*

13.8   *Perspective, after Michelangelo. Engraving by E.
Dupérac, 1569.*

13.9   *Michelangelo's project for the Capitoline Hill,
reconstruction.*

CAPITOLII · SCIOGRAPHIA · EX · IPSO · EXEMPLARI · MICHAELIS · ANGELI · BONAROTI · A · STEPHANO · DVPERAC · PARISIENSI · ACCVRATE · DELINEATA
ET · IN · LVCEM · AEDITA · ROMAE · ANNO · SALVTIS · ꝂꝀDLXIX

midair. In actuality, one cannot grasp the composition from a distance; it unfolds only upon arrival at the level of the piazza, as upon entering a huge *salone*. So Michelangelo did not continue the palace façades around the buildings; they stop short at the corners as if to indicate that they belong properly to the piazza. Consequently, the Palazzo Nuovo was planned simply as a portico with offices; the present interior court is a seventeenth-century interpolation. Michelangelo built the niched wall that appears in figure 13.6 just at the rear of the offices (note the shallow roof in figure 13.8).

Another explanation for the apparent artificiality of the solution is the immemorial function of the Campidoglio as the site of solemn public ceremonies performed in the open air. The piazza was to be the chief locus of civic events, rather than the conference halls, prisons, and tribunal within the palaces. The average citizen would come to the hill only to witness some ritual that demanded an awesome and spectacular setting. Perhaps the project was visualized as a translation into permanent materials of those arches, gates, and façades of wood and canvas erected in the sixteenth century for the triumphal entries and processions of great princes. Indeed, an occasion of this kind prompted the renovation of the Capitol. When the Emperor Charles V entered Rome in 1536, the lack of a suitable access and the disreputable condition of the piazza combined with political considerations (it was only nine years after the sack of the city by his troops) to frustrate the enactment on the hill of the traditional climax to an imperial triumph. The Pope's determination to acquire the statue of Marcus Aurelius for the Campidoglio in 1537 appears to have been the initial reaction to the embarrassment of the previous year.

In order to place the equestrian statue properly when it arrived in 1538, an overall plan was needed, since it had to be purposefully related to the existing buildings. Michelangelo's plan must have been produced at that time since the oval statue pedestal, which mirrors the proposed form of the piazza, bears an inscription of 1538, and appears in a drawing made shortly after by Francisco d'Ollanda (fig. 13.10). The oval area, with its vigorous stellate pattern (fig. 13.7), is one of the most imaginative innovations of the Renaissance: set off by a ring of three steps descending to its depressed rim, it rises in a gentle domical curve to the level of the surrounding piazza at the center. The oval was almost unknown in earlier architecture: Michelangelo had proposed it in projects for the interior of the tomb of Julius II, and it appears in church and villa sketches by Baldassarre Peruzzi; but humanistic distaste for "irregular" figures discouraged its use.[8] Further, it was traditional to treat pavements—particularly in outdoor spaces—in rectilinear patterns, either in grid form (fig. 13.1) or, in the courts

13.10 *Francisco d'Ollanda, statue of Marcus Aurelius with Michelangelo's projected base, 1538–39. Library, Escorial. After Tormò.*

13.11 *Statue of Marcus Aurelius on Michelangelo's base.*

of large palaces, as bands radiating out from the center. But neither solution was adaptable to the trapezoidal boundary of the Campidoglio. The problem, so elegantly solved by the oval, was to find an organizing figure that would emphasize the center where the statue was to be set, and yet not counteract the longitudinal axis of both the piazza and the statue itself. While the circles, squares, and regular polygons that formed the vocabulary of the quattrocento could meet only the first condition, the oval combined in one form the principles of centrality and axiality; it was this dual character that later made it so popular in church design. As a pure oval, however, Michelangelo's figure would have conceded nothing to its trapezoidal frame, but it contains a further refinement: three concave recessions formed in the surrounding ring of steps suggest to the visitor entering from the cordonata the expansion of the piazza toward the rear, and at the same time introduce him to the choice of two ascents to the Senators' palace.

The offer of alternative routes imposes an unclassical ambivalence: while the visitor enters the piazza, and later the Senators' palace, on axis, his direct progress is barred first by the statue, and then by the entrances to the double-ramped stairway. He is not only forced to choose between two equally efficient routes, but is distracted by an emphatic stellate pavement that suggests movement of a different sort, along curvilinear paths toward and away from the center. He thereby becomes intensely involved in the architectural setting to a degree never demanded by earlier Renaissance planning. By forcing the observer into a personal solution of this paradox, Michelangelo endowed movement, which usually is just a way of getting from one place to another, with aesthetic overtones.

The stairway to the Senators' palace (figs. 13.8, 13.9), though also anticipated in Peruzzi's sketches, was the first of its kind to be adapted to a palace façade. Like the oval, this form solved several problems at once: it preempted a minimum of space in the piazza, it gave direct access to the great hall on the *piano nobile,* and it was the perfect setting for the reclining river gods that had previously blocked the entrance to the Conservators' palace (fig. 13.3). Its purpose was expressive as well as practical; the dynamic effect of the triangular form, which so powerfully coordinates the three façades and masks their inequality in height, had been evoked by Michelangelo in organizing the figures of the Medici chapel and in his fortification drawings; perhaps it was initially suggested by the analogy of the river gods to the reclining allegories in the chapel. The baldachin at the summit of the flights, which may have been devised as a ceremonial setting for the appearance of dignitaries, diverts the angular accents of the stairway into the mainstream of the central axis, echoing the form of the campanile above.

13.12   *Palazzo de' Conservatori, view.*

As the stairway covered most of the lower story behind and raised the entrance to the level of the *piano nobile*, the façade could not conform to the three-story Florentine tradition exemplified by the Farnese Palace. The lower story had to be treated as a basement distinct from the upper floors; its drafted facing emphasized this distinction and also expressed the rude character of the prisons behind. In effect, the palace became a two-story structure like those on either side, so that it proved possible to harmonize the composition by adapting to all three palaces the colossal order with its heavy cornice and crowning balustrade; within this syntax the central palace could be differentiated by the design of its apertures.

The open porticoes of the lateral palaces belong, like the loggia of Brunelleschi's Foundling Hospital in Florence and the Procuratie of St. Mark's Square in Venice, as much to the square as to the buildings (figs. 13.12, 13.13). They even favor the piazza by screening the entrance portals within, so as to increase the dominance of the

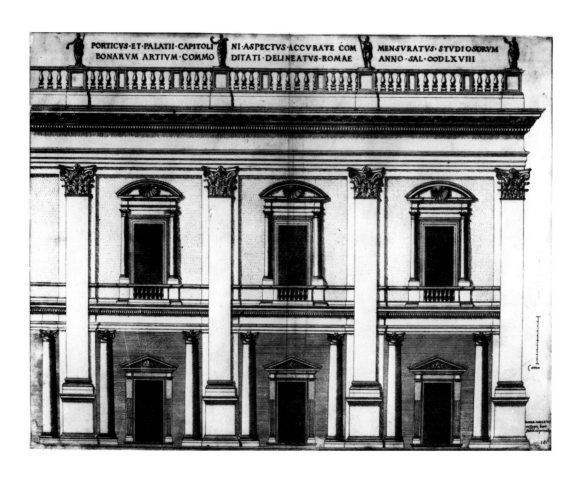

13.13   *Palazzo de' Conservatori, partial elevation.*

Engraving published by B. Faleti, 1568.

longitudinal axes over the crossaxes. They are extraordinary in structure as well as in form. Early Renaissance porticoes had been a succession of vaults supported by arches. Though Alberti insisted that antique precedent demanded that arches be sustained by piers while columns should carry only lintels, his advice was ignored before 1500; quattrocento arcades are generally columnar. Bramante reintroduced the column-and-lintel system in open loggias in the Cloister of Santa Maria della Pace and in the Vatican façade (now Cortile di San Damaso), but only in upper stories, where the interior could be spanned in wood. Peruzzi's entrance to the Massimi palace of 1535 was perhaps the first revival of the ancient technique of spanning a portico with stone beams, though on a much more modest scale than at the Campidoglio. Michelangelo's combination of column and pier provided sufficient bracing to allow expansion of the system to monumental scale. The scale actually precluded the use of arches; openings as broad as those of the Conservators' palace could not have been arched without penetrating into the preexisting second story. Furthermore, Michelangelo preferred the effects of post-and-beam construction; in 1548 he walled up Sangallo's arch over the central window of the Farnese Palace to replace it with a lintel, and on the one occasion when he used structural arches on the exterior of a building—at the Porta Pia, where they were imperative—he disguised the form. Semicircular arches have a static effect uncongenial to Michelangelo's powerful interplay of horizontal and vertical forces. Although Michelangelo used monolithic lintels or beams over the columns of the piazza façade of the Conservatori, the portico itself is spanned by flat "arches"—horizontal members composed of three separate voussoir stones doubtless joined internally by iron braces; these are made to look as much as possible like monoliths (fig. 13.14).

In the Conservators' palace, this interplay recalls the effects of a framed structure; the façade construction is as close to a skeletal frame as it is possible to attain in stone. Where the columns, pilasters, and entablatures of San Lorenzo and St. Peter's merely express stresses of load and support that actually are absorbed by the wall mass, here they really do the work that they appear to do. The cornice is supported by the pilaster-piers and the lower entablature by the columns; the façade wall is no longer a major bearer of loads; it is itself supported on beams and takes so little stress that della Porta was able to replace almost an entire section with glass (fig. 13.12). Consequently, so little wall is left that attention is drawn to the members, where it is held by the contrast of their rugged texture and light, advancing color to the smooth surface and receding color of the brick wall plane. But the stability of the portico (fig. 13.14) and façade is not wholly due to the "skeleton"; it requires stiffening by internal walls perpendicular to the principal axis—those in the rooms above, and especially by those of the lower floor (fig. 13.7), which Michelangelo ingeniously calculated to work both as buttresses and as partitions between the guild offices.

Because the Conservatori design gives the antique order a structural as well as a decorative function, it may be used profitably to illustrate the relationship of building techniques to expression in Michelangelo's architecture. The decision to unify the three palaces by a continuity of horizontal accents indicated lintel construction and emphatic cornices. In the final design it appears that Michelangelo intended to keep the potentially overwhelming horizontal accents in check by applying verticals of equal power: the colossal pilasters which, in embracing two stories, interrupt the continuity of the lower entablature and, together with the columns, window colonnettes, and balustrade figures, establish a tense equilibrium of forces. But a structural analysis reverses the process, proving that ingenious devices were necessary to prevent *verticals* from dominating the façade. The loads are concentrated in heavy masses of masonry extending from the foundations to the cornice, out of which the pilasters are carved (figs. 13.7, 13.12). To deemphasize these, Michelangelo made it appear that the pilasters alone sustain the weight. The remaining surfaces of the pier mass on either side of the pilasters he disguised as superficial decorative bands—first, by covering them with horizontal relief elements that make them seem discontinuous, and second, by applying to the wall surface above the windows horizontal bands of the same dimensions, so that the recessed pier surfaces should be read as part of an applied wall frame. So the colossal pilaster order functions as a means of diminishing rather than of emphasizing the preponderant verticality of the piers; perhaps Bramante had a similar purpose when he first used the colossal order on the piers of St. Peter's. Conversely, the horizontals had to be exaggerated to maintain an equilibrium, and again Bramante's inventions were called into service: the crowning balustrade, which appeared first in the Tempietto of 1502, augments the crown of the building to nearly six meters without substantially increasing its weight; the window balconies which Bramante had used in the House of Raphael diminish the verticality of the apertures without obstructing light.

When the vocabulary of the Conservators' palace was adapted to the Senators' façade it became purely expressive, since there were no structural problems in facing the existing medieval structure (fig. 13.6). Now the pier surfaces, which had originally masqueraded as ornament, became honestly ornamental; and it is this change in function which suggests that the design of the lateral palaces preceded that of the Senators'. Moreover, it strengthens the hypothesis that the Campidoglio façades were designed in

13.14   Palazzo de' Conservatori, interior of portico.

tentative sketches if not in their final form before the elevations of St. Peter's (1546–47); a similar motif appears there in a context that must be ornamental, since the structure depends wholly on wall masses and not on surface members.

To appreciate fully the significance of the Campidoglio design we must understand what might be called its subject matter as well as its architectural character. Like the Cortile del Belvedere, which was built to rival the great villas of antiquity, the Campidoglio was a monumental symbol in which the haunting dream of ancient grandeur became concrete. Like paintings of their time, both communicated a specific content of a more complex sort than is usually found in architecture.[9]

Sculpture played a peculiarly formative role in the evolution of the Belvedere and the Campidoglio. Distinguished collections of antiquities assembled in the fifteenth and early sixteenth centuries stimulated the urge to build; the statues had priority, and the architecture took shape around them. The Belvedere was planned as a setting for and approach to the papal museum, and the resurgence of the Capitol awaited the arrival of its equestrian centerpiece.

The ancient bronzes donated to the people of Rome by Sixtus IV and Innocent VIII in the fifteenth century were chosen more for their associations than for their beauty. They were objects of almost totemic power which the medieval mind had endowed with the responsibility for sustaining the legal and imperial symbolism of antiquity. A figure of the mother wolf which had nursed Romulus and Remus, mythical founders of Rome, was placed over the entrance of the old Conservators' palace (fig. 13.3)—and to emphasize her significance, a pair of suckling infants was added by a quattrocento sculptor. A colossal Constantinian head, and a hand from the same figure bearing a sphere, were placed in the portico (fig. 13.4); the medieval pilgrim's guidebook called the *Mirabilia urbis Romae* identified these as the remains of a colossal "Phoebus, that is, god of the Sun, whose feet stood on earth while his head touched heaven, who held a ball in his hand, meaning that Rome ruled the whole world." Both stood by the Lateran, near the *Marcus Aurelius,* throughout the Middle Ages, in a spot of which the *Mirabilia* says "There the law is final." A third figure of Hercules, whose relation to the city was less firmly established, was installed on a base pointedly inscribed "IN MONUMENTUM ROMANAE GLORIAE." Further additions were made in the sixteenth century: Leo X installed the colossal statues of two river gods before the Conservators' portico (fig. 13.3) and donated reliefs depicting the triumphal procession of Marcus Aurelius onto the hill.

Some of these pieces were integrated into Michelangelo's scheme, and others were moved indoors, but the theme *Romanae gloriae* was reinforced by new acquisitions and made explicit by inscriptions. A tablet alongside the portal of the Conservators' palace reads: "S.P.Q.R., imitating as far as possible its ancestors in spirit and deed, restored the Capitolium decayed by the ravages of time, the year 2320 after the founding of the city." But on the opposite side of the portal, a similar inscription, dated "in the year of our salvation 1568," consigns "to Jesus Christ, author of all good" the care of the people of Rome and of the Campidoglio "once dedicated to Jove." The twin tablets are a clue to hidden meanings in the design of the Campidoglio and a reminder that a Christian motivation underlies the pagan splendor.

It was Pope Paul III rather than the city fathers who insisted that the statue of Marcus Aurelius be brought to the hill against the wishes of its proper owner, the Chapter of St. John in the Lateran. Michelangelo opposed the project, but managed only to dissuade the Pope from expropriating the statues of Jupiter's twin sons, Castor and Pollux, with their rearing horses, that had stood throughout the Middle Ages on the crown of the Quirinal Hill. It is difficult to explain the choice of the *Marcus Aurelius,* not because the meaning of the transfer is unclear, but because it had so many meanings. The most important, perhaps, is that the statue, one of the finest and best preserved ancient bronzes known to the Middle Ages, had grown, rather like the *Wolf,* into a symbol of law and government, so that executions and punishments regularly took place before it. Consequently, once it was in place, two hallowed legal symbols were removed from the piazza: the *Wolf,* and the group with an attacking lion on the steps of the Senators' palace which marked the spot for the sentencing of criminals far back into the Middle Ages. In this penal role, the equestrian group was known from the earliest records in the tenth century as the *Caballus Constantini.* The convenient misnomer, which combined imperial power and Christianity, survived throughout the Renaissance.

But another legend, nearly as old, identified the rider as *il gran' villano* ("villein" in English); it was fostered for political reasons in the twelfth century, at a moment when the Holy Roman Emperor was in bad repute in Rome. It told of a low-born folk hero in republican—not imperial—days who, singlehanded, captured a besieging army and its royal general and was honored with a statue. So the figure came to symbolize a mixture of republican, antimonarchial *virtù* and romantic heroism that reminds one of the iconography of the French Revolution. The *villano* tradition may have led to the type of Early Renaissance equestrians: Simone Martini's *Guidoriccio,* Uccello's *Hawkwood,* Donatello's *Gattamelata,* Verrocchio's *Colleoni,* and others—all soldier adventurers of low birth rather than prelates or princes.

The inscription designed for the statue by Michelangelo identifies the rider as Antoninus Pius (fig. 13.10); though the correct identification had been made in the fifteenth century, it still was not accepted generally. But in any case, both Antoninus and his adopted son and successor Marcus Aurelius were represented by Renaissance humanists as the ideal emperor—the *exemplum virtutis:* peacemaker, dispenser of justice, and maecenas. Paul III must have stolen the statue both to capitalize on the public pride in the Roman heritage and its medieval glosses and to suggest that his rule of the Roman people and of the Papal States reflected the virtues of a heroic antecedent. This would explain why there was no thought of commissioning a new statue from Michelangelo or another contemporary sculptor, and why *Marcus Aurelius* was not merely set into the piazza but inspired its very shape.

In Michelangelo's design (figs. 13.7, 13.8) the two river gods were given a more imposing setting before the triangular stairway, the form of which must have been influenced by their characteristic attitude of fluvial repose. Yet, if the decision to use the pair was made for formal reasons, it was essential to give it an iconic rationale. One was the Nile, supported by a sphinx; the other was the Tigris, identified by his crouching tiger; but before being reinstalled by the steps, he became the Tiber, Rome's own river, by the ingenious expedient of replacing his Mesopotamian prop with a new wolf suckling the two founding fathers. According to Pirro Ligorio, the exchange was made "through the ignorance of a poor councillor," meaning Michelangelo, one supposes. Its purpose, however, was not to please such testy antiquarians as Ligorio, but to suggest the scope of Roman culture by linking great rivers at home and abroad.

If Rome is symbolized as the Tiber, it is incongruous that the figure in the central niche should be *Roma,* an ancient *Minerva* supplied with urban attributes. Her presence is, in fact, a makeshift solution; Michelangelo's plan was to place a *Jupiter* in the niche. The statue would have called to mind the temple of Jupiter Optimus Maximus which had stood on the Capitoline in antiquity, and which appears in the background of the triumphal relief displayed in the Conservators' palace. Had the god been in the center of a triangle flanked by the two rivers, the composition might have suggested the temple pediment, with the titular deity in the dominant position.

Attention is also attracted to this area of the piazza by a baldachin or canopy over *Jupiter's* head at the top of the stairs, a curious appendage to a Renaissance façade. In late antiquity and in the Middle Ages it was one of the most universally used symbols of imperial power. But it could be Christian, too: in the sixteenth century one would have seen such a baldachin only over the main altar of a large church.

A visitor's first impression on ascending the hill is of the statuary along the forward edge. In the earlier engraving of Michelangelo's project (cf. fig. 13.9) four male figures adorn the balcony: they are all imperial state portraits, and the two in the center, who carry spheres, are Constantinian figures found for Paul III in about 1540. The second version (fig. 13.8) replaces two emperors by a pair of horse trainers. They appear to be the Quirinal *Castor and Pollux* sought by the pope thirty years before; but in this respect the engraving is inexact. A second, more relaxed version of the twins, found near the Capitol in 1560, was ready for mounting (fig. 13.2). So the pope's wish came true posthumously without despoiling the Quirinal of its traditional monuments. We may ask why Paul had so coveted the Dioscures. Contrary to my interpretation in earlier editions, it has been shown that the twins had not been identified as Dioscures in the mid-sixteenth century, but were believed to be paired portraits of Alexander the Great carved in competition by Phidias and Praxiteles. Paul III, Alexander Farnese, used references to his great namesake frequently in the ubiquitous self-glorifying artistic programs of his pontificate.[10] Opposition to his effort to put his personal stamp on the hallowed hill was sufficiently strong to preserve the two groups in their original site to be incorporated by Michelangelo into an urban design of a later pope.

After the pope's death in 1549 the Conservators gained a greater control of the acquisition of symbolic statuary. The antiquarian-architect Pirro Ligorio identified the Dioscures set up in 1560 as coming from the ancient Curia of Pompey, and the association with that republican hero would have made the two horse tamers appealing to the representatives of the people, if not to the pope. Next to the Dioscures on the forward balcony were placed, in 1590, two still lifes on a military theme, of imperial origin, taken from an aqueduct near the city walls. They were acquired—again no doubt at the instigation of the Conservators—because they were believed to be trophies of the victories of the republican, antipatrician leader Marius, which ancient sources located on the Capitoline. The original Capitoline, moreover, had been the goal of all great triumphal processions. The tradition was revived in 1571, when Marcantonio Colonna, the victor over the Turks at Lepanto, was given a glorious triumph in the antique mode which ended in ceremonies on the piazza.[11]

The outermost decorations of the balcony crowd together as many symbolic overtones as is possible in so little space. They are columns, symbolic of power, carrying spheres, symbolic of Rome's worldwide rule. To clarify the point, the columns are mileposts from the Via Appia. The theme so abundantly illustrated on the piazza was continued in the palace courts, and in the halls of the Conservators' palace, frescoed with scenes from republican Roman history.

13.15   *Anonymous fresco*, Pagan Worship on the
Capitoline Hill. *Rome, Palazzo Massimo alle Colonne.*

To support the foregoing analysis, which may appear to discover more allusion than the cinquecento intended, we may call on a contemporary witness whose interpretation took the form of a frescoed vignette in the salone of a Roman palace (fig. 13.15).[12] The painter of about 1550–60 depicted the oval piazza with Marcus Aurelius in the center, the cordonata and the rear stairway as Michelangelo had planned them. But in place of the Senators' palace are three huge chapels of pagan divinities, the central one in baldachin form. There the herm of Jupiter is the object of unreserved adoration on the part of two Romans not yet imbued with the spirit of the Counter-Reformation. Yet it is inconceivable that Christian imagery was absent from the iconographic program. Our knowledge of Michelangelo's deep religious convictions following the period of his association with Vittoria Colonna tempts us to see the central Jupiter figure as an anagogical reference to Christ; the presence of the baldachin overhead and the absence of any other member of the Roman pantheon admits such an interpretation.

Furthermore, the arrangement of the piazza unites the ancient Rome of the forum and the New Rome of the church, a connection suggested in the inscriptions quoted above as well as in the engravings which pointedly show the ruins behind the Senators' palace (fig. 13.8), although they are not actually visible from any standpoint in or before the piazza (fig. 13.2).[13]

We come finally to the most intriguing and original feature of Michelangelo's design, the central oval which supports *Marcus Aurelius* at the apex of a gentle domical mound. Tolnay has persuasively suggested that the design may be connected with the medieval designation of the Campidoglio as the *umbilicus* or *Caput Mundi;*[14] but his belief that the convex form is intended to represent the curve of the terrestrial globe is not similarly supported by tradition or texts. The curvilinear grid dividing the pavement into twelve compartments recalls a symbolism commonly used in antiquity on the interior of cupolas, where the twelve signs of the zodiac were used to suggest the dome of Heaven or the music of the spheres;[15] in Christian architecture the twelve Apostles surrounding a central figure of Christ sometimes took the place of the signs. The twelve-part division appeared almost as often in circular pavements as a kind of counter-dome. Vitruvius (V, 6) advised that the circular pavement of theater orchestras be inscribed with four interlocking triangles forming a twelve-pointed star, since "in the number twelve the astronomy of the celestial signs is calculated from the musical concord of the stars." These parallel traditions were fused in Cesariano's Vitruvius edition of 1521, where an entire theater is reconstructed as a round, domed "Tholos" inscribed within a twelve-pointed star.[16]

While the duodecimal division in these examples is usually formed by radiating lines or by triangles, Michelangelo's complex curvilinear construction is found among a class of medieval *schemata* in circular form used to coordinate the lunar cycle with other astronomical inferences of the number twelve, such as the hours and the zodiac. Figure 13.16 is only one of many, from a tenth-century (?) manuscript of *De natura rerum* of St. Isidor of Seville, in which the lunations and signs appear in a form that differs from Michelangelo's chiefly in not being oval. The manuscript *schemata* of Isidor were reproduced in early printed books, establishing a contact with the sixteenth century.[17]

The fact that the prototypes were round, rather than oval, may be explained as an aesthetic prejudice: the circle was preferred in architecture prior to the sixteenth century—and in astronomy, until Kepler's time; Michelangelo introduced the oval in a project of the early years of the century, and the first oval dome was built by Vignola shortly after the foundation of the Campidoglio.[18]

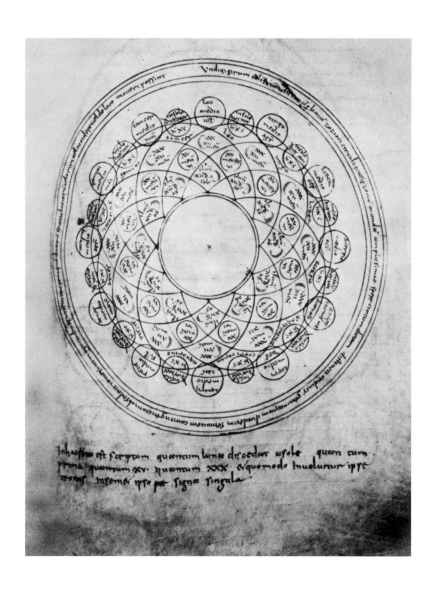

13.16 *Cosmological schema. From a tenth-century (?)*
manuscript.

The cosmological pavements and schemata do not explain the moundlike rise of Michelangelo's oval; its convexity adds a new dimension to the tradition in meaning as well as in form. The exception to the ancients' distaste for the oval may be found in a type of military shield that was well known to Michelangelo since it not only was represented in the vault stuccoes of the Conservators' portico and on the *"Trofei di Mario,"* but had been adopted by the commune as the coat of arms of the S.P.Q.R.— it appears in wooden ceilings of the Conservators' palace dated 1516–18 and 1544.[19] As was customary with the ornamental arms of the sixteenth century, these ovals are convex in shape. While ornamental shields cannot be associated with the twelve-part division of Michelangelo's pavement, there was a type of ancient shield upon which the zodiac was represented. The legendary shield of Achilles was adorned with the celestial signs, and Alexander the Great adopted the Achillean type along with the epithet Kosmokrator—ruler of the universe.[20] The title, and the shield along with it, was transferred to Roman Emperors. Another attribute of certain Kosmokrator portraits is a corona simulating the rays of the sun, indicating the resplendent powers of Apollo; and armored imperial portraits where the corona is not used have images of Apollo on the breastplate.

Usually the snake Python appears at the center of these shields, as it does in non-military representations of the zodiac. The myth of Python is associated with the shrine of Apollo at Delphi, where the snake reportedly dwelt under a moundlike stone known as the *omphalos* or *umbilicus,* which marked the center of the cosmos.[21] (So the central boss on military shields came to be called the *umbilicus.*) The *omphalos* stone became an attribute of Apollo, who appears seated upon it in Greek vases and Roman coins.

The ancient Romans moved the *umbilicus mundi* figuratively from Delphi to the Forum, where it remained until medieval legend shifted it once more to the Campidoglio.[22] Here it was permanently fixed in Michelangelo's pavement, which combined its zodiacal inferences with its moundlike form. *Marcus Aurelius,* mounted at the center, might have been a foreign element if iconic tradition had not permitted his association with the *umbilicus.* As Kosmokrator, he succeeded to Apollo's position upon the mound, and since the ancient sculptor had not equipped him with the requisite attributes, Michelangelo placed around his base the corona of Apollo: the twelve pointed rays which also serve as the starting points of the zodiacal pattern.

Notes

1. A. Graf, *Roma nella memoria e nelle immaginazioni del medio evo*, 2d ed. (Turin, 1923); P. Schramm, *Kaiser, Rom u. Renovatio* (Leipzig, 1925); F. Schneider, *Rom und Romgedanke im Mittelalter* (Munich, 1926).

2. On Italian Renaissance urbanism, see G. Giovannoni, *Saggi sull'architettura del Rinascimento* (Milan, 1935), 265–304; W. Lotz, "Italienische Plätze des 16 Jahrhunderts," *Jhb. der Max-Planck Gesellschaft* (1968), 41–58; L. Benevolo, *Storia dell'architettura nel Rinascimento* (Bari, 1968); G. Simoncini, *Città e società nel Rinascimento* (Turin, 1974); E. Guidoni and Angela Marino, *Storia dell'urbanistica: il Cinquecento* (Bari, 1982); on medieval planning, see W. Braunfels, *Mittelalterliche Stadtbaukunst in der Toskana* (Berlin, 1953).

3. L. H. Heydenreich, "Pius II als Bauherr von Pienza," *Zeitschrift für Kunstgeschichte*, 6 (1937), 105–146; E. Carli, *Pienza, la città di Pio II* (Rome, 1967); Giancarlo Cataldi, "Pienza e la sua piazza: nuova ipotesi tipologica di lettura," *Studi e documenti di architettura*, 7 (1978), 75–115.

4. See E. Lowinsky, "The Concept of Musical Space in the Renaissance," *Papers of the American Musicological Society Annual Meeting*, 1941 (Richmond, 1946), 57ff.

5. See J. Ackerman, *The Cortile del Belvedere* (Vatican City, 1954), 121ff.; and the broader treatment of planning concepts by B. Lowry, "High Renaissance Architecture," *College Art Journal*, 17 (1958), 115ff.

6. Document published by F. Gregorovius in *R. Accad. dei Lincei. cl. di scienze morali . . . , Atti*, 3 (1876–77), 314ff. Michelangelo's designs for the Campidoglio have been thoroughly studied in G. De Angelis d'Ossat and C. Pietrangeli, *Il Campidoglio di Michelangelo* (Milan, 1965), and Harman Thies, *Michelangelo: das Kapitol*, Italienische Forschungen, Kunsthistorischen Institut in Florenz, 3d ser. (Munich, 1982).

7. *Le lettere di Michelangelo Buonarroti*, ed. Gaetano Milanesi (Florence, 1875), 431. See my discussion in *The Architecture of Michelangelo*, 2d ed. (Harmondsworth and Chicago, 1986), 37ff., and that of David Summers, *Michelangelo and the Language of Art* (Princeton, 1981), 418–446.

8. For a general discussion of the oval in Renaissance architecture, see W. Lotz, "Die ovalen Kirchenräume des Cinquecento," *Rom. Jhb.*, 7 (1955), 9ff.

9. On the iconography of the Capitol, see n. 14; H. Sedlmayr, "Die Area Capitolina des Michelan-

gelo," *Jhb. d. Preuss. Kunstslg.*, 52 (1931), 176ff.; Siebenhüner, *Das Kapitol in Rom: Idee und Gestalt* (Munich, 1954), passim; W. Heckscher, *Sixtus IV . . . Aeneas Insignes Statuas Romano Populo Restituendas Censuit* (The Hague, 1955); J. Ackerman, "Marcus Aurelius on the Capitoline Hill," *Renaissance News*, 10 (1957), 69ff.; F. Saxl, "The Capitol during the Renaissance: A Symbol of the Imperial Idea," *Lectures* (London, 1957), 200ff. My analysis is improved and expanded by Tilmann Buddensieg, "Zum Statuenprogramm in Kapitolsplan Pauls III," *Zeitschrift für Kunstgeschichte*, 30 (1969), 177–228.

10. Buddensieg, "Zum Statuenprogramm," 196ff.

11. Ibid., 205f. (Dioscures), 207 (Trophies); G. Borino et al., "Il trionfo di Marc'Antonio Colonna," *Misc. della R. Dep. rom. di storia patria*, 12 (1938).

12. I know of this painting through Wolfgang Lotz, who supplied the photograph.

13. This interpretation of the siting was suggested by Richard Krautheimer.

14. "Beitrage zu den späten architektonischen Projekten Michelangelos," *Jhb. d. Preuss. Kunstslg.*, 51 (1930), 25f.; 53 (1932), 245f.

15. K. Lehmann, "The Dome of Heaven," *Art Bulletin*, 27 (1945), 1ff., with rich bibliography.

16. Cf. R. Bernheimer, "Theatrum Mundi," *Art Bulletin*, 38 (1956), 225ff.

17. Harry Bober kindly supplied the photographs and much information on medieval *schemata*.

18. See n. 8 and E. Panofsky, *Galileo as a Critic of the Arts* (The Hague, 1954), esp. 20ff.

19. C. Pietrangeli, "Lo stemma del comune di Roma," *Capitolium*, 27 (1952), 41ff., 143ff.; 28 (1953), 61.

20. O. Brendel, "Der Schild des Achilles," *Die Antike*, 12 (1936), 273ff.

21. G. Karo, "Omphalos," *Dict. des antiquités grecques et romaines*, 4, 1 (Paris, 1904); J. Fontenrose, *Python* (Berkeley, 1959), 374ff. and fig. 27, a fresco from the House of the Vetii, Pompeii, showing Python on an *omphalos* inscribed with intersecting bands forming lozenges like those of the Capitoline pavement. My attention was first drawn to the relationship of the zodiac and the *omphalos* by E. R. Goodenough, "A Jewish-Gnostic Amulet of the Roman Period," *Greek and Byzantine Studies*, 1 (1958).

22. B. Gamucci, *Le antichità della città di Roma* (Venice, 1569), fol. 10v: "Il qual colle, nell' accrescimento della città essendo restato come umbilico di quella . . ."

Postscript

Reading this study nearly thirty years after it was written I realize how differently I—and most of my colleagues—approached major architectural monuments at that time. First of all I had chosen the life works of a single architect, one who had been called "divine" during his lifetime and who has continued to be held in awe. And within that framework, I had emphasized primarily the genesis of the architectural forms both in the sense of their roots in the design of the preceding generation and in the sense of their role in the creative evolution of the architect. Finally, I attempted to interpret the iconography of the project, perhaps an inevitable decision in view of the symbolic character of the site and of its traditions. I do not repudiate these choices, but today my sympathy with tendencies throughout the field to place greater emphasis on social-political and economic factors underlying architectural enterprise would have prompted a broader interpretation. I should certainly have discussed the creative involvement of Pope Paul III, from his decision to initiate the new project with the acquisition of the statue of Marcus Aurelius to his choice of the Dioscures at the top of the *cordonata*, and I should have more clearly defined the relation of the Vatican to the city officers in fixing policy and in financing construction. I should have placed greater emphasis on the uniqueness of an urban design in which the open space, at least as much as the buildings that frame it, was re-formed by the architect.

In literature since the original publication of this chapter, the issue of the chronology of the design has been in the forefront. My position was that Michelangelo conceived the general scheme of the piazza by 1538 but that what we know of his working methods and use of architectural drawings makes it unlikely that he made clearly articulated elevations before the successive portions of the project were under way. Moreover, I cannot imagine that he would have been willing to return in 1563 to a design of a quarter century before without altering it (the drawings associable with the side palaces seem to be of the sixties).

Renato Bonelli's chapter on the Campidoglio in the publication edited by Portoghesi and Zevi (pp. 425–496) offers striking revisions to the chronology of all earlier writers. He proposes essentially that each portion of the piazza was designed as the opportunity came to build it, and that there was no unifying scheme prior to the construction of the central oval in 1561. It is basic to his argument that Francisco d'Ollanda's drawing of the equestrian statue of Marcus Aurelius (fig. 13.10), set up on an oval base by Michelangelo in 1537–38, shows that the statue was not placed in the center of the piazza but considerably to the rear and off axis, and that therefore the oval scheme could not have been considered until the '60s. In fact, Francesco displaced the statue only slightly to the rear of its ultimate position, probably because it was the only way to represent the entrance to the Conservatori Palace with its recumbent river gods. Curiously, Bonelli's thesis is torpedoed in the catalog of the same volume (pp. 886–895), written by Lionello Puppi and Franco Barbieri, who essentially share my views of the chronology.

Andrew Morrogh has called my attention to Cesare d'Onofrio's publication of an interesting fresco from the Sala delle Oche in the Conservators' Palace showing the Campidoglio early in the period of remodeling (d'Onofrio, pp. 148f.), with a group of nude dancers in the foreground. It represents the piazza from the same point as in figure 13.5, at the entrance to the Conservators' Palace, but in place of the rough retaining wall with a central niche against the Aracoeli there is a simple open loggia—either an unexecuted scheme or a fantasy of the painter. The loggia does not appear in later views. D'Onofrio dates the fresco to mid-1537 on the grounds that the statue of Marcus Aurelius, which arrived in 1537–38, is "not yet" in place, and an obelisk mentioned by Fichard as being on the hill in 1536 is "no longer" there. This would make it the earliest view of the Campidoglio in the time of Michelangelo. But I believe it to be later, because it represents the steps planned by Michelangelo, probably built in the mid-1540s, which lead to the future loggia at the side of the Aracoeli. In this kind of representation, which is not intended to observe topographical accuracy, important elements may be removed for reasons of pictorial exposition; in this case the depiction of the equestrian statue would have reduced the clarity of the foreground dancers.

Harman Thies covers every aspect of the history and design process of Michelangelo's Campidoglio and its relation to earlier and later urban architecture of the Renaissance with obsessive intensity and numbing length, but is technically sound in method and offers a more plausible chronology than Bonelli's. He proposes that the entire scheme, down to details of structure and design, was determined as a whole by the time the statue of Marcus Aurelius was placed in 1537–38, with possible modifications prior to the beginning of work on the stairway in front of the Senatori in 1546–47. The strongest support for this argument is that many of the features projected for the side palaces were used by Jacopo Sansovino at the Marciana Library in Venice, begun in 1537 (two-story elevation with a taller upper story, crowning balustrade with statues, cove vaulting in the portico, and, above all, the type of support at the two front corners, a block with engaged half-columns). While the similarities to the Biblioteca Marciana are striking, it would have been exceptional for Michelangelo to have made his studies for a project in process available to a colleague, though he did employ Aristotile da Sangallo as an assistant prior to 1547.

Leon Satkowski, in a study of the design of the Uffizi Palace in Florence written for a forthcoming book on Vasari's architecture, points out that the 1568 edition of Vasari's *Lives* (Milanesi ed., VII, 222) describes a different design from the one that at that time was under construction: "Seguitò dalla banda di mezzogiorno, dove è il palazzo di' Conservatori, per riquadrarlo, una ricca e varia facciata con una loggia da piè piena di colonne e nicchie, dove vanno molte statue antiche, ed attorno sono vari ornamenti e di porte e finestre, che già n'è posto una parte; e dirimpetto a queste ne ha a seguitare un'altra simile di verso tramontana sotto Araceli . . .". Satkowski suggests that the niched ground-floor loggia may have been a feature of an earlier design for the façade, recognizing how uncommon it was for Vasari to have ignored the evidence of building that he must have seen. No satisfactory explanations have been offered by other scholars, myself included, but I am embarrassed at having overlooked this passage in the catalog of my book.

The theme of Michelangelo's interest in the various strata of society within the city of Rome and its reflection in his design was taken up by Charles Burroughs in a paper read at the 1989 meeting of the Society of Architectural Historians, entitled "Michelangelo and the Trades: Toward the Elucidation of an Odd Order." Burroughs emphasizes the significance of the stalls for Roman guilds within the loggia of the Palazzo dei Conservatori, a factor that I did not sufficiently emphasize in defining the program for the designers. He suggests that there is a different, more organic spirit—most notably in the Ionic capitals—in the design of the loggia floor that reflects a theme of labor (recalling that this theme had been emphasized in sculpture on the lowest level of the Florentine Campanile) in contrast to the more canonical treatment of the upper floor, where the city councillors held their ceremonies and meetings. I am not wholly persuaded by the argument, but I believe it deserves being brought into the discussion.

Aiken, R. C. "The Capitoline Hill during the Reign of Sixtus V," Ph.D. diss., University of California, Berkeley, 1977.

Bruschi, Arnaldo. "Michelangelo in Campidoglio e l'invenzione dell'ordine gigante," *Storia architettura*, 4 (1979), 5–28.

Buddensieg, Tilmann. "Die Statuenstiftung Sixtus' IV im Jahre 1471," *Römische Jahrbuch für Kunstgeschichte*, 20 (1983), 33–73.

De Angelis d'Ossat, G., and C. Pietrangeli. *Il Campidoglio di Michelangelo* (Milan, 1965).

d'Onofrio, C. *Renovatio Roma: storia urbanistica dal Campidoglio al E.U.R.* (Rome, 1973).

Güthlein, Klaus. "Der Palazzo Nuovo des Kapitols," *Römische Jahrbuch für Kunstge-schichte,* 22 (1985), 83–190.

Liebenwein, Wolfgang. "Antikes Bildrecht in Michelangelo's Area Capitolina," *Mitt. des Kunsthist. Insts. in Florenz,* 28 (1984), 1–32.

Portoghesi, P., and B. Zevi, eds. *Michelangiolo Architetto* (Turin, 1964).

Thies, Harman. *Michelangelo: das Kapitol,* Italienische Forschungen, Kunsthistorischen Institut in Florenz, 3d ser., XI (Munich, 1982).

14

The Gesù in the Light of Contemporary Church Design

Never has there been any doubt that the Gesù in Rome represents one of the most significant and influential architectural statements of the Renaissance. In fact, it is usually represented as being literally incomparable, as if it had sprung full-grown from the head of Vignola without real precedent or explanation in its environment or background. We see it in a different light, as the first monumental Roman church of a formal and liturgical style adopted as widely in Italy as was the Counter-Reformation itself, and my purpose here is to reconstruct that context. When I say "we see it" this way, I am not being academic, but am acknowledging the fact that when I first presented this problem in a talk, I was only seeing half of its dimensions, and consequently interpreted it wrongly. I was set straight by Professor Milton Lewine of Columbia who, in conversations, in his dissertation of 1960, and in a more recent article, clarified both the Roman background and the liturgical implications.[1]

My theory had been that the sources of the new style were to be found in north Italy, and particularly in Milan.[2] I had two arguments for this. First, I claimed that Milan had not really experienced an architecture of the High Renaissance, so that when the new spirit of the Counter-Reformation encouraged the revival of medieval longitudinal churches with their hall-like naves suitable for preaching, provincial Milan found itself closer to the medieval tradition of liturgy and building than the principal center of religious life, Rome, and unencumbered by the shadow of the great masters

From *Baroque Art: The Jesuit Contribution*, edited by I. Jaffe and R. Wittkower (New York: Fordham University Press, 1974), 15–28.

of the early sixteenth century—Bramante, Michelangelo, and Raphael. Second, I claimed that the major High Renaissance churches of Rome were centrally planned, notably Bramante's St. Peter's. Humanist thinking had temporarily disrupted the tradition of the longitudinal church for reasons revealed by my great friend and teacher Rudolf Wittkower; architectural theory from Alberti to Palladio insisted on the preeminence of the round, polygonal, or Greek-cross plan.[3]

The shock, first of the Protestant Reformation, and second of the sack of Rome in 1527, brought about a revival of pietism and a wave of reform in the Roman Church that prompted a conservatism in architectural design which, in turn, resulted in a style of church building in what I should call the box style with barnlike naves, flat wooden roofs, a row of side chapels, and a chancel.[4] A number of instances appear in figures 14.1–14.10. These examples of the box style serve to show that the change in form was not accompanied by a new architectural vision. Architects of this generation, raised on the tradition of classical antiquity, were unprepared to respond creatively to the new demands, and their large churches were rather uninspired places.

This was the condition of large-scale ecclesiastical building when St. Francis Borgia arrived in Rome in 1550 to find St. Ignatius living and working in squalor and the Jesuits confined to a small chapel entirely inadequate to accommodate the crowds attracted by the import and vigor of their sermons. With his powerful connections in the Curia and Roman nobility, Borgia easily removed the obstacles that St. Ignatius had encountered from the city planners in attempting to gain permission to build a large church and cloister in the vicinity of the Piazza Venezia.[5] Within the same year, 1550, a grandiose scheme was developed for the general area of the present buildings. Fortunately, drawings of this earliest of all Jesuit projects are preserved, together with the hundreds of architectural plans of sixteenth- and seventeenth-century Jesuit buildings in the Bibliothèque Nationale in Paris (fig. 14.1).[6]

This complex fills a part of the area occupied by the existing buildings; it was not carried out, partly because it provided too little space for living quarters, and partly because wealthy landlords in the area began a fifteen-year battle with the Order to contain its expansion—a battle that ultimately moved from the courts to the streets.[7]

The architect of the Paris plan probably was the Florentine, Nanni di Baccio Bigio.[8] Nanni was the right-hand man of Antonio da Sangallo the Younger, who succeeded Raphael as architect of St. Peter's, and who at the time of his death was no longer in the advanced guard of his profession. The selection of Nanni in 1550 implies

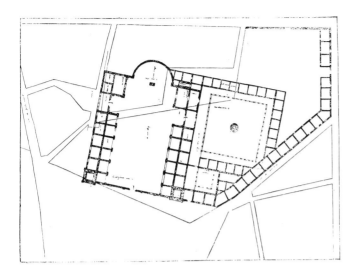

14.1   *Rome, Il Gesù, plan project attributed to Nanni
di Baccio Bigio. Paris, Bibliothèque Nationale. After
Pirri.*

the expectation of a conservative design, or at least one which might put the needs of the Order above the dictates of high style. The plan of figure 14.1 supports this interpretation.

While the conventual structures are unexceptional, the church is new in program but without any distinction or modernity architecturally. Indeed, the drawing looks like an amateur's. This is an odd combination: creativity of type is usually accompanied by creativity in design. What we see here suggests that the inventive element is not Nanni's contribution but that of Ignatius and Francis Borgia, that it was they who demanded a cross-plan with entrances in the arms of the cross, a huge open nave without a crossing, an ample apse with plenty of room for dispensing the Eucharist, and a façade flanked by towers in the manner of northern Gothic cathedrals (or should we grant Nanni the towers, under the influence of the Sangallo St. Peter model?). This church could not be vaulted; it required a wooden roof, and we know from later correspondence that Borgia argued vigorously for the wood cover on the grounds that it provided better acoustics for the sermons, since masonry vaulting produced echoes.[9]

This plan or one like it must have been the one for which a cornerstone was laid in 1550. At the time of its acceptance, the architect Giacomo Barozzi da Vignola, designer of the actual church, was on hand, perhaps as an expert judge;[10] this may indirectly illuminate something of the politics of the situation, as Vignola had become, on Sangallo's death, the favored architect of the Farnese family, and was helping Michelangelo to finish the family palace in Rome (it was the Farnese pope, Paul III, who chose Michelangelo for St. Peter's).

After the death of St. Ignatius, there emerges a picture of two camps: a Borgia camp committed to the Sangallesque architectural tradition, and a Farnese camp, under Alessandro Cardinal Farnese, supporting Vignola. Borgia must have felt, like many practical men of affairs today, that the important thing was to have a workable plant, and that a minor architect was more apt to listen to reason than a great personality in the arts. The Farnese, like the princes they were, wanted an elegant, avant-garde building by a famous architect—one that would have a Farnese "look." And they ultimately won, because it was they who had the money, and they gave lavishly. Before this happened, however, there was a moment of complete agreement when it appeared that Michelangelo might agree to design the buildings. This was in 1554, and letters of St. Ignatius and Polanco echo the elation of the Order over having secured the services of the greatest artist of the age. It was Cardinal della Cueva who approached the great Florentine, now 79 years of age, who with St. Ignatius was present at the second foundation ceremony on October 6, 1554.[11] The report says that the architect descended into the foundations to lay the stone; it does not say which architect; my guess is that it was not Michelangelo, who was too old, and too vain, to leap into muddy pits. I wonder if Michelangelo even made the design. One drawing has been published several times as his Gesù project (fig. 14.2).[12] It is identified by a later hand as being for the Gesù, and it has upon it a number of boldly stroked suggestions done in Michelangelo's favored material, red chalk, and with his characteristic bravura. But the architecture is absolutely antithetical to his; it is in the Sangallo tradition, and the ensemble actually is very like the original Nanni scheme: wood-roofed without a crossing, large apse, and short transept arms. This is clearly an alternative design by Nanni or someone close to him, and the chalk jottings, if they are Michelangelo's, are so drastically different in architectural intent that they suggest a master architect correcting the work of an amateur. This is all we hear of Michelangelo and Nanni, and fourteen years pass before the definitive design is accepted (fig. 14.3). What distinguishes the Uffizi design (fig. 14.2)

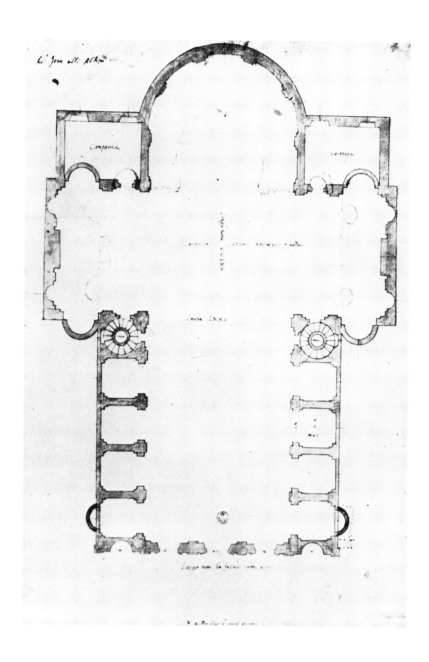

14.2   Plan project by Bartolomeo Rocchi with
corrections in red chalk by Michelangelo. Florence,
Uffizi.

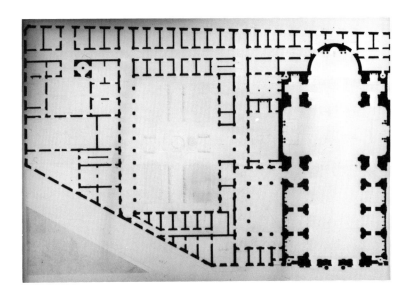

14.3   Site plan. After Pirri.

14.4   Rome, San Giovanni Decollato, plan. After Lewine.

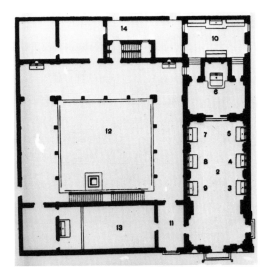

is its broad nave entered by three portals, and its large and simple apse; otherwise it has a poverty of scale and that failure to coordinate parts which characterizes the box style. It is not from this source that Vignola derived his inspiration.

It was for this reason that I was inclined to look outside Rome to find the genesis of the mature Counter-Reformation style, but I learned from Lewine that I was too hasty. He found that some of the most seminal thinking about church design was not going into big parish and conventual churches but, as might be expected, into the small chapels and oratories designed for organizations that were the center of advanced thought and action in the years before and during the Council of Trent. The church of San Giovanni Decollato is one of his major examples (fig. 14.4).[13] Its significance lies in the fact that the plan is conceived as a sequence of clearly distinguished spaces, each with a distinct function. First, one enters a vestibule marked off from the nave by heavy piers. Then there is a nave with three altar recesses to a side, which again is definitively isolated from the choir or vestigial transept by wall responds, a railing, and a rise of two steps. The chancel is separated again from the altar chapel, which is raised one more step, and finally there is a sacristy behind. This church was started in 1535, the year in which the oratory itself (marked 13 on the plan) was finished. Obviously the plan was inspired by the simple form of the oratory, but it shows an effort to separate four functions without loss of continuity. The significance of this is apparent when we compare the church to Alessi's San Barnaba in Milan, a church of 1558 to which we shall return later.

Even churches of the box style which did not provide a separation of functions with such clarity began to exhibit features influenced by this kind of thinking. In Antonio da Sangallo's church of Santo Spirito in Sassia in the Vatican Borgo (fig. 14.5), of the late 1530s, and in many other Roman churches of the period cited by Lewine, an entrance is provided in the center chapel of the nave, which has the effect of deemphasizing the longitudinal axis by creating a cross axis, and this by implication establishes the nave as an autonomous space.

It was clear to both Lewine and me that these changes were not motivated by a new aesthetic of architecture, but by a new concept of the role of the church. The reaction of Rome to the Protestant Reformation and the sack of the city was to initiate a radical reform of the liturgy, the clergy, and the monastic orders. This reform anticipated by several decades the pronouncements of the Council of Trent—it began to take vigorous effect in the 1530s—and it can now be seen that art historians have overesti-

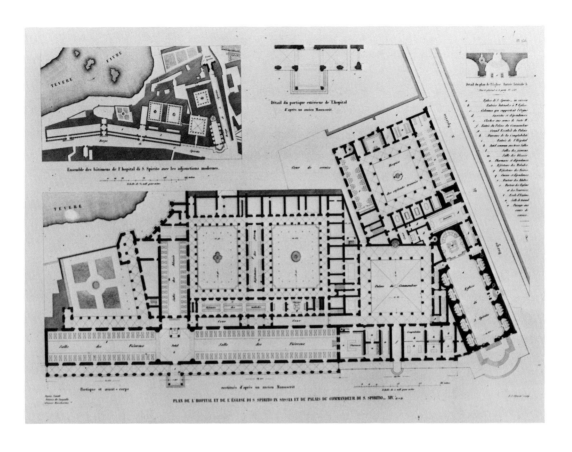

14.5   *Vatican, Hospital and Church of Santo Spirito,*
plan. After Letarouilly.

mated the Council as the influential force in the Counter-Reformation. Its principal effect was to codify practices and principles that already had been accepted a generation earlier.

Many aspects of the reform demanded radical changes in church design. The need for frequent Masses and dispensing of the Sacrament made obsolete the kind of church that, prior to 1530, had served the majority of the congregation only once or twice a year. Now, many altars were required so that Mass could be said at more than one place at once, and a main altar where the Eucharist could be devoutly enshrined in a distinct area of special holiness. The nave had to be freed from encumbrances such as tombs and screens. Because year-round preaching was seen as the most effective instrument of public reform, and because the previously empty churches began to be filled with crowds of worshipers, the nave also had to become an assembly hall. The logical place for the pulpit was at the end of the nave, and thus the hall acquired a natural terminus that tended to distinguish it from the chancel and crossing.

The preaching function affected not only the form of the nave, but its structure as well, since it stimulated a search for effective acoustical design. At first, the experts claimed that a flat and coffered wooden ceiling provided the best distribution of sound—this was the advice given by Francesco Giorgi to the builders of San Francesco della Vigna in Venice in 1535:

I recommend that all the chapels and the choir be vaulted because the word or song of the minister echoes better from the vault than it would from rafters. But in the nave of the church, where there will be sermons, I recommend a ceiling (so that the voice of the preacher may not escape, nor re-echo from the vaults). I should like to have it coffered with as many squares as possible with their appropriate measurement and proportions, which squares should be treated in a workmanlike manner with gray paint.[14]

As I have already mentioned, Giorgi's conservative solution was urged for the Gesù by Francis Borgia.

Giorgi's suggestion that the coffering be a uniform gray fits the requirement of the new pietism that the church as well as the clergy be pure and devoid of mundane references or distractions; an asceticism of decoration, particularly in the nave hall, was a significant feature of the new architecture.

The spirit of the Roman reform movement was exported to northern Italy as early as 1524, when Gian Matteo Giberti was named Bishop of Verona.[15] Giberti's stewardship of this diocese reached into every aspect of ecclesiastical practice; he set out to reform the clergy and the liturgy and to attract and discipline the lay public; his efforts extended even to certain aspects of church design. The principles of his episcopal visits were codified in his *Costituzioni,* published in 1542, a work that strongly influenced the conciliar deliberations. St. Charles Borromeo regarded him as a saint, and when St. Charles arrived in Milan in 1565, he modeled his own pastoral visits and rules on the *Costituzioni.* The design and decoration of churches was the subject of Borromeo's third Provincial Council in 1573, and the regulations decided on at that time were the source of Borromeo's famous book of 1577, the *Instructionum fabricae et supellectilis ecclesiasticae libri duo.*[16] This book and its author have long been identified as a major stimulus to the creation of a Counter-Reformation ecclesiastical style; but a close examination of the north Italian churches themselves proves that he was not the creator of a new style but the spokesman and codifier of a style already fully matured during the third quarter of the century.

My earlier reference to the elimination of decoration from the church interior prompts me to start our north Italian probe close to Giberti's Verona, with the interiors of Palladio's two great churches in Venice, San Giorgio Maggiore of 1568 (fig. 14.6) and the Redentore of 1577 (fig. 14.7), where absolute whiteness prevails.[17] Moreover, at San Giorgio, designed three years before the Gesù, the other new tendencies have matured into a design advanced beyond the box churches of the first half of the century. Here the several functions of the church are distinctly separated. There is a distinct nave, with three shallow altar chapels to a side, and a transept with semicircular terminations marked at the crossing by a notably elevated cupola. A chancel or altar area is elevated three steps above the nave and is structurally self-contained; behind, a columnar screen separates it from the claustral choir designed to keep the monks isolated from the lay public, as they had been earlier in Giorgi's San Francesco della Vigna in Venice. There is an awkwardness in this first attempt to piece together self-sufficient parts which Palladio overcomes in his second experiment in the basilical genre. At the Redentore, the elements are better integrated without compromising the concepts of the separation of functions, but since the later date of that church and its unique votive function remove it from our present concerns, I note only that the nave is literally separate, and that the chapels, raised from the nave floor, are distinct spaces linked by internal passages.

We have already seen that Palladio was not the first north Italian architect to seek new solutions to the new demand. The Perugian Galeazzo Alessi had left home at the age of 24 in 1536 to spend six years in Rome as a member of the household of two

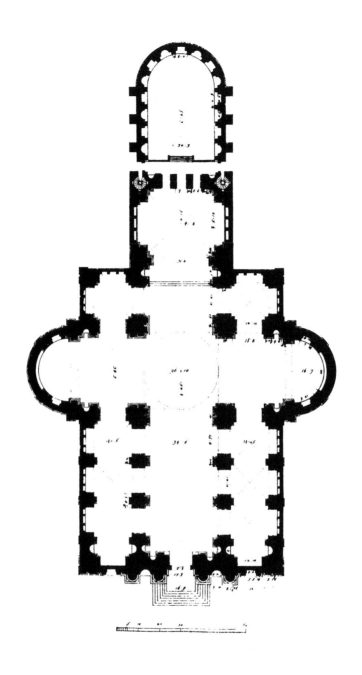

14.6   Venice, San Giorgio, plan. After Bertotti
Scamozzi.

14.7   Venice, Il Redentore, nave interior.

cardinals. We know nothing of any architectural training there, but an apprenticeship must be assumed from the fact that he was called for important commissions in 1548 to Genoa and that from the start his work was of a stature to place him alongside his great contemporaries Palladio and Vignola. By 1555 he had begun to spend part of each year in Milan, and was commissioned to design the Palazzo Marino.[18] In 1560 he appears in the documents of the rebuilding of two churches that are central to our present interest: San Barnaba and San Vittore al Corpo.

San Barnaba (fig. 14.8) was designed probably in 1558,[19] the year in which the Barnabites appealed to the city for permission to expand their church slightly into the public right-of-way, since the street on one side and the monastery on the other left a constricted space which explains the peculiarity of the plan. Alessi was forced to invent a dwarfed transept covered by a curious transverse barrel vault with a central lantern. The design is based on the separation of the functions of nave, chancel, and choir, each with a distinct covering in masonry, not coffering. The chancel is raised three steps above the nave and the altar rail is placed on the top step, and the lateral chapels are also raised, as in Palladio's Redentore, which also is anticipated in the narrow passages connecting the chapels. Paul Frankl explained these passages as an aspect of the new aesthetic of the period,[20] in which there was a tendency to create connections among isolated units, but I believe that the motivation is again liturgical, to permit the celebrant to reach his altar without mixing with the laity. These passages are also a feature of the final Gesù design. Finally, the interior is illuminated by windows borrowed from Roman baths, which were adopted by both Palladio and Vignola at mid-century.

Though many individual features of San Barnaba anticipate Palladio, the total configuration of San Vittore al Corpo (fig. 14.9) more effectively conveys the relationship.[21] The remodeling of the medieval basilica of San Vittore had been in the hands of the local architect Vincenzo Seregni, who built the conventual structures between 1553 and 1559. His numerous projects for the church of 1559–60 were rejected in favor of Alessi's for reasons that are apparent when we compare one of them with the final Alessi design. Seregni's is retrospective. His attempt to add a nave onto a domed central-plan structure is an effort to solve a problem which Leonardo and Bramante had posed sixty years earlier, notably for the Cathedral of Pavia. Parts are added together ineffectually and without an articulated approach to function. By comparison, Alessi's design (fig. 14.9) is a simple and clear statement of a new program that achieves everything I have ascribed to Palladio: it revives the three-aisled Latin cross and estab-

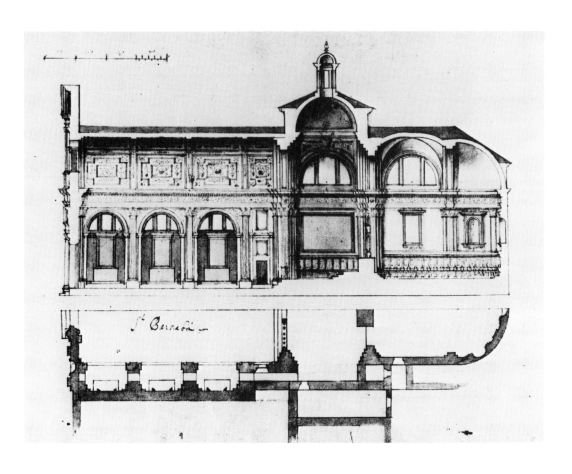

14.8 Milan, SS. Paolo and Barnaba, plan and
elevation. Milan, Raccolta Bianconi.

14.9 Milan, San Vittore al Corpo, plan. Milan,
Raccolta Bianconi.

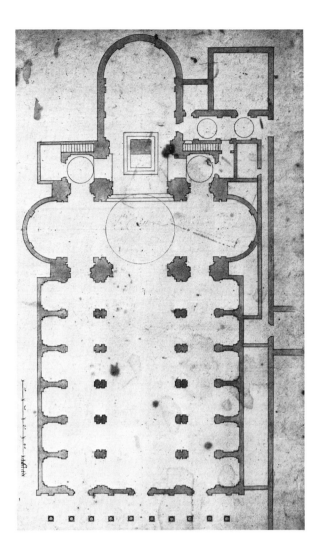

lishes a four-part division of nave, transept, elevated chancel, and choir. The crossing is dominated by a dome on a high drum supported on four freestanding piers aided by heavy masses in the transept arms. This is the San Giorgio plan in embryo, but a peculiarly mature embryo that achieves a better integration of transept terminations and sacristies, anticipating the Redentore. Palladio, however, far outstripped his predecessor in building on the plan; his shorter nave, ample fenestration, and undecorated creamy surfaces resulted in a moving, light-bathed interior that contrasts with Alessi's cavelike and overdecorated basilica.

Alessi's plan was not entirely unprecedented. The Milanese architect Domenico Giunti, author of the extraordinary Villa Simonetta, designed the church of Sant' Angelo in 1552 (fig. 14.10),[22] in which many of the new elements are anticipated: the linked chapels of San Barnaba, the culminating dome and the distinct transept and choir of San Vittore. Only the cohesion of the whole is lacking.

Features of the new scheme appeared in Rome at the same moment as they were adopted by Palladio. The earliest evidence is in Vignola's unexecuted project of 1565 for Santa Maria in Traspontina, where the nave and transept are of the same design as San Vittore.[23] Although the church was also a monastic foundation, the architect, like his Roman contemporaries, was not interested in the specialization of other functions as the northerners were; it lacks the cloistered choir of the preceding examples. Another Alessian invention which reappears here and in other Vignola designs is the use of a domed area behind the crossing piers to help support the major dome. Alessi put it alongside the chancel, while Vignola moved it forward to the end of the aisles. This project by Vignola—which, incidentally, includes the lateral nave portal we have seen earlier in Rome—is the direct forerunner of the Gesù, to which I shall now return.

Four years after the failure of the second Gesù project of 1554, the Jesuits appointed a member of the Order, Giovanni Tristano, as architect-in-chief for all Italian projects.[24] But when Cardinal Farnese agreed in 1561 to underwrite the costs of the Roman church, Tristano was gently forced into the background by the cardinal's architect, Vignola, who measured the site in 1562. However, the combination of real estate problems and the cardinal's reluctance to start paying caused another delay. Father Tristano was not recalled from supervising in the provinces to Rome to attend to the new Gesù until 1566, and even then it was two years before the excavations began. Throughout the summer of 1568 a series of negotiations took place between Farnese and Vignola on one hand, and Father General Borgia, Polanco, and Tristano on the other.[25] These resulted in two letters of instruction from the cardinal to Borgia and to Vignola on August 26 which specify, first, that the cost is not to exceed 25,000 scudi; second, that there must be only one nave with side chapels, not a nave with side aisles; third, that the nave is to be vaulted (in answer to Borgia's plea for wood roofing, Farnese says that it is simply not true that masonry vaulting causes echoes, as may be seen in churches of much larger dimensions than this, where one hears perfectly); fourth, that the façade of the church must face west, as it does today; and finally that, these stipulations being met, Vignola is to choose whatever form he thinks best for the

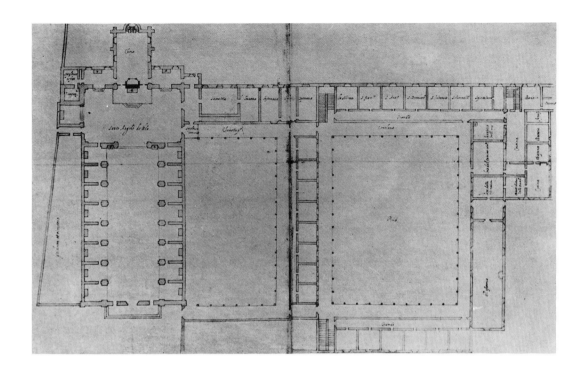

14.10 Milan, San Angelo, plan. Milan, Raccolta
Bianconi.

church.[26] The cardinal drove a hard bargain, and the only instruction that seems to be a contribution from the Order is the elimination of side aisles. This conflict arose over the orientation and appears from his letter of the same date to Borgia: ". . . the choir and high altar should stand toward San Marco, and thus I instructed the architect; and I wish you would acquiesce and not think about altering my resolution into something different." Two weeks later, Vignola and Tristano again went together to visit the cardinal in his country villa at Caprarola, and thereafter the design of the church proper must have been settled.[27] The façade was still indeterminate; Vignola was paid for a new façade model in 1569, another in 1570, for façade drawings in the same year, and finally, unable to satisfy the cardinal, he was dismissed in 1571.

The plan that presumably was presented to the cardinal does not look precisely like any of those we have seen, but the elements are familiar (fig. 14.3). From the earlier Gesù projects it preserves the three entrances into a wide nave and the ample open chancel; the nave, transept, and chancel are clearly distinguished but well coordinated with each other. The transept has flat rather than rounded ends, probably for the same reason as in Alessi's San Barnaba: a street runs along the left side, permitting only a token projection. As in San Barnaba (fig. 14.8) and the Redentore (fig. 14.6), the nave chapels are linked by passages; they are segregated from the nave not by steps but by low railings. The break between the nave and the transept is marked by a low domed area that is similar to the chapels but serves two entirely different functions: first, it is a passage to the exterior on both sides, like the nave portals we have seen before, and, second, it is part of the buttressing system for the central dome; there is a heavier mass of masonry here than over the chapels: the entrance is much smaller, and the surrounding piers thicker. The great contribution which Vignola has made to the style I have been discussing is in having found a way to create unity without sacrificing the distinctiveness of parts. He uses the domed crossing as a module; the nave is two modules long, the chancel one, and the height of the dome three. The noble cohesiveness of this conception explains why Farnese preferred Vignola to other Roman designers, and why the Gesù became the model for most subsequent basilical churches in Rome in the following generations.

This was not Vignola's first and only proposal for the Gesù. Nearly twenty years ago I visited the Siena library to look at a sketchbook of a Sienese architect of the later part of the sixteenth century, Oreste Vannocci Biringucci, and discovered in it a sequence of pages that had been copied from some lost drawings by Vignola. It was in this book that the Traspontina design appeared, and I vividly recall the excitement of turning the page to find a drawing obligingly labeled "Il Vig.ª per il Jesu" (fig. 14.11).[28] There are two drawings on the page, and they draw our attention from the plan to the façade. The lower one, which is the one specifically labeled "Jesu," originally struck me as a fascinating novelty in façade design, but Maria Casotti, in a monograph on Vignola, discovered that this is not really a whole façade but merely the *upper story* of the final Vignola project which was published in a well-known engraving (fig. 14.14).[29] The upper sketch is much more interesting, as one can deduce from close inspection, because it is for an *oval* church, domed, with a chapel on axis; you can see the flying buttresses all round. Similar oval churches, conceivably planned for the Gesù, appear on another folio of the Vannocci sketchbook. One of these plans has a portico on the façade, a feature which we have seen in Alessi's San Vittore. At first I discounted the connection of the oval projects with the Gesù, arguing that Vannocci's inscription could apply only to the lower of the two sketches, but then Wolfgang Lotz, with whom I published the drawings, pointed out that the façade is almost the same as the one appearing on the foundation medal (fig. 14.12) of 1568.[30] Furthermore, the two-tower elevation is reminiscent of the Ignatian plan of 1550 (fig. 14.1). This project, then, must be close to the medal of June 1568, but it certainly was done before the instructions were received from the cardinal in August, in which a nave and side chapels are discussed. It probably is the earliest in a series, and it is intriguing because it has nothing in common with the cruciform churches except the façade. I refer to a series, because the foundation medal shows a façade that does not fit the final plan; its two side portals do not lead into the nave, but into the file of side chapels, which must have been designed quite differently if they were to accommodate circulation.

The façades of the drawing and of the medal, with their colossal order below and low attic above, together forming a rectangle crowned by a pediment, are not in the Roman tradition, but revive Michelangelo's unsuccessful project for San Lorenzo in Florence. Roman churches usually had an upper story restricted to the width of the nave and connected to the lower story by the volutes. But the north Italian Serlian or Palladian window in Vignola's medal suggests that a more direct source was a church we have already seen: Alessi's San Barnaba in Milan (fig. 14.13). Alessi's connection with the Gesù is not merely circumstantial; in January 1570, a year before Vignola's façade was rejected, Alessi was invited to submit a façade project.[31] The fact that he was asked to do so without being required to visit Rome is evidence of his exalted reputation as a church designer.

il Vig.° il Gesu

14.11   *Oreste Vannocci Biringucci, two projects after*
Vignola. Siena, Biblioteca Comunale.

14.12   *Rome, Il Gesù, foundation medal of 1568.*

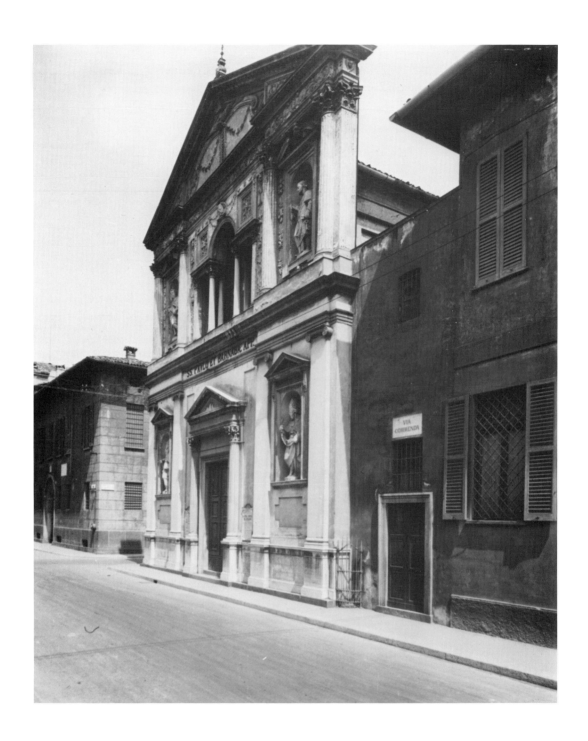

14.13   Milan, SS. Paolo and Barnaba, façade.

Vignola's final façade plan of 1570 was engraved by Cartaro in 1573 (fig. 14.14). Appropriately, the inscription celebrates the imperious cardinal and not the Jesuits. This façade abandons the planar simplicity of the medal project for an intricate, even ambiguous interplay of forms that lacks the cohesion of the inspired plan. It is this, no doubt, that explains the decision of the cardinal to reject Vignola's façade model in favor of one by a young pupil of Michelangelo, Giacomo della Porta (fig. 14.15). The Farnese were not sentimental; they had fired Sangallo in order to get Michelangelo to design the cornice of their palace, and now again they were listening for the *dernier cri*. In both cases they guessed correctly; the shift to della Porta constituted a commitment to the style that became the germ of the Baroque. Vignola was paid 40 scudi compensation and disappeared until his death in 1573.[32] Della Porta also replaced him at the Farnese palace, but perhaps after his death.[33]

Comparing the two façades in these engravings, we clearly see that della Porta's is brilliantly knit together in a fashion which focuses attention at the center in a dramatic way. While Vignola's suggests a rectangular center with subsidiary wings, della Porta's creates a crescendo, accentuating the main portal by the invention of a pediment within a pediment, and, by drawing all the niches into the central area, leaving the outer wings bare. His volutes, moreover, softly link the two stories and emphasize their oneness. Of course, della Porta leans on Vignola's ideas in many respects, but simplifies and enriches them in the spirit of Michelangelo.

In subsequent generations, della Porta's solution was tenacious; it impressed itself on church façades throughout the world.[34] Della Porta's façade was finished in 1575, as we can read after the Farnese name on the entablature. In 1577, in accordance with a traditional mason's custom, a grand feast was held on the top of the main vault for the workmen, to celebrate the completion of the nave.[35]

The year in which the façade was finished was the year of Giovanni Tristano's death, which reminds us that he had been on the job as supervisor and co-architect all along. Presumably, he might have made important contributions to the design, in which case his relative obscurity would be unjust treatment, so it is worth examining one of the innumerable independent architectural projects that he designed and built in the period 1556–75. The largest and finest of these is the church of the Gesù in Tristano's home town, Ferrara, designed in 1570.[36] The façade is the work of a distinct and inventive personality, but it is as somber as penitence itself. The interior is richer and more inventive, but it is disjointed, lacking in cohesive forces, and this can be seen as well in the awkward plan, which is no more mature than those of the '30s and '40s. This is

14.14 *Vignola, façade project of 1570, engraved by Mario Cartaro, 1573.*

14.15 *Giacomo della Porta, façade project with nave alteration.*

FACIES EXTERNA CVM PROSPECTV INTERIORIS TEMPLI AB ALEXANDRO
CARDINALI FARNESIO SOCIESV AEDIFICATI

PARS EXTERIOR *Iacobo de la Porta Architecto* PARS INTERIOR *Iacobo Barozo à Vinola Architecto*

Scala palmorum

20

quite characteristic of Tristano's work, and it surely suggests that he cannot have played a significant part in the design either of the façade or of the interior of the Roman church. The examples we have seen also show that it would be impossible to distinguish a Jesuit style; if anything, the examples reflect Tristano's Ferrarese roots. Just how impossible it would be to distinguish a Jesuit style is perhaps best illustrated by reference to a sheet of plan studies drawn in the '80s by Tristano's successor as chief architect of the Order, Father Giovanni de Rosis.[37] They seem to have almost nothing in common except an unimpeded central space. Even side aisles are now allowed. Vignola's oval was not forgotten; it appears there, again with a vestibule. These plans may have been circulated in the provinces as models to be followed by affiliates without architects of their own. And the variety is characteristic of the great collection of plans in Paris. The freedom of choice was intentional, since, beginning in 1565 on the election of Borgia, it became obligatory for every affiliate to submit for review in Rome any building proposal no matter how small.[38] Since strict control would have been possible within this system, the absence of it must have been purposeful; in Flanders, for example, new churches actually were built in the Gothic style.

It is odd, then, to discover that the architect and painter Giuseppe Valeriani, co-author of the Jesuit College in Rome, composed a treatise on the Jesuit style—"nostra consuetudine," the source says. Another document speaks of the "modo che usa la compania." But this must have been meant only in the most general sense—in short, the characteristic Jesuit church should be on a square accessible to the populace, and yet within the members' living compound; it should dispense with side aisles; where possible, it should have tribunes for private attendance at services on the part of the Fathers within the cloister: screened passages called by the Italians *coretti,* such as those in the Roman church, the first of their kind.[39]

Having returned thus to Rome with the conclusion that the Jesuit style exists, but in so general a sense that it does not affect the significant forms of the architecture, let us conclude with a tour through the mother church, which remained the most imposing of all Renaissance buildings of the Order (fig. 14.16).

In the engraving after della Porta's project, the interior appears in its original state: austere, even dour, with its great barrel vault crowning the cool classicism of Vignola's design. When we enter the Gesù today we get a quite different experience; Vignola's calm voice is lost in the brilliance of exuberant High Baroque stucco, sculpture, veneer, and painting; it is as if a Palestrina motet had to compete for attention

14.16   Rome, Il Gesù, façade.

14.17   Interior.

with Vivaldi's *Gloria* (fig. 14.17). The conflict emerged by degrees; at first the Baroque spirit was applied on festive occasions, such as the splendid celebration of the first centenary of the Order in 1639, portrayed in a painting by Andrea Sacchi and assistants. Here decorations in the form of hangings are simply draped on and over Vignola's orders. The next stage—in which Giovanni Battista Gaulli, called Baciccio, a pupil of the great Bernini, was commissioned to decorate the nave and dome, together with sculptors and stuccoists under Antonio Raggi—came in 1672–85, and permanently altered the aspect of the interior.[40] In the longitudinal section, engraved while Gaulli was still at work, the dome and apse decorations are still incomplete, but we can see how Vignola's intentions were altered. The spirited mobility of Gaulli's motives is characterized by the detail nearest the observer in the nave, acanthus clusters that leap up the socle of the vault like flames. The formerly sober window frames have been remodeled in the image of altarpieces, as if we should witness actual rather than painted miracles by looking through them into heaven. The fresco at the crown of the vault

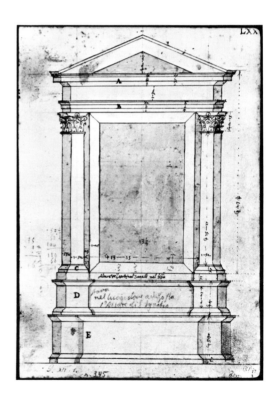

14.18 *Giacomo della Porta, drawing of Savelli Altar in Gesù transept. Vienna, Albertina.*

also does its best to persuade us that the architecture has suddenly dissolved to reveal a vision. The engraving shows at the base of the transept arm a splendid altarpiece with a spectacular sunburst at its crown. This also was erected in the later part of the seventeenth century, together with its companion across the transept, the altarpiece of St. Ignatius, by Father Pozzo. This is vastly different from the one designed for Cardinal Savelli by Giacomo della Porta sometime before 1587 which it replaced (fig. 14.18).[41] I discovered della Porta's design when leafing through the Italian architectural drawings in the Albertina in Vienna where there is a set of measured drawings taken from the original. It follows the sober spirit of Vignola's design, and shows the versatility of della Porta who also completed much of Michelangelo's work. Of course, this belongs to an era when everyone could remember Ignatius as a quiet priest who probably would have looked with suspicion on images inflamed by passion, no matter how spiritual, and with horror on such an altar dedicated to himself. The causes of differences between the Vignola and the Baroque Gesù could be explained fully only by theologians, but the change illustrates to laymen a fundamental contrast in the concept of religious art between the later sixteenth and the seventeenth century, when the reform character changes to a propaganda character, and the mood of contemplation gives way to a mood of excitation. This change is most evident in painting, and it can be seen in the altarpieces in the several chapels.

Finally, I should like to add that these observations affect the prevailing characterization of the Gesù as it appears in all the handbooks of architecture, where it is represented as the fountainhead of Baroque architecture. It is true that many of Vignola's inventions which were realized here for the first time were accepted by seventeenth-century architects, but I believe that if the Gesù had come down to us in its original simplicity it would have been praised not for its anticipation of the Baroque but for its vigorous statement of the spirit of its own time, when the arts were only beginning to emerge from the shadow of the giants of the High Renaissance, and when the Jesuit Order was just beginning to emerge from its early struggles for survival.

Notes

1. See Milton Lewine, "The Roman Church Interior, 1527–1580," Ph.d. diss., Columbia University, 1960; "Roman Architectural Practice During Michelangelo's Maturity," *Stil und Überlieferung in der Kunst des Abendlandes*, Acts of the 21st International Congress for the History of Art, 1964 (Berlin, 1967), 20–26.

2. Outlines of the history of Milanese architecture in the first half of the sixteenth century may be found in E. Arslan, "L'architettura milanese del primo Cinquecento," *Storia di Milano*, 7 (1954), 533–563; P. Mezzanotte, "L'architettura milanese dalla fine della signoria sforzesca alla metà del Seicento," ibid., 10 (1957), 559–645; C. Baroni, *L'architettura lombarda da Bramante al Richini* (Milan, 1941).

3. R. Wittkower, "The Centrally Planned Church and the Renaissance," *Architectural Principles in the Age of Humanism*, Part I (London, 1949), and later editions. See also E. Sinding Larsen, "Some Functional and Iconographical Aspects of the Centralized Church in the Italian Renaissance," *Inst. Romanum Norwegiae, Acta*, 2 (1965), 203–253.

4. Churches of this type are discussed by Giuseppe Zander, "A proposito di alcune chiese napoletane anteriori al Gesù di Roma," *Palladio*, n.s. 3 (1953), 41–46. Zander convincingly challenges the proposal by Georg Weise ("Chiese napoletane anteriori al Gesù del Vignola," *Palladio*, n.s. 2 [1952], 148–152) that a group of Neapolitan churches deriving from Spanish Gothic models were influential in the formation of Vignola's plan.

5. P. Tacchi Venturi, "Note storiche e topografiche di Roma nel sec. XVI: Le case abitate in Roma da S. Ignazio di Loyola . . . ," *Studi e documenti di storia e diritto*, 20 (1899), 287ff.; P. Pirri, "La topografia del Gesù di Roma e le vertenze tra Mutio Muti e S. Ignazio," *Archivum Historicum Societatis Iesu*, 10 (1941), 178f.; Tacchi Venturi, *Storia della compagnia di Gesù in Italia*, 2d ed. (Rome, 1951), 2:546ff.; P. Pecchiai, *Il Gesù di Roma* (Rome, 1952), 3–9.

6. See Jean Vallery-Radot, *Le recueil des plans d'édifices de la compagnie de Jésus conservés à la Bibliothèque Nationale de Paris* (Rome, 1960). Pirri, "La topografia del Gesù," 177ff., discovered the plan of 1550 presumably by Nanni, and published it in the hand-drawn copy reproduced in figure 14.1. I attempted to get a photograph of the original, but the folio cited by Pirri (Paris, B.N., Cabinet des estampes, Cod. Hd-4D, fol. 82) has

drawings for other structures, and was obviously misquoted.

7. Pirri, "La topografia del Gesù," 177–204.

8. Pirri, "La topografia del Gesù," and his *Giovanni Tristano e i primordi della architettura gesuitica* (Rome, 1955), 138 and note. A document of 1554 (p. 213) may refer to a later plan by Nanni ("disegno che ho fatto della chiesa nova, che vole fare la comp.ª di Jesu"). The Paris plan is not signed, but since Nanni was the architect at the time, he presumably was the author. On Nanni's active but undistinguished career, see R. Wittkower, "Nanni di Baccio Bigio and Michelangelo," *Festschrift für Ulrich Middeldorf* (Berlin, 1968), 248ff.; M. Lewine, "Nanni, Vignola and S. Martino de' Svizzeri in Rome," *Journ. Soc. Archit. Historians*, 28 (1969), 27ff.

9. Pirri, *Tristano*, 147.

10. Ibid., 138n.; Pecchiai, *Il Gesù di Roma*, 10f.

11. Tacchi Venturi, "Note storiche e topografiche," 326f., and *Storia*, 2:545ff.; Pirri, "La topografia del Gesù," 20f.; Pecchiai, *Il Gesù di Roma*, 14f.; J. Ackerman, *The Architecture of Michelangelo*, 2d ed. (London, 1964), 2:145f.; *Michelangelo architetto*, ed. Portoghesi and Zevi (Turin, 1964), 944ff.

12. Uffizi, Arch. 1819, published and first attributed to Michelangelo by A. Popp, "Unbeachtete Projekte Michelangelos," *Münchner Jhb.*, n.s. 4 (1927), 389–477.

13. M. Lewine, "Roman Architectural Practice," 20ff.

14. The text is reproduced in translation by R. Wittkower, *Architectural Principles*, 155ff.

15. On Giberti, see Angelo Grazioli, *Gian Matteo Giberti* (Verona, 1955), esp. 76ff.; E. Cattaneo, "Influenze veronesi nella legislazione di San Carlo Borromeo," *Problemi di vita religiosa in Italia nel Cinquecento*, Atti del convegno di storia della chiesa in Italia, Bologna, 1958 (Padua, 1960), 123–166. Prof. Lewine and Wolfgang Lotz drew my attention to these sources and to Giberti's role.

16. St. Charles's book is most easily accessible in the Italian translation of C. Castiglione and C. Marcora, *Arte sacra, De fabrica ecclesiae* (Milan, 1952). The original is published in *Acta Ecclesiae Mediolanensis . . .* (Milan, II. 1890; III. 1892), ed. A. Ratti (Milan, 1892), esp. 561–638. A richly annotated edition of the Latin text is in Paola Barocchi, *Trattati d'arte del Cinquecento*, vol. 3 (Bari, 1962). See A. Deroo, *Saint Charles Borromée* (Paris, 1963), and C. Baroni, *L'architettura*

lombarda, 86ff. Baroni cites the volume *Echi di S. Carlo Borromeo* (Milan, 1937–38) for further commentary on the influence of the Saint on the arts. I have not found this volume. For the Milanese background, see F. Chabod, "Per la storia religiosa dello stato di Milano durante il dominio di Carlo V," *Annuario dell' Ist. ital. per l'età moderna e contemporanea,* 2–3 (1936–37) (Bologna, 1938); C. Marcora, "La chiesa milanese nel decennio 1550–60," *Storia della diocesi di Milano,* 7 (Milan, 1960), 254–501.

17. On Palladio's churches, see W. Timofiewitsch, *Die sakrale Architektur Palladios* (Munich, 1968); G. Zorzi, *Le chiese e i ponti di Andrea Palladio* (Vicenza, 1966), and general observations in my *Palladio* (Harmondsworth and Baltimore, 1967). The peculiar problems involved in the development of the Redentore plan and its possible origins as a central-plan church have been revealed by E. Larsen, "Palladio's Redentore, a Compromise in Composition," *The Art Bulletin,* 47 (1965), 419–467.

18. On Alessi in Milan, see Hanns Hoffmann, "Die Entwicklung der Architektur Mailands von 1550–1650," *Wiener Jhb. für Kunstgeschichte,* 9 (1934), 69–73; Giovanni Rocco, "Galeazzo Alessi a Milano," *Atti del IV convegno nazionale di storia dell'architettura* (Milan, 1939), 185–198; P. Mezzanotte, "L'architettura milanese," 577ff.

19. C. Baroni, *Documenti per la storia dell'architettura a Milano nel Rinascimento e Barocco* (Florence, 1940), 1:87ff.; Nancy A. Houghton Brown, "The Church of S. Barnaba in Milan," *Arte lombarda,* 9 (1964), 62–93; 10 (1965), 65–98.

20. Paul Frankl, *Principles of Architectural History* (Cambridge, Mass., 1968), 31ff. (published 1914 as *Entwicklungsphasen der neueren Baukunst*).

21. C. Baroni, *L'architettura lombarda,* 123f.; P. Mezzanotte, "L'architettura milanese," 572ff.

22. C. Baroni, *L'architettura lombarda,* 122; P. Mezzanotte, "L'architettura milanese," 565ff.

23. Vignola's presence at Santa Maria in Traspontina is known only through a drawing of ca. 1580 by Oreste Vannocci Biringucci showing a (competition?) project for the church and inscribed "Trasp.ⁿᵃ Vig.ᵃ," which I published with W. Lotz, "Vignoliana," *Essays in Memory of Karl Lehmann, Marsyas,* suppl. 1 (New York, 1964), 3–7, figs. 1–2.

24. P. Pirri, *Tristano,* 10ff.; 40ff.

25. The chronology of the design and construction of the church is summarized with reference to the documents and secondary sources by W. Lotz in Ackerman and Lotz, "Vignoliana," 14–18. Cf. the documents in Pirri, *Tristano,* 248ff.

26. The letters are transcribed in Pirri, *Tristano,* 228f., docs. XXIV, XXV.

27. Ibid., p. 249, doc. XLIV; Pecchiai, *Il Gesù di Roma,* 43.

28. Ackerman and Lotz, "Vignoliana," 7–10. The project and the plan mentioned below were first published, with my approval, by Lotz, "Die ovalen Kirchenräume des Cinquecento," *Römisches Jahrbuch für Kunstgeschichte,* 7 (1955), 45–48, and republished by Maria Casotti, *Il Vignola* (Trieste, 1960), 209ff.

29. Casotti, *Il Vignola,* 209ff.

30. Ackerman and Lotz, "Vignoliana," 8f., 18, fig. 7.

31. A. Ronchini, "La chiesa del Gesù in Roma," *Atti e memorie delle RR. dep. di storia patria per le prov. modenesi e parmensi,* 7 (1874), 30; Ackerman and Lotz, "Vignoliana," 16, 19f.

32. Pecchiai, *Il Gesù di Roma,* 43; Pirri, *Tristano,* 252, doc. XLIV: "Sua Signoria s'è resoluta di non fare la facciata secondo il disegno di detto Vigniuola ma pigliare quello di m. Jac.° della Porta."

33. Ackerman, *The Architecture of Michelangelo,* 2:84.

34. See H. Wölfflin, *Renaissance and Baroque* (London, 1964), 93–108 (first ed., 1888); G. Giovannoni, "Chiese della seconda metà del Cinquecento in Roma," *Saggi sull'architettura del Rinascimento,* 2d ed. (Milan, 1935), 177ff.; W. Lotz in Ackerman and Lotz, "Vignoliana," 22ff.

35. Pirri, *Tristano,* 255, doc. XLIV.

36. Ibid., 118–126, pls. XIX–XXIII.

37. Ibid., pl. VI, from Bibl. Estense, Modena, fondo Campori; Vallery-Radot, *Le recueil des plans,* 7.

38. Vallery-Radot, *Le recueil des plans,* 6ff.; P. Moisy, *Les églises des Jésuites de l'ancienne assistance de France* (Rome, 1958), 1:45ff.

39. Vallery-Radot, *Le recueil des plans,* 7, 68–75; Moisy, *Les églises des Jésuites,* 61ff., 303ff.; F. de Dainville, "La légende du style jésuite," *Études,* 287 (1955), 3ff.; C. Galassi Paluzzi, *Storia segreta dello stile dei Gesuiti* (Rome, 1951).

40. Cf. Robert Enggass, *The Paintings of Baciccio* (University Park, Pa., 1964), 3–74.

41. J. S. Ackerman, "Della Porta's Gesù Altar," *Essays in Honor of Walter Friedlaender, Marsyas,* suppl. II (New York, 1965), 1f.

Postscript

This article, written for a symposium organized by Rudolf Wittkower with Irma Jaffe at Fordham University, was the first of several studies I devoted to the influence of reformed liturgy on church planning. My teacher Richard Krautheimer had been a major contributor to the study of the interaction of liturgy and design. The theme of the symposium—"Baroque Art: The Jesuit Contribution"—was a symptom of a tendency in architectural history to reach beyond the characteristically formalistic treatment of buildings to find social, economic, and political motivations for design choices.

The period of the Catholic Reformation and the Counter-Reformation stimulated a profound rethinking of the liturgy, of the participation of the clergy and the congregation in the Mass, of the role of preaching, and other issues that had a potential for radically altering the articulation of spaces within the church. The opportunity to address the design of the Gesù was particularly appealing because it had been so extensively discussed in the purely formal terms of its position in the evolution of Renaissance, Mannerist, and Baroque style.

I'm embarrassed that in this paper I too was still in the thrall of formal interpretation and followed earlier literature on the Gesù in overlooking a fundamental innovation of the Jesuit order with respect to past monastic practice: that Mass is not sung communally. There is no choir and, in the design of churches, no need to provide space for stalls. (Note, however, that Cardinal Farnese, in his letter quoted in the essay at n. 26, refers to the "choir.") This, more than aesthetic preferences, accounts for the simple form of the eastern end of the Gesù, where the expected spatial distinction of presbytery and choir is replaced by a unified space accommodating a single function. Further (and this point had always been emphasized), the church must accommodate resident members of the order by providing sequestered cubicles, out of public view, from which services may be heard. Vignola provided these in *coretti*, chambers behind screens placed in a sort of attic over the nave arcade.

Klaus Schwager's excellent study of the Gesù proposes that Giacomo della Porta made a fundamental change in the design of the interior of the church as well as of the façade. Because della Porta's façade was elevated by 2 meters over that of Vignola, the interior elevation of the nave had to be raised accordingly, which was done by adding an attic over the nave cornice; this attic is clearly delineated in the engraving reproduced in my figure

14.15, and it would have helped to achieve a *meravigliosa vaghezza* (the term used by Alessi, who himself offered more elevated façade designs at this time) on the interior. Below this level, the nave elevation remained as Vignola had designed it.

Schwager was led to this conclusion by an unpublished letter of 1570 addressed to Cardinal Alessandro Farnese (which, curiously, he neither identifies nor transcribes). The letter, he reports, criticizes a design by an unidentified author in which, as in that of Vignola, the entablature of the main façade order is lower than that in the nave. 1570 was also the date at which Vignola produced a *secondo modelo della facciata*, perhaps because Cardinal Farnese was dissatisfied with the initial design, recorded in the medal (fig. 14.12). We cannot know whether Vignola refused to meet the new demands, or whether the cardinal was dissatisfied with his proposals, but in any case the architect was dismissed in 1571. Clearly, the controversy that culminated in the commission to della Porta for the façade design and the vault elevation was over issues of architectural style (probably relating principally to the appearance of the interior), and did not involve the interests of the Jesuits.

Schwager presents the Uffizi plan reproduced in figure 14.2—now attributed to Bartolomeo Rocchi—as an awkward reflection of the project by Michelangelo referred to in 1554. I rejected that association except for the pentimenti in red chalk, which I thought to be Michelangelo's effort to control the vast spaces proposed in the drawing. He also brings into consideration a drawing for the cupola from the della Porta workshop that appears to be transitional between Vignola's design and the final project, which, like the nave vault, had to be elevated.

Alan Ceen, in tracing the history of the Via Papalis, shows how the planning of this major Roman street affected the designs of the Gesù. In 1538 the Via Papalis was rerouted at the point at which it reached the Piazza Alteriorum on the west side of the church of Santa Maria Alteriorum—the future site of the Gesù. The new route veered to the right and passed through this square directly toward the Capitoline Hill, crossed the Capitoline piazza, and descended to the Forum. While the church of Santa Maria had faced north onto the old route (which continued past the Palazzo Venezia and San Marco, skirting the Capitoline), the Gesù, as later stipulated in the instructions of Cardinal Farnese, was to be oriented to face west onto the new papal route as it turned toward the Capitoline Hill. Michelangelo was commissioned in 1537 to make the civic center accessible, and this may have encouraged the pope to reroute his triumphal way (thus underscoring his power over the city government)—which ultimately influenced the orientation and the siting of the Gesù.

Ackerman, James S. "Della Porta's Gesù Altar," *Essays in Honor of Walter Friedlaender* (New York, 1965), 1–2.

Ackerman, James S. "Il contributo dell'Alessi alla tipologia della chiesa longitudinale," *Galeazzo Alessi e l'architettura del Cinquecento* (Genoa, 1975), 461–466.

Ackerman, James S. "Observations on Renaissance Church Planning in Venice and Florence," *Florence and Venice, Comparisons and Relations,* vol. 2 (Florence, 1980), 287–308.

Ackerman, James S. "Palladio e lo sviluppo della concezione della chiesa a Venezia," *Bollettino del Centro Internazionale di Studi di Architettura,* 19 (1977), 9–26 (published 1980).

Ackerman, James S. "Pellegrino Tibaldi, San Carlo Borromeo e l'architettura ecclesiastica del loro tempo," *San Carlo e il suo tempo: Atti del Convegno internazionale* (Rome, 1986), 574–586.

Bosel, Richard. *Jesuitenarchitektur in Italien (1540–1773). I: Die Baudenkmaler der römischen und der neapoltanischen Ordensprovinz,* 2 vols. (Vienna, 1985); 1:160–179 relates to the Gesù. A thorough treatment of the chronology and authorship of designs for the Gesù, without interpretation.

Carboneri, Nino. "Le chiese del Alessi," *Bollettino del Centro Internazionale di Studi di Architettura,* 19 (1977), 191ff.

Ceen, Alan. *The Quartiere de' Banchi: Urban Planning in Rome in the First Half of the Cinquecento* (New York and London, 1986).

Foscari, Antonio, and Manfredo Tafuri. *L'armonia e i conflitti: la chiesa di San Francesco della Vigna nella Venezia del '500* (Venice, 1983).

Isermeyer, C. A. "Le chiese di Palladio in rapporto al culto," *Bollettino del Centro Internazionale di Studi di Architettura,* 10 (1968), 42–59.

Isermeyer, C. A. "La concezione degli edifici sacri palladiani," *Bollettino del Centro Internazionale di Studi di Architettura,* 14 (1972), 105–135.

Milone, Marinella. "La facciata di Santa Maria dell'Orto di J. Barozzi da Vignola," *Quaderni dell'Istituto di storia dell'architettura,* 22 (1975), 127–142.

Moore, Derek. "Pellegrino Tibaldi's Church of S. Fedele in Milan: The Jesuits, Carlo Borromeo and Religious Architecture in the Late Sixteenth Century," Ph.D. diss., New York University, 1988.

Schurhammer, G. *Francis Xavier: His Life, His Times,* tr. M. J. Costelloe, S. J., 3 vols. (Rome, 1973), esp. 1:iv, 443–456.

Schwager, Klaus. "La chiesa del Gesù del Vignola," *Bollettino del Centro Internazionale di Studi di Architettura,* 19 (1977), 251–271.

Scotti, Aurora. "Architettura e riforma cattolica nel Milano di Carlo Borromeo," *L'arte,* 19/20 (1972), 55–90.

Stankowski, Martin. "Der römische Gesù und die Jesuiten. Ein methodischer Versuch," *Ars Bavarica,* 23–24 (1981), 89–122.

15

The Geopolitics of Venetan Architecture
in the Time of Titian

An approach to architecture based on political, social, and economic history has emerged in the last fifteen years as the dominant critical-historical method in the study of Renaissance architecture in Venice and the Veneto.[1] The method is peculiarly suited to the situation in the Venetian Republic because so much of its major building was conceived either for the government or for patricians who served in state or local councils. The method has a wider application, and I believe it will in time become preeminent in the criticism of the architecture of all times and places for which adequate documentation has survived. I have found it to be an aid to a deeper and broader view of architecture than the traditional critical approaches of Western art history, which often have been restricted to tracing and analyzing the history of forms, within or without a context of the history of ideas.

The deeper view derives from the examination and criticism not only of buildings but of the programs that brought them into being. Works of architecture inevitably are generated by the expressed needs and desires of patrons, whose visions are formed in the context of the group of which they are members; they are not simply the product of the creative inspiration of designers, as they appear in so many traditional studies, but of the interaction of a program framed by the individual client and by the traditions of his group and the responses of an architect selected by the client. The broader view stems from this commitment to reconstruct the program, since it requires knowledge

From *Titian: His World and His Legacy,* edited by David Rosand (New York: Columbia University Press, 1982), 41–71. Copyright © Columbia University Press.

not only of the life, the interests, and the building intentions of the client, but also of his immediate and wider circle and its traditions and ideology. Since an ideology is characteristically absorbed unconsciously, the critic-historian also has to use the advantages of historical perspective to identify and interpret motivations not expressed or articulated in the framing of programs in the past. A similar knowledge of the architect and of his background and responses to his culture is also needed, and finally, whatever can be found of the needs and habits of those other than the patron who use and are affected by buildings being investigated, especially insofar as such needs and habits diverge from those of the patron and the designer. In this way, the understanding of architecture derives from and contributes to the understanding of a culture as a whole.

Venice and the Veneto: Two Renaissances

The particular dependence of Venetan architecture on political-economic determinants was the result initially of a war and its aftermath, which impeded the evolution of an architectural style for such a long period that the style was obsolete by the time a real resurgence had become possible. In 1509 the League of Cambrai—which included the Papal States, the Holy Roman Empire, the French monarchy, and the Duchy of Milan— was formed to oppose Venetian advances in the Terraferma by military force; their armies overran the mainland territories of the Republic and penetrated as far as the shores of the Lagoon, within sight of the city itself. Though the threat of total defeat soon subsided and ultimately little territory was lost, the war dragged on until 1516– 17, and the Venetian government remained sufficiently alarmed during the ensuing decade to allot virtually all of its resources for public construction to the fortification of the Terraferma, starting with Treviso and Padua in 1517, and the colonies in the eastern Mediterranean.

Private as well as public patronage was restrained. While some major projects initiated in the years immediately preceding the war (Villa Giustinian at Roncade, 1508; San Salvatore, 1506) were not halted, and the Procuratie Vecchie in Piazza San Marco was rebuilt immediately after a fire of 1512, the effort of recovery during the following decade permitted almost no architectural enterprise. By the time equilibrium had been restored in the late 1520s and early '30s, Venetian ambitions had shifted away from the support of a vigorous local style toward the model of the so-called High Renaissance in Rome, which had flourished precisely in the years of Venice's greatest difficulties. The surviving Venetian architects were then brushed aside from the councils of wealth and power, to be picked up, as Scarpagnino was, by the conservative, non-noble citizens who managed the *scuole* of Venice, or by lesser government offices, while the prestigious commissions went to new personalities imported from abroad or created instantly out of local talent in allied crafts.

The Venetian Renaissance did not evolve, it broke in two: the first Renaissance concluded with the close of the war, and the second burst forth nearly full grown about the time of the sack of Rome. It was the counterpart of a resurgence in the political theater—encouraged by Venice's miraculous emergence from the war without serious loss of property or independence—of the "myth" of Venice, according to which the Republic surpassed even republican Rome in the perfection of its constitution. The claim was based on the permanence of Venice over the centuries, its assurance of liberty, and the sharing of power among its competent inhabitants (a spurious assertion); two of the most influential statements of the myth, those of the patrician Gasparo Contarini and of the Florentine historian Donato Giannotti, were written in the period 1523–31.[2]

Because of the extended architectural famine, the second Renaissance was exceedingly indebted to Roman innovations of the intervening years, not only for the training of Sansovino and the Veronese Sanmicheli, the two distinguished architects who left the papal city to work in the Veneto, but for the definition of humanist architectural orthodoxy in general. The Roman Renaissance prior to 1526 and its offshoot in the Mantuan buildings of the Roman architect Giulio were the seedbeds of the second, Venetian style. But from the time Sansovino and Sanmicheli set foot in the north, the Golden Age of Rome crystallized in the Venetian imagination into that quarter century prior to the sack of 1527. Sebastiano Serlio, another refugee to Venice from the sack, turned to publishing popular illustrated books on architecture, the first of which (Book IV), appearing a decade later, asserted his dependence on Raphael's contemporary Baldassarre Peruzzi. Serlio's illustrations of contemporary architecture in his subsequent Book III (1540) include no designs later than 1520. Few central Italian architectural innovations after that time had much impact on the architects of the Republic—neither those of Michelangelo or Vignola, Alessi, Ammanati, Vasari, or any other central Italian. When Palladio made his Roman pilgrimages in the 1540s and '50s, the papal city had fully recovered from the sack and was building vigorously and imaginatively; but the greatest of Venetan architects noticed only the works of Bramante and Raphael.[3]

I call this second Renaissance Venetan rather than Venetian because its only contributor who worked consistently in the capital city was Sansovino, who brought a mature style from abroad, and this style was not exported into the provinces as Venetian design had been before the war. Apart from Sansovino, the generating monuments of sixteenth-century architecture are either in the Terraferma or by Terraferma architects bringing their matured manner into Venice. In this sense, the flow of culture had been reversed. That this occurred in architecture and not in the other arts is largely because of the nature of the profession. Buildings will settle down wherever there is money—as we know from those in Ronchamps, France; Brno, Czechoslovakia; and Oak Park, Illinois.

The political-social forces that generated the new architecture were not significantly different in the capital and in the Terraferma cities (fig. 15.1). Public building was generated by the Venetian Senate and councils, and in the Terraferma by Venetian government order (though local council halls, like Palladio's Basilica, were built or refurbished by the cities themselves). Most of the major private commissions were given to architects also employed by the government; either type of patronage could ease an entry into the other. But in a sense the two spheres were one: the patricians who built palaces and chapels served in the governing bodies and building commissions.

Each of the Terraferma towns had a Venetian *podestà* and captain supervising its affairs and the collection of taxes for the capital.[4] Some towns, like Padua, were under more repressive rule, but all had councils like that of Venice, open to adult males of the patriciate and, with decreasing frequency, to occasional wealthy citizens. "Citizens," members of the professional, civil servant, and merchant classes, largely disenfranchised, were rarely responsible for the patronage of major buildings except through the *scuole* of Venice, which were charitable clubs and cooperatives that absorbed some of the nonpatrician citizen's ambition to do something significant in his society.[5]

The distribution of power made for a radically different approach to architecture from that found in contemporary Florence or Rome, where power was centered in a court and filtered down to satellites of that court. There, each individual or family would strive egoistically in patronage for personal distinction and often grandiosity within generally accepted limits of decorum. In the Veneto, competition was also a factor, but within a context of civic and class pride. The procurators of San Marco, the many commissioners (or *savi*) of other offices, the ambassadors abroad worked hard out of affection for the Republic and for its greater splendor, and private patrons sought seriously to contribute to the magnificence of the city as a whole. In Vicenza,

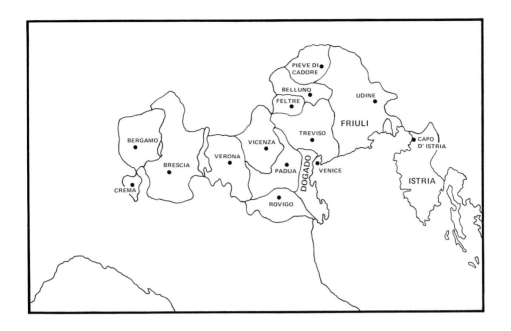

15.1   The mainland dominions of the Venetian
Republic, ca. 1550–1620.

where the nobility was exceedingly rich from land holdings, there seems to have been a communal decision to assign to Palladio the decoration of the entire city with their palaces, each of which was individualistic, even idiosyncratic—much more so than Roman or Florentine palaces—and yet in harmony with the whole. In the provinces, however, that harmony did not reflect love of the state—Venice was the exploiter—but the class cohesion of an aristocracy of imperial origins that no doubt felt itself superior to the merchant nobles of the Lagoon.[6]

The Terraferma aristocracy was well educated and free-thinking: not only architecture but religious thought had a second renaissance, which on one hand extended to militant Protestantism and on another to radical Catholic reform, like that of Giberti in the diocese of Verona. The Theatine Order was founded by a Vicentine nobleman, San Gaetano Thiene, and, at another extreme, the Accademia Olimpica was established to promote a variety of humanist interests, including, as we know from the surviving Teatro, the revival of classical drama. Palladio was a member of this ambitious organization; the presence of a craftsman was an uncommon occurrence in a closed society, but consistent with a type of patronage that began not by hiring him in the usual manner but literally by creating him. Palladio was simply a stonemason from Padua, Andrea di Pietro, when Giangiorgio Trissino picked him out and made him a humanist and a scholar. The nobles felt a need for a voice and, finding none around, fashioned it out of a talent that proved to be far more exceptional than they could have known.[7] This education was the inspiration of a remarkable humanist, Giangiorgio Trissino, who was central to the formation of the Academy; it was later supplemented by the patrons of the villa of Maser, the influential Venetian brothers Daniele Barbaro, Patriarch-elect of Aquileia and commentator on Vitruvius in an edition on which Palladio collaborated, and Marcantonio Barbaro, an outstanding political figure and ambassador of the Republic. They provided Palladio with a bridge to commissions in Venice, steering his later career as surely as Trissino had charted his beginnings.[8] This may explain partially why the celebrated *Quattro libri dell'architettura,* which Palladio published toward the end of his career in 1570, is unique among Renaissance architectural treatises in its insistence on associating his designs with the specific needs (and social rank) of the patrons for whom they were conceived. The patrons are named, and often relevant facts about the family are recorded; Palladio was the first architectural writer to represent the design process as the outcome of a dialogue between the architect and real individuals in specific situations.[9]

The making of Palladio, whose very name was an invention of Trissino, mirrored the re-creation in Padua of Falconetto, from a pedestrian painter to the herald of the second Renaissance style in the Veneto under the tutelage of Alvise Cornaro. Cornaro, like Trissino the guiding spirit of the intellectuals in his town, was the patron of the innovative comic-satiric theater of Ruzante and the spearhead of an agricultural renaissance based on land reclamation. Cornaro used architecture to express his innovative ideas and wrote about it, as no other humanist had done, with great concern for the accommodation of practical functions. Modern critics have seen him as partly responsible for most of Falconetto's buildings.[10]

In Florence and Rome this kind of tutorial relationship between architects and patrons could not have occurred; there, major patrons selected architects who had made a reputation in minor commissions or in the figural arts, as the popes came upon Bramante, Raphael, and Michelangelo. But the phenomenon of renewal I have described was not itself renewed in the Veneto: once the second Renaissance style had been created, it became as fixed and sometimes as ossified as the aristocratic class that initiated it and the government of the Serenissima itself. With occasional exceptions, such as the great Longhena, the principles of Sansovino and Palladio were codified into the law of later generations, as if they were being held in escrow for neoclassical Britons.

The Terraferma and the Villa

The greatly increased importance of the Terraferma was obviously the result not of its architectural inventiveness but of an economic evolution, which made land and its architectural products more important economically to Venice of the sixteenth century than it had been in earlier periods.[11] Venetian patrician families had had large Terraferma holdings long before this time, in many cases for centuries, and had earned income from agriculture; and a large number of modest villa-residences in addition to a few great *castelli* of the fifteenth and early sixteenth centuries attest to the increasing number of landholders who found it worthwhile to spend at least part of their time supervising work on their farms.[12] A superficial manifestation of the change was the rapidly developing taste for the relaxing charms of the country, seen as an escape from the city, to which Girolamo Priuli referred scornfully when he wrote in his diary early in the century:

Since the noblemen and citizens of Venice had enriched themselves, they wished to enjoy their success and to live in the Terraferma and elsewhere, devoting themselves to pleasure, delight and the country life, meanwhile abandoning navigation and maritime activities. These were certainly more laborious and troublesome, but it was from the sea that all benefits came. We can judge the damage inflicted by the Terraferma on the city of Venice from the way in which her intoxicated nobles, citizens and people bought estates and houses on the Terraferma and paid twice as much as they were worth. They paid 20–25 ducats per campo *of land, which yielded 3–4% per annum, and subsequently erected palaces and houses on these estates which consumed large sums of money. . . . Nonetheless, there was no man of means, among nobility, citizenry, or populace, who failed to buy at least one estate and house on the Terraferma, especially in the Padovano and Trevigiano, for these were nearby regions, and they could go and stay there and return in a day or two.*[13]

Priuli's view was jaundiced; he longed for the great age of Levantine trade when Venice was a city of daring merchants, before she had to compete with Atlantic powers who sailed around Africa or cope with the Turkish advance. What he failed to anticipate was that in an inflationary age land would become the best available investment and the reclamation of marginal land the most profitable industry; and, in an age of expanding territory and population, maintaining an adequate food supply without having to resort to costly purchases from abroad would become one of the preeminent concerns of the Republic. Ultimately, much greater profits might be had off the land than off the sea.[14]

But it was not merely profit that enticed Venetians onto the land, nor, Priuli notwithstanding, did they merely go to rest on weekends or to escape the plague. An attitude was becoming more common that made the countryside worthy on its own account rather than simply as an antithesis of the city; it was not Arcadian fantasy that brought this about,[15] but rather an increasing sympathy with the landholder's responsibility toward his properties in cultivation, that awareness which had been expressed by ancient Roman authors such as Vergil and more relevantly by those more practical farmers cited by Daniele Barbaro in his commentary on Vitruvius's villa chapter (VI,9): "Columella, Varro, Cato, and [Rutilio] Palladio."[16] Those writers depicted agriculture and horticulture as occupations worthy of a gentleman and, in contrast to urban occupations, capable even of promoting moral betterment. A generation after Priuli, the Venetan nobleman Roberto di Spilimburgo, in his *Cronaca* of 1540, called land investment "the finest and most suitable commerce, that proper to gentlemen."[17] Consistent with this reappraisal is the depiction of peasants and shepherds in Venetian painting as convincing and worthy people; in all other parts of Renaissance Europe the worker is portrayed as either comic or villainous. The Venetian landlord depended on and associated with farm laborers.[18]

Alvise Cornaro, who coined the term *santa agricoltura*,[19] was the herald of this realist-humanist reappraisal:

At this very time [his eighty-third year] I still go every year to revisit some of these neighboring cities, and to enjoy my friends whom I find there, and I take pleasure being with them and conversing with them, and through them with others who are there, men of fine intellect: with architects, painters, sculptors, musicians, and farmers, since our age is rich in such men.

I see the works they have recently made and see again earlier works, and I always learn things that I take pleasure in knowing. I see the palaces, gardens, the collections of antiquities. . . . But above all I take pleasure in the voyage going and coming, as I consider the beauty of the sites and landscapes through which I pass. Some on the flat, others hilly, near rivers or springs, with many beautiful habitations and gardens around them.[20]

It came naturally to this technologist of a new era, the pioneer of modern land reclamation,[21] to class farmers with artists as the practitioners of the manual arts whose fine intellects elevated them above the common herd, and Cornaro's love of the cultivated landscape was consistent with his belief that nature awaited the improving hand of man. Few aristocrats would have shared such radical views, but increasing numbers in Venice and the Terraferma cities were purchasing farmland or adding to inherited holdings and building there a kind of villa unknown in central and southern Italy, capable of accommodating both a life of luxury and the functions of a farm.[22] The combination was not itself new: early Venetan villa complexes, like that of the Castello Giustinian in Roncade (1508ff.),[23] were palaces combined with farm enclosures, all encircled by walls like a castle—not defensive in the military sense, but expressing rather what I suppose to be ambivalence toward the charms of the countryside, an ambivalence rarely expressed in Palladio's generation.

The Villa Garzoni at Pontecasale south of Padua (fig. 15.2) was built by Sansovino some time after 1537, one of his earliest private commissions.[24] We know that Alvise Garzoni was of a wealthy Venetian citizen family that had purchased extensive lands in the area in the mid-fifteenth century, and that, together with the monks of the Abbey of Santa Giustina in Padua and with the canons of Candiana and Alvise Cornaro, he took part in a pioneering consortium to carry out land reclamation in the area in 1540.[25] The Garzoni obviously encouraged the architect to propose a quite new type

15.2   *Pontecasale, Villa Garzoni, by Jacopo Sansovino.*

15.3   *The villas of Palladio.*

of design, and Sansovino attempted to oblige, but he had some difficulty in deciding what a villa ought to be, since he had probably never before stayed long enough in the farmlands of the Terraferma to become aware of the traditions there. He picked up enough of them to surround the area with a wall reminiscent of the *castelli* and to build majestic *barchesse* alongside the villa in a different, simpler style. But the villa itself is a grandiose palace, the façade of which is Venetian on the flanks and Roman in the middle. It is one of the most breathtaking buildings of its time, but somewhat out of tune with its function, and Sansovino was not drawn into any further villa commissions. Sanmicheli was the first to come to terms definitely with the new exigencies of the country seat for great landholders. His villa structures—of which two, both destroyed, were recorded by Vasari: La Soranza in Treville di Castelfranco Veneto (before 1540) and that of Girolamo Cornaro in Piombino Dese (after 1539)—were by contrast simple cubic structures, the former with a central arched loggia, separated by a short distance from the *barchesse,* as in the main structure at Villa Garzoni. They were without classical articulation and are closely related in conception to Palladio's contemporary design of Villa Godi in Lonedo.[26]

Whether or not Palladio took the clue from Sanmicheli, he soon found the way to satisfy the new need with his perfect balance of magnificence and agricultural function, of Venetan villa tradition and ancient Roman elegance, and his excitingly varied solutions cover much of the map of the Terraferma, responding to calls from both Venetian and provincial patricians (fig. 15.3).

The Barbaro villa at Maser (figs. 15.4–15.6) is not just a palace in the country, but a complex in which dwelling and farm functions are integrated into the building itself: the upper floor of the villa is for habitation and is on the level of a rear terrace adorned with a richly sculpted nymphaeum and a pond, while the lower floor—an adaptation of the arched *barchesse* traditional in the Veneto—is intended for the storage of farm implements and feed, while the flanking towers contain stable, a winery, and, above, dovecots for raising edible fowl.[27] The walled gardens designed for the slopes on either side of the broad central access were irrigated by water that flowed from the nymphaeum at the rear through the kitchen.[28] Palladio later provided a separate chapel inspired by the Pantheon.

The villa shows a sensitivity to the environment, reflecting in its varied forms and extended horizontality the forested foothill site, and nestling into the gradual slope of the land by stepping down from a one-story elevation at the rear to two at the front. Yet it is distinctly a member of a class of like structures invented by Palladio to express

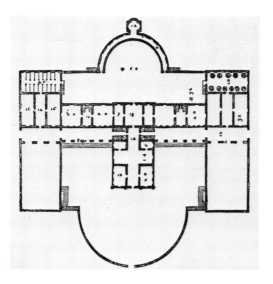

15.4   *Maser, Villa Barbaro, plan. From Andrea Palladio,* I quattro libri dell'architettura, *1570.*

15.5   *Maser, Villa Barbaro.*

15.6   *Maser, Villa Barbaro, view from the* salone.

the relationship of luxurious and classicized aristocratic life and practical agricultural industry peculiar to this time and place.[29] From the front window of the grand cruciform *salone,* behind the central temple front, the owners could look down over the low encircling walls on their lands in cultivation (fig. 15.6). A view of plowed fields and growing grain had taken precedence over formal parterres (which presumably were preserved in the garden enclosures on either side).

If at Maser domestic and economic functions are kept in equilibrium, there was one villa, of Mario Repeta at Campiglia, in which they were entirely fused, as both the dwelling and the farm were screened by a uniform portico. "The part for the habitation of the patron," Palladio explained, "and that for the villa use have the same order; whatever the former loses in grandeur in not being more eminent than the latter, the latter—farm—portion gains in proper ornament and dignity, becoming equal to that of the patron and [contributing to] the beauty of the whole work."[30]

Palladio adjusted his established villa types to the peculiar requirements and personality of his patrons, as at the famed Villa Rotonda outside Vicenza, which differs from all the others—most notably in not being adapted to farming—to such an extent that Palladio included it among the palaces in his *Quattro libri.* He designed it as a place of entertainment for a distinguished prelate and put temple porticoes on all four sides and a domed circular room at the center "because there are beautiful vistas in every direction."[31] He goes on to describe the hill on which it is perched, together with a ring of like hills about, as having "the aspect of a very grand theater." The adaptation of the temple front to many of the villas is an imposing way of underscoring the classical heritage that suggested a sacralization of the country life.[32] Palladio was apparently convinced that the great palaces of Roman times had templelike façades, because one is shown in the elevation, presumably drawn by him, illustrating the sixth book of Barbaro's Vitruvius commentary.

Urban Architecture

Vicenza in particular is surrounded by villas because the Vicentine aristocracy was particularly well off; they also built more in town than did the aristocracy in the other provincial centers. In fact, it is essential to the analysis of Venetan architecture to realize that there were significant differences among the capacities of the several towns to support an architectural Renaissance.

Padua, for example, in spite of being the seat of Italy's greatest university, suffered a political and economic depression in Titian's time. It was a battleground during the war, and afterward it was punished by Venice for disloyalty, the powers of its council being so weakened that the aristocracy lost interest in exercising what little authority was left to it. Following the war, the Republic leveled the suburbs for a mile outside the old fortifications to aid defense against further attack—which came only with Napoleon—creating what they called a *guasto* around the town. Worst of all, by expropriating rebel property and taking other estates for defaulted loans, Venetians came to control one third of the Padovano while the church held another third.[33]

Padua's only architect of the second Renaissance was Giovanni Maria Falconetto, whose commissions came both from the city government, doubtless aided by Venice, and from Alvise Cornaro, whose great wealth, unique among Paduans, derived from the acquisitions of an ecclesiastical uncle in the days before church reform. Apart from the two city gates, in the ring of government-sponsored fortification and the Monte di Pietà, a civic commission, all of Falconetto's work was connected with Cornaro, who built for himself in 1524 a loggia and later what he called an Odeon as paradigms of the new *all'antica* style (fig. 15.7). Cornaro also helped Falconetto obtain his most lavish commission, for the Villa Vescovile at Luvigliano.[34] The loggia, in fact, was the first monument of the new style. It is pedantically proper and probably was conceived more by Cornaro than by Falconetto, who had only just been transformed from a painter into an architect. In the court where Cornaro built his two model structures, the plays of his protégé Ruzzante were performed, forerunners of the Commedia dell'Arte, in which, in harmony with Cornaro's convictions, peasants and servants are depicted as real people and the provincial dialect is spoken authentically enough to make the works almost inaccessible to the outsider. The ambivalence in Cornaro between a humanist and a realist or populist culture is consistent with that of the other villa builders who tried to combine the intellectual and the agricultural life.

Symptomatic of the difference in patronage between Padua and Vicenza is the contrasting treatment of Padua's Sala della Ragione and the Vicentine Basilica—both fourteenth-century buildings of similar design (fig. 15.8). While the Paduans simply saw to it that the irregular medieval exterior was kept in repair, the Vicentines went to extraordinary lengths to have their hall—which already had been modernized in the fifteenth century—newly refaced in the most modern classical style, seeking in turn the counsel of the most distinguished designers in north Italy: Sansovino, Serlio, Sanmicheli, and Giulio Romano.[35]

15.7   *Padua, Loggia and Odeo Cornaro, by Giovanni
Maria Falconetto, 1524–.*

15.8   *Vicenza, Basilica, by Andrea Palladio, 1549–.*

Palladio apparently was not yet regarded as the equal of these visitors; when he and his partner presented a design in 1546, the Council had them erect an entire bay to full scale in wood for closer study, and even three years later the final vote on the award of the commission involved a choice between the models of Palladio, of the fifteenth-century designer, and of Giulio Romano. In the interim, Palladio had become established as the author of some major villa projects, and by this time his Vicentine residence and education by Trissino made him appear the supremely qualified interpreter in architecture of the ideals of the local nobility.

The design was severely circumscribed by the nature of the existing building: the old portico vaults had to be kept, and their lowness forced the architect to produce a low external arcade. This, more than aesthetic predilections, accounts for the choice

*15.9   Venice, Library of St. Mark, by Jacopo
Sansovino, 1537–.*

of the Palladian motif, in which the arch springs from columns well inside the piers that divide the major bays and thus can be kept relatively low. The motif also helps adjustment to substantial differences in width from bay to bay, since the span of the arch can be kept uniform while the columns can be as near to or as far from the piers as a particular bay width dictates.

Palladio's vocabulary is taken rather from recent Roman architecture than from antiquity—even the so-called Palladian motif was borrowed from Bramante and his circle.[36] But the fact that the Vicentine Palazzo della Ragione was called a basilica indicates an intention to give the civic center the character of an ancient forum. The forum function was reflected also in the two piazzas flanking the basilica: the Piazza dei Signori, "destined for the use of the nobility" and accented with a great column, of 1464, bearing the winged lion of the Serenissima facing toward the principal east-west artery, and the lower Piazza delle Erbe on the opposite side, which functioned as a market. Under the arcades were (and still are) shops for commerce and crafts. The bringing together of all the classes in one central civic space was anticipated in the earlier history of the center and was thus as much a matter of survival as of willed revival of antiquity: it was Palladio's task to bring the heritage into the public consciousness.

The extended Vicentine Piazza dei Signori must have intentionally reflected the Piazzetta in Venice, just as the basilica is a reflection of the Venetian Library of San Marco,[37] designed by Jacopo Sansovino from 1537 on (fig. 15.9).[38] The library was a project of the Procurators of San Marco, a state committee that served as trustees of the vast sums that came to the government through gifts and bequests and whose members were among the most influential nobles of the Senate. This body was disposed in its architectural commissions to promote expression of the wealth and magnificence of the state, and it envisaged the library less as a place to consult books (its very position is unfavorable to that purpose) than as the completion of the majestic entranceway to the city, complementing the Palace of the Doges.[39] In this respect, the library is also a kind of basilica overlooking a forum; it too housed offices of the government and shops for commerce and craft, and it was surrounded in the Renaissance by the stalls of a cheese and salami market. It also anticipated Palladio's building in rejecting the tradition of Venetian design that then dominated the Piazza San Marco to adopt the vocabulary of modern Roman architecture (specifically that of Antonio da Sangallo).[40]

It is apparent that the rulers of Vicenza sought to echo the enterprise of the Procurators; indeed, it was Sansovino whom they first called as a consultant, in 1538, the year after he had begun to build the Library. That Palladio was impressed by Sansovino's building is indicated by the fact that it is the only modern Venetan design mentioned in the *Quattro libri,* where it is characterized as "il più ricco et ornato edificio, che forse sia stato fatto da gli Antichi in qua."[41] This description is probably expressing not simply admiration but the suggestion that Sansovino is the master of a rhetorical lavishness that Palladio wishes to distinguish from his own ethical and more reserved classicism.[42] Sansovino, however, was uniquely skilled at adopting whatever form of address appealed to his patrons: in his church designs he was conservative and even respectful of quattrocento Venetian tradition; and in one commission from the Procurators of San Marco for a poorhouse—Ca' di Dio, 1545—he designed the most anonymous known work of any major architect of his time.[43] Sansovino's career cannot be properly understood without considering the relationship of architectural genre to the aims of his several private and public patrons.

As the protracted negotiations for the design of the Basilica continued, palace building became the fashion in Vicenza; the wealthiest of the nobility seem to have felt that the status of their families would be tarnished if they did not contribute to the ring of splendid mansions that was rising about the center (fig. 15.10). The enterprise changed the face of the medieval city, setting a standard of elegance for its time and for future generations. We are still not sure whether the initial stage of the first of the grand mansions, started for the Thiene family about 1542, was designed by Giulio Romano while he was consulting on the Basilica or by Palladio.[44] The palace for Iseppo Porto, of the later 1540s, however, represents the mature, Romanized master and makes a sharp contrast to the fifteenth-century Venetian Gothic Palazzo Colleoni-Porto nearby on the same street; it symbolizes both a new era and a new independence from Venetian style. The façade design is dependent on an early sixteenth-century Roman model, the Palazzo Caprini by Bramante, which profoundly influenced palace design throughout Italy, but in every other respect Palladio's palace is strikingly original.[45] Palladio divided the plot, a long rectangle that extends through a city block to another street, into three equal cubes. The two outer cubes contain matching palaces with like street façades, one destined for "the use of the patron and of his women" and the other for guests: between them is a majestic court surrounded by a covered loggia whose colossal Corinthian columns support a balustraded balcony on the upper story. The palaces, of which only one was built, are entered, like many of Palladio's later works, through square vaulted entrance atria in imitation of Roman domestic architecture.[46]

15.10   *Vicenza, Palazzo Iseppo Porto, 1549–, by*
Andrea Palladio.

15.11   *Vicenza, Palazzo Chiericati, 1551–, by Andrea*
Palladio.

But, having invented this remarkable new type, Palladio was able to sweep it aside a year or two later in designing a palace for Girolamo Chiericati.[47] The needs were different; the place was to be on a large open area called the Isola near the principal access to the town from the east, and the client apparently did not want to plan lavishly for guests (fig. 15.11). There are no obvious reflections of the ancient house or of the Roman Renaissance in the plan or the façade, though the relationship of the palace to the site invites comparison to Michelangelo's design for the Capitoline Hill in Rome. Only the *all'antica* vocabulary links the Chiericati and the Porto designs. The most striking innovation in private palace design is the open portico on the ground floor and on the wings of the upper floor. It is the subject of a revealing petition of the patron to the City Council of March 19, 1551, which eloquently illustrates how much the Vicentines considered their new residences to be contributions to the public welfare:

Since I, Gerolamo Chiericati, have decided to rebuild from the foundations my house located on the Piazza dell'Isola, having been advised also by expert architects and by many honorable citizens that a portico should be made along the façade of this house over the Isola for my greater convenience and for the ornament of the whole city . . . [the portico, thirteen feet wide, would cost much more, he says, but would be much better, so that he requests a concession]. This being not only for the benefit of the public and of no harm or offense to anyone, but rather convenient and useful to the neighbors as is well known to all, and with all this, if I may add an obligation to my country I will remain eternally obligated and particularly tied by loving devotion.[48]

The nature of the site prompted the architect and the patron to give even a private dwelling the public character reminiscent of the ancient forum-basilica.

A similar though less expensive campaign of renewal had been launched in the territory of Verona twenty years earlier. Michele Sanmicheli, a Veronese who had been working as an architect and military engineer in the Papal States with Antonio da Sangallo the Younger, returned to Verona in 1527 and was employed shortly after by the Venetian government to design new fortifications for Legnago and Verona.[49] Six years later, after he had been loaned by the government as a gesture of good will to design fortifications for the Duke of Milan, he was appointed chief military architect of the Republic, responsible for the defense of Venice itself and of all parts of the Venetian empire.

The Veronese defenses were a milestone in the history of fortification, the first in which the bastions in their definitive form replaced towers. And the two majestic gates, the Porta Nuova and the Porta Palio, were equally innovative in bringing true

Roman classicism—in contrast to the bookish efforts of Falconetto in the Gates of Padua—to the Veneto for the first time. Again, private and public patronage moved hand in hand. As Sanmicheli's thirty-year career as state architect was launched, he was carrying out the first of his Venetan commissions, the Cappella Pelligrini in San Bernardino in Verona, and a recent discovery by Douglas Lewis makes it seem likely that he was the designer in 1528 of a huge palace—never executed—on the site of the Ca' del Duca in Venice for Vettor Grimani, the Procurator who was Sansovino's chief supporter in Venice.[50] Immediately after, wealthy Veronese began to commission new palaces.

The first of the palaces, for the Canossa and the Bevilacqua families, faced a street that became a major thoroughfare only after the construction of Sanmicheli's city gates (Porta Nuova, 1533–, and, at the entrance to the street, Porta Palio, finished by 1557), both of which are on the southwest side of the city at the road leading to Lombardy, suggesting that the private and state ventures were allied in Sanmicheli's planning.[51] The façade of the Palazzo Canossa (fig. 15.12), like Palladio's design for the Porto family, is a more severe and more grandiose version of Bramante's Palazzo Caprini in Rome, with a three-arched loggia at the entrance. The plan, however—basically a U-form, the open end of which overlooks the river and the countryside beyond—is neither Roman nor Venetian; it is derived in some respects from the abortive project for Vettor Grimani, the Roman elements of which are more distinct, but I am not yet confident that I understand the motivations for the vast space allotted to the two entrance atria, or for the open prospect to the rear, which must have influenced Sansovino's Villa Garzoni. Like Palladio, Sanmicheli provided very different buildings for different clients: the Bevilacqua palace has been used as a model of Mannerist ambiguity,[52] and the Palazzo Lavezola (Pompei), on the far side of the river,[53] apparently designed ca. 1555, was paradoxically the closest to Bramante's model. Sanmicheli's two great family palaces in Venice itself—the Grimani of 1556 and the Cornaro at San Polo of before 1564—were most closely tied to the Venetian tradition in planning,[54] though the façades were more personal and less reflective of Rome than were their Veronese predecessors, and markedly less than those of Sansovino.

In Venice, the identity of purpose of the government and the aristocracy was assured; they were the same, and there was no external power (such as Venice herself exerted on provincial towns) to divide them. It was possible even for an exceptionally rich family to petition the Senate successfully for financial assistance in building a magnificent palace, as the Cornaro did in 1539 when planning their home on the Grand Canal on a scale far surpassing that of preceding palaces (fig. 15.13).[55] The design was

15.12   *Verona, Palazzo Canossa, by Michele*
Sanmicheli, ca. 1532.

15.13   *Venice, Palazzo Corner Ca' grande, by Jacopo*
Sansovino, 1539–.

Sansovino's; its rhetoric was quite close to that of the Library of St. Mark, and the basic form is a Romanization of the traditional Venetian palace type. The grandeur of size and conception was challenged in the sixteenth century only by Sanmicheli's Palazzo Grimani. The two architects—though they remained friendly enough to collaborate on a proposal for the Doge's Palace[56]—must have responded to such commissions in a spirit of intense competition, and I imagine that Sanmicheli moderated the classic Roman flavor of his earlier work partly in order to distinguish his style from that of his colleague. The patrons, it goes without saying, were also competitive and probably encouraged this tendency.

Apart from differences rooted in individual style, there were differences resulting from attitudes in the several state offices that commissioned buildings. The Procurators sought the sort of magnificence represented in the Library and in the Loggetta.[57] A more commercially oriented and economically inclined body such as the Proveditori sopra la Fabrica del Rialto obtained from the same architect a project for the Fabbriche Nuove in about 1554 that was both more conservative (it actually reflects the Monte di Pietà in Padua by Falconetto of twenty years before) and of simpler construction.[58] Sansovino was not permitted to supervise construction, with the result that the orders and proportions were incompetently handled. I have mentioned the most striking instance of the relationship of style to patronage in the Ca' di Dio, a poorhouse that the Procurators asked Sansovino to design, not with the customary elegance of its commissions, but in a style suitable to the indigence of its intended inhabitants and to the obligation of state officers to expend public funds prudently.[59] The building is quite without ornament or classical reference; it adopts the vernacular style and is distinguishable from builders' housing only in niceties of its proportions and rhythms.

Ecclesiastical Building

So long as Sansovino and Sanmicheli were able to carry out major governmental commissions, the officials saw no need to turn to other designers. Palladio was effectively shut out from official commissions while the others were active, and when his chance came, in the late 1550s, economic depression had put an end to ambitious private patronage. Palladio got his start in Venice through support from the Church, though he had not previously established himself as a designer of ecclesiastical buildings. His first commission was for the cloister of the Lateran canons at Santa Maria della Carità, and this was followed by one for the façade of the cathedral, San Pietro in Castello, which probably came to him through the intercession of the Barbaro family.[60]

The commission that signaled his full acceptance in the capital came in 1562 for the façade of San Francesco della Vigna, an astonishing event in view of the fact that Sansovino had been the architect of that church since 1533 and had designed two versions of a façade that appear on the foundation medals. Sansovino's design had come to seem old-fashioned in the course of nearly thirty years—the interior was already conservative in the 1530s: the nave design had been taken from the church of San Salvatore in Florence of ca. 1493, which Cronaca had built for the same order of Observantist Franciscans (fig 15.14)[61]—and Sansovino was not an artist whose work kept up with current shifts of style. Decisions about the commissioning of architects and the distribution of chapels were not made principally by the friars, but were in the control of the Grimani family—throughout the Renaissance, minor churches were financed by wealthy families seeking rights to the use of chapels and tomb sites, and the proliferation of chapels in fifteenth- and sixteenth-century architecture is attributable more to this tradition than to liturgical exigencies. Vettor Grimani, who as Procurator of San Marco had a major voice in hiring Sansovino for five state commissions, was the major executor: he kept Sansovino's two models of the church in his own home. Vettor and his brother Cardinal Marin bought an important chapel at a cut rate, and in 1542 the two were granted the rights to the decoration of the outer and inner faces of the façade (in two separate negotiations) without payment, and with rights to adorn the inner face with a monument to a forebear, Doge Antonio Grimani. After Vettor's death in 1558, his younger brother, the Patriarch Zuanne, having prevented Vettor's body from being buried in his own chapel, abandoned Sansovino for Palladio.[62]

Palladio's façade for San Francesco was paradoxically more in the lavish Romanizing genre of Sansovino's Library than Sansovino's own façade had been, and it better represented the purposes of the patrons. The response must have been favorable, because the architect projected another version of it for the church of San Giorgio Maggiore, built for the Benedictine monks on the island across from the Piazzetta San Marco and the mouth of the Grand Canal.[63] The Benedictines were exceedingly wealthy land owners in the Veneto and suffered less from inflation than private families or even than the state itself, and it is no surprise that theirs should have been the most extravagant program of its time, involving the redesign of the entire island settlement.[64] Here again the façade was quite separated from the body of the church, which was built in different materials and designed in a traditional Venetian style with virtually no references to antique architecture. The façade functions today as a fixture in the

15.14   *Venice, S. Francesco della Vigna, interior, by*
Jacopo Sansovino.

theatrical scenery at the entrance to the city; whether it was originally intended to do so is not certain, since the view was blocked, until the seventeenth century, by a row of monastery buildings on the San Marco side of the island.[65]

The plan of San Giorgio was derived from that of the head church of the Cassinese branch of the Benedictine Order, to which San Giorgio belonged: Santa Giustina in Padua, started in 1521. Santa Giustina was not the work of a major architect; its innovations are attributable to the regulation that every church design had to be submitted to the annual convention of all houses in the order, and they reflected the advanced reform views of the Cassinese.[66] The most significant was the adoption of a change that originated in various reformed monastic establishments in the later fifteenth century; it involved shifting the choir from its position behind a screened enclosure in the crossing and the nave, which hid the altar from public view, to a vaulted space behind the altar. This was accompanied by the isolation of the altar in a separately vaulted or domed chancel raised by steps above the level of the nave so that it became visually more accessible to the congregation.[67] These innovations were also adopted by Sansovino in the planning of San Francesco della Vigna; they were to become standard forms in churches of the Counter-Reformation. In addition, Palladio adopted from Santa Giustina an openness of planning and an amplitude of light on bright surfaces. The awkwardness of Palladio's plan is due to the difficulty of incorporating the new ideas of Santa Giustina while replacing its Byzantinizing vestiges with modern *all'antica* elements and proportions.

A decade later, at the church of the Redentore (figs. 14.6, 15.15), the conflicts were satisfactorily resolved; but they were of a different sort, because even for this state, which had stubbornly retained its independence from the papacy, the program of the Redentore was unique in its time. The church was a commission of the Venetian Senate resulting from a vow made during the most acute phase of the devastating plague of 1575–76.[68] No cleric was involved in the decision, so that a commission of distinguished senatorial officials had to be delegated to seek a site and a monastery or convent that would serve the church. Finally the choice devolved on three sites and three monastic orders, and the Senate elected the Capuchins on the Giudecca, who later bitterly complained that the lavishness of the design was incompatible with their convictions.

The senators even had a hand in determining the form of the church; on February 9, 1577, a debate took place on the proposal to "Far principiar essa chiesa in forma quadrangular," in which a minority argued for Marcantonio Barbaro's proposal of a plan "in forma rotonda."[69] A further political determinant in the design was the Senate's obligation to go as a body annually to attend Mass at the Redentore, for which purpose a pontoon bridge had to be constructed across the Giudecca Canal. The requirements of an extended processional space and of an assembly place to accommodate the crowd of senators[70] account for two major divisions within the church, the long nave and the unusually spacious area under the dome (fig. 14.6), which cannot be called a crossing or transept but rather, following Italian usage, a tribune, designed for the seating of the doge and all the senators. Because the church was assigned to a monastic order, a third major division had to be the monks' choir behind the altar, following the tradition launched in the churches just discussed. These adjustments to the Senate's program were fused with other features drawn from contemporary exper-

15.15   *Venice, Il Redentore, interior, by Andrea*
Palladio, 1575.

iments throughout Italy inspired by the principles of the Counter-Reformation, one being the raising of the chapels above the level of the nave and connecting them by passages that permit the officiating priest to get to and from any altar without mixing with lay persons; to this Palladio added his own refinement, a passage outside the tribune walls that preserved the priest's privacy all the way to the sacristy. Whereas in most churches of the time, the chancel is elevated and clearly separated, here it is somewhat fused with the tribune to bring the annual state worshipers nearer to the mystery of the Mass, and the sharp division comes at the entrance of the tribune area, marked off by steps and by the responds at the end of the nave. Palladio managed to draw the disparate parts of the church together by a sensitive treatment of color and light that somehow makes the white walls and columns seem rich and warm.

I conclude with the Redentore because it offers the clearest justification of the critical method I have tried to illustrate. It shows first how political, social, and religious aims of the Venetian aristocracy and government led not only to state support of an ecclesiastical project, but even to a major role in determining its design. Second, it shows how a new religious impulse and reform of liturgy within Italy as a whole led to experiments and innovations in church design to which Palladio was a contributor and from which he was a receiver. Lastly, it shows, perhaps particularly in the design of the façade, the impact of the architect's humanist education, in the adaptation of the Roman temple front to church use, at last perfectly equilibrated and proportioned in Palladio's major Venetian church. But Palladio, while moved by such powerful external forces, always remained the prime mover, inspired rather than pressed by the constraints imposed by society, nature, and tradition. He grew in force and conviction and his late style, like that of Titian, not only challenged the ancients he admired, but surpassed them in humanity through the manipulation of light, color, and texture.

Painting is less well adapted than architecture to "geopolitical" criticism, since it is portable and so less closely tied to custom and to institutions. In particular, sixteenth-century Venetan painting was not so adversely affected as architecture by the war of 1509–16, though its impact deserves study. The Terraferma contributed less for the obvious reason that provincial painters could move to the capital for the stimulus and contacts it offered without having to give up work elsewhere in the Veneto—Veronese painted in the villa at Maser. But much can be learned by further investigation of the patrons of the figural arts in an effort to see their impact on genre and style. We may be able to distinguish the sort of works commissioned by aristocrats from those commissioned by citizens or by the *scuole,* and Venetian from Venetan. I have mentioned the unique treatment of the laborer/peasant in Venetian art, a theme that lack of interest in social criticism has left undeveloped, one of a sort that could bridge the gulf between the history of art and of literature. The passing reference to the impact of the Counter-Reformation on church design is a reminder that the religious upheaval that raged across the peninsula in the sixteenth century was particularly violent in the Veneto, which because of its historical distance and independence from the Holy See became a center of pastoral reform, of radical Catholicism, and of Lutheranism, all of which must have had a greater impact on the arts than has been recognized. The potential of a new criticism promises not only a deeper insight into the motivation of works of art, but greater opportunity to bring the historical criticism of art into step with the other disciplines seeking to understand and to better appreciate the cultures of the past.

Notes

I am using the term *Venetan* to mean "of the Veneto" (including Venice) as distinct from *Venetian* "of the city of Venice." "Terraferma" defines the mainland area of the Veneto.

Many of the improvements in this essay made after its presentation at the Bampton Lectures are due to the extensive and generous advice of Dr. Douglas Lewis, some but not all of which is acknowledged in the notes.

1. Some characteristic examples are: Michelangelo Muraro, *Civiltà delle ville venete* (Venice, privately duplicated, 1964; revised as a course outline for the University of Padua, 1975); Muraro, "Palazzo Chiericati 'villa marittima,'" *Arte veneta,* 32 (1978), 187–194; James S. Ackerman, *Palladio* (Harmondsworth and Baltimore, 1966); M. Tafuri, *Jacopo Sansovino e l'architettura del '500 a Venezia* (Padua, 1969); Tafuri, "Committenza e tipologia nelle ville palladiane," *Bollettino del Centro Internazionale di Studi di Architettura 'Andrea Palladio'* (hereafter, BCISA), 11 (1969), 120–136; Angelo Ventura, "Aspetti storici-economici della villa veneta," *BCISA,* 11 (1969),

65–71; Reinhard Bentmann and Michael Müller, *Die Villa als Herrschaftsarchitektur* (Frankfurt am Main, 1970); Lionello Puppi, *Michele Sanmicheli architetto di Verona* (Padua, 1971); Puppi, *La Villa Badoer di Fratta Polesine* (Vicenza, 1972); Howard Burns, *Andrea Palladio, 1508–1580: The Portico and the Farmyard,* exhibition catalog (London, 1975); Deborah Howard, *Jacopo Sansovino: Architecture and Patronage in Renaissance Venice* (New Haven and London, 1975); Giuseppe Franco Viviani, ed., *La villa nel veronese* (Verona, 1975).

2. See Franco Gaeta, "Alcune considerazioni sul mito di Venezia," *Bibliothèque d'humanisme et Renaissance,* 23 (1961), 55–78; Myron Gilmore, "Myth and Reality in Venetian Political Theory," in J. R. Hale, ed., *Renaissance Venice* (London and Totowa, N.J., 1973), 431–444; W. J. Bouwsma, *Venice and the Defense of Republican Liberty* (Berkeley and Los Angeles, 1968). Contarini's *De magistribus et republica venetorum* was written in 1523–32 and published in 1543; Giannotti's *Li-*

bro della republica de' viniziani was written in 1526–27 and published in 1540; see Felix Gilbert, "The Date of the Composition of Contarini's and Giannotti's Books on Venice," *Studies in the Renaissance,* 14 (1967), 172–184. Contarini's presumption of a distribution of power among the inhabitants of Venice was predicated on the clouded premises that the *popolo* should be regarded as only servants of the upper classes and that citizens (roughly speaking, the middle class) had access to posts that actually wielded power. Later promulgators of the myth, such as Paolo Paruta, admitted that power was effectively restricted to the patrician class.

3.   After Michelangelo's death (1564), Palladio occasionally adopted details from his work, such as the drafted embrasures of the lower windows of the Palazzo Valmarana in Vicenza (from the portal of Michelangelo's Porta Pia) or the bracket supports of the balconies at the Loggia del Capitaniato in Vicenza (apparently invented by Michelangelo to support the blind niches of the Laurentian Library vestibule in Florence). But Palladio's occasional borrowings from Michelangelo never were used in a Michelangelesque syntax.

4.   For an account of the Terraferma aristocracy, their power and attitudes, see Angelo Ventura, *Nobiltà e popolo nella società veneta del '400 e '500* (Bari, 1964). In reviewing the work, Alberto Tenenti suggested that its polemical antiaristocratic position is distorting (*Studi storici,* 7 [1966], 401–408).

5.   This role of the *scuole* is suggested by an important recent study of their role and structure, Brian Pullan, *Rich and Poor in Renaissance Venice* (Cambridge, Mass., 1971).

6.   In Vicenza, however, though the aristocracy demonstrated solidarity in their urban planning and building programs, violent antagonism frequently broke out among the leading families: their private bands roamed the streets in search of trouble. The situation is summarized by Lionello Puppi, *Scrittori vicentini d'architettura del secolo XVI* (Vicenza, 1973), 20ff.

7.   On Palladio's relationship to his Vicentine patrons, see: Ackerman, *Palladio,* chs. 1, 3; Tafuri, "Committenza e tipologia"; Lionello Puppi, *Andrea Palladio* (Boston, 1975), introduction. On Trissino's role in particular, see Rudolf Wittkower, *Architectural Principles in the Age of Humanism* (London, 1962), pt. 3; Guido Piovene, "Trissino e

Palladio nel umanesimo vicentino," *BCISA,* 5 (1963), 13–23; Lionello Puppi, "Un letterato in villa: Giangiorgio Trissino a Cricoli," *Arte veneta,* 25 (1971), 72–91.

8.   Daniele and Marcantonio Barbaro were named as sureties for Palladio's contract to design the façade of San Pietro in Castello for Vincenzo Diedo, Patriarch of Venice (Puppi, *Andrea Palladio,* 322, from A. Magrini, *Andrea Palladio* [1845], 573), the architect's first commission from the Venetian establishment. Douglas Lewis (*in litteris*) pointed out that Giorgio Corner, Francesco Pisani, Alvise Foscari, and Leonardo Mocenigo, for whom Palladio designed villas, would have supported the architect.

9.   Book II, pp. 3f., of the *Quattro libri* emphasizes the adjustment of the design to the rank and wealth of the client, citing Vitruvius's Books I and VI. Commenting in 1556 on the latter book, Daniele Barbaro wrote, "I want . . . to exhort architects and *Proti* not to flatter and give in to their clients, but rather that they tell them the truth, counsel them well and lovingly, and that they think twice before having them spend money, as is said elsewhere, because in that way they truly merit praise and a name worthy of their profession"; as quoted by Elena Bassi, *The Convento della Carità* (Corpus Palladianum, VI; University Park and London, 1976), 36n.

10.   On Alvise Cornaro, see Roberto Cessi, "Alvise Cornaro e la bonifica veneziana del secolo XVI," *Accademia dei Lincei, classe scienze morali* . . ., 6th ser., 13 (1936), 301–323; Giuseppe Fiocco, "Alvise Cornaro e i suoi trattati sull'architettura," *Accademia dei Lincei, Atti,* ser. 8, *Memorie,* 4 (1952), 195–222; Fiocco, *Alvise Cornaro, il suo tempo e le sue opere* (Vicenza, 1965); Emilio Menegazzo, "Ricerche intorno alla vita e all'ambiente del Ruzante e di Alvise Cornaro," *Italia medievale e umanistica,* 7 (1964), 180–220. I have not seen the major study of Falconeto, Gunther Schweikhart's "Studien zum Werk des Giovanni Maria Falconetto," *Bollettino del Museo Civico di Padova,* 57 (1968), 17ff.

11.   Douglas Lewis (*in litteris*) takes vigorous issue with the view expressed here, pointing out that Venetian patricians had had vast land holdings—in the case of the Cornaro family reaching back to 1175—and had always regarded them as worthy of close attention and as a protection against misfortune in trade. My view, echoing that of the economic historians cited in n. 12, is admittedly the fashionable one and may be overturned as more

evidence is published; for now, I believe that the literary, economic, and architectural evidence supports the thesis that there was a substantial change during the second quarter of the century of both attitude and practice on the part of wealthy Venetians and Venetans, which in many cases made agriculture and reclamation their primary occupation and source of income.

12. On the widespread shift of Venetian wealth from trade to agriculture in the sixteenth century and its economic and political implications, see: Daniele Beltrami, *Saggio di storia dell'agricoltura nella repubblica di Venezia durante l'età moderna* (Venice and Rome, 1955); Fernand Braudel, "La vita economica di Venezia nel secolo XVI," *La civiltà veneziana del Rinascimento* (Florence, 1958), 81ff.; Ventura, *Nobiltà e popolo;* S. J. Woolf, "Venice and the Terraferma: Problems of the Change from Commercial to Landed Activities," in Brian Pullan, ed., *Crisis and Change in the Venetian Economy of the 16th and 17th Centuries* (London, 1968), 172ff. (first published 1962); Brian Pullan, "The Occupations and Investments of the Venetian Nobility in the Middle and Late Sixteenth Century," in ibid., 379ff.; Angelo Ventura, "Considerazioni sull'agricoltura veneta, sulla accumulazione originaria del capitale nei secoli XVI e XVII," *Studi storici,* 9 (1968), 674–722; Ugo Tucci, "The Psychology of the Venetian Merchant in the Sixteenth Century," in Hale, ed., *Renaissance Venice,* 346ff.

13. Priuli, *Diarii,* as quoted by Alberto Tenenti, "The Sense of Space and Time in the Venetian World," in Hale, ed., *Renaissance Venice,* 11 (an important article for understanding Venetian state policy at this time).

14. Tucci, "The Psychology of the Venetian Merchant," 356, cites lists of shipowners at three stages in the sixteenth century that show a drop in the proportion of vessels owned by noblemen from 73 percent to 11 percent. He suggests that the cutthroat competition did not appeal to aristocrats who were accustomed to genteel trading. Woolf ("Venice and the Terraferma," 187ff.), however, warns against the common conclusion that a decline in the number of traders is matched by an increase in the number of farmers; a small group of Venetian patricians and citizens may have done the bulk of land acquisition and reclamation.

15. See Bernhard Rupprecht, "Villa: zur Geschichte eines Ideals," in *Probleme der Kunstwissenschaft* (Berlin, 1966), 2:210–250, and Bentmann and Müller, *Die Villa,* passim.

16. *I dieci libri dell'architettura di M. Vitruvio tradotti e commentati da Mons. Daniele Barbaro* (Venice, 1567), 298. The references are to Marcus Porcius Cato, *De agricultura* (third and second centuries BC); Marcus Terentius Varro, *Res rusticae* (first century BC); Lucius Junius Moderatus Columella, *Rei rusticae* (first century CE); Rutilius Taurus Aemilianus Palladius, *Opus agriculturae* (fourth century CE?).

17. As quoted by Ventura, in *BCISA* 11 (1969), 66.

18. The arrangement between landholders and farm workers had not become standardized. Some workers were salaried (*boaria*) and worked under a bailiff (*gastaldo*), some rented land (*fittavoli*), and some shared evenly with the landlord what they produced in lieu of rent (*mezzadria*). See ibid., 68ff.

19. "Ho acquistato la roba, senza la quale nacqui, se ben gli miei furono richissimi, e l'ho acquistata con il migliore mezzo e il più lodevole di ogni altro, che è il mezzo della santa agricoltura; e non con mezzo di armi e sforzi, e danni d'altrui, ne con il mezzo di passare i mari con infiniti pericoli dalla vita, ovvero con altri mezzi pieni di contrarii . . ."; from a letter to Sperone Speroni published in the latter's *Opere* (Venice, 1740), 5:329 as quoted by Giuseppe Fiocco, "La lezione di Alvise Cornaro," *BCISA,* 5 (1963), 33.

20. From *Discorsi intorno alla vita sobria,* 1, in Fiocco, *Alvise Cornaro,* 179. I know of the passage from Muraro, *Civiltà delle ville venete,* n. 53.

21. See above, n. 10.

22. In my earlier writings on the villa style of the mid-sixteenth century—"Sources of the Renaissance Villa" [reprinted in this volume]; *Palladio's Villas* (Locust Valley, N.Y., 1967)—I overstated the novelty of elegant patrician building in the Terraferma, and was heartily criticized for it by several scholars who pointed to widespread villa building and farming enterprise by the upper classes in the fifteenth and early sixteenth centuries. The strongest case was made by Marco Rosci, "Forme e funzioni delle ville venete prepalladiane," *L'arte,* n.s. 2 (1968), 27–54, who pointed to a large and varied body of elegant Venetan portico-villas built before 1550 that apparently were used for both farming and luxurious residence. See also Wolfram Prinz, "Studien zu den Anfängen des oberitalienischen Villenbaues," *Kunst in Hessen und am Mittelrhein,* 13 (1973), 7–45; Kurt Forster, "Back to the Farm," *Architec-*

tura, 1 (1974), 1–12. I have revised recent editions of *Palladio* to account for this material, but I am convinced that the villas of Sansovino, Sanmicheli, and Palladio represent a significant difference in conception from the earlier buildings, that the refinement and splendor of the life for which they were designed makes them the descendants rather of the *castello* villas than of the portico type.

I also have reservations about the significance of the two villas cited by Rosci, in which the basic features of Palladian design allegedly appear prior to Palladio. The Villa Fagiuoli in the Veronese was significantly remodeled after the initial construction in 1504: G. F. Viviani, ed., *La villa nel veronese,* 414; and I suspect that the same was true of the Villa Tiretta in the Trevigiano, initiated in the same period.

23. M. Botter, *La villa Giustinian di Roncade* (Treviso, 1955); Carolyn Kolb Lewis, *The Villa Giustinian at Roncade* (New York, 1977).

24. Lionello Puppi, "La villa Garzoni di Pontecasale di Jacopo Sansovino," *Prospettive,* 24 (1961), 51–62, and *BCISA,* 11 (1969), 95–112; Bernhard Rupprecht, "Die Villa Garzoni des Jacopo Sansovino," *Mitteilungen des Kunsthistorischen Institutes in Florenz,* 11 (1963), 1–32; Tafuri, *Jacopo Sansovino,* 99–131. The literature on Villa Garzoni has referred to the family as noble. Douglas Lewis (*in litteris*) has informed me that he has found documents that securely establish their citizen status.

25. Documents on the reclamation consortium are discussed by Aldo Stella, "La proprietà ecclesiastica nella Repubblica di Venezia dal secolo XVI al XVII," *Nuova rivista storica,* 42 (1958), 66ff.

26. On La Soranza, see: Piero Gazzola, ed., *Michele Sanmicheli,* exhibition catalog (Venice, 1960), 153ff.; Bernhard Rupprecht, "Sansovino's Villa Soranza," *Festschrift Ulrich Middeldorf* (Berlin, 1968), 324–332. See also C. Douglas Lewis, "The Rediscovery of Sanmicheli's Palace for Girolamo Corner at Piombino," *Architectura,* 6 (1976), 29ff. The Villa delle Trombe in Agugliaro (Vicentino) is generally accepted as Sanmicheli's: see Renato Cevese, *Ville della provincia di Vicenza* (Milan, 1971), 2:285ff.

My comments on Sanmicheli represent a revision of my original text prompted by the advice of Dr. Lewis.

27. Dr. Lewis questioned whether the incorporated *barchesse* of Maser and other villas were actually used as Palladio intended, for basic agricultural functions other than storage. I would not be surprised to find that, like the functional innovations of many imaginative architects of later centuries, they were ignored or assigned to other uses.

28. Details of the functions of the villa are given by Palladio in his paragraph of description in the *Quattro libri,* book II, p. 51.

29. My emphasis on Palladio's response to the site and to the patron diverges from Tafuri's interpretation (in his penetrating paper on "Committenza e tipologia") that Palladio developed for the ruling class a villa type that was distinguished more for its common traits than for individual solutions adjusted to the site and to the client. He specifically speaks of a *triangulazione formale* that binds into one concept the network of Palladio's villas throughout the central area of the Veneto (see fig. 15.3).

30. Palladio, *I quattro libri,* II, xv, 61. The significance of the passage was indicated by Tafuri, "Committenza e tipologia," 132.

31. *I quattro libri,* II, iii, 18.

32. The adaptation of the dome as well as the temple front to this design gives sacral overtones to the Villa Rotonda, as pointed out by Wolfgang Lotz, "La Rotonda, edificio civile con cupola," *BCISA* 4 (1962), 69–73, who observed also that, like most centralized domed churches of the Renaissance, the Villa Rotonda is separated from other buildings and is visible from all sides.

33. Venice already held a third of Paduan land in the mid-fifteenth century, according to a complaint of the Council, as a result of expropriation of the holdings of the former *signori,* the Carrara. More expropriation of rebel holdings followed during the war of the League of Cambrai, so that by 1585 Paduans retained only 25 percent of their territory. Woolf, "Venice and the Terraferma," 181ff.; Ventura, *Nobiltà e popolo,* 337. By contrast, Venetians held only 3 percent of Vicentine territory in the mid-sixteenth century. A report on Church holdings in 1584 stated that "Nadal Donado ritornato podestà di Padoa disse che il terzo del territorio padoano è del clero il quale ne cava quattro cento mille ducati all'anno" (cited by Stella, "La proprietà ecclesiastica," 73n.).

34. For bibliography on Cornaro, see n. 10. The Villa dei Vescovi, of about 1535, is unique among the Terraferma villas; a square, two-story structure set on a high podium on the slope of a hill, it resembles Lorenzo de' Medici's Poggio a Caiano in conception.

35. See Giangiorgio Zorzi, *Le opere pubbliche e i palazzi privati di Andrea Palladio* (Venice, 1965), 43–75, esp. 44, and Franco Barbieri, *La Basilica palladiana* (Corpus Palladianum, vol. 11, Vicenza, 1968), esp. 37–43.

36. Earlier uses of the "Palladian" motif, also called the "Serliana" (it appears in Serlio's treatise), are found, e.g., in Bramante's work at Genazzano (Christoph L. Frommel, "Bramante 'Ninfeo' in Genazzano," *Römisches Jahrbuch für Kunstgeschichte*, 12 [1969], 137ff.); at Sant'Eligio degli Orefici in Rome by Raphael and Peruzzi; and at the Sala Regia of the Vatican, by Bramante or an associate under Julius II.

37. As indicated by the erection in 1640 of a second monumental column (supporting a statue of the Redeemer) in imitation of the pair at the Lagoon end of the Piazzetta in Venice. Franco Barbieri, Renato Cevese, and Licisco Magagnato, *Guida di Vicenza* (Vicenza, 1956), 99.

38. The relationship is discussed by Wolfgang Lotz, "Palladio e Sansovino," *BCISA*, 9 (1967), 13–23, and M. Tafuri, "Sansovino 'versus' Palladio," *BCISA*, 15 (1973), 149f. On the Library, see Howard, *Jacopo Sansovino*, 17–28, and Tafuri, *Jacopo Sansovino*, 47–67.

39. See Wolfgang Lotz, "La trasformazione sansoviniana di Piazza San Marco e l'urbanistica del Cinquecento," *BCISA*, 7 (1966), 114–122, where the forum aspect is suggested; Lotz, "Sansovinos Bibliothek von S. Marco und die Stadtbaukunst der Renaissance," *Kunst des Mittelalters in Sachsen: Festschrift für Wolf Schubert* (Weimar, 1967), 336–343.

40. Wolfgang Lotz, "The Roman Legacy in Sansovino's Venetian Buildings," *Journal of the Society of Architectural Historians*, 22 (1963), 3–12; reprinted in his *Studies in Italian Renaissance Architecture* (Cambridge, Mass., 1977), 140–151.

41. *I quattro libri*, Proemio, p. 5. Palladio calls the building the Procuratia, indicating that it was seen more as a government building than as a library.

42. As suggested by Lotz, "Palladio e Sansovino," 13–23; Tafuri, "Sansovino 'versus' Palladio," 149f.

43. See the Howard and Tafuri monographs on Sansovino, passim. On the Ca' di Dio, see Howard, *Jacopo Sansovino*, 112ff.

44. Palazzo Thiene appears in the *Quattro libri* (Book II, pp. 12–15) and is claimed by Palladio, but Inigo Jones was told by Scamozzi when he visited in 1613 that "these designs were of Giulio Ro-

mano, but adjusted by Palladio," a rumor that is supported by the style, particularly of the exterior, which is more highly developed than other Palladio works of this time (Palladio, moreover, was employed by the Thiene in 1542 as a *lapicida*). This opinion, which I suggested in 1966 (*Palladio*, 94), has been supported by Puppi (*Andrea Palladio*, 253), Burns (*Andrea Palladio, 1508–1580*, 36), and Kurt Forster and Richard Tuttle, "Giulio Romano e le prime opere vicentini del Palladio," *BCISA*, 15 (1973), 107–112.

45. Bernhard Rupprecht, "Palladios Projekt für den Palazzo Iseppo Porto in Vicenza," *Mitteilungen des Kunsthistorischen Institutes in Florenz*, 15 (1971), 289–314; Erik Forssman, *Il Palazzo da Porto Festa* (Corpus Palladianum, vol. VIII; Vicenza, 1973).

46. Palazzo Thiene, Palazzo Porto, and the majority of Palladio's palaces and villas remain in an unfinished condition partly because the clients' ambitions outstripped their means and partly because of depressed economic conditions in the 1560s and 1570s, exacerbated by the plague of 1575, which decimated the agricultural work force.

47. Franco Barbieri, *Il Museo Civico di Vicenza*, vol. 1 (Venice, 1962); M. Muraro, "Palazzo Chiericati."

48. Document transcribed in Zorzi, *Opere pubbliche e palazzi privati*, 203.

49. See the works cited below, n. 51.

50. The discovery of the remarkable Grimani palace plan, its attribution to Sanmicheli, and a date of 1528 (the year that Vettor purchased the site of the Ca' del Duca for which it was drawn) is announced by C. Douglas Lewis, "Un disegno autografo del Sanmicheli e la notizia del committente del Sansovino per San Francesco della Vigna," *Bollettino dei Musei Civici Veneziani*, 17 (1972), 7–36.

51. The most revealing discussion is that of Lionello Puppi, *Michele Sanmicheli, architetto da Verona* (Padua, 1971), 44–69; see also Eric Langenskiöld, *Michele Sanmicheli* (Uppsala, 1938), 54ff., 61ff., and Gazzola, ed., *Michele Sanmicheli*, 118ff., 121ff.

52. First by Nikolaus Pevsner, "The Architecture of Mannerism," in Geoffrey Grigson, ed., *The Mint* (London, 1946), 119ff.

53. Gazzola, ed., *Michele Sanmicheli*, 108; Puppi, *Michele Sanmicheli*, 112ff. The date is contested. Gazzola and other scholars have held to a traditional date of around 1530. Lotz, initially in

a review of Langenskiöld's book on Sanmicheli, and more recently in *Architecture in Italy, 1400–1600* (with L. Heydenreich; Harmondsworth and Baltimore, 1974), 217, proposes 1555, and Puppi c. 1551, on grounds of comparison to works immediately preceding those dates.

54. Rodolfo Gallo, "Sanmicheli e Venezia," *Michele Sanmicheli: Studi raccolti dall' Accademia di Agricoltura, Scienze e Lettere di Verona* (Verona, 1960), 112ff. (Palazzo Corner at San Polo), 120ff. (Grimani at San Luca); Puppi, *Michele Sanmicheli,* 109ff., 136ff.

55. Gallo, "Sanmicheli a Venezia," 114ff.; Howard, *Jacopo Sansovino,* 136f. The family, however, claimed that their petition was justified by a debt owed by the government to Caterina Cornaro, exiled queen of Cyprus.

56. Gallo, "Sanmicheli a Venezia," 134–136, 149; Puppi, *Michele Sanmicheli,* 130f., and bibliography in n. 333, and (Palladio's rejected proposal) *Andrea Palladio,* 302f.

57. On the Procurators as patrons, see Howard, *Jacopo Sansovino,* 8ff.

58. According to Howard (47ff.), the commission was troubled by interference from the Senate and the Council of Ten. The nominal clients were the Proveditori sopra la Fabrica del Ponte del Rialto. The Ten refused to vote Sansovino permission or salary to execute the building for which he had provided a model.

59. Ibid., 112ff.

60. For the Carità, see Bassi, *Il Convento della Carità,* ch. 1, and for San Pietro in Castello, Puppi, *Andrea Palladio,* 321–323. The cloister was commissioned in 1555 and the façade in 1558 by Vincenzo Diedo, Patriarch of Venice. The façade was executed in part or wholly by Francesco Smeraldi in 1594–96, who seems to have altered or replaced the original design to conform to the solution of Palladio's Redentore façade of 1576. For the role of the Barbaro brothers, see above, n. 8.

61. As observed by Howard, *Jacopo Sansovino,* 72.

62. The data on the patronage of San Francesco is from the study of Lewis, "Un disegno autografo," 25ff., which apparently was not available to Dr. Howard when she wrote her correct but less complete account.

Vettor and Marin Grimani were awarded rights to the façade as commissioners of the will of their uncle, Cardinal Domenico; I am not sure why this absolved them from the obligation to pay. The award was made by the monastic chief of the works, Zuanne Barbaro, an uncle of the brothers who patronized Palladio and supported his first commission for a church façade in Venice.

63. See Gino Damerini, *L'isola e il cenobio di S. Giorgio Maggiore* (Venice, 1956); Wladimir Timofiewitsch, *Die sakrale Architektur Palladios* (Munich, 1968), ch. 1; Puppi, *Andrea Palladio,* 362–369.

64. In 1551, for example, the monks of San Giorgio bought six hundred *campi* at once in the Padovano (Stella, "Proprietà ecclesiastica," 68). Stella estimates the price of a *campo* at this time as being thirty ducats.

65. The question was raised by Timofiewitsch (*Die sakrale Architektur Palladios,* 34), who reproduced (his fig. 2) a detail from a late sixteenth-century group portrait of the school of Tintoretto showing only the upper portion of the façade behind a row of two-story structures. Palladio probably would have wanted an unimpeded view of his façade; he wrote in 1570 (*I quattro libri,* IV, i, p. 5): "The façades of temples are to be made looking toward the most important part of the city so that Religion may seem to be placed as a custodian and protector of the Citizens." The façade shown in the painting, still without its stone veneer, has a rose window, as planned by Palladio (see Christian Isermeyer, "La concezione degli edifici sacri palladiani," *BCISA,* 14 [1972], 105–133, and my comments in "Palladio e lo sviluppo della concezione della chiesa a Venezia," *BCISA,* 19 [1977], 12). In addition, Frommel ("Palladio e la chiesa di S. Pietro a Roma," *BCISA,* 19 [1977], 107–123) proposes that it was to have been completed with a freestanding porch on four columns. The existing façade, built in 1597–1610, therefore differs significantly from what Palladio intended, though said to be "in tutto et per tutto conforme al modello fatto."

66. The connection is suggested in Timofiewitsch, *Die sakrale Architektur Palladios,* 34ff. See G. Alvarez in G. Fiocco et al., *La Basilica di Santa Giustina* (Castelfranco Veneto, 1970), 133ff.

67. Interpretation of Palladio's churches in the light of liturgical innovations has begun only recently. See Christian Isermeyer, "Le chiese del Palladio in rapporto al culto," *BCISA,* 10 (1968), 42–58; Isermeyer, "La concezione degli edifici sacri palladiani." References to Palladio in my paper "Il contributo dell'Alessi alla tipologia della chiesa longitudinale," in *Galeazzo Alessi e l'architettura del Cinquecento* (Genoa, 1975), 461–466, will be revised in forthcoming papers to take greater account of liturgical reform in the century prior to the Counter-Reformation.

68. Staale Sinding-Larsen, "Palladio's Redentore: A Compromise in Composition," *Art Bulletin*, 47 (1963), 419–437; Wladimir Timofiewitsch, *La chiesa del Rendentore* (Corpus Palladianum, vol. 3; Vicenza, 1968).

Palladio's letter about the design written to Giulio Capra refers to the different demands of the Republic and the monks. (Giovanni Bottari, *Raccolta di lettere* [Milan, 1822], 1:560.)

69. According to the document of February 9, orders were given "che [i Proveditori] debanno far principiar essa chiesa in forma quadrangular, siccome meglio parerà alla maggior parte del Collegio nostro con intervento e ballottation di detti Proveditori." Palladio's patron Marcantonio Barbaro, however, with a number of other Terraferma officials, moved "che dove dice sia fatta la chiesa in forma quadrangulare, sia detto sia fatto in forma rotonda." A compromise was proposed by Zorzi Contarini, another Terraferma official, that models be made of both schemes so the Council could compare them. The final vote was 19 to 6 in favor of the quadrangular form. See G. G. Zorzi, *Le chiese i ponti di Andrea Palladio* (Vicenza, 1966), p. 133, doc. 7, from the Senato Terra archive, vol. 51, p. 155; see also Timofiewitsch, *Die sakrale Architektur Palladios,* 67ff.

70. On the occasion of the first procession of the Senate to the site on July 20, 1577, when the foundations were complete, an altar was set up on a high podium and, facing it, "un' luogo in forma di Teatro," with a throne for the doge and banks of benches for the "ser.ma Signoria et altri Senatori"; Zorzi, *Le chiese e i ponti di Andrea Palladio*, p. 135, doc. 15.

Postscript

This paper is an example of a kind of contextual approach that has characterized the study of Venetian Renaissance architecture by scholars on both sides of the Atlantic since the early '60s. Its representation of the political, economic, and social forces that motivated the evolution of design in the early sixteenth century remains valid in general, though many studies of particularly high caliber have appeared in the past decade that refine and fill out the account more completely.

I want to call attention, however, to one work, Tafuri's *Venezia e il Rinascimento,* which has injected a startling hypothesis into discussions of the subject. Tafuri examines the motives and ideologies of Venetian patrician patrons in the sixteenth century. He poses the paradox that the political and religious liberals sided with traditional, understated native Venetian architectural styles since they symbolized opposition to the heavy hand of papal Rome, while the conservatives were proponents of the modern style—imported from Rome by Sansovino and Sanmicheli—because they were pro-Roman and revered the humanist tradition. The first group, whose members were primarily *Giovani*—members of families who had gained patrician status only in the later Middle Ages—gained the upper hand only after 1582–83, at a time when, for economic reasons, building activity slowed down.

Michelangelo Muraro's studies of Palladio's patrons, the Repeta of Campiglia, have focused attention on the fact that the purchase of feudal fiefs by non-nobles could result in the transfer of the aristocratic privileges and title as well as of the land, and that the authority to authorize such transfers had been vested by the Holy Roman Emperor in the Doge of Venice—who was not himself an imperial vassal. This added the attraction of social advancement to that of economic investment in agriculture.

My book *The Villa* contains a chapter "The Image of Country Life in Sixteenth-Century Villa Books" relevant to this theme.

Ackerman, James S. *The Villa: Form and Ideology of Country Houses.* (Princeton and London, 1990), esp. 108–133.

Atti del Convegno "Venezia e la Terraferma attraverso le Relazioni dei Rettori" (1980) (Milan, 1981), esp. 509–530 ("Possesso fondario e agricolturale nelle relazioni dei rettori veneziani in terraferma").

Barbieri, F. "Giangiorgio Trissino e Andrea Palladio," *Convegno di studi su Giangiorgio Trissino* (Vicenza, 1980).

Cevese, R., and A. Chastel, eds. *Andrea Palladio: Nuovi contributi* (Milan, 1990).

Cevese, R., et al., eds. *L'architettura militare veneta del Cinquecento* (Milan, 1988).

Finlay, R. *Politics in Renaissance Venice* (New Brunswick, 1980).

Foscari, A., and M. Tafuri. *L'armonia e i conflitti* (Turin, 1983).

Lewis, D. "Patterns of Preference: Patronage of Sixteenth Century Architecture by the Venetian Patriciate," in G. F. Lytle and S. Orgel, eds., *Patronage in the Renaissance* (Princeton, 1981), 354–378.

Lieberman, Ralph. "Venetian Church Architecture around 1500," *Bollettino del Centro Internazionale di Studi di Architettura,* 19 (1977), 35–48.

Marini, P., ed. *Palladio e Verona* (Verona, 1980).

Muraro, Michelangelo. "Feudo e ville venete," *Bollettino del Centro Internazionale di Studi di Architettura,* 20 (1978), 203–223.

Muraro, Michelangelo. "La villa palladiana dei Repeta a Campiglia dei Berici con documenti sulla persistenza del feudalesimo nel Veneto," *Campiglia dei Berici: storia di un paese veneto* (Campiglia, 1980).

Muraro, Michelangelo. *Civiltà delle ville venete* (Udine, 1986).

Puppi, Lionello. "Un letterato in villa: Giangiorgio Trissino a Cricoli," *Arte veneta,* 25 (1971), 72–91.

Puppi, Lionello, ed. *Alvise Cornaro e il suo tempo* (Padua, 1980).

Puppi, Lionello, ed. *Architettura e utopia nella Venezia del Cinquecento* (Milan, 1980).

Puppi, Lionello. "Venezia; architettura, città e territorio fra la fine del '400 e l'avvio del '500," *Florence and Venice: Comparisons and Relations, II, Cinquecento* (Florence, 1980), 341–355.

Tafuri, M. "Commitenza e tipologia delle ville palladiane," *Bollettino del Centro Internazionale di Studi di Architettura*, 11 (1969), 120–169.

Tafuri, M., ed. *Renovatio Urbis: Venezia dell'età di Andrea Gritti (1523–1538)* (Rome, 1984), esp. 9–55, M. Tafuri, "Renovatio urbis venetiarum: Il problema storico."

Tafuri, M. "'Pietas' repubblicano, neobizantinismo e umanesimo: Giorgio Spavento e Tullio Lombardo nella chiesa di S. Salvador," *Ricerche di storia dell'arte,* 19 (1985), 5–20.

Tafuri, M. *Venezia e il Rinascimento* (Turin, 1985). In English as *Venice and the Renaissance,* tr. Jessica Levine (Cambridge, Mass., 1989).

Timofiewitsch, Vladimir. "Bemerkungen zur venezianischen Sakral-architektur der Renaissance," in Klaus Ertz, ed., *Festschrift für Wilhelm Messerer* (Cologne, 1980), 193–203.

16

The Tuscan/Rustic Order:

A Study in the Metaphorical Language of Architecture

Sebastiano Serlio begins his account of the orders with a description of the Tuscan order that associates it with the practice of rustication, implying that the two should be joined because both originated in Tuscany.

Now, in order better to proceed in a logical fashion, I shall give precedence to the solidest and least ornate order, namely the Tuscan, which is the most rustic and the strongest and has less thinness and gracefulness.

The ancients dedicated buildings to the Gods in consideration of their nature, whether it be robust or delicate . . . [here Serlio follows Vitruvius's association of the three canonical orders to the range of godly attributes from masculine/warlike to virginal]. But in these modern times it seems to me proper to proceed otherwise, though not deviating from the Ancients—I mean to say, according to our Christian customs, and I should dedicate as far as possible sacred edifices according to their species to God and to His saints and profane edifices, whether public or private, to men according to their rank and profession.

They say, then, that the Tuscan manner [opera], as I see it, is suitable to fortified places, such as city gates, fortresses, castles, treasuries or where ammunition and artillery are kept, prisons, seaports, and other similar structures used in war. It is indeed true that the rustic manner, namely of varied bonding and stone roughly hewn [abozzata]—and at times interspersed with blocks more delicately worked because of the pleasure sculptors found in it—was sometimes joined by the Ancients to the Doric manner and at times even to Ionic and Corinthian. Nonetheless, because the Tuscan manner is truly the roughest and least ornate of all, it seems to me that the rustic is best suited to it and more in conformity to the Tuscan than to any other. This one can readily see to have been observed by the Tuscans both in their major and principal city, which is Florence, and in their villas, in as many beautiful and rich edifices, made indeed of rustic work, as may be found in all the rest of Christendom—with a mixture, however, of that rusticity with delicacy, which is pleasing to architects. And it is for this reason that I say that such work is more suited to the Tuscan than to the other types. Therefore, assembling some examples from the antique and some others of our own, I shall show in diverse modes of such works how city gates may be made, fortresses and also public and private places, façades, Loggias, Porticoes, Windows, Niches, Bridges, Aqueducts, and other various ornaments that may be useful to the good architect.[1]

The key points in this passage from Sebastiano Serlio's *Fourth Book of Architecture* of 1537 are:

1) He is beginning with the Tuscan order because it is the most rustic and the strongest.

2) The ancients matched the orders expressively to the personality and physique of their gods. In modern times, we should accordingly adapt them, in religious architecture, to our one God and to the saints, and, in domestic architecture, to the status and profession of the patron.

3) Replacing the *ordine toscano* with *opera toscana*, he now stealthily switches from the columnar order to rustication and associates it with military and protective functions. This extraordinary linkage he justifies on two unrelated grounds. The first is iconographic and etymological: the most rustic order is suited to the rusticated treatment of masonry walls and apertures. The second is historical and ethnographic: both are identified with Etruria/Tuscany.

Like every other Renaissance writer and practitioner of architecture, Serlio based his discussion of the ancient orders on Vitruvius's treatise of the first century BC. Vitruvius did not discuss the Tuscan order in his chapters on the three canonical orders of antiquity (Doric, Ionic, and Corinthian), but peripherally, in his description of the Etruscan temple in Book IV, vii.[2] Vitruvius suggested no connection between the order and rustication, since rustication was not employed until after his death. Though Vitruvius incorporated many elements indigenous to the Italian peninsula into his summation of Hellenistic architectural practice, he stopped short of appropriating the Etruscan vocabulary into the canon, probably because the orders were the most inviolable and semantically loaded aspect of the entire architectural repertory.

Table 16.1

Heights of Components of the Tuscan Order

(figures represent fractions of the module of one-column width at its base)

	Vitruvius	Serlio	Barbaro	Palladio	Vignola
Column:					
(incl. base and capital)	7	6	7	7	7
Base	½	½	½	½	½
plinth or socle	¼	¼	¼	¼	¼
torus	} ¼	$\frac{1}{6}$	} ¼	$\frac{3}{16}$	$\frac{5}{24}$
collar		$\frac{1}{12}$		$\frac{1}{16}$	$\frac{1}{24}$
Capital	½	½	½	½	½
abacus		$\frac{1}{6}$	$\frac{1}{6}$	$\frac{1}{6}$	$\frac{1}{6}$
echinus		$\frac{1}{8}$	$\frac{1}{6}$	$\frac{1}{6}$	$\frac{1}{8}$
ring		$\frac{1}{24}$		$\frac{1}{42}$	$\frac{1}{24}$
frieze		$\frac{1}{6}$	$\frac{1}{6}$	$\frac{1}{7}$	$\frac{1}{6}$
astragal		$\frac{1}{18}$		$\frac{1}{21}$	$\frac{1}{24}$
necking		$\frac{1}{36}$		$\frac{1}{40}$	$\frac{1}{48}$
Architrave		½		$\frac{7}{12}$	$\frac{5}{12}$
fascia		$\frac{1}{12}$		$\frac{1}{12}$	$\frac{1}{12}$
frieze	width of cap. at neck	½		$\frac{13}{30}$	$\frac{7}{12}$
cavetto				$\frac{3}{20}$	
ovolo		$\frac{1}{8}$		$\frac{3}{20}$	$\frac{1}{6}$
corona		¼		$\frac{1}{6}$	¼
cyma		$\frac{1}{8}$		$\frac{1}{6}$	$\frac{1}{16} + \frac{1}{8}$

The Vitruvian description of the Tuscan order is much less specific than that of the canonical orders. It gives only a few indications of the modular proportions of the base and the overall height of the column and of the capital (table 16.1). The only specific clues to the appearance of the column are the statements that the plinth is circular (on the other orders it is square) and that the base moldings are limited to a single torus and a collar. The nature of the capital and of the entablature is not divulged.

The Tuscan order was, so far as I know, forgotten by Roman architects of the late imperial period and throughout the Middle Ages. With the "rediscovery" of Vitruvius in the fifteenth century there came a renewed interest in the orders as the kernel of antique architectural design. Alberti, in his *De re aedificatoria* composed in the years just prior to 1452, followed the basic outlines of the Vitruvian system, but made adjustments at will. For example, his Doric column has a base with a high plinth and two torus moldings, though Vitruvius, following Greek practice, makes no reference to a base for that order.[3] Alberti obviously found Vitruvius's text on the Tuscan order incomprehensible. He did not mention it in discussing the plan of temples *Etruscorum more*.[4] He does describe an "Italic" capital but it is unequivocally that which later writers came to call Composite.[5] Probably he made a connection between the failure of Vitruvius to mention the Composite order, which he knew to be widely used by the Romans, and the fact that Vitruvius's fourth order was "Tuscan."

Alberti, however, grasped one feature of the Tuscan order from his manuscript of Vitruvius: its circular plinth. But that did not solve the problem, because he admitted: "The Etruscans are said to have used a round rather than a square plinth. I have never found that sort of base in ancient buildings."[6] That he refers to one type of non-canonical usage as "Italic" and another as "Etruscan" indicates his puzzlement. To further complicate the interpretation, he says that the Doric order had been in use "apud vetustissimos Etruscos."[7]

Alberti's fifteenth-century successors did not acknowledge this innovation: Filarete spoke of only three orders[8] as did Francesco di Giorgio,[9] and neither of them had a clear idea of how they should be designed.

No Renaissance theorist before Serlio was prepared to say much about the Tuscan order, though its existence was known from the many manuscripts and editions of Vitruvius, and some commentary and efforts to depict the order were unavoidable. The earliest attempt to visualize the order was made in Fra Giocondo's 1511 edition of Vitruvius, the first to be printed with illustrations—in crudely executed woodcuts (fig. 16.1).[10] Giocondo's text of Vitruvius's passages on the order is almost exactly what is found in modern editions, so the inaccuracy of his illustrations is not due to flaws in the transmission of the source but to Giocondo's failure to locate actual ancient examples of the Tuscan style. That problem even affected Vignola a generation later, who informed his readers that he could not find models of the order in Rome.[11]

The Tuscan base follows Vitruvius in being circular *(habeat spirae earum plinthum ad circinum)*, but is shown, without authorization from ancient remains, as curving in toward the torus. Giocondo's capital (p. 42v: fig. 16.1), with its egg-and-dart echinus, repeats his illustration of the Doric capital (p. 36v), except that it lacks a cyma molding at the top of the abacus.

A quite similar rendition of the Tuscan capital appears in a sketch illustrating the order in the margin of the manuscript translation of the *Ten Books* by Fabio Calvo made for Raphael Sanzio in 1514–15.[12] Raphael made marginal notes throughout the manuscript; possibly he drew the capital as well. He must have known Giocondo while the latter was involved in the planning of St. Peter's prior to his death in July of 1515, so it is likely that they exchanged ideas on ancient architecture, of which both were serious students. In any event, Giocondo is the likely source of this interpretation of the Tuscan capital, and we can assume that Raphael accepted or even contributed to the overly ornamental reconstruction.

A few years later, in the Como Vitruvius commentary of 1521, Cesare Cesariano illustrated the order with a correctly cylindrical plinth, but with the elaborately carved capital proposed by Giocondo and the Raphael manuscript (fig. 16.2).[13]

The 1524 Durantino translation of Vitruvius contains illustrations copied from Fra Giocondo and a text copied from Cesariano, while Giambattista Caporale's translation of 1536 copied the plates from Cesariano.[14]

Serlio's Book IV was the first book of his treatise to be published, in 1537; it contains illustrations of the Tuscan column (figs. 16.3, 16.28): there is a second illustration showing methods for establishing the entasis of the column with and without a pedestal and entablature. Though his version differs in certain respects from the more influential ones of Palladio (figs. 16.8, 16.9) and Vignola (figs. 16.6, 16.7), it is essentially the order that later centuries were to accept as Tuscan. The entablature (fig. 16.4) is divided into two parts, with a simpler left side and a more ornate right side having an architrave with two fascias and more elaborate moldings. These illustrations raise the intriguing question of the sources of Serlio's apparently unprecedented knowledge of the order; but before attempting to trace them it would be profitable to examine the versions offered by his contemporaries.

in abaco,detur,altera echino,tertia hypotrachelio cum apophygi.

a. abacus.
b. echinus
c. hypotra-
chelium cum
apophygi

d. ima craffi
tudo colūnæ

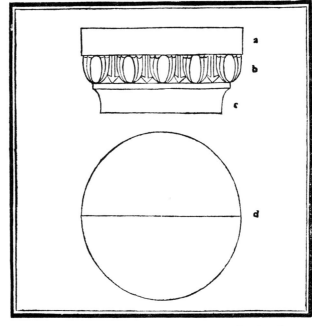

Supra columnas trabes compaétiles imponantur,vti fint altitudinis modu
lis iis,qui a magnitudine operis poftulabútur,Eæq; trabes compaétiles po/
nátur , vt tantam habeant craffitudinem,quanta fummæ colūnæ erit hypo
trachelium,& ita fint cópaétæ fubfcudibus & fecuriclis,vt cópaétura duo/
rum digitorum habeat laxationem,Cum enim inter fe tangunt & non fpi/
ramentum & perflatum venti recipiūt,concalefaciunt, & celeriter & putre
fcunt,Supra trabes & fupra parietes traieéturæ mutilorum parte quarta al/
titudinis columnæ proiiciantur,Item in eorum frontibus antepagmenta fi
gantur,fupraq; ea tympanum faftigii exftruétura feu de materia colloce//
tur,Supraq; id faftigium columen, canterii,templa ita funt collocanda, vt
ftillicidium teéti abfoluti tertiario refpondeat,Fiunt autem ædes rotundæ,
e quibus aliæ monopteræ fine cella columnatæ conftituuntur,aliæ peripte/
ræ dicuntur,Quæ fine cella fiunt,tribunal habent & afcéfum ex fuæ diame/
tri tertia parte,infuper ftylobata columnæ conftituantur tam altæ , quanta
ab extremis ftylobatarum parietibus é diametros,craffæ altitudinis fuæ cū
capitulis & fpiris decumæ partis,Epiftilium altum columnæ craffitudinis
dimidia partæ,Zophorus & reliqua quæ infuper imponuntur,ita vti in ter
tio volumine de fymmetriis fcripfi.

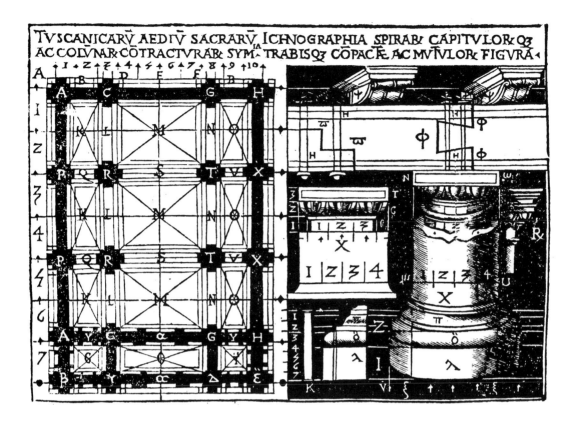

16.1   Fra Giocondo, Tuscan capital. From 1511
Vitruvius edition.

16.2   Cesare Cesariano, Tuscan temple and order.
From 1521 Vitruvius commentary.

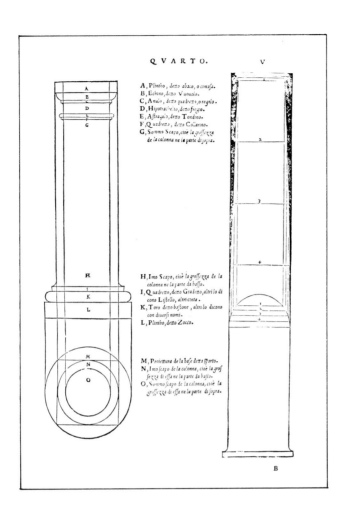

QVARTO. V

A, Plintho, detto abaco, o cimasa.
B, Echino, detto Vuouolo.
C, Anulo, detto quadretto, o regolo.
D, Hipotrachelio, detto fregio.
E, Astragalo, detto Tondino.
F, Quadretto, detto Collarino.
G, Sommo Scapo, cioè la grossezza
   de la colonna ne la parte di sopra.

H, Imo Scapo, cioè la grossezza de la
   colonna ne la parte da basso.
I, Quadretto, detto Gradetto, altri lo di
   cono Listello, altri cinta.
K, Toro detto bastone, altri lo dicono
   con diversi nomi.
L, Plintho, detto Zocco.

M, Proiettura de la base detta sporto.
N, Imoscapo de la colonna, cioè la gros
   sezza di essa ne la parte da basso.
O, Sommoscapo de la colonna, cioè la
   grossezza di essa ne la parte di sopra.

B

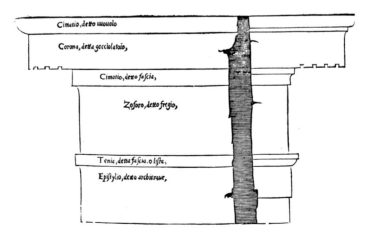

Cimatio, detto uuouolo.
Corona, detta gocciolatoio,
Cimatio, detto fascia,
Zoforo, detto fregio,
Tenia, detta fascia, o lista,
Epistylio, detto architrave,

16.3 *Sebastiano Serlio, Tuscan column. From* Regole generali di architettura, *1537.*

16.4 *Sebastiano Serlio, two versions of the Tuscan entablature. From* Regole generali di architettura, *1537.*

16.5 *Andrea Palladio?, Tuscan base and capital. From Daniele Barbaro's Vitruvius commentary of 1556.*

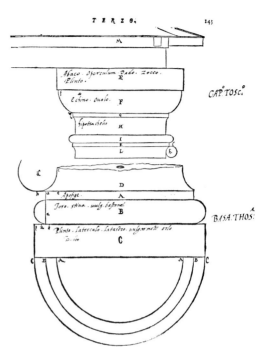

The next significant work following Serlio's came from the ambience in which he had moved during his years in Venice[15]—the Vitruvius commentary of the Venetian patrician Daniele Barbaro, for whom Palladio built the villa at Maser.[16] Palladio also aided his patron by providing the major illustrations for the commentary, so it seems likely that the presentation of the Tuscan order in this work represents Palladio's interpretation of it 16 years before he published his own architectural treatise in 1570. The illustration (fig. 16.5) closely follows that of Serlio except with respect to the entablature, which is greatly simplified, having only a quite plain architrave topped by a narrow band, essentially an eave, with joist ends projecting: this conforms better to Vitruvius's *trabes compactiles*—beams bolted or mortised together and not an entablature at all.

Between Barbaro's commentary and Palladio's *Quattro libri dell'architettura* there appeared Vignola's enormously influential thin volume on the orders, with engravings that set the standard for later generations (figs. 16.6, 16.7).[17] These meticu-

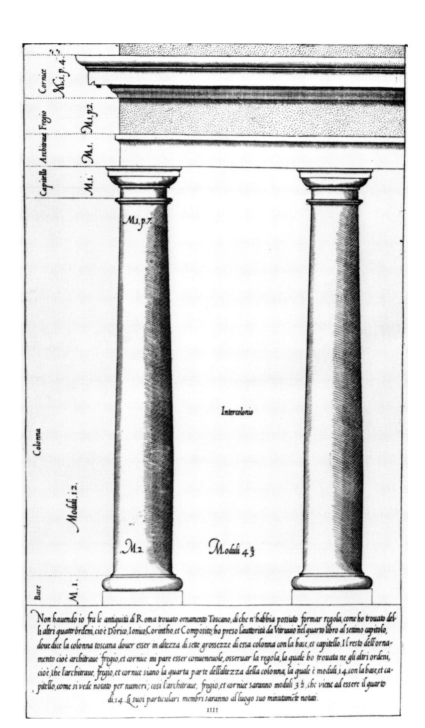

16.6   *Giacomo Barozzi da Vignola, Tuscan order.*

From La regola delli cinque ordini di architettura,

1562.

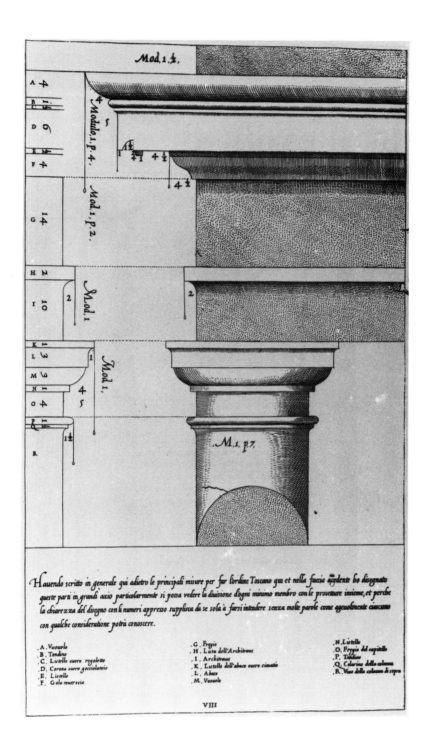

Haueñdo scritto in generale qui adietro le principali misure per far l'ordine Toscano qui et nella faccia aññedente ho disegnato queste parti in grandi accio particolarmente si possa vedere la diuisione dogni minimo membro con le proietture insieme, et perche la chiarezza del disegno con li numeri appresso supplica da se sola à farsi intendere senza molte parole come agenolmente ciascuno con qualche consideratione potrà conoscere.

.A . Vuouolo
.B . Tondino
.C . Listello ouero regoletto
.D . Corona ouero gocciolatoio
.E . Listello
.F . Gola rouerscia

.G . Fregio
.H . Luta dell'Architraue
.I . Architraue
.K . Listello dell'abaco ouero cimabò
.L . Abaco
.M . Vuouolo

.N . Listello
.O . Fregio del capitello
.P . Tondino
.Q . Colarino della colonna
.R . Viue della colonna di sopra

VIII

16.7 *Giacomo Barozzi da Vignola, Tuscan capital and entablature.* From La regola delli cinque ordini di architettura, *1562.*

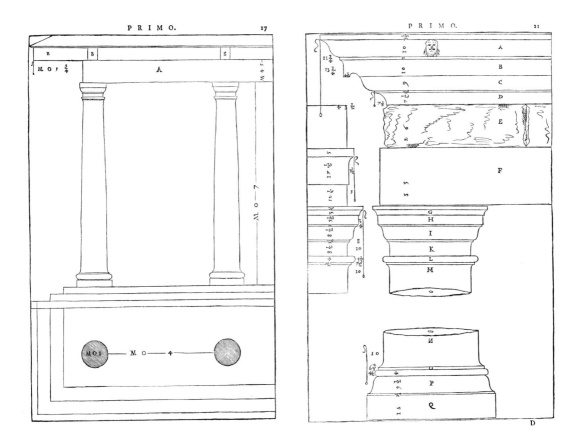

16.8   *Andrea Palladio, Tuscan order. From* I quattro
libri dell'architettura, *1570.*

16.9   *Andrea Palladio, details of the Tuscan order.*
From I quattro libri dell'architettura, *1570.*

lous, clear, and inimitable plates contain a short text (since it had to be engraved by hand) which, apart from explaining the measurements of the Tuscan order, gives only the information already cited, that Vignola had seen no examples of it in Rome.

Palladio's *Four Books of Architecture* was published in 1570, eight years after Vignola's work on the orders, and represents 30 years of intensive study of the antiquities of Rome and of northern Italy.[18] The orders are discussed in the first Book, and the Tuscan is accorded a chapter and four woodcuts of its own (XIII, 15–21). "The Tuscan order," Palladio says, "according to Vitruvius, and as seen in practice, is the barest and simplest of all the architectural orders since it retains its original antique character, and lacks all those ornaments that render the others worthy of attention and beautiful. It originated in Tuscany, the noblest part of Italy, whence it acquired its name." The expressive and symbolic role of the order is much more limited than Serlio suggested: "The Tuscan, being rough, is rarely used above ground except in one-story buildings like villa barns or in huge structures like Amphitheaters and the like which, having many orders, can take this one in place of the Doric, under the Ionic." Palladio's first illustration (fig. 16.8) is a reconstruction of the elevation of the Etruscan temple that presents, in different form, the same information as the illustration in Barbaro's Vitruvius commentary (fig. 16.5), except that the architrave is higher. There are two more detailed cuts of the base, capital, and entablature; one, the more archaeological, being also close to Barbaro, though with a more elegant carved stone entablature. The other (fig. 16.9) is an elegant modern version, the base of which replaces the traditional thick torus with a cyma topped by a narrow torus. A striking feature of the entablature is the rusticated stone frieze resting upon an absolutely plain architrave that reflects the primitive structural origins of this element.[19]

Palladio indicates the source of his knowledge of the order: "some antique edifices may be seen that may be said to be made in this order: because they have in part the same measurements, namely the Arena of Verona, the Arena and Theater of Pola, and many others: from which I have taken the templates for the Base, the capital, the frieze, and the cornice found in the last plate of this chapter . . ." (fig. 16.9).[20]

Establishing a Canon for the Tuscan Order

The main purpose of the treatment of the order in the four publications cited above was to instruct the reader on how to determine the proportions of its constituent parts, primarily for application in building design. The systems proposed by each author and by Vitruvius appear in table 16.1, expressed in fractions of the module: the width of the column at its base.[21] The most striking feature of the table is the limited extent of the information provided by Vitruvius; obviously the authors had to get most of their calculations from examining surviving ancient examples of the order. This partly explains why the figures of all the writers correspond where Vitruvius was the source, and differ where he was silent: the figures either were taken from different monuments or represent differing degrees of accuracy in measuring the same monuments. The duodecimal system underlies all the numbers, a natural result of measurement based on the foot. Vignola subdivided the basic module into 12 "parts" (Serlio called such subdivisions *oncie*—inches); Palladio into 60 "minutes."[22] Contrary to what we might expect given his modern reputation as the greatest master of proportion, Palladio's measurements do not all observe the duodecimal framework: he allows multiples of 7 and extremely awkward figures such as the frieze of 13/30 of a module (26 minutes: cf. fig. 16.9).

The contrast between the simplicity of Vignola's figures and the complexity of Palladio's is due to differences of purpose. Vignola's intention was to assimilate the conflicting evidence from ancient structures into a system calculated to simplify the design process and execution on the site, while Palladio valued the accurate imitation of the ancient source: witness the latter's claim, quoted above, to have taken his profiles from ancient monuments. Palladio's archaeological passion may also explain his choice of the 60-minute module, as better adapted to recording the small differences found in the ancient models—the use of minutes was standard procedure during the Renaissance. Though the proportional differences between the orders of the two architects would be imperceptible in an executed building, they illustrate a significant theoretical contrast. Palladio was heir to that aspect of the classical theory of imitation which obliged the artist to adhere closely to the model; Vignola moved closer to a Mannerist-Platonic approach to imitation which gave precedent to the *concetto* in the artist's mind, whereby many single experiences of the objective world are subsumed into an original *invenzione*. The difference is apparent in the style of their buildings: Palladio's are more "naturalistically" antique. Though the books of both authors enjoyed phenomenal success, Vignola's interpretation of the orders prevailed, not only because it was easier to use, but also because later architects rarely were as devoted as Palladio to archaeological precision.

Judging from the evidence of their drawings as well as from their writings, sixteenth-century architects found few examples of the Tuscan order among the ruins. Palladio's statement that he took the details of his Tuscan plates from the amphitheaters of Pola and Verona and the theater at Pola suggests that, like Vignola, he had not found models in Rome. Serlio was the first to publicize these northern monuments; his attention may have been drawn to Verona by his master Baldassarre Peruzzi (1481–1536), who made drawings of the amphitheater (fig. 16.21).[23] In his Book III, each is assigned a plate copied, as he admits, from the drawings of an anonymous architect who used the Veronese foot.[24] Palladio's early drawings of Pola antiquities appear to be copies, too, though a later drawing with detailed measurements was probably executed on the site.[25] Both architects appear to have based their reconstructions of the order on northern monuments—even ones they had not measured—because they were the only ones they knew that provided models. They were not optimal examples because, being arcuated buildings, they did not offer models of the freestanding column and temple-like entablature and cornice that I have been discussing.

Where else can Tuscan columns and entablatures have been seen by Serlio and his younger contemporaries? I know of only two other drawings showing an order in which the Tuscan is combined with rustication—both being from models in Rome that have not been located in modern topographical studies. One, by an anonymous draftsman working in Rome around 1530, comes from an unpublished sketchbook.[26] It is identified "dello ospitio di costantino ī Roma" and shows a single portal (fig. 16.10) framed by a Tuscan pilaster bound to the wall by rough *bozze*. The lower part of the frieze is rusticated, the upper smooth—a unique treatment in Roman architecture. Perhaps this otherwise unknown monument inspired the rusticated frieze in Palladio's representation of the order. The meticulous measurements of the entablature make it unlikely that this drawing is imaginary.

A drawing by Sallustio Peruzzi labeled "Aqueductus ī Viridario bulbalino del aqua Virgine" does not correspond to any other representations of that aqueduct.[27] It shows, in plan, an absidal nymphaeum or grotto with niches, similar to that of Bramante in the Cortile del Belvedere; in elevation this is framed by two rusticated Tuscan columns flanking niches on either side; the arch is also rusticated. The style is that of the Claudian arches that support the Aqua Virgo.

Equivocal evidence of the unrusticated Tuscan order survived in the remains of a temple identified in a key drawing, again by Baldassarre Peruzzi, as being "in carcer tulliano" (Uffizi, A536: fig. 16.11).[28] This was the sixteenth-century designation of the site of the three temples in the Roman Forum Holitorium alongside the Theater of Marcellus, the central one of which had been remade into the church of San Nicola in Carcere.[29]

al b) ospitio d costarino Roma

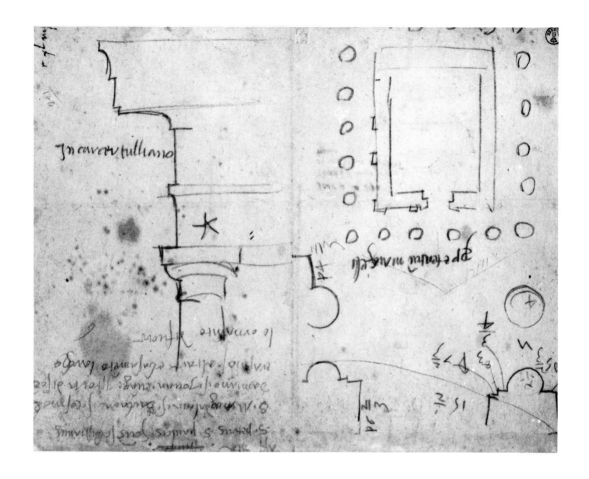

16.10   Anonymous, ca. 1530, "Ospizio di
Costantino" (unidentified Roman monument).
Montreal, Canadian Centre for Achitecture.

16.11   Baldassarre Peruzzi, sketches from the Roman
remains near San Nicola in Carcere and the Theater of
Marcellus, Rome, ca. 1530. Florence, Uffizi, 536A.

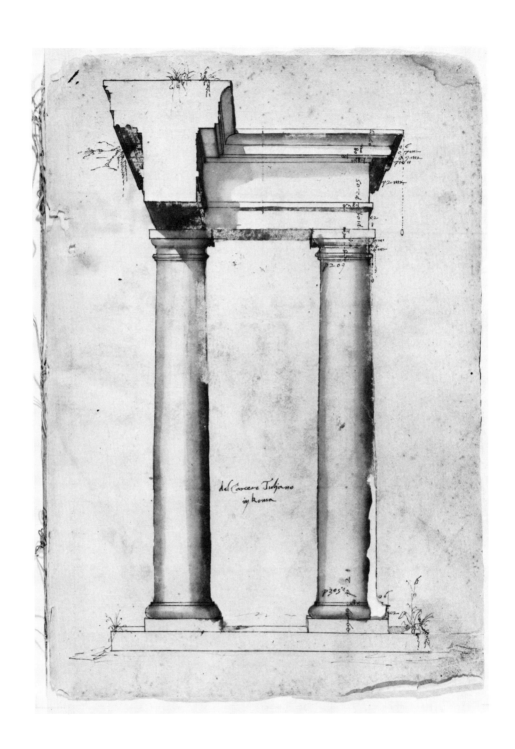

16.12   *Anonymous, ca. 1530, reconstruction of the
order of the early temple under S. Nicola in Carcere,
Rome. Montreal, Canadian Centre for Architecture.*

Though the temple was Doric, with baseless columns, Peruzzi was not alone in interpreting it as Tuscan; the columns must have been partly interred in his time and the anonymous author of fig. 16.12, in a drawing of two columns and the entablature labeled "del carcere Tuljano in Roma," also shows the Tuscan base, though Serlio correctly represents it as Doric.[30] But the confusion was not yet settled at this point: Giovanni Battista da Sangallo drew plans of the three temples, perhaps in the 1540s, and labeled the southernmost "lo toscano acanto asanto nicola incharcere le colonne sonalte." The entablature he identifies: "cornicone dello edifitio do toscano."[31] The cancellation of the first two letters of what obviously was to be the word "dorico" indicates that even architects familiar with the ancient remains were, in the absence of thorough excavation, uncertain of the borderline distinguishing the two orders.

Confusion could occur even when characteristic Tuscan bases were discovered. One from a different site appears on Uffizi A1535v, attributed to Fra Giocondo, with the identification "a mōte chavallo nel pallazo Sabini bassa doricha"; two others by the same architect identified as at San Pietro in Vincoli are also labeled Doric.[32] In spite of this statement, Giocondo drew the single-torus profile shown in all illustrations of the Tuscan order.[33]

Vincenzo Scamozzi, Palladio's pupil and an important late Renaissance theorist, compiled a list of ancient uses of the Tuscan/Rustic order. It does not distinguish instances of the column and entablature from the use of rustic masonry, but it includes two important Roman monuments inexplicably overlooked by earlier writers: the columns of Trajan (fig. 16.13) and of Marcus Antonius. What iconographic justification the use of the order for celebratory columns may have had for the Romans is uncertain, and Scamozzi did not speculate on the subject.[34]

The only drawing I know that shows the Tuscan order with the circular plinth mandated by Vitruvius is Palladio's early, carefully executed elevation of the upper terrace wall of the theater at Verona (fig. 16.14), where columns without a proper entablature are engaged to a brick wall with a central niche; this sheet seems to have been executed from studies done on the site.[35] The wall has been excavated in modern times, but the columns are almost completely destroyed.[36]

Obviously, these observations are only a preamble to a serious search for examples of the Tuscan order in Roman architecture, which I hope it will stimulate.

654 - ROMA - LA COLONNA DI TRAIANO

16.13   Rome, Trajan's column.

16.14   *Andrea Palladio, upper terrace of the theater,*
Verona. R.I.B.A., Burlington-Devonshire Collection,
no. X, 13.

The Use of the Tuscan Order in the Renaissance

The Tuscan order was also rarely employed by Renaissance architects before the publication of Serlio's book. Paradoxically, in view of Serlio's association of the order with Florentine rustication, no example of the order that I know of is found in Tuscan fifteenth- or early sixteenth-century architecture. Perhaps the earliest conscious use occurred in the columns of the spiral staircase of the Court of the Belvedere in the Vatican Palace by Bramante, in 1504 or shortly after; Bramante used the staircase as a museum of the orders, starting with Tuscan at ground level and rising through the hierarchy, one order merging imperceptibly into another.[37]

The order appears several times in palaces designed by Raphael and his circle in Rome: in Raphael's own façade of the Palazzo Branconio d'Aquila of 1514–15 (destroyed), the ground-floor order is represented by most contemporary draftsmen as Tuscan. The court piers of the Palazzo Caffarelli-Vidoni by Lorenzetti, of ca. 1524 (fig. 16.15), observe the order, as do those designed by Giulio Romano or another member of Raphael's circle for the Palazzo Alberini-Cicciaporci on the Via de' Banchi, of ca. 1518.[38] Giulio was the chief exploiter of the order prior to Serlio's publication. He used it for the entrance portal of his own house in Rome, of 1523–24 (now known only from drawings: fig. 16.16), fastening down the shafts of the pilasters with rusticated blocks so that only the bases and capitals are visible, and, in a very similar fashion, on the portal and in the court of Palazzo Stati-Maccarani (fig. 16.17; ca. 1520–24).[39]

I do not know of any use of the order in surviving ecclesiastical structures, but the elevation project for the well-known central plan project for the church of San Giovanni de' Fiorentini in Rome of ca. 1518–20 by Antonio da Sangallo the Younger proposes Tuscan for the engaged columns and pilasters of the major and minor orders of the single-story exterior.[40] Ionic and Corinthian are projected for the interior. Antonio's choice probably was prompted by the fact that the church was conceived to celebrate the presence of the Florentine "nation" in Rome.

The one work of the classic period that is entirely Tuscan is the Nymphaeum at Genazzano, an imposing garden structure now in ruins in a small hill town southeast of Palestrina (fig. 16.18). The design was attributed to Bramante by Frommel, who first published the monument, proposing a possible commission from Cardinal Pompeo Colonna and a date of 1508–11. It seems to me too inelegant in detail for the architect of St. Peter's, and more likely to be derived from the conception of the garden loggia of the Villa Madama in Rome (begun 1518–19): a date in the 1520s seems more suitable.[41]

16.15 Rome, Palazzo Caffarelli-Vidoni, court, ca.
1524.

16.16 *Rome, house of Giulio Romano, 1523–24.*
Drawing by Giovannantonio Dosio. Florence, Uffizi,
2691A.

16.17   Rome, Palazzo Stati-Maccarani, portal, by
Giulio Romano, ca. 1520–24.

16.18   Genazzano, Nymphaeum.

16.19   *Vicenza, Palazzo Thiene, atrium, ca. 1549.*

I have not found examples of the Tuscan order in the Renaissance architecture of northern Italy prior to Serlio's publication, but this may be due only to the fact that I have not had a chance to seek them out *in situ* since starting to work on the subject. The earliest case I know of is in the columns of the lateral atria of the Thiene palace in Vicenza, built by Palladio, possibly on the basis of designs by Giulio Romano, in 1549 (fig. 16.19; only one of the two projected atria was built).[42] These have refined bases and capitals and rough-hewn rustic shafts; they obviously derive from the Doric columns in the entranceway to Giulio's Palazzo del Te in Mantua.

The Tuscan order was used increasingly after this time; perhaps its most effective advocate was Vignola, who adopted it in some of his most influential buildings: the façade of the papal Villa Giulia in Rome of 1551, the Palazzo Bocchi in Bologna of 1555 (main portal), the spiral staircases at Villa Giulia (after 1551) and at the Farnese villa in Caprarola, (1565–), and the façade of Sant'Anna dei Palafrenieri in the Vatican, 1565.[43] While many architects after 1550 did not employ the Tuscan order, its use became sufficiently widespread to be no longer of special significance.

The Marriage of the Tuscan to the Rustic "Order"

Serlio, after introducing the union of Vitruvius's Tuscan order and rustication in the passage quoted as the introduction to this study, fills the remainder of chapter V of his fourth book with a variety of rustic apertures: arches, portals, gateways, retaining walls, niches, a pair of mantlepieces (one "delicate" and one *a bozze*), each with an illustration and a text. He concludes with a page showing six ways of carving a rusticated wall (fig. 16.20), from stones *"abozzate grossamente"* to those "worked with more *pulitezza.*" Indeed, his chief concern is with the juxtaposition of roughness and elegance. In an important passage where he repeats the observation that the ancients joined the three canonical orders with rustication as well as the Tuscan, he states:

It would be no error if within one manner one were to make a mixture, representing in this way partly the work of nature and partly the work of artifice: thus columns bound down [fasciate] by rustic stones & also the architrave and frieze interrupted by voussoirs [cf. fig. 16.28] reveal the work of nature, while capitals and the parts of the columns & also the cornice and pediment represent the work of the hand; and this mixture, according to my judgment, greatly pleases the eye and represents in itself great strength.

& in this mixture, Giulio Romano took greater delight than anyone, as Rome testifies in several places, and also Mantua in the very beautiful Palazzo del Te a little way out of town, a true example of the architecture and painting of our time.[44]

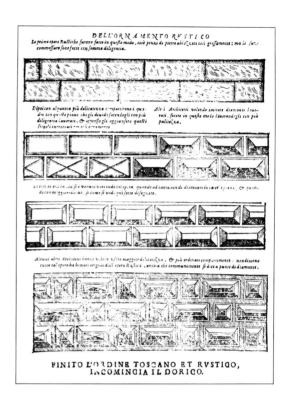

16.20 *Sebastiano Serlio, varieties of rusticated masonry.* From Regole generali di architettura, *1537.*

Serlio's reference to Giulio points to a fact apparent from figure 16.16, that the union of the Tuscan order with rustication already had been consummated in practice long before Serlio's publication—but in the '20s and '30s Giulio was as yet its only vigorous promoter. Serlio's advocacy constituted, one might say, an effort to legitimize Giulio's fantasy.

We have seen that the justification for the marriage in ancient practice was limited. The amphitheaters and theaters of Pola and Verona provided the only well-documented precedents (fig. 16.21). There were amphitheaters elsewhere in which rustication was combined with Tuscan detailing—at Capua, Arles, Nîmes, and no doubt in other sites as well—but these were not known in the centers where the principles of Renaissance architectural practice were being formulated.[45]

Thus, what prompted Serlio to proclaim that the use of the Tuscan order implied rustication was not so much his respect for the precedent of Roman antiquity as his wish to join the language of the ancient Etruscans to that of the modern Tuscans.

16.21 *Baldassarre Peruzzi, Verona amphitheater, ca.*

1530. Florence, Uffizi, 606A.

Façade rustication had been a feature of the earliest surviving civic and private palaces of Tuscany from the mid-thirteenth century, especially in Florence; originally it had served there as a symbol of communal pride and power, and was employed at the Palazzo del Podestà and the Palazzo dei Priori (fig. 16.22). In the fifteenth century it was adopted by the magnates for private palaces in the new Renaissance style, now with that *mistura* of roughness and delicacy to which Serlio referred. The rustic or partly rustic façade was the preferred fashion of Renaissance palace patrons up to the time of the expulsion of the Medici in 1494.[46] Between that time and the preparation of Serlio's book there were too few commissions for public and private palace building to keep the best Tuscan architects from being tempted away to the more vital environments of Rome and Venice. The Tuscan rusticated style expired with the fifteenth century, to return later altered by the experience of early sixteenth-century Rome.[47]

16.22   *Florence, Palazzo Salviati, ca. 1370–80.*

16.23   *Gioia del Colle, Apulia, thirteenth century.*

It is hard to say whether the initial use of rustication in the Tuscan communes of the thirteenth century was inspired more by the fortresses of the Hohenstaufen emperors in southern Italy and in Prato (in Tuscany) or by ancient Roman antecedents. The Tower of the Palazzo dei Priori in Florence and contemporary civic buildings of the mid-1200s in Florence are executed in a masonry style that might have derived from the early thirteenth-century *rocche* of Frederick II at Bari and at Gioia del Colle (fig. 16.23)[48] If so, the technique probably was taken up first by the Ghibelline lords and then adopted by the commune as a sign of its inheritance of the powers of the feudal era.

Rustication *a bozze* became more refined in the course of the fifteenth century and came to express elegance rather than defensive strength, as at the Strozzi Palace in Florence, of the 1480s and 1490s.[49]

The earliest Renaissance palaces often combined or substituted the naturalistic roughness of *bozze* with a plane, usually stuccoed surface imitating ashlar masonry, each fictive block being bordered by a sharply cut channel of a [-shaped profile. The technique was adopted for the *piano nobile* of the Medici Palace (late 1440s) and the entire façade of the Rucellai Palace (ca. 1455).[50] This also is commonly referred to as rustication, though the implications of the present discussion demonstrate how improper such a usage is: not only did the practice—which I prefer to call drafted masonry—not serve as a metaphor of the natural condition of stone (note its absence from fig. 16.20), but its structural and perhaps its historical roots were different. Drafted masonry was, I believe, employed for surface veneers; it would not make sense to use it, as rustication normally was used, for wall-bearing ashlar construction. It was employed already at the Palazzo Davanzati in the later fourteenth century;[51] there is no way of knowing whether Florentine architects adopted it from the only surviving earlier medieval precedent, the castle of Frederick II at nearby Prato, or from the many examples of drafted veneering preserved among the Roman ruins.[52]

It was the study of ruins in Rome in the first quarter of the sixteenth century that led Renaissance architects to a new view of the expressive potentialities of rustication. Not many of the surviving ancient buildings were rusticated, but those that were possessed a grandeur in harmony with the aspirations of the generation of architects that learned the profession in the workshop of St. Peter's. I have found no instances of rustication in Roman architecture that do not appear in the drawings and prints of sixteenth-century architects and print makers—except on buildings that were not yet excavated—and a number of examples recorded in the Renaissance have since been destroyed. The following brief list of the rusticated buildings most often recorded in the visual documents of the time (and consequently all in Rome) is intended only to introduce the study of the reinterpretation of rustication; it is the result of an initial, selective survey of the principal sources and would no doubt be expanded by further research.

Forum of Augustus, exterior rear wall (fig. 16.24). This tall and massive structure at the rear of the Temple of Mars Ultor was the most accessible and best preserved example of an ancient rusticated wall, being in the heart of the medieval city. It offered Renaissance architects not only a model for masonry *a bozze* but of arches with great voussoirs linking into the masonry courses of the kind adopted by Giulio Romano, Serlio, Vignola, and others (fig. 16.16). Renaissance draftsmen rarely identified this

16.24   *Rome, Forum of Augustus, rear of perimeter*
wall.

16.25 *Giovannantonio Dosio, podium of the temple of Claudius on the Celian Hill. Florence, Uffizi, 2518A.*

16.26 *Giuliano da Sangallo, eastern side of the Septizonium, Rome. From Vatican Library, MS. Barb. Lat. 4428.*

structure correctly: their drawings are labeled "foro Transitorio" or "foro di Traiano," though Palladio (*I quattro libri,* I, ix, 13) illustrates as an example of Roman ashlar masonry the wall "ove era la piazza & il Tempio di Augusto."[53]

Temple of Claudius on the Celian Hill, arches of the podium (fig. 16.25). These eight arches, built over linteled apertures of equal height and span, attracted more attention from Renaissance architects than any other ancient rusticated structure. They are the best preserved examples of the extraordinary imagination of Claudius's architect(s) in the use of rustication, and are the earliest surviving instances of the *mistura* of natural blocks with refined treatment of the order recommended by Serlio. The order is baseless; the capitals could be Tuscan or Doric.[54] Renaissance architects almost invariably identified this structure by its location alongside the church of SS. Giovanni e Paolo.

Septizonium, north wall (fig. 16.26). The rustication of this structure, which was destroyed in the later sixteenth century by Sixtus V, was highly refined, with broad planar courses carved between regularly modeled *bozze;* the relative elegance may explain the fact that only two drawings of this façade have survived (one being by Giuliano da Sangallo, a master of the Florentine style which sought similar effects): rougher and less rational treatments like that of the Claudianum were more frequently sought out.[55]

Forum Pacis (identified in the sixteenth century as "SS. Cosma e Damiano") (fig. 16.27). The drawings represent the southern perimeter wall of the temple, later called Forum of Peace, a precinct to the northeast of the Basilica of Maxentius alongside the Forum Romanum that is still little understood by archaeologists. It has a boldly rusticated wall of volcanic blocks and a travertine portal with both a lintel and an arch. The wall was used as a foundation for the medieval church of SS. Cosmas and Damian.[56]

Porta Maggiore (the commonly used name for the Porta Praenestina). This structure, which originally constituted two of the extensive sequences of arches supporting the Aqua Claudia and was remodeled by Aurelius as a gate in the city wall, is another example of the bold rustication of Claudian architecture. Its function as a major city gate assured that nearly every Renaissance architect in the city would be familiar with it.[57]

Arches of the Aqua Virgo. The aqueduct emerged from underground and crossed the Via Nazareno, on heavily rusticated arches, apparently also Claudian. Today only a portion of the attic is visible; in the sixteenth century the arches were exposed.[58]

16.27   *Rome, podium of the Forum Pacis, portal.*

A few other rusticated monuments, mostly outside of Rome, were recorded by sixteenth-century architects, but less frequently than these.[59] Since there is a large corpus of drawings and prints after ancient monuments, the very small number suggests that rustication was exceptional in Roman architecture—an impression confirmed by subsequent archaeological evidence. Thus, while the great Renaissance passion for rustication stirred up by Giulio Romano and Serlio was surely stimulated by ancient buildings—almost exclusively of the early years of the empire—they were eccentric buildings that strained to break the grip of classical rules. It should be no surprise that the second generation of sixteenth-century architects, seeking to establish its own position in an environment dominated by the classicism of its predecessors, should have been attracted to this Roman anticlassicism.

Conclusion

Although Serlio depended primarily on Vitruvius for his description of the orders, his fourth book established for them a new hierarchy, incorporating the Composite (justified by its frequent appearance in surviving antique structures) at the top of the scale, and displacing the Tuscan to the start of the sequence from its peripheral position in Vitruvius as a bit of antiquarian information. The result is a progression of five rather than three orders, arranged in a sequence from the simplest, roughest, and least ornate to the most decorative and complex—endowed with a corresponding expressive range from ruggedness, power, and civic/military solidity to urbanity, elegance, and suitability to the symbolization of the most revered deities (fig. 16.28). The use of orders in buildings had to follow the hierarchical sequence: lower stories were assigned lower orders, etc. That system, which Serlio first presented in print, must have been worked out by Bramante in the first years of the sixteenth century.[60] It became the unshakable canon of the classical tradition. But Serlio, in reviving the Tuscan order, went not only beyond Vitruvius's intention but beyond the classical rules of Bramante and his circle, because he sought not only to revive an antique usage but to bind it to the medieval and quattrocento one of rustication. His strategy was to give the language of architecture roots in the same native soil as the Italian language—that of Etruria/Tuscany. Indeed, the Tuscan/Rustic order was to the classical orders what the vernacular was to the Latin language. In Serlio's time the vernacular was first becoming acceptable as a vehicle for learned discourse. To revive the order of the Etruscans was to honor native

Italians as opposed to Roman immigrants, just as to revive rustication was to refer to a medieval practice of Italian, as opposed to transalpine origin (Gothic architecture had been called the "Maniera tedesca").

The Vitruvian system had evolved in the context of Greek post-and-lintel construction in Greek and Hellenistic architecture; the column and entablature had to carry the structural as well as the symbolic burden of the building. In Roman architecture the wall often became the principal structural element, but it rarely usurped the expressive function of the orders (the widespread use of veneer in any case discouraged expression of the supporting role of the wall), and this partly explains the rarity of rustication in antiquity. Rustication, indeed, emerged in full force only when the orders were abandoned, affirming the wall as the essential element in structure. The medieval and quattrocento rusticated civic and private palaces were quintessential wall structures, inhospitable to ornament; where the orders appeared, as in the Rucellai Palace in Florence, the rustication gave way to drafted masonry.[61]

With the awakening of a renewed interest in the orders in Bramante's circle, rustication had to be tamed. At the entrance to the Court of the Belvedere in the Vatican, the portal of rusticated stone is set into a smoothly finished brick wall. At Bramante's Caprini Palace in Rome and its innumerable imitations the ground floor was rusticated and the *piano nobile* was smooth and had a classical order with engaged columns. Raphael, in the façade of the Palazzo Pandolfini in Florence, eliminated the order on both stories, but restrained the rustication to the entrance portal and the corner quoins. The appearance of vigorously sculpted quoins (here for the first time in palace design?) draws our attention to the role of rustication as an indicator of wall-bearing structure.

Rustication appears in all the classical Renaissance buildings I have cited as a reinforcement of those elements that bear particular stress:[62] the portal, the lower floor, the corner. These are, of course, the elements that had to be made in stone as against brick. This pragmatic and purely architectural use of rustication characterized the classical moment of the first years of the sixteenth century.

Giulio Romano broke out of the confines of classical practice, seeing an opportunity to dramatize the dialectic oppositions in the history of rustication (ancient *vs.* medieval/quattrocento; column *vs.* wall; delicate *vs.* rough) by bringing the polarities together to battle for preeminence. Where Bramante and Raphael had scrupulously kept the orders isolated from the rusticated surface, Giulio caused them to be overrun by rusticated blocks that pin them like prisoners against the wall (figs. 16.16, 16.17),

16.28 *Sebastiano Serlio, the five orders. From* Regole
generali di architettura, *1537.*

setting up a Michelangelesque physical conflict. This conflict dramatizes the anomaly
of Renaissance architecture: its revival of the post-and-lintel vocabulary of antiquity to
articulate wall-bearing structures.

Moving from Rome to Mantua, Giulio, doubtless reflecting on the implications of Claudian architecture (figs. 16.12, 16.25), carried his conception a step further
by transforming the sharply chiseled *bozze* of his Roman palaces into rough blocks
and, most evocatively, column shafts (cf. fig. 16.19, based on those at the Palazzo del
Te) that appear to have been put in place just as they came from the quarry. This
innovation adds to the polarities of his early work the juxtaposition of nature (the
"unworked" stone) and art so greatly admired and so successfully publicized by Serlio.
At the same time, it moves architectural metaphor out of the purely architectural sphere
to which it had been confined by the previous generation of classical architects into the
sphere of contemporary poetry, philosophy, and critical theory, where the art-nature
dialectic was a central theme. Giulio's injection of nature into architecture also helped

16.29   *Sebastiano Serlio, gate. From* Estraordinario
libro, *1551.*

to bind architecture to garden design, just at the dawn of the golden age of the Italian villa garden. It is perhaps for this reason that Serlio chose to expand his celebration of the *mistura* of natural roughness and artificial delicacy by publishing, in 1551 in Lyons, his *Estraordinario libro . . . Nel quale si dimostrano trenta porte di opera Rustica mista con diversi ordini: e venti di opera dilicata. . . .* The majority of these gates (fig. 16.29), to judge from their fantastic and comic invention, were not conceived for palaces, public buildings, or even villas, but for gardens, the ideal locus of the contest of art against nature.

To the extent that these observations have revealed the genesis of Serlio's presentation of the Tuscan/Rustic order, they should help to reveal what an impressive metaphorical burden the language of architecture supported in the Renaissance. An architectural order was seen as an expression of actual or virtual structure and as an affirmation of the traditions and capacity for invention of a social group and of its culture. It seems to me timely to ponder this message at this moment, when many of the architects of our time are employing the classical orders as if they were intended merely for decoration and diversion.

Notes

1.   Sebastiano Serlio, *Regole generali di architettura di Sebastiano Serlio Bolognese sopra le cinque maniere degli edifici, cioe, Thoscano, Dorico, Ionico, Corinthio, e Composito, con gli esempi dell'antiquità, che con la maggior parte concordano con la dottrina di Vitruvio* (Venice, 1537): published as Book IV of the Venice 1584 edition of *Tutte le opere d'architettura*, fol. 126. Serlio's theoretical restriction of rustication to fortified structures does not conform with his citation of private palaces and villas, but in practice, defensive overtones did play a part in determining the rustic style of early domestic architecture, especially in Tuscany.

Serlio's radical association of rustication with the Tuscan order was common usage a generation later; Giorgio Vasari, writing of Cronaca's work on the Strozzi Palace in Florence, says: "condusse il guscio di fuori . . . il quale guscio è d'ordine rustico e graduato; perciochè la parte de' bozzi dal primo finestrato in giù insieme con le porte, è rustica grandemente; e la parte ch'è dal primo finestrato al secundo, è meno rustica assai. . . . Fecevi dunque il Cronaca, oltra la bellezza di fuori *con ordine toscano,* in cima una cornice corintia molto magnifica." The passage was pointed out to me by Nicholas Adams.

2.   Vitruvius, *De architectura,* IV, vii, 2–3: "Eaeque sint ima crassitudine altitudinis parte VII; altitudo tertia parte latitudinis templi; summaque columna quarta parte crassitudinis imae contrahatur. Spirae earum altae dimidia parte crassitudinis fiant. Habeant spirae earum plinthum ad circinum, altam suae crassitudinis dimidia parte, torum insuper cum apophysi crassum quantum plinthus. Capituli altitudo dimidia crassitudinis. Abaci latitudo quanta ima crassitudo columnae. Capitulique crassitudo dividatur in partes tres, e quibus una plintho, quae est in abaco, detur, altera echino, tertia hypotrachelio cum apophysi. Supra columnas trabes compactiles ponantur ut eam habeant crassitudinem, quanta summa columnae erit. . . ."

3.   Alberti, *L'architettura (De re aedificatoria)*, tr. G. Orlandi, ed. P. Portoghesi (Milan, 1966), 555–557. The two torus moldings divided by a scotia, proposed by all Renaissance theoreticians, are significant for this study because the Vitruvian Tuscan order has only one torus and no scotia. See R. Krautheimer, "Alberti's Templum Etruscum," *Studies in Early Christian, Medieval and Renaissance Art* (New York, 1969), 333–344.

4.   Alberti, *L'architettura*, Book VII, iv, 555–557.

5.   Ibid., Book VII, vi, viii, 565–567, 585: "Italici quotquot in caeteris ornamenta sint, suis capitulis adiunxere. . . ."

6.   Ibid., Book VII, vii, 573. He goes on to speculate (apparently attempting to interpret Vitruvius's specifications) that the circular base could be the continuous round plinth that runs under all the columns on some ancient round temples with porticoes.

7.   Ibid., Book VII, vi, 565.

8.   *Filarete's Treatise on Architecture,* tr. and ed. by John Spencer (New Haven, 1965), Bk. 1, fol. 3r, in Florence, B. N., Magl. II, 1, 140.

9.   See Richard Betts, "On the Chronology of Francesco di Giorgio's Treatises: New Evidence from an Unpublished Manuscript," *Journal of the Society of Architectural Historians,* 26 (1977), 3–14. Betts demonstrates the difficulty Francesco experienced in interpreting the Vitruvian orders, especially in his early writings. This is borne out by his translation of Vitruvius's passage on the Tuscan order (Florence, B.N., II.1.141, fol. 128v), which shows his inability to visualize its essential characteristics. He omits the round form of the plinth and, describing the capital, he renders "hypotrachelio cum apophysi" as "epatra chuclio." I am most grateful to Dr. Beverly Brown for transcribing the passage.

10.   *M. Vitruvius per iocundun solito castigatior factus cum figuris et tabula ut iam et intelligi possit* (Venice, 1511).

11.   Giacomo Barozzi da Vignola, *La regola delle cinque ordini d'architettura* (Rome, n.d. [1562]), iiii: "non havendo io fra le antiquità di Roma trovato ornamento toscano . . . ho preso l'autorità da vitruvio. . . ."

12.   Bayerische Staatsbibliothek, Cod. ital. 37, fol. 39, in Vincenzo Fontana and Paolo Morachiello, eds., *Vitruvio e Raffaello: Il de architettura di Vitruvio nella traduzione inedita di Fabio Calvo ravennate* (Rome, 1975). The date is established by Raphael's correspondence (pp. 28–29).

At the close of the manuscript, Raphael is named as the instigator and Calvo as the executor of the translation.

The first reference I have found to a canon of five orders appears as a postscript to the well-known letter attributed to Raphael and addressed to Leo X (therefore written in the period 1514–20), now recognized as being in the hand of Baldassare Castiglione. The postscript appears only in the copy of the letter appended to Calvo's translation. The canon, however, is not yet Serlio's (Attic appears in place of Composite), and it is hard to make the case for Raphael's authorship of the postscript as strong as it is for the letter. The observations on the orders are not specific or accurate. The nature of the Attic is quite unclear ("L'Attica ha le colonne facte a quattro faccie"), and the author says of the Tuscan only that it is "assai simile alla Dorica" and that among the ancient buildings in which different orders were used together, there are examples of Tuscan and Doric combinations, which does not seem to have been true. I have used the text in Julius Vogel, *Bramante und Raffael* (Leipzig, 1910), 114. The extensive literature on the attribution of the letter proper is reviewed in Fontana and Morachiello, 25ff.

13.   *Di Lucio Vitruvio Pollione de architettura libri decem traducti de latino in vulgare affigurati* (Como, 1521), LXX. See also LXII.

14.   *M. L. Vitruvio Pollione traducto di latino in volgare dal vero exemplare* (Venice, 1524); *Vitruvio in volgar lingua raportato per M. Gianbatista Caporale di Perugia* (Bologna, 1536).

15.   On Serlio and his circle in Venice, see the richly documented study of Hubertus Günther, "Studien zum venezianischen Aufenthalt des Sebastiano Serlio," *Münchner Jahrbuch für Kunstgeschichte,* 32 (1981), 42–94; and M. Rosci, *Il trattato di architettura di Sebastiano Serlio* (Milan, n.d.), 25ff.

16.   *I dieci libri dell'architettura tradotti e commentati da Mons. Daniel Barbaro* (Venice, 1556) (142–144 in the 1567 ed.).

17.   See n. 11. Christof Thoenes's valuable new study, "Vignolas 'Regola delli cinque ordini'" is scheduled for publication in the *Römisches Jahrbuch für Kunstgeschichte,* 1982; I am indebted to him for the opportunity to read it in proof.

18.   *I quattro libri dell'architettura di Andrea Palladio, ne' quali, dopo un breve trattato de' cinque ordini, & di quelli avertimenti, che sono piu necessarii nel fabricare; si tratta delle case privati, delle Vie, de i Ponti, delle piazze, de i Xisti, et de' Tempii* (Venice, 1570).

19. Palladio's caption to figure 16.8 reads: "A, Architrave di legno," while the caption to figure 16.9 reads: "F, Architrave . . . Al dritto dell'architrave segnato F, vi è la sacoma d'un Architrave fatto più delicatamente." Drawing Royal Institute of British Architects, X/8, by Palladio or an assistant, showing the Tuscan order as a freestanding trabeated colonnade and as applied to an arcade, may have been made in preparation for the publication of the *Four Books* (Hans Spielmann, *Andrea Palladio und der Antike* [Munich and Berlin, 1966], cat. no. 26). Palladio (*Quattro libri*, I, xiii, 15f.) incorporated the discussion of the different styles of intercolumniation in Vitruvius III, iii into his canon of the orders, associating the Tuscan with aerostyle, which could have an intercolumniation of three or more column diameters since the architrave is of wood (see E. Forssman, "Palladio e le colonne," *Boll. del Centro Internazionale di Studi di Architettura,* 21 [1978], 71–88).

20. *I quattro libri,* I, xiiii, 19.

21. Vignola's module is half the column base, so his figures have been halved to conform with the others. The Palladian figures are taken from his text, but since it is incomplete I have filled in the gaps from the plates.

22. Serlio does not use modular subdivisions in this case; he does propose a geometrical system for calculating the diminution of the column thickness toward the top that seems complicated for use on the site.

For a discussion of the several systems of measurement in this period, see Wolfgang Lotz, "Sull' unità di misura nei disegni di architettura nel Cinquecento," *Boll. del Centro Internazionale di Studi di Architettura,* 21 (1979), 223–232.

23. Uffizi, A605, 606, 3033 (see the catalog *Palladio e Verona* [Venice, 1980], nos. III, 40–41). Serlio acknowledged his debt to Peruzzi in the preamble to Book IV (fol. 126 in 1584 ed.): "Di tutto quello, che voi trovarete in questo libro che vi piaccia, non darete gia laude a me, ma si bene al precettor mio Baldassar Petruccio da Siena. . . ." According to Vasari (*Vite,* ed. Milanesi, IV, 606f.), Peruzzi planned to publish an illustrated commentary on Vitruvius.

24. As observed by Günther, "Studien," 63; Serlio, Book III, 72v: "queste cose di Pola furono misurate da uno miglior disegnatore; che intendente di misure e di numeri." The Pola monuments are illustrated on fols. 72 and 85. Günther also notes that, according to Sarayna (*De origine et amplitudine civitatis Veronae* . . . [Verona, 1540], fol.

iv), Serlio did not know the Verona amphitheater at first hand: "quia ipse non vidit . . . aut non recte designavit. . . ."

25. Palladio's drawings of the theater and amphitheater in Pola are: London, Royal Institute of British Architects, Burlington-Devonshire Collection, nos. VIII/21r, v; 22r, v; 23 (amphitheater); X/3 (theater) (Giangiorgio Zorzi, *I disegni delle antichità di Andrea Palladio* [Venice, 1959], 93, 97f., figs. 216, 235–239; Spielmann, *Palladio und der Antike,* cat. nos. 119, 130–132, figs. 69–70, 78, 79). That Palladio's early Pola drawings were copies (VII/22, 23: dated in the 1540s or earlier by Spielmann and by Douglas Lewis, *The Drawings of Andrea Palladio,* exhibition catalog [Washington, D.C., 1981], cat. nos. 17, 18) is indicated by the fact that the measurements are the same as those of Serlio (in some cases more complete, which suggests a common source), in Veronese feet (Günther, "Studien," 65), and are shown in perspective, a technique Palladio did not use in original drawings. The later drawings are on R.I.B.A. VIII/21 (after 1560). Palladio's drawings of the Verona amphitheater are R.I.B.A. VIII/18, 19 (Zorzi, 97; Spielmann, cat. nos. 126–127).

26. Fol. 6r in a sketchbook of ca. 1530 acquired recently by the Canadian Centre for Architecture in Montreal (as yet uncataloged), knowledge of which I owe to Arnold Nesselrath, who also guided me to the publication cited in n. 30. The date has been suggested by Dr. Nesselrath in consultation with Howard Burns.

27. Reproduced by A. Bartoli, *I monumenti antichi di Roma nei disegni degli Uffizi di Firenze,* 6 vols. (Rome, 1914–22), IV, pl. 385, fig. 675. Although the draftsman identifies the structure with the Aqua Virgo, it cannot be identified with the supporting arches discussed below (at n. 58).

28. Ibid., II, pl. 129. Another Peruzzi sketch that appears to represent the Tuscan order appears on Uffizi A632r (ibid., pl. 183, fig. 318). It is labeled "Basamēto di san Pietro in la parte exteriore" and appears to be a podium supporting a major Doric order. Franz Metternich associated it with Raphael's design for the peripheral walls of the apses, and dated it 1520–27, but without further explanation (*Der Erbauung der Peterskirche zu Rom im 16. Jahrhundert* [Vienna, 1972], 50, fig. 64).

29. See Livia Crozzoli Aite, "I tre templi del foro Olitorio," *Atti della Pontificia Accademia romana di Archeologia,* ser. III, *Memorie,* XIII (Rome, 1981), 12ff. Here, as in earlier archaeological literature, the southernmost temple from which Pe-

ruzzi drew is properly identified as Doric since it lacks a base; Aite, however, in reviewing 50 drawings and prints made between the time of Peruzzi and that of Piranesi (pp. 26–46, with illustrations of the majority), does not discuss the problem of the confusion with Tuscan.

30. Fol. 3r (the two previous folios are lost) in the Canadian Centre sketchbook cited in n. 26. Serlio shows the temple in *Tutte le opere,* 59v-60, as baseless Doric. His entablature, however, is remarkably close to his model for the Tuscan order in figure 16.3.

31. Uffizi A1657 (Bartoli, *Monumenti,* IV, pl. 306, fig. 503; Aite, "I tre templi," fig. 44).

32. V. Fontana and P. Morachiello, *Vitruvio e Raffaello,* pl. 23; Bartoli, *Monumenti,* I, pl. 34, fig. 61: Uffizi, A1542v. The same occurs in a drawing by Bastiano da Sangallo labeled "basa di cholonna doricha" (Bartoli, IV, pl. 341, fig. 578: Uffizi, A1743v).

33. An unidentified sketch by Beccafumi shows two Tuscan bases and, separately, an entablature with a two-fascia architrave and a quite simple cornice. This might, however, be an invention for a modern building. (Fol. XLII from the sketchbook of the Coghlan Briscoe collection in London, illustrated in R. de Liphart Ratshoff, "Un libro di schizzi di Domenico Beccafumi," *Riv. d'arte,* 17, ser. 2, 7 [1935], fig. 43.) The sketchbook has been dated prior to Beccafumi's departure from Rome in 1512 by Donato Sanminiatelli ("The Beginnings of Domenico Beccafumi," *Burlington Magazine,* 99, no. 657 [1957], 401ff.), but I am convinced on the basis of the figural and architectural style that it was at least partly executed during the 1530s. A group of drawings of rustic gateways attributed to Beccafumi in the drawing archive of the Avery Library in Columbia University (cf. *Sebastiano Serlio: An Exhibition in Honor of the 500th Anniversary of his Birth,* by Myra N. Rosenfeld [Columbia University, New York, 1975], 5) is, in my opinion, copied from the plates of Serlio's Book IV by a later sixteenth-century draftsman and has nothing to do with Beccafumi.

34. Vincenzo Scamozzi, *L'idea del tempio dell'architettura* (Venice, 1611), 2:53–55. The Arcadius column in Constantinople is also Tuscan (G. Beccati, *La colonna coclide istoriata* [Rome, 1960]). Although the Roman columns were frequently illustrated by the engravers of views, they did not attract much attention from architects; Antonio da Sangallo the Younger, however, made two sketches of the bases (Bartoli, *Monumenti,* II,

pls. 222, 274, figs. 379, 459: Uffizi, A1204, A1153). Scamozzi mentions the remains of a temple of Hercules near Lucca, another called the Vetulonio temple, amphitheaters in Popolonia, now Piombino, and at the site of the ancient Vitulia; and the Labyrinth of King Porsena there. He closes with a list of bridges, gates, tombs, and other monuments where rustication was used.

35. London, R.I.B.A., X/13v: Zorzi, *Disegni,* 94, fig. 222; Spielmann, *Andrea Palladio,* cat. 116, fig. 66; Lewis, *Drawings,* cat. 10.

36. See Luigi Beschi, "Verona romana: i monumenti," in *Verona e il suo territorio* (1960), 1:429, fig. 18 (photograph of the terrace drawn by Palladio); *Palladio e Verona,* cat. III, 37.

37. J. Ackerman, *The Cortile del Belvedere* (Vatican City, 1954), 38f.; Arnaldo Bruschi, *Bramante Architetto* (Bari, 1969), 417–433, figs. 276–280, pl. 3. My reference to the "conscious use" of the order is meant to distinguish Bramante's Tuscan from the system of such unsophisticated designs as that of Casa Turchi in Rome, of the first years of the sixteenth century, which, though it qualifies as Tuscan, is hard to locate within the movement of advanced antiquarian learning with which I have been concerned. I should also like to acknowledge the generous assistance of Christof Frommel in locating Renaissance examples of the order.

38. Christof Frommel, *Die römische Palastbauten der Hochrenaissance,* 3 vols. (Tübingen, 1973), 2:13–22, 3: pls. 10–14 (Branconio d'Aquila); 2:53–61, 3: pls. 25–27 (Caffarelli-Vidoni; ascribed to Lorenzetti by Vasari, the palace came to be known as the work of Raphael in the seventeenth century); 2:1–12, 3: pls. 1–6 (Alberini-Cicciaporci; ascribed to Giulio by Vasari). The pilasters of the *piano nobile* of the façade are also a version of Tuscan, but an idiosyncratic one in which the bases and capitals merge with the entablatures.

39. Frommel, *Palastbauten,* 2:216–223, 3: pl. 86 a–c (house of Giulio); drawings representing the house are preserved by Aristotile da Sangallo (Uffizi, A2692), Giovannantonio Dosio (Uffizi, A2691), and two anonymous contemporaries, one in Florence, Biblioteca Nazionale (this and the two preceding illustrated by Frommel) and the one at Chatsworth (recently reproduced by Howard Burns in *Boll. del Centro Internazionale di Studi di Architettura,* 21 [1979], fig. 7, and Lewis, *Drawings,* cat. 50). For Palazzo Stati-Maccarani, see Frommel, 2:322–326, 3: pls. 139–142.

40. The drawing, from Antonio's shop, is Uffizi A233 (G. Giovanoni, *Antonio da Sangallo il giovane* [Rome, n.d. (1959?)], fig. 166); Antonio Labacco, *Libro appartenente all'architettura* (Venice, 1576), illustrates the same design, but with an Ionic order.

41. Frommel, "Bramantes 'Ninfeo' in Genazzano," *Römisches Jahrbuch für Kunstgeschichte,* 12 (1969), 137–160; the attribution has been questioned by Christof Thoenes, "Note sul 'ninfeo' di Genazzano," *Studi bramanteschi* (Rome, 1974), 575–583, and Bruschi, *Bramante,* 1048ff.

42. L. Puppi, *Andrea Palladio* (Boston, 1975), 251ff.; K. W. Forster and R. J. Tuttle, "Giulio Romano e le prime opere vicentine del Palladio," *Boll. del Centro Internazionale di Studi di Architettura,* 15 (1973), 107–120 (here the atrium design is assigned to Palladio and the columns to Giulio). Palladio says in the *Quattro libri,* II, 12–15: "Due altre entrate vi sono ne' fianchi, le quali hanno le colonne nel mezo, che vi sono poste non tanto per ornamento, quanto per rendere il luogo di sopra sicuro, e proportionare la larghezza all'altezza." Although the use of the Tuscan order in atria was no more common than its use elsewhere, it had a special justification for Palladio: his mentor Daniele Barbaro, commenting on Book VI, iii of Vitruvius (*I dieci libri:* "De i Cavedi delle case"), speaks of the "Tuscan" atrium: "Prima è la Toscana, che è la piu semplice delle altre, dallaquale forse sono gli Atrii nominati, perche erano in Toscana i popoli Atriensi." Another instance of the use of the Tuscan order in the Veneto is at the Palazzo degli Honorij in Verona, by Sanmicheli; the ground-floor arcade is based on the order of the amphitheater (fig. 16.21). (*Michele Sanmicheli, catalogo a cura di Piero Gazzola* [Venice, 1965], 171f., figs. 168–169.)

43. Vv.aa., *La Vita e le opere di Jacopo Barozzi da Vignola (1507–1573) nel quarto centenario della morte* (Vignola, 1974), figs. 3, 12, 16, 51, 86, 93, which include, in addition to those cited above, the parish church at S. Oreste al Soratte and the Porta Faulle in Viterbo. Galeazzo Alessi also frequently used the order: at Palazzo Marino in Milan, the Sacro Monte in Varallo, the lantern of Sta. Maria in Carignano in Genoa, and the villas delle Peschiere and Cambiaso in Genoa (*Galeazzo Alessi e l'architettura del '500: Atti del convegno* [Genoa, 1975], figs. 38, 153, 254, 261ff., 415).

44. Serlio, *Fourth Book,* 133v (1584): "& di tal mistura se ne è piu dilettato Iulio Romano, che alcun'altro, come ne fa fede Roma in piu luoghi, & anco Mantoa nel bellissimo palazzo detto il Te fuori di essa poco discosto, esempio veramente di Architettura, & di pittura a nostri tempi." The passage is discussed by Marco Rosci, *Il Trattato,* 1:47ff. Serlio's role as a propagator of Giulio's innovations in the rustic style was ably discussed and interpreted by Ernst Gombrich in a seminal article on Mannerism in architecture ("Zum Werke Giulio Romanos, II: Versuch einer Deutung," *Jahrbuch der kunsthistorischen Sammlungen in Wien,* n.s. 7 [1936], 121–150). See also E. Kris, "'Der Stil *Rustique,'* Die Verwendung des Naturabgusses bei Wenzel Jamnitzer und Bernard Palissy," *Jahrbuch der kunsthistorischen Sammlungen in Wien,* n.s. 1 (1926), 137–208; M. Tafuri, "Il mito naturalistico nell'architettura del '500," *L'Arte,* 1 (1968), 6–36.

45. On the Pola amphitheater, see: Stefan Mlakar, *Das Amphitheater in Pula* (Pola, 1969); on Verona, L. Beschi, "Verona Romana," who cites the similar use of the order at Arles and Nîmes; Stefano Ricci, *Il teatro romano di Verona* (Venice, 1895). Plate V in Ricci shows vigorous rustication at the base of the lowest level of the theater that would have delighted Giulio and Serlio had it been excavated in their time.

46. The history of rustication through the Renaissance is surveyed by Emil Roth, *Die Rustika der italienische Renaissance und ihre Vorgeschichte* (diss., Munich; published Vienna, 1917). See also L. H. Heydenreich, "Il bugnato rustico," *Boll. del Centro Internazionale di Studi di Architettura,* 2 (1960), 40ff. The best account of its origins in thirteenth- and fourteenth-century Florence is that of S. Sinding Larsen, "A Tale of Two Cities," *Acta ad Archaeologicam et Artium Historiam Pertinentia,* 6 (1975), 163ff.

47. Already in Raphael's Pandolfini Palace of 1516, where the rustication was restricted to corner quoins and the enframement of the portal (Frommel, *Palastbauten,* 2:355–365, 3: pls. 156–160; S. Ray, *Raffaello architetto* [Bari, 1974], 207ff., 329ff.).

48. Roth, *Rustika,* p. 4. Sinding Larsen, "Tale of Two Cities," challenges the proposal of Juergen Paul (*Der Palazzo Vecchio in Florenz. Ursprung und Bedeutung seiner Form* [Florence, 1969], 84–89) that the rustication of the Palazzo Vecchio in Florence and of later trecento palaces derives from Hohenstaufen models on the grounds that the blocks are treated quite differently.

49. On the assessment of the entirely rusticated Strozzi Palace of the 1480s/1490s as elegant, see E. H. Gombrich, "The Early Medici as Patrons of

the Arts," *Italian Renaissance Studies,* ed. E. F. Jacob (London, 1960), 308f.; F. W. Kent, " 'Più superba di quella de Lorenzo': Courtly and Family Interest in the Building of Filippo Strozzi's Palace," *Renaissance Quarterly,* 40 (1977), 311–323.

50. See Brenda Preyer, "The Rucellai Palace," *Giovanni Rucellai ed il suo Zibaldone, II: A Florentine Patron and His Palace* (London, 1981), 155–225. Circa 1455 is proposed as a probable moment (p. 182) within the documented limits of 1452 and 1458. It has occurred to me that the so-called *spalliera,* a pattern of incised hatching at the base of the façade, could be a reference, not to Roman *opus reticulatum,* as is usually assumed, but to similar large-scale hatching appearing in a like position on some of the Etruscan funerary urns made in the form of a house (A. della Seta, *Italia antica* [Bergamo, 1928], 234, fig. 247). We do not know, however, if such objects were known to Renaissance antiquarians or, if so, whether they were recognized to be Etruscan. The example of antique rustication closest to the practice of early Renaissance Florentine palace designers is a house depicted on an early Christian sarcophagus in the Grotte Vaticane, cited and illustrated by Howard Burns, "Quattrocento Architecture and the Antique," *Classical Influences on European Culture, A.D. 500–1500,* ed. R. Bolgar (Cambridge, 1971), 264, pl. 6c.

51. Preyer, 185, cites also the Minerbetti and della Stufa palaces in Florence.

52. The best-known surviving example is the republican tomb of Cecelia Metella on the Appian Way. Sixteenth-century architects also recorded the drafted wall at the base of the portico of the Temple of Mars Ultor in the Forum of Augustus; e.g., Peruzzi in Uffizi A632: "in foro transitorio/di marmo tucti" (Bartoli, *Monumenti,* fig. 325); Serlio, *Tutte le opere,* fol. 89; and Palladio (Vicenza, Mus. Civico, no. 5r: Zorzi, *Disegni,* fig. 75). It was used at the round temple in the Forum Boarium and on the base of Hadrian's tomb in Rome (*Il libro di Giuliano da Sangallo: codice vaticano Barb. Lat., 4428,* ed. C. Hülsen [Leipzig, 1910], fols. 39r, v), on the cella wall of the temple of Antonius and Faustina (Bartoli, *Monumenti,* III, pl. 290, fig. 477, Uffizi 1166v, by Antonio da Sangallo the Younger; Antonio Labacco's *Libro,* pls. 15, 16). Serlio, fol. 86, shows it at the amphitheater at Pola and again at a "palace" on the Quirinal Hill (fol. 87). See also Peruzzi's drawing, Uffizi A532r: a tomb with a round tower of drafted masonry on a monumental base identified "p(er)

lauia di tiuoli"; A532 (Bartoli, pl. 151, fig. 281; see also Sallustio Peruzzi, pl. 388, fig. 680: Uffizi, A665r).

53. G. Lugli, *Roma antica: il centro monumentale* (Rome, 1946), 258–269; E. Nash, *A Pictorial Dictionary of Ancient Rome* (Tübingen, 1961), 1:401–409, fig. 502. Illustrations: Peruzzi, Uffizi A633r/632v: "muro exterior del foro transitoro di peperigno"; Antonio da Sangallo the Younger, Uffizi A1141 (Bartoli, *Monumenti,* II, pl. 183, fig. 318; III, pl. 275, fig. 460); Serlio, *Tutte le opere,* III, fol. 89; Labacco, *Libro,* pl. 7.

54. A. M. Colini, "Storia e topografia del Celio nell'antichità," *Atti della Pontificia Accademia romana di Archeologia: Memorie,* 7 (1944), 137–162; A. Prandi, *Il complesso monumentale della basilica celimontana di SS. Giovanni e Paolo* (Vatican City, 1950), 373–420; Nash, *Dictionary,* 1:243–247, figs. 284–286. The uniqueness of the monument was recognized already in the fifteenth century. Francesco di Giorgio Martini drew one of the arches in his manuscript treatise completed by 1486 (*Trattati di architettura ingegneria e arte militare,* ed. C. Maltese [Milan, 1967], I, fol. 78v, pl. 144, from Turin, Cod. Saluzziano, 148). Later illustrations include: *Libro di Giuliano da Sangallo,* fol. 3v; G. A. Dosio, *Roma antica e i disegni di architettura agli Uffizi,* ed. F. Borsi et al. (Rome, 1976), cat. 49, 123: Uffizi A2518, 2030; Salvestro Peruzzi, Uffizi, A661v, 689r; Ciro Ferri, Uffizi A4376 (Bartoli, *Monumenti,* IV, pls. 382, 374, figs. 669, 654; V, pl. 497, fig. 920); Piranesi, *Antichità romane* (Rome, 1756), IV, pls. LIII ff.

55. T. Dombart, *Das palatinische Septizonium zu Rom* (Rome, 1922); C. Hülsen, "Septizonium," *Zeitschrift für Geschichte der Architektur,* 5 (1911–12), 1–24. Illustrations: *Libro di Giuliano da Sangallo,* fol. 32r (my fig. 16.26); A. Bartoli, "I documenti per la storia del Settezonio severiano e i disegni inediti di Marten van Heemskerk," *Boll. d'arte,* 3 (1909), 261, fig. 4 (Vienna, Hofbibliothek: anonymous sixteenth-century draftsman who shows rustication only on the ground floor).

56. Lugli, *Centro,* 269–273; Nash, *Dictionary,* 2:439–445. Illustrations: Fra Giocondo, Uffizi A1534; Peruzzi, Uffizi 382, 383; A. da Sangallo Younger, Uffizi A992 (Bartoli, *Monumenti,* I, pl. 25, fig. 52; II, figs. 215f.; III, pl. 297, fig. 485).

57. I. A. Richmond, *The City Wall of Imperial Rome* (Oxford, 1930), 205–217; Nash, *Dictionary,* 1:225–228. Illustrations: *Il libro di Giuliano da Sangallo,* fol. 5; Fra Giocondo, Uffizi A1881; A. da Sangallo Younger, Uffizi A1369; Sallustio

Peruzzi, Uffizi A690 (Bartoli, *Monumenti,* I, pl. 35, fig. 62; III, pl. 215, fig. 362; IV, pl. 383, fig. 670); G. A. Dosio, Uffizi A2527 (*Roma antica,* cat. no. 32; Bartoli, pl. 473, fig. 872).

58. Thomas Ashby, *The Aqueducts of Ancient Rome* (Oxford, 1935), 167–182; E. Van Deman, *The Building of the Roman Aqueducts* (Washington, D.C., 1934), 167–178; Nash, *Dictionary,* 1:55f. Illustrations: Sallustio Peruzzi, Uffizi A666v. The drawing does not show the arches represented by Piranesi, *Antichità,* I, xii; *Campus Martius,* XX.

59. Among other documents recorded, tombs appear most often, e.g., *Il libro di Giuliano da Sangallo,* fol. 75v; Giuliano was exceptionally interested in Roman rustication, perhaps because he had emphasized the technique in his Florentine period, and some of his examples (fols. *v, 2*) may be his own inventions. As Scamozzi says (*Idea,* 2:54), many Roman bridges were rusticated, but they do not appear frequently among the drawings (but see Serlio, *Tutte le opere,* III, fols. 89v, 90); a catalog of surviving Roman bridges has been compiled by Piero Gazzola, *Ponti romani,* vol. 2 (Florence, 1963). For bridges in and around Rome, see Rome, Gabinetto Nazionale delle Stampe, *I ponti di Roma* (Rome, 1975).

60. Serlio, in his sixth Book, on domestic architecture, employed the Tuscan order for the articulation of ideal schemes distinguishing the grades of country houses from that of the merchant to the least elaborate of the nobleman's villas. Dwellings of the lower classes are of wood construction without orders. Other orders are employed on those of higher rank, but the Tuscan appears on certain of their elevations, indicating that it is not strictly class-bound. The same is true of the urban structures in the manuscript (*Sebastiano Serlio on Domestic Architecture,* ed. Myra Rosenfeld [New York and Cambridge, 1978], pls. I–XVII). Bramante illustrated the sequence of the orders in the spiral staircase of the Belvedere court in the first decade of the century (see above).

61. The tension between the expression of the wall and that of the orders is illustrated in such imitations of the Rucellai palace as the Piccolomini Palace in Pienza and S. Michele all' Isola in Venice, where the channels of the drafting overrun the pilasters.

62. As noted by Roth, *Rustika,* 35.

Postscript

The interests of Postmodern architects must have played a large part in making the subject of the orders hot in the late '70s and early '80s. Maybe we historians were trying to protect the classical tradition from the undiscriminating embraces of its new admirers. I think my principal motivation was to demonstrate with one example how the orders mean, with the hope of discrediting their use in a purely decorative and unmetaphorical way. But, for whatever reason, the bibliography below, most of which comes from that period—and which represents only a small portion of the new literature on the five orders in the Renaissance—is symptomatic of a sudden excitement in a subject that might have seemed academic a short time before. This study was researched and written in a brief period, and I knew when I sent it out for publication that a lot of details could be added to document its points more thoroughly—for example, more instances of reference to the Tuscan and Rustic modes in the literature of the time, and more ancient Roman examples—but I believed that they would not substantially alter the major points, and I was for some reason in a hurry.

Hubertus Günther's exemplary study (1985) of the varying definitions of the Tuscan order in the Renaissance documents a much greater confusion than I was aware of among Renaissance architects in interpreting Vitruvius's text and in identifying actual examples of the order among Roman remains. His evidence, which includes many texts and drawings that I did not cite, demonstrates that the majority of architects could not distinguish clearly between the Doric and Tuscan orders, though Bramante had attempted to juxtapose the two in the spiral staircase of the Cortile del Belvedere (Thoenes, 1977). This was due mostly to Vitruvius's imprecision: the only Tuscan features that he clearly differentiates from the Doric are the round plinth and the base with a single torus. Moreover, Vitruvius was discussing architecture in wood, and Renaissance architects sought a standard for stone architecture. Serlio's illustrations of the Tuscan order (figs. 16.3, 16.4) are largely inventions; his trabeation is essentially Doric without metopes and triglyphs. Paradoxically, later writers frequently used Serlio to "elucidate" Vitruvius's text. The interpretations of Barbaro and Palladio, Günther suggests, are closest to what Vitruvius meant.

Morolli's article in *Natura e artificio,* a collection that reached me only after my essay had been sent off, is a thorough study of the textual sources for the Tuscan/Rustic order. It documents a consistent tendency, which I failed to emphasize, to maintain a distinction between the Tuscan order, which fits plausibly into the classical canon of orders, and the Rustic, a vaguely defined naturalistic mode that may be allied with or applied to not only the Tuscan (to which Serlio says it is best fit) but also the other orders (as in Serlio's book of gates), and may even be a quasi-order of its own, as in the use of column shafts imitating tree trunks with lopped-off limbs (Bramante's court at Sant'Ambrogio in Milan; Philibert de l'Orme, *Architecture de Philibert de l'Orme* [Paris, 1648], fol. 213v). Vasari, however, in extensive comments in chapter III of the *Proemio* to his *Lives* that should have been included in my essay, uses "Rustic" to define the Tuscan order as well. Scamozzi, as documented by Morolli, was the strictest classicist of the theorists and stands at the opposite pole, attacking those who claim that "I ligamenti rustici sia un' ordine per se" (*Idea*, VI, i, 3).

Both Morolli and John Onians, in his excellent chapter on Serlio in *Bearers of Meaning* (1988), make the point that the use of rustic elements caused considerable uneasiness among designers and theorists because it invites irrationality and because its classical justification is limited. Serlio, apologizing for the uncanonic character of his *Libro estraordinario* on gates (1551), explains that it was first conceived in Fontainebleau forest, in a *furore architettonico* experienced while the author was surrounded by wild beasts—the designs were the product of poetic transport. His excuse is that most people have an insatiable hunger for novelty, and that if it were not for the *bizaria* of some men, we would not recognize the modesty of others (text for Gate xxvii). Serlio represents rustic design, moreover, as suited "alla villa . . . ancora nella città ad un edificio di un letterato o mercante di vita robusta" (Book IV, vii, 164r), in other words, to the bourgeoisie, or what the Venetians would have called a "citizen," rather than to the aristocracy. Onians perceptively interprets the distinction as applicable to Serlio's famous illustrations of sets for the satiric, comic, and tragic theater in Book II. The satiric set, a wild landscape with rustic huts, may be associated with *gente vitiosa e rustica;* the comic, which has partially wooden construction and some Gothic buildings, represents an ordinariness of civic building that may be seen as bourgeois in character; and the tragic, with pure classical palaces and public buildings, is suited to the *nobile* or patrician class.

Onians also cites Serlio's unpublished Munich manuscript on gates and fortifications (Codex Icon. 190): the text accompanying the drawing of an ancient bridge calls attention to a Corinthian arch facing the city and a rusticated Tuscan one facing the barbarians.

The work of Luigi Polacco, which escaped my attention earlier, offers ample evidence (esp. 55ff.)—in painting as well as in architectural fragments—for locating the origins of the Tuscan order in Etruscan architecture, perhaps as early as the sixth or seventh century BC. There is no indication, however, that any of the examples cited were known in the Renaissance. Polacco also discusses (p. 136) Vitruvius's reference (IV.6, 6) to an architectural mode that he called the "tuscanicae dispositiones," and suggests that this was meant only in the sense of *priscus* rather than as a synonym for "Etruscan." He cites other passages in Vitruvius referring to "tuscanicus mos" (III.3, 5), "tuscanica genera" and "tuscanica opera" (IV.8, 5), and "atrium tuscanicum" (VI.3, 1).

Belluzzi, A. "L'opera rustica nell'architettura italiana del primo Cinquecento," in M. Fagiolo, ed., *Natura e artificio* (Rome, 1979), 98–111. This article traces the use of heavy rusticated blocks in the façade design of the sixteenth century.

Boëthius, Axel. "Of Tuscan Columns," *American Journal of Archaeology,* 66 (1962), 249–254.

Denker, C. "Die Säulenordnungen bei Bramante. Untersuchung zum architektonischen Detail," Ph.D. diss., Bonn, 1984.

Forssman, E. *Dorico, ionico, corinzio nell'architettura del Rinascimento* (Bari, 1973).

Günther, Hubertus. "Gli ordini architettonici: rinascità o invenzione?, II," *Roma e l'antico nell'arte e nella cultura del Cinquecento* (Rome, 1985), 272–310 (for part I of this study, see Thoenes, 1985).

Günther, Hubertus. "Die Lehre von den Säulenordnungen," in H. Günther, ed., *Deutsche Architekturtheorie zwischen Gotik und Renaissance* (Darmstadt, 1986), 89–98. Traces the definition of the orders in northern Europe and the nature of "national" orders.

Günther, Hubertus. "Serlio e gli ordini architettonichi," *Sebastiano Serlio: Sesto seminario internazionale di storia dell'architettura* (Vicenza, 1987; published Milan, 1989), 154–168.

Juren, Vladimir. "Une traité inédite sur les ordres de l'architecture et le problème des sources du libre IV de Serlio," *Fondation Eugène Piot: monuments et mémoires,* 64 (1981), 193–239.

Morolli, Gabriele. "'A quegli idei selvestri': interpretazione naturalistica, primato e dissoluzione dell'ordine architettonico nella teoria cinquecentesca sull' opera rustica," *Natura e artificio* (Rome, 1979), 55–97.

Onians, John. *Bearers of Meaning: The Classical Orders in Antiquity, the Middle Ages, and the Renaissance* (Princeton, 1988).

Onians, John. "The System of the Orders in Renaissance Architectural Thought," *Les traités d'architecture de la Renaissance (Actes du colloque de Tours)* (Paris, 1988), 169–178.

Polacco, Luigi. *Tuscanicae dispositiones* (Padua, 1952). The use of the Tuscan order in antiquity.

Thoenes, Christof. "Bramante und die Saülenordnungen," *Kunstchronik,* 30 (1977), 62f.

Thoenes, Christof. "Vignolas 'Regola delli cinque ordini,'" *Römisches Jahrbuch für Kunstgeschichte,* 20 (1983), 347–376.

Thoenes, Christof. "Gli ordini architettonici: rinascità o invenzione?, I," *Roma e l'antico nell'arte e nella cultura del Cinquecento* (Rome, 1985), 261–271.

Tönnesmann, A. "Palatium Nervae, ein antikes Vorbild für florentiner Rustikafassaden," *Römisches Jahrbuch für Kunstgeschichte,* XI, 1984, 61–70.

Zanni, Nicoletta. "Giulio Romano e l'istituzione dell'ordine rustico come sistema." *Bollettino del Centro Internazionale di Studi di Architettura,* 24 (1982–87), 221–235.

Photograph Credits

4.6: Cambridge, Fitzwilliam Museum

5.4: Vatican Library

5.8, 15, 16: by gracious permission of Her Majesty the Queen

6.1: London, National Gallery

6.2: Naples, Soprintendenza beni artistici

6.3: Art Resource, Inc.

6.4: Vienna, Österreichische Nationalbibliothek, Lichtbildwerkstatt Alpenland

6.5, 7: Art Resource, Inc.

6.6: Harvard University, Fogg Museum

7.1: Paris, Museé du Louvre

7.2: Rotterdam, Boymans–van Beuningen Museum

7.3: Vienna, Albertina Gallery

7.4, 5: by gracious permission of Her Majesty the Queen

7.9: Bern Botanical Institute

7.10: The Wellcome Trustees

8.1: G. E. Kidder Smith

9.2, 12, 13, 16, 17, 18: Art Resource, Inc.

9.6, 9: London, The British Architectural Library

9.8: Milan, Istituto per la storia dell'arte Lombarda

9.10: Harvard University, Fogg Museum, Arthur Kingsley Porter Collection

9.15: Harvard University, Fogg Museum

9.16, 18: Art Resource, Inc.

10.3: Milan, Electa S.P.A.

10.6, 8: author

10.7: Art Resource, Inc.

11.2, 6, 7: Musei Vaticani

11.4: Florence, Soprintendenza beni artistici

11.8: Rome, Fototeca Unione

11.9: Harvard University, Fogg Museum

12.1, 2, 3, 5, 8, 9: Florence, Soprintendenza beni artistici

12.4, 6, 7: author

13.2: courtesy Leonard von Matt

13.7, 8: New York, Metropolitan Museum of Art

13.9: author

13.12, 14: John Vincent

13.15: W. Lotz

14.7: Phyllis Massar

14.8, 9, 10: Milan, Biblioteca Trivulziana

14.11: author

14.14, 15: Vienna, Albertina Gallery

14.16: G. E. Kidder Smith

14.17: Art Resource, Inc.

15.2, 14: Harvard University, Fogg Museum

15.5, 8, 10, 11, 15: Phyllis Massar

15.6: Vicenza, Foto Giacomelli

15.7, 9, 12: author

15.13: Art Resource, Inc.

16.11, 16, 21: Florence, Soprintendenza beni artistici

16.10, 12: Montreal, Canadian Centre for Architecture

16.13: E. Richter

16.14: London, British Architectural Library

16.15, 17: Rome, Istituto per il Catalogo e la Documentazione

16.18: Rome, Biblioteca Hertziana

16.19: Vicenza, Centro Internazionale per gli Studi di Architettura

16.22, 24, 27: author

16.23: Harvard University, Fogg Museum

Index of Names

Note: Italicized page numbers indicate illustrations.

Democritus, 115

Descartes, René, 104, 111, *112*

Diedo, Vincenzo, 490(n60)

Dilg, Peter, 205

Diocletian, 312

Dioscures, 407, 413

Dioscurides, 195

Dixon, Jehan de, 266

Doge's Palace (Venice), 471, 479

Domus Augustiana (Rome), 347

Domus Aurea (Rome), 337, 342, 347

Donatello, 13, 64, 76, 84, 94(n61), 153, 405

Doni, Anton, 317(n20)

D'Onofrio, Cesare, 414

Dosio, Giovanni Antonio, 332, *333*, 358, *528*, 538(n39)

Duccio di Buoninsegna, 16

Du Cerceau family, 378

Duchamp, Marcel, *54*

Durantino, 499

Dürer, Albrecht, *75, 77, 79*, 91(n41), 156–157, 187, 188, *189, 190*

Dyggve, Ejnar, 312

Edgerton, Samuel, 87(n4), 90(nn24, 27, 29, 31)

Eisenman, Peter, 34

Ellenius, Allan, 205

Ensingen, Ulrich von, 222, 230

Epicurus, 115

Estienne, Charles, 199

Euclid, 62, 64, 74, 103

Evans, Walker, *54*

Falconetto, Giovanni Maria, 459, 467, *468*, 476, 479

Farnese, Alessandro (Cardinal), 364, 420, 432–434, 439, 448, 449. *See also* Paul III (Pope)

Farnese, Pierluigi, 368

Farnese family, 348–349

Farnese Palace (Rome), 364, *365*, 368–370, *371*, 399, 401

Ferdinand (King of Naples), 307

Ferrara, Miranda, 301

Fichard, Johannes, 414

Fiesole

Badia, 305

Medici villa at, 318(n31), 322

Filarete (Antonio Averlino), 182(n43), 277–281, *279–280*, 304, 358, 363, 386, 498

Fiocco, G., 315, 319(n43)

Firimburg, Annas de, 220, 222, 258(n21)

Florence, cathedral, 261(nn50, 51), 364, 373

Focillon, Henri, 20

Fondaco dei Turchi (Venice), 312, *313*, 315, 318(n31)

Fontainebleau, 378, 543

Fontana, Carlo, 281

Fontana, Vincenzo, 536(n12), 538(n32)

Forster, Kurt, 321, 539(n41)

Forum of Augustus (Rome), 526, *527*

Forum Pacis (Rome), *529, 530*

Foundling Hospital (Florence), 399

Fouquet, Jean, 92–93(n50)

Francesco di Giorgio, 363, 382, 386, 389, 498

Frankl, Paul, 218, 245, 258(n19), 429

Frederick II (Emperor), 11, *525, 526*

Frey, Dagobert, 352(nn21, 24), 353(n28), 355(n53)

Frey, Karl, 380(n21), 381(n26)

Frommel, Christof, 317, 321, 538(nn38, 39), 539(n41)

Fuchs, Leonhart, 200, 202

Gaddi, Taddeo, 160

Gaillart, Jehan, 266

Galantic, I., 94(n63)

Galeata, palace of Theodoric at, *315, 316*

Galen, 62, 66, 103–104, 119, 142(n43), 205

Gallo, Rodolfo, 490(nn54, 55, 56)

Garzoni, Alvise, 461–463

Gaulli, Giovanni Battista, 444

Gavel, Jonas, 183

Gazzaniga, M. S., 53(nn9, 10, 11, 12)

Gazzola, Piero, 488(n26), 489–490(n53)

Geese, Uwe, 357

Gessner, Konrad, 205

Gesù, Church of the (Ferrara), 439

Gesù (Rome), 417–451, *419, 421, 422, 437, 443*

Ghiberti, Lorenzo, 59, 63, 64, 84, 153

Giannotti, Donato, 455

Giberti, Gian Matteo, 425–426, 458

Gil de Hontañon, Rodrigo, 256(n2), 266

Giocondo, Fra, 369, 498, *500, 513*

Gioia de Colle (Apulia), *525*

Giorgi, Francesco, 425

Giorgione, 176

Giotto di Bondone, 16, 55, 177

Giuliano da Maiano, 307

Giunti, Domenico, 432

Goedicke, C., 322

Goldthwaite, Richard, 382

Gombrich, E. H., 93(nn50, 56), 539(n44), 539–540(n49)

Goodenough, E. R., 412(n21)

Gozzoli, Benozzo, 304, 305

Grayson, Cecil, 87(nn1, 3, 6), 90(nn27, 29, 31), 178(n1)

Greco, El (Domenikos Theotokopoulos), 17, 43

Greenberg, Clement, 39, 45, 55

Grimaldi, F. M., 125

Grimani, Antonio (Doge), 480

Grimani, Domenico (Cardinal), 490(n62)

Grimani, Marin (Cardinal), 480, 490(n62)

Grimani, Vettor, 476, 480, 490(n62)

Grimani, Zuanne, 480

Grimani family, 480, 489(n50)

Grosseteste, Robert, 63, 107–108, 116, 141(n35)

Guarino of Verona, 180(n23)

Guasti, Cesare, 216(nn50, 51)

Gundissalinus, Dominicus, 267

Günther, Hubertus, 536(n15), 537(nn24, 25), 542

Haitham, Ibn-al-. *See* Alhazen

Hall, Marcia B., 183

Heemskerk, Marten van, 353(n27), 358, *391*

Heilige Kreuz (Schwäbisch-Gmünd), 264

Heinz, Marianne, 382

Held, Richard, 142(n54)

Helmholtz, H. L. F., 104

Hesperides, garden of, 358

Heydenreich, L. H., 277, 307, 318(n26), 321, 412(n3), 489–490(n53), 539(n46)

Heyman, Jacques, 267

Hills, Paul, 95, 183

Hoeniger, F. David, 205

Holbein, Hans, 102

Horti Sallustiani (Rome), 347

House of Seven Gables (Salem), 28

Howard, Deborah, 385(n1), 489(n43), 490(nn57, 58, 59, 61)

Hugh of St. Victor, 267

Huygens, Constantin, 125

Luzi, Luzio, 349

MacCurdy, Edward, 137, 138(n2), 142(n48), 143(nn63, 67, 70, 73)

McMahon, A. Philip, 136, 138(n1), 180(n25)

Magenta, Carolo, 298(nn8, 10), 299(n32)

Magi, Filippo, 357

Maltese, C., 147(n109), 148–149, 183

Manet, Edouard, 13, 43

Mansfield Woodhouse (England), villa at, 312, *314*

Mantegna, Andrea, 86, 156, 195

Marcus Aurelius, statue of, 390, 396, *397, 405–406*, 411, 413

Maretto, Paolo, 318(n30)

Marius, Gaius, 407

Martini, Francesco di Georgia, 321

Martini, Simone, 405

Masaccio (Tommaso Guidi), 64, 76, 84, 95, 158, 159, 165, 177, 183

Maurolyco, Francesco, 142(n42)

Maurolycus, 132

Mayen (Germany), villa at, 312

Medici, Cosimo de', 64, 304

Medici, Lorenzo the Magnificent, 307

Medici, Pietro de', 278

Medici family, 364
  palace of, 526
  villas of, 304

Megalotti, Francesco, 368

Meiss, Millard, 87n

Meleghino, Jacopo, 368–369

Melzi, Francesco, 136, 165

Michelangelo, 39, 55, 176, 381(n25)
  as architect, 32, 332, 362, 364, 365, 379(n3), 380(n17), 386–415, 420–421, 435, 449, 486(n3)

as painter, 10, 17, 42, 81, 337, 362

Michelozzo di Bartolommeo, 277, 281–282, 301, 304, 316

Mignot, Jean, 230–240, 241, 265, 267

Milan, cathedral, 212–267, 271, 365, 373

Mlakar, Stefan, 539(n45)

Monaco, Lorenzo, 156

Mondeno de' Luzzi, 111, 142(n42)

Mondrian, Piet, 46

Monte de Pietà (Padua), 479

Monza, cathedral, 213, 215, 271

Morachiello, Paolo, 536(n12), 538(n32)

Morolli, Gabriele, 542–543

Morragh, Andrew, 414

Morresi, Manuela, 322

Morscheck, Charles R., Jr., 300, 301

Mungersdorf, villa at, 312

Munoz, U., 299(nn16, 17, 18, 20, 21, 24)

Muraro, Michelangelo, 318, 485(n1), 492

Murray, Stephen, 266

Naldini, Battista, 358

Nanni de Baccio Bigio, 381(n25), 418–420, *419*

Naumachia, at Vatican, 340–341

Nesselrath, Arnold, 537(n27)

Niccoli, Niccolò, 64

Nicolas de Bonaventure, 215–218, 241, 264

Nymphaeum (Genazzano), 516, *519*

Ollanda, Francisco d', 396, *397*, 413

O'Malley, C. D., 100, 102, 143(n60), 146(n97)

Onians, John, 543

Oresme, Nicholas, 71

Orsenigo, Simone de, 223, 229, 247

Orvieto, well at, 365

420, 429, 432–434, 439, 440, 445, 448–449, 497, *503–508*, 521, 526

Villa alle Volte (Siena), 307, *309*

Villa Barbaro (Maser), 463, *464–465*, 466, 503

Villa Cornaro (Piombino Dese), 463

Villa Farnesina (Rome), 305, 321

Villa Garzoni (Pontecasale), 461, 462, 476

Villa Giulia (Rome), 304, 521

Villa Giustinian (Roncade), 454

Villa Godi (Lonedo), 463

Villa Lante (Bagnaia), 322

Villa Madama (Rome), 303, 516

Villa Porto Colleoni (Thiene), 307, *308,* 322

Villa Repeta (Campiglia), 466

Villa Simonetta, 432

Villa Tusculana (Tivoli), 322

Villa Vescovile (Luvigliano), 322, 467, 488(n34)

Ville Radieuse, 35

Vimercanti, Count Gasparo, 284

Vincenzo, Antonio di, 216, *219,* 224, 264, 298(n4)

Viollet-le-Duc, Eugène-Emmanuel, 211, 228

Visconti, Gian Galeazzo, 213, 256–257(n6), 266, 270, 271, 275, 277, 285

Vitruvius (Marcus Vitruvius Pollio), 21, 23, 303, 363, 409, 496–499, 507–508, 532, 542, 543

Volpaia, Bernardo della, 358

Vos, Martin de, 358

Weidlitz, Hans, 199, *201,* 202, 205

Weitz, Morris, 21

White, John, 93(n54)

William of Morbeke, 109

Witelo, 63, 71, 104, 109, *110,* 141(n26)

Wittkower, Rudolf, 418, 448

Wölfflin, Heinrich, 8, 9

Woolf, S. J., 486(nn12, 14), 487(n14), 488(n32)

Wright, Frank Lloyd, 35

Wyeth, Andrew, 46

Zeri, Federico, 300

Zeuxis, 85

Zevi, B., 413

Zorzi, Giangiorgio, 489(n35), 491(nn69, 70)